CW00348383

FEET OF FINES
FOR ESSEX

FEET OF FINES
FOR ESSEX

VOLUME V
1547–1580

Edited by
MARC FITCH, C.B.E., M.A., D.Litt., Hon. F.B.A., F.S.A.
and
FREDERICK EMMISON, M.B.E., D.U., F.S.A.

LEOPARD'S HEAD PRESS
1991

1991
Published by
LEOPARD'S HEAD PRESS LIMITED
2a Polstead Road, Oxford OX2 6TN

ISBN 0 904920 18 6

Printed in Great Britain by Blackmore Press, Longmead, Shaftesbury, Dorset

CONTENTS

ACKNOWLEDGEMENTS

Those who use this volume have every reason to be grateful to Dr. F. G. Emmison, who has given hundreds of hours over several years to the compilation in an entirely honorary capacity. The originals were calendared seventy years ago by the great scholar, R. C. Fowler (an Assistant Keeper, P.R.O.), and the balance by myself.

M.F.

Grateful thanks are due to Dr. Marc Fitch (apart from his editorial burden) for bearing the cost of printing, except for small but appreciated grants by the Friends of Historic Essex and Miss Anne Barker; also to Mr. Roy Stephens for dealing with various problems in seeing the book through the press.

F.G.E.

INTRODUCTION

The property market

The present calendar reveals how the 'New Men' who had acquired Essex monastic lands at the Dissolution were creating larger estates. The Fines show Sir Richard Rich, Lord Rich, who bought Leighs Priory from the Crown, later becoming possessed of numerous manors in central and east Essex. Sir William Petre's gradual and extensive enlargement of his Ingatestone Hall estate is similarly evidenced.[1] Other big estates were built up by successful Crown officers. We see the purchases of many manors by Sir Anthony Browne, Chief Justice of Common Pleas, and Sir Thomas Mildmay, Auditor of the Court of Augmentations, and of several manors by Thomas Mildmay, Auditor of the same court, and of other manors by Thomas Fanshawe, an Exchequer official, and John Southcote, William Ayloffe, and Thomas Meade, all judges, who came to live in the county, the last also being active J.P.s. Among the lesser London luminaries, William Bendlowes, serjeant-in-law, by a long series of Fines acquired much property around his home (still surviving) at Place Farm, Great Bardfield.

Thus the Fines testify to a volatile property market, in which some purchases, like Sir William Cecil's, were apparently for investment only. Several magnates appear as purchasers or vendors or both. Robert Dudley, Earl of Leicester, bought the manor of Wanstead, which was to be his chief country residence, and a neighbouring manor, both in 1579. Two Fines in the following year (pp.234, 236) suggest his having sold them, but they were in fact mortgaged.[2] In 1578 an adjacent manor, Aldersbrook in Little Ilford and Wanstead, became the home of Henry Herbert, Earl of

---

1. Details in F. G. Emmison, *Tudor Secretary* (reprint 1970), pp.266–70.
2. Essex Record Office, D/DCw T3.

Pembroke, but only for two years, when he sold it. William Cecil, Lord Burghley, who never lived in Essex, purchased several manors in 1574–76; but his predecessor as Secretary of State, Sir Thomas Smyth, had confined himself to possessing the manor of Theydon Mount, on which he built, to his own advanced designs, the remarkable Hill Hall (now ruined by fire). The names of John Paulet, Marquis of Winchester, Francis Russell, Earl of Bedford, and Sir Nicholas Bacon occur occasionally; none apparently was resident in Essex. Thomas Sackville, Lord Buckhurst, is seen mostly as a vendor. Sir William Waldegrave of Smallbridge, just over the Suffolk border, purchased the manor of Stanstead Hall in Halstead in 1566; followed by a succession of sales, 1572–76, and finishing with Wormingford. The Fines disclose the loss in his last four years of the extensive estates of the ill-fated Walter Devereux, Earl of Essex, perhaps to defray the expenses of his Irish ventures.

Among the outstanding features, although known from other sources, is the dismemberment of virtually all the vast Essex estates of Edward de Vere, seventeenth Earl of Oxford. By 1580 he had lost twenty large and small properties. Contrary to the truth, there is the oft-repeated story that, when Burghley refused Oxford's request to save the Duke of Norfolk from execution (1572), he at once took the foolish revenge of dissipating his estates in order to ruin his wife Anne, Burghley's daughter. The account was completely disproved over seventy years ago by B. M. Ward, Oxford's biographer.[3] He elicited from the unpublished Patent Rolls that the estates remained unaffected until four years later (1576), when selling started, as a result of his costly foreign travel and his loss through investing in Frobisher's voyages. In 1580 Oxford revived his fathers's company of actors; this and the heavy maintenance expenses led to further major sales extending throughout the year. The end of the present volume (Michaelmas term 1580) coincides with the last of this series, except for a manor on the Cambridge-Essex border. A resumption after nearly two years saw him divesting himself of almost all that remained of his lands. But Ward's refutation of the revenge allegation has apparently not been seen by several recent historians, who have maintained the false story.

The rise of yeomen to the ranks of the gentry is apparent from the numerous transactions. It is best studied more fully by including the evidence in the previous volume (ending in 1547), supplemented from that in the Fines for the rest of Elizabeth's time, which it is hoped may be published similarly within a few years as

3. B. M. Ward, *The Seventeenth Earl of Oxford* (1928), pp.331, 353–54.

Volume VI of the series. One family on which much research has already been done is that of Fitch of north Essex.[4] The earliest Fitch Fines (from 1523)[5] in the present book indicate yeoman status. Although William Fitch had purchased the manor of Little Canfield in 1538, he was not accorded gentlemanly rank until 1540; after which the family gradually added to their properties for the rest of the Tudor period. Likewise William Beryff, who acquired half the manor of Bentons in Witham in 1553, was not recorded as 'gentleman' until his purchase of further property in the following year.

The evidence of Fines for manorial history

The record of Tudor Fines is a historian's happy hunting ground for the minor manors and late pseudo-manors in which Essex abounded. The present volume therefore supplements the two main printed sources, Morant's *History of Essex* (1768, reprint 1978) and Reaney's *Place-Names of Essex* (1935), for those parts of the county not yet covered by the *Victoria History of Essex*. A typical instance (p.5) is the sale in 1547 by Sir Anthony Hevenyngham of the manors of Flete Hall in Sutton and Barrow Hall in Eastwood. The Fine corrects Morant (i, p.292), who says that Flete Hall manor 'passed by Fine in 1557' and furnishes a useful reference to what is now Westbarrow Hall, not to be confused with the Domesday manor of Barn Hall in neighbouring Little Wakering. The manor of High Hall in Tolleshunt D'Arcy (p.212) does not occur in Morant, nor is the minute 'manor' of 'Le Lyon' or 'Red Lyon' in Hornchurch (pp.88, 113). Morant (ii, p.19) does not give manorial status to Seabrights in Great Baddow although he found the 'Hall' suffix under 1544; it is only 'a messuage' and lands in a Fine of 1547.

The Fines refer to some manors of earlier date than those cited in *Place-Names of Essex*. A few obscure manors, such as Mary Hall in Belchamp Walter (p.17), are not readily found in *PNE*, which gives it present name of St. Mary Hall with only a 13th-century source. The Fine of the 'manor' of Pyersyes in Halstead (pp.13, 36), quoted as the earliest reference in *PNE*, is found as a house called Perces in Morant. Of the manor of Bacons with Flories in Great Tey (pp.96, 106), Bacons finds no place in *PNE* and the site has

---

4. Sir Anthony Wagner, *English Genealogy* (1960), pp.192—6.
5. The family in fact occurs in Volume IV (very frequently) and in Volume III (1404).

apparently not been located. The same remark applies to the little manor of Pounte *alias* Benets in Bulmer, to which the industrious Morant managed to find three references. Unlike the Fines (pp.26, 41), he rightly refused manorial status to the four houses of Paslowes, Imbers, Falconers and Bowers in Good Easter. Occasionally the attorney who gave the details to the court was in doubt: Stock Hall in Matching is termed 'the manor or messuage' (p.19) but a manor later (p.37); and Gayshams Hall, a sub-manor in the great lordship of Barking, appears as a messuage in the Fines, and it seems that a few other small estates, each recorded in the Fines as a messuage and lands, should have been termed manors.

The owership of a few manors had been subdivided into moieties and even moieties of moieties (i.e. a fourth part); of the latter, the manor of Otes in High Laver is a good example, supplementing Morant (i, p.140–1) with five Fines. Other fractions occur, e.g. two-thirds of Waltham Hall in Takeley (p.20), later unified (p.189). Extreme instances are one-seventh of a non-manorial estate (p.5) and of 4 acres (p.2), where it may be possible that the wife was one of seven daughters and co-heirs. Two such daughters joined with their husbands to sell two-fifths of what may be (p.13), although not so termed, the manor of Boons in Bocking (Morant, ii, p.387).

Obsolete forms of place-names, misleading or highly inaccurate spellings, and places which have finally evaded positive identification are discussed at the end of the Preface.

Manorial appurtenances

The important right to hold a market or fair, granted by the Crown, is associated with a few manors. The market and two annual fairs attached to the manor of Abells in Halstead were held by royal grant of 1467; two Fines (pp.126, 209) refer to them, the latter adding the term *ferie* (holy-days). Brentwood market and fairs went with the manor of South Weald (p.187). The transaction of 1580 regarding the manor of Fingrith Hall in Blackmore (p.238) includes the fair at Fingrith, which Morant linked with the manor of Blackmore Priory. A common appurtenance was the liberty of free warren or chase — the right to keep and hunt beasts of the chase (see Index of Subjects under 'warrens'). Fishery rights, not all manorial, were also fairly common (see Index), and a single 'free fishpond in Fobbing water' is mentioned (p.107). Most were freshwater fisheries. Coastal fishery rights appear as 'weirs', often spelt 'wares', and in other contemporary documents sometimes known as keddles or kiddles, which were nets attached to permanent stakes.[6] Weirs were recorded off the north bank of the Blackwater estuary (e.g. p.196, but 'without fishing rights'), off the south bank at Bradwell-juxta-Mare (p.96), where unusually it is called the 'Pounte' (Pant generally being reserved for the upper part of the river), and off 'Walletts' (Wallasea island). Other coastal features include wharves, quays, a salthouse, and a fish-store, all at Harwich, a wharf at Stanford-le-Hope, and rent paid in salt from Stow Maries or Woodham Ferrers saltcotes.[7] The Thames ferries were manorial, but not Fambridge ferry. The Fines add to our imperfect knowledge of the title to advowsons[8] and also give a few details of tithes in some parishes.

In medieval times the possession of a dovecote was restricted to lords of manors; some manors, e.g. Arnolds in Mountnessing (pp.148, 152, 221), had two. But by the Tudor period the law seems to have been much overlooked, as one sees many non-manorial dovecotes, even on a very small property (e.g. pp.56, 102). Of the few parks specifically mentioned, little is known of Ramsden (Bellhouse) Park apart from its being shown on Chapman and André's Map of Essex (1777).

To many properties was attached 'common of pasture', or grazing rights. These existed over areas ranging from village 'greens' to great heaths, especially those in east Essex, such as Tiptree Heath, and those around Colchester. Of middle-size commons one finds Farewood Common in Great Leighs (p.2) and Stock Common (p.182). Grazing rights are noted, e.g., for '2 horses, 2 cows and 30 sheep' at Hockley and Rawreth (p.30) and for 5 'animals' at Nazeing (p.64). Rights in the forest areas are exemplified by grazing for 100 sheep and feeding (pannage) for 12 pigs at Theydon Garnon and Mount (p.99). 'Faldage', the privilege attached to certain manors, obliged the tenants to set up folds in which their sheep manured the stubble after harvest. Such sheep-walks are found in six Fines, all relating to the chalk lands in north-west Essex — the area of the wide common (or open) fields, clearly shown on Chapman and André's Map of Essex (1777) — the highest figures being for 300 sheep (p.45) and for 600 sheep (p.96). Other large flocks of sheep fed on the coastal marshlands (p.12).

6. Details in F. G. Emmison, *Elizabethan Life: Home, Work and Land* (1976), pp.70—72.

7. *Ibid.*, pp.88—90.

8. Newcourt, *Repertorium* (1710).

Miscellaneous items

Among other valuable facts are the references to mills, a majority specifying whether water, wind, or fulling-mills.[9] But where the Fine covers more than one parish, one cannot always identify the relevant parish. Most of the water-mills are those shown on Chapman's Map and on, or their sites on, modern maps. The location of windmills *may* correspond with those on the same map (1777), e.g. Canewdon (p.215), but some may have vanished, e.g. that in the manor of Prestons in South Hanningfield (p.152), before 1777. Of the few fulling-mills 'Walbury mill' in Great Hallingbury (p.79) was the predecessor of the 'silk mill' on Chapman, the frontispiece plate of which, showing a fulling-mill, is a source of perennial delight. Fines add to our otherwise imperfect knowledge of the title to advowsons,[10] also some details of tithes in various parishes. Non-pecuniary rents (token only in some cases) paid to certain manors comprise apples, fowls, cloves, cumin, wax, salt, cartloads of wood from Waltham Forest, two pairs of gilt spurs, and two red roses.

Description of property

In the method of recording the property, Fines differ greatly from Deeds (conveyances, mortgages, etc.). Whereas the latter may furnish much detail or virtually nothing beyond 'messuage and the appurtenant lands', the post-medieval Fines follow a standardised form employing a limited number of terms. The regular order, subject to slight variation, is as follows, the words italicised being commonest: *messuage* (dwelling house), toft (site of a former dwelling), cottage, curtilage (yard), barn, stable, *garden, orchard,* mill, dovecote; *land* (arable), *meadow, pasture, wood,* furze and heath (probably rough pasture), moor, fresh marsh, and salt marsh. A few additional words may occur: shop, kitchen (often a separate outhouse to reduce fire risk), and wharves, etc. (in coastal properties).

Acreages

A matter of some interest is the degree of accuracy of the acreages given in Fines. Two otherwise authoritative pamphlets about Deeds

9. Essex is fortunate in having two recent works of outstanding interest: H. Benham, *Some Essex Windmills* (1976) and K. G. Farries, *Essex Windmills, Millers and Millwrights* (1981—86).

10. There are many gaps in the clergy-lists in Newcourt's *Repertorium* (1710).

cast doubt. One avers that 'acreages are approximate only', the other that 'details of land are usually conventional, the acreages given are too large'.[11] Neither writer stated that he had based his generalisation on a detailed study of individual Fines. The present writer felt that the problem justified some research. The result[12] was based on collation of Fines with Deeds, where both relate to the same property. The article cites eighteen 16th- and 17th-century examples drawn from documents in the Essex Record Office. The conclusion is that the acreages and also the qualities (arable, wood, etc.) in the majority of Tudor Fines are fairly reliable, even where all figures end in '0'. It must suffice to quote only one passage. The two authors' dismissive comments about acreages undoubtedly arose from two facts: (1) many Fines, especially those for the bigger estates, give round figures, and (2) some seem at first sight to enumerate the qualities according to a sort of normal ratio as 30 a. land, 10 a. meadow, 20 a. pasture and 5 a. wood. Many farms of course had such proportions. But a short study would have shown (1) that numerous Fines give acreages not ending in noughts, and (2) that the quasi-standard ratios have plenty of exceptions. That round figures appear in Fines of big estates is only natural, as few pre-1700 descriptive surveys and large-scale maps were available; and area estimates were often made also in Deeds.[13] If the recent article has established reliability, the corollary follows that, where the Fine is the *sole* known record of a property trans-action, its topographical facts are valuable to the local historian. Indeed, as the article exemplifies, it is not uncommon for a Fine to contain more detail than its related feoffment or similar con-veyance. One should however emphasise that Fines dealing with very large properties, especially those in the 'Divers Counties' series covering many counties (unlike those of average-size prop-erties on the borders of two counties, e.g. p.51), express only roughly estimated acreages.

Types of Fines

The curious terminology used in Fines needs some explanation. What is their effect on the parties' title to the property? They were resorted to for various reasons, the chief being to render the title

11. A. A. Dibben, *Title Deeds, 13th–19th Centuries* (Histl. Assoc., 1968), and J. Cornwall, *How to Read Old Title Deeds, XVI–XIX Centuries* (1963).
12. F. G. Emmison, 'Final Concords' (*The Local Historian*, August 1981, pp.414–16).
13. *Ibid.*, p.412.

more secure by their being recorded in the Court of Common Pleas. A Fine barred the wife's right of dower. A few were linked with marriage settlements. The 'use', or title resulting from the Fine, cannot be definitely deduced; even in the simplest form of Fine the deforciant and the plaintiff are not necessarily, though nearly always, the vendor and the purchaser respectively. The intended effect was often ensured by a 'Deed to lead the uses of a Fine' or a 'Deed to declare the uses', made before or after the Fine was 'levied'; such a document frequently being found in company with a Final Concord in a bundle of deeds.

In the absence of such an explanatory document, one must study the language of the record itself. Our Fines, unlike those of earlier date, belong to relatively few types. The best description is found in the 'formulary' section of the late C. A. F. Meekings' introduction to Tudor Fines.[14] A brief summary follows.

1. Plaintiff secures his title from deforciant. (The normal type.)
2. Plaintiff secures the reversion to the property on the death of deforciant(s), who is/are the life tenant(s); the latter may be the deforciant's wife (e.g. p.22, no. 7, p.23, no. 26), his mother-in-law (p.2, no. 13), etc., or plaintiff secures the reversion at end of lessee's term (p.4, no. 45.)
3. Plaintiff 'renders back' to deforciant(s) for his/their life/lives, with remainder(s) to named person(s) (e.g. p.21, no. 2, heir apparent, p.12, no. 19, p.13, no. 32, or husband, p.25, nos. 73, 74).
4. Plaintiff renders back to deforciant(s) in fee simple (e.g. p.21, no. 91, p.27, no. 30).
5. Plaintiff renders back to deforciant(s) in fee tail (e.g. p.2, no. 25, p.4, no. 50, p.5, no. 80, p.16, no. 21).

A few other versions are found (e.g. p.2, no. 23, p.19, no. 63), some being too complicated for discussion in this Preface.

Family history

In a period for which the earliest parish register is not uncommonly lost, Fines are a useful secondary source for a wife's christian, though not maiden, name. Relationships are sometimes given, e.g. p.1, no. 2, p.2, no. 5, or suggested, e.g. p.2, no. 21.

14. *Abstracts of Surrey Feet of Fines, 1509–1558* (Surrey Record Society, 1946).

Spellings

A number of unusual place-names occur, in particular, Thambridge (for Fambridge), Gooster (Good Easter), Standishe (Stambridge), Chestover (Chesterford), Aldorney (Althorne), and Ravensden Bellows (Ramsden Bellhouse). Such spellings are certainly errors of the court scribes. Essex readers may be surprised to find that the distinctive prefixes or suffixes to some parish names differed from those in later and modern use. Examples are Chignall Trench-foyle (now Chignall Smealy), Tey Godmer (now Little), and Roothing Masy (now Margaret). The 'Ginge' or 'Inge' group of parishes in central Essex were known in medieval and Tudor times as Ing Berners or Ing Hospital (for Fryerning), (G)yng Margaret, Gyng Mountney, 'Gyngraff', rightly Gyng Ralph (Ingrave), and Ging ad petram (probably so-called from the milestone on the Roman road to Colchester, still preserved at Ingatestone cross-roads), and the prizewinner (G)ing Joyberd Laundry, named after two twelfth-century tenants (the alternative of Buttsbury).[15] In other cases forms which might be misleading (e.g. 'Bures', for Bowers Gifford, not Bures in north Essex) have been correctly indexed. Identification is a time-consuming task. In the end the following place-names still remain elusive, though their approximate location is generally deducible: Austeyns, Bustes, Crawlese, Duxworth, Gyps, Hamptons, Horewood, Leylofte Hall, Stulpes, Tolkelones and Wrestes. Suggestions are invited.

Since this Introduction was written several years ago, much new material for 16th-century social history and Essex local and family history is in 5,000 detailed abstracts in *Essex Wills, 1558–1603*, vols. 1–5 (1982–89) and *Elizabethan Life*, vols. 1–5 (1970–80), all edited by F. G. Emmison, obtainable from E.R.O., County Hall, Chelmsford; another 7,000 wills abstracts have been made for vols. 6–12 (1991–97?).

F.G.E.

---

15. See *Place-Names of Essex*, pp.253–4. etc.

FEET OF FINES FOR ESSEX

When there are two or more deforciants (vendors), the names of the principal one(s) are given *in italics*.

Abbreviations: a.—acre; ar.—land (generally = arable); cott.—cottage; def.—deforciant (see page xvi); gdn.—garden; kt.—knight; mess.—messuage (dwelling house); mks.—marks; mw.—meadow; pa.—pasture; pl.—plaintiff (see page xvi); rt.—rent; w.—wife; wid.—widow; wd.—wood.

CP25(2)/57/418   EASTER, 1 EDWARD VI   1547

1. Rd. Archer, pl. Tho. Deryng, def. 4 a. mw. in Theydon Garnon. 40 mks.

2. Jn. Rolles, pl. Jn. Richardson & w. *Joan*, dau. & heir of Tho. Parker, decd., def. A third part of a mess. & 9 a. ar. in Little Chysshall & Great Chysshall. £40.

3. Jn. Cole, pl. *Tho.* Paston, knight, & w. Agnes, def. 20 a. ar., 35 a. pa. & 16 a. wd. in Bulmer. £40.

4. Jn. Hamond, pl. Wm. Fuller & w. *Agnes*, def. A moiety of a mess., 12 a. ar., 3 a. mw. and 14 a. pa. in Fobbyng. £30.

5. Tho. Campe, pl. Tho. Myners, gent., & w. Alice, def. 2 mess., 40 a. ar., 10 a. mw. & 10 a. pa. in Roydon, Nasyng & Great Parndon. £40.

6. Tho. Peycok, Jn. Clerke, Edm. Clerke & Reg. Hyghgate jun., pl. *Jn.* Sowthwell and w. Eliz., def. 4 a. ar., 3 a. mw. & 5 a. marsh in Feryng. Def. quitclaimed to pl. & the heirs of Tho. £30.

7. Robt. Arthur, gent., pl. Jn. Spelman & w. Margt., Robt. Parmafaye & w. *Joan* & Wm. Teryngton & w. Eliz., def. 1 mess., 30 a. ar., 12 a. mw. & 30 a. pa. called Sabryghts in Great Badowe. 200 mks.

8. Robt. Shether, clk. & Wm. Harby, pl. *Ralph* Naylyngherst, esq., & w. Eliz., def. 80 a. ar., 6 a. mw., 30 a. pa. & 4 a. wd. in Brayntre. Def. quitclaimed to pl. & the heirs of Robt. 160 mks.

9. Jn. Wyseman of London, esq., pl. Wm. West, knight, & w. *Frances*, def. The manor of Tendering *alias* Tewes & 12 mess., 10 gdns., 500 a. ar. 40 a. mw., 200 a. pa., 10 a. wd., 66s. 8d. rt. of ½ lb. of wax & 1 lb. of cumin in Tendering, Depden, Amberden, Wymbysshe, & Thaxsted. £300 (*altered from* £200).

10. Jn. Mounford, pl. Walter Scotte, esq., & w. *Eliz.*, def. The manor of Langtons & 1 mess., 240 a. ar., 24 a. mw., 100 a. pa., 10 a. wd. & 10s. rt. in Little Canfelde, Great Canfelde & Great Dunmowe. £200.

11. Rd. Hyckys, pl. Geo. Daniell, gent., def. 1 mess., 2 tofts, 2 curtilages, 12 a. ar., 10 a. mw. & 20 a. pa. in Westhangyngfeld. 100 mks.

12. Edm. Moigne, pl. Jn. Lygett & w. *Alice*, def. 1 mess., 1 gdn., 1 orchard, 40 a. ar., 6 a. mw., 30 a. pa., 4 a. swamp (*stagn'*) & 4 a. wd. in Tolshunt Mauger, Totham & Goldhanger. 50 mks.

13. Hy. Holland & Jas. Holland, pl. Jn. Myche & w. Alice, def. 1 mess., & 1 gdn. called Drakes & 6 a. mw., in Rayley, which Juliana Myche, wid., late the w. of Jn. Myche sen. holds for life without impeachment of waste of the inheritance of the said Jn. Miche jun. Pl. & the heirs of Hy. to hold the reversion of the chief lords. £40.

14. Kath. Okey, wid., pl. Hugh Browne, def. 12 a. pa. in Moose. 20 mks.

15. Wm. Eve, pl. Rd. Savage & w. *Eliz.*, def. A seventh part of 4 a. pa. in Masshebury. 40s.

16. Rd. Riche, knight, lord Ryche, pl. *Jn.* Ingland of Great Lighes sen., 'husbondman', & w. Eliz., def. 1 mess., 1 toft, 1 dovecote, 1 gdn., 60 a. ar., 4 a. mw., 20 a. pa., & 10s. rt. in Great Lighes & common of pa. in 'Farewood Comen' in Great Lighes. £140.

17. Geo. Sayer, pl. *Hy.* Fortescue, esq., & w. Eliz., def. The manor of Motes and 4 mess., 100 a. ar., 30 a. mw., 100 a. pa., 30 a. wd., 20 a. alder & 5s. rt. in Lexden, Colchester, Stanweye, Fordam & Bergholt Sakevyle. £140.

18. Wm. Jennyn, pl. Simon Tomlynson & w. *Joan*, def. A fourth part of 2 mess., 25 a. ar., 4 a. mw. & 10 a. pa. in Abbes Rodyng. £20.

19. Rd. Hasylwood, pl. *Tho.* Paston, knight, & w. Agnes, def. The manor of Ketchyn & 3 mess., 240 a. ar., 4 a. mw., 30 a. pa., 6 a. marsh & 30s. rt. in Bulmer. £120.

20. Tho. Myldemaye, esq., pl. Jn. Spylman & w. *Margt.*, Robt. Parmafaye & w. *Joan* & Wm. Teryngton & w. *Eliz.*, def. 1 mess., 50 a. ar., 14 a. mw., 34 a. pa., 2 a. wd. & 2s. rt. in Chelmesford, Mulshame & Great Badowe. £148.

21. Rd. Taverner, esq., Roger Taverner & Robt. Taverner, gent., pl. *Robt.* Gurdon, gent., & w. Rose, def. The manors of Hanhams *alias* Bulleyns & Whelars & 6 mess., 6 gdns., 400 a. ar., 50 a. mw., 500 a. pa., 200 a. wd. & 40s. rt. in Tenderyng, Fratyng, Great Bentley & Thoryngton. Def. quitclaimed to pl. & the heirs of Rd. 620 mks.

22. Walter (Kember), pl. *Clement* Robartes & w. Mary, def. The manor of Little Braxsted, 4 mess., 1 (water)mill, (80 a.) ar., 10 a. mw., 10 a. pa., 40 a. wd., 22s. rt. & a rt. (of 1 lb. of pepper) in Little Braxsted, & the advowson of the church of Little Braxsted. Def. quitclaimed to pl. & his heirs. And for this pl. gtd. two parts of the manor, tenements & rt. to def. for their lives (with remainder to the right heirs of Clement, & the third part to Clement & his heirs), to hold of the chief lords.

CP25(2)/66/545　　　　　　　DIVERS COUNTIES

5. Mich. 38 Henry VIII & Eas. 1 Edward VI. Jn. Goldynge, esq., & Thos. Goldynge, gent., his son & heir apt., pl. Jn. Talbott, knight, & w. Eliz., def. Manors of Thykkoo & Londres & 4 mess., 150 a. ar., 30 a. mw., 150 a. pa., 40 a. wd. & 50s. rt. in Thykkoo, Londers, Aston & Stevynton, co. Essex, & property in Bartelowe, co. Cambridge. Def. quitclaimed to pl. & the heirs of Jn. £46 — Essex, Cambs.

6. Tho. Danyell, pl. Bart. Turner & *Wm.* Turner, def. Manor of Grendon in Bulmer & 3 mess., 1 cott., 100 a. ar., 80 a. mw., 100 a. pa., 40 a.wd. & 13s. rt. in Grendon, Bulmer, Baladon, Great Henney & Little Henney, co. Essex, & property in Sudbury, co. Suff. £110 — Essex, Suff.

CP25(2)/57/418　　　　　TRINITY, 1 EDWARD VI　　　　　1547

23. Eas. & Trin. Hy. Hardson & Tho. Oules, citizens & skinners of London, pl. Tho. Holles, knight, & w. Anne, Rd. Taverner, esq., Roger Taverner & Robt. Tavener, def. Manor of Westhurroke *alias* Westhall in Westhurroke *alias* le Vynyard & 26 mess., 12 tofts, 20 gdns., 1 dovecote, 1 windmill, 600 a. ar., 100 a. mw., 370 a. pa., 100 a. wd., 100 a. marsh, 200 a. furze & heath & £10 rt. in Westhurroke, Duddynghurste, Harmyrys, Orsed, Styfford, Grace, Aulflye & Gorys. Def. quitclaimed to pl. & the heirs of Hy., with separate warranties for the heirs of Anne & Rd. £1,960.

24. Eliz. Kyngesman, pl. Jn. Osborne & w. *Denise*, def. 1 mess., 1 toft, 10 a. ar., 6 a. mw. & 20 a. pa. in Althorn. £60.

25. Jn. Dalton, pl. Tho. Wryght, def. 1 mess., 20 a. ar., 12 a. mw. & 12 a. pa. in Sowthweld & Brendwood. Def. quitclaimed to pl. & his heirs. And for this pl. granted the same to def. to hold for one month, with remainder to Anne Tanner late the w. of Adam Tanner for life & then to Jn. Tanner son of the said Adam & his heirs, to hold of the chief lords.

26. Tho. Petyte, pl. Jn. Alsop & w. Alice, def. A moiety of 1 mess., 40 a. ar., 10 a. mw., 20 a. pa. & 30 a. furze & heath in Staunford Ryvers. Def. quitclaimed from themselves & the heirs of Alice to pl. & his heirs, with warranty from themselves & the heirs of Jn. £20.

27. Eas. & Trin. Tho. Bysshop & Wm. Holte, pl. *Walter* Scotte, esq., & w. Eliz., def. Manor of Stapulford Tawney & 12 mess., 40 a. ar., 60 a. mw., 40 a. pa., 100 a. wd. & 40s. rt. in Stapulford. Def. quitclaimed to pl. & the heirs of Tho. And for this pl. granted the same to def. & the heirs of Walter to hold of the chief lords.

28. Eas. & Trin. Lau. Porter, pl. Rd. Sampfurth & w. *Joan*, def. Manor of Beremans & 1 mess., 1 cott., 100 a. ar., 4 a. mw., 6 a. pa., 4 a. wd. & 10s. rt. in Chygenhale Smelye *alias* Chygenhale Trenchefoyle, & the advowson of the church of Chygenhale Smelye *alias* Chygenhale Trenchefoyle. £100.

29. Wm. Stonard, pl. Lau. Porter & w. *Eliz.*, def. 4 a. pa. in Chygenhale Trenchefoyle *alias* Chygenhale Smelye. £10.

30. Jn. Eweley, pl. Jn. Corbett, gent., def. 1 mess. and 1 gdn., in le Castlestrete, Walden. £20.

31. Robt. Taverner, gent., pl. Walter Celye, gent., & w. Eliz., def. 2 mess., 2 gdns., 50 a. ar., 20 a. mw. and 50 a. pa. in Stapylford Abbots. Def. quitclaimed from themselves & the heirs of Walter to pl. & his heirs, with warranty for themselves & the heirs of Eliz. £80.

32. Jn. Haukyn, pl. *Hy.* Spelman, gent., & w. Anne, def. 1 mess., 1 cott., 1 gdn. (*orto*), 6 a. ar., 3 a. mw. and 4 a. pa. in Borndewoode. 100 mks.

33. Rd. Harbye & w. Cristina, pl. Jn. Eweley, def. 3 mess., in le Goldestrete, Walden, & 12 a. ar. in Walden. Def. quitclaimed to pl. & the heirs of Rd. 40 mks.

34. Jn. Smyth, gent., p!. Robt. Stowe, def. 1 mess., 2 gdns., 20 a. ar., 20 a. pa. & common of pasture in Ardeleigh. £36.

35. Eas. and Trin. Jn. Vaus, pl. *Tho.* Vaus and w. Agnes, def. 1 mess., 1 gdn. & 3 a. pa. in Westham. £30.

36. Eas. & Trin. Rd. Newman, pl. Tho. Whepyll & w. Margt., def. 1 mess., 2 cotts., 2 barns (*orreis*), 1 toft, 2 gdns. & 1 orchard in Branktre. Def. quitclaimed from themselves & the heirs of Tho. to pl. & his heirs, with warranty from themselves & the heirs of Margt. £20.

37. Robt. Taverner, gent., pl. Anth. Broune, gent., & w. Joan, def. 3 mess., 6 gdns., 200 a. ar., 20 a. mw., 200 a. pa., & 20 a. wd. in Lamborne, Stapleford & Navystok. Def. quitclaimed from themselves & the heirs of Anth., with warranty from themselves & the heirs of Joan. £360.

38. Tho. Eve son of Jn. Eve, decd., pl. *Jn.* Dormer, gent., & w. Eliz., Tho. Dormer, esq., son & heir of Mich. Dormer, kt., & Ambrose Dormer, gent., def. 1 mess., 56 a. ar., & 2 a. mw. in Goodester, Chyknall Seynt James & Bromefeld. £60.

39. Eas. & Trin. Wm. Foster, pl. Rd. Sampfurth & w. *Joan*, def. 20 a. ar., 2 a. mw. & 5 a. pa. in Wyllynghale Spayne. £40.

40. Eas. & Trin. Wm. Gregyll, pl. Jas. Holmested & w. Beatrice, def. 6 a. ar. in Branketre. Def. quitclaimed from themselves & the heirs of Jas. to pl. & his heirs, with warranty from themselves & the heirs of Beatrice. £20.

41. Geo. Thomson, pl. Wm. Dalyson and w. *Agnes*, def. 1 cott. & 1 gdn. (*orto*) in Westham. £10.

42. Eas. & Trin. Rd. Byrle, pl. Jn. Canon & w. Eliz., def. 6 a. ar. in Black Notley. Def. quitclaimed from themselves & the heirs of Jn. to pl. & his heirs, with warranty from themselves & the heirs of Eliz. 20 mks.

43. Robt. Somerford & Wm. Hynks, pl. Nich. Robynson, def. 10 mess., 4 cotts., 500 a. ar., 60 a. mw., 500 a. pa., & 80 a. wd. in Fulchars, Goodster, Rothing Masy, Rothing Margarett & Roxwell. Def. quitclaimed to pl. & the heirs of Robt. 200 mks.

44. Trin. 38 Henry VIII & Trin. 1 Edward VI. Wm. Harrys, esq., pl. Jn. Clerke & w. *Joan*, def. 1 mess., 120 a. ar., 40 a. mw. & 120 a. pa. in Maylond & Southmynster. 160 mks.

3

45. Hil. 38 Henry VIII & Trin. 1 Edward VI. Tho. Spryng, pl. Wm. Parke, gent., def. 1 mess., 100 a. ar., 20 a. mw., 60 a. pa. & 10 a. wd. in Great Saylyng, Felsted & Little Raygn, which Geo. Maxye, gent., holds for a term of years. Pl. & his heirs to hold the reversion of the chief lords. £100.

46. Wm. Lukyn, pl. Lau. Porter & w. *Eliz.*, def. 1 gdn. & 15 a. ar. in Chygenhale Trenchefoyle *alias* Chygenhale Smelye. 40 mks.

47. Hy. Chyverton & Geo. Ryche, pl. Ranulph Cholmondeley, esq., & w. *Eliz.*, def. 4 mess., 50 a. ar., 16 a. md., 30 a. pa., & 16 a. wd. in Hornedon on le Hill. Def. quitclaimed to pl. & the heirs of Hy. 200 mks.

48. Jn. Bowyer, pl. Tho. Burges, gent., def. 2 mess., & 2 gdns. in Branktre. £40.

49. Eas. & Trin. Wm. Cotton, pl. Tho. Okeley, def. 1 mess., 1 barn, 1 gdn., 50 a. ar., 8 a. mw., 30 a. pa., & 3 a. wd. in Kyrby & Walton. £100.

50. Eas. & Trin. Rd. Heydon, esq., & Nich. Rokewode, esq., pl. *Jn.* Huddelstone, esq., & w. Bridget, Tho. Darcy, esq., & Robt. Bedyngfeld, def. Manor of Typtre & 12 mess., 12 tofts, 12 gdns., 1 dovecote. 300 a. ar., 60 a. mw., 400 a. pa., 60 a. wd., 20 a. marsh, 60 a. furze & heath & £6 rt. in Typtre, Braxstedd, Tolshunt Tregos, Little Tolshunt, Maldon, Wyteham, Colchester, Tutham, Falbarne, Terlyng, Ingard, Tolshunt Knyght, Goldynger & Stanwey. Def. quitclaimed to pl. & the heirs of Rd. And for this pl. granted the same to Robt. & his assigns for one week, with remainder to Tho. & w. Eliz. & his heirs male of her body & his right heirs.

51. Nich. Collyn, pl. Wm. Ayloff, esq., & w. *Anne*, def. Manor of Brenthall & 200 a. ar., 20 a. mw., 60 a. pa., 20 a. wd. & 20s. rt. in Fynchyngfeld. £100.

52. Eas. & Trin. Wm. Gent, pl. Chris. Fytche & w. Joan, def. 1 mess., 8 a. ar., 10 a. pa., & 1 a. wd. in Bompsted at the Steeple. Def. quitclaimed from themselves & the heirs of Chris. to pl. & his heirs, with warranty from themselves & the heirs of Joan. 40 mks.

53. Eas. & Trin. Nich. Collyn, pl. Rd. Sampfurth & w. *Joan*, def. 1 mess., 70 a. ar., 2 a. mw. & 13 a. pa. in Willynghale Doo & Wyllynghale Spayne. 100 mks.

CP25(2)/66/545   DIVERS COUNTIES

21. Eas. & Trin. Jn. Hawkysshall & Wm. Lemer sen., pl. Rd. Frende & w. *Clement*, Robt. Stansby & w. *Joan*, Clement Fen & w. *Rose* & Wm. Royston & w. *Alice*, def. Property in Suffolk, & 1 mess., 1 gdn., 14 a. ar., 2 a. mw. & 8 a. pa. in Pentlowe & Lyston, co. Essex. Def. quitclaimed to pl. & the heirs of Jn. £240 — Suff., Essex.

CP25(2)/57/418   MICHAELMAS, 1 EDWARD VI   1547

54. Jn. Willett, pl. Tho. Malle & w. *Denise*, def. A moiety of 1 mess., & 27 a. ar. in Brendwood & Shenvyld. £50.

55. Robt. Sawnderson & w. Anne, pl. Jn. Smyth, gent., def. 10 mess., 6 tofts, 1 dovecote, 200 a. ar., 60 a. mw., 140 a. pa., 20 a. wd. & 40s. rt. in Stapylford Tawnye, Northwyeld Bassett, Theydon Gernon & Theydon att Mount. Def. quitclaimed to pl. & the heirs of Anne. £200.

56. Wistan Parker, pl. Tho. Byggs & w. Alice & *Robt.* Parker, def. 1 mess., 2 curtilages, 1 gdn. & 3½ a. mw. in Chelmesford & Mulsham within the parish of Chelmesford. 100 mks.

57. Jas. Wilkynson & w. Dorothea, pl. *Chris.* Smythe, gent., & w. Margt, def. 1 mess., 1 cott., 1 gdn., 40 a. ar., 10 a. mw. & 20 a. pa. in Eastham & Ilford. Def. quitclaimed to pl. & the heirs of Dorothea. £40.

58. Jn. Bekwyth of Stysted, pl. *Jn.* Feld & w. Joan, def. 2 mess., & 3 gdns. in Bokyng. £20.

59. Hy. Baker, pl. Robt. Smythe, gent., & w. *Eliz.*, def. 1 mess., 2 cotts., 100 a. ar., 20 a. mw., 30 a. pa., & 4 a. wd. in Rawreth, Wyckford & Raleigh. 130 mks.

60. Jn. Gardener, pl. Hy. Donham & w. *Margt.*, def. 4 a. ar.,in Great Wenden. £10.

61. Tho. Wolmer & w. Alice, pl. Tho. Turner & w. *Anne*, dau. & heir of Wm. Debenham, gent., def. 1 mess. & 1 gdn. in Billerica. Def. quitclaimed to pl. & the heir of Tho. Wolmer. £30.

4

62. Robt. Mors, pl. Wm. Cristion son & heir of Jn. Cristion, decd., def. 1 mess. & 6½ a. ar. in Barlyng. £30.

63. Tho. Emery, pl. Wm. Warren & w. *Alice*, def. 1 mess., 1 gdn., 12 a. ar. & 12 a. pa. in Danbury & Ronsale. £40.

64. Tho. Mildemay, esq., pl. Oliver Hyde, gent., & w. *Thomasina*, def. 80 a. ar., 18 a. mw., 50 a. pa., & 8 a. wd. in Mulseham, Chelmesford, Wydford & Great Baddowe. £100.

65. Tho. Kyng son of Robt. Kyng, pl. *Tho.* Lawrens & w. Agnes, def. 27 a. ar. & 2 a. mw. in Magdelene Laver & Norwelbasset. £40.

66. Rd. Smart, pl. *Anth.* Hevenyngham, knight, & w. Mary, def. Manors of Fletehall & Barrowehall & 4 mess., 160 a. ar., 40 a. mw., 300 a. pa., 100 a. marsh, 60 a. wd. & £6 rt. in Sutton, Estwood, Rocheford, Lee, Royley, Asshedon, Showbery, Hawkewell, Hadley & Canewedon. £480.

67. Alice Jenour, wid., pl. *Robt.* Broune, esq., & w. Eliz., def. 1 mess., 16 a. ar., 3 a. mw., 74 a. pa., & 9 a. wd. in Wykford, Rowndell, Downham & Sowthanyngfeld. 260 mks.

68. Rd. Gybbes, pl. *Robt.* Taverner, gent., & w. Eliz., def. 4 a. ar. & 16 a. mw. in Stapleford Abbott. £40.

69. Tho. Cornwaleys, esq., pl. Tho. Sampforde, def. A seventh part of 1 mess., 100 a. ar., 10 a. mw., 20 a. pa., & 5 a. wd. in Rammesdon Belhous, Downham, Wykeford, Runwell & South Hannyngfeld. £30.

70. Rd. Glascock, pl. *Jn.* Mountford & w. Joan, def. Manor of Keers & 2 mess., 2 cotts., 100 a. ar., 10 a. mw., 10 a. pa., & 30s. rt. in Eythropp & Rothyng. £106.

71. Jas. Anderkyn, pl. Wm. Ambros & w. *Joan*, def. A third part of 1 mess., 1 gdn., 8 a. pa., & 2 a. marsh in Cryxsey. £20.

72. Launcelot Madyson, pl. Jn. Pascall, gent., def. 1 mess., 1 gdn. (*orto*), 1 gdn. (*gardino*), 30 a. ar., 10 a. mw. & 40 a. pa. in Sandon. £80.

73. Jn. Sorrell, pl. *Edm.* Stane & w. Agnes, def. 16 a. ar. in Great Donmowe. 40 mks.

74. Tho. Westbrome sen., pl. Tho. Gardener, def. 4 mess., 100 a. ar., 20 a. mw., 100 a. pa., & 20 a. wd. in Great Clacton & Little Clacton. £100.

75. Jn. Ausop, pl. Jn. Smyth & *Rd.* Smyth, gent., def. 40 a. ar., 10 a. mw., 20 a. pa., & 10 a. wd. in Grenestede, Bobyngworth & Stanford Ryvers. £100.

76. Rd. Godfrey, pl. Jn. Seyntcler, esq., def. 1 mess., 100 a. ar., 20 a. mw., 60 a. & 20 a. wd. in Chyche Regis *alias* Chyche St. Osithe. £100.

77. Trin. & Mich. Geo. Broke, knight, lord Cobham, pl. *Rd.* Riche, knight, lord Riche, & w. Eliz., def. Manor of Bendysshall & 15 mess., 15 gdns., 400 a. ar., 500 a. mw., 400 a. pa., 300 a. wd. & £20 rt. in Radwynter & Ayston. £860.

78. Tho. Holywell, pl. Tho. Josselyn, knight, def. 2 mess., 2 gdns. (*gardinis*), 1 gdn. (orto), 40 a. ar. & 2 a. mw. in Manewden. £40.

79. Tho. More & w. Eliz., pl. *Chris.* Aleyn & w. Agnes, def. 2 mess., 60 a. ar., 20 a. mw., 100 a. pa., & 4 a. wd. in Thaxsted. Def. quitclaimed to pl. & the heirs of Tho. £120.

80. Hy. Symond, clerk, pl. Francis Clopton, esq., & w. Lora & *Hy.*, Ererd, gent., def. Manor of Smeton & 300 a. ar., 40 a. mw., 60 a. pa., 20 a. wd., 40 a. furze & heath & 40s. rt. in Smeton, Waterbelcham, & Bulmere. Def. quitclaimed to pl. & his heirs, with warranty against the bishop of Norwich & his successors. And for this pl. granted the same to Francis for one week, with remainder to Hy. & w. Joan & the heirs of his body, Jn. Ererd & the heirs of his body, & the right heirs of Hy., to hold of the chief lords.

81. Wm. Broun, pl. Tho. Turner & w. *Anne*, dau. & heir of Wm. Debenham, gent., def. 1 mess., 1 barn, 52 a. ar., 100 a. marsh & 5s. 4d. rt. in Fobbyng & Stanford. Def. quitclaimed to pl. & his heirs. And for this pl. granted the same to Tho. & his heirs to hold of the chief lords.

82. Robt. Southwell, knight, pl. Jn. Watton sen. & w. *Joan* & Geo. Watton, their son & heir apt., def. 3 mess., 3 gdns., 100 a. ar., 40 a. mw., 100 a. pa., 10 a. wd., 40 a. furze & heath, 40 a. marsh & 20s. rt. in Raynam *alias* Rayneham. £160.

5

83. Tho. Benton, pl. *Tho.* Lawrens & w. Agnes, def. 2 mess., 63 a. ar., 3 a. pa., & 2 a. mw. in Harlowe, Magdelene Laver & Machyng. 70 mks.

84. Trin. & Mich. Jn. Glascok sen. & Wm. Glascok, pl. Rd. Riche, knight, lord Riche, def. 1 mess., 1 barn, 1 gdn., 40 a. 1 rood of ar., 7 a. mw., 16 a. 3 roods of pa. & 3 a. wd. in Moreton, Mawdelen Lavgre & Bobyngworthe. Def. quitclaimed to pl. & the heirs of Wm. £70.

85. Robt. Bedyngfeld, pl. Robt. Sawnderson, gent., & w. *Anne*, def. 10 mess. (etc., as in 55) in Stapilford Tawnye, North Wyeld Bassett, Theydon Gernon & Theydon at Mount. Def. quitclaimed to pl. & his heirs. And for this pl. granted the same to def. & the heirs of their bodies, with remainder to the heirs of the body of Robt. and the right heirs of Anne, to hold of the chief lords.

86. Tho. Reve, pl. Wm. Warde & w. *Margt.*, def. 2 a. ar. & 8 a. wd. in Ardeley. £10.

87. Jn. Cracherode sen. and w. Margery, pl. *Miles* Spylman, gent., Jn. Goldwell, gent., & w. Anne, Jn. Carter & w. Alice, def. 1 gdn. (*orto*), 2 gdns. (*gardinis*), 10 a. ar., 2 a. mw., 8 a. pa. and 18d. rt. in Thaxsted. £40.

88. Jn. Onywyn & w. Joan, pl. Nich. Uncle & w. Margery, def. 1 mess., 1 gdn. & 6 a. ld. in Great Horkessleygh. £20.

89. Jn. Wright & w. Margt., pl. Jn. Lebarde, def. 1 mess. in Barkyng. Def. quitclaimed to pl. & heirs of Jn. £40.

90. Trin. and Mich. Jn. Sampfurth, pl. Rd. Sampfurth & w. *Joan*, def. 1 mess., 1 gdn. (*gardino*), 1 gdn. (*orto*), 160 a. ar., 10 a. mw., 60 a. pa., 10 a. wd. and 20s. rt. in Good Ester, Rothyng Masye, Rothyng Margarett and Roxwell. Def. quitclaimed to pl. & his heirs. And for this pl. granted the same to Rd. for one month, with remainder to Denise Lukyn for life without impeachment of waste and Jn. Lukyn & his heirs, to hold of the chief lords.

91. Steph. Bekyngham, esq., pl. Rd. Merke, def. 1 mess., 1 gdn. 10 a. ar. & 10 a. pa. in Tolleshunt Maior. £20.

92. Jn. Paycock, pl. Jn. Sowthwell, esq., def. 1 mess., 2 cott., 3 curtilages, 40 a. ar., 16 a. mw. and 30 a. pa. in Kelvedon, Feryng & Ryvenhale. 200 mks.

93. Jn. Symon, pl. Robt. Thomas & w. *Eliz.*, def. 6 a. pa. in Buttysbury £20.

94. Wm. Cracherode jun., pl. Wm. Cracherode sen. & w. *Margt.*, def. 1 mess., 1 gdn. & 2 a. pa. in Toppesfeld. £20.

95. Jn. Lucas, esq., pl. Jn. Deane, def. 3 mess., 15 a. ar., 2 a. mw., 20 a. pa., & 10 a. wood in Great Horkesley & Little Horkesley. £30.

CP25(2)/57/419   HILARY, 1–2 EDWARD VI   1548

1. Mich. & Hil. Jn. Spreynger, pl. Jn. Hawmonde & w. *Margery*, def. 1 mess., 7 a. ar. & 1 a. mw. in Fyfhide. £30.

2. Tho. Myldemaye, esq., pl. Baldwin Dale and w. *Margt.*, late the w. of Rd. Love, decd., def. 1 mess., 1 cott., 2 barns, 1 stable, 4 gdns. and 12 a. ar. in Mulsham in the parish of Chelmesford. 55 mks.

3. Mich. & Hil. Wm. Goodwyn, pl. *Jn.* Ussher & w. Grace & Wm. Ussher, def. The manor of Boones & 100 a. ar., 15 a. mw., 60 a. pa., 20 a. wd. and 8s. rt. in Bokkyng and Gosfell. 85 mks.

4. Hy. Rockaden, pl. Jn. Tylney & w. *Denise*, def. 5 mess., 16 a. ar., 4 a. mw., 4 a. pa. and 4 a. marsh in West Thorock. £40.

5. Rd. Pety & w. Eliz., pl. Walter Cely & w. *Eliz.*, def. 1 mess., 1 gdn., 200 a. ar., 10 a. mw., 20 a. pa. & 10 a. wd. in Kelweydon and Navestoke. Def. quitclaimed to pl. & the heirs of Rd. £180.

6. Mich. & Hil. Wm. Gregyll, pl. Rd. Carable, son & heir of Cristina Carable, def. 2 mess. and 2 gdns. in Branktre. £20.

7. Rd. Heton, pl. Wm. Grey, def. 1 mess., 1 gdn., 1 orchard, 6 a. ar. & 6 a. pa., in Dagenham. 40 mks.

8. Jn. Osborn, gent., pl. Walter Dennys, knight, & *Hugh* Dennys, esq., & w. Kath., def. Manors of Snorham & Peverells & 4 mess., 2 dovecotes, 200 a. ar., 100 a. mw.,

400 a. pa., 200 a. marsh, 20 a. wd. & £6 6s. 8d. rent in Snorham, Lachyndon & Lytell Lachyndon, & the advowson of the church of Snorham *alias* Lyttell Lachyndon. £200.

9. Mich. & Hil. Hy. Parker, knight, lord Morley, & Hy. Parker, knight, his son & heir apt., pl. Jn. Abbott, def. 1 mess., 100 a. ar., 6 a. mw. and 16 a. pa. in Halyngbury Morley, Halyngbury Burcher & Bylchehanger. Def. quitclaimed to pl. & the heirs of Hy. the son. 130 mks.

10. Tho. Lawrens, pl. *Jn.* Lucas, esq., & w. Eliz., def. Manor of Harbardys *alias* Harbartys & 6 mess., 6 gdns., 6 orchards, 500 a. ar., 40 a. mw., 300 a. pa., 30 a. wd., 40 a. furze & heath & 60s. rt. in Raylegh, Rawreth & Great Hokley. 400 mks.

11. Jn. Wryght & w. Margt., pl. *Jn.* Lybarde & w. Margt., def. 1 mess. in Barkyng. Def. quitclaimed to pl. & the heirs of Jn. £20.

12. Wm. Pascall, pl. Wm. Camper, def. A moiety of 8 a. ar., 4 a. mw., 8 a. pa. & ½ a. wd. in Retyngdon. £25.

13. Wm. Kyng, pl. Jn. Osborne, gent., & w. *Denise*, def. 114 a. pa. in Althorn. £200.

14. Geo. Tuke, esq., pl. *Tho.* Darcye, knight, & w. Eliz., Robt. Gurdon, gent., & w. Rose, def. Manors of Layer Marney & Gybgrakys & 60 mess., 10 gdns., 1 dovecote, 2,000 a. ar., 500 a. mw., 1,500 a. pa., 600 a. wd., 300 a. marsh, 800 a. furze & heath & £20 rent in Layer Marney, Gybgrakys, Great Totham, Little Totham, Inforth, Feryng, Great Braxsted, Kelvedon, Messyng, Copford, Layer Breton, Wygbarought, Salcote Vyrle & Haybridge, & the advowson of the church of Layer Marney. £140.

15. Mich. and Hil. Wm. Seborough & Alice Gate, wid., pl. Jn. Salmond, def. 2 mess., 1 barn, 2 gdns., 1 a. mw. & 10 a. pa. in Pakelsham. Def. quitclaimed to pl. & the heirs of Wm. £38.

16. Tho. Lawrens & Jn. Lawrens, pl. Jn. Brett sen., son & heir apt. of Giles Brett, def. 1 mess., 24 a. ar., 5 a. mw. and 6 a. pa. in Tolleshunt Maior. Def. quitclaimed to pl. & the heirs of Tho. £40.

17. Rd. Ivett, citizen & grocer of London, pl. *Jn.* Osborne, gent., & w. Denise, def. 3 mess., 3 gdns., 40 a. ar. and 10 a. pa. in Rayleigh. 80 mks.

18. Joan Ballard, wid., & Jn. Ballard, pl. *Jn.* Freman & w. Alice, def. 1 mess., 1 cott., 1 orchard, 1 gdn., 20 a. ar., 18 a. mw. and 16 a. pa. in Kelvedon & Navetoke. Def. quitclaimed to pl. & the heirs of Jn. 80 mks.

19. Tho. King, pl. *Anth.* Hungerford, knight, & w. Dorothy, def. 16½ a. ar. and 55 a. wd. in Estham & Westham. £40.

20. Steph. Bekyngham, esq., pl. Geo. Badcok, def. 2 mess., 2 gdns., 1 orchard, 40 a. ar., 20 a. mw., 60 a. pa. and 3 a. wd. in Goldhanger, Little Totteham & Tolleshunt Maior. £40.

21. Geoff. Lukyn, pl. Denise Lukyn, wid., Jn. Lukyn her son & *Wm.* Palmer, def. 1 mess., 1 gdn. (*gardino*), 1 gdn. (*orto*), 10 a. ar., 2 a. mw., 8 a. pa. and 12d. rent in Goodester & Masshebury. £30.

CP25(2)/66/545   DIVERS COUNTIES

39. Mich. & Hil. Wm. Levesey, pl. Tho. Eve & w. *Ellen*, def. 1 mess., 16 a. ar., 5 a. mw., 4 a. pa. and 2 a. wd. in Great Halyngbury, Byrchanger & Storteforde, co. Essex, & property in Storteforde, co. Herts. Def. quitclaimed from themselves & the heirs of Tho. to pl. & his heirs, with warranty from themselves & the heirs of Ellen. £60. — Essex, Herts.

CP25(2)/57/419   EASTER, 2 EDWARD VI   1548

22. Jn. Collyn & Steph. Collyn, pl. *Jn.* Pryor & w. Ellen, def. 20 a. ar., 6 a. mw., 30 a. pa. and 6d. rt. in Bockyng. Def. quitclaimed to pl. & the heirs of Jn. £40.

23. Jn. Byrde, pl. *Jn.* Welles & w. Joan, def. 15 a. ar. in Tolleshunt Knights. £40.

24. Anth. Barbour, pl. Roger Parker & w. Anne, def. 20 a. ar., 4 a. mw., 60 a. pa. & 2 a. wd. in Halsted. Def. quitclaimed from themselves & the heirs of Roger, with warranty from themselves & the heirs of Anne. 100 mks.

25. Jn. Pryour, pl. *Ralph* Nalynghurst, gent., & w. Eliz., def. 20 a. ar., 6 a. mw., 30 a. pa. & 6d. rt. in Brancktree & Bockyng. £40.

26. Rd. Styleman & Wm. Sorrell, pl. Jn. Aynolff *alias* Ellys, def. 12 a. ar. in High Rothyng. Def. quitclaimed to pl. & the heirs of Rd. £20.

27. Tho. Sulman, pl. Jn. Cleydon & w. *Agnes*, dau. of Wm. Coo of Great Sampford, decd., def. 1 mess., 1 barn, 3 gdns., 20 a. ar., 1½ a. mw., 5 a. pa. and 2 a. wd. in Great Sampford & Little Sampford. £40.

28. Rd. Godfrey, pl. Jn. Seyntclere, esq., def. 30 a. ar., 30 a. pa. & 10 a. wd. in Weleigh. £40.

29. Rd. Kenynden & w. Margt., pl. *Tho.* Hobson, gent., & w. Adriana, def. 2 mess. & 2 gdns in Barkyng. Def. quitclaimed to pl. & the heirs of Rd. £20.

30. Hil. and Eas. Jn. Cornell son & heir of Wm. Cornell, pl. *Steph.* Cobbe of London, 'haberdassher', & w. Helen, def. The manor of Omystyde & 1 mess., 40 a. ar., 20 a. mw., 60 a. pa., & 12 a. wd. in Radwynter. Def. quitclaimed to pl. & his heirs. Warranty against Mary Bendysshe, wid., & the heirs of Wm. Bendysshe, decd. £80.

31. Jn. Wyseman, esq., pl. Jn., earl of Oxford, def. 1 mess. & 260 a. ar. called Moche Canfelde Parke in Great Canfelde, Takeley, Little Canfeld & Hatfeld Regis. £200.

32. Wm. Petre, knight, the king's chief secretary, pl. *Giles* Capell, knight, Hy. Capell, knight, & Edw, Capell, esq., def. Manor of Bacons & 10 mess., 5 tofts, 240 a. ar., 30 a. mw., 200 a. pa., 60 a. wd. & £4 rent in Bacons, Gyng Mounteney, & Yngatstone. 400 mks.

33. Steph. Nytyngale sen., pl. Nich. Jeppes *alias* Gyppes & w. *Margt.*, def. 1½ a. ar. in Widdyngton. £10.

34. Wm. Petre, knight, pl. *Oliver* Hyde & w. Thomasina, def. Manor of Gyng Margarett *alias* Margett Ing & 10 mess., 10 cotts., 6 tofts, 324 a. ar., 100 a. mw., 50 a. pa., 66 a. wd., 130 a. furze & heath & £10 rt. in Gyng Margarett *alias* Margett Ing, Nynges, Little Burstede & Great Burstede. £400.

35. Anth. Sparrowe, pl. Robt. Andrewe, gent., & w. *Eliz.*, def. 1 mess., 1 gdn. & ½ a. ar. in Maldon. £40.

36. Wm. Petre, knight, pl. *Wm.* Sabryght and w. Joan (and Edm. . . . .) def. 1 mess., 6 a. ar., 4 a. mw., 12 a. pa., & 6d. rt. in Gyng Mountney. £40.

37. Robt. Hunte, pl. Tho. Serle sen., def. 4 mess., 100 a. ar., 5 a. mw., 10 a. pa. & 5 a. wd. in Elmedon, Arkesden, Wenden & Lowghtes. Def. quitclaimed to pl. & his heirs. And for this pl. granted the same to def. & his heirs to hold of the chief lords.

38. Rd. Archer, pl. Tho. Deryng, def. 2 a. mw. in Theydon Garnon. £10.

39. Jn. Wiseman, esq., pl. Edm. Mordaunt, esq., & w. *Agnes*, def. Manor of Yardley Hall & 138 a. ar., 5 a. mw., 40 a. pa., 5 a. wd. and 10s. rt. in Thaxsted, Wymbysshe & Depden. £260.

40. Tho. Knyght, pl. Agnes Cock, def. 1 mess., 1 kitchen, 1 gdn. & 12 a. ar. in Bradwell by the Sea. 50 mks.

41. Jn. Brydges, pl. *Hy.* Tyrrell, knight, & w. Thomasina, def. 2 mess., of which one is called 'le Bores Hedd', 2 curtilages, 1 barn, 5 gdns. & 10 a. mw. in Chelmesford, Mulseham & Spryngfeld. £120.

42. Edw. Ley, pl. Tho. Powlter & w. Joan, Jn. Halle & w. Kath., & Chris. Blefytt & w. *Alice*, def. 2 mess., 3 a. ar., 5 a. mw. & 6 a. pa. in Blacke Nottley. 80 mks.

43. Hil. & Eas. Jn. Jeffrey, pl. *Wm.* Rydgeley, citizen & merchant tailor of London, & w. Alice, def. 5 mess., 50 a. ar., 30 a. mw., 40 a. pa., 20 a. wd., 20 a. furze & heath & 4s. 10d. rt. in Great Warley *alias* Warley Abbatisse, Craneham & Upmynster *alias* Upmyster. £140.

44. Hil. & Eas. Rd. Evererd, pl. Jn. Haukyn sen. & Jn. Haukyn jun., his son & heir apt., def. 4 a. mw. in Great Waltham. £20.

45. Clement Smyth, knight, pl. Hy. Sheldon, esq., & w. *Alice*, one of the kinswomen & heirs of Rd. (Ratclyff, gent., def. A moiety of manor of Terlynge *alias* Terlynghall *alias*) Margeries and 10 mess., 600 a. ar., 20 a. mw., 100 a. pa., (40 a. wd. & £10 rt. in Terlyng,) Fayersted, Boreham, Great Leyes & Hatfeld Peverell; a moiety of 6 mess.,

FEET OF FINES FOR ESSEX

2 tofts, (300 a. ar., 40 a. mw., 100 a. pa., 60 a. of) wd., 20 a. furze & heath & 40s. rt. in Halsted, Playstowe, Colne (Engyne & Stysted; a moiety of 2 mess., 100) a. ar., 20 a. mw., 100 a. pa., 20 a. wd. & 40s. rt. (in Runwell; & a moiety of 6 mess., 6 gdns. & 10) a. ar. in Maldon. £340.

CP25(2)/66/546   DIVERS COUNTIES

9. Hil. & Eas. (The King's uncle Edward, duke of Somerset, Mich. Stanhoppe, kt.,) Tho. Darcy, kt., & Jn. Lucas, esq., pl. John, earl of Oxford, def. Honour (*honore sive honorie*) of Henyngham at the Castle, the manors of Tylbury by Clare, Douneham, (Maldon, Flaunnerswyke *alias* Flaunderswyke, Bounches,) Flaxlond, Stanstede Mont- fychett, Burnels, Bentfyld Bury, Burylodge, Netherhall in Gestyngthorp, Garnons in Tenderynge, Toppysfyld, Wyvenhoo, Newors Batelswyke, Great Canfyld, Great Bentley, Dodyngherste, Lammarshe, Grayes in Henyngham Sybble, Prayours, Little (Geldham *alias* Little Yeldham, Earls Colne, Crepynghall, Warehylls,) Jepcrake, Parkys in Gestyng- thorp, Nether Yeldham, Great Yeldham, Barwyks, Scotnes in Toppysfyld, Shreves in Gaynes Colne, Paynes in Pentlowe, Peppers, Pevers, Estonhall, Fynggerett, Vaws, Colne Wake, Countesmede in Bumpstede with members, (Waltons in Purley, Waltons in Mok- kyng, Gubbyns in Tylbury *alias* East Tylbury,) Mountnessyng, Wennyngton, Kennyngton, Tenderynghall, Erlesfee in Bures Gyfford, Battelshall in Stapleford Abbotts, Hayes in Stowe, & Crustwyche, & 2,000 mess., 20 mills, 20 dovecotes, 2,000 gdns., 2,000 (orchards, 20,000 a. ar., 2,000 a mw., 15,000 a. of) pa., 3,000 a. wd., 5,000 a. furze & heath & £200 rent in Henyngham at the Castle, Tylbury by Clare, Downeham, Maldon, Flaunderwike, Bounches, Flaxlond, Stanstede Monfychett, Burnells, (Bentfyld Bury, Burylodge, Gestyngthorpe, Wyvenhoo, Newers, Battelswyke, Alresford, Grynstede, Est) donyland, Great Canfyld, Little Canfyld, High Rodyng, Hatfyld Regis, Great Bentley, Thurryngton, Little Bentley, Fratyng, Dodynghurst, Shenfyld, Lammarshe, Great Hennay, Alphamston, Henyngham Sybble, (Great Yeldham, Little Yeldham, Earls Colne, Crepyng, Great Fordham, Little Fordham, Chapell Parishe, Gestyngthorp), Nether Yeldham, Toppesfeld, Gaynes Colne, Pentloo, Fynggerett, Blakamore, Vaws, Colne Wake, Gosfyld, Hawstede, Wormyngford, Bumpsted at the Steeple, Helyon Bumpstede, Hempstede, Purley, (Mokkyng, Est Tylbury, Mountenessyng, Wennyngton, Kennyngton, Raynam, Alvelegh, Tenderyng, Buresgyfford, Stapleford) Abbott, Stowe & Fambrydge, co. Essex; & property in other counties. Def. quitclaimed to pl. & the heirs of the duke. 40,000 mks. — Wilts., Suff., Bucks., Salop, Devon, Cornw., Essex, N'thants., Leics., Norf., Herts., Cambs., Kent, Berks.

CP25(2)/57/419   TRINITY, 2 EDWARD VI   1548

46. Eas. & Trin. Philip Mordaunt, Robt. Mordaunt, gentlemen, Wm. Westley & Tho. Crofte, pl. Margt. Westley, wid., def. 1 mess., 8 a. ar., 10 a. pa. & 2 a. wd. in Great Barde- felde & Thaxsted. Def. quitclaimed to pl. & the heirs of Philip. £36.

47. Hil. & Trin. Roger Hygham & w. Alice, pl. *Tho.* Dyer, esq., & w. Frances, def. 1 mess., 1 barn, 200 a. ar., 40 a. mw., 200 a. pa., 40 a. wd., 50 a. furze & heath & 20s. rt. in Hayleff *alias* Haysley, Leigh, Purleigh, Woodham Mortymer, Maldon & Jenkynmaldons. Def. quitclaimed to pl. & the heirs of Roger. £396.

48. Eas. & Trin. Tho. Tyler, pl. *Wm.* Barnes & w. Eliz., def. 12 a. ar. & 8 a. pa. in Rocheford & Hawkewell. £33.

49. Jn. Fauns, pl. Tho. Staples & w. *Anne*, def. 1 mess. & 1 gdn. in Streteford Lang- thorne in the parish of Westham. Def. quitclaimed to pl. & his heirs. And for this pl. granted the same to def. & the heirs of Tho. to hold of the chief lords.

50. Tho. Malyn, pl. Tho. Wallys, def. 2 mess., 2 gdns., 2 a. ar. & 2 a. pa. in West- mersey. £40.

51. Hy. Burman, pl. Robt. Kegyll & w. *Anne*, def. 2 mess., 1 gdn. & 1 quay in Har- wich. £40.

52. Eas. & Trin. Edm. Wyndesor, esq., Hy. Hampden, gentlemen, Jn. Wylforde sen. & Jn. Wylford jun., pl. Jn. Hampden, knight, & w. Philippa & *Edw.* Ferers, gent., def. Manor of Theydon on the Mount & 60 mess., 1 dovecote, 60 gdns., 1,000 a. ar., 200 a. mw., 300 a. pa., 200 a. wd., 200 a. furze & heath & 100s rt. in Theydon on the Mount & the advowson of the church of Theydon on the Mount. Def. quitclaimed to pl. & the heirs of Edm. £600. (Notes at foot.) Certified in Chancery, Easter, 18 Eliz. Theydon for Thedon amended by mandate in court, Trinity, 18 Elizabeth.

9

53. Robt. Smyth, pl. Jn. Damsell & w. Margt., def. 1 mess., 30 a. ar., 2 a. mw. & 8 a. pa. in Elmested. £40.

54. Eas. and Trin. Anth. Broun, gent., pl. *And.* Corbett, knight, & w. Joan, def. Manor of Hobrughall and 10 mess., 200 a. ar., 30 a. mw., 40 a. pa., 60 a. wd. & 20s. rt. in Hobrughall, Little Hobruge, Great Braxsted, Little Braxsted & Wyttam. £240.

55. Eas. & Trin. Giles Capell, knight, pl. *Jn.* Dormer, gent., & w. Eliz., def. 60 a. ar., 20 a. mw. & 60 a. pa. in Little Reigne & Bockyng. 130 mks.

56. Wm. Sapurton, gent., & Edw. Maxye, gent., pl. Rd. Fan, def. 2 mess., 2 gdns. (*gardinis*), 2 gdns. (*ortis*), 20 a. ar., 4 a. mw. & 16 a. pa. in Thaxsted. Def. quitclaimed to pl. & the heirs of Wm. £100.

57. Eas. & Trin. Rd. Ryche, knight, lord Ryche, chancellor of England, pl. Geo. Tuke, esq., Walter Celye, gent., & w. Eliz., def. Manor of Southweld, except 1 mess. & 1 gdn. in Southweld, & 20 mess., 200 a. ar., 20 a. mw., 200 a. pa., 100 a. wd. & £20 rt. in Southweld & Brentwood, the rectory of Southweld & the advowson of the vicarage of Southweld. Def. quitclaimed to pl. & his heirs. Warranty by Geo. against all men. Warranty by Walter & Eliz. against themselves & the heirs of Walter. £1,190.

58. Rd. Tull, pl. Jn. Goodwyn & w. Anne, def. 1 mess., 1 barn, 1 orchard & 3 gdns. in Barkyng. Def. quitclaimed from themselves & the heirs of Jn. to pl. & his heirs, with warranty from themselves & the heirs of Anne. £40.

59. Eas. & Trin. Jn. Aburfurth & Wm. Spylman, pl. *Jn.* Ewen & w. Agnes, def. 1 mess., 1 cott., 60 a. ar., 4 a. mw., 30 a. pa. & 6 a. wd. in Thaxsted. Def. quitclaimed to pl. & the heirs of Jn. £80.

60. Baldwin Dales, pl. Chris. Heton & w. *Joan*, def. A moiety of 1 mess. & 1 gdn. in the hamlet of Mulsham in the parish of Chelmesford & a moiety of 2 a. ar. in Harvardstock. £40.

61. Eas. & Trin. Jn. Mountgomery, gent., pl. Tho. Hogate & w. *Margt.*, def. 2 mess., 2 gdns., 92 a. ar., 5 a. mw., 8 a. wd., 54 a. marsh & 7s. rt. in Assyngdon & Southfambrige. Def. quitclaimed to pl. & his heirs. And for this pl. granted the same to def. & the heirs of their bodies with remainder to the heirs of the body of Margt. & the right of Tho., to hold of the chief lords.

1548   MICHAELMAS, 2 EDWARD VI

62. Trin. & Mich. Jn. Lucas, esq., pl. Margt. Waspe, wid., def. 4 mess., 4 gdns., 100 a. ar., 20 a. mw., 100 a. pa., 6 a. wd. & 40 a. marsh in Frynton & Walton. 100 mks.

63. Jn. Buck, pl. Jn. Parker, def. 1 mess., 1 gdn. (*orto*) 1 gdn. (*gardino*), 8 a. ar. & 2 a. pa. in Ryckelyng, Ugley & Berden. £20.

64. Wm. Gosse, pl. Wm. Jackson & w. *Margt.* & Mich. Trenchefelde & w. *Joan*, def. 9 a. pa. in the parish of Ramsey. 10 mks.

65. Trin. & Mich. Charles Radclyff, gent., pl. *Nich.* Rossheton & w. Joan, def. 1 mess., 60 a. ar., 40 a. pa. & 10 a. mw. in Great Mapilsted. 40 mks.

66. Jas. Harrys of Great Bursted, pl. Robt. Cheke of Debenham and w. *Mary*, def. 1 mess., 80 a. ar., 20 a. mw., 50 a. pa. & 10 a. wd. in Great Bursted & Little Bursted. 80 mks.

67. Jas. Harvy, pl. Hy Tyrell, knight, def. 1 mess., 2 curtilages & 1 gdn. in Chelmesford & Spryngffeld. 40 mks.

68. Wm. Goodwyn, gent., pl. Tho. Turner & w. *Margt.*, def. Manor of Boones & 100 a. ar., 15 a. mw., 60 a. pa., 20 a. wd. & 8s. rent in Bockinge, Gosfelde, Stysted, & Haulsted. 200 mks.

69. Tho. Marvyn, pl. Robt. Kegyll & w. Anne, def. 2 mess. in Harwich (*Harwico*). £20.

70. Wm. Pascall, pl. *Rd.* Reynolde & w. Joan, def. A moiety of 8 a. ar., 4 a. mw., 8 a. pa. & ½ a. wd. in Retyngdon. 80 mks.

71. Wm. Goodwyn, gent., pl. Rd. Waulter & w. *Margt.*, dau. & heir of Tho. More, def. 13s. 8d. rt. in Stysted, Halsted, Branktre & Bockinge. 20 mks.

72. Jas. Harryson and w. Grace, pl. *Tho.* Wallys & w. Alice, def. 1 barn, 20 a. ar., 8 a. pa. & 2 a. wd. in South Wokenden. £40.

73. Jn Sowtherne, pl. *Jn.* Dey & w. Alice, def. 2 mess. & 2 a. pa. in Wyvenho. £20.

74. Jas. Lorde, pl. *Jn.* Bote & w. Joan, def. 1 tenement, 2 tofts, 2 gdns., 20 a. ar., 30 a. pa., 10 a. mw., 6 a. wd., & 10 a. furze & heath in Danbury. 50 mks.

75. Wm. Broke, pl. *Robt.* Thomas, citizen & merchant tailor of London, & w. Eliz., def. 7 a. ar. & 8 a. pa. contained in three several closes called 'Fysshes', 'Little Berds' and 'Brokefeld' and ½ a. mw. in Chygwell. Def. quitclaimed to pl. and his heirs. £20.

76. Tho. Thrustill, pl. Robt. Higham, gent., def. 4 a. ar., 35 a. pa. & 4 a. wd. in Purleigh. 50 mks.

77. Wm. Sydey, gent., pl. Jn. Mayston, def. 1 mess., 2 gdns., 24 a. ar., 2 a. mw., 10 a. pa. & 6 a. alder in Wythermundford *alias* Wormyngford. £36.

78. Jn. Freman, pl. Tho. Sulman & w. *Joan*, def. 4 a. ar. in Hadstocke. £10.

79. Jn. Nele, pl. Wm. Samwell and w. *Joan*, def. 5 a. ar. called 'Hobbysdone Stall' in Hatfeld Peverell. £10.

80. Eas. & Mich. Robt. Turnor, pl. Rd. Barcker & w. *Isabel*, def. 1 mess., 1 gdn., 15 a. ar. & 2 a. mw. in Wymbysshe. £80.

81. Trin. & Mich. Jn. Lucas, esq., pl. *Francis* Jobson, esq., & w. Eliz., def. Site of the late monastery of St. John Baptist, Colchester, & 20 mess., 2 dovecotes, 20 gdns., 3 orchards, 100 a. ar., 15 a. mw., 100 a. pa., 10 a. wd. & 7 a. marsh in West Donyland, Colchester (*Colcestria*), Grensted & Wevenhoo. £132.

82. Rd. Ryche, knight, lord Ryche, chancellor of England, Hy. Pygott, Edm. Mordaunte & Walter Farr, gentlemen, pl. Hy. Carye, esq., def. Manor of Leigh *alias* Lye & 10 mess., 10 gdns., 200 a. ar., 40 a. mw., 200 a. pa., 200 a. wd., 100 a. marsh, 200 a. furze & heath & 100s. rt. in Leigh *alias* Lye, Middelton *alias* Mylton, Prytelwell and Hadley, & the advowson of the church of Leigh *alias* Lye. Def. quitclaimed to pl. & the heirs of Rd. £200.

83. Aubrey Williams & Wm. Hunt, pl. Simon Wyllyams and w. *Margt.*, def. 1 mess., 2 gdns., 10 a. ar. and 6 a. pa. in Toppesfelde. Def. quitclaimed from themselves & the heir of Margt. to pl. & the heirs of Aubrey, with warranty from themselves and the heirs of Simon. £20.

84. Trin. & Mich. Robt. May, pl. *Tho.* Fannyng jun. and w. Clemencia, def. 2 a. mw. in Little Canfelde. 20 mks.

85. Tho. Crawley, esq., pl. Jn. Spylman & w. *Margt.*, Robt. Parmafay & w. *Joan*, & Wm. Teryngton & w. *Eliz.*, def. 1 mess., 2 cotts., 3 curtilages, 250 a. ar., 10 a. mw., 60 a. pa., 12 a. wd. & 20s. rent in Great Chyssell, Little Chyssell & Heydon. £160.

CP25(2)/57/420   HILARY, 2-3 EDWARD VI   1549

1. Jn. Gatys, pl. *Jn.* Higham & w. Eliz., def. 1 mess., 16 a. ar., 2a. mw., 6 a. pa., 2 a. wd. & 8 a. marsh in Tollesbury. £40.

2. Walter Myldemay, knight, pl. Wm. Myldemay & w. *Agnes* dau. & heir of Wm. Paschall, def. 2 mess., 100 a., mw., 100 a. pa. & 40 a. wd. in Woodham Ferrers. £80.

3. Jn. Heethe, pl. Geo. Harper, knight, def. 20 mess., 1 mill, 4 tofts, 16 gdns., 200 a. ar., 100 a. mw., 200 a. pa., 60 a. wd., 70 a. furze & heath & £10 rt. in Lacton *alias* Latton, Eppyng & Harlowe, a moiety of the manor of Lacton, & the advowson of the vicarage of Latton. £900.

4. Jn. Brokes sen., pl. Robt. More sen., def. 1 mess., 1 gdn., 4 a. mw. & 14 a. pa. in Brendwod, Weld & Shenfeld. £80.

5. Robt. Rochester, esq., brother of Wm. Rochester, pl. Said Wm. Rochester, esq., def. Manor of Mylles & 2 mess., 1 toft, 100 a. ar., 10 a. mw., 100 a. pa., 20 a. wd. & 20s. rt. in Stysted. £140.

6. Wm. Huett, pl. Tho. Ayleward & w. *Agnes*, def. 2 mess., 2 gdns., 2 orchards, 60 a. ar., 20 a. mw., 30 a. pa. & 20 a. wd. in Gosfeld, which Joan Bykner, wid., holds for life. Pl. & heirs to hold the reversion of the chief lords. £60.

11

7. Wm. Hogge, pl. *Wm.* Pawne & w. Ellen, def. 2½ a. mw. in Blakemore. £10.

8. Mich. & Hil. Rd. Hewett *alias* Luter, Jn. Hewett *alias* Luter & Jn. Collyn, pl. Robt. Saunderson, gent., & w. *Anne*, def. 2 mess., 1 cott., 1 gdn. (*gardino*), 2 gdns. (*ortis*), 80 a ar., 16 a. mw., 20 a. pa. & 4 a. wd. in Stapleford Tawney, Weyld Gullett & North Weyld Bassett. Def. quitclaimed to pl. & the heirs of Rd. £140.

9. Tho. Purcas, pl. *Jn.* Gyon & w. Margt. & Tho. Aylewood & w. Agnes, def. 1 mess., 2 tofts, 1 gdn., 60 a. ar., 5 a. mw. & 20 a. pa. in Great Yeldham, Toppesfyld, & Tylbery. £80.

10. Geo. Crymble, pl. Jn. Crymble & w. *Grace*, def. 1 mess., 1 gdn., 2 a. mw. & 10 a. pa. in Inworth. 40 mks.

11. Mich. & Hil. Geo. Frith, pl. *Humphrey* Shawe & w. Agnes, def. 30 a. ar. in North Wokyngdon called Westland. £40.

12. Mich. & Hil. Francis Wyatt, esq., pl. Robt. Sawnderson & w. *Anne*, def. 1 mess., 40 a. ar. & 80 a. mw. in Thaydon Garnon. £220.

13. Rd. Ryche, knight, lord Ryche, chancellor of England, Robt. Ryche, esq., & Anth. Broun, gent., pl. Hy. Carye, esq., def. Manors of Foulnes, Nesshewyke, Arundells Marshe, Newewyke, Estwyke, Southwyke *alias* Foulnes Hall, Rogworth, Mounkyngbarne *alias* Monkenbarne & Tyllett in Walletts, & 20 mess., 30 gdns., 5,000 a ar., 1,000 a. mw., 7,000 a. pa., 1,000 a. wd., 8,000 a. marsh, 6,000 a. salt marsh, 2,000 a. furze & heath & £10 13s. 4d. rt. in Foulnes etc. (*as above*), & the advowson of the church of Foulnes. Def. quitclaimed to pl. & heirs of Anth. £2,000.

14. Mich. & Hil. Rd. Ryche, knight, lord Ryche, chancellor of England, & w. Eliz., pl. Wm. Marquess of Northampton, def. Manors of Patchyng Hall & Woodhall le Hyde & 500 a. ar., 100 a. mw., 300 a. pa., 300 a. wd., 500 a. furze & heath & 100s. rent in Bromefelde, Chelmesford, Wryttell, Chignall, Great Waltham & Little Waltham. Def. quitclaimed to pl & the heirs of Rd. £400.

15. Mich. & Hil. Tho. Fyggys & w. Joan, pl. Jn. Braunche & w. *Agnes*, one of the daus. & heirs of Jn. Mays, decd., def. 1 mess., 1 barn, 1 gdn. and 2 a. ar. in Great Burstede. Def. quitclaimed to pl. & the heirs of Tho. £40.

16. Mich. & Hil. Rd. Tanner, pl. Wm. Harres & *Agnes*, def. 1 mess., 3 a. ar., & 3 a. pa. in Little Rane. 50 mks.

17. Mich. & Hil. Robt. Breten sen., pl. Rd. Byknold & w. *Margt.*, def. 20 a. ar. in Mokkyng & a moiety of 6 a. ar. & 30 a. heath in Mokkyng & Orsett. £40.

18. Mich. Welbore & Tho. Sampfurth, pl. Wm. Nevell, def. 1 mess., 1 gdn., 1 a. mw. & 5 a. pa. in Stowe Marrys. Def. quitclaimed to pl. & the heirs of Mich. And for this pl. gtd. the same to def. & his heirs to hold of the chief lords.

19. Mich. & Hil. Wm. Rutte, pl. Simon Stonerd & w. *Joan*, def. 1 mess., 1 cott., 2 gdns. (*ortis*), 2 gdns. (*gardinis*), 10 a. ar., 6 a mw., 20 a. pa. & 4 a. wd. in Wodeham Ferrers. Def. quitclaimed to pl. & his heirs. And for this pl. gtd. the same to def. for life, with remainder to Jn. Stonerd their son & the heirs of his body & the right heirs of Joan, to hold of the chief lords.

20. Trin. & Hil. Jn. Coker sen., pl. *Robt.* Higham of Stragell, co. Suffolk, gent., & w. Margt., def. Manor of Wychams & 10 mess., 10 gdns., 60 a. ar., 30 a. mw., 80 a. pa., 30 a. wd., 20 a. furze & heath, & 50s. rent in Wodham Ferrys, Stowe, Purley, Danbury (&) Wodham Mortymer. 200 mks.

CP25(2)/66/546   DIVERS COUNTIES

31. Clement Smyth, knight, & Thos. Curties, pl. Hy. Serle & w. *Alice*, def. Property in Cambs. & Mdx. & 1 mess., 140 a. ar., 60 a. mw., 200 a. pa. & 160 a. wd. in Wycke, Stebeneth, Boxsted & Myleende, co. Essex. Def. quitclaimed to Clement Smyth & his heirs. £2,240 — Cambs., Mdx., Essex.

35. Hy. Turnour, esq., & Jn. Parfey, pl. *Tho.* Barnardiston, knight, & w. Mary & Anne Barnardiston, wid., def. Manors of Ketton *alias* Kedyngton & Barnardyston & other property in Suff., & manor of Ketton *alias* Kedyngton & 15 mess., 600 a. ar., 100 a. mw., 400 a. pa., 60 a. wd., 200 a. furze & heath & £6 rent in Ketton *alias* Kedyngton & Sturmer, co. Essex. Def. quitclaimed to pl. & his heirs of Hy. And for this pl. gtd. the same to Anne for life, with remainder to Tho. & his heirs, to hold of the chief lords — Suff., Essex.

21. **Wm. Abell**, pl. *Jn.* Crystmasse, esq., & w. Muriel & Geo. Crystmasse, gent., his son & heir apt., def. 1 mess., 2 curtilages, 3 cotts. and 1 gdn. in the new hithe within the parish of St. Leonard, Colchester. £40.

22. **Wm. Browne**, pl. Def. (as in the last). 4 mess., 3 curtilages & 2 gdns. within the parishes of SS. Runwold & Martin in the town of Colchester. £100.

23. **Jn. Lawe**, pl. *Robt.* Gardyner & w. Joan, def. 1 mess., 1 gdn. (*gardino*), 1 barn & 1 gdn. (*orto*) in Chepyng Walden. £40.

24. **R. Upcher**, pl. *Rd.* Osborne & w. Agnes, def. 1 mess., 1 gdn. & 1 orchard in Bokkyng. £40.

25. **Jn. Nicolls**, pl. Jn. Jennynges, gent., & w. *Parnell*, def. 3 a. ar. in Chepyng Walden. £10.

26. **Jn. Moygne sen.**, pl. Robt. Browne & w. Eliz., def. Manor of Pyersyes & 2 mess., 2 cotts., 4 tofts, 2 gdns., 2 orchards, 1 dovecote, 100 a. ar., 30 a. mw., 200 a. pa., 20 a. wd., 20 a. marsh & heath & 30s. rt. in Stansted & Halsted. £140.

27. **Jn. Chase**, pl. *Wm.* Steven & w. Anne, def. 2 a. mw., & 2 a. wd. in Elmested. £20.

28. **Tho. Geslyng** & w. Ellen, pl. Tho. Cawston, gent., def. 1 mess., 1 gdn., 2 orchards, 1 toft, 20 a. ar., 4 a. mw., 6 a. pa. & 2 a. wd. in Rayley. Def. quitclaimed to pl. & the heirs of Tho. And for this pl. gtd. to def. & his heirs a yearly rt. of mks. from the same, payable at the Annunciation & Michaelmas, with power of distraint.

29. **Wm. Goodwyn**, gent., pl. Jn. Beald & w. *Margt.* & Rd. Upcher & w. *Ellen*, def. Two fifth parts of 20 mess., 10 gdns., 10 orchards, 200 a. ar., 80 a meadow, 100 a. pa. & 13s. 4d. rt. in Bokkyng, Branketre, Stysted, Halsted, Gosfeld, Panfeld & Felsted. 100 mks. (See no. 59.)

30. **Jas. Northon**, son & heir of Rd. Northon, pl. Jn Crystmasse, esq., & w. Muriel & Geo. Cristmasse his son & heir apt., def. 2 mess., 4 curtilages, 3 cotts., 2 orchards, 3 gdns. & 2 a. ar. within the parishes of St. James & Grensted in the town of Colchester. £30.

31. **Hil. & Eas. Anth. Coke**, kt., pl. Wm. Shelton, esq., & w. *Joan*, def. Advowson of the church of Mawdlen Laver. £40.

32. **Wm. Wolbar** & Jn. Smyth, pl. Hy. Northey, gent., & w. *Eliz.*, def. 6 mess., 4 cotts., 8 gdns., 1 dovecote, 200 a. ar., 50 a. mw., 50 a. pa. & 20 a. wd. in Alveley. Def. quitclaimed to pl. & the heirs of Wm. And for this pl. gtd. the same to def. for their lives, with remainder to Geo. Northey, son & heir apt. of Hy., for life, & the right heirs of Eliz., to hold of the chief lords.

33. **Jn. Stephyn**, pl. *Jn.* Cristmasse, esq., & w. Muriel & Geo. Cristmasse, gent., his son & heir apt., def. 2 mess., 4 curtilages, 3 cotts. & 2 gdns. in the new hithe in the parish of St. Leonard, Colchester. £100.

34. **Rd. Locke**, pl. *Wm.* Steven & w. Anne, def. 20 a. ar., 3 a. mw., 20 a. pa. & 10 a. wd. in Elmested, Alsford & Thoryngton. £40.

35. **Margt. Cock**, pl. *Jn.* Crystmasse, Muriel & Geo. (*as in* 33), def. 1 mess., 2 curtilages & 1 gdn. in the new hithe within the parish of St. Leonard, Colchester. £20.

36. **Hil. & Eas. Tho. Porter**, pl. *Wm.* Pawne, esq., & w. Ellen, def. 9 a. ar. in Stondon. 40 mks.

37. **Jn. Churche**, gent., pl. Joan Murfyn, wid., def. 1 mess., 1 kitchen (*coquina*), 1 barn, 1 gdn., 12 a. ar., 12 a. pa., 3 a. wd., 4 a. mw., 2 a. moor & common pasture in Great Totham which Tho. Sawen holds for his life. Def. quitclaimed to pl. & his heirs. And for this pl. gtd. the same to def. & her heirs, with remainder to Jn. & his heirs. 40 mks.

38. **Hil. & Eas. Jn. Cornell**, pl. Tho. Sylesden, gent., def. 1 mess., 18 a. ar., 4 a. mw. & 24 a. pa. in Bumpsted at the Steeple & Byrdebroke. £60.

39. **Tho. Goldyng**, esq., pl. Roger Strutt & w. *Eliz.*, def. 1 mess. called 'Adams', 100 a. ar., 20 a. mw., 100 a. pa. & 20 a. wd. in Belcham St. Paul. £40.

40. Hil. & Eas. Jn. Harryngton & Edm. Harryngton, pl. Tho. Ayleward & w. Agnes, Jn. Guyon & *Robt.* Guyon, def. 2 mess., 100 a. ar., 6 a. mw., 20 a. pa. & 11d. rt. in Great Maplested & Henyngham Syble. Def. quitclaimed to pl. & the heirs of Jn. 100 mks.

41. Hil. & Eas. Jn. Alsop, pl. Robt. Saunderson, gent., & w. *Anne*, def. 3 mess., 3 gdns., 1 orchard, 9 a. ar. & 4 a. mw. in North Wyelde Bassett, Stapleforde Tawney (and) Theydon att Mountt. £36.

42. Steph. Bentley, pl. *Jn.* Talbott, kt., & w. Eliz., def. 1 toft, 10 a. ar., 4 a. mw., 6 a. pa. & 2 a. wd. in Bumstede Helyon. £30.

43. Jn. Fowle & w. Margery, pl. *Jn.* Cristmasse, esq., & w. Muriel, & Geo. Cristmasse, gent., his son & heir apt., def. 1 mess., 4 curtilages, 3 cotts., 1 dovecote & 4 gdns. in the new hithe within the parish of St. Leonard, Colchester. Def. quitclaimed to pl. & the heirs of Margery. £40.

44. Jn. Hudelston, esq., pl. *Jn.* Cutt, kt., & w. Sibbella, def. Manor of Overhall & 1 mess., 1 mill, 90 a. ar., 20 a. mw., 155 a. pa., 25 a. wd. & 40s. rt. in Berkelowe & Asshedon. £200.

45. Hil. & Eas. Wm. Reynold, pl. Jn. Brown, esq., & w. *Cristiana*, def. 4 mess., one of which is called 'le Swanne', 16 a. ar., 3 a. mw., 15 a. pa. & ½ a. wd. in Chelmesford, Mulsham & Springefeld. £180.

CP25(2)/66/546   DIVERS COUNTIES

45. Wm. Webbe, pl. *Edm.* Scotten & w. Joan, def. Property in Nayland, co. Suff., & 8d. rt. in Great Horkysley, co. Essex. £80.

CP25(2)/57/420   TRINITY, 3 EDWARD VI   1549

46. Mich. Welbore & Jn. Mortelake, pl. Lewis Mortelake, def. 2 mess., 3 cotts., 2 barns, 2 gdns., 50 a. ar., 8 a. mw., 20 a. pa. & 4 a. wd. in Burdebroke & Steple Bumpsted. Def. quitclaimed to pl. & the heirs of Mich. And for this pl. gtd. the same to def. & his heirs, to hold of the chief lords.

47. Eas. & Trin. Wm. Noke, pl. *Wistan* Parker & w. Mary & Robt. Parker & w. Joan, def. 1 mess., 2 curtilages, 1 gdn & 4 a. mw. in Chelmesford & Mulseham. £(10).

48. Eas. & Trin. Jn. Joyer, pl. Jn. Crasson & w. *Joan*, def. 1 mess., 1 gdn., 1 barn, 5 a. ar., & 2 a. pa. in Manwden. 40 mks.

49. Eas. & Trin. Rd. Godfrey, pl. *Robt.* Taverner, gent., & w. Eliz., def. 10 a. ar., 2 a. mw. & 8 a. pa. in Stapleford Abbott. £40.

50. Eas. & Trin. Jn. Westwyke & w. Eliz. & Rd. Westwyke their son, pl. Rd. Poole sen., def. 1 mess., 1 orchard, 10 a. ar. & 8 a. pa. in Boreham called 'Trowers'. Def. quitclaimed to pl. & the heirs of Eliz. £40.

51. Eas. & Trin. Jas. Baker, esq., pl. Wm. Draywood, def. 1 mess., 52 a. ar. & 7 a. marsh called 'le Horse' in Bowers Gifford. £116.

52. Eas. & Trin. Wm. Draywood, pl. Jas. Baker, esq., def. 1 mess., 1 cott., 80 a. ar. & 180 a. salt marsh called 'Southstynkneys' and 'Wykehowse' in South Bemflete & Bowers Gifford. £234.

53. Jn. Webbe, clerk, pl. *Rd.* Bury, gent., & w. Eliz., def. Manor of Barlands & 7 mess., 200 a. ar., 100 a. mw., 200 a. pa., 40 a. wd. & 20s. rt. in Pryttelwell, Shopland & Sutton. £400.

54. Wm. Cardynall, gent., pl. Jn. Seyntclere, esq., def. Manors of Moveromes & Colehall & 6 mess., 4 cotts., 6 gdns., 20 a. ar., 30 a. mw., 200 a. pa., 30 a. wd., 100 a. furze & heath & 40s rt. in Great Bromeley, Fratyng, Elmested, Allesford & Great Bentley. £86.

55. Edm. Markaunt, gent., pl. Tho. Spycer & w. *Joan*, def. 2 mess. & 2 gdns. in Earl's Colne. £20.

56. Eas. & Trin. Wm. Clerke & w. Joan, pl. Rd. Poole sen., def. 1 mess., 1 barn, 2 gdns., 20 a. ar., 2 a. mw. & 4 a. pa. in Goodester called 'Omedes'. Def. quitclaimed to pl. & the heirs of Joan. £30.

14

FEET OF FINES FOR ESSEX

57. Tho. Willett, pl. *Hy.* Everard, gent., & w. Agnes, def. Manor of Smeton *alias* Smeton Halle & 300 a. ar., 40 a. mw., 100 a. pa., 40 a. wd., 40 a. furze & heath & 40s. rt. in Smeton, Bulmer, Water Belcham, Borley, Brondon & Little Henny. £200.

58. Jn. Hunwicke & Alan Hunwicke, pl. Jn. Puckyll, def. 2 mess., 2 gdns., 18 a. ar. & 3 a. mw. in Henyngham Syble, Hennyngham at the Castle & Great Maplestede. Def. quitclaimed to pl. & the heirs of Jn. £40.

59. Wm. Goodwyn, gent., pl. Wm. Whythed & w. *Margery,* def. A fifth part of 20 mess. etc. (as in 29). £40.

MICHAELMAS, 3 EDWARD VI   1549

60. Wm. Harrys, esq., pl. *Tho.* Darcy, kt., and w. Eliz., Wm. Cardynall, gent., & w. Lettice, def. Manor of Cryckesey, the advowson of the church of Cryckesey, & 5 mess., 200 a. ar., 30 a. mw., 200 a. pa., 200 a. marsh, 20 a. wd., 100 a. furze & heath & £5 rt. in Cryckesey, Aldorney & Burnham. £400.

61. Tho. Fretton, pl. Jn. Tabur & w. *Joan,* def. 1 mess., 20 a. ar., 2 a. pa. & 2 a. wd. in Great Waltham. £40.

62. Eas. & Mich. Nich. Colyn, pl. *Tho.* Sorrell & w. Joan, def. 1 toft, 1 gdn., 1 barn, 10 a. ar., 2 a. mw. & 6 a. pa. in Hyeghester. £20.

63. Anth. Stapleton & Wm. Pyreson, gent., pl. Jn. Dypdale & w. *Joan, Margt.* Peryman, *Alice* Peryman & Jn. Logson, def. 1 mess., 1 barn, 16 a. ar. & 6 a. mw. in Daggenham. Def. quitclaimed to pl. & the heirs of Anth. And for this pl. gtd. the same to Jn. Logson for life without impeachment of waste, with remainder to Eliz. Logson & the heirs of her body & the right heirs of Jn. Logson, to hold of the chief lords.

64. Rd. Smarte, pl. Rd. Townesende & w. *Kath.*, def. Manor of Hampton Barnes & 1 mess., 100 a. ar., 80 a. mw., 160 a. pa., 30 a. wd., 30 a. furze & heath & £4 rt. in Great Stambredge, Hadleygh, Asingdon & Thambrydge (*sic*). £220.

65. Mich. Welbore, pl. Tho. Burges, gent., def. 2 mess., 2 gdns., 30 a. ar., 2 a. mw. & 10 a. pa. in Branktre & Bokkyng & a moiety of 1 mess., 140 a. ar., 10 a. mw. & 40 a. pa. in Branktre & Black Notley. Def. quitclaimed to pl. & his heirs. And for this pl. gtd. the same to def. & his heirs, to hold of the chief lords.

66. Robt. Mascall & David Mascall, sons of Joan Mascall, wid., pl. The said Joan, def. 2 mess., 20 a. ar., 20 a. mw., 20 a. pa. & 2 a. wd. in Fynchyngfyld. Def. quitclaimed to pl. & the heirs of Robt. And for this pl. gtd. the same to def. for life without impeachment of waste, with remainder to pl. & the heirs of Robt., to hold of the chief lords.

67. Eas. & Mich. Wm. Gregyll & Gober (Roger) Fitche, pl. *Jn.* Beeld & w. Margt., def. 3 mess. & 4 gdns. in Branketre. £40.

68. Jn. Badcok, pl. Jn. Quylter sen., def. 24 a. ar., 30 a. pa. & 3 a. wd. in Colne Wake & Mounte Bures. 20 mks.

69. Wm. Harrys, esq., pl. *Rd.* Ryche, kt., lord Ryche, chancellor of England, & w. Eliz., def. 500 a. marsh & 50 a. salt marsh in Sutton & Little Stambryge in the island of Fowlnes. £400.

70. Tho. Symon, pl. *Tho.* Colford & w. Alice, def. 1 mess., 1 gdn., 1 orchard, 1 barn, 1 a. mw. & 14 a. pa. in the parish of Stondon. £40.

71. Wm. Pyrton, kt., pl. *Robt.* Gurdon, gent., & w. Rose, def. 60 a. ar., 8 a. mw., 60 60 a. pa. & 4 a. wd. in Tendryng, Little Bentley, Great Bentley, Wykkes & Mysteley. £40.

CP25(2)/57/421   HILARY, 3-4 EDWARD VI   1550

1. Wm. Smyth & w. Clemencia, pl. Rd. Kenenden & w. *Margt.*, def. 1 mess. & 1 gdn. in Barkyng. Def. quitclaimed to pl. & the heirs of Wm. £40.

2. Tho. Whyte, pl. Rd. Whythe, def. 2 mess. & 2 gdns. in Upmynster. £40.

3. Jn. Bendyshe, pl. Robt. Mordant, esq., def. 10 a. pa. called 'Rolves' in Bumsted at the Steeple. £20.

4. Hamo Amcotes, pl. Jn. Vaus, def. 3 a. pasture in Westham. £10.

5. Tho. Eve, pl. *Rd.* Ivat & w. Joan, def. 1 barn, 40 a. ar., 6 a. mw., 4 a. pa. & 6 a. wd. in Rayleygh. £40.

15

6. Edw. Sulyard, gent., son & heir of Eustace Sulyard, esq., decd., & Margt. Sulyard, wid., mother of Edw. & late w. of Eustace, pl. *Tho.* Cornewaleys, kt., & w. Anne, def. 1 mess., 100 a. ar., 40 a. mw., 100 a. pa. & 20 a. wd. in South Hanyngfeld, Est Hanyngfeld, West Hanyngfeld & Downhan. Def. quitclaimed to pl. & the heirs of Edw. £150.

7. Tho. Horlock, pl. *Hy.* Baker, son & heir of Wm. Baker, *Jn.* Nokes & w. Ellen, def. 3 mess. & 1 gdn. in Harwyche. 40 mks.

8. Mich. & Hil. Jn. Moteham, pl. Rd. Draper & w. *Joan*, def. 1 mess., 40 a. ar., 1 a. mw. & 20 a. pa. in Great Tey (&) Tey Godmer. £80.

9. Wm. Raynolde, pl. Jn. Cornewell, def. A moiety of 1 mess., 1 cott., 1 barn, 1 dovecote, 2 gdns., 80 a. ar., 10 a. mw., 40 a. pa., 10 a. wd. & 6d. rent in Boreham, Terlinge, Great Lighes & Little Badowe. 80 mks.

10. Mich. & Hil. Wm. Archer, pl. *Jn.* Newman & w. Eliz., def. 1 mess., 1 cott., 1 gdn. (*gardino*) & 1 gdn. (*orto*) in Brentwode. £30.

11. Wm. Sumpner, pl. Jn. Wyseman, esq., & w. Joan & *Robt.* Tyrrell, gent., son & heir of Humphrey Tyrrell, decd., def. 1 mess., 2 gdns., 60 a. ar., 20 a. mw., 40 a. pa. & 10s. rt. in Orsett. £160.

12. Mich. & Hil. Rd. Pynnell & w. Benedicta, pl. Rd. Draper & w. *Joan*, def. 1 mess. & 1 curtilage in Coksale. Def. quitclaimed to pl. & the heirs of Rd. £40.

13. Tho. Walleis, pl. Tho. Eve & w. *Juliana*, def. A fourth part of 6 a. mw. & 12 a. pa. in Bulfan. £13.

14. Jn. Churche sen., gent., & his son, Jn. Churche jun., pl. *Wm.* Cole & w. Edith, def. 1 mess., 40 a. ar., 40 a. pa., 30 a. fresh marsh & 140 a. salt marsh within the parish of St. Mary, Maldon. Def. quitclaimed to pl. & his heirs. Warranty against Wm. & his heirs & Anth. Cole, Rd. Cole & Robt. Cole & their heirs. £80.

15. Rd. Ryche, kt., lord Ryche, chancellor of England, pl. Hy. Carye, esq., def. Manors of Packelsam, Esthall, Southall & Wakeryngs & 20 mess., 10 tofts, 1,000 a. ar., 100 a. mw., 2,000 a. pa., 500 a. wd., 1,000 a. marsh, 2,000 a. salt marsh & 60s. rt. in Packelsam, Esthall, Southall & Wakeryngs. £1,120.

16. Wm. Cardynall, esq., pl. Jn. Seyntclere, esq., def. Manors of Moverons & Coldhall & 4 mess., 6 cotts., 6 curtilages, 300 a. ar., 40 a. mw., 200 a. pa., 30 a. wd., 200 a. fresh marsh, 50 a. salt marsh & 20s. rt. in Bryghtlynsey, Allesford, Thoryngton & Great Bromley. £400.

17. Mich. & Hil. Wm. Sorrell, pl. *Jn.* Wyseman, esq., & w. Joan, def. 1 mess., 2 gdns., 60 a. ar., & 10 a. pa. in High Ester. £80.

18. Mich. & Hil. Jn. Goldan, pl. *Anth.* Broun, esq., & w. Joan, def. 12 a. ar. in South Weld. £10.

19. Mich. & Hil. Edw. Chisshall, gent., Tho. Algor, Jn. Richard & Rd. Wynterflod, pl. Wm. Chisshall, esq., & w. Eliz., def. 5 a. ar., 3 a. pa. & 8s. 8d. rt. in Little Berdefeld & Great Berdefeld. Def. quitclaimed from themselves & the heirs of Wm. to pl. & the heirs of Tho., with warranty from themselves & the heirs of Eliz. 40 mks.

20. Jn. Godsalve, kt., & Tho. Gawdye, esq., pl. *Jn.* Brokeman, esq., & w. Anne, def. Manors of Powers & Bovyllys & 6 mess., 6 curtilages, 8 cotts., 6 gdns., 1 dovecote, 500 a. ar., 40 a. mw., 500 a. pa. & £6 rt. in Witham, Falkebourn, Fayersted, Terlyng, Hatfeld Peverell, Little Claston & Bockyng. Def. quitclaimed to pl. & the heirs of Jn. And for this pl. gtd. the same to def. & the heirs of the body of Jn. Brokeman, with remainder to his right heirs, to hold of the chief lords.

21. Tho. Franke sen., esq., pl. Wm. Marche, gent., def. Site of the late monastery of Bylegh, manor of Bylegh, & 5 mess., 1 dovecote, 2 mills, 100 a. ar., 300 a. mw., 1,000 a. pa., 80 a. wd., 100 a. moor, 100 a. furze & heath & 40s. rt. in Maldon, & the rectories of the churches of St. Peter & All Saints, Maldon, with all tithes & profits & the advowsons of the vicarages. Def. quitclaimed to pl. & his heirs. And for this pl. gtd. the same to def. & the heirs of his body, with successive remainders to Tho. Franke, son & heir apparent of pl., Jn. Franke, second son, & Francis Franke, third son, & the heirs male of their bodies, and pl. & his heirs, to hold of the chief lords.

CP25(2)/66/547   DIVERS COUNTIES

3. Hy. Payne, gent., pl. *Rd.* Martyn, esq., & Roger Martyn, his son & heir apt., def. Manor of Mary Hall & 1 mess., 140 a. ar., 14 a. 1 rood of mw., 12 a. pa., 18 a. wd. & 60s. rt. in Walter Belchampe & Gestyngthorpe, co. Essex, & prop. in Suff. Def. quitclaimed to pl. & his heirs. And for this pl. granted the same to def. & the heirs of Rd., to hold of the chief lords. — Essex, Suff..

CP25(2)/57/421   EASTER, 4 EDWARD VI   1550

22. Hil. & Eas. Jn. Collyn, pl. *Jn.* Jennyns, gent., & w. Joan, def. A fourth part of the manor of Otes & 6 mess., 6 cotts., 500 a. ar., 50 a. mw., 200 a. pa., 50 a. wd. & £10 rt. in High Laver, Little Laver, Matchyng & Harlowe. £103.

23. Hil. & Eas. Hy. Saye & Jn. Campynett, pl. Robt. Trappes sen., esq., & w. *Joan*, Robt. Trappes, jun., their son & Francis Trappes, another son, def. Manor of Takeley *alias* Bassingborns & 16 mess., 16 tofts, 16 orchards, 16 gdns., 1,000 a. ar., 400 a. mw. 1,300 a. pa., 200 a. wd., 800 a. furze & heath & 40s. rt. in Takeley, Bassyngbornes, Trendles, Rawrethe, Asshelden, Norpett, Caneuden, Hollande, Hockeley, Hadley & Trownderlysse. Def. quitclaimed to pl. & the heirs of Hy. And for this pl. granted the same to Robt. sen. & Joan for life without impeachment of waste, with successive remainders to Robt. jun. & Francis & the heirs male of their bodies, Joyce Saxe, dau. of Robt. sen. & Joan, & the heirs of her body, & the right heirs of Robt. sen., to hold of the chief lords.

24. Rd. Ryche, kt., lord Ryche, chancellor of England, pl. Hy. Fortescewe, esq., & w. *Eliz.*, def. Manors of Chatham *alias* Chatham Hall & Bromefeld & 10 mess., 6 tofts, 300 a. ar., 60 a. mw., 200 a. pa., 60 a. wd. & £6 rt. in Chatham, Bromefeld & Little Waltham. £620.

25. Jn. Whiter, pl. *Tho.* Spryng, esq., & w. Juliana, def. 1 mess., 80 a. ar., 20 a. pa. & 10 a. wd. in Great Horkisleigh, Little Horkisleigh & Berholt Sakvile. 100 mks.

26. Hil. & Eas. Jn. Mayster, pl. *Robt.* Taverner, esq., & w. Eliz., def. 3 a. mw. & 7 a. pa. in Stapleford Abbott. £20.

27. Jn. Lytle, pl. Robt. Browne, esq., def. 1 mess., 1 curtilage, 1 barn, 40 a. ar. & 2 a. mw. in Stysted, Pattvswyke, Coggeshall & Bradwell. £65.

28. Rd. Grene, pl. *Clement* Tusser, gent., & w. Ursula, def. 3 mess., 2 cotts., 2 barns, 3 gdns., 40 a. ar., 8 a. mw., 20 a. pa., & 5s. rt. in Cressyng. £100.

29. Tho. Mott, pl. Oliver Wryght & w. Collett, def. 1 mess., 1 gdn., 5 a. ar., & 1 a. wd. in Rocheford. £20.

30. Wm. Goodwyn, pl. *Roger* Wentworth & w. Alice, def. 2 mess., 2 gdns., 200 a. ar., 40 a. mw., 200 a. pa., 40 a. wd., 20 a. furze & heath & 40s. rt. in Bokkyng. £146.

31. Jn. Peppys & Jn. Wylde, pl. Philip Byrde, def. 10 mess., 8 cotts., 6 shops, 4 barns, 1 dovecote, 60 a. ar., 10 a. mw., 10 a. pa., & 10s. rt. in Walden, Lyttelburye & Debpden. Def. quitclaimed to pl. & the heirs of Jn. Peppys. And for this pl. granted the same to def. & his heirs, to hold of the chief lords.

32. Jas. Anderkyn, pl. Wm. Anderkyn & w. *Margt.*, def. 1 mess., 16 a. ar. & 8 a. pa. in Canneudon & Cryckesey *alias* Cryxheth. £30.

33. Edm. Mordaunt, gent., pl. Jn. Cutt, kt., def. Manor of Roos *alias* Rose & 200 a. ar., 100 a. pa., 20 a. mw., 100 a. wd. & £7 rt. in Walden *alias* Broke Walden, Thunderley & Depden. £300.

34. Mich. Welbore & Wm. Fowke, pl. Wm. Robynson, def. 1 mess., 1 gdn. (*gardino*), 1 gd. (*orto*), 160 a. ar., 10 a. mw., 60 a. pa., 10 a. wd. & 20s. rt. in Goodester. Rothyng Masye, Rothyng Margarett & Roxwell. Def. quitclaimed to pl. & the heirs of Mich. £140.

35. Gilbert Nevell, Tho. Josselyn & Jn. Asshedon, pl. *Ralph* Nalyngherst, esq., & w. Eliz., def. Manor of Nalyngherst Hall & 1 mess., 80 a. ar., 10 a. mw., 80 a. pa., 2 a. wd. & £3 rt. in Branketre *alias* Great Reygnes, Little Reygne, Felsted, Stysted & Bokkyng. Def. quitclaimed to pl. & the heirs of Gilbert. £140.

36. Tho. Richmund, pl. Jn. Cristemas. Cuthbt. Dawson & w. *Emma*, def. 1 mess., in Manytre. £20.

37. Clement Smyth, kt., Jn. Ackeleane & w. Margt., pl. *Simon* Trendell & Jn. Compton, def. 5 mess., 3 barns, 1 gdn., 100 a. ar., 40 a. mw., 100 a. pa., 60 a. wd. & 40s. rt. in Halsted, Stysted & Colne Engeain. Def. quitclaimed to pl. & the heirs of Jn. Ackelane. £164.

38. Wm. Haywood, pl. *Jn.* Clerke & w. Anne, def. 1 mess., 6 a. ar., 2½ a. mw. & 2 a. pa. in Harwardstoke *alias* Stock. £32.

39. Wm. Harrys, esq., pl. Wm. Anderkyn & w. *Margt.*, def. 50 a. ar. in Cryckesey *alias* Cryxheth. £80.

40. Wm. Rochester, pl. Rd. Elkyn & w. *Joan*, def. 1 mess., 1 gdn., 1 (a.) ar. & 1 a. pa. in Terlynge. £30.

41. Hil. & Eas. Wm. Stane, pl. *Tho.* Wytham & w. Alice, def. 1 mess., 30 a. ar., 7 a. mw., 10 a. pa. & 3. a. wd. in Norton Maundevile. £40.

42. Robt. Maynard, pl. *Jn.* Davy & w. Joan, def. 24 a. ar. and 2 a. wd. in Ardeleygh & Grynsted. £20.

43. Geo. Crede, pl. Jn. Tilney, esq., & w. *Denise*, def. 8 mess., 6 cotts., 300 a. ar., 60 a. mw., 300 a. pa., 6 a. wd., 20 a. marsh, 300 a. furze & heath & 5s. rt. in Hornechurche, Wennyngton, Barwik, Reynham & Alvithley. £80.

44. Tho. Pomfrett, pl. *Jn.* Glover sen. & w. Agnes & Jn. Glover jun., def. 1 mess., 1 curtilage & 1 gdn. in Chepyng Walden. £60.

45. Jn. Jenyns, gent., & w. Joan, pl. *Jn.* Wyseman, esq., & w. Joan, def. Manors of Olyves & Waldraines & 160 a. ar., 20 a. mw., 100 a. pa., 40 a. wd. & 100s. rt. in Great Dunmowe & Berneston. Def. quitclaimed to pl. & the heirs of Jn. 240 mks.

46. Anth. Broun, esq., & w. Joan, pl. *Rd.* Riche, kt., lord Riche, chancellor of England, & w. Eliz., def. Manor of South Weld & 20 mess., 200 a. ar., 20 a. mw., 200 a. pas., 100 a. wd. & £20 rt. in South Weld & Brentwood. £1,300.

47. Walter Bantoft, pl. Rd. Haymer & w. *Margery*, def. 1 mess., 1 barn & 1 gdn. in Hedyngham at the Castle. 40 mks.

48. Jn. Charvell, pl. Wm. Norman & w. *Eliz.*, def. 1 mess. & 1 gdn. in Pryttelwell. £20.

49. Wm. Draper & Tho. Cocke, pl. Hy. Vaughan & w. *Agnes*, & Wm. Dowe & w. *Agnes*, def. 1 mess., 1 gdn., 3½ a. ar. & 1½ a. mw. in Great Dunmowe. Def. quitclaimed to pl. & the heirs of Tho. £40.

50. Rd. Ryche, kt., lord Ryche, chancellor of England, pl. Hy. Carie, esq., def. Manors of Rotcheforde, Doggatts *alias* Dukketts, Upwyke, Strodewyke, Swayne, Myttons, Hawkwell & Commes *alias* Combes & 20 mess., 20 tofts, 20 curtilages, 2,000 a. ar., 500 a. mw., 3,000 a. pa., 1,000 a. wd., 1.000 a. marsh, 2,000 a. furze & heath & £20. rt. in Rotcheforde, Hawkwell, Upwyke, Strodewyke, Swane, Myttons, Lyttell Standysshe, Comines & Doggetts, & the advowsons of the churches of Rotcheforde & Lyttell Standysshe. £2,000.

51. Jn. Peryert, kt., & w. Eliz., pl. Ralph Nalyngherst *alias* Nauyngherst, def. Manor of Sir Hewghes & 2 mess., 400 a. ar., 50 a. mw., 100 a. pa., 80 a. wd. & £4 rt. in Great Baddo, Westhanfeld & Sondon. Def. quitclaimed to pl. & the heirs of Jn. £500.

52. Jn. Tomson, pl. Jn. Braunche & w. *Ellen*, def. 1 mess., 60 a. ar., 80 a. mw., 66 a. pa., 40 a. wd. & £10 rt. in (Theydon Garnon and) Garnon Hall; a moiety of the manor of Garnon Hall, 18 mess., 200 a. ar., 100 a. mw., 100 a. pa. & 20 a. (wd.) & waste in (Theydon Garnon & Garnons) Hall; a moiety of a third part of the advowson of the church of Theydon Garnon (this clause is in error repeated). Def. quitclaimed to pl. & his heirs the tenements, rts. & third part, & granted to them the reversion of the moieties, which Edw. Bysshop holds for life. And for this pl. gtd. the same to def. for life, with remainder to the right heirs of Jn. Braunche, to hold of the chief lords.

53. Wm. Rutter, pl. Jn. Motham & w. *Agnes*, Jn. Newton & w. *Grace*, & Roger Strutte & w. *Eliz.*, def. 2 mess., 1 curtilage, 2 gdns., 10 a. ar., 14 a. pa. & ½ a. wd. in Langenho & Westmersey. Def. quitclaimed to pl. & his heirs. And for this pl. gtd. the same to Roger & his heirs, to hold of the chief lords.

54. Jn. Bowtell, pl. Tho. Thurstell & w. Grace, def. 1 tenement, 1 gdn. & 2 a. ar. in Danbury. £20.

18

55. Jn. Turnour, pl. Simon Tompson & w. *Joan*, def. 2 mess. in Chelmesford. £20.

56. Wm. Fynkell, pl. Jn. Fanne & w. *Alice*, one of the sisters & co-heirs of Hy. Hedyche, & Tho. Grene & w. Joan, another sister & co-heir, def. 3 mess., 1 barn, 20 a. ar. & 20 a. pa. in Great Totham, Little Totham, Goldanger & Tolleshunt Maior. £30.

57. Rd. Esterford, pl. Tho. Humfrey & w. Margery, & Wm. Smyth & w. *Agnes*, def. 1 mess., 1 barn & 1 gdn. in Halsted. £20.

58. Ralph Warren, kt., pl. *Rd.* Fermour & w. Anne, def. Manor of Newporte Pounde *alias* Newporte Ponde & 40 mess., 200 a. ar., 60 a. mw., 200 a. pa., 40 a. wd., 100 a. furze & heath & £5 rt. in Newport Pounde *alias* Newport Ponde. £460.

59. Jn. Lucas, esq., & Wm. Markaunt, gent., pl. Rd. Sandes, gent., & w. *Kath.*, def. 5 mess., 20 cotts., 4 gdns., 3 orchards, 30 a. ar., 5 a. mw., 20 a. pa. & 8 a. wd. in Wyttham & Cressyng. Def. quitclaimed to pl. & the heirs of Jn. £40.

CP25(2)/66/547   DIVERS COUNTIES

15. Tho. Barnardeston, kt., pl. Jn. Barnardeston, gent., def. Property in Kedyngton *alias* Ketton, Barnardeston, Great Wrattyng & Hunden, co. Suff., & 4 mess., 10 tofts, 10 cotts., 50 a. ar., 10 a. mw., 20 a. pa., 2 a. wd. & 10s. rt. in Kedyngton *alias* Ketton, Haveryll & Styrmer, co. Essex. £140. − Suff., Essex.

CP25(2)/57/421   MICHAELMAS, 4 EDWARD VI   1550

(There were no fines in Trinity term. The session of the Common Bench was adjourned.)

60. Jn. Lynne, pl. Tho. Leightonby & w. *Joan*, def. A moiety of 1 mess., 40 a. ar., 20 a. mw., 20 a. pa. & 3 a. wd. in Fayrestede & Great Lees *alias* Moche Lees. £40.

61. Hy. Locke, pl. *Tho.* Ballard & w. Alice, def. 1 mess. & 13 a. ar. in Althorne. £40.

62. Trin. & Mich. Jn. Rogers, pl. Jn. Hawkyns & w. *Agnes*, def. A fourth part of 1 mess., 1 curtilage & 1 gdn. in Mowsham in the parish of Chelmesford. £18.

63. Hil. & Mich. Oliver Schuthilworth, pl. Jn. Baynham & w. Margt., def. Manor or mess. called 'Stockhaule' & 300 a. ar., 100 a. mw., 300 a. pa., 20 a. wd., 40 a. furze & heath & 5s. rt. in the parishes of Matchyng, Hatffeld Brodocke & Lytle Lavour. Def. quitclaimed to pl. & his heirs 100 a. ar. & the mess., mw., pa., wd., furze & heath, & gtd. to them the reversions of 200 a. ar., which Jn. Collyns holds for the life of the said Jn. Baynham, & the rt., which Wm. Stob holds for a term of 21 years, to hold of the chief lords. £280.

64. Wm. Castelman & Wm. Fox, pl. Wm. Olyff *alias* Lambert, def. 3 mess. & 1 gdn. in Harwiche. Def. quitclaimed to pl. & the heirs of Wm. Castelman. £100.

65. Jn. Ayle(tt) sen., pl. *Edm.* Sworder & w. Eliz. & Wm. Sworder & w. Denise, def. 1 mess., 1 gdn., 1 orchard, 4 a. ar. & 2 a. pa. in Ledon Rothyng. £20.

66. Bart. Averell, gent., pl. *Jn.* Lucas, esq., & w. Eliz., def. Manor of Bretton *alias* Bretton Hall *alias* Barton Hall & 5 mess., 200 a. ar., 50 a. mw., 300 a. pa., 300 a. marsh, 100 a. alder, 200 a. furze & heath, 100 a. wd. & £3 rt. in Great Stanbrygge & Little Stanbrygge. £280.

67. Tho. Devenyssh, pl. *And.* Broman & w. Agnes, def. 2 mess. & 1 a. ar. in Alvythley. £30.

68. Simon (R)use & Jn. Pecock, pl. Wm. Smethe, def. 1 mess., 1 cott., 2 gdns. & 1 a. ar. in Bumpsted at the Steeple. Def. quitclaimed to Jn. & his heirs. 40 mks.

69. Jn. Lucas, esq., pl. Geoff. Weyld & w. *Anne*, def. 4 mess., 4 gdns., 100 a. ar., 20 a. mw., 100 a. pa., 6 a. wd. & 40 a. marsh in Frynton. £80.

70. Wm. Colman, pl. Jn. Bredge & w. *Beatrice*, def. 3 mess., 1 dovecote & 6 gdns. in Coggeshall. £40.

71. Geoff. Vaughan of London, merchant tailor, & Wm. Hales, gent., pl. *Hy.* Bernes, gent., & Jn. Tyrrell, esq., def. Manor of Malgraves & 30 mess., 300 a. ar., 100 a. mw., 200 a. pa. & 20 a. wd. in Horndon on the Hill. Def. quitclaimed to pl. & the heirs of Geoff. And for this pl. gtd. a yearly rt. of 40 mks. from the manor & tenements, payable at the Annunciation & Michaelmas, to Hy. & his heirs, with power of distraint; & also gtd. the manor & tenements to Jn. & his heirs, to hold of the chief lords.

72. Emma Ower, wid., Robt. Ower, Wm. Ower & Roger Ower, pl. Jn. Goodeve & w. *Joan*, dau. & heir of Rd. Haukyn, decd., def. 1 toft, 1 gdn., 12 a. ar. & 1 a. pa. in Great Lyeghes. Def. quitclaimed to pl. & the heirs of Robt. £20.

73. Jn. Brokeman, gent., & Jn. Moigne jun.. gent., pl. Hy. Frankelyn & w. *Cecily*, Vincent Pett & w. *Mary*, Jn. Hardyng & w. *Joan*, def. 1 mess., 1 dovecote, 1 gdn., 1 orchard, 6 a. ar. & 8 a. mw. in Wyttham & Boreham. Def. quitclaimed to pl. & the heirs of Jn. Moygne. £40.

74. Wm. Harrys, pl. *Wm.* Anderkyn & w. Margt., def. 1 mess., 2 orchards, 6 a. mw. & 8 a. pa. in Cryxsey. £40.

75. Jn. Raymond, esq., pl. *Anth.* Staplton, esq., & w. Joan, def. 1 mess., 60 a. ar., 10 a. mw., 40 a. pa., 4 a. wd. & 5s. rt. in Fayersted. 100 mks.

76. Tho. Miller, & w. Alice & Jn. Miller their son, pl. *Tho.* Colte, gent., & w. Magdalen, def. Two parts of the manor of Takeley *alias* Waltham Hall, & two parts of 15 mess., 1 cott., 1 windmill, 16 gdns., 130 a. ar., 20 a. mw., 130 a. pa., 20 a. wd. & £6 rt. in Takeley. Def. quitclaimed to pl. & the heirs of Jn. 160 mks.

77. Trin. & Mich. Rd. Costen *alias* Nodes, pl. Bart. Tate, gent., def. 6 mess., 6 tofts, 20 gdns., 100 a. ar., 20 a. mw., 40 a. pa., 100 a. wd. & 10s. rt. in Barkyng. 400 mks.

78. Jn. Lucas, esq., pl. Wm. Bolter & w. *Denise*, def. 2 mess., 10 a. ar., 2 a. mw., 30 a. pa. & 8 a. wd. in Ardeleigh & Colchester. £40.

79. Wm. Scott, citizen & 'haberdassher' of London, pl. Alvered Michell, gent., & w. *Marion*, def. 6 mess., 100 a. ar., 30 a. mw., 30 a. pa., & 6 a. wd. in Stifford & Raylegh. 160 mks.

80. Jn. Lygett, pl. Hy. Frankelyn & w. *Cecily*, Vincent Pett & w. *Mary*, Jn. Hardyng & w. *Joan*, sisters & co-heirs of Tho. Chylde, decd., def. 8 mess., 6 gdns., 1 orchard, 18 a. ar., & 1 a. mw. in Wyttham. £100.

81. Tho. Legate sen., pl. Tho. Turke & w. *Mary*, def. 1 mess., 40 a. ar., 20 a. mw., 20 a. pa. & 6 a. wd. in Stapulforde Tawny, which Agnes Grene, wid., holds for life. Def. gtd. the reversion to pl. & his heirs. And for this pl. gtd. the same to def. & the heirs of their bodies with remainder to the heirs of the body of Mary & the right heirs of Tho. Turke, to hold of the chief lords.

82. Eas. & Mich. Wm. Parker, pl. *Geo.* Baldok & w. Agnes, def. 1 mess., 1 gnd., 12 a. ar., 4 a. mw., 20 a. pa. & 10 a. wd. in Leighton. 80 mks.

83. Tho. Dyer, pl. *Jn.* Pery & w. Joan, def. 1 mess., 1 gdn. & 3 a. ar. in Manewden. £40.

84. Jn. Rogers, pl. Hy. Osbourn & w. *Philippa*, one of the daus. & co-heirs of Jn. Warner & w. *Agnes*, dau. & heir of Jn. Tompson, & Chris. Fytche & w. *Joan*, another of the daus. & co-heirs, def. 1 mess., 2 cotts. & 2 gdns. in Mulsham within the parish of Chelmesford. £40.

85. Rd. Costen, pl. And. Wadham, gent., & w. *Anne*, def. 6 mess., 6 cotts., 4 barns, 1 dovecote, 5 orchards, 6 gdns., 140 a. ar., 14 a. mw., 40 a. pa. & 140 a. wd. in Barkyng & Ilford. 200 mks.

86. Eas. & Mich. Jn. Wyseman, esq., & w. Joan, pl. Agnes Smyth, wid., late the w. of Jn. Smyth, kt., decd., & *Francis* Smyth, esq., def. Manor of Asshewell Hall & 1 mess., 200 a. ar., 16 a. mw., 40 a. pa., 50 a. wd. & 10s. rt. in Fynchyngfeld, Wethersfeld, (Shalford) & Great Berdefeld, & 1 mess., 40 a. ar. & 10 a. pa. in Wethersfeld. Def. quitclaimed to pl. & the heirs of Jn. £300

87. Tho. Darcye, esq., pl. Edm. Moygne, gent., Jn. Lygett & w. *Alice*, def. 3 mess., 40 a. ar., 6 a. mw., 20 a. pa. & 4 a. wd. in Tolshunt Maior, Totham & Goldyngham. £60.

88. Jn. Wyseman, esq., pl. *Jn.* Holte, gent., & w. Anne & Robt. Holte, gent., def. Manor of Brokholes alias Roos & 3 mess., 300 a. ar., 100 a. mw., 300 a. pa., 100 a. wd., 20 a. marsh & 40s. rt. in Radwynter, Great Sampford, Little Sampford, Wyndbysshe & Hempstede. £400.

89. Jas. Anderken, pl. Jn. Borman, def. A third part of 1 mess., 20 a. ar., 6 a. mw. & 7 a. marsh in Cryxseth & Althorne. £40.

90. Tho. Thurstell, pl. *Jn.* Ultyng & w. Emma, def. 12 a. ar., 4 a. mw. & 4 a. wd. in Danbury. £40.

91. Trin. & Mich. Jas Dryland & Roger Holden, gentlemen, pl. Ralph Nalynghurst, gent., def. 3 mess., 3 gdns., 160 a. ar., 12 a. mw., 60 a. pa., 8 a. wd. & 50 a. salt marsh in Goldhanger, Great Totham, LittleTotham, Tolston, Tollesbury, Tolston Maior, Tolston Darcy & Great Badowe. Def. quitclaimed to pl. & the heirs of Jas. And for this pl. granted the same to def. & his heirs, to hold of the chief lords.

92. Tho. Sampford, pl. Geo. Jeffrey, 'yoman', def. 1 mess. & 34 a. ar. in Willinghale Doo & Barners Rodyng. £80.

93. Wm. Splyman, pl. Jn. Kent *alias* Reignold & w. *Margt.*, def. 1 cott. & 5 a. 3 roods pa. in Thaxsted. £30.

94. Jn. Ewcley, pl. Wm. Shipman, def. 2 mess. & 1 cott. in le Castlestreate in Walden. Def. quitclaimed to pl. & his heirs. And for this pl. gtd. the same to def. and his heirs, to hold of the chief lords.

95. Wm. Sumpner, pl. *Jn.* Burton & w. Joan, def. 2 mess., 20 a. ar., 10 a. mw. & 10 a. pa. in Eppyng. £80.

96. Wm. Spylman, pl. Robt. Goldyng & w. *Adrea*, def. 1 mess. called 'le Cage' & 1 gdn. in Thaxsted. £30.

97. Ankerius Merytt, pl. Tho. Stoughston, def. 1 mess. & 1 gdn. in Ging Hospitall *alias* Ingatestone *alias* Ingberners. £40.

98. Tho. Lodge, pl. Jas Atkynson & w. *Isabel*, def. 1 mess. & 6 a. ar. in Lordwenstrete in Westham. £36.

99. Hamo Amcotes, pl. Jn. Vaunce, def. 2 mess. in Westham. £40.

100. Jn. Jankyns, pl. Roger Warren, gent., def. 2 mess. & 2 tofts in Colchester. £40.

101. Jn. Yorke, kt., & w. Anne, pl. *Tho.* Harman, esq., & w. Kath., def. 1 mess., 2 gdns., 60 a. ar., 40 a. mw., 30 a. pa., 100 a. marsh & 20 a. furze & heath in Barkyng & Westham. Def. quitclaimed to pl. & the heirs of Jn. £360.

CP25(2)/66/547   DIVERS COUNTIES

34. Rd. Dobbys, citizen & alderman of London, pl. Alexander Coton, gent., & w. Mary, def. 3 mess. & 3 gdns. in Southwarke, co. Surr., & 1 mess., 1 barn, 1 gdn. & 1 orchard in Great Ilford, co. Essex. Def. quitclaimed to pl. for the life of Mary. £150. — Surr., Essex.

CP(2)/57/422   HILARY, 4-5 EDWARD VI   1551

1. Wm. Horne, pl. Nich. Jennyng *alias* Genyng, def. 1 mess., 1 gdn. & 1 orchard in Walden. £40.

2. Jn. Keyme, pl. Juliana Norwiche, wid., def. Manor of Kensyngton & 6 mess., 6 cotts., 100 a. ar., 40 a. mw., 100 a. pa., 40 a. wd., 120 a. furze & heath & 30s. rt. in Kensyngton, Dodynghurst, Shenifeld, Standen & Keldon. Def. quitclaimed to pl. & his heirs. And for this pl. gtd. the same to def. for life without impeachment of waste, with remainder to Wm. Peter, kt., & his heirs, to hold of the chief lords.

3. Mich. & Hil. Jn. Foxton, pl. *Tho.* Tyrtyll & Nich. Gresswell, def. 1 mess., 1 cott., 2 barns, 20 a. ar., 6 a. mw. & 20 a. pa. in Chepyng Walden & Wymbysh. Def. quitclaimed to pl. & his heirs. And for this pl. gtd. the same to Tho. for life, with remainder to Nich. & Joan Tyrtyll & the heirs of their bodies & the right heirs of Nich., to hold of the chief lords.

4. Trin. & Hil. Tho. Lodge, pl. Dame Isabel Gressham, wid., def. 4 mess., 4 gdns., 1 curtilage, 26 a. mw. & 4 a. pa. in Westham & Estham. £160.

5. Rd. Ryche, kt., lord Ryche, chancellor of England, & w. Eliz., pl. *Rd.* Smyth, gent., & w. Alice, def. 1 mess., 200 a. ar., 20 a. mw., 100 a. pa., 40 a. wd. & 20s. rt. in Bobyngworth, Castell Onger, High Onger, Stanford Ryvers, Grensted & Shelley. Def. quitclaimed to pl. & the heirs of Rd. £160.

6. Mich. & Hil. Margt. Sylyarde, wid., pl. *Arthur* Clerke, gent., & w. Alice, def. 1 mess., 2 cotts., 3 curtilages, 1 orchard, 2 gdns., 20 a. ar., 5 a. mw. & 30 a. pa. in Southanyngfeld, (Ron)well & Ramysdon Bellhouse. Def. quitclaimed to pl. & her heirs. 100 mks.

7. Mich. & Hil. Jn. Carowe, pl. Robt. Tyrrell, son & heir of Humphrey Tyrrell, def. 6 mess., 50 a. ar., 20 a. mw., 50 a. pa., 10 a. wd. & 5s. rt. in Shenvyld, which Francis Chauncy & w. Alice hold for her life. Def. gtd. the reversion to pl. & his heirs, to hold of the chief lords. £200.

8. Arthur Clerke, gent., pl. Geo. Cristemas, esq., def. 1 mess., 6 tofts, 4 a. ar. & 4 a. moor in Colchester. £40.

9. Mich. & Hil. Wm. Broke, pl. *Martin* Bowes, kt., & w. Anne, def. 7 mess., 1 curtilage, 5 gdns., 1 barn & 41 a. ar. in Great Ilford & Berkyng. £130.

10. Tho. Lynsell jun. & Lewis Lambard, pl. Rd. Fytche, gent., def. 4 mess., 4 gdns., 140 a. ar., 8 a. mw., 40 a. pa. & 8 a. wd. in Lynsell & Little Bardfeld. Def. quitclaimed to pl. & the heirs of Tho. £220.

11. Mich. & Hil. Launcelot Madyson & Jn. Glascocke, pl. Ralph Nalynghurst, gent., def. Manor of Frewells *alias* Cobbes & 3 mess., 3 gdns., 160 a. ar., 12 a. mw., 60 a. pa., 8 a. wd., 50 salt marsh & 10s. rt. in Goldangar, Great Totham, Little Totham, Tolleshunt Darcy, Tollyshunt Mauger, Tollesbury & Sandon. Def. quitclaimed to pl. & the heirs of Launcelot. £206.

12. Wm. Fensclyff, gent., pl. *Jn.* Androwe & w. Anne, def. 4 a. mw., 4 a. pa. & 8 a. wd. in the hamlet of Upshere & Waltham Holy Cross. £20.

CP25(2)/57/422   EASTER, 5 EDWARD VI   1551

13. Wm. Eve, pl. Tho. Bedyll, gent., def. 10 a. ar. in Chiknall Trenchefoyle. £20.

14. Robt. Clark, pl. Rd. Shorte & w. *Joan*, def. 1 mess. & 1 gdn. in Walden. 40 mks.

15. Roger Parker, gent., pl. Wm. Cracherode, gent., & w. Eliz., def. 1 mess., 1 gdn. & 2 a. ar. in Gosfeld. Def. quitclaimed from themselves & the heirs of Wm. to pl. & his heirs of Eliz. £30.

16. Wm. Petre, kt., pl. Robt. Collens & w. *Sibil* & Tho. Hatteler & w. *Joan*, def. 10 mess., 20 a. ar., 10 a. mw., 15 a. pa., 8 a. wd. & 10s. rt. in Harward Stoke & Buttesbury. 100 mks.

17. Tho. Carre, pl. *Wm.* Gente & w. Agnes, def. Manor of Moynes, 1 dovecote, 60 a. ar., 20 a. mw., 40 a. pa., 10 a. wd. & 10s. rt. in Bompsted at the Steeple & Byrdebroke. £100.

18. Jn. Malle, pl. Wm. Waldegrave, kt., def. 1 mess., 40 a. ar., 4 a. mw. & 40 a. pa. in Bures at the Mount & Wormyngforde. Def. quitclaimed to pl. & his heirs, at a yearly rt. of 18s. 4d. to def. & his heirs, payable at the Annunciation & Michaelmas, with power of distraint.

19. Robt. Monke, pl. Wm. Poley & w. *Alice*, def. 1 mess. & 1 gdn. in Chelmysford. £40.

20. Anth. Aspelond, gent., & Wm. Rutter, pl. Wm. Hoye, gent., def. 1 mess., 1 gdn., 2 barns, 2 orchards, 10 a. ar., 15 a. mw. & 12 a. pa. in Peldon & Aberton. Def. quitclaimed to pl. & the heirs of Wm. And for this pl. gtd. the same to def. for life, with remainder to pl. & the heirs of Wm., to hold of the chief lords.

21. Jn. Wyseman, esq., pl. *Edm.* Mordaunt, esq., & w. Agnes, def. Manor of Brodeokes & 1 mess., 200 a. ar., 6 a. mw., 40 a. pa., 10 a. wd. & 10s. rt. in Wymbysh, Thaxsted & Depden. £400.

22. Tho. Raine, pl. Tho. Bedyll, gent., def. 24 a. ar. & 2 a. pa. in Bromefeld. £30.

23. Hil & Eas. Wm. Beste, pl. *Jn.* Wyseman, esq., & w. Joan, def. 1 mess., 7½ a. ar., 7½ a. pa. & 4 a. fresh marsh in Chaldwell & Little Thurrocke. £40.

24. Hil & Eas. Robt. Sawyer, pl. *Jn.* Taylour & w. Agnes, def. 1 mess. & 2 gdn. in Leghe. £20.

25. Tho. Parker, pl. Roger Parker, gent., son & heir of Hy. Parker, gent., decd., & w. *Anne*, def. 1 mess., 20 a. ar. & 4 a. pa. in Wethersfeld. £80.

26. Geoff. Lorkyn, pl. Robt. Tyrell, gent., def. 1 mess., 2 orchards, 5 dgns., 100 a. ar., 60 a. pa., 20 a. mw. & 20 a. wd. in Shenfeld & Dodynghurst, which Alice Chansye, w. of Francis Chansye, holds for life. Pl. & his heirs to hold the reversion of the chief lords. £200.

27. Hy. Becher, pl. *Jn.* Lynge, gent., & w. Anne, def. 2 mess., 2 barns, 2 stables, 2 gdns., 2 orchards & 7 a. ar. in South Welde & Brentwood. 100 mks.

28. Robt. Poole, pl. Roger Parker, gent., son & heir of Hy. Parker, gent., decd., & w. *Anne*, def. 1 mess., 1 toft, 26 a. ar., 6 a. mw. & 16 a. pa. in Toppesfeld. £60.

29. Wm. Aylett, pl. Edm. Harrison & w. *Cristina*, def. 1 mess., 1 orchard, 1 gdn., 20 a. ar., 2 a. mw., 10 a. pa. & 16d. rt. in Cressyng & Wyttam. £60.

30. Wm. Crackerode, gent., pl. Roger Parker, gent., son & heir of Hy. Parker, gent., decd., & w. Anne, def. Manor of Hosyes & 3 mess., 52 a. ar., 7 a. mw., 32 a. pa., 2 a. & 21s. 8d. rt. in Toppesfeld, Hengham Syble & Little Yeldham. Def. quitclaimed from themselves & the heirs of Roger to pl. & his heirs, with warranty from themselves & the heirs of Anne. 160 mks.

31. Jn. Haryngton, pl. Def. as in last. 1 mess., 40 a. ar. & 2 a. mw. in Wethersfeld & Hengham Syble. Def. quitclaimed to pl. & his heirs, with warranty from themselves & the heirs of Anne. £60.

32. Wm. Pownsett & w. Ellen, pl. Jn. Burre, def. 20 a. ar., 10 a. mw., 12 a. pa. & 10s. rt. in Barkyng. Def. quitclaimed to pl. & the heirs of Wm. £160.

33. Tho. Rooper & w. Anabel, Jn. Pumfrett & w. Joan, Tho. Erswell & w. Margt. & Rd. Goodwyn & w. Agnes, pl. Francis Wryght & w. *Anne*, kinswoman & heir of Tho. Albery, def. 1 mess. & 1 curtilage in Walden. Def. quitclaimed to pl. & the heirs of Tho. Rooper. £52.

34. Edm. Markaunt, gent., pl. Jn. Beall, def. 1 mess., 1 gdn. & 4 a. ar. in Dovercourt. £40.

35. Rd. Peverell, pl. Wm. Poley & w. *Alice*, def. 2 mess. & 2 gdns. in Chelmysford. 80 mks.

36. Roger Hadstock, pl. Wm. Leevyng & w. *Eliz.*, kinswoman & heir of Jn. Bowbank, decd., def. 1 mess., 1 gdn. & 1½ a. ar. in Shalford. £20.

37. Robt. Sprynge, pl. Hy. Sheperde & w. *Alice* & Tho. Brette & w. *Agnes*, def. A moiety of 1 mess., 2 cotts., 3 curtilages, 10 a. ar. & 2 a. mw. in Great Yeldham. 40 mks.

38. Edm. Powcebye, pl. Tho. Crowder & w. *Agnes*, def. 1 mess. in Walden in Castelstrete. £40.

39. Tho. Willowes of Hadstok, pl. Robt. Trygge & w. *Agnes* & *Anne* Mason, one of the daus. of Nich. Mason, decd., def. 2 mess., 1 toft, 1 gdn., 2 barns, 10 a. ar., 5 a. mw., 30 a. pa. & wd. in Hadstok. 200 mks.

40. Hil. & Eas. Wm. Stamer, pl. Jn. Elesford, def. 1 mess., 1 gdn., 8 a. ar., 3 a. mw. & 10 a. pa. in Leghe. £40.

41. Rd. Everard sen., pl. Tho. Bedyll, gent., def. 1 mess., 1 barn, 1 gdn., 3 a. ar., 4 a. mw. & 5 a. pa. in Great Waltham. £30.

42. Hil. & Eas. Ranulph Lynne, gent., pl. Wm. Tadelowe & w. *Alice*, def. 1 mess., 1 dovecote, 100 a. ar., 20 a. mw., 40 a. pa., 20 a. wd. & 5s. rt. in Nether Yeldham. £80

43. Tho. Wrothe, kt., & Ralph Standysshe, gent., pl. *Tho.* Audeley, esq., & w. Juliana, def. Manor of Pryours Maner & 6 mess., 500 a. ar., 60 a. mw., 300 a. pa., 200 a. wd. & £10 rt. in Pritewell *alias* Prittelwell, Estwoode, Hadley & Lee, & the rectory of the parish church of Pritewell alias Prittelwell & the advowson of the church & vicarage. Def. quitclaimed to pl. & the heirs of Tho. £400.

CP25(2)/66/548   DIVERS COUNTIES

3. Steph. Hales, pl. Wm. Garnett & w. *Agnes*, def. Property in Broxborne, co. Herts. & 8 a. mw. & 2 a. fresh marsh in Nasyng, co. Essex. Def. quitclaimed to pl. & his heirs.

And for this pl. gtd. the same to Wm. & his heirs, to hold of the chief lords. — Herts., Essex.

CP(2)/57/422   MICHAELMAS, 5 EDWARD VI   1551

44. Eas. & Mich. Rd. Hart, pl. *Wm.* Westwyck & w. Dorothy, def. 1 mess., 1 barn, 1 gdn. & 1 a. ar. in Plecy & Great Waltham. (*There were no fines in Trinity term. The session of the Common Bench was adjourned.*) £20.

45. Eas. & Mich. Tho. Gregyll, pl. Jn. Vaunce, kinsman & next heir of Joan Wylford, decd., def. 1 mess., 1 gdn., 1 archard & 10 a. ar. in Branketre. £80.

46. Eas. & Mich. Jn. Paschall, gent., pl. Robt. Kyng, gent., & w. *Lettice*, def. 1 mess., 2 gdns. & 1 a. mw. in Great Badewe. £20.

47. Eas. & Mich. Robt. Stevyn, pl. *Jn.* Lydgeard & w. Alice, def. 1 mess., 1 gdn. & 1 orchard in Witham. £20.

48. Jn. Kyngsman, gent., pl. Tho. Rampston sen., gent., def. 1 mess., 3 curtilages, 1 barn, 2 orchards, 2 gdns., 12 a. ar., 10 a. mw., 10 a. pa. & 2 a. wd. in Great Braxsted. 80 mks.

49. Wm. Hylles & w. Agnes, pl. Tho. Woodward & w. *Joan*, dau. & heir of Walter Ryppyngale, decd., def. 1 mess., 1 gdn. & 1 orchard called 'Body Deyes' in Aldham. Def. quitclaimed to pl. & the heirs of Wm. £20.

50. Wm. Pounsett & w. Ellen, pl. *Rd.* Tull & w. Margt., def. 1 mess., 1 barn, 1 stable & 1 gdn. in the town of Barkyng. Def. quitclaimed to pl. & the heirs of Wm. £40.

51. Jn. Howe, pl. Jn. Langley, def. 2 mess., 2 gdns., 3 tofts, 20 a. ar., 2 a. mw., 20 a. pa. & 1 a. wd. in Great Clacton. £40.

52. Jas. Myller & w. Agnes, pl. Joan Tanner, wid., def. 1 mess. & 1 curtilage in Barkyng. Def. quitclaimed to pl. & the heirs of Jas. £20.

53. Eas. & Mich. Jn. Bridges, pl. Robt. Kyng, gent., & w. *Lettice*, def. 12 mess., 4 curtilages, 1 barn, 20 gdns., 2 orchards, 5 a. mw., 7 a. pa., 1 a. wd. & 5s. rt. in the hamlet of Mulsham in the parish of Chelmefford, Bromeffeld & Great Badewe. £200.

54. Eas. & Mich. Wm. Gate, pl. Tho. Moore of the City of London, 'mercer', & w. *Eliz.*, def. 1 mess., 2 gdns., 16 a. ar. & 4 a. pa. in Thaxsted. £20.

55. Jas. Thurnebecke, pl. Tho. Woodward & w. *Joan*, def. 1 mess., 1 gdn. & 2½ a. pa. in Aldham. £30.

56. Joan Salter, wid., pl. Hy. Fortescue, esq., def. 1 barn, 2 a. mw. & 3 a. pa. called 'Whyghtts' in Terlyng. £10.

57. Rd. Enewes & Geo. Chaterton, pl. Robt. Grene, def. 1 mess., 1 gdn., 4 a. ar., 3 a. mw. & 4 a. pa. in Earls Colne & Colne Engayne. Def. quitclaimed to pl. & the heirs of Rd. £40.

58. Rd. Wood, pl. *Jn.* Hunte jun. & w. Marion, def. 1 mess., 2 curtilages, 1 barn, 1 gdn., 8 a. ar. & 4 a. pa. in Ardelegh. £20.

59. Wm. Walgrave, pl. Tho. Bynder & w. *Thomasina*, def. 30 a. ar., 6 a. mw. & 8 a. wd. in Fratyng. £30.

60. Tho. Sorrell, pl. Humphrey Bagsha, gent., & w. *Agnes*, def. 3 mess. & 6 gdns. in Chelmesford & Mulsham. £20.

61. Robt. Smyth, pl. Robt. Tottenham, son & heir of Wm. Tottenham, decd., def. 1 mess., 6 a ar., 10 a. mw. & 4 a. pa. called 'warrens' in Great Sampfford & Hempsted. 40 mks.

62. Jn. Burnam, pl. Jn. Rowe & w. *Eliz.* & Edw. Wood & w. *Joan*, def. 1 mess. & 5 roods land in Westham & Westham Marshe. £20.

63. Jn. Heyward, pl. Wm. Ayloff, esq., def. 1 mess. & 1 a. salt marsh in Ramesey. £20.

64. Jn. Warren & w. Joan, pl. Nich. Fann, def. 1 barn & 14 a. ar. in Thaxsted called 'Dryvers', 'Bretts' & 'Hungerwells'. Def. quitclaimed to pl. & the heirs of Joan. £30.

65. Eas. & Mich. Rd. Meade, pl. *Tho.* Grey & w. Alice, def. Manor of Chamberlyns & 60 a. ar., 15 a. mw., 10 a. pa. & 10s. rt. in Claveryng. £80.

66. Jn. Machell, citizen & 'haberdassher' of London, pl. *Anth.*Fabyan & w. Thomasina, def. 1 mess., 1 gdn., 30 a. ar., 10 a. mw. & 10 a. pa. in Estham, Westham, Estwestham, Placeys, Estham Burnells, Westham Burnells & Leyghton. £40.

67. Eas. & Mich. Humphrey Frith & w. Roburga, pl. *Geo.* Tuke, esq., Anth. Broun, esq., & Jn. Lyndesell, def. 1 mess., 1 orchard, 2 gdns., 1 barn, 40 a. ar., 12 a. mw., 70 a. pa. & 4 a. wd. in Southwell called 'Bowells' *alias* 'Cok a Bowells'. Def. quitclaimed to pl. & the heirs of Humphrey. £60.

68. Jn. Mersshe, pl. Jn. Taverner & w. *Margt.*, def. A third part or purparty of 6 a. mw. & 12 a. pa. in Great Stanbridge. £40.

69. Jn. Richards *alias* Baker & w. Lucy, pl. *Jn* Stanys & w. Millicent, def. 4 mess., 2 gdns., 2 orchards, 2 barns, 20 a. ar., 1 a. mw., 2 a. pa. & 4 a. wd. in Henham. Def. quitclaimed to pl. & the heirs of Jn. £100.

70. Eas. & Mich. Jn. Core & w. Anne, pl. *Tho.* Everard & w. Margt. & *Geo.* Baye & w. Marion, def. 1 mess., 1 gdn., 1 orchard, 1 barn, 120 a. ar., 24 a. mw., 60 a. pa. & 8 a. wd. in Hatfeld Brokeoke *alias* Kyngis Hatfeld. Def. quitclaimed to pl. & the heirs of Jn. £140.

71. Trin. & Mich. Nich. Stuard, pl. Tho. Johnson, def. 1 mess., 1 gdn., 1 orchard, 6 tofts, 20 a. ar., 8 a. mw., 60 a. pa. & 6 a. wd. in Bradfeld & Wyckes, which Cecily Johnson, wid., holds for life, with remainder to def. & the heirs of his body. Pl. & his heirs to hold the remainder of the chief lords. £40.

72. Wm. Goodwyn, gent., pl. Jn. Sherpe & w. *Joan*, def. 3 mess., 3 gdns., 3 orchards & 16d. rt. in Bokkyng. £40.

73. Wm. Lawrens & Robt. Damsel, pl. Rd. Aulfeld jun. & w. *Joan*, one of the sisters & heirs of Chris. Stede, def. A moiety of the manor of Benyngtons & a moiety of 1 mess., 60 a. ar., 10 a. mw., 20 a. pa. & 4 a. wd. in Wyttham, Wyckham & Hatefelde Peverell. Def. quitclaimed to pl. & the heirs of Wm. And for this pl. gtd. the same to def. for their lives without impeachment of waste, with remainder to the right heirs of Rd., to hold of the chief lords.

74. Wm. Lyonell & Jn. Pyreson, pl. Steph. Lyonell & w. *Anne*, def. 1 mess. & 1 gdn. in Barkyng. Def. quitclaimed to pl. & the heirs of Wm. And for this pl. gtd. the same to def. & the heirs of their bodies, with remainder to the right heirs of Steph., to hold of the chief lords.

75. Mary Parker, wid., pl. Jn. Parker, def. A third part of the rectory & church of Claveryng; a third part of 240 a. ar., 10 a. mw., 20 a. wd. & 20s. rt. in Claveryng & Langeley; & a third part of the advowson of the vicarage of Claveryng. Def. quitclaimed to pl. & her heirs. 200 mks.

76. Tho. Colte, gent., pl. Rd. Banester, gent., def. 3 mess., 2 gdns., 2 orchards, 1 dovecote, 3 barns, 40 a. ar., 60 a. mw., 60 a. pa. & 10 a. wd. in Waltham Holy Cross *alias* Waltham 'of the Holy Crosse' & Halifelde, & common of pasture for 28 sheep in the same places. £220.

77. Philip Mordaunt, son & heir apt. of Robt. Mordaunte, esq., & w. Mary, pl. The same Robt. & w. *Barbara*, def. Manor of Barneys Rodyng & 10 mess., 6 cotts., 4 tofts, 1 dovecote, 10 gdns., 300 a. ar., 30 a. mw., 200 a. pa., 100 a. wd., 100s. rt. & a rt. of 12 capons in Barneys Rodyng. Def. gtd. the same to pl. for their lives, with remainder to the heirs male of Philip of the body of Mary, the heirs male of the body of Philip & the heirs of the body of Philip, to hold of Robt. & his heirs at a yearly rt. of £6 13s. 4d. to Robt. for his life, payable at the Annunciation & Michaelmas; with reversion to Robt. & his heirs, to hold of the chief lords.

78. Wm. Moore, clk., & Arthur Kemp, pl. *Wm.* Poore, gent., & w. Joan, def. 4 mess., 1 toft, 5 gdns., 126 a. ar., 6 a. mw. & 50 a. pa. in Great Byrche, Little Byrche, Stanwey, Esthorp, Copforth & Langenho. Def. quitclaimed to pl. & the heirs of Wm. And for this pl. gtd. to def. & the heirs of Wm. 1 mess. called 'Goodwyns', 1 gdn. & 50 a. ar. in Great Byrche, Little Byrche, Stanwey & Copforth & 1 mess. called 'Lucassys', 1 gdn. & 12 a. ar. in Great Byrche, parcel of the above, to hold of the chief lords; & to Wm. & his heirs 2 mess., 1 toft, 3 gdns., 64 a. ar., 6 a. mw. & 50 a. pa., in Great Byrche, Little Byrche, Esthorp & Langenhoo, the residue, to hold of the chief lords.

79. Law. Warren, citizen & goldsmith of London, pl. *John* Seyntclere, esq., & Wm. Cardynall, esq., def. Manor of Moverone *alias* Morehams & 10 mess., 10 gdns., 1,000 a. ar., 200 a. mw., 800 a. pa., 400 a. marsh, 30 a. wd. & 20s. rt. in Moverons, Morehams, Bryghtlynsey, Thoryngton & Allesford, & free warren in Bryghtlynsey. £550.

80. Wm. Austyn & w. Juliana, pl. Tho. Moyle, kt., and w. *Kath.* def. Manor of Gerpyns & 3 mess., 2 gdns, 2 orchards, 1 dovecote, 2 barns, 160 a. ar., 9 a. mw., 30 a. pa., 6 a. wd. & 9s. 1d. rt. in Reynham. Pl. & the heirs of their bodies to hold of the chief lords, with remainder to the first born son of the body of Juliana for life & the right heirs of Wm. £140.

81. Trin. & Mich. Jn. Machyn & Arthur Kempe, gentlemen, pl. *Jn.* Paschall, gent., & w. Mary, def. 1 mess., 2 curtilages, 1 barn, 1 dovecote, 2 gdns., 1 orchard, 20 a. ar., 6 a. mw., 37 a. pa. & 7 a. wd. called 'Sabryghtes' in Great Badewe. Def. quitclaimed to pl. & the heirs of Jn. And for this pl. gtd. to Jn. Paschall a yearly rt. of 15s. from the same, payable at Michaelmas & the Annunciation, with power of distraint; & also gtd. the tenements to Mary for one month, with remainder to (Robt.) Kynge & his heirs, to hold of the chief lords.

CP25(2)/66/548   DIVERS COUNTIES

36. Eas. & Mich. Robt. Bewyk, pl. *Francis* Pryour & w. Margt., def. Property in Suss., & 2 mess., 1 barn, 1 gdn., 1 orchard & 6 a. ar. in Daggenham, co. Essex. Def. quitclaimed to pl. & heirs. And for this pl. gtd. the same to def. for their lives, with remainder to the heirs of Francis of the body of Margt. & the right heirs of Francis, to hold of the chief lords. — Suss., Essex.

CP25(2)/57/423   HILARY, 5–6 EDWARD VI   1552

1. Robt. Wythe, gent., pl. Paul Wylkynson, gent., def. 1 mess., 1 barn, 1 gdn., 40 a. ar., 20 a. mw., 20 a. pa. & 20 a. furze & heath in Esthame & Little Elleforde. £100.

2. Wm. Marcoll & Tho. Wolman, 'shomaker', Jn. Bysshoppe *alias* Peryn, def. 1 mess., 2 gdns., 9 a. ar. & 3 a. pa. in Stansted Mountfychet. Def. quitclaimed to pl. & the heirs of Wm. £60.

3. Jn. Cutter, pl. Jn. Hunton *alias* Harper & w. *Annastacia* def. 1 mess., 1 toft & 1 gdn. in the parish of St. Botulph within the town of Colchester. £40.

4. Jn. Starkey, pl. Tho. Brende & w. Margery & *Francis* Pryor & w. Margt., def. 2 mess., 1 barn, 1 gdn., 1 orchard & 4 a. ar. in Daggenham. £40.

5. Robt. Alman, pl. Rd. Wylde and w. *Alice*, kinswoman & heir of Wm. Hale, decd., def. 1 mess., 1 gdn. & ½ a. mw. in Thaxsted. £12.

6. Simon White, pl. Tho. Eve & w. *Juliana*, def. 1 mess. & 1 gdn. in Brentwood. £30.

7. Mich. & Hil. Tho. Marshe, gent., pl. *Rd.* Ryche, kt., lord Ryche, chancellor of England, & w. Eliz., def. Manors of Great Bursted, Whytes, Gurneys, Bukwynes, Lowbryge, Chalwedon, Newerkes, Passelowes, Imbers, Fawconers & Bowres; the rectories of Great Bursted & Goodester; 30 mess., 2 mills, 1,000 a. ar., 100 a. mw., 1,000 a. pa., 300 a. wd., 1,000 a. furze & heath & £50 rt. in Great Bursted, Little Bursted, Billerica, Gyngmountney, Mountnesing, Barstyldon, Langdon & Goodester; & the advowsons of the vicarages of Great Bursted & Goodester. Def. quitclaimed to pl. & his heirs. And for this pl. granted the same to def. for their lives without impeachment of waste for the life of Rd., with remainder to Robt. Ryche their son and the heirs male of his body & the right heirs Rd., to hold of the chief lords.

8. Jn. Tynley, pl. Francis Broke, gent., def. 2 tofts, 20 a. ar. & 10 a. pa. in Dovercourt. £40.

9. Hy. Stapylton, gent., pl. Robt. Tyrrell, esq., def. Manor of Shenefelde *alias* Shenevyle & 6 mess., 6 gdns., 6 orchards, 5 tofts, 200 a. ar., 40 a. mw., 300 a. pa., 40 a. wd., 100 a. furze & heath & £5 rt. in Shenefelde *alias* Shenevyle, Brentwode, Welde, Gyngraverd Landye & Herford Stok in the parish of Buttysbery, & the advowson of the church of Shenefelde *alias* Shenevyle. Def. quitclaimed to pl. & his heirs. And for this pl. gtd. the same to def. for life without impeachment of waste, with remainder to Anne w. of def. for life without impeachment of waste, to hold of the chief lords, with reversion to pl. & his heirs.

10. Giles Capell, kt., pl. *Wm.* Dormer, gent., & Geoff. Dormer, gent., sons of Mich. Dormer, kt., decd., def. 60 a. ar., 20 a. mw. & 60 a. pa. in Little Reigne & Bockyng. 130 mks.

EASTER, 6 EDWARD VI 1552

11. Jn. Lucas, esq., pl. *Geo.* Crystemas & Edm. Markaunt, gentlemen, def. 3 mess., 3 gdns., 3 orchards, 3 tofts, 200 a. ar., 20 a. mw., 200 a. pa. & 40 a. wd. in Colchester, Myleende & Grensted. £120.

12. And. Fuller, 'yoman', pl. *Law.* Morse & w. Agnes, def. 1 mess., 1 gdn. & 1 orchard in Barkyng. £40.

13. Wm. Armystedde & w. Wenefrida, pl. *Jn.* Starkye & w. Margt., def. 2 mess., 1 gdn., 1 orchard & 2 a. ar. in Daggenham. Def. quitclaimed to pl. & the heirs of Wm. £40.

14. Hil. & Eas. Reg. Sumpner & Chris. Sumpner, pl. Jn. Hanchett, gent., & w. Bridget, def. 60 a. ar., 2 a. mw. & 10 a. pa. in Great Parndon, parcel of the manor of Cannons. Def. quitclaimed to pl. & the heirs of Reg. 80 mks.

15. Hil. & Eas. Jn. Adams, pl. Robt. Fan, def. 1 mess., 1 gdn., 20 a. ar., 4 a. mw. & 12 a. pa. in Little Laver, High Laver & Abbes Rodyng. 50 mks.

16. Matthias Bradbury, pl. Jn. Buk & w. Kath., & *Oliver* Frohoke, def. 30 a. ar., 6 a. mw., 30 a. pa. & 3 a. wd. in Arkysden & Elmedon. £80.

17. Edw. Combe, pl. Rd. Pomell & w. *Kath.*, Hy. Lawrence & w. Joan, def. 1 mess. & 3 a. pa. in West Bargholte. £20.

18. Jn. Josselyn, pl. Jn. Holmested & w. *Alice,* def. Manor of Nalynghurst Hall & 3 mess., 2 cotts., 1 orchard, 1 gdn., 100 a. ar., 20 a. mw., 40 a. pa., 4 a. wd. & 60s. rt. in Braynktre & Great Rayne. 130 mks.

19. Mich. & Eas. Geo. Tuke, esq., pl. Jn. Stede, def. 1 mess., 1 barn, 1 orchard, 15 a. ar. & 12 a. pa. in Layer Marney & Messyng. 50 mks.

20. Jn. Myller, pl. Geo. Raymonde, gent., & w. *Anne,* def. 3 mess., 2 curtilages, 3 gdns., 10 a. ar., 4 a. mw., 6 a. pa., 3 a. wd. & 4 a. fresh marsh in Paklesham, Great Stambredge, Pryttelwell & Canewdon. 50 mks.

21. Roger Parker, gent., pl. *Jn.* Wyncoll & w. Anne, def. 1 mess., 2 curtilages, 2 gdns., 40 a. ar., 12 a. mw., 50 a. pa. & 4 a. wd. in Bockyng. 100 mks.

22. Tho. Arnold, pl. *Jn.* Sylverwood & w. Agnes, def. 1 mess., 1 gdn., 20 a. ar., 4 a. mw. & 6 a. pa. in Hadley. £40.

23. Hil. & Eas. Rd. Bysshoppe *alias* Peryn, pl. *Rd.* Savell & Jn. Savell, def. 1 mess., 2 gdns., 22 a. ar., 1 a. mw. & 2 a. pa. in Stansted Mountfychet. £60.

24. Wm. Shypman, pl. Robt. Stacey & w. *Alice,* def. 1 mess. & 1 cott. in Walden. £40.

25. Roger Parker, gent., pl. *Tho.* Wylton & w. Joan, def. 1 mess., 1 curtilage, 10 a. ar., 2 a. mw. & 8 a. pa. in Wydfford & Wryttell. 50 mks.

26. Hil. & Eas. Jn. Foxton, pl. Jn. Seyntclere, esq., def. Manors of Seyntclereshall & Frowyke & 10 mess., 5 tofts, 700 a. ar., 40 a. mw., 1,000 a. pa., 500 a. wd., 300 a. furze & heath, 1,000 a. marsh & £5 rt. in Seynt Osees & Weleygh. Def. quitclaimed to pl. & his heirs. And for this pl. gtd. the same to def. for life, with remainder to Margt. his w. for life & Wm. Cardynall, gent., & his heirs, to hold of the chief lords.

27. Hil. & Eas. Geo. Frythe, pl. *Armigil* Wade & w. Alice, def. 2 mess., 2 gdns., 80 a. ar. & 40 a. mw. in Dagnam. £80.

28. Tho. Pechy, pl. Jn. Pavett, def. 1 mess., 1 curtilage & 1 gdn. in Malden. £40.

29. Hil. & Eas. Jn. Hasteler, pl. Wm. Marche, esq., *Tho.* Franke sen., esq., & Tho. Franke, gent., his son & heir apt., def. 80 a. ar., 1 a. mw., 20 a. pa. & 6 a. wd. in Maldon, Ultyng, Woodham Water & Woodham Mortymer. Def. quitclaimed to pl. & his heirs, with warranty against Jn. Franke & Francis Franke, sons of Tho. sen., & their heirs. £220.

30. Jn. Parker, pl. Wm. Armested & w. *Wenefrida,* def. 8 a. ar. & 3 a. pa. in Little Waltham. £40.

31. Jn. Law & Tho. Eryswell, pl. Wm. Strachye & w. Annabilla, Rd. Stockwell & w. Joan, *Jn.* Smythe & w. Eliz., Tho. Wyllyamson & w. Kath., Wm. Bowlyng & Robt. Half-hed, def. 1 mess., & 7½ a. ar. in Walden. Def. quitclaimed to pl. & the heirs of Jn. Lawe. And for this pl. gtd. the mess. & 6 a. ar. to Wm. Bowlyng & his heirs & 1½ a. ar. to Robt. & his heirs. to hold of the chief lords.

32. Robt. Turnor, pl. *Rd.* Stockwell & w. Joan, def. 1 mess. & 2 a. ar. in Walden. £40.

33. Jn. Jackson, pl. *Wm.* Boyton & Jn. Boyton, def. 1 mess., 1 barn, 1 stable, 1 orchard & 1 gdn. in Walden. £40.

34. Nich. Brodewater, pl. Wm. Dryffylde & w. *Agnes* dau. & heir of Jn. Myller, def. 1 gdn., 2 a. ar. & 1 a. mw. in Rayleigh. £40.

35. Rd. Goldyng, gent., pl. *Jn.* Harecrofte & w. Kath., def. 1 mess., 1 gdn., 34 a. ar., 4 a. mw. & 6 a. pa. in Pebmersche & Colne Engayne. £40.

36. Rd. Upchare, pl. Tho. Sparrowe & w. *Alice*, dau. & heir of Rd. Yeldham, def. 2 mess., 2 tofts, 2 curtilages, 4 gdns. & 4 a. ar. in Bockyng. £60.

37. Rd. Everard sen., pl. Wm. Armested & w. *Wenefrida*, dau. & heir of Jn. Rolf, decd., def. 2 a. mw. & 6 a. pa. in Great Waltham. £20.

38. Tho. Freman, pl. Wm. Armysted & w. *Wenefrida*, def. 1 barn, 70 a. ar. & 2 a. wd. in Terlyng & Hatfeld Peverell. Def. quitclaimed to pl. & his heirs. And for this pl. gtd. the same for one week, with remainder to Jn. Paxton & w. Gertrude & her heirs, to hold of the chief lords.

39. Tho. Helley, pl. Tho. Tryttell & w. *Eliz.*, def. 1 mess. & 1 gdn. in Pryttelwell. £40.

40. Robt. Fannyng, pl. *Jn.* Bullocke & w. Margery, def. 1 mess. & 1 gdn. in Raleygh. £20.

41. Tho. Sparrowe & w. Alice, pl. *Rd.* Upchare & w. Ellen, def. 1 mess., 2 curtilages & 2 gdns. in Bokkyng. £20.

(Hil. & Eas. Mathias Bradbury, gent., pl. *Jn.* Wyseman, esq., & w. Agnes, def. 1 mess. called Venowrys, 1 gdn., 1 orchard, 100 a. ar., 14 a. mw., 40 a. pa., 10 a. wd. & 10s. rt. in Tacksted & Esthame 'at the Hill' *alias* Eston 'at the Hill' *alias* Eston 'at the Mount'. £80.

Wm. Downes & Wm. Blage, pl. Jn. Vygarus & w. Margery, dau. & heir of Rd. Garrard, decd., def. 2 mess., 3 gdns., 4 a. ar. & 1 a. mw. in Bokkyng & Great Maplested. Def. quit-claimed to pl. & the heirs of Wm. Downes. And for this pl. gtd. the same to def. for their lives, with remainder to the right heirs of Jn., to hold of the chief lords.)

(These two fines are taken from the Notes, the Feet being missing.)

CP25(2)/66/549   DIVERS COUNTIES

2. Jn. Alyngton & Jn. Webbe jun., pl. Jn. Webbe sen. & w. *Alice*, def. Prop. in Hyn-keston, co. Cambs., & 1 mess., 1 gdn. & 8 a. ar. in Claveryng, co. Essex. Def. quitclaimed to pl. & the heirs of Jn. Alyngton. £80. — Cambs., Essex.

CP25(2)/57/423   TRINITY, 6 EDWARD VI   1552

42. Eas. & Trin. Rd. Raynold, pl. Jn. Peryman & w. *Eliz.*, def. 14 a. ar., 3 a. mw. & 1 a. wd. in Great Bursted. £30.

43. Wm. Pounsett, esq., pl. Edm. Beamond & w. *Kath.*, def. 36 a. ar. in Barkyng. £40.

44. Edw. Waldegrave, esq., pl. Wm. Rochester, esq., def. A moiety of the manor of Babyngworth & 9 mess., 3 tofts, 1 mill, 300 a. ar., 30 a. mw., 180 a. pa., 60 a. wd. & £3 rt. in Babyngworth, High Onger, Stanford Ryvers, Welde, Northwelde Bassett & Harlowe, & the advowson of a mediety of the church of Babyngworth. £240.

45. Rd. Frende sen., pl. Nich. Parker & w. *Margery*, def. 7 a. pa. & 5 a. wd. in Bel-champe St. Paul, Stubbyng & Wyllowhedge. £40.

46. Jn. Cokerell, pl. Tho. Chamber & w. *Alice*, def. 1 mess. called Brownes & 20 a. ar., 4 a. mw., 20 a. pa. & 15 a. fresh marsh in Fordham. £80.

47. Law. Dalton, gent., & w. Dorothy, pl. Geo. Whetenhall, gent., def. 1 mess., 1 croft, 1 gdn., 1 orchard & 4 a. ar. in Stanforde le Hope, & the advowson of the churches of Stanforde le Hope & Fange. Def. quitclaimed to pl. & the heirs of Law. £30.

48. Robt. Myddelton sen., pl. Francis Jobson, kt., def. 2 mess. & 2 gdns. in Colchester, with Margt. Hyll, wid., holds for life. Pl. & his heirs to hold the reversion of the chief lords. £100.

49. Jn. Maykyn & w. Agnes, pl. Tho. Clerke & w. *Isabel*, def. A moiety of 1 mess., 1 gdn. & 10 a. ar. in Langenhoo. Def. quitclaimed to pl. & the heirs of Agnes. £40.

50. Mich. & Trin. Rd. Dale, pl. Jn. Love, def. 1 mess., 1 barn & 6 a. ar. in Hardford Stock. £30.

51. Eas. & Trin. Jn. Playell, pl. Wm. Byott & w. Margery & *Tho.* Osmond, def. 1 water-mill & 1 a. ar. in Stebbyng. 100 mks.

52. Eas. & Trin. Jn. Raymond, gent., pl. Robt. Reymond, gent., & w. *Agnes*, def. 1 mess., 2 gdns., 1 orchard, 1 a. ar. & 1 ar. mw. in Great Dunmowe. £20.

53. Eas. & Trin. Rd. Wllys, pl. Edw. Palmer & w. *Margt.*, def. 4 mess., 5 gdns., 2 a. ar. & 3 a. pa. in Bokkyng. £60.

54. Rd. Saunderson, pl. *Jn.* Freman & w. Alice, def. 1 mess., 1 gdn., 1 orchard & 6 a. ar. in Keldon *alias* Kelwedon. £20.

55. Eas. & Trin. Jerome Songer, gent., pl. Steph. Rose & w. Joan, def. 1 mess., & 1 gdn. in Terlyng. £20.

56. Eas. & Trin. Jn. Raymond, gent., & Geo. Raymond, pl. Hy. Longe & w. *Alice*, def. 1 mess. & 1 gdn. in Great Dunmowe. Def. quitclaimed to pl. & the heirs of Jn. £40.

57. Eas. & Trin. Wm. Kynge, citizen & 'grocer' of London, pl. Walter Farre, gent., & w. Fredeswida, def. 1 mess., 1 gdn., 15 a. ar., 15 a. pa., 10 a. salt marsh & ½ a. wd. in Stanford le Hope & Curryngham. £140.

58. Eas. & Trin. Walter Farre, gent., & w. Fredeswida, pl. Jas. Harrys & w. *Dorothy*, def. 14 a. ar. & 2 a. mw. called 'Paddes' *alias* 'Poddesbroke' in Great Bursted. Def. quitclaimed to pl. & the heirs of Walter. £40.

59. Eas. & Trin. Robt. Alleyn, pl. *Robt.* Westley & w. Alice, def. 1 mess., 2 gdns., 4 a. ar. & 6 a. pa. in Bumsted at the Steeple. £(40).

60. Jn. Lucas, esq., pl. Rd. Sands, gent., & w. Kath., def. Manor of Ramesey *alias* Reydon Hall *alias* Westhall *alias* Parkers Hall & 10 mess., 300 a. ar., 40 a. mw., 300 a. pa., 100 a. marsh, 40 a. alder, 40 a. furze & heath, 200 a. wd. & 40s. rt. in Ramesey, Dovercoort, Little Okeley, Wrabnes, Wykes, Bradfeld & Great Okeley, which def. holds for the life of Kath. with remainder to Mary Roydon & her heirs. Def. gtd. to pl. whatever they had in the above for the life of Kath., to hold of the chief lords. £2(20).

61. Wm. Gent & Edw. Short, pl. Jn. (Moreton), gent., & w. *Mary* & Jn. Thurston, def. Manor of Frynton & 3 mess., 3 gdns., 3 orchards, 500 a. ar., 100 a. mw., 500 a. pas., 30 a. wd., 10 a. salt marsh & 20s. rt. in Frynton & Kyrby; except 30 a. pa. lying in 6 little enclosures called 'the pyghtels', 16 a. wd. called 'Whytton Wood' & the advowson of the church of Frynton in Frynton. Def. quitclaimed to pl. & the heirs of Wm. And for this pl. gtd. the same to Jn. Thurston to hold from Michaelmas last for 52 years, rendering to pl. & the heirs of Wm. £20 yearly, payable at the Annunciation & Michaelmas, with powers of distaint after 9 days & penalty of 40s. for each payment in arrear; & the reversion of def. & the heirs of Mary, to hold of the chief lords.

DIVERS COUNTIES

24. Rd. Lacy, pl. *Pet.* Wentworth & Wm. Holland, def. Property in Oxon., London & Bucks., & 1 mess., 60 a. ar., 10 a. mw. & 200 a. pa. in Great Standbridge, North Subery, Pecclesham, Little Wakeryng & Berlyng, co. Essex. Def. quitclaimed to pl. & his heirs. And for this pl. gtd. the same to Wm. for one week, with remainder to Pet. & his heirs, to hold of the chief lords. — Oxford, London, Essex, Bucks.

FEET OF FINES FOR ESSEX

CP25(2)/57/423 MICHAELMAS, 6 EDWARD VI 1552

62. Wm. Bowlyng, pl. *Edm.* Mordaunt, esq., & w. Agnes, def. 1 barn, 1 gdn., 5 a. mw. & 4 a. pa. in Walden. £40.

63. Jn. Gooddaye, pl. *Wm.* Michell, gent., & w. Anne, def. The rectory of Branktre & 40 a. ar., 10 a. mw., 40 a. pa. & 10 a. wd. in Branktre, & the advowson of the vicarage & church of Branktre. £200.

64. Tho. Wyllyamson, pl. *Edm.* Mordaunt, esq., & w. Agnes, def. 2 mess., 50 a. ar., 10 a. mw., 30 a. pa. & 10 a. wd. in Wymbysshe & Thunderley. £140.

65. Nich. Colyn, pl. *Ralph* Nalynghurste, esq., & Jas. Dryland, gent., def. 4 a. ar., 8 a. mw. & 8 a. pa. in Gt. Badowe & Sondon. £40.

66. Jn. Bulle, pl. *Jn.* Nicolles & w. Cecily, def. 1 mess., 2 curtilages, 2 gdns., 20 a. ar., 10 a. pa., 15 a. wd. & 20 a. furze & heath in Elmestede. £40.

67. Tho. Wyseman, pl. *Edm.* Heygate & w. Constance, def. A moiety of 1 mess., 1 toft, 1 barn, 1 orchard, 1 gdn., 30 a. ar., 12 a. mw., 60 a. pa. & 2 a. wd. in Great Badowe. 200 mks.

68. Wm. Fytche, pl. Wm. Copsey & w. *Margt.*, def. 1 mess., 1 garden, 12 a. ar., 4 a. mw., 26 a. pa. & 1 a. wd. in Stamborne. £40.

69. Alan Ingram, pl. Ralph Malkyn & w. *Joan*, def. 1 mess., 1 kitchen & 1 gdn. in Mulsham. £20.

70. Jn. Gate, kt, vice-chamberlain of the King's household, pl. Wm., earl of Pembroke, lord Herberte of Cardyffe, kt, of the Garter, def. The advowson of the church of Bernston. £40.

71. Rd. Weston, esq., & w. Wiburga, pl. Robt. Maye & w. *Margt.*, def. 1 mess., 1 gdn. & 1 orchard in Great Dunmowe. Def. quitclaimed to pl. & the heirs of Rd. £20.

72. Jn. Harte, pl. Rd. Harte, def. 1 mess. & 3 gdns. in Thaxsted. 40 mks.

73. Wm. Fytche, gent., pl. *Robt.* Maye & w. Margt., def. 2 mess., 4½ a. ar. & 3 a. mw. in Little Canfeld. £30.

74. Tho. Godfrey, gent., pl. *Steph.* Cowper & w. Dorothy, def. 1 mess., 1 barn, 1 gdn. 1 orchard, 16 a. ar., 12 a. pa. & 10 a. mw. in Hokley & Rawrethe, & common of pa. for 2 horses, 2 cows & 30 sheep in Hokley & Rawrethe. 100 mks.

75. Philip Honwyke, pl. Wm. Ynde & w. *Marion*, def. 2 mess. & 2 gdns. in Halsted. £20.

76. Jn. Holmested, pl. *Wm.* Archer & w. Kath., def. 1 mess., 1 water-mill, 2 a. ar., 2 a. mw. & 4 a. pa. in Belchampe William *alias* Belchampe Water. 100 mks.

77. Robt. Creffyld, pl. *Jn.* Mooteham, son & heir of Jn. Mooteham, decd., & w. Margery, def. 12 a. ar., 6 a. mw. & 6 a. pa. in Great Tey. 80 mks.

78. Roger Appulton, esq., pl. Wm. Hayward & w. *Helen*, def. A moiety of 1 mess., 40 a. ar. & 20 a. pa. in Sowthbemeflete. £40.

79. Roger Grome, pl. *Jn.* Osborne, gent., & w. Joan, def. Manor of Snorham & 4 mess., 2 dovecotes, 160 a. ar., 60 a. mw., 360 a. pa., 20 a. wd. & £6 6s. 8d. rt. in Snorham, Lachyndon & Lytell Lachyndon, & the advowson of the church of Snorham *alias* Lytell Lachyndon. £280.

80. Hy. Stapilton, gent., pl. Robt. Tyrrell, esq., def. Manor of Porters & 5 mess., 500 a. ar., 60 a. mw., 300 a. pa., 30 a. wd., 60 a. marsh & £4 rt. in Barkyng & Daggenham £400.

81. Robt. Martyn, pl. Wm. Androwes *alias* Paynter & w. *Eliz.*, def. 1 mess., & 4 a. ar. in Lytell Ocley. £20.

82. Roger Parker, gent., pl. *Tristrian* Fytche, gent., & w. Margt., def. 1 mess., 2 cotts., 2 barns, 1 gdn., 50 a. ar., 6 a. mw., 30 a. pa. & 8 a. wd. in Lyndsell. 70 mks.

83. Robt. Potter, pl. Wm. Aresmyth & w. *Margt.*, def. A third part of 1 mess., 2 cotts., 1 barn, 1 gdn., 30 a. ar., 10 a. mw., 30 a. pa. & 8 a. wd. in Fordham, which Eliz. Badcock, wid., holds for life. Pl. to hold the reversion of the chief lords. £20.

30

84. Jn. Tebolde, pl. Wm. Cotton, esq., def. 40 a. ar., 100 a. pa. & 10 a. mw. in Hempsted. Def. quitclaimed to pl. & his heirs. And for this pl. gtd. the same to def. for life without impeachment of waste, with remainder to Agnes Cotton his w. for life & the right heirs of def. to hold of the chief lords.

85. Wm. Salmon & w. Joan, pl. Francis Archer & w. *Joan*, def. 6 a. ar., 3 a. mw., 5 a. pa. & 1 a. wd. in Great Stambredge. Def. quitclaimed to pl. & the heirs of Wm. 40 mks.

86. Wm. Huett, citizen & alderman of London, pl. *Jn.* Clerke & w. Frances, def. 3 mess. & 2 gdns. in Wryttell. £40.

87. Tho. Adam, pl. Hy. Johnson & w. *Margt.*, dau. & heir of *Jn.* Turner, decd., def. 1 mess., 1 gdn. 4 a. ar. & 3 a. mw. in Takeley & Hadfeld Brodioke. £30.

88. Tho. Wyllyamson, pl. Nich. Rutland, def. 2 mess., 1 toft, 1 gdn. & 2 a. ar. in Walden. £40.

89. Wm. Reynold, pl. *Jn.* Cornwell & w. Kath., def. A moiety of 1 mess., 1 cott., 1 barn, 1 dovecote, 2 gdns., 80 a. ar., 10 a. mw., 40 a. pa., 10 a. wd. & 6d. rt. in Boreham, Terlyng, Great Lyghes & Little Baddowe. 80 mks.

90. Wm. Cardynall, gent., pl. Jn. Brokeman, esq., def. Manor of Brevilles *alias* Bovelles & 4 mess., 4 curtilages, 6 cotts., 40 gdns., 200 a. ar., 20 a. mw., 50 a. pa. & 20s. rt. in Little Clafton & Great Clafton. £200.

91. Hy. Brettyn, pl. Tho. Haygate & w. *Margt.*, def. 1 mess. & 1 gdn. in Prytwell. 20 mks.

92. Tho. Whyte *alias* Cowper, pl. Jn. Whyte *alias* Cowper & w. *Juliana*, def. 1 mess., 1 gdn. & 1 a. pa. in Stysted. £20.

93. Wm. Buxston, pl. *Greg.* Smythe & w. Welthiana, def. 3 mess., 3 gdns., 3 orchards, 40 a. ar., 10 a. mw., 40 a. pa. & 4. wd. in Westmersey. £100.

CP25(2)/57/424   HILARY, 6–7 EDWARD VI   1553

(Several Feet of this term are damaged or missing.)

1. Robt. Dennes, pl. *Jn.* Glascock jun. & w. Joan, def. 12 a. ar. & 16 a. pa. in Hatfyld Regis *alias* Hatfeld Brodock. £40.

2. Jn. Baynbrigge, pl. Clement Tusser, gent., def. 2 a. mw. & 5 a. pa. in Kelwydon. 55 mks.

3. Hy. Pynell, pl. Robt. Studde & w. *Margery*, def. 1 mess. & 1 gdn. in Maldon. £20.

4. Jn. Marven & Chris. Allen, pl. Robt. Broke, gent., def. 3 tofts, 30 a. ar., 30 a. pa. & 200. a. marsh in Dovercourt & Ramesey. Def. quitclaimed to pl. & the heirs of Jn. £140.

5. Jn. Samborn, pl. *Tho.* Lawrence & w. Lucy, def. 2 mess., 1 orchard, 2 gdns., 20 a. ar., 10 a. mw. & 10 a. pa. in Sowthwelde. Def. quitclaimed to pl. & his heirs. And for this pl. gtd. the same to Tho. & his heirs, to hold of the chief lords.

6. Rd. (Westwoode), pl. *Tho.* (Halmer, gent.,) & w. Margt., def. (1 mess., 16) a. ar., (10) a. mw. & 6 (a. pa.) in Harlowe. (70 mks.)

7. Jn. Pyreson & Jn. (Upney), pl. Wm. (Pyreson) & w. *Agnes*, def. (1 mess.,) 4 a. ar. (and 6 a. mw. in Barkyng). Def. quitclaimed to pl. & the heirs of Jn. Pyreson. And for this pl. gtd. the same to def. & the heirs of their bodies, with remainder to the right heirs of Agnes, to hold of the chief lords.

8. Mich. & Hil. Rd. Peverell, pl. Jn. Fuller & w. Margt., def. 1 tenement, 20 (a. ar. & 20) a. pa. in Mysley. Def. quitclaimed to pl. & his heirs. And for this pl. gtd. the same to (Jn. & his heirs), to hold of the chief lords.

9. Jn. Thurston, pl. *Jn.* Lucas (esq.,) & w. Eliz., def. 4 mess., 4 gdns., 100 (a. ar., 20 a.) mw., 100 a. pa., 6 a. wd. & 40 a. (marsh) in Frynton & Walton. £80.

10. Wm. Wykylsworth & w. Joan, pl. *Tho.* (Mall) & w. Denise, def. 1 mess., 1 barn & 1 orchard in Shenfeld. Def. quitclaimed to pl. & the heirs of Wm. £40.

11. Wm. (Bowlynge) and Jn. Vawdey, pl. Jn. Lawe, def. Manor of Dudno Graunge & 10 mess., (6 tofts, 300) a. ar., 100 a. mw., 100 a. pa., 100 a. wd. & £3 rt. in (Loughtes, Curseall,) Elmedon, Heydon, Great Chissell, Langley & Chepynge Walden. Def. quitclaimed to pl. & the heirs of Jn. And for this pl. gtd. the same to def. & his heirs, to hold of the chief lords.

(Rd. Brody, pl. *Tho.* Mall & w. Denise, def. 10 a. ar. in Shenfeld. £40.)

Geo. Stonerd, esq., pl. Humphrey Bagsha & w. *Agnes,* def. A moiety of 12 a. ar., 4 a. mw. & 20 a. pa. in Steple. £30.

Jn. Purvey, pl. Jn. Burre, gent., def. 3 mess. & 3 gdns. in Berkyng. £40.

(*These three fines are taken from the Notes, the Feet being missing.*)

EASTER, 7 EDWARD VI 1553

12. Jn. Laurence, esq., pl. Robt. Hasylrygge & w. *Alice,* def. 1 mess., 1 barn, 1 gdn., 1 orchard, 40 a. ar., 40 a. mw., 40 a. pa., 40 a. salt marsh, 40 a. fresh marsh, 10 a. wd. & common of pa. for 70 sheep in Estylbery & Westylbery. £100.

13. Wm. Cordell & Wm. Myldemay, gentlemen, pl. *Ralph* Nalinghurst & Jas. Dryland, def. 12 a. mw. in Great Badowe. Def. quitclaimed to pl. & the heirs of Wm. Cordell. £80.

14. Jn. Johnson, pl. *Tho.* Sebroke & w. Barbara, def. 4 a. ar., 66 a. pa. & 20 a. wd. in Ashldon. £60.

15. Margery Godbolde, wid., pl. Tho. Cordall & w. *Emma,* def. A moiety of a third part of 2 mess., 140 a. ar., 30 a. mw., 100 a. pa., 10 a. wd. & 10s. rt. in Willynghale Doo, Wyllynghale Spayne & Willynghale Roke. 65 mks.

16. Ralph Nalynghurst, gent., pl. *Jn.* Pascall, esq., & w. Mary, def. 1 gdn., 5 a. ar., & 2 a. pa. in Great Baddowe. £30.

17. Hil. & Eas. Jn. Stock & w. Margery, pl. Edw. Concedew & w. *Marion,* def. 1 mess., 12 a. ar. & 1½ a. mw. in Estham. Def. quitclaimed to pl. & the heirs of Jn. £40.

18. Geo. Daye jun., pl. *Jn.* Daye & w. Joan, def. 1 mess., 1 gdn., 6 a ar. & 5 pa. in Claveryng. £40.

19. Jn. Page *alias* Baxter & w. Anne, pl. Tho. Cordall & w. *Emma,* def. A moiety (as in 15) in Willynghale Doo, Willynghale Spayne & Willynghale Rokell. Def. quitclaimed to pl. & the heirs of Anne. 65 mks.

20. Jn. Strang, pl. Jn. Baker & w. *Margery,* dau. & heir of Wm. Hilpe, def. 1 mess. & 6 a. ar. & common of pa. for 20 sheep (*bidentes*) & 2 bullocks in Thorynton. 20 mks.

21. Wm. Aylett, pl. *Reg.* Heygate, gent., & w. Constance & Eliz. Heygate his sister, def. 4 mess., 2 curtilages, 1 barn, 1 water-mill, 90 a. ar., 10 a. mw., 40 a. pa. & 10 a. wd. in Earls Colne, Colne Engayne & Kelwedon. 230 mks.

22. Jn. Traves, pl. *Jn.* Tooke, gent., & w. Isabel, def. 1 mess., 1 curtilage, 1 gdn., 8 a. mw., 40 a. pa., 3 a. wd. & 5s. rt. in Daggenham & Barkyng. £100.

23. Launcelet Madyson, pl. *Reg.* Heygate, gent., & w. Constance, def. 2 mess., 2 tofts, 3 curtilages, 2 barns, 1 dovecote, 2 gdns., 40 a. ar., 16 a. mw., 70 a. pa., 4 a. wd. & 3s. rt. in Sandon & Danbury. £236.

24. Wm. Ewsdon, pl. Wm. Totnam, def. 1 mess., 1 gdn. & 1 orchard in Great Wenden. £40.

25. Nich. Collyn, pl. *Tho.* Bedyll, gent., & w. Eliz., def. 1 mess., 60 a ar., 10 a. mw., 20 a. pa. & 2s. rt. in Wyllyngale Doo, Fyfyld & Bechampe Rodyng. £100.

26. Leonard Gill, pl. *Tho.* Isbell & w. Helen, def. 1 mess. in Walden. £20.

27. Hil. & Eas. Jerome Songer, pl. *Edm.* Mone, gent., & w. Susan, def. 50 a. ar., 10 a. mw., 60 a. pa. & 10s. rt. in Wytham, Falborne & Revenall. £60.

28. Hil. & Eas. Robt. Salmon & Jn. Cooke, pl. Tho. Malle & w. *Denise,* def. A moiety of 2 mess., 4 gdns., 2 barns, 20 a. ar., 10 a. mw. & 10 a. pa. in Brentwood & Shenfeld. Def. quitclaimed to pl. & the heirs of Robt. And for this pl. gtd. the same to def. & the heirs of their bodies, with remainder to the right heirs of Tho., to hold of the chief lords.

29. Tho. Pyreson, pl. Tho. Holcrofte, kt., & w. *Juliana*, def. 1 mess., 1 cott., 1 barn, 1 dovecote, 1 orchard, 20 a. ar. & 1 a. mw. in Barkyng. £40.

30. Jerome Songer, gent., pl. Jn. Crofte & w. *Rose*, def. 1 mess., & 1 gdn. in Wytham. £20.

31. Jn. Gilder, pl. Geo. Cristemas, esq., def. 2 mess., 2 gns., 1 dovecote & 1 a. ar. in the parish of St. Martin of the town of Colchester. £40.

32. Jn. Collyn, pl. *Rd.* Ryche, lord Ryche, & w. Eliz., def. 2 mess., 80 a. ar., 5 a. mw. & 10 a. pa. in Little Laver & High Laver. 130 mks.

33. Tho. Walker, pl. Wm. Walker, def. 2 mess., 2 gdns., 7 a. ar., 4 a. mw. & 4 a. pa. in Rayleygh. Def. quitclaimed to pl. & his heirs. And for this pl. gtd. a yearly rt. of 5 mks. from the same to def. & his assigns for life, payable at Michaelmas & the Annunciation, with power of distraint.

34. Jn. Wyseman, esq., pl. *Edm.* Mordaunt, esq., & w. Agnes, def. Manor of Weldebernes & 12 mess., 200 a. ar., 20 a. mw., 200 a. pa., 6 a. wd. & £8 rt. in Depden, Thunderley & Wymbysshe. 530 mks.

35. Jn. Collyn, pl. Jn. Burre, gent., son & heir of Jn. Burre, decd., def. 1 mess., 20 a. ar., 10 a. mw., 10 a. pa. & 70 a. wd. in Barkyng. £80.

36. Steph. Craske, Hy. Smyth & Thomasina Bretten, pl. Francis Cheveley & w. Anne, def. 2 mess., 2 gdns., 2 orchards, 20 a. ar., 10 a. mw. & 20 a. pa. in Ramesdon Bellowes & Ramesdon Crayes, which Francis & Anne hold for her life, with remainder to Thomasina & Alice Bretten & Eliz. Bretten & their heirs. Def. gtd. whatever they had to pl. & the heirs of Steph., to hold for the life of Anne of the chief lords. £40.

37. Hil. & Eas. Robt. Noke jun., pl. Robt. Noke sen., def. 10 a. ar. & 4 a. mw. in Great Halyngbury. 80 mks.

38. Hy. Browne, gent., & Robt. Thrope, pl. *Ralph* Nalynghurst, esq., & w. Eliz. & Jas. Dryland, gent., def. Manors of Syr Hughes *alias* Hughes & Stisteds & 6 mess., 2 barns, 1 stable, 660 a. ar., 68 a. mw., 440 a. pa., 210 a. wd. & £13 9s. rt. in Great Badowe, Westhanyngfeld, Sondon, Stisted, Brayntre, Bokkyng, Hawsted & Gosfeld. Def. quitclaimed to pl. & the heirs of Hy. And for this pl. gtd. to Ralph & his heirs the manor of Sir Hughes *alias* Hughes & 3 mess., 200 a. ar., 30 a. mw., 300 a. pa., 40 a. wd. & 100s. rt. in Great Badowe, Westhanyfeld & Sondon, & the manor of Stisteds & 3 mess., 2 barns, 1 stable, 460 a. ar., 38 a. mw., 140 a. pa., 140 a. wd. & £8 9s. rt. in Stisteds, Brayntre, Bokkyng, Hawsted, Gosfeld, & Great Badowe, & the manor of Stisteds & 2 mess., 1 barn, 240 a. ar., 20 a. mw., 100 a. pa., 100 a. wd. & £8. 9s. rt. in Stisted, Brayntre, Bokkyng, Hawsted & Gosfeld & 5 a. mw. & 9 a. pa. in Great Badowe, to hold of the chief lords; & also gtd. to Ralph 1 mess., 1 barn, 1 stable, 220 a. ar., 13 a. mw., 31 a. pa. & 30 a. wd. in Great Badowe, the residue, to hold for 14 years from Michaelmas last at a yearly rt. of £12 to pl. & the heirs of Hy., payable at the Annunciation & Michaelmas, with power of distraint, & the reversion of the same to def. & the heirs of Ralph, to hold of the chief lords.

39. Gerard Shelbury, pl. Geo. Cristemas, esq., def. 1 mess. called 'a warehouse' in the new hithe of the town of Colchester. £20.

40. Tho. Wyseman, pl. Robt. Penycoke, gent., def. 1 mess., 1 orchard, 1 gdn. & 10 a. ar. in Great Waltham & Felsted. £20.

41. Hil. & Eas. Tho. Mylksoppe, pl. *Robt.* Tyrrell, esq., & Tho. Tyrrell his son & heir apt., def. 1 mess., 20 a. ar., 1 a. mw. & 10 a. pa. in Redeswell, Stamborn, Redeswell Norton, Fynchyngfelde & Bumpsted at the Steeple. 50 mks.

42. Jn. Swallowe, pl. *Wm.*, marquess of Northampton, & w. Dame Eliz., def. 1 mess., 1 barn, 1 gdn., 40 a. ar., 10 a. mw., 60 a. pa., 40 a. wd., 10 a. marsh & 10 a. alder & furze in Halsted & Gosfeld. 70 mks.

CP25(2)/66/549   **DIVERS COUNTIES**

51. Tho. Metcalff & w. Alice, pl. *Guy* Wade, gent., & w. Kath., def. Property in Stratford at Bowe & Stebenhethe, co. Mdx., & 2 tofts, 1 gdn., 10 a. ar., 12 a. mw., 15 a. pa., 5 a marsh, 1 a. wd. & a free fishery in Stratford at Bowe, Stebenheth & Westham, co. Essex. Def. quitclaimed to pl. & the heirs of Tho. £120. – Mdx., Essex.

54. Robt. Bedyngfeld, gent., pl. Jn. Watson, 'glover', def. Property in Stoke by Clere & Wyxhoo, co. Suff., & 5 mess., 4 cotts., 6 gdns. & 10 ar. in Ballyngton by Sudbury, co. Essex. Def. quitclaimed to pl. & his heirs. And for this pl. gtd. the same to def. for life without impeachment of waste, with remainder to Agnes his w. for life without impeachment of waste & Rd. Hasylwood sen. & his heirs, to hold of the chief lords. — Suff., Essex.

CP(2)/57/424 **TRINITY, 7 EDWARD VI** 1553

43. Jn. Eve jun., pl. Jn. Pond, def. 1 mess , 2 barns, 1 stable, 80 a. ar., 2 a. mw., 10 a. pa., 1 a. wd. & 2s. rt. in Margarett Rodyng. 160 mks.

44. Simon Josselyn, pl. Robt. Kyng, gent., & w. *Lettice*, def. 1 mess., 3 a. ar. & 2 pa. in Great Badowe. 40 mks.

45. Eas. & Trin. Tho. Glascock, pl. Jn. Johnson & w. *Agnes*, def. A moiety of 2 mess., 2 gdns., 2 orchards, 60 a. ar., 5 a. pa. & 4 a. mw. in Chycknall Smely, Chycknall Saynt James, Bromefeld & Moche Waltham. 100 mks.

46. Geo. Crymble, pl. And. Bedeman & w. *Alice*, def. 1 mess. & 1 gdn. in Rocheforde. £20.

47. Eas. & Trin. Geo. Barnes, kt., citizen & alderman of London, pl. *Pet.* Johnson of London, gent., & w. Mary, def. 10 a. mw. in Westham. £100.

48. Wm. Sumpner, pl. *Rd.* Westwood & w. Margery, def. 1 barn, 1 orchard, 10 a. ar., 15 a. mw. & 12 a. pa. in Harlowe & Latton. 100 mks.

49. Jn. Gate, kt., pl. *Edw.* Fynes, kt. of the Garter, lord Clynton & Saye, great admiral of England, and w. Eliz., def. Manor of Ronewell Hall *alias* Ronewell & 6 mess., 5 tofts, 6 gdns., 400 a. ar., 100 a. mw., 400 a. pa., 100 a. wd. & £20 rt. in Ronewell. £660.

50. Robt. Eyton & Wm. Smalwood, pl. Robt. Smythe, gent., def. 2 mess., 1 gdn., 1 orchard & 3 a. ar. in Chelmysford & Spryngfeld. Def. quitclaimed to pl. & the heirs of Robt. £40.

51. Roger Thatcher & *Jn.* Thatcher, pl. Jn. Coke & w. Isabel, def. 2 mess., 2 barns, 2 gdns., 50 a. ar., 10 a. mw., 20 a. pa. & 6 a. wd. in Chaldwell & Dagenham. Def. quitclaimed to pl. & the heirs of Roger. £90.

52. Eas. & Trin. Jn. Dygby, pl. Wm. Ayloff, esq., def. 2 mess., 60 a. ar., 6 a. mw. & 50 a. pa. in Felsted, Gosfeld & Hengham Syble. 160 mks.

53. Jn. Smyth, esq., son & heir of Clement Smythe, kt., pl. Jn. Akelane, esq., & w. *Margt.*, one of the kinswomen & heirs of Rd. Ratclyff, gent., def. A moiety of the manor of Tyrlyng *alias* Tyrlynghall *alias* Margeryes & 24 mess., 2 tofts, 6 gdns., 1,000 a. ar., 80 a. mw., 300 a. pa., 120 a. wd., 20 a. furze & heath & £14 rt. in Terlynge, Fayrsted, Boreham, Great Leyes, Hatfeld Peverell, Halsted, Playstowe, Colne Engyne, Stysted, Runwell & Maldon. £420.

54. Jn. Garrard, pl. Jn. Grene & w. *Eliz.*, def. A moiety of 3 mess., 2 barns, 1 stable, 2 orchards, 60 a. ar. & 6 a. mw. in Wytham. £40.

55. Robt. Lotte, pl. Robt. Wytton & w. Grace & *Wm.* Daye, def. 1 mess., 1 gdn., 1 orchard, 4 a. ar., 2 a. mw., 4 a. pa. & 1 a. wd. in Cryseseyght. £40.

56. Wm. Cardynall, gent., pl. *Jn.* Brokeman, esq., Anth. Brokeman, gent., & Tho. Brokeman, gent., def. Manor of Bovyldes *alias* Boveldes & 4 mess., 4 curtilages, 6 cotts., 4 gdns., 100 a. ar., 20 a. mw., 300 a. pa., 20 a. wd., 40 a. marsh & 10s. rt. in Little Clafton & Great Clafton. 460 mks.

57. Eas. & Trin. Anth. Roo, pl. *Jn.* Paschall, gent., & w. Mary, def. 1 mess., 2 tofts, 1 barn, 1 gdn., 10 a. ar., 8 a. mw., 12 a. pa. & 1 a. wd. in Nevyndon *alias* Nevyngdon. 50 mks.

58. Robt. Aylett, pl. *Wm.* Johnson & w. Agnes, def. 1 mess., 1 gdn., 1 orchard, 3 a. ar. & 3 a. mw. in Willinhale Doo & Shellowe Bowellys. £30.

59. Eas. & Trin. Rd. Gilbert, pl. *Reg.* Heygate, sent., & w. Constance, def. 60 a. ar., 5 a. mw. & 2 a. wd. in Sandon. £140.

60. Eas. & Trin. Wm. Bendlowes, gent., Tho. Unwyn & Rd. Algor, pl. *Wm.* Chysshull, esq., & w. Eliz., def. 2 mess., 3 gdns., 38 a. ar., 10 a. mw. & 64 a. pa. in Little Sampford, Great Sampford, Great Berdefeld & Little Berdefeld. Def. quitclaimed to pl. & the heirs of Rd. 230 mks.

FEET OF FINES FOR ESSEX

61. Robt. Geyre & Jn. Poley, gentlemen, pl. Wm. Wood, *Wm.* Rolff & w. Eliz., Geo. Johnson & w. Kath. & Wm. Salyng, def. Manor of Lytilbury & 2 mess., 120 a. ar., 50 a. mw., 100 a. pa., 50 a. wd. & 20s. rt. in Stanford Ryvers, Kelvedon, High Honger & Grenestede. Def. quitclaimed to pl. & the heirs of Jn. Separate warranty by Wm. Salyng against himself & his heirs. And for this pl. gtd. to Wm. Salyng & his heirs 2 mess. & 20 a. ar. in Highonger, parcel of the above, & to Wm. Wood & his heirs the residue, to hold of the chief lords.

62. Wm. Brownyng & w. Rose, pl. Jn. Munde & w. Anne, def. A moiety of 1 mess., 2 curtilages, 4 a. ar., 1 a. mw. & 4 a. pa. in Chelmesford & Bromeffeld. Def. quitclaimed to pl. & the heirs of Wm. £30.

63. Jn. Dormer, pl. Tho. Holmes, def. 2 mess., 30 a. ar., 14 a. mw. & 10 a. pa. in Ramysdon Belhowse, Ramysdon Cray & Downeham. £80.

64. (Wm.) Markaunt, pl. (Jn.) Grene & w. *Eliz.*, one of the sisters & heirs of (Chris.) Stede, def. (A moiety (sic)) of the manor of Benyngtons (*alias* Bentons & 6 mess.) 6 gdns., (200 a. ar., 20 a. mw., 200 a. pa., 6) a. wd. & (40s. rt. in Wytham, Wyckham, Bradwell and) Hatfyld Peverell. (Def. quitclaimed the moities (sic) to pl. & his heirs. And for this pl. gtd. the moieties (sic) to pl. & the heirs of Jn., to hold of the chief lords.)

65. Jn. Cornelius *alias* Johnson & w. Alice, pl. *Jn.* Machell & w. Margt., def. 1 mess., 1 gdn., 30 a. ar., 10 a. mw. & 10 a. pa. in Estham, Westham, Estwestham, Placeys, Estham Burnell, Westham Burnell & Leighton. Def. quitclaimed to pl. & the heirs of Jn. £40.

CP25(2)/66/549   DIVERS COUNTIES

59. Eas. & Trin. Gilbert Gerrard, gent., & Rd. Chysnall, pl. Tho. Holcrofte, kt., & w. *Juliana*, def. Property in London, Mdx. & Beds., & 4 mess., 4 gdns., 20 a. ar., 4 a. mw., 20 a. pa. & 10 a. wd. in Ilforde & Barkyng, co. Essex. Def. quitclaimed to pl. & the heirs of Gilbert. And for this pl. gtd. the same to Tho. & his heirs, to hold of the chief lords. — London, Mdx., Essex, Bedford.

60. Robt. Catlyn, esq., & Jn. Machell, citizen & 'clotheworker' of London, pl. *Tho.* Lodge, citizen & grocer of London, & w. Anne, def. Property in the co. of Salop, & 5 mess., 1 curtilage, 4 gdns., 10 a. ar., 26 a. mw. & 4 a. pa. in Westham & Estham, co. Essex. Def. quitclaimed to pl. & the heirs of Robt. And for this pl. gtd. the same to def. & the heirs of Tho., to hold of the chief lords. — Salop, Essex.

CP25(2)/70/577   MICHAELMAS, 1 MARY   1553

1. Trin. & Mich. Clement Clerke, pl. Wm. Turnour *alias* Turner, def. 6 a. ar., 6 a. pa. & 2 a. wd. in Bokkyng. £20.

2. Jn. Watkyns, gent., & Tho. Wallynger, pl. Jn. Broke & w. *Margt.*, one of the daus. of Wm. Merke of Lagenhoo, def. 1 mess., 1 curtilage, 12 a. ar., 4 a. mw. & 24 a. pa. in Great Totham, Little Totham & Wyckham. Def. quitclaimed to pl. & the heirs of Tho. And for this pl. gtd. the same to def. & the heirs male of their bodies, with remainder to the feminine heirs of the body of Margt. & her right heirs, to hold of the chief lords.

3. Wm. Goodwyn, pl. Wm. Whytehed & w. *Margery*, def. 10 mess., 10 gdns., 20 a. ar., 3 a. mw. & 8 a. pa. in Bokkyng. £40.

4. David Amye, pl. *Jn.* Smyth, esq., & Oliver Shutilworth, gent., def. Manors of Haleys & Takeles & 2 mess., 100 a. ar., 30 a. mw., 60 a. pa. & 10 a. wd. in Eppyng, Hyghonger, Northwelbassett & Mawdelyn Lavour. Def. quitclaimed to pl. & his heirs. And for this pl. gtd. the same to Oliver for one month, with remainder to Jn. & his heirs, to hold of the chief lords.

5. David Sympson, gent., & Rd. Durant, gent., pl. Tho. Sammes sen., def. 1 toft, 6 a. ar., 2 a. mw., 36½ a. pa. & 12 a. salt marsh in Great Totham, Little Totham, Goldhanger & Heybrydge. Def. quitclaimed to pl. & the heirs of David. And for this pl. gtd. the same to def. to hold for life without impeachment of waste. with remainder to Hy. Sammes his son & the heirs of Hy., to hold of the chief lords.

6. Jn. Garrard, pl. Rd. Aulfeld & w. *Joan*, def. A moiety of 3 mess., 2 barns, 1 stable, 2 orchards, 60 a. ar. & 6 a. mw. in Wytham. £40.

35

7. Trin. & Mich. Edw. Ryche, esq., pl. Tho. Mathew & w. *Emma* & Jn. Thressher & w. *Joan*, def. A mess. called 'Salmons', 40 a. ar., 5 a. mw., 4 a. pa. & 1 a. wd. in Horndon 'upon the Hyll'. £80.

8. Jn. Newe, pl. Jn. Cressenor, esq., & w. *Sibil*, def. 1 mess. & 1 gdn. in Maldon. £40.

9. Joan Egglesfeld, wid., pl. *Arthur* Darcye, kt., & w. Mary, def. 30 a. mw. & 10 a. marsh called 'Tun Marshe'*alias*Newtones in Eastham. 260 mks.

10. Rd. Maynard & Wm. Archer, pl. *Wm.* Fitzwilliam, kt., & w. Anne, def. 140 a. ar., 20 a. mw., 60 a. pa. & 20 a. wd. in Theydon Garnon, Theydon Mount & Theydon Boyes. Def. quitclaimed to pl. & the heirs of Rd. £220.

11. Jn. Drywood jun., pl. *Jas.* Baker, esq., & w. Mary, def. 25 a. pa. & 5 a. mw. called 'Brettens' in Southbeflett. £80.

12. Jn. Lyndesell, pl. *Clement* Roberdys, gent., & Jerome Songer, gent., & w. Mary, def. 1 mess., 1 curtilage, 20 a. ar., 10 a. mw. & 16 a. pa. in Ultyng, Hatfeld Peverell & Boreham. 130 mks.

13. Trin. & Mich. Tho. Mathewe, pl. Jn. Thressher & w. *Joan*, def. 11 a. ar. & 1 a. pa. in West Tylbery. £20.

14. Trin. & Mich. Jn. Hunwycke, Wm. Hunwicke & *Wm.* Goodwyn, pl. Wm., marquess of Northampton, & w. Dame Eliz., def. 1 mess., 3 cotts., 1 barn, 2 gdns., 160 a. ar., 26 a. mw., 70 a. pa., 30 a. wd. & 30 a. moor & marsh in Halsted, Great Maplested, Little Maplested, Henyngham Sible & Gosfylde. Def. quitclaimed to pl. & the heirs of Wm. Hunwicke. £80.

15. Wm. Beryff, pl. *Rd.* Aulfeld jun. & w. Joan, one of the sisters & heirs of Chris. Stede, def. A moiety of the manor of Bentons *alias* Benyngtons & 6 mess., 6 gdns., 4 orchards, 200 a. ar., 20 a. mw., 200 a. pa., 6 a. wd. & 40s. rt. in Wytham, Wyckham, Bradwell & Hatfeld Peverell. £80.

16. Robt. Thurgood, pl. *Wm.* Fitz Willyam, kt., & w. Anne, def. 2 mess., 3 curtilages, 2 barns, 4 gdns., 100 a. ar., 12 a. mw. & 40 a. pa. in Northweld Bassett. £160.

17. Jn. Grene, pl. *Wm.* Fitz William, kt., & w. Anne, def. Manor of Madellys & 6 mess., 4 cotts., 140 a. ar., 30 a. mw., 100 a. pa., 10 a. wd. & 100s. rt. in Eppyng, Great Parndon & Little Parndon. £300.

18. Wm. Spilman & Rd. Purcas, pl. *Tho.* More & w. Eliz. & Chris. Aleyn, merchant of the staple of Calais, def. 1 mess., 29 a. ar. & 2 a. pa. in Thaxsted. Def. quitclaimed to pl. & the heirs of Wm. £140.

19. Hy. Rede, pl. *Ralph* Rede & w. Alice, def. 1 mess. & 5 a. ar. in Toppesfeld. £20.

20. Tho. Cotton, gent., & w. Joan, pl. *Nich.* Rookes & w. Joan & Robt. Watson, def. The rectory & church of Great Wendon *alias* Wenden & 1 toft, 1 barn, 1 orchard, 40 a. ar., 10 a. mw., 10 a. pa. & 40s. rt. in Great Wendon, Little Wendon & Newporte Ponde, all tithes of sheaves, grain & corn in Great Wendon. Little Wenden & Newporte Ponde, & the advowson of the vicarage of the church. Def. quitclaimed to pl. & the heirs of Tho. 130 mks.

21. Edm. Harryngton, pl. *Nich.* Bragg & w. Helen, def. 1 mess., 40 a. ar., 5 a. pa. & 5 a. wd. in Hengham Syble. £60.

22. Trin. & Mich. Jn. Pygrom, pl. *Reg.* Moygne, gent., & w. Margt., def. Manor of Pyersyes & 1 mess., 100 a. ar., 12 a. mw. & 40 a. pa. in Halsted & Stansted. 230 mks.

23. Jn. Benton, pl. Wm. Holwey & w. *Joan*, dau. & heir of Wm. Kyng, decd., def. 1 mess., 1 gdn., 10 a. ar. & 2 a. mw. in Moreton. £40.

24. Jn. Serle, pl. *Wm.* Fitz William, kt., & w. Anne, def. Manor of Marshalls & 1 barn, 1 gdn., 60 a. ar., 12 a. mw., 20 a. pa., 3 a. wd. & 60s. rt. in Northweld Bassett & Theydon Garnon. 160 mks.

25. Joan Egglesfeld, wid., pl. *Anth.* Hungerford, kt., & Jn. Hungerford his son & heir apt., def. 28 a. marsh called 'Tun Marshe' in Eastham. 230 mks.

26. Jn. Lyttell, pl. *Jn.* May & w. Lucy, def. 20 a. ar., 10 a. mw., 20 a. pa. & 4 a. wd. in Hedyngham Syble. £40.

27. Tho. Darcy, esq., pl. *Tho.* Laurens & w. Eliz., def. 1 mess., 60 a. ar., 4 a. mw., 10 a. pa. & 6 a. wd. in Fayrested. £40.

28. Tho. Armiger sen., gent., pl. *Tho.* Darcy, kt., lord Darcy of Chyche, & w. Eliz., def. Manor of Canewndon *alias* Canewdon *alias* Canedon & 20 mess., 20 gdns., 20 orchards, 500 a. ar., & £15 rt. in Canewndon *alias* Canewdon *alias* Canedon, Hakwell, Asshedon, Pakylsham, Little Stambryge, Hokeley, Rocheford, Great Wakeryng & Little Wakeryng. £360.

29. Rd. Johnson, 'grocer', pl. *Jas.* Harryson & w. Grace, def. 1 mess., 20 a. ar., 6 a. pa. & 3 a. wd. in South Wokyngdon. £30.

30. Tho. Darcy, esq., pl. *Jas.* Langbroke & w. Grace, def. 1 mess., 1 barn, 1 gdn., 1 orchard, 40 a. ar., 40 a. mw., 300 a. pa., 10 a. wd. & 20s. rt. in Tolson Darcye. 200 mks.

31. Rd. Twede, pl. Wm. Draper sen., gent., def. 1 mess., 1 toft, 1 cott., 1 orchard, 1 gdn., 6 a. ar. & 8 a. pa. in Aldham. 40 mks.

32. Jas. Dryland, gent., pl. Tho. Burges, gent., def. 2 mess., 2 gdns., 2 orchards, 30 a. ar. & 2½ a. mw. in Branktree & Bokkyng, & a moiety of 1 mess., 1 gdn., 1 orchard, 140 a. ar., 10 a. mw. & 40 a. pa. in Braynktree & Black Notley. £80.

33. Tho. Sumpner, pl. Hy. Parker, lord Morley, & w. Dame Alice, def. 1 mess., 1 barn, 1 stable, 2 gdns., 80 a. ar. & 10 a. mw. in Eppyng. 130 mks.

34. Trin. & Mich. Tho. Whyte, pl. Tho. Chycheley, esq., & w. Marion, Jn. Hager, gent., & w. *Beatrice*, def. 12 mess., 6 cott., 40 a. ar., 20 a. mw., 80 a. pa., 60 a. marsh, 3 a. wd. & 10s. rt. in Upmynster, Raynham, Wennyngton, Alveley, East Tylbury, West Tylbury & Hornechurche. £200.

35. Walter Cupper, gent., pl. Paul Wilkynson, gent., def. 1 mess., 1 toft, 1 barn, 1 stable, 1 gdn., 1 orchard, 20 a. ar., 30 a. mw., 40 a. pa., 30 a. marsh & 2s. rt. in Estham & Little Elford. £100.

36. Trin. & Mich. Eliz. Bisshopp, wid., pl. Robt. Albright, citizen & 'carpenter' of London, & w. Agnes, def. 1 mess., 1 barn & 1 gdn. in Leightonston. £40.

CP25(2)/70/577   HILARY, 1 MARY   1554

37. Wm. Nevyll, pl. Jn. Sandys, gent., def. 2 mess., 1 curtilage, 1 cott. & 1 gdn. in Woddham Ferrers. 40 mks.

38. Hy. Leader, pl. *Jn.* Byrles & w. Joan, def. 2 mess., 2 tofts, 1 gdn. & 1 a. ar. in Saffron Walden. £40.

39. Trin. & Hil. Edw. Mulleynes & Jn. Holmested, pl. *Wm.*, marquess of Northampton, & w. Dame Eliz., def. 1 mess., 1 cott., 2 gdns., 6 a. ar., 6 a. wd., 4 a. marsh & alder & 7s. rt. in Halsted, Stansted & Pebmersshe. Def. quitclaimed to pl. & the heirs of Edw. 59 mks.

40. Mich. & Hil. Tho. Shelton & Jn. Hewes, pl. *Joan* Shelton, wid., & Humphrey Shelton, gent., def. Manor of Oungar called 'Batells Manour' in Oungar & 1 mess., 1 gdn., 2 barns, 1 orchard, 1 dovecote, 280 a. ar., 200 a. mw., 400 a. pa., 220 a wd. & 20d. rt. in Highe Oungar, Standford Ryvers & Stapleford Tawny. Def. quitclaimed to pl. & the heirs of Tho. £1,200. This agreement was made by precept of the Queen.

41. Mich. & Hil. Jn. Gresham, kt., & alderman of London, & Jn. Southcote, gent., pl. Tho. Leveson, citizen & mercer of London, & w. Ursula, def. 8 mess., 8 gdns., 40 a. ar., 10 a. mw. & 20 a. pa. in Walden & Saffrone Walden. Def. quitclaimed to pl. & the heirs of Jn. Gresham. And for this pl. gtd. the same to Ursula for life, with remainder to Tho. & his heirs, to hold of the chief lords.

42. Mich. & Hil. Jn. Lyndesell & Tho. Aylett, pl. *Humphrey* Brown, kt., one of the justices of the Bench, & w. Agnes, def. Manor of Stockhall & 100 a. ar., 30 a. mw., 60 a. pa., 5 a. wd. & 15 s. rt. in Matchyng, Hatfyld Brodeoke & Little Laver. Def. quitclaimed to pl. & the heirs of Jn. £220.

43. Geo. Barne, kt., alderman of London, pl. *Hy.* Burman & w. Joan, def. 8 mess., 1 salt-house (*domo salsaria*) and 1 fish-house (*domo piscaria*), 5 gdns., 1 quay, 3 a. ar. & 2 weirs in Harwich (*Herwico*) and the port of Orwell. £120.

44. Mich. & Hil. Clement Robertys, gent., pl. Jas. Thornebake & w. *Ellen*, Wm. Bery & w. *Margt*. & Geo. Hubbe & w. *Alice*, def. 3 mess., 3 gdns., 3 orchards, 30 a. ar., 8 a. mw., 10 a. pa., 4 a. heath & 12d. rt. in Wytham, Falborne & Little Braxsted. £100.

45. Jn. Lyncolne, pl. Edw. Colver, 'yoman', & w. *Alice*, def. 1 mess. & 1½ a. mw. in Brentwood. £40.

46. Trin. & Mich. Wm. Hunwyke, pl. Tho. Hunwyke, def. 1 mess., 1 gdn., 15 a. ar., 4 a. mw. & 20 a. pa. in Great Leyghes. 50 mks.

47. Robt. Maye, pl. *Jn.* Glascok, gent., & w. Mary, def. 1 mess., 2 tofts, 2 curtilages, 2 barns, 2 gdns., 50 a. ar., 12 a. mw. & 20 a. pa. in Little Canfeld. 160 mks.

48. Mich. & Hil. Tho. Stocks & w. Alice, pl. *Geo.* Gille, gent., & w. Anne, def. 52 a. ar., in Stansted Mountfytchett. Def. quitclaimed to pl. & the heirs of Tho. 100 mks.

49. Wm. Clerke, pl. Wm. Marler, gent., def. 3 mess., 4 cott. & 3 gdns. in Coggeshale. 50 mks.

50. Edw. Gryffyn, esq., attorney general of the Queen, Wm. Cordall, esq., solicitor general of the Queen, & Jn. Marshe, esq., pl. Wm. Tanfyld, gent., and w. *Eliz.*, def. The manor of Vang atte Noke, Peverells & Coptfolde Hall *alias* Coldehalle & 4 mess., 4 cott., 10 gdns., 800 a. ar., 200 a. mw., 500 a. pa., 300 a. wd., 80 a. marsh & £12 rent in Gyng Margarett, Vang atte Noke & Westhannyngfelde. Def. quitclaimed to pl. & the heirs of Edw. £400.

51. Mich. & Hil. Wm. Enyver, pl. *Jn.* Swallowe, gent., & w. Anne, def. 1 mess., 2 gdns. & 8 a. ar. in Panfeld 40 mks.

52. Rd. Large, pl. Tho. (Eg)lam *alias* Knyght & w. *Margery*, def. 1 mess. & 1 gdn. in Prittelwell. 10 mks.

53. Mich. & Hil. Robt. Whetstons, pl. *Edw.* Fynes, lord Clynton & Say, & w. Eliz., def. The lordship or manor of Woodworth & Hylhowse & 40 mess., 30 cott., 40 tofts, 500 a. ar., 30 a. mw., 500 a. pa., 200 a. wd., 30 a. furze & heath & £7 rent & the advowson of the church of Woodforth in Woodforth & Hylhowse. £640.

CP25(2)/83/709   DIVERS COUNTIES

11. Edw. Wyndsore, kt., & Hy. Hampden, gent., pl. Robt. Oxynbridge, kt., & w. Alice & *Wm.* Scott, esq., def. Manor of Synkcleris & 4 mess., 6 cott., 6 gdns., 200 a. ar., 80 a. mw., 300 a. pa., 10 a. wd., 120 a. marsh & 3s. 4d. rt. in West Tylbery & Est Tylbery, co. Essex, & property in Sussex & Kent. Def. quitclaimed to pl. & the heirs of Edw. 1,390 mks. — Sussex, Essex, Kent.

CP25(2)/70/578   EASTER, 1 MARY   1554

1. Jn. Freer of Clare (co. Suffolk), pl. *Jn.* Lamberde of Heleyns Bumsted & w. Joan, def. 20 a. ar., 5 a. mw., 30 a. pa. & 4 a. wd. in Bumsted at the Steeple *alias* Steple Bumsted. 130 mks.

2. Jn. Wale & Tho. Sorrell, pl. Tho. Smyth, def. 4 mess., 2 barns, 2 stables, 3 gdns., 2 orchards, 40 a. ar., 2 a. mw., 12 a. pa. & 2 a. wd. in Great Dunmowe. Def. quitclaimed to pl. & the heirs of Jn. £40.

3. Wm. Harrys, esq., pl. *Tho.* Darcy, kt., lord Darcy, & w. Eliz., def. Manors of Stockys, Lytteryn, Dykers & Algaays & 1 mess., 2 tofts, 1 cott., 1 barn, 1 gdn., 1 orchard, 100 a ar., 40 a mw., 300 a. pa., 3 a. wd., 100 a. fresh marsh, 40 a. salt marsh, 50 a. furze & heath & 100s. rent in Althorn, Maylond & Cryxseyght. £700.

4. Wm. Lynne, pl. Wm. Walgrave, kt., def. 2 mess., 2 barns, 1 stable, 1 bakery, 2 curtilages, 30 a. ar., 14 a. mw., 100 a. pa. & 2 a. wd. in Wormyngford, Mont Bures & Chapel Paryshe. £80.

5. Tho. Crawley, esq., pl. *Tho.* Josselyn, kt., & w. Dorothy, def. Manor of Manewden Hall & 20 mess., 6 cott., 400 a. ar., 30 a. mw., 60 a. pa., 10 a. wd. & £20 rent in Manewden, Farneham, Ugley & Stansted Mountfychett. £553.

6. Robt. Gooddaye, pl. Def. as in preceding. 84 a. ar., 7 a. mw., 30 a. pa. & 2 a. wd. in Sheryng. 200 mks.

7. Hy. Clerke, pl. *Wm.* Fitzwillyam, kt., & w. Anne, def. 8 a. ar., 2 a. mw., 4 a. pa. & 8 a. wd. in Theydon Garnon. 50 mks.

8. Tho. Darcye, esq., pl. Jn. Seyntclere, esq., def. 1 mess., 1 gdn., 100 a. ar., 100 a. mw., 100 a. pa., 240 a. fresh marsh, 40 a. salt marsh & 5 a. wd. in Saynt Osyth. 830 mks.

9. Jas. Pargeter, gent., pl. *Jn.* Collyns and w. Joan, def. 1 mess., 20 a. ar., 10 a. mw., 10 a. pa. & 70 a. wd. in Barkyng. £80.

10. Jn. Maynard, pl. *Geo.* Cristemas, esq., & w. Bridget, def. 2 mess., 2 gdns., 1 water-fulling-mill called 'Est Myll', 2 a. ar., 10 a. mw., 2 a. pa. & 2s. rent in Colchester. 160 mks.

11. Wm. Norman, pl. Edm. Hurry and w. *Eliz.*, def. 3 a. ar. in Legh. £20.

12. Wm. Beryff, gent., pl. *Wm.* Draper sen., gent., & Wm. Draper jun., gent., his son and heir apt. def. 3 mess., 4 tofts, 3 curtilages, 2 cotts., 2 barns, 1 dovecote, 2 gdns., 2 orchards, 140 a. ar., 20 a. mw., 120 a. pa. & 20 a. wd. in Aldham, Great Tey, Little Tey, Tey Maundevyle *alias* Marks Tey. £200.

13. Tho. Josselyn, kt., pl. *Wm.* Stafford, kt., & w. Dorothy, def. The manor of High Rothyng *alias* High Rodyng & 160 mess., 1,000 a. ar., 200 a. mw., 200 a. pa., 200 a. wd. & £7 rt. in High Rodyng. £620.

14. Mich. 4 Edward VI & Eas. 1 Mary. Jn. Gyllett, pl. Hy. Wynter & w. *Alice*, one of the daus. and co-heirs of Wm. Gosse, decd., Wm. Jacson & w. *Margt.*, dau. & one of the co-heirs of Margt. Davy, another dau. & co-heir of Wm., Mich. Trenchefeld and w. *Joan*, another dau. & co-heir of Margt. Davy, & Tho. Cambridge & w. *Joan*, one of the daus. & co-heirs of Tho. Hawle, decd., def. 1 mess., 1 gdn. & 3 a. ar. in Ramsey. 40 mks.

15. Wm. Archer, pl. Wm. Atkynson & w. *Thomasina*, def. A fourth part of 20 a. ar., 6 a. mw. & 20 a. pa. in Gyng Margarett. 40 mks.

16. Bart Averell, gent., pl. *Tho.* Darcy, kt., lord Darcy, & w. Eliz., def. The manor of Pudsey *alias* Pudsey Hall & 2 tofts, 2 curtilages, 4 cotts., 1 barn, 2 gdns., 1 orchard, 80 a. ar., 20 a. mw., 120 a. pa., 6 a. wd., 60 a. fresh marsh, 60 a. salt marsh & £7 rent in Canewdon *alias* Canewden, Little Stambredge, Asschyngdon, Hockeley, Hawkwell & South Fambredge. £400.

17. Tho. Mee & Rd. Bulleyn, pl. Tho. Harryson & w. *Eliz.*, def. 2 mess., 1 gdn. & 1 shop in Chepyng Walden. Def. quitclaimed to pl. & the heirs of Tho. And for this pl. granted the same to def. & the heirs of Tho., to hold of the chief lords.

18. Wm. Serle & Hy. Polsted, esq., pl Tho. Ford, Wm. Stokes & w. *Margt.*, Jn. Hodgeson & w. Joan, def. 1 mess., 1 toft, 2 gdns. & 1 a. ar. in Great Berdefeld & Fobbyng. Def. quitclaimed to pl. & the heirs of Wm. £36.

19. Tho. Darcy, esq., pl. *Wm.* Beryff & w. Kath., def. A moiety of the manor of Bentons etc. (as in 15 of Michaelmas term, 1553). £140.

20. Tho. Rooper, pl. Jn. Po(mfr)ett and w. *Joan*, def. 1 mess. in Walden. £40.

21. Hil. and Eas. Jn. Drywood of Dunton Halle, 'yoman', pl. Tho. Eyon *alias* Jen and w. *Alice*, def. 40 a. ar. & 6 a. wd. in Gyngejaybardlaundrey, which Wm. Sylbanke holds for life. Pl. and his heirs to hold the reversion of the chief lords. £60.

22. Tho. Erswell, pl. Tho. Roper & w. Anabel & Jn. Pomferett & w. *Joan*, def. 1 mess., 1 gdn. (*gardino*) and 1 gdn. (*orto*) in Walden. £40.

23. Trin. & Eas. Tho. Gutter, pl. *Wm.*, marquess of Northampton, & w. Dame Eliz., def. The manor of Hipworth & 84 a. ar., 27 a. mw., 70 a. pa., 20 a. moor & marsh & 47s. 5d. rt. in Halsted, Henyngham Syble, Little Maplested & Great Maplested. 530 mks.

24. Tho. Gregill & Wm. Prowe, pl. Jn. Tyler & w. *Agnes*, def. 1 mess. & 2 gdns. in Branketre. Def. quitclaimed to Tho. & his heirs. £200.

25. Wm. Bowlynge, pl. Hugh Tompson *alias* Saunder and w. *Mgt.*, def. 2 a. ar. in Walden. £20.

26. Tho. Docwra, esq., pl. Wm. Scott, esq., def. Manor of Oldehall & 1 barn, 1 gdn., 1 orchard, 40 a. ar., 5 a. mw., 100 a. pa., 60 a. marsh & £9 rent in Curringham, Fobbyng, Fange, Bursted, Stanford le Hope, Estylbury, Westylbury & Chaldwell. 400 mks.

27. Tho. Copland & Jn. Bryges, pl. *Anth.* Hungerforde & Wm. Gowge, def. 1 mess., 1 barn, 40 a. ar. & 44 a. fresh marsh in Estham. Def. quitclaimed to pl. & the heirs of Tho. And for this pl. gtd. the same to Wm. to hold from the Annunciation, 1566, for 30 years, rendering £12 yearly at SS. Simon & Jude & St. George Martyr, with power of distraint, with reversion to Anth. & the heirs of his body, to hold of the chief lords.

28. Trin. & Eas. Jn. Hubbard, pl. *Wm.*, marquess of Northampton, & w. Dame Eliz., def. 1 mess., 1 toft, 3 barns, 3 gdns., 100 a. ar., 12 a. mw., 20 a. pa., 10 a. wd. & 10 a. moor & marsh in Halsted. £168.

29. Same dates. Philip Hunwicke & Wm. Hunwicke, pl. Def. as in preceding. The manor of Slohouse & 2 mess., 2 cotts., 2 barns, 2 gdns., 160 a. ar., 10 a. mw., 100 a. pa., 60 a. wd. & 20 a. moor & marsh in Halsted & Gosfylde. Def. quitclaimed to pl. & to the heirs of Philip. £220.

30. Wm. Ayllett & w. Margt., Robt. Wortham & w. Eliz., Rd. Rought & w. Philippa, Jn. Franke of Little Waltham & w. Joan, Jn. Franke jun. & w. Thomasina, Tho. Eardeley & w. Bridget & Joan Smyth, pl. Wm. Rochester, esq., def. 1 mess., 100 a. ar., 20 a. mw., 20 a. pa., 10 a. wd. & 10s. rent in Little Waltham & Great Leyghes. Def. quitclaimed to pl. & the heirs of Margt. £80.

31. Philip Hunwicke, pl. *Jn.* Hubbard & w. Anne, def. 1 toft, 3 gdns., 2 barns, 70 a. ar., 5 a. mw., 40 a pa. & 10 a. moor & marsh in Halsted called 'Blacknams', 'Balaams' and 'Jernigams'. 130 mks.

32. Robt. Turner, pl. *Hy.* Carter, Humphrey Carter, Rd. Carter & Jn. Carter, def. 1 mess., 1 orchard. & 1 a. ar. in Stapleford Tawney. £40.

33. Robt. Forster & Mich. Forster, gentlemen, pl. Geo. Cristemas, esq., def. Manor of Barnhams & 10 mess., 6 tofts, 3 dovecotes, 10 gdns., 300 a. ar., 30 a. mw., 200 a. pa., 60 a. wd. & 10s. rt. in Beamonde, Wheleighe, Thorpe, Colchester, Boxsted, Myleende, Lexden & Great Horseley. Def. quitclaimed to pl. & the heirs of Robt. £220.

1554   TRINITY, 1 MARY

34. Jn. Prentyce jun., pl. Tho. Sewalle, def. 1 mess., 2 cott., 2 curtilages, 1 barn, 1 gdn. & 4 a. ar. in Halsted. 40 mks.

35. Jn. Marsshe sen., citizen & mercer of London, pl. Tho. Hales, gent., & w. *Eliz.*, def. 1 mess. called 'Adyncars', 1 orchard, 1 gdn., 12 a. ar., 10 a. mw. & 10 a. pa. in Dagenham £40.

36. Tho. Love, pl. *Walter* Vesey & w. Agnes, def. 1 mess., 1 gdn., 30 a. pa. & 4 a. wd. in Ardeleigh. £40.

37. Robt. Bredge, pl. Steph. Hache & w. *Margt.*, and *Eliz.* Beryff, def. 1 mess., 2 tofts, 1 barn, 1 gdn, 1 orchard, 5 a. ar. & 4 a. pa. in Stysted. 40 mks.

38. Margt. Whytyng, wid., late w. of Jn. Whytyng, pl. Tho. Archer & w. *Agnes*, def. 1 mess. & 1 gdn. in Thaxsted. £20.

39. Eas. and Trin. Tho. Stocks, pl. Jn. Turner & w. Maud, def. 1 mess., 1 gdn. & 1 orchard in Great Berdefeld. £30.

40. Garrett Harman, pl. *Edw.* Barker and w. Frances, def. 8 a. mw. in Westham Burnells. £40.

41. Tho. Darcy, esq., pl. Jn. Huddylston, kt., & w. Bridget, def. Manor of Wekes *alias* Wek & 2 mess., 2 gdns., 60 a. ar., 30 a. mw., 120 a. pa., 12 a. wd., 160 a. furze & Heath & 25s. 9d. rt. in Tolshunte Maior, Norton, Mondene & Branston. Def. quitclaimed from themselves & the heirs of Jn. to pl. & his heirs, with warranty from themselves & the heirs of Bridget. £145.

42. Eas. and Trin. Tho. Lyndesell & Robt. Wright, pl. Chris. Aleyn, esq., & w. *Agnes*, def. A pension of £4 yearly out of (*extra*) the vicarage of Depden. Def. quitclaimed to pl. & the heirs of Tho. £80.

43. Jn. Ducke, pl. Robt. Abbott & w. *Alice*, def. 1 mess. & 1 gdn. in Haverhyll. £20.

44. Jn. Hamond, pl. *Hy.* Spender & w. Kath., def. A moiety of 1 mess., 40 a. ar., 4 a. mw. & 5 a. pa. in Fobyng. £40.

45. Eas. and Trin. Jn. Dawby, pl. *Jn.* Clerke and w. Joan, def. 1 mess. & 1 curtilage in Harwich ('Harwico'). £40.

46. Jn. Barnard, pl. Rd. Darby & w. *Margt.*, def. 1 mess., 1 gdn. & 6 a. ar. in Fayersted. £40.

47. Steph. Craske, gent., pl. Jas. Athelham, def. 2 mess., 100 a. ar., 20 a. mw., 20 a. pa. & 3 a. wd. in Rothyng Aythorp & High Ester. £100.

48. Eas. & Trin. Jn. Cowland, pl. *Tho.* Josselyn, kt., & w. Dorothy, def. The manor of Highams & 1 mess., 140 a. ar., 12 a. mw., 4 a. wd. & 15s. rt. in Rothyng Aythorp. 260 mks.

49. Jn. Love jun., pl. Wm Walker & *Tho.* Walker & w. Cristina, def. 2 mess., 1 toft, 1 curtilage, 2 gdns, 7 a. ar. & 5 a. mw. in Raylegh. 110 mks.

50. Eas. & Trin. Jn. Cooke, pl. Jn. Trayford, def. 1 mess., 1 barn & 1 gdn. in Raylegh, which Jn. Radyshe & w. Agnes hold for her life. Pl. & his heirs to hold the reversion of the chief lords. £20.

51. Rd. Saunders, pl. Wm. Weston, gent., & w. *Mary*, one of the daus. & heirs of Agnes Wryghtyngton, def. A moiety of 1 mess., 2 tofts & 3 curtilages called 'Persons' in Walden. 40 mks.

52. Oswald Davye, pl. Edw. Fabyon, def. 1 mess., 22 a. ar., 1 a. mw. & 2 a. wd. in Brodwell, Stistede, Fering & Kelden. £40.

53. Wm. Bendlowes, gent., & Tho. Ford, pl. *Wm.* Stokes and w. Margt., def. 30 a. ar. & 7 a. wd. in Great Berdefeld. Def. quitclaimed to pl. & the heirs of Wm. 100 mks.

54. Eas. & Trin. Wm. Spylman, pl. *Robt.* Barker and w. Agnes, def. 1 mess. & 1 gdn. in Thaxsted. £40.

55. Chris. Snelog & Hy. Snelog, pl. *Rd.* Putto and w. Eliz., def. 1 mess., 1 curtilage, 1 gdn., 20 a. ar., 4 a. mw. & 10 a. pa. in Finchingfeld & Toppesfeld. Def. quitclaimed to pl. & the heirs of Chris. £60.

56. Rd. Stonard & w. Margt., pl. Robt. Gerves & w. *Anne*, def. A moiety of 1 mess., 12 a. ar., 2 a. mw. & 2 a. moor in Gyngemargarett. Def. quitclaimed to pl. & the heirs of Margt. £40.

CP25(2)/70/579   MICHAELMAS, 1 AND 2 PHILIP AND MARY   1554

1. Wm. Aylett, pl. *Hy.* Rochester & w. Agnes, def. 1 mess., 1 orchard., 1 barn, 30 a. ar., 4 a. mw., 12 a. pa. & 3 a. wd. in Great Leyghes. £80.

2. Thomasina Cornewall, wid., pl. Robt. Cornewall, gent., def. Manor of Curpayles and 10 mess., 6 tofts, 6 gdns., 1 water-mill, 100 a. ar., 40 a. mw., 80 a. pa., 12 a. wd. & 30s. rt. in Haverhyll, Sturmer, Kedyngton & Bumstede. £220.

3. Jn. Clare, gent., pl. *Jn.* Seyntclere, esq., & w. Margt., def. 1 mess., 1 gdn., 2 tofts, 16 a. ar., 6 a. pa., 1 a. wd. & 8 a. marsh in Chiche Regis *alias* Chyche St. Osythe. £40.

4. Jerome Songer, gent., pl. Jn. Dar'yng *alias* Broun, def. 1 mess. & 1 gdn in Walden. £40.

5. Jn. Holmested, pl. Jn. Belcham & w. *Joan*, def. 1 mess., 4 a. land & 4 a. ar. in Little Maplested & Halsted. 40 Mks.

6. Geoff. Snaggs & Jn. Snaggs, pl. Anth. Rigbye, gent., def. 1 mess., 1 curtilage, 1 orchard, 50 a. ar., 12 a. mw., 20 a. pa. & 30 a. wd. in Barkyng & Dagenham. Def. quitclaimed to pl. & the heirs of Geoff. £80.

7. Rd. Ryche, kt., lord Ryche, pl. *Wm.* Strangman, gent., & w. Mary, def. 2 a. pa. in Hadley Castell & a moiety of 100 a. salt marsh in Hadley Castell. £30.

8. Jn. Chappeleyn, pl. Jn. Gaynesford, esq., & w. *Cicilia*, def. 40 a. ar., 16 a. pa. and 6 a. wd. in Toppesfeld, Wethersfeld & Hengham Syble. £140.

9. Jn. Freer, pl. Robt. Perker & w. *Joan*, late the w. of Tho. Hawkyn, decd., def. 1 mess., 13 a. ar., 3 a. mw., 2 a. pa. & 3 a. wd. in Bumpsted at the Steeple. £40.

10. Edw. Gryffyn, esq., attorney general, Wm. Cordell, esq., solicitor general, Edw. Brockett, esq., & Geo. Hadley, pl. Wm. Clopton, esq., def. The manors of Whetleygh & Downhall & 14 mess., 2 cotts., 2 tofts, 140 a. ar., 50 a. mw., 30 a. pa., 110 a. wd., 40 a. furze & heath & £9 rent in Reylegh, Thundersley & Hadleygh. Def. quitclaimed to pl. & the heirs of Wm. And for this pl. gtd. the same to def. to hold for life of the chief lords without impeachment of waste, with remainder to Tho. Clopton & w. Dorothy & the heirs of Tho. of the body of Dorothy, the heirs of the body of def. & the right heirs of Eliz. Wethersby, mother of def.

11. Tho. Shorry, pl. Rd. Jenyn & w. *Joan*, def. 10 a. ar. in High Ester. £30.

12. Tho. Darcye, esq., pl. *Jn.* Sentcler, esq., & w. Margt., def. 1 mess., 1 gdn., 100 a. ar., 100 a. mw., 100 a. pa., 5 a. wd., 240 a. fresh marsh & 40 a. salt marsh in Sent Osyth. 400 mks.

13. Jn. Busshe, pl. Tho. Bett & w. *Joan* & Wm. Reynold & w. *Margt.*, def. 1 mess. & 1 gdn. in Shenfyld. £20.

14. Rd. Bryce, pl. Jn. Duckett & w. *Alice*, def. 1 mess. & 1 gdn. in Thaxsted. 40 mks.

15. Tho. Pytteman, pl. Tho. Moyse & w. *Etheldreda*, def. 1 mess., 1 gdn. & 10 a. ar. in St. Osithe. £30.

16. Giles Alyngton, kt., pl. *Robt.* Cornewell, gent., & Rd. Cornewell, gent., def. 2 mess., 2 tofts, 2 gdns., 80 a. ar., 40 a. mw., 120 a. pa., 40 a. wd. & 20s. rt. in Haverill, Sturnmere, Kedyngton & Bumstede. £80.

17. Robt. Pollard, pl. *Ranulph* Lyn, gent., & w. Eliz., def. 1 mess., 1 dovecote, 1 gdn., 100 a. ar., 10 a. mw., 60 a. pa., 20 a. wd. & 10s. rt. in Netheryeldam, Stamborne & Toppysfeld. £80.

18. Jerome Songer, gent., & w. Mary, pl. Jerome Grene, gent., def. 1 mess., 2 dovecotes, 1 gdn., 1 orchard, 100 a. ar., 12 a. mw., 100 a. pa., 12 a. wd., 10 a. marsh & 10s. rt. in Wytham & Falborne. Def. quitclaimed to pl. & the heirs of Jerome. £240.

19. Jn. Ayland, pl. *Wm.* Sawyer *alias* Draper & w. Margt., def. 1 mess. & 1 gdn. in Moche Dumowe. £20.

20. Roger Fytche, pl. *Roger* Perker, gent., & w. Anne, def. 1 mess., 1 gdn., 30 a. ar., 6 a. mw., 16 a. pa. & 3 a. wd. in Bokkyng. £80.

21. Wm. Petre, kt., pl. *Wm.* Lukyn & w. Joan & Tho. Lukyn & w. Eleanor, def. The manors of Maysburye *alias* Marshebury Hall and Matching & 300 a. ar., 40 a. mw., 140 a. pa., 30 a. wd. & £12 rent in Marshebery *alias* Masbuerye, Goodester, Chyknall St. James and Matching, and the advowson of the church of Mashbury. £440.

22. Jn. Lyttell, pl. Anth. Rigby, gent., def. 1 mess., 1 gdn., 1 barn, 24 a. ar., 10 a. mw. & 1 a. wd. in Barkyng. £40.

23. Wm. Stubbyng, pl. *Jn.* Gaynsford, esq., & Cicilia, def. The manor of Gaynsfords and 2 mess., 2 gdns., 2 tofts, 2 barns, 140 a. ar., 20 a. mw., 200 a. pa., 2 a. wd. & 20s. rent in Toppesfeld, Wethersfeld, Finchefeld & Syble Henyngham. £140.

24. Wm. Cooke, 'cooper', pl. *Wm.* Wynde & w. Kath., def. 1 mess., 1 gdn & 1 orchard in Hawsted. £20.

25. And. Fuller, pl. Anth. Rigbye, gent., def. 1 mess., 1 curtilage, 1 gdn., 1 barn, 20 a. ar., 6 a. mw. & 3 a. wd. in Barking & Dagnam. £40.

26. Wm. Lukyn, pl. Tho. Lyster & w. *Eliz.*, def. 1 mess., 1 orchard & 3 a. ar. in Felsted. £20.

27. Jn. Ballard, pl. Tho. Legatt, esq., & w. *Petronilla*, def. 40 a. ar., 20 a. pa. & 10 a. wd. in Kelwedon. £40.

28. David Sympson, gent., pl. Wm. Lathum, def. The manor of Beachamps & 1 mess., 2 tofts, 3 curtilages, 2 gdns., 1 orchard, 60 a. ar., 30 a. mw., 110 a. pa., 6 a. wd. & 40s. rt. in Ronwell & Wyckford. £320.

29. Robt. Bonham, gent., pl. Margt. Fabyan, wid., def. 2 mess., 3 tofts, 2 curtilages, 2 barns, 2 gdns., 1 orchard, 20 a. land, 5 a. mw., 30 a. pa. & 4 a. wd. in Coggeshale, Bradwell by Coggeshale & Stysted. £60.

(*Note*: the scribe wrote *sexaginta* and *sexaginta libras* twice.)

30. Edw. Brokett and Geo. Hadley, pl. Wm. Barley, esq., and w. *Joyce*, def. A moiety of the manors of Mulsham and Leyer Breten *alias* Leyer Barley & a moiety of 20 mess., 10 cotts., 10 tofts, 10 orchards, 66 a. ar. 100 a. mw., 200 a. pa., 40 a. wd., 60 a. furze & heath & £4 rent in Mulsham, Salcott, Leyer Breten *alias* Leyer Barley & Wygbourow, & a moiety of the advowson of the church of Salcott. Def. quitclaimed to pl. & the heirs of Edw. And for this pl. granted the same to def. to hold for their lives of the chief lords without impeachment of waste, with remainder to Tho. Clopton, gent., & w. Dorothy & the heirs of her body by him, the said Wm. Barley & the heirs of his body, the heirs of the body of Hy. Barley, esq., decd., his father, & the right heirs of Wm.

31. Robt. Ardeley, pl. Jn. Payne & w. *Ellen*, def. 3 a. mw. in Wormyngforde. 50 mks.

32. Jn. Adyngton & Chris. Adyngton, pl. *Agnes* Syke, wid., Ellen Adyngton & Margery Adyngton, daus. of Wm. Adyngton late of Banbury, co. Oxon., def. Manor of Harlowe *alias* Harlowe Bery & 20 mess., 2 barns, 1 water-mill, 500 a. ar., 40 a. mw., 500 a. pa., 100 a. wd., 60 a. furze & heath & £10 rt. in Harlow, Sheryng, Latton, Great Ilford, Little Ilford, Chigewell & Wansted, & the advowson of the church of Harlowe. Def. quitclaimed to pl. & the heirs of Jn. £800.

33. Tho. Pullyver, pl. Margt. Garrard, wid., & *Geo.* Symcotts, gent., def. 1 mess., 1 barn, 1 pond (*stagno*), 10 a. ar., 10 a. mw., 20 a. pa., 10 a. marsh, & a free fishery in Westham, Estham & Berkinge, & 13½ a. marsh, 10 a. reed (*arundinis*) & a free fishery in Estham, Westham & Berking. £80.

34. Wm. Rychardson, pl. *Nich.* Everard, gent., & w. Cecily, def. 1 mess., 1 barn, 10 a. ar. & 10 a. pa. in Copford. 50 mks.

35. Francis Benson, pl. Jn. Sandys, gent., def. 1 mess., 2 tofts, 1 barn, 1 gdn., 1 orchard, 20 a. ar., 6 a. mw. & 16 a pa. in Wodham Ferrers. £40.

36. Trin. & Mich. Jn. Wyseman, esq., pl. *Matthias* Bradburye, gent., & w. Margt., def. 1 mess., 1 gdn., 1 orchard, 160 a. ar., 12 a. mw., 20 a. pa. & 6 a. wd. in Thaxsted & Easton. £240.

37. Rd. Prowe, pl. *Geo.* Bacon & w. Margt., def. 1 mess. & 1 barn in Walden. £30.

38. Jn. Rogers, pl. Nich. Merell & w. *Eliz.*, def. A fourth part of 1 mess., 1 curtilage and 1 gdn. in Mulsham in the parish of Chelmesford. £30.

39. Barthelet Grene, pl. *Nich.* Wolvur *alias* Albar & w. Joan, def. 1 mess., 1 gdn., 1 orchard & 15 a. 1 rood ar. in Stanstede Myll in the parish of Bartechanger. 40 mks.

40. Robt. Pole, pl. Roger Perker, gent., & w. Anne, *Roger* Fytche & w. Margery, & Tho. Woodam & w. *Agnes*, def. 1 mess., 2 cotts., 2 barns, 1 gdn., 52 a. ar., 6 a. mw., 30 a. pa. & 8 a. wd. in Lyndesell and Brokeshed. £80.

41. Robt. Taverner, gent., pl. Hy., earl of Sussex, viscount Fitz Water, lord Egremond & Burnell, def. The manor of Priors and 2 mess., 2 tofts, 1 gdn., 3 orchards, 30 a. ar., 20 a. mw. & 20 pa. in Lamborn. £80.

42. Rd. Skelton, pl. Rd. Johnson & w. Eliz. & Jn. Brett & w. Lettice, def. 1 mess., 1 toft, 1 cott., 1 gdn., 1 orchard & 4 a. pa. in Hadleygh. 40 mks.

43. Tho. Darcy, esq., pl. Lau. Waren & w. Joan, def. Manor of Moverons *alias* Morehams & 10 mess., 10 gdns., 1,000 a. ar., 200 a. mw., 800 a. pa., 30 a. wd., 400 a. marsh and 20s. rt. in Moverons, Morehams, Bryghtlynsey, Thoryngton & Alresford, & free warren in Bryghtlynsey. Def. quitclaimed from themselves & the heirs of Lau. to pl. & his heirs, & granted for themselves & the heirs of Joan, warranty against themselves & the heirs of Lau. £300.

44. Wm. Adams, pl. *Edw.* Cole and w. Joan, def. 1 mess., & 1 gdn. in Brayntre. £16.

45. Hy. Baker, pl. Jn. Sandys, gent., def. 18 a. ar., 2 a. mw., 16 a. pa. & 4 a. wd. in Wodham Ferrers. 100 mks.

46. Lau. Warren, gent., pl. *Jn.* Seyncler, esq., & w. Margt., def. 1 mess., 1 gdn., 100 a. ar., 20 a. mw., 200 a. pa., 10 a. wd., 100 a. marsh & liberty of warren in Bryklyngsey & Thoryngton. £300.

47. Jn. Starlyng, pl. Rd. Benson & w. Margt. & Agnes Abell, def. Two thirds of 1 mess., 20 a. ar., 2 a. mw. & 20 a. pa. in Ardeley. £40.

48. Jn. Wayman & w. Eliz., pl. Tho. Skott and w. *Ellen* and Bridget Gardener, def. Two thirds of 1 messuage, 1 garden and 1 quay in Harwyche. £40.

49. Ralph Pyke, pl. Margt. Moyse *alias* Morse, wid., *Tho.* Moyse *alias* Morse and w. Joan and Jn. Moyse *alias* Morse & w. Eliz., def. 1 mess., 1 gdn., 1 barn, 8 a. ar., 7 a. pa. & 2 a. fresh marsh in Barlyng & Little Shobery *alias* Northsobery. 50 mks.

50. Jn. Whytt, pl. *Wm.* Strache & w. Margt., Wm. Burshall & w. Margt. & Jn. Butcher and w. Kath., def. 1 mess. & 1 gdn. in Walden *alias* Saffron Walden. £40.

51. Wm. Andrewe, pl. Def. as in 48. Two thirds of 1 mess. & 1 gdn. in Harwiche. £40.

52. Rd. Harpur, esq., pl. Jn. Kynge, def. 5 mess., 2 cotts., 1 dovecote, 7 gdns., 7 orchards, 200 a. ar., 30 a. mw., 100 a. pa., 6 a. wd & 300 a furze & heath in Magdelen Leavar, North Well Bassett & Moreton *alias* Murten. 200 mks.

53. Jn. Aylyff, kt., citizen & alderman of London, pl. Humphrey Bagsha, gent., & w. *Agnes*, one of the sisters & heirs of Robt. Arthur, gent., def. A moiety of 2 mess. & 240 a. marsh in Priklewell *alias* Pritwell & Estwood. £170.

54. Rd. Weston, esq., pl. *Jn.* Dormer, gent., & w. Eliz., Wm. Dormer & Ambrose Dormer, gentlemen, def. 2 mess., 30 a. ar., 14 a. mw. & 10 a. pa. in Ramsdon Belhouse, Ramsdon Craye & Downeham. £80.

55. Wm. Humfrey, pl. *Geo.* Gille, gent., & w. Anne, def. 1 mess., 50 a. ar., 8 a. pa. & 3 a. wd. in Henham & Plegeden. £60.

56. Tho. Herde, pl. Rd. Sandes, gent., & w. Kath., def. 4 tofts, 60 a. ar., 10 a. mw. & 60 a. pa. in Wrabnesse, which def. hold for the life of Kath., with reversion to Mary Roydon & her heirs. Def. granted to pl. whatever they had in the same. £80.

57. Tho., lord Darcye of Chyche, pl. *Jn.* Seyntclere, esq., & w. Margt., def. Manor of Frowyke *alias* Frodwyke & 10 mess., 5 tofts, 500 a. ar., 40 a. mw., 400 a. pa., 300 a. wd., 200 a. furze & heath & £5 rent in Saynt Osyth & Weleigh. £400.

58. Wm. Dey, pl. Tho. Eyon & w. *Alice*, def. 4 a. ar. in Buttesburye. £10.

59. *Jn.* Thurgood, pl. Jerome Gylbert, gent., def. 2 mes., 2 gdns., 1 orchard, 30 a. ar., 10 a. mw. & 20 a. pa. in Colne Engayne. £60.

60. Jn. Savyll, pl. *Geo.* Gille, gent., & w. Anne, def. 50 a. ar., 2 a. mw. & 10 a. pa. in Stansted Mountfychett. £60.

61. Hy. Trigge, 'yoman', pl. Jn. Trigge jun., def. 1 mess., 1 curtilage, 1 gdn., 1 orchard & ½ a. ar. in Arkesden & Elmeden. Def. quitclaimed to pl. & his heirs. And for this pl. gtd. the same to def. & his heirs to hold of the chief lords.

62. Jn. Bonnar, pl. *Robt.* Haule & w. Etheldreda, def. 1 mess. & 1 gdn. in Leigh. 20 mks.

63. Godfrey Swayne, gent., pl. Jn. Heylok, def. 1 mess. & 1 gdn. in Thaksted. £16.

64. Mich. & Hil. Jn. Aylyff, kt., citizen & alderman of London, pl. *Humphrey* Bagshawe of Hippoletts, co. Hertford, gent., & w. Agnes, def. A moiety of 3 mess., 3 cotts., 40 a. ar., 100 a. mw., 120 a. pa. & 200 a. marsh in Burneham, Walletts & Alfernayshe *alias* Alfletnayshe. £163.

65. Rd. Turner, pl. *Tho.* Garrold & w. Joan, def. 1 mess. & 1 gdn. in Audleyend. £20.

66. Jn. Peryn *alias* Bysshopp, pl. *Geo.* Gille, gent., & w. Anne, def. 1 mess., 100 a. ar., 10 a. mw., 40 a. pa., 10 a. wd. & 4d. rent in Bentfeld, Stansted Mountfychet & Byrcheangre. 200 mks.

1. Hil. & Eas. Wm. Wyllowes & Jn. Wyllowes, pl. *Rd.* Tyrell, esq., & w. Grace, def. 17 a. ar. & 18 a. pa. in Asshedon & Barkelowe. Def. quitclaimed to pl. & the heirs of Wm. £60.

2. Wm. Parrett, pl. Robt. Hare and w. *Joan* and Agnes Stevens, def. 1 mess. & 1 gdn. in Waltham Holy Crosse. £12.

3. Tho. Willowes, pl. Reg. Mede & w. *Barbaria*, def. 2 mess., 1 toft, 1 gdn., 2 barns, 10 a. ar., 5 a. mw., 29 a. pa. & 4 a. wd. in Hadstooke. £80.

4. Jn. Machyn, gent., & Jn. Newe, pl. *Hy.*, earl of Sussex, Tho., lord Fytz Water, Hy. Radeclyff, kt., & w. Honora, & Wm. Clarke, def. Manor of Norton Hall *alias* Coldnorton & 3 mess., 2 tofts, 3 curtilages, 3 barns, 2 gdns., 2 orchards, 600 a. ar., 40 a. mw., 200 a. pa., 20 a. wd., 100 a. fresh marsh, 100 a. salt marsh & £20 rent in Coldnorton, Purleigh, Northfambryge, Lachyndon & Stowe Marrys. Def. quitclaimed to pl. & the heirs of Jn. Machyn. And for this pl. gtd. the same to Hy. Radeclyff & Honora to hold for 10½ years from All Saints last, rendering £30 yearly, payable at Michaelmas & the Annunciation, with power of distraint, & also the reversion of the same with rt. for their lives with reversion to the earl & his heirs, to hold of the chief lords.

5. Hil. & Eas. Geof. Athelham *alias* Alham, pl. *Steph.* Craske, gent., and w. Olive & Jas. Athelham *alias* Alham, def. 12 a. ar., 3 a. mw., 10 a. pa. & 3 a. wd. in Highester & Rothyng Aythorpe. £40.

6. Wm. Aylett, pl. Rd. Rought & w. *Philippa*, def. A seventh part of 3 mess., 100 a. ar., 20 a. mw., 20 a. pa., 10 a. wd. & 10s. rt. in Little Waltham, Great Lighes & Witham. 20 mks.

7. Hil. & Eas. Godfrey Swayne, gent., pl. Tho. Mede, 'yoman', def. Manor of Lee Bury & 2 mess., 2 tofts, 1 dovecoet, 160 a. ar., 20 a. mw., 10 a. pa., 12 a. wd., 60s. rt. & a liberty of a foldage (*faldagii*) of 300 sheep in Elmeden, Wenden, Arkesden & Lowetis. Def. quitclaimed to pl. & his heirs. And for this pl. gtd. the same to def. to hold for life of the chief lords without impeachment of waste, with remainder to Tho. Mede, gent., & the heirs of his body, & the right heirs of def.

8. Robt. Bredge, pl. Jasper Brokhoussen, esq., def. 2 mess., 2 tofts, 3 curtilages, 1 barn, 1 dovecote, 2 gdns. & 10 a. pa. in Coggeshale. £80.

9. Rd. Strode, gent., pl. *Geo.* White, gent., & w. Kath., def. 2 mess., 100 a. ar., 40 a. mw., 100 a. pa., 20 a. wd., 200 a. marsh & a free fishery in Tyllyngham & Denge. Def. quitclaimed to pl. & his heirs. And for this pl. gtd. the same to def. & the heirs of Geo. to hold of the chief lords.

10. Tho. Warner, pl. Mich. Meryll & w. *Mary*, def. 1 mess., 2 curtilages & 2 gdns. in Coggeshale. £20.

11. Hil. and Eas. Jn. Eason, esq., pl. Jn. Seyntler, esq., def. Manor of Chichridell *alias* Seyntlers Hall & 100 a. ar., 40 a. mw., 200 a. pa. & 140 a. wd. in St. Osit, Great Bentley, Custerige & Wilie. £80.

12. Hil. & Eas. Jn. Freman sen., Wm. Colle, Tho. Garner *alias* Gardyner, Jn. Garner *alias* Gardyner, Jn. Curteys, Tho. Newman, Rd. Strachon, Jn. Colle, Steph. Buck & Jn. Flack, pl. *Rd.* Tyrell, esq., & w. Grace, def. 48 a. ar., 2 a. mw. & 2 a. pa. in Asshedon & Barkelowe. Def. quitclaimed to pl. & the heirs of Jn. Freman. £80.

13. Godfrey Swayne, gent., pl. Tho. Kymbold & w. Margery, def. 2 mess. & 5 a. ar. in Walden & Wenden. Def. quitclaimed to pl. & his heirs. And for this pl. gtd. to def. to hold for their lives of the chief lords without impeachment of waste, with remainder to the right heirs of Tho.

14. Wm. Seymer, pl. *Jn.* Scotte & w. Margt., def. 2 mess., 2 gdns., 1 orchard, 20 a. ar., 10 a. mw., 30 a. pa. & 30 a. wd. in Esthannyngfelde. 200 mks.

15. Anth. Broun, esq., & w. Joan, pl. Hy. Warner, esq., def. Manor of Churchehall & 4 mess., 6 gdns., 200 a. ar., 20 a. mw., 100 a. pa., 20 a. wd., 200 a. fresh marsh, 100 a. salt marsh & 100s. rt. in Pakelsham & Great Stanbridge, & the advowson of the church of Pakelsham. Def. quitclaimed to pl. & the heirs of Anth. £440.

16. Tho. Maskall, pl. *Jn.* Wynterflode & w. Eliz., def. 1 mess., 40 a. ar., 4 a. mw., 10 a. pa. & 5 a. wd. in Little Sampforde. £40.

17. Jn. Lyndesell & w. Jane, pl. Rd. Sampforth, def. 2 mess., 4 cotts., 8 gdns., 100 a. ar., 20 a. mw., 40 a. pa. & 20s. rt. in Roxwell & Writtell. Def. quitclaimed to pl. & the heirs of Jn. £140.

18. Wm. Colyn, pl. *Tho.* More, citizen & mercer of London, & w. Eliz., def. 1 mess., 16 a. ar., 5 a. mw. & 7 a. pa. in Thaxsted. 100 mks.

FEET OF FINES FOR ESSEX

19. Tho. Washuas & w. Dorothy, pl. Tho. Lorkyn, def. 2 mess., 100 a. ar., 12 a. mw., 100 a. pa. & 100 a. marsh in Bradfeld, Wykys, Wrabness & Mistleleigh, which Margt. Alen, wid., holds for life. Pl. & the heirs of Tho. to hold the reversion of the chief lords. £170.

20. Ralph Gyfford, pl. *Rd.*, Mannocke & w. Margt., def. 1 mess., 4 a. ar., 6 a. pa. & 10 a. wd. in Boxsted. £40.

21. Jn. Brett, pl. Robt. Tenderinge, Wm. Eyer & w. *Alice* and Geo. Lylly & w. *Joan*, def. 4 mess., 2 curtilages, 2 barns, 40 a ar., 20 a. mw., 30 a. pa. & 10 a. wd. in Little Badowe & Boreham. 230 mks.

22. Jn. Brett, pl. Wm. Ayer & w. *Alice* & Geo. Lyllye & w. *Joan*, def. 3 mess., 4 gdns., 20 a. ar., 4 a. mw. & 12 a. pa. in Danberie, Sandon, Purleigh & Chelmesford. £140.

23. Tho. Thurgood, pl. Tho. Parker, gent., & w. *Eliz.* & Charles Newcomen, gent., & w. *Joan*, def. 4 mess., 4 gdns, 70 a. ar., 16 a. mw., 30 a. pa., 3 a. wd. & 8d. rt. in Shenfeld & Brentwood. Def. quitclaimed to pl. & his heirs. And for this pl. gtd. 3 mess., 3 gdns., 70 a. ar., 14 a. mw., 30 a. pa., 2 a. wd. & 8d. rt. in the said towns, parcel of the same, to Tho. & Eliz. & her heirs, to hold of the chief lords; & 1 mess., 1 gdn. & 2 a. mw. in Brentwood, the residue (*sic*), to Charles & Joan & the heirs of their bodies, to hold of the chief lords, with remainder to the right heirs of Joan.

24. Wm. Strachy, pl. Tho. Williamson, gent., & w. *Kath.*, def. 4 mess., 2 tofts, 3 gdns., 3 a. ar., 1 a. mw. & 2 a. pa. in Saffron Walden. £40.

25. Hil. & Eas. Jn. Holmested, pl. *Tho.* Gutter & w. Jane, def. Manor of Hypworth *alias* Hypworth Hall & 1 mess., 80 a. ar., 12 a. mw., 20 a. pa., 20 a. moor & 47s. 5d. rt. in Halsted, Hengham Syble, Little Maplested & Great Maplested. £200.

26. Jn. Wyseman, esq., pl. *Pet.* Wentworth, esq., & w. Eliz. & Paul Wentworth, gent., def. The manor of Mockynghall & 20 mess., 20 tofts, 2 dovecotes, 20 gdns., 200 a. ar., 60 a. mw., 400 a. pa., 40 a. wd., 100 a. salt marsh, 100 a. furze & heath & £20 rt. in Barlynge, Great Stanbrydge, Great Wakerynge, Little Wakerynge, Leighe, Shopland, Rocheforde, Pryttelwell, Bemflete, Fowlnes, Althorne, Thundersley & Hadley, & a third part of the advowson of the church of Great Stanbrydge. 800 mks.

27. Tho. Turnehatche, pl. *Jn.* Kyng & w. Joan, def. 1 mess., 1 gdn., 1 orchard & 1 a. mw. in Stapleford Tawney. £16.

28. Rd. Weston, esq., pl. Rd. Sampford, gent., def. Manor of Scrynes & 10 mess., 4 cotts., 8 gdns., 400 a. ar., 60 a. mw., 200 a. pa., 40 a. wd. & 100s. rt. in Writtell, Roxwell, Shellowe & Willingale Spayne. £280.

29. Jn. Mordaunt, kt., pl. Jn. Warde & w. *Agnes*, def. 2 mess., 2 gdns., 2 orchards, 20 a. ar., 10 a. pa. & 4 a. wd. in Westhorndon & Esthorndon. £40.

30. Hil. and Eas. Rd. Lyon, pl. Jn. Cowell, def. 1 mess. in Walden. £40.

31. Hil. & Eas. Jn. Cleydon of Stamborn, pl. *Rd.* Tyrell, esq., & w. Grace, def. 11 a. 3 roods ar. & 7 a. pa. in Asshedon. £40.

32. Tho. Hare, pl. *Wm.* Sandell, Jn. Sandell & Rd. Sandell, def. 1 mess., 1 curtilage & 1 gdn. in Lee, which Robt. Grygges & w. Joan hold for her life. Pl. & his heirs to hold the reversion of the chief lords. £40.

33. Rd. Samford, pl. Wm. Barley, esq., def. 2 mess., 42 a. ar., 5 a. mw. & 2 a. pa. in Elsenham. Def. quitclaimed to pl. & his heirs. And for this pl. granted to def. & his heirs a yearly rent of 28s. 6d. & 3 capons from the same, the money at Michaelmas & the Annunciation & the capons at Christmas, with power of distraint.

34. Rd. Sampford, pl. *Jn.* Lyndesell, gent., & w. Jane, def. 1 mess., 2 tofts 2 curtilages, 1 barn, 2 gdns., 60 a. ar., 12 a. mw., 20 a. pa., 10 a. wd. & 8s. rt. in Wyllynghale Doo & Fyffeld. £120.

35. Tho. Meade jun. of the Middle Temple, London, gent., pl. *Tho.* Crawley jun., gent., kinsman & heir of Reg. Whytbread, gent., decd., & w. Jane, def. Manor of Pygotɩs & 240 a. ar., 20 a. mw., 40 a. pa., 20 a. wd. & 40s. rt. in Elmedon. £140.

36. Hil. & Eas. Hy. Payne, esq., pl. Ralph Chamberleyn, kt., def. 30 a. ar., 4 a. mw. & 40 a. pa. in Bures St. Mary & Lammersshe. £40.

37. Jn. Newyngton, pl. Jn. Gatton & w. *Joan* & Agnes Whyte, daus. & heir of David Whyte, def. 1 mess., 1 gdn. & ½ a. ar. in Fobbyng. £40.

38. Hil. & Eas. Owin Clune, citizen & 'draper' of London, pl. Ralph Calley, gent., def. 2 mess., 100 a. ar. & 100 a. pa. in Orsett & Hornedon. £180.

39. Jn., earl of Oxford, & w. Margery, pl. *Edm.* Bewpre & Edw. Thursby, esquires, def. Manors of Barwicks & Scotneys & 20 mess., 20 gdns., 400 a. ar., 40 a. mw., 100 a. pa., 100 a. wd. & £10 rt. in Toppesfeld. £420.

40. Tho. Braynewood, pl. Tho. Boner & w. *Joan*, def. A moiety of 8 a. ar. in Great Waltham & High Easter. £10.

41. Wm. Strachy, pl. Wm. Carre & w. *Fina* dau. & heir of Wm. Belcheff *alias* Felsted, decd., def. 1 mess. in Saffron Walden. 20 mks.

42. Rd. Luter, pl. *Geo.* Skott, gent., & w. Maud, def. 2 mess., 40 a. ar., 10 a. mw., 25 a. pa. & 3 a. wd. in Stapleford Tawnye. £150.

43. Wm. Lytelberye, pl. Humphrey Hyll, gent., & w. *Joan*, def. 1 mess., 2 gdns., 6 tofts, 40 a. ar., 4 a. mw., 30 pa. & 3 a. wd. in Dedham & Ardeleigh. £40.

44. Wm. Nyghtyngale, pl. Edm. Mordaunt, esq., & w. *Agnes*, def. 28 a. ar., 5 a. pa. & 3 a. wd. in Wymbyshe & Thunderley. Def. quitclaimed to pl. & his heirs, with warranty for themselves & the heirs of Agnes against themselves & the heirs of Edm. £80.

45. Hil. & Eas. Geoff. Athelham *alias* Allam, pl. Steph. Craske, gent., & w. Olive & Jas. Athelham *alias* Allam, def. 1 mess., 60 a. ar., 8 a. mw., 12 a. pa. & 3 a. wd. in Highester & Rothing Aythrope. Def. quitclaimed to pl. & his heirs. Warranties by Steph. & Olive against themselves & the heirs of Steph. & by Jas. against all men. £80.

46. Wm. Huberde, pl. Roger Grace & w. *Margt.* & Anth. Pullen & w. Mary, def. Two thirds of 2 mess., 2 gdns., 4 tofts, 60 a. ar., 10 a. mw., 40 a. pa. & 4 a. wd. in Peldon & Little Wigborough. Def. quitclaimed to pl. & his heirs. And for this pl. gtd. the same to Roger & his heirs to hold of the chief lords.

47. Wm. Peverell, gent., pl. *Rd.* Godfrey and w. Alice, def. 1 mess., 1 gdn., 100 a. ar., 20 a. mw., 60 a. pa. & 30 a. wd. in Chyche Regis *alias* Chyche St. Osithe & Weleigh. £140.

48. Mary Scot, wid., pl. *Geo.* Whetenhall, esq., & w. Alice, def. Manor of Walbery & 40 a. ar., 30 a. mw., 200 a. pa., 40 a. wd. & £8 rt. in Hollingbery. 400 mks.

49. Rd. Sampforth, pl. *Roger* Parker, gent., & w. Anne, def. Manor of Frith Hall & 2 mess., 4 cotts., 8 gdns., 100 a. ar., 20 a. mw., 100 a. pa., 10 a. wd. & 20s. rt. in Norton Maundevile & High Onger. 460 mks.

50. Walter Crane, pl. Ralph Whytherell & w. *Joan*, def. 1 a. mw. called 'Cowbredge Medue' in Great Bromeley. £40.

51. Rd. Champion, citizen & draper of London, & w. Margt., pl. *Geo.* Whetenhall, esq., & w. Alice, def. Manor of Hassingbrooke & 2 mess., 1 gdn., 300 a. ar., 40 a. mw., 30 a. pa., 30 a. wd. & 40s. rt. in Stanford le Hoope. Def. quitclaimed to pl. & the heirs of Rd. £420.

CP25(2)/83/710   DIVERS COUNTIES

34. Jn. Elliott, citizen & merchant of London, pl. *Geo.* Whetenhall, esq., & w. Alice, def. Property in Chorley, co. Hertford; & 1 fulling mill called 'Walbery Myll', 4 a. ar., 6 a. mw. & 4 a. pa. in Great Halyngbery & Sabbesforth, co. Essex. £140. — Herts., Essex.

35. Hil. & Eas. Wm. Lawson & Geo. Collyns, pl. Jn. Broket, esq., & w. *Ellen*, def. A third part of the manor of Hopebrydgehall, & a third part of 2 capital mess., 10 tofts, 1 dovecote, 3 gdns., 300 a. ar., 50 a. mw., 100 a. pa., 20 a. wd. & 20s. rt. in Great Okeley & Little Okeley, co. Essex; & property in Herts. & Suff. Def. quitclaimed to pl. & the heirs of Wm. And for this pl. gtd. the same to def. to hold for their lives of the chief lords without impeachment of waste, with remainder to Jn. Brokett their son & the heirs male of his body & Zelanthiel Brokett, another son, & his heirs. — Herts., Essex, Suffolk.

CP25(2)/70/580   TRINITY, 1 AND 2 PHILIP AND MARY   1555

52. Wm. Riggs, esq., pl. *Rd.* Jonson & w. Margt., def. 1 barn, 30 a. ar., 2 a. mw., 3 a. pa. & 2 a. wd. in South Wokendon. £40.

53. Eas. & Trin. Jn. Reynoldes, pl. *Wm.* Alcrofte & Walter Alcrofte, def. 1 mess., 11 a. ar., 3 a. pa. & ½ a. wd. in Little Chesterford. £16.

54. Jn. Payne, pl. *Hy.* Peyt & w. Alice, def. 1 mess. called Hoggs & 1 gdn. in Grays Thorok. £40.

55. Wm. Hunwicke, pl. *Hy.* Warner & Wm. Emerson, def. Manor of Boys *alias* Dynes & 5 mess., 2 barns, 5 cotts., 10 gdns., 500 a. ar., 40 a. mw., 100 a. pa., 80 a. wd. & £4 rt. in Halsted, Great Maplested & Little Maplested. £200.

56. Reg. Hollyngworth & Tho. Cosyn, pl. Jerome Balborowe, def. 3 mess., 3 gdns., 20 a. ar., 8 a. mw., 21 a. pa., 8 a. wd. & 5s. rt in Barkyng, Dagenham, Myleende & Colchester. Def. quitclaimed to pl. & the heirs of Reg. And for this pl. gtd. the same to def. & the heirs of his body to hold of the chief lords, with remainder to his right heirs.

57. Jn. Wright of Southweld, pl. Agnes Forger, def. 1 mess., 1 barn, 2 gdns., 2 orchards, 13 a. ar., 2 a. mw. & 3 a. pa. in Great Canfeld. £30.

58. Jn. Pragill, gent., pl. *Jn.* Lynsey & w. Joan, def. 1 mess., 1 curtilage called 'Copthall' & ½ a. ar. in a street called 'Balmestrete' in the parish of Westham & 7 a. ar. in Netherhyde in Westham. £80.

59. Rd. Luter *alias* Huett, pl. *Jn.* Parker & w. Alice, def. 1 mess., 1 gdn., 27 a. mw. & 3s. 6d. rt. in Thedongarnon. £200.

60. Tho. Darcy, esq., pl. Jn. Grene & w. *Eliz.*, def. A moiety of the manor of Bentons *alias* Benyngtons & 6 mess., 10 gdns., 6 orchards, 260 a. ar., 20 a. mw., 200 a. pa., 6 a. wd. & 60s. rt. in Wytham, Wyckham, Bradwell & Hatfeld Peverell. £140.

61. Martin Bowes, kt., citizen & alderman of London, & Jn. Southcott, gent., pl. Martin Bowes, gent., & w. *Frances*, def. Manors of Jenkyns & Malmaynes & 10 mess., 10 gdns., 10 orchards, 2 barns, 2 dovecotes, 300 a. ar., 20 a. mw., 60 a. pa., 30 a. wd., 80 a. marsh, 20 a. furze & heath & 40s. rt. in Barkyng & Dagnam. Def. quitclaimed to pl. & the heirs of Martin. And for this pl. gtd. the same to def. to hold for their lives of the chief lords, with remainder to the heirs of Martin of the body of Frances and his right heirs.

CP25(2)/83/710   DIVERS COUNTIES

52. Jn. Myllys & w. Agnes, pl. *Paul* Wylkynson, gent., & w. Anne, def. 2 a. pa. in Westham, co. Essex, & prop. in Chesthunt, co. Hertford. Def. quitclaimed to pl. & the heirs of Jn. £80. — Essex, Herts.

CP25(2)/70/581   MICHAELMAS, 2 AND 3 PHILIP AND MARY   1555

1. Geo. Kelsey and w. Joan, pl. Robt. Scrafeld & w. *Joan*, def. 6 a. ar. & 1 a. pa. in Terlyng. Def. quitclaimed to pl. & the heirs of Joan. £40.

2. Jn. Boram, pl. *Jn.* Mower and w. Kath., def. 1 mess., 12 a. ar., 4 a. (mw.) & 6 a. pa. in Haverell. 50 mks.

3. Tho. Mall, pl. Jasper Broune, def. 1 mess., 1 barn & 2 gdns. in Brentwood. £20.

4. Trin. & Mich. Jn. Whyte, pl. *Roger* Parker, esq., & w. Anne, def. 1 mess., 2 tofts, 3 curtilages, 2 barns, 2 gdns., 100 a. ar., 30 a. mw., 80 a. pa., 40 a. wd. & 20 a. alder in Gosseffeld & Halsted. £300.

5. Trin. & Mich. Edw. Neale, pl. Geo. Malle, def. 10 a. ar., 8 a. mw. & 6 a. pa. in Wyllynghale Spayne, which Eliz. Cooke, wid., holds for life. Pl. & his heirs to hold the reversion of the chief lords. 40 mks.

6. Robt. Drywoode, pl. *Jn.* Gylbert *alias* Hale & w. Joan, Tho. Arnold & w. Joan, def. 1 mess., 1 gdn., 24 a. ar., 6 a. mw. & 10 a. pa. in Hadley *alias* Hadleigh. £40.

7. Tho. Cooke, pl. Rd. Stowe, kinsman & heir of Jn. Stowe, def. 1 mess., 2 tofts, 2 curtilages, 4 a. ar., 1 a. mw. & 5 a. pa. in Aldham. 50 mks.

8. Owin Lawe, clerk, & Jn. Lawe, pl. *Jn.* Vawghen & w. Agnes, def. 1 mess., 1 gdn. & 3 a. mw. in Stapleford Abbott. Def. quitclaimed to pl. & the heirs of Owin. £40.

9. Edw. Chyld, pl. Jn. Machyn & w. *Mary*, def. 1 mess., 1 toft, 1 barn, 1 gdn., 1 orchard & 2 a. ar. in Wodham Water. 40 mks.

10. Wm. Reynold sen., pl. Robt. Byrchard & w. Helen, def. A moiety of 1 mess., 2 tofts, 2 curtilages, 1 barn, 2 gdns., 1 orchard, 12 a. ar., 4 a. mw., 10 a. pa. & 8 a. wd. & a third of 1 mess., 3 tofts, 4 curtilages, 1 barn, 1 dovecote, 2 gdns., 3 orchards, 60 a. ar., 12 a. mw., 30 a. pa. & 10 a. wd., in Great Lyghz, Terlinge, Hatfelld Peverell & Boreham. £80.

11. Jn. Moteham, pl. Robt. Brett, def. 3 a. mw. & 3 a. pa. in Fordham, which Roger Swan & w. Sabina hold for her life. Pl. & his heirs to hold the reversion of the chief lords. £20.

12. Chris. Aleyn & Giles Aleyn, pl. Jn. Aleyn, esq., def. 5 mess., 4 gdns., 1 orchard, 12 a. mw., 20 a. pa. & 1 a. wd. in Thaxsted. Def. quitclaimed to pl. & the heirs of Chris. And for this pl. gtd. the same to def. & his heirs to hold of the chief lords.

13. Jn. Fytz & Jn. Gardyner, pl. Jn. Barker & Tho. Barker, def. 3 mess., 3 gdns., 60 a. ar., 8 a. mw., 50 (a.) pa. & 6 a. wd. in Twynsted, Pedmershe, Lamemershe & Great Henny. Def. quitclaimed to pl. & the heirs of Jn. Fytz. And for this pl. gtd. the same to Jn. Barker & his heirs to hold of the chief lords.

14. Rd. Page, pl. Simon Leper, def. 1 mess., 1 gdn., 6 a ar. & 30 a. pa. in Salcotte & Tolshunt Knyghts. £40.

15. Tho. Darcy, esq., pl. Jn. Bridge, def. 1 mess., 1 gdn., 24 a. ar., 10 a. mw., 60 a. pa. & 10 a. wd. in Tolshunt Tregos *alias* Tolshunt Darcy, Tolshunt Knyghts & Tolshunt Maior. £40.

16. Tho. Sylesden, esq., pl. Tho. Cavyll, son & heir of Wm. Cavyll, def. 2 mess., 2 gdns., 40 a. ar., 10 a. mw., 20 a. pa. & 1 a. wd. in Stebbyng. £40.

17. Anne Heygate, wid., pl. Reg. Heygate, gent., def. 1 mess., 3 tofts, 4 curtilages, 1 barn, 1 dovecote, 2 gdns., 2 orchards, 6 a. ar., 4 a. mw., 6 a. pa. & 2 a. wd. in Feryng. 200 mks.

18. Rd. Horwood & Jn. Lyndesell, pl. Wm. Gylbanke & Tho. Yon & w. *Alice*, dau. & heir of Margt. Thorne, def. 1 mess., 1 gdn., 1 orchard, 16 a. ar. & 6 a. mw. in Buttysbery. Def. quitclaimed to pl. & the heirs of Rd. And for this pl. gtd. the same to Wm. to hold for life of the chief lords, with remainder to Jn. Ryggs & his heirs.

19. Jn. Hedyche, pl. Wm. Kene & w. Joan & *Tho*. Byrde sen., def. 6 a. ar. & 10 a. pa. in Tolleshunt Darsey & Tolleshunt Knyghts. 40 mks.

20. Tho. Denys *alias* Denys, pl. Jn. Wright, def. 1 mess. & 4 a. ar. in Childerdiche. £20.

21. Trin. & Mich. Jn. Byrche, gent., & Jn. Lyndesell, gent., pl. Jn. Gaynesford, gent., def. Manor of Gobions & 10 mess., 8 cotts., 200 a. ar., 60 a. mw., 300 a. pa., 40 a. wd. & 40s. rt. in Layndon, Little Bursted, Donton, Langdon, Westley & Eastley. Def. quitclaimed to pl. & the heirs of Jn. Byrche. 460 mks.

22. Tho. Lyndesell jun., pl. *Steph*. Collyn & w. Alice, def. 20 a. ar., 6 a. mw., 30 a. pa. & 6d. rt. in Bokkynge. £40.

23. Rd. Eve, pl. Rd. Burley & w. *Anne*, def. 1 mess., & 1 gdn. in Chelmesford. £20.

24. Jn. Compton & Rd. Whorwood, pl. Tho. Wellys & w. Agnes & Rd. Cowper & w. *Thomasina*, def. Two thirds of 1 mess., 1 gdn. & 1 orchard in the parish of All Saints, Sudbury. Def. quitclaimed to pl. & the heirs of Jn. And for this pl. gtd. the same to Tho. & his heirs to hold of the chief lords.

25. Roger Amyce, gent., pl. Anth. Rygbye, gent., def. 5 mess., 5 curtilages, 5 tofts, 5 gdns., 5 orchards, 3 dovecotes, 300 a. ar., 100 a. mw., 40 a. pa., 60 a. moor, 60 a. marsh, 100 a. wd., 200 a. furze & heath & £5 rt. in Barkyng, Dagenham, Great Ilford, Little Ilford, Romeford, Hornchurch & Woodford. £420.

26. Steph. Collyn, pl. *Jn*. Collyn & w. Joan, def. 1 mess., 3 gdns., 50 a. ar., 12 a. mw., & 30 a. pa. in Great Badowe. £200.

27. Tho. Stokes, pl. Jn. Boxer & w. *Joan*, def. 1 mess. & 2 a. ar. in Aythroppe Rothing. 20 mks.

28. Jn. Collyn, pl. *Tho*. Bedyll, gent., & w. Eliz., def. 1 mess., 2 curtilages, 2 barns, 3 orchards, 4 gdns., 120 a. ar., 20 a. mw., 60 a. pa., 10 a. wd. & 3s. rt. in Willingale Doo, Willingale Spayne, Norton & High Onger. £200.

29. Jn. Eve, pl. Edm. Goodewe *alias* Farthing and w. *Joan*, def. 2 a. mw. in Stock. 20 mks.

30. Jn. Collyn, pl. Jn. Clerke jun., def. 1 mess., 1 gdn., 1 orchard & 24 a. ar. in Little Laver, High Laver & Matching, which Agnes Clerke, wid., holds for life. Pl. & his heirs to hold the reversion of the chief lords. 50 mks.

31. Jerome Grene, pl. Jn. Turnor, gent., def. Manor of Berthall & 50 a. ar., 4 a. mw., 30 a. pa. & 7s. rt. in White Colne, which Thomasina Lake, wid., holds for life. Pl. & his heirs to hold the reversion of the chief lords. £60.

32. Hy. Aylett, pl. Jn. Purcas & w. *Joan*, def. 14 a. ar. in White Rothynge. £20.

33. Trin. & Mich. Jn. Stoner, Geo. Scott, Robt. Taverner, Tho. Barfote, gent., Jn. Boland, Tho. Northrope, Robt. Spakeman, Ralph Hill, Rd. Cuddard, Mich. Pott, Nich. Hill, Geo. Holmes, Jn. Wybert, Hy. Archer & Steph. Archer, pl. *Anth.* Broun, esq., & w. Joan, def. 3 a mw. & 11½ a. pa. in Chigwell. Def. quitclaimed to pl. & the heirs of Jn. Stoner. 100 mks.

34. Rd. Samford, pl. *Wm.* Pawne, esq., & w. Ellen, def. 1 mess., 1 gdn., 1 orchard & 10 a. ar. in Hye Onger. 50 mks.

35. Wm. Sumpner, pl. Edw. Campyon, gent., def. 1 mess., 2 barns, 1 orchard, 2 curtilages, 100 a. ar., 12 a. mw., 40 a. pa. & 6 a. wd. in Harlowe & Sheryng. £340.

36. Wm. Dryfeld, pl. *Chris.* Charter & w. Margt. def. 2 mess. & 2 gdns. in Legh. £30.

37. Geo. Toose, pl. Tho. Patriche & w. *Alice*, def. 8 a. pa. in Wyckes. £40.

38. Jn. Reymond, gent., pl. Wm. Crayford, def. 10 a. ar., 12 a. pa. & 3s. 6d. rt. in Woodham Ferrers & Althorne, & a moiety of 1 mess., 15 a. ar. & 15a. pa. in Halthorne aforesaid. £120.

39. Tho. Warner, pl. *Jn.* Fuller & w. Margery, def. 2 mess. & 2 gdns. in Walden. £40.

40. Robt. Middelton, pl. *Geo.* Cristemas, esq., & w. Bridget, def. 2 mess., 2 tofts & 2 gdns. in Colcestre. £40.

41. Wm. Symnell, pl. Def. as in preceding. 1 mess., 1 toft, 2 curtilages & 2 gdns. in Colcestre. £40.

42. Jn. Wentworth, kt., pl. *Jn.* Swallowe, gent., & w. Anne, def. 2 mess., 2 gdns., 2 orchards, 4 a. mw. & 12 a. pa. in Gosfeld. £40.

43. Rd. Gosnold, pl. *Tho.* Rychemond sen. & w. Alice, def. 20 a. ar., 20 a. pa. & 3 a. wd. in Great Holland. £40.

44. Tho. Richemond jun., pl. *Jn.* Hubberd, gent., & w. Anne, def. 1 mess., 1 gdn., 1 barn, 30 a. land & 20 a. pa. in Dover Courte. £40.

45. Tho. Archer, pl. Jn. Warren jun., def. 2 mess., 3 cotts., 4 gdns., 1 barn, 6 tofts, 7 crofts, 40 a. ar., 20 a. me., 20 a. pa & 1 a. wd. in Thaxsted. £40.

46. Pl. as in preceding. *Jn.* Pooley & w. Ellen, def. 2 a. mw. called 'Kentts Meade' in Thaxsted. £20.

47. Jn. Colett *alias* Davenyshe, pl. Wm. Raven, def. 1 mess., 2 tofts, 2 curtilages, 1 gdn. & 1 orchard in Cressyng. £20.

48. Rd. Wallys jun., pl. Tho. Grey, gent., & w. *Alice* & Eliz. Serle, def. 1 mess., 1 curtilage, 1 gdn., 29 a. ar., 2 a. mw., 3 a. pa. & 5 a. wd. in Great Chesell & Little Chesell. 100 mks.

(Wm. Beryff, gent., pl. *Geo.* Cristemas, esq., & w. Bridget, def. 1 capital mess. called 'le Vyne', 2 tofts, 1 gdn *(orto)* & 2 gdns *(gardinis)* in Colcester. £40.)

(Taken from the Notes, the Foot being missing.)

CP25(2)/83/711   DIVERS COUNTIES

2. Rd. Tirell, pl. Etheldreda Broun, wid., Geo. Broun, esq., & w. Eliz. & Wistan Broun, gent., his son, def. Property in Barkelowe, Aiston, Castell Camps, Citie Camps &

Horsett, co. Cambs., & 3 mess., 20 a. ar., 8 a. mw., 50 a. pa., 20 a. wd., 50 a. furze & heath & 20s. rt. in Aiston, Castell Camps, Citie Camps & Horsett. £80. − Cambs., Essex.

9. Tho. Bysshopp, pl. *Geo.* Broune, esq., & w. Eliz. & Wistan Broune, gent., his son, def. The manors of Rokewood Hall, Brounes Mannor *alias* Colvyle Hall *alias* Knyghts, Markes & Langenhoo & 40 mess., 1 mill, 2,000 a. ar., 400 a. mw., 2,000 a. pa., 1,000 a. wd., 4,000 a. marsh & £30 rt. in Abbes Rodyng, Beauchamp Rodyng, Margarett Rodyng, Little Laffour, High Laffour, White Rodyng, Aytrop Roding, Matching, Hatfeld Regis, Langenho, Aberton, Peldon, Fyngringhoo & Bere, & the advowsons of the churches of White Rodyng & Langenhoo, co. Essex, & property in Wilts. & Hants. Def. quitclaimed to pl. and his heirs. And for this pl. gtd. the manors of Rokewood Hall & Langenhoo & 10 mess., 1 mill, 1,400 a. ar., 250 a. mw., 1,400 a. pa., 400 a. wd., 4,000 a. marsh & £13 rt. in Abbes Rodyng, Beauchamp Rodyng, Margarett Rodyng, Little Laffour, High Laffour, Langenho, Aberton, Pelton, Fyngringhoo & Bere & the advowson of the church of Langenhoo to Geo. to hold for life of the chief lords without impeachment of waste, with remainder to Wistan & the heirs of his body, the heirs of the body of Geo., the heirs of the body of Jn. Broune, esq., decd., father of Geo., the heirs of the body of Wistan Broune, kt., decd., father of Jn., and the right heirs of Wistan, kt.; the manor of Brounes Mannor *alias* Colvyle Hall *alias* Knyghts & 10 mess., 200 a. ar., 50 a. mw., 200 a. pa., 100 a. wd. & 100s. rt. in White Rodding, Abbes Rodyng, Aytrop Roding, Matching & Hatfeld Regis to Geo. & Eliz. to hold for their lives of the chief lords without impeachment of waste, with remainder as before; and the manor of Markes & 20 mess., 400 a. ar., 100 a. mw., 400 a. pa., 500 a. wd. & £12 rt. in White Roding & the advowson of the church of White Roding & the property in Wilts. & Hants. to Geo. & Eliz. to hold for their lives of the chief lords, without impeachment of waste for the life of Geo., with remainder to Wistan his son & the heirs of his body & the right heirs of Geo. − Essex, Wilts, Southampton.

18. Wm. Laxton, kt., citizen & alderman of London, & w. Joan, pl. Geo. Bacon, gent., & w. Margt. & *Wm.* Holton & w. Alice, def. Property in Naylande, co. Suffolk, & 16 a. mw. in Great Horsley, co. Essex. Def. quitclaimed to pl. & the heirs of Wm. £120. − Suff., Essex.

CP25(2)/70/581   HILARY, 2 AND 3 PHILIP AND MARY   1556

49. Mich. & Hil. Wm. Sapurton, gent., pl. Tho. Nevell, kt., def. A moiety of 1 mess., 2 tofts, 4 curtilages, 2 barns, 2 gdns., 2 orchards, 40 a. ar., 20 a. mw., 80 a. pa., 20 a. wd. called 'Fowches' (in) Great Totham & Little Totham. 80 mks.

50. Mich. & Hil. Tho. Serle, citizen & mercer of London, pl. Charles Newcomen, gent., & w. *Joan,* def. 4 a. ar. & 1 a. wd. in Shenfeld, which Kath. Nytingale, wid., holds for life. Pl. & his heirs to hold the reversion of the chief lords. £40.

51. Mich. & Hil. Tho. Crawley, esq., pl. *Tho.* Docwra, esq., & w. Mildred, def. Manor of Oldehall & 1 barn, 1 gdn, 1 orchard., 40 a. ar., 5 a. mw., 100 a. pa., 60 a. marsh & £9 rt. in Curryngham, Febbynge, Fange, Bursted, Stanford le Hope, Estylbury, Westylbury & Chaldwell. 400 mks.

52. Tho. Cotton, gent., pl. *Wm.* Ryggs, esq., & w. Anne, def. 1 mess., 1 toft, 1 barn, 30 a. ar., 2 a. mw., 3 a. pa. & 2 a. wd. in South Wokyngton *alias* South Wokenden *alias* Wokyndon Rokele *alias* Wokindon at the Steeple. £40.

53. Jn. Aldriche, pl. *Tho.* Darcye, kt., lord Darcye of Chiche, & w. Dame Eliz., def. Manor of Frowike *alias* Frodwyke & 10 mess., 5 tofts, 500 a. ar., 40 a. mw., 400 a. pa., 300 a. wd., 200 a. furze & heath & £5 rent in Seint Osithe & Weleighe. £400.

54. And. Kyng, pl. *Jn.* Glascock, gent., & w. Joan, def. 2 mess., 2 orchards & 9 a. ar. in Bobingworth & Morton. £30.

55. Mich. & Hil. Jn. Jackson & Rd. Broun, pl. Wm. Aylyff, esq., & w. *Margt.,* def. 1 mess., 2 cott., 3 curtilages, 1 orchard, 2 gdns., 20 a. ar., 5 a. mw. & 30 a. pa. in South-annyngfeld, Ronwell & Ramesdon Bellhouse. def. quitclaimed to pl. & the heirs of Rd. £100.

56. Jn. Henyns, gent., pl. Jn. Herne, gent., & w. *Eliz.,* def. A moiety of manor of Blumpsters & 10 mess., 8 cotts., 200 a. ar., 20 a. mw., 100 a. pa., 10 a. wd. & 100s. rt. in Great Eyston *alias* Eiston at the Mount, Tiltey & Lynsell. £180.

57. Tho. Pullyn (*sic*), pl. *Hy.* Pullyuer, son & heir of Jn. Pullyver, & w. Agnes, def. 8 a. ar. in Barkyng. £20.

58. Mich. & Hil. Jas. Leonarde & w. Alice, pl. Lau. Morse, def. 3 mess., 7 a. ar., 6 a. mw., 5 a. pa., 3 a. marsh & 5s. rt. in Barkyng & Dagnam. Def. quitclaimed to pl. & the heirs of Jas. £100.

59. Mich. & Hil. Geo. Dene, pl. *Tho.* Barker & w. Agnes, def. 1 mess., 1 toft, 1 curtilage, 1 gdn & 1 orchard in Great Dunmowe. £40.

60. Mich. & Hil. Jn. Felde & Jn. Hethecote, pl. Jn. Grave, def. 1 mess., 30 a. ar. & 30 a. mw. in Theydon Garnon & Theydon Mont. Def. quitclaimed to pl. & the heirs of Jn. Felde. And for this pl. gtd. the same to def. & his heirs to hold of the chief lords.

61. Wm. Levet, pl. Wm. Hodge & w. Anne & *Wm.* Anderkyn, def. 4 a. ar., 2 a. mw. & 6 a. pa. in Althorn, Southmynster & Maylond. 40 mks.

62. Mich. & Hil. Bart. Averell, pl. *Tho.* Darcy, lord Darcy, and w. Eliz., def. 1 mess., 2 tofts, 1 barn, 1 gdn., 1 orchard, 50 a. ar., 10 a. mw., 60 a. pa. & 2 a. wd. in Sowthmynster, Maylond & Althorn. 230 mks.

63. Geo. Nicolles, gent., pl. Roger Newman, def. 3 mess., 100 a. ar., 20 a. mw. & 40 a. pa. in Great Wenden, Little Wenden, Arkysden & Littleburi. £60.

64. Tho. Sparowe, pl. *Jn.* Hewett & Valentine Hewett, def. 1 barn, 20 a. ar., 3. mw. & 8 a. pa. in Stysted. £40.

65. Tho. Parnell, pl. *Gabriel* Busshe & w. Margery, def. 1 mess., 1 gdn., 1 orchard & 2 tofts in Walden. £40.

66. Mich. & Hil. Wm. Reynold, pl. Wm. Dodd sen. & *Wm.* Dodd jun., def. 1 mess., 1 gdn., 1 orchard & 4 a. ar. in Great Chesterford. £30.

67. Mich. & Hil. Philip Byrde, gent., & Joan Peppys, wid., pl. Tho. Strachye sen. & w. *Agnes*, def. 1 mess., 12 a. ar. & 12 a. pa. in Depden. Def. quitclaimed to pl. & the heirs of Philip. 80 mks.

68. Mich. & Hil. Tho. Stock, pl. *Jn.* Holmested, gent., & w. Alice, def. 1 mess., 26 a. ar., 4 a. mw. & 12d. rt. in Great Berdefelde. 100 mks.

69. Mich. & Hil. Jn. Holmested, gent., pl. *Wm.* Hunwycke, gent., & w. Joan, def. 20 a. ar. in Halsted. £20.

70. Trin. & Hil. Rd. Palmer, pl. Tho. Cooke *alias* Chapman and w. *Eliz.*, def. 3½ a. ar. in Byrchanger. £40.

71. Mich. & Hil. Jn. Enyver jun. & Eliz. Enyver, wid., pl. Jn. Toland & w. *Joan*, def. 1 mess., 1 gdn. & 1 orchard in Eystanes at the Mount *alias* Eyston at the Mount. Def. quitclaimed to pl. & the heirs of Jn. £20.

72. Mich. and Hil. Jn. Baxster & Edm. Baxster, pl. *Tho.* Bradlowe *alias* Jacobbe & w. *Margery,* def. A moiety of 1 mess. called 'Rowses' & 40 a. ar., 6 a. mw., 26 a. pa., 4 a. wd. & 2s. rt. in Willynghale Doo, Wyllynghale Spayne & Wyllynghale Rokell. Def. quitclaimed to pl. & the heirs of Jn. 100 mks.

CP25(2)/83/711   DIVERS COUNTIES

78. Mich. & Hil. Jn. Cornell, pl. *Wm.* Stubbynge & w. Margt., def. 1 mess., 1 gdn., 5 a. ar., 71 a. pa., & 1 a. mw. in Haverell, co. Essex, & the same in Haverell, co. Suffolk. 80 mks. — Essex, Suffolk.

CP25(2)/70/582   EASTER, 2 AND 3 PHILIP AND MARY   1556

1. Tho. Smyth, kt., & w. Philippa, pl. *Edw.* Ferrers, esq., & (w.) Bridget, def. Manor of Theydon & 20 mess., 20 cotts., 20 tofts, 20 gdns., (1,000 a. ar., 300 a.) mw., 300 a. pa., 300 a. wd., 200 a. furze & heath, 100 a. marsh, £5 (rt. & view of frank-pledge) in Theidon commonly called Theidon on the Mount, & the advowson of the church of Theidon aforesaid. Def. quitclaimed to pl. & the heirs of Tho. And for this pl. gtd. to def. & the heirs of Edw. a yearly rt. of 5 mks. from the same for the life of Philippa,

payable at the Annunciation & Michaelmas, & another yearly rt. of £30 from the same, the first payment being at Michaelmas after the death of Philippa, with power of distraint in either case.
Endorsed that this was registered by the Chancery in 1576.

2. Geo. Songer & w. Joan, pl. *Tho.* Darcy, esq., & w. Eliz., def. 9 a. ar. in Tolleshunt Knyghts *alias* Tolleshunt Busshes. Def. quitclaimed to pl. & the heirs of Geo. £20.

3. Jn. Parmyter & Tho. Purcas, pl. *Rd.* Wynterflod & w. Cecily, def. 10 a. ar., 12 a. pa. & 40 a. wd. in Henyngham Syble & Gossefeld. Def. quitclaimed to pl. & the heirs of Jn. £60.

4. Mich. 6 Edward VI & Eas. Wm. Vernon, gent., pl. Wm. Marche, def. 1 mess., 1 barn, 20 a. ar., 1 a. 3 roods of mw., 60 a. pa. & 5 a. wd. in Malden & Woodham Water. £60.

5. Jn. Enyver & w. Eliz., pl. *Rd.* Hedge & w. Ellen, def. 2 mess., 2 orchards & 7 a. ar. in Eystanes at the Mount *alias* Great Eston. Def. quitclaimed to pl. & the heirs of Jn. 40 mks.

6. Francis Jobson, kt., pl. *Hugh* Denys, esq., & w. Kath., def. Manor of Acres Flete Marshe & 2 cotts., 100 a. ar., 20 a. mw., 100 a. pa., 200 a. fresh marsh & 100 a. salt marsh in Canowdon, Burnham & Pakelsham. £200.

7. Jn. Lawrens, gent., pl. *Jas.* Atwoode & w. Joan, def. 1 mess., 3 gdns., 40 a. ar., 20 a. mw., 40 a. pa., 6 a. wd. & 30 a. marsh in Estylbery & Mockyng. 100 mks.

8. Mich. & Eas. Wm. Kyme & Hy. Jones, pl. *Jn.* Patryk, Rd. Knyght & w. Agnes, def. Manor of Amours *alias* Heth Place & 6 mess., 2 cotts., 7 tofts, 6 gdns., 4 orchards, 600 a. ar., 140 a. mw., 300 a. pa., 30 a. wd., 100 a. furze & heath & 20s. rt. in Orsett, Shawdewell, Gyngrave & Little Thurrock. Def. quitclaimed to pl. & the heirs of Wm. And for this pl. gtd. the same to Jn. to hold for life of the chief lords without impeachment of waste, with remainder to Joan Foster, wid., for life, the heirs of the body of Jn. of the body of Joan, & the right heirs of Jn.

9. Giles Sorysbye, pl. *Wm.* Turpyn & w. Petronilla & Jn. Spruse sen., def. 1 mess. in Walden. £40.

10. Jn. Bawde, gent., pl. Robt. Tirrell, gent., def. 180 a. salt marsh in Donton. £100.

11. Jn. Mutford & Philip Muntford, pl. *Tho.* Fannyng & w. Clemencia, def. 16 a. ar. in Little Canfeld. Def. quitcalimed to pl. & the heirs of Jn. £30.

12. Tho. Darcy, esq., & w. Eliz., pl. *Geo.* Songer & w. Joan, def. 50 a. ar., 10 a. mw. & 100 a. salt marsh in West Marsey. Def. quitclaimed to pl. & the heirs of Tho. £80.

13. Pl. as in preceding. Jn. Barnard & w. *Agnes*, def. 2 mess., 2 gdns., 20 a. ar., 3 a. mw., 10 a. pa. & 5 a. wd. in Wytham, Little Braxsted & Great Braxsted. Def. quitclaimed to pl. & the heirs of Tho. £40.

14. Mich. & Eas. Edm. Markaunt, gent., pl. *Roger* Grace & w. Margt., def. Two thirds of 2 mess., 2 gdns., 4 tofts, 60 a. ar., 10 a. mw., 40 a. pa. & 4 a. wd. in Peldon & Little Wigborough. £40.

15. Jn. Holmested, gent., pl. Margt. Glassenbye, wid., Rd. Sparrowe & w. Margt., & *Jn.* Salman & w. Agnes, def. 1 gdn., 1 orchard, 15 a. ar. & 6 a. pa. in Gossefeld. 80 mks.

16. Tho. Westbrome, pl. *Tho.* Washuas & w. Dorothy, def. 12 a. ar. & 12 a. pa. in Great Clacton. £40.

17. Hil. & Eas. Rd. Noke & w. Mary, pl. Tho. Lincolne, def. 2 mess., 1 curtilage & 1 gdn. in Brentwood. Def. quitclaimed to pl. & the heirs of Rd. £40.

18. Geo. Nycolson, pl. *Wm.* Sapurton, gent., & w. Alice, def. 1 mess., 2 tofts, 1 curtilage, 1 barn, 40 a. ar., 4 a. mw., 8 a. pa. & 4 a. alder in Halsted & Gosseffelde. 100 mks.

19. Jn. Baker & w. Margery, pl. Jn. Smyth & w. *Joan* and Wm. Edwards & w. *Joan*, daus. & co-heir of Tho. Spycer, decd., def. 1 a. wd. in Woodham Ferrers. Def. quitclaimed to pl. & the heirs of Jn. 10 mks.

20. Jn. Warner, pl. Jn. Carter & w. Eliz., def. 1 mess., 10 a. ar., 2 a. mw. & 10 a. pasture in Langham. £40.
(*Note: The foot is ambiguous as to whether the heirs are of Jn. or Eliz. Carter.*)

21. Agnes Rand, wid., pl. Tho. Grene, def. 1 mess., 2 tofts, 1 barn, 1 gdn., 1 orchard, 10 a. ar. & 6 a pa. in Tey Godmer *alias* Little Tey, Tey Maundevyle *alias* Markys Tey, and Great Tey. £30.

22. Jn. Traves, citizen & merchant tailor of London, pl. Rd. Weston, esq., & w. Margt. & Jn. Addyngton, gent., son of Chris. Addyngton, def. Manor of Aldersbrooke & 3 mess., 2 curtilages, 4 gdns., 1 dovecote, 160 a. ar., 30 a. mw., 120 a. pa., 4 a. wd. & 40s. rent in Little Ilford & Wansted. Def. quitclaimed to pl. & his heirs, with separate warranties against the heirs of Margt. & against Jn. Addyngton & his heirs & Ralph Addyngton, kinsman & next heir of Tho. Addyngton late of London, decd. 820 mks.

23. Tho. Wyndsore, esq., & Edw. Stokwood, esq., pl. Wm. Palmer, gent., def. 1 mess., 1 toft, 1 gdn., 30 a. ar., 6 a. mw., 10 a. pa., 2 a. wd. & 10 a. marsh in Stanford in le Hoop. Def. quitclaimed to pl. & the heirs of Tho. 100 mks.

24. Wm. Towes, pl. *Rd.* Wynterflod & w. Cecily, def. 1 mess., 40 a. ar., 8 a. mw. & 12 a. pa. in Little Berdefeld. £100.

25. Wm. Enyuer, pl. Kath. Warner, wid., def. 1 mess., 1 barn, 2 gdns. & 3 a. ar. in Panfeld. £20.

26. Simon Passefyld, pl. *Tho.* Hardyng & w. Joan, def. 7a. ar. called 'Skynners Lande' in Wytham. £30.

27. Hil. & Eas. Tho. Baker, pl. Jerome Songer, gent., & w. Mary & *Hy.* Songer, gent., and w. Eliz., def. 2 mess., 3 tofts, 2 barns, 2 gdns., 2 orchards, 50 a. ar., 10 a. mw., 70 a. pa. & 10s. rt. in Wytham, Falkebourne & Rewenhale. £100.

28. Launcelet Madyson, pl. *Tho.* Heygate, gent., & Edm. Heygate, gent., his son & heir apt., def. 3 mess., 3 gdns., 100 a. ar., 6 a. mw., 40 a. pa., 3s. rt. & a rt. of 1 cock & 1 hen in Sandon & Danbury. £220.

29. Rd. Tebold, pl. Jn. Hatche & w. Anne, def. 1 mess. & 1 gdn. in Bockyng. £20.

30. Roger Wyncoll sen., pl. *Jn.* Laurens & w. Anne, Gilbert Hylls & w. Agnes, Rd. Sammes & Wm. Sammes, def. Manor of Herberds & 2 mess., 1 barn, 60 a. ar., 20 a. mw., 220 a. pa., 30 a. wd. & 4s. rent in Raylegh, Rawregh & Great Hokleigh. £250.

31. Wm. Fytche, gent., pl. Tho. Wentworth, kt., lord Wentworth, def. Manor of Lyndesell Hall & 6 mess., 4 cotts., 10 tofts, 600 a. ar., 100 a. mw., 300 a. pa., 20 a. wd. & 100s. rt. in Lyndesell. 470 mks.

32. Wm. Raynolde, pl. *Geo.* Saunder & w. Margery, def. A fourth part of 1 mess., 3 tofts, 4 curtilages, 1 barn, 1 dovecote, 2 gdns., 3 orchards, 60 a. ar., 12 a. mw., 30 a. pasture & 10 a. wd. in Great Lyghes, Terlyng, Hatfeld Peverell & Boreham. £40.

33. Jn. Lytell, pl. Roger Wyncoll, def. 1 mess., 2 tofts, 2 curtilages, 1 barn, 2 gdns., 1 orchard, 2 a. ar., & 2 a. pa. in Halsted. £40.

34. Geo. Woode, pl. *Lau.* Judie & w. Rose, def. 3 a. mw. in Lalford. £20.

35. Tho. Raven, pl. Hy. Fortescue, esq., def. 1 mess., 1 gdn., 1 orchard, 18 a. ar., 1 a. mw. & 10 a. pa. in Little Waltham. £40.

36. Wm. Whyte, pl. *Roger* Parker, gent., & w. Anne, def. 1 mess., 1 gdn., 10 a. ar., 60 a. pa., 4 a. wd. & 1d. rt. in Bradwell by the Sea. £140.

37. Jn. Woode, pl. *Jn.* Webbe & w. Agnes, def. 1 mess. & 12 a. mw. in Dedham. £40.

38. Francis Stacy, gent., pl. Martin Bowes, esq., & w. *Frances*, def. 1 mess., 40 a. ar., 80 a. marsh & 21s. rt. in Barkyng. 400 mks.

39. Jn. Hudson, pl. Jas. Sutton, gent., def. 2 mess., 1 barn, 1 stable, 1 gdn. & 1 orchard in Waltham Holycrosse & Weststrete. £40.

40. Hy. Graye & Jn. Mounds, pl. *Tho.* Halys & w. Eliz., def. Manor of Markes & 3 mess., 300 a. ar., 80 a. mw, 200 a. pa., 60 a. wd. & £6 13s. 4d. in Haveringe, Hornchurche, Dagenham & Barkynge. Def. quitclaimed to pl. & the heirs of Jn. £140.

41. Edw. Danyell, brother of Rd. Danyell, pl. The same Rd. Danyell, def. 8 a. ar. & 2 a. mw. in Sandon. £20.

42. Tho. Wood, pl. *Robt.* Wood & w. Joan, def. 1 mess., 1 orchard, 1 barn, 20 a. ar. & 4 a. mw. in Boreham. 100 mks.

43. Rd. Danyell, brother of Edw. Danyell, pl. The same Edw. Danyell, def. 1 mess., 1 gdn. & 2 a. ar. in Sandon. 20 mks.

44. Wm. Hare, pl. *Robt.* Wood & w. Joan, def. 1 mess., 1 gdn., 1 barn, 30 a. ar. & 6 a. mw. in Boreham. 100 mks.

45. Rd. Hamond, pl. Jn. Hamond, son & heir of Jn. Hamond, decd., def. 1 mess., 1 barn, 1 curtilage, 1 orchard, 8 a. ar. & 12 a. pa. in Depden. £60.

46. Hil. & Eas. Tho. Thurgood & Rd. Horwood, pl. Hy. Parker, kt., def. 20 a. ar., 10 a. mw. & 20 a. pa. in Latton & Harlowe. Def. quitclaimed to pl. & the heirs of Tho. And for this pl. gtd. the same to def. & his heirs to hold of the chief lords.

47. Tho. Herd & Wm. Dancaster, pl. Walter Hynton & w. *Frances*, def. 1 mess., 1 orchard & 8 a. pa. in Orsett. Def. quitclaimed to pl. & the heirs of Tho. And for this pl. gtd. the same to def. to hold for their lives of the chief lords, with remainder to the right heirs of Walter.

48. Robt. Burchard & w. Ellen, pl. *Tho.* Darcy, esq., & w. Eliz., def. 1 mess., 1 barn, 2 gdns., 1 orchard, 66 a. ar., 2 a. mw., 2 a. pa. & 1 a. wd. in Fayrested, Falkeborne, Terling & Witham. Def. quitclaimed to pl. & the heirs of Robt. £80.

49. Joan Parker, wid., pl. *Robt.* Milborn, son & heir of Wenefrida Rolffe, & w. Eliz., def. 10 a. ar., 1 a. mw. & 8 a. pa. in Great Waltham, Little Waltham & Bromefeld. £40.

CP25(2)/83/711   DIVERS COUNTIES

36. Geo. Bridge, pl. Wm. Raven & w. *Alice*, def. Property in Lynton, co. Cambridge, & 5 a. ar. in Hadstoke, co. Essex. £22. — Cambridge, Essex.

37. Hil. & Eas. Rd. Catelyn, serjeant at law, & Wm. Cordell, solicitor general, pl. *Giles* Alyngton, kt., & w. Alice, Rd. Alyngton, esq., & Wm. Alyngton, gent., their sons, def. 5 mess., 4 cotts., 10 tofts, 400 a. ar., 40 a. mw., 200 a. pa., 30 a. wd. & £5 rent in Ketton *alias* Kedyngton, Haverell *alias* Haverhyll, Sturmer, Bumsted & Wrattyng, co. Essex, & property in other counties. Def. quitclaimed to pl. & the heirs of Wm. And for this, among other settlements, pl. granted the Essex property to Giles for 1 month, with remainder to Rd. Alyngton & w. Jane & the heirs of their bodies, the heirs of the body of Ursula his late w., Wm. & the heirs male of his body, Philip Alyngton, another son of Giles, & the heirs male of his body, the heirs male of the body of Giles, Rd. Alington his brother & the heirs male of his body, Jn. Alyngton, another brother, & the heirs male of his body. Geo. Alyngton, another brother, & the heirs male of his body, the heirs of the body of Giles, & his right heirs, to hold of the chief lords. — Cambridge, Suff., Essex, Herts.

40. Jn. Colte, gent., & Jn. Gryggys, pl. *Hy.* Colte, gent., son & heir apt. of Geo. Colte, esq., & w. Eliz., def. Manor of Suffokes & property in Enfeld, co. Middlesex, & 6 a. mw. in Susan & Chynkford, co. Essex. Def. quitclaimed to pl. & the heirs of Jn. Colte. And for this pl. granted the same to def. & the heirs of Hy. to hold of the chief lords. — Mdx., Essex.

CP25(2)/70/582   TRINITY, 2 AND 3 PHILIP AND MARY   1556

50. Wm. May, pl. *Jn.* Tope & w. Joan, def. 2 mess., 2 tofts, 2 curtilages, 1 barn, 2 gdns., 4 a. ar., 2 a. mw. & 6 a. pa. in Pateswyk. Def. quitclaimed to pl. & his heirs. And for this pl. gtd. the same to def. to hold for their lives of the chief lords, with remainder to pl. & his heirs.

51. Geo. Saunder, pl. *Wm.* Reynold sen. & w. Helen, def. A moiety of 1 mess., 2 tofts, 2 curtilages, 1 barn, 2 gdns., 1 orchard, 12 a. ar., 4 a. mw., 10 a. pa. & 8 a. wd. in Boreham & Hatffeld Peverell. £40.

52. Jn. Huett *alias* Luter, pl. *Hy.* Johnson & w. Dorothy, def. 1 mess., 1 gdn., 1 orchard & 22 a. ar. in Lamborne. £76.

53. *This relates to the parish of St. Andrew, Holborn (in London).*

54. Eas. & Trin. Tho. Smyth, gent., pl. Tho., duke of Norfolk, def. The rectory of White Notley & 1 mess., 40 a. ar., 2 a. mw., 20 a. pa. & 16 a. alder in White Notley, & the advowson of the vicarage of White Notley. £80.

55. Tho. Thurstell, pl. Joan Pynell, wid., def. A moiety of 1 mess., 1 toft, 1 curtilage, 1 gdn., 1 orchard, 10 a. ar., 5 a. mw., 12 a. pa. & 2 a. wd. in Layerbretten and Great Byrche. £40.

56. Tho. Franke jun., pl. *Robt.* Lukyn, gent., & w. Joan, def. 31 a. ar. & 4 a. mw. in Hatfield Regis *alias* Hatfelde Brodeoke. £50.

57. Wm. Paschall, gent., pl. Robt. Wood, gent., & w. Joan, def. 1 mess., 2 tofts, 2 curtilages, 1 barn, 1 gdn., 1 orchard, 30 a. ar., 6 a. mw. & 20 a. pa. in Danbury & Sandon. £80.

58. Wm. Ball, pl. *Chris.* Kyng & w. Joan, def. 1 mess., 1 barn, 2 gdns., 2 orchards, 6 a. ar., 2 a. mw., 4 a. pa., 1 a. wd & 3 a. alder in Little Horkesleigh. £40.

59. Eas. & Trin. Hy. Hunt, pl. *Roger* Parker, gent., & w. Anne, def. 1 rood of mw. & 3 a. pa. in Gosfeld £40.

60. Eas. & Trin. Robt. Waspe, pl. Def. as in preceding. 1 mess., 1 gdn., 2 a. mw. & 4 a. pa. in Gosfeld. £40.

61. Eas. & Trin. Sebastian Johnson, pl. Def. as in preceding. 1 dovecote, 13 a. ar. & 5 a. mw. in Gosfeld. £40.

62. Nich. White, pl. *Tho.* Laurence & w. Eliz., def. 1 mess., 1 cott., 3 gdns., a barn, 12 a. ar., 3 a. mw., 6 a. pa. & 3s. 8¼d. rt. in Terling. 140 mks.

63. Hy. Sharyngton, esq., pl. Wm. Dunche, esq., def. 16 a. mw. in Waltham Stowe Marshe & Leyton. £213.

64. Tho. Merke, pl. *Rd.* Northey & w. Kath. & Wm. Powre & w. Joan, def. 1 mess., 2 gdns., 3 tofts, 20 a. ar., 4 a. mw., 6 a. pa. & 2. a. wd. in Langenho. £40.

CP25(2)/70/583   MICHAELMAS, 3 AND 4 PHILIP AND MARY   1556

1. Geo. Packer, pl. Alice Morrell, wid., def. 1 mess. & 2 gdns. in Stanford Rivers. £30.

2. Anth. Broun, serjeant at law, & w. Joan, pl. Tho. Phellipps, citizen & merchant tailor of London, & w. *Margery,* dau. of Thomasina Water, def. Manor of Churchehall & 4 mess., 6 gdns., 200 a. ar., 20 a. mw., 100 a. pa., 20 a. wd., 200 a. fresh marsh, 100 a. salt marsh & 100s. rt. in Pakelsham, Great Stanbridge, & the advowson of the church of Pakelsham. Def. quitclaimed to pl. & the heirs of Anth. £480.

3. Jn. Barnard, pl. *Wm.* Hunwyke, gent., & w. Joan & Philip Hunwyke & w. Marion, def. 1 mess., 2 barns, 3 gdns., 100 a. ar., 10 a. mw., 50 a. pa. & 4 a. wd. in Halsted. £140.

4. Jn. Sorrell, pl. *Jn.* Barker & w. Joan, def. 60 a. ar., 3 a. mw. & 10 a. pa. in Great Waltham. £40.

5. Tho. Blatche & Robt. Rame, pl. Tho. Sawyn, def. 3 mess., 30 a. ar., 1 a. mw., & 10 a. pa. in Little Waltham & Great Lyghes. Def. quitclaimed to pl. & the heirs of Tho. 100 mks.

6. Francis Barnam, pl. Jn. Johnson, def. 1 mess., 1 cott., 1 gdn., 1 orchard, 1 barn, 24 a. ar., 30 a. mw., 10 a. pa. & 2 a. wd. in Barkynge. £100.

7. Trin. & Mich. Tho. Savage, pl. Robt. Barker & w. *Agnes,* def. 2 a. 1 rood ar. in Thaxsted. 20 mks.

8. Hy. Aylett, pl. Jn. Purcas & w. *Joan,* def. 8 a. ar., 4 a. mw. & 6 a. pa. in White Rodyng. £40.

9. Tho. Wright, pl. *Geoff.* Athelham *alias* Allam & w. Joan, def. 1 mess., 60 a. ar., 8 a. mw., 12 a. pa. & 3 a. wd. in Highestrer & Rothing Aythorpp. £80.

10. Pl. as in 5. Wm. Sawyn, def. 1 mess., 10 a. ar., 3 a. pa. & 3 a. wd. in Little Waltham. Quitclaim as in 5. £30.

11. Jn. Starling, pl. Tho. Patmere *alias* Bryggs, def. 1 mess., 1 gdn. & 12 a. ar. in the town of Colchester & Grenested. £40.

12. Trin. & Mich. Anth. Albrough, pl. Jn. Reymont, def. 1 mess., 1 toft, 1 curtilage. 1 gdn., 1 orchard, 6 a. ar., 1 a. mw. & 6 a. pa. in Walden. Def. quitclaimed to pl. & his heirs. And for this pl. gtd. the same to def. & his heirs to hold of the chief lords.

13. Trin. & Mich. Wm. Ryche, clerk, vicar of Stebbyng, pl. *Jn.* Raymond, esq., & w. Margt., def. 1 mess., 60 a. ar., 10 a. mw., 40 a. pa., 4 a. wd. & 5s. rt. in Fayersted. £100.

14. Tho. Lathberie & Francis Jackson, pl. Hy. Moynes & w. *Alice* & Lau. Nycolson, def. 10 a. ar., 20 a. mw., 20 a. pa., 4 a. wd. & common of pa. for 50 animals in the marsh of Halyfeld in Halyfeld, Upshere & Waltham Holy Cross. Def. quitclaimed to pl. & the heirs of Tho. 160 mks.

15. Tho. Londe, pl. *Tho.* Hempsted & w. Alice, def. 1 dovecote, 7 a. ar., & 1 a. mw. in Bumpsted at the Steeple. £40.

16. Wm. Porter & w. Kath., pl. Nich. Porter & w. *Eleanor*, def. 2 mess., 1 barn, 2 gdns., 2 orchards & 2 a. ar., in Great Chesterford. Def. quitclaimed to pl. & the heirs of Wm. £40.

17. Tho. Porter, pl. *Tho.* Josselyn, kt., & w. Dorothy, def. 58. a. ar., 2 a. 1 rood mw. & 3 a. pa. in Sheringe. £96.

18. Jn. Lewes, gent., pl. Wm. Shawe & w. *Alice*, def. 2 a. pa. in Westham. 40 mks.

19. Jn. Bucke, pl. Rd. Cutt, def. A moiety of 10 a. ar. & 10 a. mw. in Ricling. £40.

20. Margt. Collynne, wid., pl. Jn. Clerke, def. 10 a. ar., 4 a. mw. & 36 a. pa. in Broxed. £40.

21. Nich. Kent, gent., & Jn. Belgrave, pl. *Bart.* Fulnetbye, gent., & w. Margt., def. Manor of Crulles *alias* Curles & 6 mess., 6 cotts., 200 a. ar., 12 a. mw., 20 a. pa., 20 a. wd. & 40s. rt. in Claveryng & Langeley. Def. quitclaimed to pl. & the heirs of Nich. And for this pl. gtd. the same to def. & the heirs of the body of Bart. of the body of Margt. to hold of the chief lords, with remainder to Chris. Fulnetby, gent., & his heirs.

22. Robt. Bedyngfeld, pl. *Edm.* Beawpre, esq., & Edw. Thursby, esq., def. Manor of Dorewards & 10 mess., 6 cotts., 1 water-mill, 10 gdns., 340 a. ar., 50 a. mw., 360 a. pa., 15 a. wd. & £7 rt. in Bockyng & Brayntre & free warren in Bockyng. Def. quitclaimed to pl. & his heirs. And for this pl. gtd. to Edm. the site of the manor, 1 gdn., 100 a. ar., 20 a. mw. & 220 a. pa. in Bockyng, parcel of the above, to Edw. for one week, with remainder to Edw. & Mary his w. & his heirs, & the residue to Edw. & his heirs, to hold of the chief lords.

23. Trin. & Mich. Wm. Ayluff, esq., pl. Geo. Badcock, def. 2 mess., 4 tofts, 4 curtilages, 2 barns, 2 gdns., 2 orchards, 40 a. ar., 6 a. mw., 80 a. pa., 10 a. wd. & 5s. rt. in Ronwell, Sowthanyngffeld & Wyckfford. 320 mks.

24. Steph. Lyonell, pl. Tho. Grenestrete & w. *Joan*, def. 1 mess., 1 curtilage & 1 gdn. in Barkyng. £20.

25. Hugh Nevyll, pl. Robt. Harrys, gent., def. 1 mess., 1 curtilage, 1 barn, 1 orchard, 1 gdn., 20 a. ar., 3 a. mw., 14 a. pa. & 3 a. wd. in Sandon & Danbury. £80.

26. Jn. Baker sen., pl. Jerome Songer, gent., & Jn. Derlinge *alias* Browne & w. *Clemencia*, def. 1 mess. & 1 gdn. in Walden. £20.

27. Philip Byrd, pl. *Tho.* Holt & Jn. Holt, def. 10 a. 1 rood ar. in Depden & Weydington. £40.

28. Jn. Harte & Simon Mayre, pl. Rd. Songer, gent., & w. Eliz., *Jerome* Songer, gent., & w. Mary, Tho. Baker, Wm. Love, clk., & Geo. Armond, def. 3 mess., 4 barns, 2 dovecotes, 3 gdns., 400 a. ar., 20 a. mw., 100 a. pa. & 20 a. wd. in Wytham, Falkeborne & Rewenhale. Def. quitclaimed to pl. & the heirs of Jn. And for this pl. gtd. a yearly rt. of £10 from the same to Eliz. for life, payable at the Annunciation & Michaelmas & beginning at the first of those feasts after the death of Rd., with power of distraint.

29. Tho. Cocke, pl. *Jn.* Jenyns, gent., & w. Jane, def. 8 a. mw., 10 a. pa. & 15 a. wd. in Eystanes at the Mount *alias* Great Eyston. Def. quitclaimed to pl. & his heirs. And for this pl. gtd. a yearly rt. of 40s. from the same to Jn. for life, payable at the Annunciation & Michaelmas, with power of distraint.

30. Hy. Coo, pl. *Jn.* Turnor sen. & w. Alice & Jn. Turnor jun., def. 2 mess. & 2 gdns. in Chelmesford. 40 mks.

57

31. Nich. Wylbor, pl. Edw. Palmer & w. *Margt.*, def. 1 mess., 1 gdn., 4 a. ar. called Bartelotts in Bockyng. £40.

32. Edm. Beawpre, esq., pl. Edw. Thursby, esq., def. Manors of Alresforde & Esthal & 20 mess., 10 cotts., 1 water-mill, 20 gdns., 500 a. ar., 30 a. mw., 500 a. pa., 260 a. wd., 100 a. furze & heath & £10 rt. in Alresforde, Fratyng, Thoryngton, Stysted & Wyvenho, view of frankpledge & free warren in Alresforde, a several fishery in the salt water called 'Alresforde Forde' in Alresforde, the advowson of the church of Alresforde, & a moiety of 1 water-mill in Alresforde & Thoryngton. £600.

33. Jn. Mede sen., pl. *Jn.* Jenyns, gent., & w. Jane, def. 20 a. ar., 7 a. mw. & 25 a. pa. in Eystanes at the Mount *alias* Great Eyston. £60.

34. Edw. Brokett sen., esq., & Jn. Kettell, gent., pl. Humphrey Bagsha, gent., & w. *Agnes*, def. A moiety of 2 mess., 20 a. mw., 200 a pa. & 4 a. wd. in Great Bado *alias* Baddo. Def. quitclaimed to pl. & the heirs of Edw. And for this pl. gtd. the same to def. to hold for their lives of the chief lords without impeachment of waste, with remainder to Jn. Bagsha their elder son & the heirs of his body, Robt. Bagsha, another son, & the heirs of his body, & the right heirs of Agnes.

35. Edw. Woode, pl. Edw. Barker, gent., def. 1 mess., 2 a. pa. & 2 a. wd. in Wansted. £40.

36. Wm. Lutlebery, pl. *Rd.* Godfrey & w. Alice, def. 4 mess., 4 gdns., 2 orchards & 4 a. pa. in the parish of Leonard in the New Hithe of the town of Colchester. £80.

37. Hy. Cocke, pl. *Jn.* Woodley & w. Anabella, def. 1 mess., 1 gdn., 1 orchard, 30 a. ar. & 2 a. pa. in Henham. £40.

38. Trin. and Mich. Jn. Webbe sen., pl. *Ralph* Freman and w. Edith, def. 7 a. ar. in Bokkyng. £20.

39. Tho. Wenden, pl. *Jn.* Turnour, gent., & w. Cristiana, def. 1 mess., 1 toft, 1 gdn., 8 a. ar., 1 a. mw. & 8 a. pa in Colne Wake, Pontesbright & Great Tey. £60.

40. Tho. Moyse, pl. *Hy.* Purlyant *alias* Purland & w. Kath., def. 1 mess. in Chaldwell in the parish of Barkyng. £40.

41. Tho. Cocke, pl. Tho. Colvyle & w. Joan & *Jn.* Colvyle, def. 30 a. ar. & 4 a. mw. in Eystanes at the Steeple *alias* Little Eyston. 100 mks.

42. Wm. Leveson, pl. *Tho.* Leveson & w. Ursula, def. 1 mess., 1 gdn., 1 orchard, 1 dovecote, 2 barns, 100 a. ar., 16 a. mw., 60 a. pa., 70 a. fresh marsh, 30 a. salt marsh, 60 a. wd., 10s. rt. & a rt. of 2 capons in Westhoroch. 400 mks.

43. Edw. Thursby, esq., pl. Edm. Beawpre, esq., def. 3 mess., 3 gdns., 2 orchards, 27 a. ar., 13½ a. mw., 42 a. pa. & 6 a. wd. in Bockynge. £200.

44. Trin. & Mich. Wm. Hone, esq., & Wm. Rutter, gent., pl Wm. Draywood & w. *Alice*, def. 2 mess., 1 barn, 80 a. ar., 10 a. mw., 200 a. marsh & two thirds of 6 a. wd. in South Bemflet, Bowers Gifford, Thunderslye & Raylighe. Def. quit-claimed to pl. & the heirs of Wm. Hone. And for this pl. gtd. the same to Wm. Dreywood & his heirs to hold of the chief lords.

45. Tho. Soole, pl. *Jn.* Turnor sen. & w. Alice & Jn. Turnor jun., def. 1 mess. in Chelmesford. £10.

46. Wm. (Gregyll) & Tho. Laurence, pl. Jn. Hewer, def. 1 mess., 1 barn, 1 gdn., 1 orchard, 8 a. ar. & 2 a. mw. in (Inford.) Def. quitclaimed to pl. & the heirs of Wm. And for this pl. gtd. the same to def. to hold for life of the chief lords without impeachment of waste, with remainder to (Mary his w.) & the heirs of her body by him and his right heirs.

47. Jas. Morley, pl. *Rd.* Nott & w. Joan & Wm. Nott, def. 3 mess., 3 tofts, 2 gdns., 1,000 a. ar., 100 a. mw., 100 a. pa., 100 a. furze and heath and 100 a. marsh in Graies Thorocke, Graies Strope, Litle Thorocke, Stifford & Chaldwell. 200 mks.

48. Geo. Maull, pl. *Roger* Torell and w. Alice, def. 10 a. ar. & 10 a. marsh in Estylbery. £40.

49. Trin. & Mich. Rd. Cosyn & Rd. Petyt, pl. Tho. Rampson, gent., & w. Jane, def. 2 mess., 240 a. ar., 12 a. mw., 50 a. pa., 5 a. wd. & 20 s. rt. in Bokkyng, Gossefeld, Little Rayne, Shalford & Branketre. Def. quitclaimed to pl. & the heirs of Rd. Cosyn. And for this pl. gtd. the same to def. & the heirs of Tho. to hold of the chief lords.

50. Trin. & Mich. Jn. Graveley, pl. *Jn.* Dune & w. Alice, def. 1 mess. & 1 gdn. in Mulsham. £20.

51. Trin. & Mich. Rd. Hamond, pl. Jn. Shell & w. *Joan*, def. A moiety of 1 mess., 1 barn, 30 a. ar., 1 a. mw., 8 a. pa. & 1 a. wd. in Depden. £36.

52. Jn. Taye, esq., Hy. Stapylton, Jasper Jones, gentlemen, & Wm. Peverell, 'yoman', pl. Edm. Pyrton, esq., def. Site of the manor of Elmysted & 3 mess., 4 gdns., 6 tofts, 2 barns, 100 a. ar., 20 a. mw., 100 a. pa. & 40 a. wd. in Elmested. Def. quitclaimed to pl. & the heirs of Jn. £400.

53. Edm. Beawpre, esq., pl. Edw. Thursby, esq., def. 1 mess., 6 gdns., 34 a. ar., 122 a. pa. & 26 a. wd. in Bockynge. £209.

54. Jn. Mountford & Robt. Anneys, pl. Tho. Colvyle & w. Joan and *Jn.* Colvyle & Tho. Cocke, def. 1 mess., 1 water-mill, 30 a. ar., 4 a. mw. & 4 a. pa. in Eystanes at the Steeple *alias* Little Eyston. Def. quitclaimed to pl. & the heirs of Jn. Mountford. And for this pl. granted to Tho. Colvyle a yearly rt. of 56s. 8d. from the same for five years from Michaelmas if he shall live so long & another yearly rt. £4 16s. 8d. for life from Michaelmas, 1561, & to Joan a yearly rt. of 33s. 4d. for life; all payable at the Annunciation & Michaelmas, with power of distraint.

55. Jn. Enyver, pl. *Jn.* Jenyns, gent., & w. Jane, def. 1 mess., 1 barn, 2 gdns. & 8 a. ar. in Eystanes at the Mount *alias* Great Eyston. £20.

56. Tho. Greye & Robt. Bryckett, gent., pl. *Robt.* Aspelond, esq., & Anth. Aspelond, gent., def. Manor of Heydon & 6 mess., 12 tofts, 600 a. ar., 30 a. mw., 100 a. pa., 30 a. wd. & £3 rt. in Heydon, Cristeshall, Great Crissall & Little Chissall, & the advowson of the church of Heydon. Def. quitclaimed to pl. & the heirs of Tho. And for this pl. gtd. the same to Robt. for three days, with remainder to him & Eliz. his w. to hold for their lives of the chief lords without impeachment of waste, Wm. Hoye & w. Mary & the heirs of their bodies, the heirs of the body of Wm. & the right heirs of Robt. Aspelond.

(Tho. Stansted & w. Joan, pl. *Tho.* Audeley sen., esq., & w. Kath., def. 1 mess., 2 tofts, 2 curtilages, 2 barns, 1 gdn., 1 orchard, 100 a. ar., 10 a. mw. & 40 a. pa. in Great Tey. Def. quitclaimed to pl. & the heirs of Tho. 40 mks.)
(Taken from the Note, the Foot being missing.)

CP25(2)/83/712   DIVERS COUNTIES

5. Jn. Wyllowes, Rd. Thurgor & Leonard Thurgor, pl. *Rd.* Tyrell, esq., & w. Grace, def. 19 a. ar. & 9 a. pa. in Asshedon & Barkelowe, co. Essex, & property in Berkelowe & elsewhere, co. Cambs. Def. quitclaimed to pl. & the heirs of Jn. £80. — Cambs., Essex.

6. Trin. & Mich. Tho. Powle & w. Jane, pl. *Jn.* Yorke, kt., & w. Anne, def. 1 mess., 2 gdns., 100 a. ar., 80 a. mw., 60 a. pa., 160 a. marsh & 30 a. furze & heath in Barkynge & Westham, co. Essex, & property in Wollwiche, co. Kent. Def. quitclaimed to pl. & the heirs of Tho. £3,800. — Essex, Kent.

CP25(2)/70/583   HILARY, 3 AND 4 PHILIP AND MARY   1557

57. Tho. Wyllyamson, pl. *Edm.* Mordant, esq., & w. Agnes, def. 16 a. pa. & 6 a. 1 rood wd., in Wymbyshe. £40.

58. Jn. Wase & w. Wenefrida, pl. *Jn.* Stuard & w. Grace, def. 5 mess., 1 gdn., 1 orchard., 30 a. ar., 13 a. mw., 16 a. pa & 3 a. wd. in Great Bursted. Def. quitclaimed to pl. & the heirs of Jn. £130.

59. Wm. Peter, kt., Wm. Coke, esq., & Edw. Napper, gent., pl. *Tho.* Baron *alias* Barne, gent., & w. Anne, def. Rectory of Barkynge & all tithes pertaining to it in Barkynge, & the advowson of the vicarage of the parish church of Barkynge. Def. quitclaimed to pl. & the heirs of Wm. Peter, with warranty against themselves & the heirs of Tho. & Robt. Thomas & And. Salter & their heirs. £200.

60. Mich. & Hil. Robt. Hyrst, gent., pl. *Tho.* Josselyn, kt., & w. Dorothy, def. Manor of Cowykebury & 4 mess., 4 barns, 4 gdns., 4 orchards, 140 a. ar., 20 a. mw., 40 a. pa., 16 a. wd. & £3 rt. in Sheringe. 400 mks.

61. Clement Cysley & Jn. (Keyle), gentlement, pl. Wm. Abbatt, esq., & w. *Margery*, def. Manor of Westbury & 4 mess., 40 tofts, 40 gdns., 1,500 a. ar., 300 a. mw., 1,000 a. pa., 200 a. fresh marsh, 200 a. wd. & 100s. rt. in Westbury, Gaysehams Hall, Barkyng, Ilford, Woodford, Dagenham & Chigwell, & tithes of corn & hay from the manor of Westbury in Barking, Ilford, Woodford, Dagenham & Chigwell. Def. quitclaimed to pl. & the heirs of Clement. 920 mks.

62. Tho. Wallys, pl. Jn. Darlyng *alias* Browne & w. *Clemencia*, def. 1 mess. & 3 a. ar. in Walden. 20 mks.

63. Humphrey Fryth & w. Robergia, pl. Jn. Hoppysley, gent., & w. *Mary*, def. 1 mess. & 16 a. pa. in Upmynster. Def. quitclaimed to pl. & the heirs of Humphrey. £40.

64. Jn. Underwode, pl. Jn. Sewall & w. *Alice*, def. 1 mess., 1 gdn., 1 barn, 10 a. ar. & 2 a. mw. in Marks Teye *alias* Tey Mandevyle. £20.

65. Hy. Hurt, pl. Jn. Tyrrell, esq., def. 1 mess., 1 curtilage, 20 a. ar., 4 a. mw., 24 a. pa. & ½ a. wd. in Northbemflete & Wykford. £60.

66. Rd. Grace, pl. Tho. Rynger, def. 1 mess., 1 gdn., 60 a. ar., 10 a. mw. & 40 a. pa. in Great Maplested, which Wm. Whyte holds for life. Pl. & his heirs to hold the reversion of the chief lords. £40.

67. Robt. Smyth, pl. Tho. Bellyngham & w. *Joan*, def. 1 mess., 1 cott., 10 a. ar. & 1 a. wd. in Harvardstocke, £40.

68. Edw. Crane, pl. Roger Crystofer & w. *Margt.*, def. 2 mess. & 2 gdns. in Harwich. £40.

69. Anth. Roo & Wm. Rogers, pl. And. Pascall, gent., def. 1 mess., 1 curtilage, 1 barn, 1 gdn., 40 a. ar., 10 a. mw., 40 a. pa., 3 a. wd. & 20 a. salt marsh in Fange *alias* Fange at Noke. Def. quitclaimed to pl. & the heirs of Anth. £80.

70. Tho. Lyndsell sen., pl. *Jn.* Wylton & w. Kath., def. 1 mess. & 2 gdns. in Thaxsted. £20.

71. Nich. Foxe, pl. *Agnes* Heydon & Margt. Jacob, wid., kinswomen & heirs of Rd. Moriss, decd., def. 1 mess., 1 barn, 50 a. ar., 4 a. mw. & 3 a. pa. in Newporte Pond & Wydyngton. £80.

72. Lancelet Maddyson & Tho. Saffowe, pl. Robt. Harrys, gent., def. 1 mess., 1 orchard, 1 barn, 13 a. ar., 7 a. mw. & 10 a. pa. in Sandon. Def. quitclaimed to pl. & the heirs of Tho. 100 mks.

73. Trin. & Hil. Robt. Thorpe, gent., pl. *Tho.* Colt, gent., & w. Magdalen, def. Manor of Colchester Hall & 20 mess., 10 tofts, 500 a. ar., 100 a. mw., 200 a. pa., 20 a. wd. & 40s. rt. in Takeley, Ellesnam, Broxsted, Little Canfeld, Eston, White Rothyng & Sabrycheworthe, co. Herts. £140.

74. Steph. Craske, pl. *Wm.* Lynnett & Hy. Smythe, def. 5 mess. 6 tofts., 3 barns, 8 gdns., 4 orchards, 30 a. ar., 20 a. mw., 15 a. pa., 6 a. moor & 30s. rt. in Branktree & Bockyng. £140.

75. Jn. Keyle, gent., pl. Wm. Abbatt, esq., & w. *Margery*, def. 4 mess., 4 gdns., 2 orchards, 4 barns, 200 a. ar., 120 a. mw., 80 a. pa., 100 a. fresh marsh & 4 a. wd. in Barking & Reple, 12 cartloads of wd. yearly in the forest of Waltham, & tithes of corn & hay from the mess., farms & tenements called Eastbury. 800 mks.

76. Hil. 2 & 3, & Hil. Wm. Frohoke, pl. Rd. Cokman & w. *Joan*, def. 3 mess., 1 toft, 1 gdn. & 1 a. ar. in Walden. £40.

77. Jas. Bacon & Augustine Curteis, pl. *Tho.* Halys, gent., & w. Eliz., def. Manor of Markes & 3 mess., 150 a. ar., 20 a. mw., 170 a. pa., 40 a. wd. & £6 13s. 4d. rt. in Hornchurche, Dagenham & Barkyng. Def. quitclaimed to pl. & the heirs of Augustine. £200.

CP25(2)/70/584   EASTER, 3 AND 4 PHILIP AND MARY   1557

1. Jn. Buck, pl. *Jn.* Woodley & w. Anabella, def. 10 a. ar., 1 a. mw. & 6 a. pa. in Henham. £40.

2. Jn. Garrard, pl. Wm. Kene & w. Joan & *Tho.* Byrde, def. 1 mess., 1 cott., 3 gdns. & 10 a. ar. in the town of St. Laurence. 50 mks.

3. Pl. as in preceding. Jn. Maye & w. *Cristina*, def. 1 mess., 1 curtilage, 1 gdn., 5 a. ar. & 1 a. mw. in Stisted. And for this pl. gtd. the same to def. to hold for their lives of the chief lords.

4. Bart. Averell, pl. *Robt.* Heigham, gent., & w. Margt., def. Manor of Herons *alias* Countysbrydge & 1 mess., 1 barn, 2 gdns., 60 a. ar., 20 a. mw., 60 a. pa., 80 a. fresh marsh, 80 a. salt marsh, 4 a. wd. & 40s. rt. in Althorne, Maylond & Lachyngdon. £340.

5. Hil. & Eas. Tho. Wyseman, pl. *Robt.* Southwell, kt., & w. Margt., Rd. Lee & w. Eliz., def. Manor of Bardfilds *alias* Bardevyles & 3 mess., 3 curtilages, 3 tofts, 3 barns, 3 gdns., 100 a. ar., 30 a. mw., 80 a. pa., 3 a. wd. & 20s. rt. in Northebemflete, Nevyngdon, Wyckford & Bardefelds. Def. quitclaimed to pl & his heirs, with separate warranties from Robt. & Rd. £280.

6. Rd. Whorwood & Hy. Jones, pl. Wm. Flemynge *alias* Saunder & w. *Margt.*, def. 1 mess., 40 a. ar., 10 a. mw. & 10 a. pa. in Great Sampford & Little Sampford. Def. quitclaimed to pl. & the heirs of Hy. And for this pl. gtd. the same to def. to hold for their lives of the chief lords without impeachment of waste, with remainder to the right heirs of Wm.

7. Hil. & Eas. Wm. Hamlyn, pl. *Hy.* Hame and w. Bridget, def. 1 mess., 1 gdn. & 1 orchard in Wytham. £30.

8. Hil. & Eas. Robt. Fannyng, pl. Jn. Sympson & w. *Joan,* def. 3 a. ar. & 3 a. pa. in Little Wakeryng. £20.

9. Hil. & Eas. Jas. Pergitor, gent., pl. Jn. Burre, def. 1 mess., 1 barn, 1 stable, 1 gdn., 1 orchard, 15 a. ar., 2 a. mw., 10 a. pa. & 10 a. wd. in Barkyng, which Kath. Bemond, wid., holds for life. Pl. & his heirs to hold the reversion of the chief lords. £80.

10. Jerome Songer, gent., & w. Mary, pl. Robt. Mylborne & Jn. Paxton & w. *Gertrude*, def. 1 barn, 70 a. ar. & 2 a. wd. in Terlyng & Hatfeld Peverell. Def. quitclaimed to pl. & the heirs of Jerome. £140.

11. Mich. & Eas. Hy. Bone, pl. Hy. Lyman sen., def. 3 mess., 3 barns, 3 gdns., 40 a. ar., 20 a. mw., 20 a. pa., 6 a. wd. & 1 a. marsh in Navestoke. And for this pl. gtd. the same to def. & his heirs to hold of the chief lords.

12. Hil. & Eas. Chris. Horner, pl. *Giles* Kynwolmarshe & w. Eliz., def. 1 mess., 1 gdn. & ½ a. ar. in Little Rayne *alias* Rignes. 20 mks.

13. Hil. & Eas. Rd. Hamond son of Jn. Hamond, decd., pl. *Nich.* Smythe, gent., & w. Margt., def. 1 mess., 1 gdn. & 5s. 8d. rt. in Walden. £40.

14. Hy. Songer, pl. Tho. Nudygate, def. A moiety of the manors of Warners & Burses & 20 mess., 10 cotts., 500 a. ar., 100 a. mw., 500 a. pa., 100 a. wd. & 100s. rt. in Great Waltham, Little Waltham, Plasshey, Felsted, Great Lighes, Little Lighes, Pakelsham, Thundersley, Halsted & Great Stambridge. £200.

15. Hil. & Eas. Nich. Wright & w. Joan, pl. *Robt.* Ryse & w. Kath., def. 8 a. ar. in Depden. Def. quitclaimed to pl. & the heirs of Nich. £40.

16. Geo. Frithe sen., pl. Steph. Moyle & w. *Joan*, def. 1 a. ar. in Daggenham. £20.

17. Rd. Page, pl. Edw. Rosse, gent., def. 2 mess., 2 gdns., 1 water-mill, 14 a. ar., 2 a. salt marsh & 12d. rt. in Great Wigbaroughe, Little Wigbaroughe, Salcott & Tolleshunt Knyghtys. £140.

18. Hy. Aylett, pl. Jn. Purcas & w. *Joan*, def. 1 mess., 1 curtilage, 1 orchard, 20 a. ar. & 10 a. pa. in White Rodynge. £80.

19. Wm. Frythe, pl. Rd. Thresshar & w. Eliz. & *Wm.* Downyng & w. Joan, def. 1 mess., 1 barn, 1 gdn. & 7 a. ar. in Horndon. £80.

20. Wm. Sidey sen., pl. *Tho.* Gray, esq., & Wm. Gray, gent., def. 1 toft, 1 gdn. & 8 a. ar. in Bures St. Mary. And for this pl. granted a yearly rt. of 8s. from the same to def. & the heirs of Tho., payable at the Annunciation & Michaelmas, with power of distraint.

21. Wm. Petre, kt., pl. Tho. Wood & w. *Joan*, def. A third of 1 mess., 2 gdns., 1 orchard, 6 a. ar. & 10 a. pa. in Mountnesing. £20.

22. Rose Trott, wid., pl. *Rd.* Houghton, gent., & w. Eliz., def. 1 mess., 120 a. ar., 50 a. mw., 200 a. pa., 12 a. wd. & 10s. rt. in Nasyng & Waltham Holy Crosse, & two thirds of the manor of Langryge *alias* Lytle Langryge *alias* Waterhall & a sewer or several fishery in the water of Luy. £440.

23. Wm. Hamond, pl. Geo. Hamond, def. 1 mess. & 1 gdn. in Arkysden. £20.

24. Robt. Halfhed & Robt. Turner, pl. Wm. Adam & w. *Margt.*, def. 6 mess., 6 gdns., 4 orchards & 2 a. ar. in Walden. Def quitclaimed to pl. & the heirs of Robt. Halfhed. And for this pl. gtd. the same to def. & the heirs of Wm. to hold of the chief lords.

25. Wm. Strache, pl. Edw. Munday & w. *Joan*, dau. & heir of Isabel Cely, def. 1 mess. & 1 gdn. in Walden *alias* Saffron Walden. £30.

26. Wm. Rastell, serjeant at law, & Jn. Newdigate, esq., pl. Wm. Bendlowes, serjeant at law, def. 5 mess., 1 cott., 4 barns, 5 orchards, 10 gdns., 34 a. ar., 3 a. mw. & 6 a. pa. in Great Berdefeld, Little Berdefeld & Panfeld. Def. quitclaimed to pl. & the heirs of Wm. And for this pl gtd. the same to def. & his heirs to hold of the chief lords.

27. Wm. Fytche, gent., pl. *Tho.* Wentworth, kt., lord Wentworth, & w. Dame Anne, def. Manor of Camoyes & 10 mess., 10 cotts., 10 tofts, 500 a. ar., 100 a. mw., 200 a. pa., 60 a. wd. & £10 rt. in Toppysfeld, Over Yeldham, Nether Yeldham, Stamborn, Reddeswell & Fynchyngfeld. £400.

28. Wm. Hunwyke, gent., & Jn. Puckkell, pl. *Jn.* Stokes & w. Frances, def. 1 mess., 1 barn, 1 gdn., 15 a. ar., 3 a. mw. & 16 a. pa. in Henyngham Sible & Gossefeld. Def. quitclaimed to pl. & the heirs of Wm. 70 mks.

29. Tho. Smyth, esq., pl. Wm. Poulett, esq., & w. *Anne*, dau. & heir of Edm. Smyth, esq., def. Manors of Cressyng Temple & Redfans & 6 mess., 10 tofts, 6 curtilages, 6 barns, 1 water-mill, 2 dove-cotes, 6 gdns., 6 orchards, 500 a. ar., 60 a. mw., 200 a. pa., 100 a. alder, 100 a. wd. & £4 rt. in Wytham, Cressyng, Rewenhale, White Notley, Black Notley, Little Waltham, Little Lyghez, Bradwell by Coggeshall, Shalford, Great Salyng, Fynchyngfeld & Great Bardfeld, & the hundred of Wytham. £760.

30. Rd. Woodcock sen., pl. Rd. Coltman & w. *Kath.*, def. 2 mess., 2 barns., 2 gdns., 3 a. ar. & 3 a. pa. in Claveryng. £40.

31. Tho. Studdalff *alias* Stodall, pl. Tho. Browne *alias* Cuckuk & w. *Eliz.*, def. 1 mess., 1 barn, 1 gdn. & 1 orchard in Wytham. 100 mks.

32. Robt. Spryng, pl. *Ralph* Freman & w. Edith, def. 1 mess., 1 barn, 1 gdn., 4 a. ar., 6 a. mw. & 4 a. pa. in Bockyng. 80 mks.

33. Robt. Longe, pl. *Jn.* Jenyns, gent., & w. Jane & Wm. Enyver & w. Agnes, def. 16 a. ar., in Great Dunmowe. 50 mks.

34. Rd. Dey, pl. *Tho.* Andrewes *alias* Payntour & w. Eliz., def. 1 mess. & 1 gdn. in Harwiche. £40.

35. Robt. Bryckett & Tho. Payne, pl. Tho. Cooke, def. 2 mess., 2 gdns, 200 a. ar., 40 a. pa., 10 a. mw. & 10 a. wd. in Great Chyshull & Little Chysull. Def. quitclaimed to pl. & the heirs of Robt. 160 mks.

36. Wm. Loughton & w. Eliz., pl. Tho. Phypp & w. *Alice* & *Margery* Hastynges, wid., def. 1 mess., 1 toft, 3 gdns., 2 orchards & 5 a. ar. in Waltham. Def. quitclaimed to pl. & the heirs of Eliz. £40.

37. Wm. Longe, pl. *Tho.* Bemysshe & w. Kath., def. 1 mess. & 1 gdn. in Great Dunmow. £20.

38. Hil. & Eas. Wm. Lawrence, pl. Jn. Tyrrell, def. 1 mess., 1 toft, 1 barn, 1 gdn., 10 a. ar. & 10 a. pa. in South Okendon. £40.

39. Jn. Ayleward, pl. *Nich.* Smyth, gent., & w. Margt., def. 1 mess. in Walden. £36.

40. Geo. Neele, pl. *Tho.* Hawys & w. Joan, def. 1 mess., 1 barn, 1 gdn., 8 a. ar., 1 a. mw. & 3 a. pa. in Little Badowe & Boreham. 50 mks.

41. Tho. Bealle, pl. Simon Fawce, def. 1 mess. & 1 gdn in Aburton. £40.

42. Jas. Haledaye, pl. Jn. Tyrrell, def. 1 mess., 1 barn, 1 gdn., 20 a. ar., 5 a. mw., 12 a. pa. & 5 a. marsh in Alveley. 70 mks.

43. Wm. Glascock, gent., pl. *Jn.* Jenyns, gent., & w. Jane, def. 18 a. ar., 1 a. mw. & 2 a. pa. in Great Dunmowe. 100 mks.

44. Rd. Marchall, pl. *Augustine* Thayer & w. Anne, def. 1 mess., 1 barn, 2 gdns., 10 a. ar. & 6d. rt. in Little Waltham. 50 mks.

45. Wm. Scotte, pl. *Jn.* Coppyn & w. Gresilda, def. 1 mess., 2 gdns., 1 orchard, 12 a. ar., ½ a. mw. & 3 a. wd. in Pebmerishe *alias* Pedmarsshe. £40.

CP25(2)/83/712   DIVERS COUNTIES

35. Chris. Hyll, clk., & Robt. Ley, clk., pl. Jn. Mayer, def. 4 mess., 3 tofts, 4 gdns., 100 a. ar., 12 a. md., 100 a. pa. & 10 a. wd. in Foxherd *alias* Foxerth, Oton, Belcham Albrytt, Belcham Wyllyams & Lyston, co. Essex, & prop. in Milford *alias* Long Milford, co. Suff. Def. quitclaimed to pl. & the heirs of Chris. £40. − Essex, Suff.

36. Jn. Yorke, kt., & w. Anne, pl. *Tho.* Powle, esq., & w. Jane, def. 1 mess., 2 gdns., 100 a. ar., 80 a. mw., 60 a. pa., 160 a. marsh & 30 a. furze & heath in Barkyng & Westham, co. Essex, & the same in Wollwiche, co. Kent. Def. quitclaimed to pl. & the heirs of Jn. £1,700. − Essex, Kent.

37. Hugh Griffith, gent., & Rd. Gwyn, gent., pl. Hy. Fortescew, esq., def. Manors of Powrsshall *alias* Pooryshall & Walley Hall & 20 mess., 10 tofts, 20 gdns., 500 a. ar., 160 a. mw., 700 a. pa., 150 a. wd., 300 a. furze & heath & £10 rt. in Wytham, Fawlkeborne, Terlyng, Feyrsted & Revynhall, co. Essex; & prop. in Hertfordshire & Mdx.. Def. quitclaimed to pl. & the heirs of Hugh. £800. − Essex, Herts., Mdx.

48. The K. & Q., pl. *Jn.* Cheke, kt., & w. Mary, def. Manors of Clare, Claretthall, Hunden, Assheton & Pytley *alias* Pightley & 100 mess., 40 tofts, 60 cotts., 80 gdns., 60 orchards, 4 dovecotes, 6 mills, 1,000 a.ar., 300 a. mw., 800 a. pa., 300 a. wd., 2,000 a. furze & heath & 100s. rt. & free fishery, free warren, liberties & franchises in Stoke, Esse, Thacksted, Byrbroke, Rudgwell *alias* Redeswell, Pitley, Toppesfelde, Sturmyr, Stoke, Ayshe, Clarett Halle, Assheton, Clare & Bradefelde, & the advowsons of the churches of Clare, Hunden & Asheton, co. Essex; & prop. in other counties. Def. quit-claimed to the Q. & her heirs & successors. £3,000. − Suff., Essex, Cambs., Hunts., Suss., Lincs., Norf.

CP25(2)/70/584   TRINITY, 3 AND 4 PHILIP AND MARY   1557

46. Wm. Luckyn & Geoff. Luckyn, pl. *Ralph* Nalynghurst, gent., & w. Eliz. & Lancelot Madyson, def. Manor of Frevells *alias* Cobbes & 3 mess., 3 gdns., 100 a. ar., 12 a. mw., 60 a. pa., 8 a. wd., 40 a. salt marsh, 40 a. fresh marsh, 1,000 a. common, 10s. rt. & 2 weirs (*waris sive piscat'*) in Goldanger, Great Totham, Little Totham, Tolleshunt Mauger, Tolleshunt Darcye & Tollesburye. Def. quitclaimed to pl. & the heirs of Geoff. Separate warranties by Ralph & Lancelot. £100.

47. Geo. Palmer & Robt. Lee, pl. Francis Michell, gent., & w. *Joan* & Jn. Braunche & w. *Ellen*, def. Manor of Garnonshall & 1 mess., 3 barns, 2 gdns., 2 orchards, 200 a. ar., 100 mw., 200 a. pa., 100 a. wd. & £12 rt. in Theydon Garnon, Theydon Boys & Theydon at the Mount, view of frank-pledge in Theydon Garnon, & the advowson of the church of Theydon Garnon. Def. quitclaimed to pl. & the heirs of Geo. And for this pl. gtd. the manor, mess., 3 barns, 2 gdns., 2 orchards, 100 a. ar., 50 a. mw., 100 a. pa., 100 a. wd., rt. of £12, view of frank-pledge & advowson to Jn. & Ellen to hold for their lives of the chief lords, with remainder to the right heirs of Jn., & the residue to Francis & Jane & the heirs of Francis to hold of the chief lords.

48. Wm. Kynge, pl. Rd. Reynolds & w. *Anne*, def. 17 a. pa. called 'Typtoes' in Great Bursted. £80.

49. Rd. Northen, pl. Rd. Sandys, gent., & w. Kath., def. 40 a. ar., 4 a. mw. & 20 a. pa. in Mystelleigh. Pl. to hold for the life of Kath. £40.

50. Eas. & Trin. Tho. Serle, citizen & mercer of London, pl. Charles Newcomen, gent., & w. *Joan*, def. 1 capital mess., 1 gdn., 1 orchard, 1 barn & 3 a. mw. in Brentwood, which Kath. Nytingale, wid., holds for life. Pl. & his heirs to hold the reversion of the chief lords. 130 mks.

51. Rd. Tanner, pl. Rd. Derbye, gent., & w. *Margt.*, def. 1 mess., 1 gdn., 1 orchard, 14 a. ar., 2 a. mw. & 8 a. pa. in White Notley & Black Notley. £40.

52.   Tho. Knolles & w. Mary, pl. Tho. Heyrde & w. *Margt.*, def. A fifth pt. of 20 mess., 10 cotts., 20 gdns., 20 orchards, 300 a. ar., 200 a. pa., 60 a. mw., 40 a. wd. & £10 rt. in Chigwell. Def. quitclaimed to pl. & the heirs of Tho. And for this pl. gtd. a moiety of the same to def. & the heirs of Margt. to hold of the chief lords.

53.   *(This relates to Wallyngton (? in Norfolk)).*

54.   Jas. Spender, pl. Beatrice Twedey, wid., & *Rd.* Twedey, gent., def. 1 mess., 1 gdn., 1 curtilage, 10 a. ar., 6 a. mw., 10 a. pa. & 1 a. wd. in West Hannyngfeld. £40.

55.   Ambrose Gilberde *alias* Gilbert, gent., Edw. Watkinson, clk., & Hy. Crowther, pl. *Edm.* Tyrrell, esq., & w. Susan, def. Manor of Ockeley *alias* Hockeley & 1 mess., 2 cotts., 2 gdns., 160 a. ar., 40 a. mw., 300 a. pa., 20 a. wd. & 20s. rt. in Great Hockeley *alias* Great Ockeley & Little Hockeley *alias* Little Ockeley. Def. quitclaimed to pl. & the heirs of Ambrose. £400.

56.   Simon Cawston, pl. *Robt.* Feyldys & w. Rose, def. 1 mess. & 1 gdn. in Manitre. £40.

57.   Tho. Campe, pl. *Polidor* Rosse, gent. & w. Joan, def. 1 mess., 11 a. ar. & common of pa. for 5 animals in Nasyng. £40.

58.   Jn. Mordaunt, kt., pl. Roger Cholmeley, kt., Tho. Russhell, kt., & w. *Frances*, def. 1 mess., 100 a. ar., 30 a. mw., 20 a. pa., 60 a. wd. & 4 a. furze & heath in Gingeraff. £40.

59.   Eas. & Trin. Wm. Vernon, gent., pl. Tho. Frank, gent., def. 1 mess., 1 barn, 20 a. ar., 1 a. 3 roods mw., 60 a. pa., & 5 a. wd. in Maldon & Woodham Water. £160.

60.   Jn. Southcot, gent., & Giles Hill, gent., pl. *Jn.* Ayleff, esq., & w. Susan & Erkenwald Ayleff, gent., def. The rectory of Great Wakeryng *alias* Moche Wakeryng & a moiety of 1 mess., 40 a. ar., 100 a. mw., 100 a. pa. & 200 a. marsh in Great Wakeryng *alias* Moche Wakeryng, Estwood & the island of Walletts. Def. quitclaimed to pl. & the heirs of Jn. And for this pl. gtd. the same to Jn. & Susan to hold for their lives of the chief lords, with remainder to the heirs male of the body of Jn. Erkenwald & the heirs male of his body, & the right heirs of Jn.

61.   Jn. Lufkyn, pl. Humphrey Hyll, gent., & w. *Joan*, def. 2 a. mw. in Dedham. £40.

62.   Rd. Barnard, pl. *Wm.* Fytche, gent., & Francis Mannock, gent., & w. Mary, def. 1 mess., 1 gdn., 1 orchard, 100 a. ar., 9 a. mw., 21 a. pa., 5 a. wd., 5s. rt. & a rt. of ¾lb. of pepper in Little Berdefeld & Great Berdefeld. £200.

63.   Eas. & Trin. Wm. Bendlowes, serjeant at law, pl. Hy. Veysey, gent., def. 5 mess., 4 tofts, 60 a. ar., 12 a. mw., 100 a. pa., 10 a. wd. & 12d. rt. in Great Berdefeld, Little Berdefeld, Great Sampford, Little Sampford & Hengham Sible *alias* Sybbelhennyngham. 400 mks.

64.   Hy. Courteman, pl. Roger Coker, clk., def. 1 mess., 1 gdn., 6 a. ar., & 1 a. mw. in Woodham Mortymer. £30.

65.   Wm. Rastell, serjeant at law, pl. Leonard Sandell, gent., & w. Eliz. & *Jn.* Pylbarough, gent., son of Jn. Pylbarough, esq., decd., def. 3 mess., 134 a. ar., 15 a. mw., 40 a. pa., 14 a. wd. & 2s. 8d. rt. in Hatfeld Peverell & Boreham. And for this pl. gtd. the same to Leonard & Eliz. to hold for their lives of the chief lords without impeachment of waste, with remainder to Jn. the son & the heirs of his body, the heirs of the bodies of the said Jn. the father & Eliz., & the right heirs of Jn. the father.

66.   Tho. Crawley, esq., pl. Edm. Mordant, esq., & w. Agnes, def. 1 mess., & 60 a. wd. in Thunderley & Wymbysshe. £200.

67.   Roger Groome, pl. *Steph.* Beckyngham, esq., & w. Jane, def. Manor of Hyllhouse *alias* Hellhouse & 2 tofts, 2 barns, 2 gdns., 100 a. ar., 30 a. mw., 150 a. pa., 100 a. wd., 200 a. fresh marsh 100 a. salt marsh & 20s. rt. in Lachyngdon, Lawlyng & Althorn. £300.

CP25(2)/83/712   DIVERS COUNTIES

54.   Wm. Goodwyn, citizen & mercer of London, & w. Margt., pl. *Jn.* Ellyott & w. Margt., def. Prop. in Stortford, Albury & Farnsham, co. Hertford, & 16 a. ar. in Farneham, co. Hertford, & 16 a. ar. in Farneham, co. Essex. Def. quitclaimed to pl. & the heirs of Wm. £220. — Essex, Herts.

CP25(2)/70/585   MICHAELMAS, 4 AND 5 PHILIP AND MARY   1557

1.   Trin. & Mich. Robt. Baker, pl. Hy. Pascall & w. Margt., def. 1 mess., 1 barn, 1 gdn., 16 a. ar., 2 a. mw., 8 a. pa. & 3s. 4d. rt. in Burneham. 100 mks.

2.   Jn. Machyn, pl. *Jn.* Bonar, citizen & barber-surgeon of London, & w. Eliz., Joan Bonar, Jn. Chamberleyn & w. Eliz. & Anne Bonar, def. 1 mess., 1 gdn., 1 orchard & 9 a. pa. in Cryxhythe. £40.

3.   Wm. Sphere, pl. *Robt.* Gurdon, esq., & w. Rose, def. 32 a. wd. called 'Aungevynes' in Langham & Boxsted. £40.

4.   Clement Cisley & Jn. Keyll, gentlemen, pl. Wm. Abbotte, esq., & w. *Margery*, dau. & heir of Wm. Denham, kt., def. 1 mess., 1 toft, 1 gdn., 1 orchard, 200 a. ar., 100 a. mw., 100 a. pa., 50 a. fresh marsh & 40 a. wd. in Gayshams Hall & Barkyng, & tithes of corn & hay from them. Def. quitclaimed to pl. & the heirs of Clement. £200.

5.   Rd. Packman, pl. Eliz. Wayman, wid., def. 1 mess. & 1 gdn. in Harwyche. £40.

6.   Robt. Banester & Tho. Freman, pl. *Jn.* Ferrers & w. Barbara & Rd. Dale, def. Manor of Champyons Pryors & Joys & 1 mess. called 'Burres', 20 mess., 400 a. ar., 100 a. mw., 500 a. pa., 200 a. wd. & 40 a. furze & heath in Woodham Ferrers. Def. quitclaimed to pl. & the heirs of Robt. And for this pl. gtd. the same to Rd. to hold from Michaelmas, 1563, for 21 years, at a yearly rt. of £27 6s. 8d. to pl. & the heirs of Robt., payable at Michaelmas & the Annunciation, with power of distraint; with remainder to Jn. & Barbara & the heirs of Jn., to hold of the chief lords.

7.   Robt. Halfehed, pl. *Leonard* Gylle & w. Eliz., def. 1 mess., 1 gdn. & 1 orchard in Walden. £40.

8.   Hy. Stapilton, gent., pl. Rd. Aburfourth, gent., def. 2 mess., 2 gdns., 3 orchards, 5 tofts, 40 a. ar., 16 a. mw. & 60 a. pa. in Thaxsted. Def. quitclaimed to pl. & his heirs. And for this pl. gtd. the same to def. & his heirs to hold of the chief lords.

9.   Jn. Lucas sen., pl. *Jn.* Lynge, gent., & w. Anne, def. 1 mess., 1 gdn. & ½ a. ar. in Brentwood. £40.

10.   Tho. Love, Rd. Horsepyt & Ranulph Weleigh, pl. Rd. Hansard & w. *Frances*, def. 3 mess., 3 gdns., 3 orchards, 60 a. ar., 3 a. reed (*iuncarie*) & 10 a. wd. in Great Horkesley. Def. quitclaimed to pl. & the heirs of Tho. 160 mks.

11.   Tho. Sammys, pl. *Rd.* Hyll & w. Bena, def. 4 a. ar., 4 a. mw. & 2 a. pa. in Great Totham. £40.

12.   Robt. Belde, pl. Robt. Walker & w. *Eliz.*, def. 1 mess., 12 a. ar., 2 a. mw., 3 a. pa., & 1 a. alder in Laumershe. £40.

13.   Rd. Durant & w. Kath., pl. *Jn.* Page & w. Mary, def. 1 mess., 1 gdn., 1 orchard, 60 a. ar., 20 a. mw., 40 a. pa., 10 a. wd. 40 a. furze & heath & £4 rt. in Great Totham & Little Totham. Def. quitclaimed to pl. & the heirs of Rd. £76.

14.   Rd. Hubberd, gent., pl. Wm. Auncell & w. *Joan*, def. 3 mess., 3 gdns. & 3 orchards in Tacley. £40.

15.   Wm. Hulke, pl. Ralph Tirell, gent., def. 1 mess., 1 orchard, 1 gdn., 6 a. mw. & 30 a. pa. in Nevenden & Basseldon. £80.

16.   Wm. Payn, pl. Tho. Brome & w. *Margery*, dau. & heir of Wm. Doryvall, def. 1 mess. & 9 a. ar. in Elmysted. £40.

17.   Trin. & Mich. Edw. Waldegrave, esq., pl. Jn. Bowyer, gent., def. 10 a. pa., & 150 a. wd. in Boxstid, Langham, Colchester, Dedham & Horseley. £80.

18.   Tho. Love & Rd. Horsepytt, pl. Rd. Hansard & w. *Frances*, def. 1 mess., 1 gdn., 40 a. ar., 20 a. mw. & 12 a. pa. in Wormingford. Def. quitclaimed to pl. & the heirs of Tho. 160 mks.

19.   Jn. Lucas jun., pl. Jn. Lynge, gent., & w. Anne, def. 1 mess., in Brentwood. Def. quitclaimed from themselves & the heirs of Jn. to pl. & his heirs, with warranty against Jn. & his heirs & against Margery Foxley, w. of Ralph Foxley, & Anne. £40.

20.   Trin. & Mich. Tho. Spilman, gent., & w. Kath., pl. *Roger* Higham, gent., & w. Joan, def. Manor of Bodneke & 200 a. ar., 30 a. mw., 16 a. pa., 20 a. wd. & 40s. rt. in Asshlden & the parish of St. Laurence adjacent. Def. quitclaimed to pl. & the heirs of

Tho. And for this pl. gtd. the same to def. to hold for their lives of the chief lords, with remainder to the right heirs of Roger.

21. Owin Clunne, citizen & 'draper' of London, pl. Ralph Calley, gent., & w. *Eleanor*, def. 2 mess., 100 a. ar. & 100 a. pa. in Orsett & Hornedon. £160.

22. Jn. Sylverwoode & w. Joan, pl. Robt. Sayre & w. *Alice*, dau. & heir of Ursula Assheley, def. 1 mess., 1 stable & 1 gdn. in Alveley. Def. quitclaimed to pl. & the heirs of Jn. £30.

23. Rd. Everard sen., pl. *Jn.* Everard & w. Eliz., def. Manor of Haverings & 3 mess., 2 gdns., 100 a. ar., 12 a. mw., 60 a. pa., 12 a. wd. & 13s. 4d. rt. in Little Rayne & Felsted. £200.

24. Trin. & Mich. Hy. Archer & Wm. Astlett, pl. Francis Kyrton, def. 6 mess., 200 a. ar., 20 a. mw., 300 a. pa., 16 a. marsh & 80. a. wd. in Hadley *alias* Hadley at the Castle, Thundersley & Lyghe. Def. quitclaimed to pl. & the heirs of Hy. And for this pl. gtd. the same to def. & the heirs of his body to hold of the chief lords, with remainder to his right heirs.

25. Jn. Clerke, pl. Jn. Wincoll & w. Anne, *Tho.* Sewall & w. Eliz., def. 2 mess., 1 gdns., 16 a. ar. & 2 a. marsh in Alphamston & Halsted. £40.

26. Hil. & Mich. Wm. Harvy, pl. Jn. Thorpe & w. *Rose*, def. 2 mess., 2 curtilages, 2 barns, 20 a. ar., 2 a. mw. & 2. a. pa. in Hatfeld Bradoke & Takeleygh. £40.

27. Wm. Bretten, pl. Jn. Sawyn, def. 1 toft, 1 curtilage, 10 a. ar., 1 a. mw. & 3 a. pa. in Boreham. £40.

28. Trin. & Mich. Rd. Hewett *alias* Lutter, pl. *Rd.* Glascock & Jn. Glascock & w. Margt., def. 1 mess., 1 gdn., 30 a. ar., 6 a. mw., 20 a. pa. & 12s. rt. in Stapylford Tawny. 130 mks.

29. Trin. & Mich. Wm. Strachie jun., pl. Edw. Elryngton, esq., def. 5 a. mw. in Wyddyngton. £40.

30. Tho. Brend, pl. Robt. Tyrrell, esq., def. 6 a. fresh marsh in Berkynge. £40.

CP25(2)/83/713   DIVERS COUNTIES

3. Hil. & Mich. Edw. Howseden, pl. Robt. Symond & Geo. Saywer, def. Prop. in Hynxston, co. Cambridge, & 44 a. ar. in Great Chesterford, co. Essex. £80. — Cambridge, Essex.

8. Trin. & Mich. Jn. Goodwyn, esq., & Wm. Fletewood, gent., pl. Tho. Lyttyll, esq., & w. *Eliz.*, def. A third of the manor of Hopebrydgehall & 2 mess., 10 tofts, 1 dovecote, 3 gdns., 300 a. ar., 50 a. mw., 100 a. pa., 20 a. wd. & 20s. rt. in Great Okeley & Little Okeley, co. Essex, & prop. in other counties. Def. quitclaimed to pl. & the heirs of Jn. And for this pl. gtd. the same to def. to hold for their lives of the chief lords without impeachment of waste, with remainder to the heirs of the body of Tho. & the right heirs of Eliz. — Herts., Essex, Suff.

17. Edw. Lytelton, esq., & Robt. Byddell, pl. Francis Cokayn, gent., & w. *Mary*, def. Manors of Little Bromley *alias* Overhall, Bramehall, Badleyhall, Ardeley, Laulford, Skyrmans Fee in Clakton & Frynton & 100 mess., 100 tofts, 100 gdns., 100 orchards, 5,000 a. ar., 400 a. mw., 4,000 a. pa., 200 a. wd., 60 a. furze & heath & £10. rt. in Little Bromley, Bramhall, Little Bentley, Badleyhall, Ardeley, Laulford, Skyrmans Fee in Clakton, Burton, Godmaston & Frynton, & the advowsons of the rectories & churches of Little Bromley & Frynton, co. Essex; & prop. in other counties. Def. quitclaimed to pl. & the heirs of Edw. And for this pl. gtd. the same to def. & the heirs of the body of Francis by Mary, with remainder to Tho. Cokayn, kt., for 3 days, the heirs of the body of Mary, & the right heirs of Francis. — Dorset, Northampton, Warwick, Essex.

CP25(2)/70/585   HILARY, 4 AND 5 PHILIP AND MARY   1558

31. Mich. & Hil. Jn. Sewall, pl. *Jn.* Williams & w. Anne, def. 1 mess., 2 gdns., 6 a. ar., 1 a. mw. & 4 a. pa. in Hengham Syble *alias* Sybbell Hennyngham. £30.

32. Mich. & Hil. Robt. Harte, pl. *Jn.* Walkelyn & w. Alice, def. 1 mess., 14 a. ar., & 6 a. pa. in Hempsted. £60.

33. Mich. & Hil. Jn. Reymond, gent., pl. *Jn.* Golyng & w. Joan, def. 1 mess., 1 gdn., 1 orchard, 10 a. ar., 2 a. mw. & 6 a. pa. in Depden. £40.

34.   Mich. & Hil Robt. Came, pl. *Jn.* Aburforth, son & heir apt. of Jn. Aburforth, decd., & w. Anne, def. 1 mess., 1 gdn., 1 orchard, 4 a. mw. & 9 a. pa. in Thaxsted. £50.

35.   Robt. Kettell & w. Kath., pl. *Hy.* Miller & w. Rose, def. 1 mess., 1 gdn. & ½ a. ar. in Wickham St. Paul *alias* Wickham Pole. Def. quitclaimed to pl. & the heirs of Kath. £40.

36.   Jn. Clerke, pl. *Hy.* Turnor, esq., & w. Anne, def. Manor of Plegeden *alias* Plechden & 12 mess., 400 a. ar., 30 a. mw., 40 a. pa., 40 a. wd. 30s rt. & a rt. of 1 capon in Plegeden, Henham, Elsenham & Brokeshed. 400 mks.

37.   Wm. Pylstone & w. Agnes & Geo. Pylstone, pl. *Augustine* Thaywer, gent., & w. Anne, def. Manor of Fowchyns *alias* Howchyns & 300 a. ar., 20 a. mw., 200 a. pa. & 53s. 4d. rt. in Feryng, Little Tey, Great Tey & Coggeshall. Def. quitclaimed to pl. & the heirs of Wm. £200.

38.   Jn. Thomas, pl. *Chris.* Welshe, gent., & w. Anne & Hy. Standyshe, def. 9 a. mw. & 20 a. pa. in Waltham Holy Cross. Def. quitclaimed to pl. & his heirs. And for this pl. gtd. the same to Hy. from Michaelmas last for 21 years, rendering yearly to pl. & his heirs £3 for the first 11 years & 1d. for the residue, at the Annunciation & Michaelmas, with power of distraint; with remainder to def. & the heirs of *Chris.*, to hold of the chief lords.

39.   Steph. Page, pl. *Rd.* Curlyng & w. Joan, def. 2 mess., 2 gdns., 1 orchard, 30 a. ar., 8 a. mw. & 12 a. pa. & 6 a. wd. in Alresford. 160 mks.

40.   Mich. & Hil. Robt. Barker, pl. *Tho.* Archer & w. Agnes, def. 1 mess. & 1 gdn. in Thaxsted. £20.

41.   Mich. & Hil. Jn. Buk sen., pl. *Rd.* Cutt, gent., Hy. Cutt sen., gent. & Hy. Cutt jun., gent., son & heir apt. of the latter, def. 20 a. ar., 3 a. mw. & 8 a. pa. in Ugley & Berden. Def. quitclaimed to pl. & his heirs. And for this pl. gtd. to def. & their heirs a yearly rt. of 18s. 8d. from the same & 18s. 8d. in the name of relief at the dec. of each tenant, payable at the Annunciation & Michaelmas, with power of distraint.

42.   Mich. & Hil. Jn. Heron, gent., & w. Eliz., pl. *Jn.* Jenyns, gent., & w. Jane, def. A moiety of the manor of Hersted Hall & 6 mess., 200 a. ar., 20 a. mw., 100 a. pas., 40 a. wd. & 100s. rt. in Byrdebroke, Fynchyngfeld, Bumsted at the Steeple, Redeswell, S(t)amborn & Hempsted. Def. quitclaimed to pl. & the heirs of Eliz. £200.

43.   Mich. & Hil. Tho. Lyndesell, pl. Jn. Crackenell & w. Joan, Robt. Basse & w. *Agnes*, dau. of Tho. Thake, decd., def. 1 mess., 1 barn, 3 gdns. & 4 a. ar. in Great Dunmowe. £36.

44.   Mich. & Hil. Tho. Archer & w. Agnes, pl. *Robrt.* Barker & w. Agnes, def. 1 mess., 1 barn, 1 gdn. & 1 orchard in Thaxsted. Def. quitclaimed to pl. & the heirs of Tho. £20.

45.   Mich. & Hil. Wm. Rayln, pl. *Jn.* Morsse & w. Eliz., def. 1 mess. & 1 gdn. in Legh. £40.

46.   Rd. Goldyng, gent., pl. *Jn.* Cole & w. Eliz., def. 3 mess., 3 tofts, 2 gdns., 80 a. ar., 4 a. mw., 40 a. pa. & 3. a. wd. in Bulmer. £100.

47.   Mich. & Hil. Wm. Hoye, gent., pl. Robt. Mullyngs & w. *Joan*, dau. & heir of Geo. Senewe, def. 2 mess., 3 tofts, 2 barns, 3 gdns., 2 orchards, 20 a. ar., 6 a. mw. & 16 a. pas. in Peldon, Aburton & Little Wygbaroughe. £80.

48.   Hy. Somersam, pl. Robt. Cocke & w. *Anne*, def. 1 mess., 1 curtilage & 1 gdn. in Chelmesford *alias* Chemysford. £80.

49.   Trin. & Hil. Rd. Gwyn & Hugh Gryffith, pl. Hy. Fortescue, esq., def. Manors of Falkeborn & Blumsall & 10 mess., 1 dovecote, 10 tofts, 12 gdns., 1,000 a. ar., 200 a. mw., 600 a. pa., 300 a. wd., 20 a. marsh & 40s. rt. in Fawlkeborn, Blumsall, Wittam, Terling, Feyersted, Hatfeld Peverell & Revenhall, & the advowson of the church of Fawlkeborn. Def. quitclaimed to pl. & the heirs of Rd. £220.

50.   Rd. Bradye, pl. Tho. Ball & w. *Joan*, def. 5 a. ar. & 1 a. mw. called 'Alstonys' in Blakemore. 40 mks.

51.   Tho. Barrington, esq., & Tho. Hanchett, gent., pl. *Hy.* Parker, kt., lord Morley, & w. Eliz. & Tho. Bedyll, gent., def. 1 capital mess. called Barwaldon Hall *alias* Barnedon

Hall and 100. a. ar., 100 a. mw. & 400 a. pa. in Tolleshunt Knyghtes, Salcotes Vyrley & Wigbarowght. Def. quitclaimed to pl. & the heirs of Tho. Barryngton. And for this pl. gtd. the same to Tho. Bedyll for 21 years from Michaelmas last at a yearly rent of £68; payable at the Annunciation and Michaelmas, with power of distraint; with remainder to Hy. & Eliz. & the heirs of the body of Hy., to hold of the chief lords.

52.   Mich. & Hil. Jn. Morsse, pl. Joan Ryngland, wid., def. 1 mess. & 2 gdns. in Legh. £40.

53.   Mich. & Hil. Tho. Clayton, gent., pl. Jn. Clearke jun. and w. *Alice*, def. 1 mess. & 1 gdn. in Bokkyng. £20.

54.   Jn. Thomas, pl. *Chris.* Welche, gent., & w. Agnes & Wm. Browne, def. 40 a. pa. in Uppeshere in the parish of Waltham Holy Cross. Def. quitclaimed to pl. & his heirs. And for this pl. gtd. the same to Wm. for 30 years from Michaelmas last, at a yearly rt. of £4 payable at the Annunciation & Michaelmas, with remainder to pl. & the heirs of Chris. to hold of the chief lords.

CP25(2)/83/713   DIVERS COUNTIES

19.   Edw. Blakwell, gent., & w. Alice, pl. *Wm.* Blakwell, gent., & w. Margt., def. 1 mess., 1 gdn., 6 a. ar. & 6 a. mw. in Waltham Holy Cross & Sywardston, co. Essex, & prop. in Mdx. Def. quitclaimed to pl. & the heirs of Edw. 220 mks. – Essex, Mdx.

21.   Jn. Wysse & Geo. Yeo, pl. Jn. Broke, son & heir apt. of Jn. Broke, def. 4 a. ar., 3 a. mw., 8 a. pa. & 5 a. wd. in Seynt Lawraunce of Waltham, co. Essex, & prop. in London, Mdx. & Herts. Def. quitclaimed to pl. & the heirs of Geo. £160. – London, Essex, Mdx., Herts.

CP25(2)&70/586   EASTER, 4 AND 5 PHILIP AND MARY   1558

1.   Hy. Fanshawe, pl. *Wm.* Clarke, esq., & w. Anne, def. 1 mess., 1 cott., 1 orchard, 1 gdn., 10 a. ar., 10 a. mw., 50 a. pa. & 8 a. wd. in Barkynge. 130 mks.

2.   Lancelet Speere and Robt. Bossall, pl. Edw. Roosse, gent., def. 100 a. ar., 8 a. mw. & 200 a. pa. called 'Herkes' and 'Paynes' in Salcott Virly, Great Wigborow & Leyre Marney. Def. quitclaimed to pl. & the heirs of Lancelet. And for this pl. gtd. the same to def. for one month, with remainder to Isabel his w. for life & him & his heirs, to hold of the chief lords.

3.   Hy. Trigge, pl. Tho. Crawley jun., gent., son & heir of Robt. Crawley, decd., def. 2 mess., 2 gdns., 1 orchard, 100 a. ar., 10 a. mw., 20 a. pa., 2 a. wd. & common of pasture for 10 animals & 200 sheep in Christhall, Heydon & Wenden Loughts. £140.

4.   Hil. & Eas. Wm. Glascock, pl. Wm. Aylyff, esq., def. 1 mess., 1 curtilage, 1 orchard, 20 a. ar., 6 a. mw. & 14 a. pa. in Dagenham. 100 mks.

5.   Jerome Gylberd, pl. Edw. Maynard & w. *Anne*, def. 20 a. ar., 6 a. mw., 6 a. pa., 5 a. wd. & 10 a. furze & health in Ardeley & Grynsted. £40.

6.   Jn. Mede, pl. Jn. Shedde & w. *Joan*, def. 10 a. ar. in Berden. £40.

7.   Hil. & Eas. Robt. Chatterton, gent., pl. Wm. Barlee, esq., def. Manor of Wyckyn *alias* Wyckyn Bonant & 8 mess., 8 tofts, 10 cotts., 40 dovecotes, 10 gdns., 10 orchards, 500 a. ar., 100 a. mw., 200 a. pa., 40 a. wd, 100 a. furze & heath & 8s. rt. in Wyckyn *alias* Wyckyn Bonant, & the advowson of the church of Wyckyn. Def. quitclaimed to pl. & his heirs. And for this pl. gtd. the same to def. for life, with remainder to Tho. Leventhorp & w. Dorothy & the heirs of their bodies, the heirs of the body of Dorothy, & the right heirs of Tho., to hold of the chief lords.

8.   Tho. Love, pl. Jn Barnabe, gent., def. 1 mess., 2 barns, 1 gdn. & 16 a. ar. in Little Horkesleigh & Great Horkesleigh. £40.

9.   Tho. Parke & Wm. Hardyng, pl. *Jas.* Bretten, son & heir of Anne Bretten, one of the daus. & co-heirs of Jn. Clovyle of Dunton, decd., & *Margt.* w. of the said Jas., Tho. Fynche & w. *Margt.*, another dau. & co-heir, and *Joan* Clovyle, another dau. & co-heir, def. 2 mess., 1 barn & 41 a. ar. in Little Bursted & Great Bursted. Def. quitclaimed to pl. & the heirs of Tho., with warranty against Jn., abbot of St. Peter, Westminster, and his successors. And for this pl. gtd. the same to Jas. & his heirs, to hold of the chief lords.

10.   Same parties. 12 a. ar. in Great Bursted. Similar settlement on Tho. Fynche & w. Margt. & her heirs, to hold of the chief lords.

11.   Same parties. 2 mess. & 34 a. ar. in Bilerica & Great Bursted. Similar settlement on Joan & her heirs, to hold of the chief lords.

12.   Hugh Apparrye, pl. Edm. Stokes & w. *Bridget*, def. 1 mess., 1 curtilage, 1 gdn., 6 a. mw. & 10 a. pa. in Westham. £80.

13.   Hil. & Eas. Rd. Chapman, pl. Robt. Benne, def. 1 mess., 1 barn, 1 stable, 1 gdn., 1 orchard & 6 a. ar. in Walden *alias* Chepyng Walden. £40.

14.   Jn. Baron sen., pl. Jn. Long & w. *Marion*, def. A moiety of 1 mess., 1 gdn., 1 toft, 10 a. ar., 10 a. pa., 5 a. mw. & 5 a. furze & heath in Layer Bretton. £40.

15.   Wm. White, pl. *Wm.* Ayer jun. & w. Alice, def. 1 mess., 1 barn, 1 gdn. & 3 a. ar. in Chelmesford, which Wm. Ayer sen. holds for life. Pl. & his heirs to hold the reversion of the chief lords.

16.   Hy. Stonard, pl. *Jn.* Reymond, gent., Wm. Trayford & w. Jane, def. 20 a. ar., 10 a. pa. & 3 a. salt marsh in Woodeham Ferrers. £40.

17.   Wm. Chapleyne, pl. Jn. Webbe & w. *Anne*, def. 1 mess., 1 gdn. & 3 a. ar. in Foxherth. £30.

18.   Hil. & Eas. Hy. Rede & Tho. Rede, pl. Tho. Campe & w. *Ellen*, dau. & co-heir of Rd. Tagell, decd., def. A moiety of 2 mess., 3 cotts., 24 a. ar. & 16 a. pa. in Matching & High Laver. Def. quitclaimed to pl. & the heirs of Tho. £40.

19.   Hil. & Eas. Jn. Beste, pl. *Geo.* Cristmas, esq., & w. Bridget, def. 4 mess., 1 dovecote, 1 barn, 2 orchards, 4 gdns., & 4 a. pa. in the parish of St. James of the town of Colchester. 160 mks.

20.   Bart. Averell, gent., pl. Hy. Songar, gent., & w. *Eliz.* & Tho. Philippes & w. *Margery*, def. Manor of Burces *alias* Burshes *alias* Burses & 3 mess., 2 gdns., 1 orchard, 1 dovecote, 120 a. ar., 16 a. mw., 40 a. pa., 10 a. wd. & 10s. rt. in Thundersley & Rayley. £144.

21.   Hil. & Eas. Edw. Brokyt, Geo. Gyll, Geo. Hadley, esquires, & Anth. Asplande, gent., pl. Wm. Barlee, esq., def. A moiety of the manors of Leyre Barlee *alias* Breten & Moulsham, a moiety of 20 mess., 12 cotts., 12 tofts, 10 dovecotes, 30 gdns., 10 orchards, 1,000 a. ar., 100 a. mw., 400 a. pa., 100 a. wd. 100 a. furze & heath & £6. rt. in Leyre Barlee *alias* Breton, Moulsham, Saltcott & Wigborough, and a moiety of the advowson of the church of Saltcott. Def. quitclaimed to pl. & the heirs of Geo. Hadley. And for this pl. gtd. the same to def. to hold for life of the chief lords without impeachment of waste, with remainder to Joyce his w. for life, Dorothy w. of Tho. Leventhorpe & the heirs of her body, the heirs of the body of def. & the right heirs of Hy. Barlee, esq.,

22.   Hil. & Eas. Rd. Southwell, kt., & Jn. Best, gent., pl. Geo. Cristmas, esq., def. 1 water-mill, 2 mess., 20 a. ar., 6 a. mw. & 20 a. pa. in Bergholt Sakevyle. Def. quitclaimed to pl. & the heirs of Rd. 160 mks.

23.   Hil. & Eas. Roger Barney, gent., pl. Tho. Fyrmyn, def. 1 mess., 16 a. ar., 4 a. mw. & 10 a. pa. in Hatfeld Brodedoke *alias* Kyngs Hatfeld. Def. quitclaimed to pl. & his heirs. And for this pl. gtd. the same to def. & his heirs to hold of the chief lords.

24.   Wm. Rudde & Rd. Putto, pl. *Jn.* Tyler & Roger Platt, def. 1 mess., 1 toft & 1 gdn. in Brancktree. Def. quitclaimed to pl. & his heirs of Wm. And for this pl. gtd. the same to Roger for 7 years from the Annunciation last, at a rt. of a red rose yearly at the Nativity of St. John Baptist, with remainder to Agnes Haynes & the heirs of her body & Roger & his heirs, to hold of the chief lords.

25.   Jn. Gates, pl. *Rd.* Gates & w. Agnes, def. 1 wind-mill, 1 gdn. & 2 a. ar. in Rotyngdon. £40.

26.   Mich. & Eas. Robt. Kempe, pl. Jn. Heron & w. *Eliz.*, def. 5 roods mw. in Fynchyngfeld. 10 mks.

27.   Jn. Lyndesey & Hy. Bone, pl. Tho. Malle & w. *Denise*, def. 2 mess., 2 tofts, 4 curtilages, 4 gdns., 4 orchards, 2 barns, 30 a. ar., 10 a. mw., 20 a. pa. & 10 a. wd. in Brentwood, Shenfeld & Ardley. Def. quitclaimed to pl. & the heirs of Jn. And for this pl. gtd. the same to def. & the heirs of Denise, to hold of the chief lords.

CP25(2)/83/713   DIVERS COUNTIES

31.   Mich. & Eas. Francis Jobson, kt., pl. Jn. Alen, gent., def. The site of the late priory of Hatfeld Peverell & the manor of Hatfeld Peverell & 20 mess., 20 tofts, 20 curtilages, 20 barns, 8 dovecotes, 20 gdns., 20 orchards, 500 a. ar., 100 a. mw., 500 a. pa., 100 a. wd., 100 a. alder & £20 rt. in Hatfeld Peverell, Wytham, Utynge, Woodham Mortymer, Woodham Water, Great Totham, Little Totham, Westham, Tolshunt Darsey, Terlyng, Boreham, Little Badowe, Debden, Bradwell by Coggeshale, Bradwell by the Sea, Nantwych, Blomsham Hall, Little Waltham, Hasylle, Margarett Rothyng, Fayersted & Stratford Langthorn, the rectory of Hatfeld Peverell & the advowson of the parish church of Hatfeld Peverell & pensions of 60s. for tithes in Nantwich in Terlyng, 20s. 8d. for 2 portions of tithes in Blomsham Hall alias Blonteshaull in Falbourn, 40s. from the parish church of Little Waltham, £4 from the parish church of Debden, 7s. from the parish church of Fayersted, 3s. 4d. from a portion of tithes in Wytham & 60s. from the late dissolved monastery of Stratford, co. Essex; & prop. in Suff.; which Jn. Alen, esq., father of def., holds for life. Pl. & his heirs to hold the reversion of the chief lords. 800 mks. — Essex, Suff.

CP25(2)/70/586   TRINITY, 4 AND 5 PHILIP AND MARY   1558

28.   Eas. & Trin. Anth. Broun, serjeant at law, pl. Tho. Parker, gent., and w. Eliz., def. 1 mess., 1 curtilage & 1 orchard in Brentwood. £40.

29.   Jn. Lynsey, pl. Jn. Wyllet & w. Agnes, Tho. Stonestrete & w. Joan, def. 2 mess., 2 curtilages, 1 gdn. & ½ a. ar. in Westham,. £20.

30.   Law. Grene, pl. Charles Browne, Wm. Browne & Jn. Browne, def. 4 a. 3 roods ar. in Estham. £40.

31.   Eas. & Trin. Robt. Sparke & Robt. Emery, pl. Jn. Mathew & w. Cecily, def. 1 mess., 1 gdn., 1 orchard & 2 a. pas. in Wydýton alias Wyddyngton. Def. quitclaimed to pl. & the heirs of Robt. Sparke. £40.

32.   Tho. Hewett alias Litter, pl. Tho. Wright & w. Joan, def. 2 mess., 2 gdns., 60 a. ar., 10 a. mw., 20 a. pa. & 3 a. wd. in Highester & Aythrope Rothing. £180.

33.   Eas. & Trin. Jas. Wooddall & w. Joan, pl. Wm. Calton & w. Cath., def. 1 mess. in Walden alias Cheping Walden. Def. quitclaimed to pl. & his heirs of Jas. £40.

34.   Tho. Muschampe, citizen & goldsmith of London, pl. Rd. Pese jun. & w. Margery, def. A moety of 1 mess., 30 a. ar., 10 a. mw. & 20 a. pa. in Spryngfelde. £50.

35.   Tho. Mustean, pl. Tho. Loveday & w. Alice, def. 1 mess., 1 curtilages, 1 gdn. & 3 a. mw. in Bockyng. £40.

36.   Eas. & Trin. Tho. Mede, gent., pl. Jn. Dryver, 'yoman', def. 10 a. ar., & 12 a. wd. in Elmedon & Wendon Losse. Def. quitclaimed to pl. & his heirs. And for this pl. gtd. the same to def. & the heirs of his body, to hold of the chief lords, with remainder to his right heirs.

37.   Eas. & Trin. Hy. Purchase pl. David Portwey, def. 10 a. ar., & 4 a. mw. in Stebbynge. £20.

38.   Wm. Clerke, pl. Peter Fygge, gent., & w. Joan, def. 4 a. ar. in Chelmesford. 40 mks.

39.   Matthew Smythe, gent., pl. Edm. Mordaunt, esq., def. 36 a. mw. in Wymbysshe. 200 mks.

40.   Eas. & Trin. Jas. Bacon & Augustine Curtes, pl. Tho. Hales, gent., & w. Eliz. def. Manor of Markes & 3 mess., 150 a. ar., 20 a. mw., 170 a. pa., 40 a. wd. & £6 13s. 4d. rt. in Hornechurche, Dagenham, Barkynge & Haveryng at Bower. Def. quitclaimed to pl. & the heirs of Augustine. £520.

41.   Steph. Page, esq., pl. Jn. Teye, esq., & w. Constance, def. 1 mess., 1 barn, 1 gdn., 100 a. ar., 40 a. mw., 100 a. pa. & 100 a. marsh in Peldon. £240.

42.   Jn. Sterlyng, pl. Wm. Mannok sen., gent., and Francis Mannok, gent., def. 20 a. ar. & 12 a. pa. in the suburb of the town of Colchester & in Colchester. £40.

43.   Robt. Lambert & Jn. Fowle, pl. Tho., duke of Norfolk, def. 3 mess., 3 cotts., 3 barns, 3 gdns. & 30 a. ar. in Colchester. Def. quitclaimed to pl. & the heirs of Robt. £220.

44.   Eas. & Trin. Jn. Lyndsey sen., pl. *Jn.* Pragell & w. Ellen, def. 1 mess., 1 curtilage, 1 gdn. & 3 roods ar. in Westham. £40.

45.   Rd. Whorwood & Wm. Walter, pl. Hy. Halmer, esq., def. Manor of Chambers & 1 mess., 1 barn, 200 a. ar., 30 a. mw., 150 a. pa., 40 a. wd. & 40s. rt. in Eppyng. Def. quitclaimed to pl. & the heirs of Rd. And for this pl. gtd. the same to def. to hold for life of the chief lords without impeachment of waste, with remainder to Alice Welbecke, wid., for life, & the right heirs of def.

46.   Wm. Sydey sen., gent., pl. Jn. Paycok & w. Margt. & *Rd.* Enew, def. 1 mess., 1 toft, 2 gdns. & 6 a. ar. in Coggeshale. Def. quitclaimed to pl. & his heirs. And for this pl. gtd. the same to Jn. & Margt. & the heirs of their bodies, to hold of the chief lords, with remainder to Jn. & his heirs.

47.   Tho. Smyth, esq., pl. Wm. Cardynall, esq., def. Manor of Copped Kechyn & 2 mess., 1 barn, 2 tofts, 4 gdns., 20 a. ar., 20 a. mw., 100 a. pa., 4 a. wd. & 10s. rt. in Mundon & Purleigh. £220.

48.   Eas. & Trin. Wm. Bendlowes, serjeant at law, pl. *Robt.* Hall & Rd. Hall & w. Joan, def. 2 mess., 1 cott., 3 gdns., 2 orchards, 1 a. ar. & 1 a. mw. in Great Berdefelde & Finchingfeld. £40.

49.   Jn. Collyn, pl. Edw. Lymsey, esq., def. A moiety of the manor of Otes & 6 mess., 6 cotts., 1 dovecote, 500 a. ar., 50 a. mw., 200 a. pa., 50 a. wd. & £10 rt. in High Laver, Magdalen Laver, Littillaver, Miching & Harlowe. £140.

CP25(2)/00/000   MICHAELMAS, 5 AND 6 PHILIP AND MARY   1558

50.   Jn. Elyott, pl. *Geo.* Gyll, esq., & w. Anne, def. 3 mess., 3 orchards, 100 a. ar., 5 a. mw., 40 a. pa. & 3 a. wd. in Farnham. £40.

51.   Jn. Dymok, pl. *Robt.* Stepneth, gent., & w. Joan, def. 10 a. mw. in Westham. 160 mks.

52.   Wm. Stedeman, pl. *Miles* Leeds & w. Cristiana, def. 1 barn, 1 gdn., 3 a. ar., & 6 a. pa. in Barkyng. £40.

53.   Wm. Brown, pl. Steph. Wynter, def. 2 mess., 2 barns, 2 stables, 2 gdns., 140 a. ar., 10 a. mw., 40 a. pa., 10 a. wd., 6 a. marsh & 2s. rt. in Wethermondford *alias* Wormynford, Little Horkesleigh, West Bergholt & Fordeham. 260 mks.

54.   Eliz. Cocke, wid., pl. Tho. Kenester & w. *Anne,* one of sisters & heirs of Kath. Lame late w. of Edw. Lame, def. A moiety of 1 mess. & 1 croft in Brentwood. £40.

55.   Trin. & Mich. Tho. Myldmay, esq., pl. Hy. Fortescue, esq., def. Manor of Little Waltham & 20 mess., 10 cotts., 1 dovecote, 300 a. ar., 40 a. mw., 140 a. pa., 100 a. wd., 20 a. moor & 60s. rt. in Little Waltham, Great Waltham, Bromefeld, Great Lighes, Little Lighes, Spryngfeld & Boreham. £400.

56.   Wm. Gasley, pl. Tho. Wyllyamson & w. *Kath.*, def. 2 mess. & 2 shops in Saffron Walden *alias* Chepyng Walden. £40.

57.   Trin. & Mich. Wm. Enyver & w. Agnes, pl. *Jn.* Jeyns, gent. & w. Jane, def. 1 mess., 1 gdn., 1 orchard, 16 a. ar., 4 a. mw. & 12 a. pa. in Eystanes at the Mount *alias* Great Eyston. Def. quitclaimed to pl. & the heirs of Wm. £40.

58.   Chris. Westwood, pl. Tho. Clarke & w. *Mary,* def. 1 mess., 1 gdn. & 8 a. ar. in Goldhanger. £10.

59.   Hy. Fuller, pl. *Tho.* Potter & w. Agnes, def. 7 a. ar. & 3 a. mw. in Chigwell. £20.

60.   Jn. Reymond, esq., & Tho. Beck, pl. Joan Beck, def. 1 mess., 1 curtilage, 1 barn, 1 gdn., 10 a. ar., 4 a. mw. & 6 a. pa. in Ralegh. Def. quitclaimed to pl. & the heirs of Tho. £40.

61.   Trin. & Mich. Jn. Kyng & Ambrose Leder, pl. *Jn.* Jenyns, gent. & w. Jane, def. 1 cott., 1 gdn. & 8 a. ar. in Einstanes at the Mount *alias* Great Eston. Def. quitclaimed to pl. & the heirs of Jn. £20.

71

FEET OF FINES FOR ESSEX

62. Trin. & Mich. Wm. Peaveyrell, gent., pl. Jn. Raynsforthe, kt., def. 1 mess., 1 toft, 1 croft, 1 gdn., 1 orchard, 30 a. ar., 10 a. mw., 40 a. pa., 6 a. wd. & 40 a. furze & heath in Owltyng, Hatfeld Peaveyrell & Mawdon. £40.

63. Tho. Swallowe, pl. Jn. Repken & w. *Eliz.*, def. 30 a. ar., 1 a. mw. & 1½ a. wd. in Great Clacton. £40.

64. Nich. Steward, pl. *Anth.* Russhe, esq., & w. Eleanor, def. A moiety of the manor of Dangewell Hall, & a moiety of 2 mess., 2 gdns., 3 orchards, 2 barns, 300 a. ar., 20 a. mw., 200 a. pa., 60 a. wd., 20 a. furze & heath & 10s. rt. in Great Ocle & Wyckes. 70 mks.

65. Geo. Tuke, esq., pl. Hy. Rockyngham, def. 1 mess., 3 gdns., 20 a. ar., 20 a. mw., 30 a. pa. & 10 a. wd. in Layr Marney, Much Wigborough & Tolsent Knyghts. £80.

66. Edw. Cole, pl. *Wm.* Haye, 'yoman', & w. Joan, def. 20 a. ar. & 1 a. mw. called 'Hulwoods' in Great Bentley, Frating & Wyvenhoo. £40.

67. Trin. & Mich. Geoff. Vaughan, pl. *Jn.* Patrick & w. Jane, def. 3 mess., 3 gdns., 2 orchards, 16 a. ar. & 10 a. marsh in Thorok & Orsett. 130 mks.

68. Trin. & Mich. Jn. Mordaunt, kt., pl. Roger Cholmeley, kt., & w. *Cristiana*, def. 1 mess., 100 a. ar., 30 a. mw., 20 a. pa., 6 a. wd. & 4 a. furze & heath in Gynge Raffe. £40.

69. Wm. Dalton, pl. Jas. Croseley & w. *Grace*, one of the daus. & heirs of Jn. Danyell, def. A moietry of 1 mess., 1 curtilage, 2 tofts & 4½ a. ar. in Westham. £40.

70. Anth. Jebbe, pl. Wm. Danwood & w. *Eliz.*, def. A moiety of 1 mess. & 6 a. ar. in Brentwood & Shenfeld. Def. quitclaimed to pl. & his heirs. And for this pl. gtd. the same to def. & the heirs of Wm. to hold of the chief lords.

71. Eas. & Mich. Hy. Browne, pl. Paul Wylkynson & w. *Anne*, def. Manor of Northend & 1 mess., 2 barns, 1 stable, 20 a. ar., 30 a. mw., 10 a. pa., 20 a. furze & £7 rt. in Estham & Lytle Ilford. £140.

72. Arthur Harrys, gent., pl. Wm. Harrys, gent., def. 1 mess., 40 a. mw., 40 a. pa., & 10 a. wd. in Stowe Marrys & Cold Norton, which Margery Cooke, wid., holds for life. Pl. & his heirs to hold the reversion of the chief lords. £60.

73. Tho. Haymer, pl. Edm. Pyrton, esq., def. 18 a. pa. called 'Wilonds' in Tenderyng. £40.

74. Tho. Fuller, pl. *Tho.* Knolles & w. Mary, def. A moiety of a fifth pt. of 20 mess., 10 cotts., 20 gdns., 20 orchards, 30 a. ar., 200 a. pa., 60 a. mw. & 40 a. wd., & a moiety of a fifth pt. of £10 (rt.) in Chyggwell. £80.

75. Wm. Kynge & Anth. Jebbe, pl. *Tho.* Browne & w. Eliz., Eliz. Lovelake, wid., & Robt. Cage & w. Margt., def. 1 mess., 1 orchard, 40 a. ar., 5. a. mw., 10 a. pa. & 5 a. wd. in Little Bursted. Def. quitclaimed to pl. & the heirs of Wm. And for this pl. gtd. the same to Tho. to hold for life of the chief lords with remainder to pl. & the heirs of Wm.

CP25(2)/83/713   DIVERS COUNTIES

49. Jn. Wynterflod & Robt. Frauncys, pl. *Robt.* Jordon & w. Joan, def. 3 mess., 3 gdns. & 10 a. ar. in Borham & Bures St. Mary, co. Essex, & prop. in Bures St. Mary, co. Suff. Def. quitclaimed to pl. & the heirs of Jn. And for this pl. gtd. the same to def. & the heirs of Robt. to hold of the chief lords. — Essex, Suff.

72

1.   Robt. Pake, pl. Tho. Yen & w. *Alice*, def. 1 mess., 80 a. ar., 20 a. mw., 40 a. pa., & 6 a. wd. in Layndon & Estlee. £140.

2.   Robt. Middelton, pl. *Francis* Jobson, kt., & w. Eliz., def. 1 a. mw. & 26 a. wd. in Westbergholt & Lexden. £40.

3.   Mich. 5 & 6 Philip & Mary & Hil. 1 Elizabeth. Jn. Chapman, pl. Jn. Passefeld & w. *Maud*, late the w. of Wm. Stratffeld, def. 7 a. ar. in Springfeld. 40 mks.

4.   Mich. & Hil. Hy. Standysshe, pl. Jn. Herd & w. Eliz., def. 2 mess., 1 barn, 2 gdns. & 1 orchard in Waltham Holy Cross. £40.

5.   Mich. & Hil. Francis Archer, pl. Edw. Palmer & w. *Margt.*, def. 1 mess., 2 tofts, 3 curtilages, 1 barn, 1 orchard, 4 gdns. & 12 a. ar. in Bockyng. £40.

6.   Robt. Veysye, pl. Jn. Darnell, def. 1 mess., 6 tofts, 3 a. mw. & 30 a. pa. in Misseley. £80.

7.   Hy. Archer, pl. Rd. Archer, def. 3 mess., 2 gdns., 30 a. ar., 10 a. mw., & 10 a. pa. in Theydon Garnons *alias* Cowpersale. £40.

8.   Jn. George, pl. Edw. Hawke, def. 1 mess., 1 gdn, 1 orchard, 10 a. ar., 1 a. mw. & 2 a. pa. in Langenho which Tho. Holde & w. Eliz. hold for her life. Pl. & his heirs to hold the reversion of the chief lords. £40.

9.   Tho. Powle, esq., pl. *Rd.* Flower, gent., & w. Margt., def. 12 a. ar., 6 a. mw., 12 a. pa. & 2 a. wd. in Ilford *alias* Great Ileford & Barkynge. 100 mks.

10.   Wm. Brown, pl. Jn. Wynter, def. 1 mess., 1 barn, 2 stables, 1 gdn., 70 a. ar., 6 a. mw., 26 a. pa., 5 a. wd., 4 a. marsh & 12d. rt. in Wethermondeford *alias* Wormyngford, Little Horkesleigh & West Bergholt. 130 mks.

11.   Mich. & Hil. Hy. Broun, esq., & Philip Browne, pl. Mich. Brysley, def. 2 mess., 2 barns, 2 stables, 2 gdns., 1 orchard, 8 a. ar., 8 a. mw., 1 a. wd. & 5s. rt. in Estham & Lytle Ilforde. Def. quitclaimed to pl. & the heirs of Hy. £140.

12.   Jn. Warner, pl. Jn. Raven & w. *Margt.*, def. 3 mess. & 9 a. ar. in Witham. £40.

13.   Mich. & Hil. Tho. Chappelayn, pl. *Jn.* Skynner & w. Eliz., def. 1 mess., 1 gdn., 24 a. ar. & 4 a. pa. in Depden. £30.

14.   Wm. Bowlyng, pl. Nich. Ereswell & w. *Joan*, def. 12½ a. pa. in Saffron Walden *alias* Cheping Walden. £20.

15.   *A fine marked Essex but relating to Suffolk.*

16.   Wm. Bambrough & Tho. Bambrough, pl. Edm. Heyghgate, def. A moiety of 160 a. fresh marsh & 20 a. salt marsh called 'Alfletnes' & two weirs within the island of Walletts in the parishes of Estwoode & Pryklewell. Def. quitclaimed to pl. & the heirs of Wm. £200.

17.   Jn. Wynterflod & Tho. Lyndesell, pl. Francis Mannocke, esq., def. Manors of Carbonells, Bellowes & Powers & 10 mess., 5 tofts, 4 mills, 3 dovecotes, 4 gdns., 1,000 a. ar., 200 a. mw., 1,000 a. pa., 300 a. wd., 400 a. heath, 200 a. marsh & £6 rt. in Wyckes, Ramsey, Bradfeld, Manston & Heigh Ester. Def. quitclaimed to pl. & the heirs of Jn. £280.

18.   Tho. Wyseman, gent., pl. *Wm.* Legatt, gent., & w. Joan, def. 1 mess., 20 a. ar., 10 a. mw., 20 a. pa. & 10 a. wd. in Lachendon. £100.

19.   Mich. & Hil. Jn. Reymond, esq., & Rd. Bramley, pl. Francis Reymond, gent., & w. *Anne*, def. 4 mess., 4 gdns., 80 a. ar., 10 a. mw., 40 a. pa., 2 a. wd., 6 a. marsh, 10 a. furze & heath & 10s. rt. in Great Dunmowe, Eistanes et the Tower *alias* Little Eiston & Little Canfeld. Def. quitclaimed to pl. & the heirs of Jn. And for this pl. gtd. the same to def. & the heirs of Francis to hold of the chief lords.

20.   Mich. & Hil. Tho. Sampford, pl. Jn. Fyfhide *alias* Fyfelde, def. 1 mess., 1 gdn., 20 a. ar., 6 a. mw., 4 a. pa., 1 a. wd. & 2s. rt. in Fifhide *alias* Fyfelde. £40.

1. Hy. Petyveer, pl. Jn. Godfrey, def. 1 mess., 1 gdn. (*gardino*), 1 gdn. (*orto*), 20 a. ar., 3 a. mw. & 8 a. pa. in Theydon Garnon. £40.

2. Tho. Bennett, pl. Robt. Weston & w. *Juliana*, def. 1 mess., 1 gdn., 1 orchard, 10 a. mw. & 6 a. pa. in Wytham & Wyckham. And for this pl. gtd. the same to def. & the heirs of Robt. to hold of the chief lords.

3. Roger Marten of Long Melford, pl. Wm. Clopton of Lyston, esq., def. 6½ a. mw. in Lyston. £80.

4. Wm. Lepyngwell, pl. Rd. Oates & w. *Rose*, def. 1 mess., 1 gdn. & 1 a. ar. in Gynghospytall *alias* Ingatstone *alias* Imverners. £40.

5. Mich. & Eas. Wm. Frythe, pl. *Jn.* Mountgomery, clk., & Alice Mountgomery, wid., def. 2 mess., 1 curtilage, 1 toft, 1 gdn. & 3 a. ar. in Hornedon. £40.

6. Tho. Awborowe, pl. *Ralph* Nalynghirste, gent., & w. Eliz., def. 1 mess., 1 gdn., 1 orchard & 3 a. ar. in Great Badowe. £40.

7. Hil. & Eas. Nich. Ereswell, pl. *Tho.* Ereswell & w. Margt., Jn. Totnam & w. Margery & Wm. Calton & w. Anne, def. 10 a. ar. in Saffron Walden *alias* Chepyng Walden. £40.

8. Hil. & Eas. Tho. Ereswell, pl. *Nich.* Ereswell & w. Joan, def. 1 mess. & 1 shop in Saffron Walden *alias* Chepyng Walden. 20 mks.

9. Mich. & Eas. Tho. Eve & Wm. Stonard, pl. Geoff. Athelham *alias* Alham & w. *Joan*, def. 1 mess. (1 gdn., 3 a. ar., 2 a.) mw. & 2 a. pa. in Plecy *alias* Playsshey & Great Waltham. Def. quitclaimed to pl. & the heirs of Tho. And for this pl. gtd. the same to def. to hold for their lives of the chief lords, with successive remainders to Robt. (Horsenayle), Jn. Horsenayle jun. & Tho. (Horsenayle) & the heirs of their bodies, & Joan & her heirs.

10. Jn. Danyell, pl. *Miles* Leeds & w. Cristiana, def. 1 mess., & 1 gdn. in Barkyng. £40.

11. Tho. Browne, pl. *Jn.* Melborne & w. Eleanor, def. 1 mess., 1 barn, 1 dovecote, 1 gdn., 1 orchard, 90 a. ar., 6 a. mw., 10 a. pa. & 7 a. wd. in Gestyngthrope *alias* Gesthorpe & Bulmer. £100.

12. Hil. & Eas. Rd. Serle & Rd. Algor, pl. Tho. Algor, brother & heir of Robt. Algor, decd., & son & heir of Jn. Algor late of Bures, decd., & Anne, w. of Tho., & *Alice*, wid., late w. of the said Jn., def. 11 a. ar. in Great Berdefeld & Little Berdefeld. Def. quitclaimed to pl. & the heirs of Rd. Serle. £40.

13. Tho. Glascock, pl. Tho. Nevell & w. *Eliz.*, def. A moiety of 2 mess., 2 gdns., 2 orchards, 60 a. ar., 4 a. mw. & 5 a. pa. in Chycknall Smeley, Chycknall Seint James, Bromefyld & Muche Waltham. £40.

14. Jn. Freman *alias* Mounds, pl. *Jerome* Grene & w. Jane, def. Manor of Berthall & 60 a. ar., 6 a. mw., 40 a. pa. & 8s. rt. in White Colne. £60.

15. Jn. Collyn, pl. Rd. Riche, kt., lord Riche, def. Manor of Bowsers *alias* Litle Laver Halle & 1 mess., 1 barn, 1 gdn., 1 orchard, 160 a. ar., 15 a. mw., 43 a. pa., 16 a. wd. & 8s. rt. in Lyttle Laver, High Laver, Abbys Rothing & Wyllynghall Doo, & the advowson of the church & rectory of Lyttle Laver. £215.

16. Chris. Goodryck, pl. Rd. Goodryck, esq., def. 5 mess., 4 cotts., 5 tofts, 200 a. ar., 100 a. mw., 100 a. pa. & 20 a. wd. in Newport Pond & Wyddyngton. £220.

17. Hil. & Eas. Hy. Leder, pl. *Tho.* Ereswell & w. Margt., def. 1 mess., 1 curtilage, 1 barn, 1 stable & 1 gdn. in Saffron Walden *alias* Chepyng Walden. £40.

18. Hil. & Eas. Nich. Chapman, pl. Edw. Palmer & w. Margt. & Jn. Swallowe, gent., def. 4 a. mw. in Bockyng called 'le Teynter Leyes'. And for this pl. gtd. the same to Jn. to hold from Michaelmas last for 59 years, rendering 26s. 8d. yearly to pl. & his heirs at the Annunciation & Michaelmas, with reversion to Edw. & Margt. & her heirs to hold of the chief lords.

19. Anth. Jebbe, pl. Robt. Carter & w. *Margt.*, def. 1 mess. & 1 curtilage in Branktree. £20.

74

20. Hil. & Eas. Tho. Parke & Miles Lakyn, pl. Wm. Marshall, clk., def. 2 mess., 2 gdns., 9 a. ar. & 11 a. pa. in Canewden & Hakewell. Def. quitclaimed to pl. & the heirs of Tho. And for this pl. gtd. the same to def. and his heirs to hold of the chief lords.

21. Tho. Hall, clk., pl. Wm. Fitche, 'yeoman', and w. *Margt.*, def. 1 mess. & 1 gdn. in Esse *alias* Asshen. £10.

22. Hil. & Eas. Jn. Lambard, pl. *Wm.* Stokes & w. Margt., def. 1 mess., 2 gdns., 2 orchards & 16 a. ar. in Great Berdefeld. £40.

23. Hy. Wyberd, son of Jn. Wyberd & w. Joan, pl. The same *Jn.* and Joan, def. 1 mess., 1 gdn., 1 orchard, 20 a. ar., 3 a. mw. & 2 a. pa. in Great Halyngbury. And for this pl. gtd. the same to def. to hold for their lives of the chief lords.

24. Mich. & Eas. Jn. Cooke, gent., pl. Jn. Strangman, gent., def. 10 mess., 3 tofts, 3 barns, 10 gdns., 100 a. ar., 20 a. mw., 100 a. pa., 4 a. wd., 140 a. marsh, a common fishery & 3s. 4d. rt. in Raylegh, Hadlegh, Rocheford, Lachingdon & Thunderslegh. Def. quitclaimed 1 mess., 1 toft, 1 gdn. & 26 a. ar. in Ralegh & Thunderslegh to pl. & his heirs; & gtd. to the same the reversions of 1 mess., 1 barn, 1 gdn. & 6 a. ar. in Ralegh which Agnes West, wid., holds for life, 6 mess., 1 barn, 6 gdns., 10 a. ar. & 3s. 4d. rt. in Hadlegh which Margt. Strangman, wid., holds for life, & 2 mess., 2 tofts, 1 barn, 2 gdns., 58 a. ar., 20 a. mw., 100 a. pa., 4 a. wd., 140 a. marsh & a common fishery in Lachindon & Rocheford which the said Margt. holds until she has fulfilled the testament & last will of Edw. Strangman, gent., decd.; to hold of the chief lords. 400 mks.

25. Wm. Crayford, son of Jn. Crayford, pl. *Jn.* Currall *alias* Hunte & w. Alice, def. 1 mess. called 'le Cocke' & 1 gdn. in Brendwood. £20.

26. Paul Jeffrey, pl. Wm. Wykylsworth, def. 10 a. ar., 17 a. pa. & 3 a. wd. in Shenfelde. £20.

27. Wm. Serle, pl. *Wm.* Smyth, Jn. Smyth, Robt. Smyth & w. Eliz. & Jn. Whytley & w. Margt., def. 1 mess. & 3 gdns. in Great Berdefeld. £36.

28. Hil. & Eas. Jn. Frith, pl. *Roger* Nicolson & w. Agnes, def. 1 mess. & 4 a. a. in Little Warley. £40.

29. Hil. & Eas. Tho. Unwyn *alias* Onyon, pl. Robt. Mordaunte, esq., & w. Barbara & *Philip* Mordaunte, gent., his son & heir apt., def. 1 mess., 1 gdn., 40 a. ar., 3 a. mw. & 14 a. pa. in Fynchingfeld. 160 mks.

30. Tho. Smythe, gent., pl. *Edw.* Barker, gent., & w. Frances, def. 1 mess., 6 a. ar. & 4 a. pa. in Wansted. £60.

31. Hil. & Eas. Tho. Lytley, gent., & Francis Bright, pl. Hy. Nuttall & w. *Eliz.*, def. 1 mess. called 'Courts', a third party of a mess. called 'Banks', & 1 dovecote, 1 barn, 1 stable, 1 orchard, 2 gdns., 40 a. ar., 20 a. mw., 40 a. pa., 10 a. wd. & 20 a. marsh called 'Spaynes Mershe' & 'Randes' in Alvithley *alias* Alveley *alias* Auveley. Def. quitclaimed to pl. & the heirs of Tho. And for this pl. gtd. the same to def. to hold for the life of Eliz. of the chief lords, with successive remainders to the heirs of her body by the body of Hy., Felicia Kyng & Susan Kyng, her daus., & the heirs of their bodies, & Hy. & his heirs.

32. Tho. Allen, gent., pl. Tho. Peke, def. 1 mess., 1 cott., 1 gdn., 1 orchard, 10 a. pa. & 4 a. wd. in Wyckforde & Rawrey. And for this pl. gtd. the same to def. & his heirs to hold of the chief lords.

33. Rd. Riche, kt., lord Riche, pl. Tho., duke of Norfolk, def. Manor of Erles Hall *alias* Erles Fee & 30 mess., 10 cotts., 200 a. ar., 20 a. mw., 200 a. pa., 10 a. wd., 100 a. marsh & £24 rt. in Pritwell *alias* Prittillwell, Southchurche, Estwoode, Leigh, Sutton Temple & Milton. £640.

CP25(2)/126/1607   TRINITY, 1 ELIZABETH   1559

1. Jn. Stonerd, esq., pl. *Francis* Saunders, esq., & Margt. Valentyne, wid., def. Manor of Loughbroughes & 2 mess., 2 tofts, 2 barns, 1 dovecote, 3 gdns., 20 a. ar., 100 a. pa. & 1 a. wd. in Chygwell & Woodford. £150.

2. Jn. Fraunces, pl. *Tho.* Harryson & w. Agnes, def. 1 mess. & 1 gdn in Rocheford. 20 mks.

3. Wm. Fytz Williams, kt., pl. Edm. Norryngton, def. 1 mess., 1 barn, 1 gdn., 10 a. ar., 4 a. mw. & 8 a. pa. in Theydon Garnon. £40.

4. Tho. Wylforde, pl. Tho. Serle, def. 1 mess., 1 cott., 1 gdn., 1 orchard & 1 a. ar. in Brentwood. £40.

5. Jn. Thurston, pl. *Roger* Parker, gent., & w. Anne, def. Manor of Colbrands & 4 mess., 4 tofts, 4 gdns., 100 a. ar., 30 a. mw., 200 a. pa., 30 a. wd., 100 a. marsh & 40s. rt. in Great Clacton & Little Clacton. £140.

6. Jn. Dyer, pl. Wm. Pascall, def. 1 mess., 1 gdn., 1 orchard, 100 a. ar., 10 a. mw., 20 a. pa. & 2 a. wd. in Fyfhide, Rothing Beauchampe & Willinghale Doo. £200.

7. Jn. Whyte, pl. *Roger* Parker, gent., & w. Anne, def. 50 a. ar., 10 a. mw., 20 a. pa., 20 a. wd. & 4s. 8d. rt. in Gosfeld, Halsted & Bokkynge. £40.

8. Jn. Coker, gent., son of Tho. Coker of Mapowder, co. Dorset, esq., decd., pl. Jn. Bedell, def. Manor of Wybrigge *alias* Standes Wibrigge & 10 mess., 10 tofts, 10 gdns., 100 a. ar., 100 a. mw., 60 a. pa., 5 a. wd. & £5 rent in Hornechurche & Haveryng in le Bower. £200.

9. Tho. Gregyll, pl. Hy. Songer, gent., & w. *Eliz.*, Tho. Phillipps & w. Margery & Tho. Newdygate, def. 2 mess., 8 gdns., 60 a. ar. & 2 a. mw. in Great Waltham, Highester & Plecy *alias* Playsshey. £80.

10. Anth. Herde, pl. Robt. Herde, son & heir of Tho. Herde, decd., def. 3 mess., 3 gdns., 3 orchards, 20 a. ar. & 3 a. mw. in Fynchyngfeld. 80 mks.

11. Tho. Unwyn *alias* Onyon & Tho. Sulman, pl. Wm. Chisshull, esq., & *Roch* Grene, esq., 31 a. ar., 1 a. mw. & 9 a. pa. in Little Sampford. Def. quitclaimed to pl. & the heirs of Tho. Unwyn. £40.

12. Jn. Cocke, pl. *Wm.* Brockes and w. Ursula, def. 1½ a. ar. called Gallowcrofte in Shenfeld. 40 mks.

13. Robt. Newman, gent., pl. *Tho.* More of London, mercer, & w. Eliz., def. 12 a. mw. in Thaxsted. £80.

14. Tho. Baker, gent., pl. Humphrey Cornewall, gent., def. 1 mess., 200 a. ar., 20 a. mw., 200 a. pa. & 10 a. wd. in Walden & Assheton. £160.

15. Wm. Browne, pl. *Jn.* Hilton & w. Mary, def. 2 mess. & 2 gdns. in Stratford Langthorne. £40.

16. Tho. Serle, pl. Geo. White, esq., def. 30 a. ar., 20 a. mw., 20 a. pa. & 20 a. wd. in Shenfeld. 160 mks.

17. Edw. Baesshe, esq., & w. Thomasina, pl. Robt. Webbe, gent., def. Manor of Barlands & 7 mess., 200 a. ar., 100 a. mw., 200 a. pa., 40 a. wd. & 20s. rt. in Prittelwell, Shopland & Sutton. Def. quitclaimed to pl. & the heirs of Edw. £460.

18. Wm. Danwood, pl. Tho. Gryggs *alias* Grygle & w. *Olive,* def. A moiety of 1 mess., 4 a. ar. & 4 a. mw. in Brentwood & Shenfeld. £40.

19. Roch Grene, wsq., pl. Wm. Chisshull, esq., def. 2 mess., 2 gdns, 22 a. ar., 5 a. mw. & 3 a. pa. in Little Sampford & Great Sampford. £40.

CP25(2)/126/1608   MICHAELMAS, 1 AND 2 ELIZABETH   1559

1. Jn. Grene, pl. *Rd.* Day & w. Eliz., def. 2 mess. & 2 gdns. in Harwiche. £40.

2. Trin. & Mich. Jn. a Ware, pl. *Rd.* Penyfather & w. Margery, def. 2 mess., 2 gdns., 2 barns, 2 orchards & 3 a. mw. in Wryttell. 100 mks.

3. Trin. & Mich. Jn. Howe jun., pl. Tho. Luffkyn & w. Joan, def. 16 a. ar. & 6 a. wd. in Ardeley. £40.

4. Hy. Aylett, pl. Wm. Snellyng & w. *Joan*, def. 1 mess., 1 curtilage, 1 orchard, 30 a. ar., 6 a. mw. & 16 a. pa. in White Rodyng. £80.

5. Eliz. Paveley, wid., pl. Jas. Burley & w. *Joan,* def. 1 mess., 1 gdn. & 1 orchard in Chepyng Onger. £40.

6. Lau. Lytle, pl. Jn. Wells & w. *Mary*, Tho. Hawcks & w. *Agnes*, def. 2 mess. & 2 gdns. in Mannyngtre & Mystleye. £40.

7. Wm. Bowlyng, pl. Jn. Warman & w. *Mary*, Joan Adam, wid., & Agnes Seman, def. 4½ a. ar. in Walden. £40.

8. Jn. Garrard, pl. *Jn.* Stane & w. Bridget, def. 40 a. ar. called 'Wrights' in Canewdon *alias* Canydon. 100 mks.

9. Jn. Goodaye, pl. *Tho.* Burges & w. Agnes, def. 1 mess., 1 cott., 1 gdn., 1 orchard, 100 a. ar., 10 a. mw., 20 a. pa. & 4 a. wd. in Branktre & Blacknotley. £220.

10. Hy. Broke, pl. Wm. Tyndall, gent., & w. *Anne*, def. 2 mess. & 1 gdn. in Great Dunmowe. £40.

11. Jn. Lamme, pl. *Jerome* Songer, gent., & Jn. Stonnard, def. 2 mess., 2 gdns., 2 orchards & 6 a. ar. in Kelwydon. £40.

12. Trin. & Mich. Tho. Smythe, esq., pl. Wm., marquess of Northampton, def. Manor of Langford & 30 mess., 10 tofts, 1 dovecote, 1 fulling mill, 30 gdns., 20 orchards, 200 a. ar., 100 a. mw., 500 a. pa., 30 a. wd., 30 a. marsh & £12 11s. rt. in Langford, Ultyng, Revenhale, Hatfeld Peverell, Woodham Mortymer, Heighbridge, Wykham & Great Maldon, & the advowson of the church of Langford. £720.

13. Eas. & Mich. Jn. Abell, esq., pl. Rd. Coringe & w. Anne, def. 3 mess., 20 a. ar., 20 a. mw. & 60 a. pa. in Colchester & Mileend, which def. hold for their lives with remainder to Tho. Coring son of Tho. Coring, decd., & the heirs of his body & the right heirs of Rd. Def. quitclaimed to pl. for their lives. 160 mks.

14. Robt. Lamberd, pl. Tho. Levesham, def. 3 mess., 2 tofts, 3 gdns., 1 orchard & 3 a. pa. in the parish of St. Leonard, Colchester. 130 mks.

15. Rd. Hall & Tho. Stysted, pl. Tho. Dawson, def. 30 a. ar., 20 a. mw., 40 a. pa., 5 a. marsh, 4 a. wd., 2s. rt. & a rt. of 1 lb. of pepper in Rocheford, Asshyngdon & Hawkwell. Def. quitclaimed to pl. & the heirs of Rd. £60.

16. Edw. Alston, pl. Tho. Whight & w. *Alice*, def. 1 mess., 1 water-mill, 8 a. ar. & 10 a. mw. in Great Henney & Twynsted. £40.

17. Trin. & Mich. Jn. Lawe, pl. Edw. Pollard, def. 1 mess., 3 gdns., 20 a. ar., 10 a. mw. & 10 a. pa. in Berdfeld Salyng. £40.

18. Tho. Wyseman, gent., pl. *Jn.* Rochester, esq., & w. Philippa, def. Manor of Mylleys & 2 mess., 2 tofts, 100 a ar., 10 a. mw., 100 a. pa., 20 a. wd. & 20s. rt. in Stysted. 170 mks.

19. Jn. Mylborne, pl. *Jn.* Ferrers, esq., son & heir of Humphrey Ferrers, kt., decd., & w. Barbara, def. Manor of Merkes & 5 mess., 300 a. ar., 30 a. mw., 300 a. pa., 80 a. wd., £6 rt. & a rt. of 3 capons in Great Dunmowe, Little Dunmowe, Highester & Great Waltham. £400.

20. Wm. Stedman, pl. *Rd.* Forker & w. Agnes, def. 2 mess., 1 gdn & 1 a. ar. in Barkyng. £40.

21. Hy. Maxey, gent., & Rd. Fytche of Bockyng, pl. *Jn.* Goodhey & w. Mary & Margery Fytche, wid., def. Manor of Panfeld called 'Panfeld Pryory' & 12 mess., 12 gdns., 300 a. ar., 16 a. mw., 100 a. pa., 30 a. wd. & £6 rt. in Panfeld. Def. quitclaimed to pl. & the heirs of Rd. And for this pl. gtd. the same to Margery to hold from Michaelmas for 32 years at a yearly rt. of £15 payable at the Annunciation & Michaelmas, with power of distraint, with reversion to Jn. & Mary & the heirs of Jn. to hold of the chief lords.

22. Wm. Nutbrowne, pl. *Robt.* Mylborne & w. Helen, def. 1 mess., 80 a. ar., 10 a. mw., 80 a. pa., 12 a. wd. & 8s. rt. in Dounham, Runwell, Rammesdon Belhowse, Westhanyngton, Esthanyngton & Southanyngton. £100.

23. Wm. Danwood *alias* Beane & w. Eliz., pl. *Jn.* Haukyn & w. Agnes, def. 1 mess. & 1 gdn. in Brentwood. Def. quitclaimed to pl. & the heirs of Wm. £40.

24. Geo. Cooke *alias* Barker & w. Mary, pl. Rd. Cooke *alias* Barker & w. Eliz., def. 1 mess., 1 barn & 1 gdn. in Feryng. Def. quitclaimed to pl. & the heirs of Geo. £40.

25. Robt. Bragge, pl. *Jn.* Cole, gent., & w. Eliz., def. 16 a. ar., 13 a. pa. & 15 a. wd. in Bulmer. £80.

26. Edw. Bell, gent., pl. *Jn.* Loraunce & w. Agnes, def. 2 mess., 1 curtilage & 3 a. ar. in Harvardestock. £40.

27. Jn. Shyngton *alias* Lee, pl. *Robt.* Shyngton *alias* Lee 'yoman', and w. Anne, def. 1 mess., 1 cott., 1 orchard, 1 gdn., 8 a. ar., 1 a. mw. & 14 a. pa. in Stanford Ryvers. £40.

CP25(2)/259/ Mich. 1–2 Eliz.   DIVERS COUNTIES

2. Trin. & Mich. Jn. Mordaunt, kt., & Robt. Johns, gent., pl. Wm. Aprice, esq., def. 5 mess., 4 tofts, 5 gdns, 100 a. ar., 40 a. mw., 100 a. pa., 20 a. wd. & 10s. rt. in Walthamstowe, co. Essex, & property in other counties. Def. quitclaimed to pl. & the heirs of Jn. And for this pl. granted the Essex prop. to def. to hold for one month, with successive remainders to Robt. Aprice & w. Joan & the heirs male of his body of her body, the feminine heirs of his body by her, the heirs male of the body of Robt., Edm. Aprice, second son of Wm., & the heirs male of his body, Lewis Aprice, third son of Wm., & the heirs male of his body, Jn. Aprice, fourth son of Wm., & the heirs male of his body, & the said Wm. & his heirs, to hold of the chief lords. — Beds., Essex., Hunts., Norf..

CP25(2)/126/1609   HILARY, 2 ELIZABETH   1560

1. Mich. & Hil. Edm. Harryngton, pl. *Jn.* Harryngton & w. Cecily, def. A moiety of 1 mess., 2 gdns., 1 orchard, 20 a. ar., 3 a. mw. & 2 a. pa. in Great Gelham *alias* Great Yeldham & Toppefeld. £40.

2. Wm. Cracherode, gent., pl. *Jn.* Kyrkby, gent., & w. Eliz., def. 6 a. ar., 3 a. mw. & 13 a. pa. in Hedyngham Syble. £40.

3. Jas. Pargeter, pl. Jn. Gessam, def. 4 a. pa. & 4 a. wd. in Barkynge. 5 mks.

4. Rd. Redley, pl. Jn. Machyn & w. *Mary,* def. 2½ a. pa. in Woodham Water. £40.

5. Mich. & Hil. Wm. Bellowe, pl. *Jn.* Thake & w. Agnes, Robt. Poynyerd, gent., & w. Bridget, def. 1 mess., 1 barn, 1 gdn., 1 orchard, 30 a. ar., 6 a. mw., 10 a. pa. & 2d. rt. in Clavering. 200 mks.

6. Edw. Isaak, esq., pl. Tho. Nevyle, kt., def. Manor of Oldholt & 6 mess., 6 tofts, 6 gdns., 6 orchards, 2 dovecotes, 600 a. ar., 40 a. mw., 300 a. pa., 20 a. wd & 25s. rt. in Little Birche, Great Birche, Leyer Marney, Leyer Bretton, Messinge, Copford & Rewenhale. £1,000.

7. Mich. & Hil. Robt. Spryng, pl. *Tho.* Garrold *alias* Butcher & w. Joan, def. 1 mess., 1 barn, 2 gdns., 9 a. ar. & 3 roods mw. in Great Gelham *alias* Great Yeldham & Tylbury. £24.

8. David Sympson, gent., pl. *Jas.* Baker, esq., son & heir of Edw. Baker, esq., decd., & w. Mary, def. 4 a. mw. in Wyckford. £10.

9. Mich. & Hil. Robt. Parker, pl. *Jn.* Loveday, Tho. Barker & w. Kath. & Wm. Stourton & w. Eliz., def. 1 mess., 1 barn & 2 gdns. in Great Dunmowe. £20.

10. Mich. & Hil. Tho. Denys, pl. Wm. Fulston & w. *Agnes*, & Edm. Valantyne & w. *Joan,* def. Two thirds of 1 mess. & 4 a. pa. in Gynge Mounteney. £40.

11. Tho. Cole, pl. Jn. Heidon & w. *Agnes* & Robt. Woodd, def. A moiety of 3 mess., 60 a. ar., 4 a. mw. & 10 a. pa. in Newport Pond, Wyddyngton & Rycklyng. 100 mks.

12. Mich. & Hil. Robt. Wright, pl. *Jn.* Mounes & w. Eliz., def. 1 mess., 1 barn, 1 gdn., 1 orchard, 10 a. ar., 2 a. mw., 6 a. pa. & ½ a. wd. in Southwelde. 130 mks.

13. Mich. & Hil. Jn. Harryngton, pl. *Robt.* Walford & w. Jane & Robt. Kempe, def. 1 mess., 2 gdns, 10 a. ar. & 1 a. mw. in Fynchyngfeld. £40.

14. Mich. & Hil. Tho. Londe, pl. *Jn.* Hempsted & w. Kath., def. 1 mess., 1 barn, 1 gdn., 1 orchard, 8 a. ar. & a a. mw. in Bumpsted at the Steeple. 40 mks.

15. Mich. & Hil. Tho. Unwyn *alias* Onyon, pl. *Wm.* Fytche & w. Joan & Jn. Fytche, his son & heir apt., def. 1 mess., 2 barns, 2 gdns., 1 orchard, 22 a. ar., 4 a. wd., 16 a. pa. & 3 a. wd. in Little Sampford & Great Sampford. £80.

16. Roger Gyttons & w. Emma, pl. Jn. Heygham, gent., & w. *Eliz.*, def. 1 mess., 16 a. ar., 2 a. mw. & 2 a. pa. in Ramysden Belhous. Def. quitclaimed to pl. & the heirs of Roger. £40.

17. Rd. Durant, gent., pl. Wm. Newman, def. 1 mess., 1 gdn., 1 orchard, 2 a. ar., 1 a. mw. & 2 a. pa. in Warley Waylett *alias* Warley Abbisse *alias* Great Warley. £40.

18. Edw. Chylde, pl. Jn. Machyn & w. *Mary,* def. 2½ a. pa. in Woodham Water. £40.

19. Philip Hunwycke, pl. *Jn.* Choppyn, gent., & w. Grace, def. Manor of Holts & 140 a. ar., 10 a. mw., 100 a. pa., 10 a. wd., 20 a. marsh & 30s. rt. in Esthorpe, Great Birche, Little Birche & Copford. £280.

CP25(2)/259/(Hil. 2 Eliz.)   DIVERS COUNTIES

3. Mich. & Hil. Tho. Wentworth, kt., lord Wentworth, Chris. Heydon kt., Giles Alyngton, kt., Tho. Cornewaleys, kt., Wm. Chyssell, esq., & Wm. Cotton, esq., pl. *Jn.* Wentworth of Gosfeld, kt., Jn. Wentworth of Baconsthorppe, co. Norfolk, esq., Hy. Wentworth, esq., brother of the last, & Hy. Wentworth of Steple Bumpsted, esq., def. Manors of Wethersfeld, Little Horkesley, Coddham, Shorne Hall & Nicols & 500 mess., 100 tofts, 5 mills, 100 gdns., 5,000 a. ar., 1,000 a. mw., 5,000 a. pa., 1,000 a. wd., 3,000 a. furze & heath & £30 rt. in Wethersfeld, Little Horkesley, Great Horklesley, Bockyng, Shalford, Syble Henyngham *alias* Syble Heddyngham, Brayntre, Little Reyne, Great Bardfeld & Little Bardfeld, & property in Suffolk. Def. quitclaimed to pl. & the heirs of Giles. £4,400. — Essex, Suff..

CP25(2)/126/1610   EASTER, 2 ELIZABETH   1560

1. Wm. Cotton, esq., & Robt. Rede *alias* Davy, pl. Jn. Byggyn *alias* Byggyng sen., def. 1 mess., 1 gdn., 1 orchard, 60 a. ar., 4 a. mw. & 10 a. pa. in Bokkyng. Def. quitclaimed to pl. & the heirs of Wm. And for this pl. gtd. the same to def. to hold of the chief lords for life without impeachment of waste, with remainder to Rd. Byggyn *alias* Byggyng, his son & heir apt., & his heirs.

2. Jn. Atkynson, pl. Geo. Clerson & w. *Eliz.*, def. 1 mess. in Bylleryca. £20.

3. Anth. Cooke, kt., pl. *Roger* Capstock, gent., & w. Anne, def. 100 a. pa., 300 a. wd. & 200 a. heath in Waltham Stowe. £80.

4. Hil. & Eas. Tho. Hawkyn, pl. *Wm.* Rotheman & w. Margt., def. 10 a. ar., 2 a. pa., & 2 a. wd. in Great Leighes. £40.

5. Hil. and Eas. Jn. Smythe, pl. *Tho.* Clayton, gent., & w. Anne, def. 1 mess., 1 barn & 1 gdn. in Bockyng. £20.

6. Hil. & Eas. Wm. Walker, pl. Wm. Symsonne & w. *Joan*, Tho. Whyte & w. *Margt.* & Rd. Ram & w. *Margery*, sisters & heirs of Hy. Swallowe, def. 1 mess., 4 a. ar. & 6d. rt. in Felsted. £40.

7. Hy. Pasmere, gent., pl. Tho. Stuckle, esq., & w. *Anne*, def. 3 mess., 3 orchards, 3 gdns., 60 a. ar., 10 a. mw., & 12 a. pa. in Waltehamstowe, Waltehamstowe Tone & Hygham Bensted. And for this pl. gtd. the same to def. & the heirs of their bodies, with remainder to the heirs of the body of Anne & the right heirs of Tho., to hold of the chief lords.

8. Wm. Walker, pl. *Geo.* Savage & w. Maud, def. 3 a. ar. in Good Ester. 10 mks.

9. Hil. & Eas. Tho. Lawsell, pl. Robt. Thressher & w. *Margt.*, one of the daus. of Hy. Gyler *alias* Spendlove, decd., def. A moiety of 1 mess., 1 barn, 2 gdns., 1 orchard & 16 a. ar., in Great Waltham. £30.

10. Rd. Westwood, pl. Jn. Terlyng & *Giles* Terlyng, def. 1 mess., 20 a. ar., 10 a. mw., 12 a. pa. & 2 a. wd. in Latton. £70.

11. Kath. Browne, wid., pl. *Wm.* White & w. Eliz., def. 1 mess., 1 gdn. (*gardino*), 1 gdn. (*orto*), 10 a. ar., 2 a. mw., 8 a. pa. & 12d. rt. in Goodester & Masshebury. £40.

12. Anth. Jebbe, pl. Wm. Poley, esq., & w. *Alice* and Tho. Shaa, esq., def. Manors of Great Stambrige, Little Stambrige, Seynt Laurence Hall, Colmans, Shelford & Bradworth & 40 mess., 2,000 a. ar., 500 a. mw., 2,000 a. pa., 1,000 a. marsh, 1,000 a. wd. & £20 rt. in Great Stambrige, Little Stambrige, Seynt Laurence, Tillingham, Bradwell by the Sea, Great Wakering, Little Wakering, Shopland, Sutton, Pritwell *alias* Prittilwell, Leigh, Estwood, Raleigh, Thundersley, Rocheford & Fulnes. And for this pl. granted the same to Tho. & the heirs male of his body, with remainder to Robt. Shaa & the heirs male of his body & the right heirs of Jn. Shaa, kt., to hold of the chief lords.

13. Hil. & Eas. Rd. Glascock, pl. *Jn.* Glascock & w. Margt., def. 1 mess., 1 gdn. (*gardino*), 1 gdn. (*orto*), 60 a. ar., 15. mw., 30 a. pa. & 4 a. wd. in Little Laver & High Laver. 130 mks.

14. Arthur Malby, citizen & fishmonger of London, pl. Tho. Malby, kinsman & heir of Tho. Malby, decd., def. Manor of Chalkewell & 6 mess., 6 gdns., 100 a. ar., 100 a. mw., 100 a. pa., 40 a. wd., 200 a. marsh & £6 3s. rt. in Chalkewell, Pritt(i)llwell, Haveryng, Mylton, Lachyngdon, Eastwood, Great Stambridge, Little Stambridge, Leigh, Hornechurch & Thundersley. £480.

15. Tho. Bennett, pl. *Wm.* Barlee, esq., & w. Joyce & Wm. Danyell, def. Manor of Mulsham & 2 mess., 2 barns, 2 gdns., 100 a. ar. 200 a. mw., 300 a. pa., 15 a. wd. & 40s. rt. in Great Wigborowe, Leir Marney, Leyr de la Haye & Salcott Furley. And for this pl. gtd. the same to Wm. Danyell to hold from Michaelmas & the Annunciation, with reversion to Wm. Barlee & Joyce & the heirs of Wm., to hold of the chief lords.

16. Jn. Meke, pl. Tho. Wells, def. 1 mess., 1 gdn. & 1 a. ar. in Rocheford. £40.

17. Hugh Full, citizen & 'draper' of London, & w. Fredeswida, pl Anne Byrd, wid., def. 3 mess., 1 barn, 3 gardens, 6 a. ar., 2 a. mw. & 4 a. pa. in Black Notley & Little Lyes. Def quitclaimed to pl. & the heir of Fredeswida. £40.

18. Rd. Riche, kt., lord Ryche, Robt. Riche, kt., & Tho. Franke, esq., pl. *Eliz.* Fane, wid., & Roland Clerke, kt., def. Manor of Butlers, a moiety of manor of Shopland Hall, 20 mess., 10 cotts., 10 tofts, 300 a. ar., 100 a. mw., 200 a. pa., 60 a. wd., 160 a. marsh, 100 a. furze & heath & 40s. rt. in Butlers, Shopland, Sutton, Prittelwell, Leigh, Hadley, Greate Wakerynge, Showbery, Rochford, Hackwell, Rawreth & Crycksheth, & the advowsons of the churches of Butlers & Shopland. Def. quitclaimed to pl. & the heirs of Rd. £600.

19. Rd. Weston, one of the justices of the Common Bench, & w. Margt., pl. Tho. Farmer, esq., & w. *Frances*, dau. & sole heir of Tho. Harde & w. Dorothy, one of the daus. & co-heirs of Jn. Harper of Russhall, kt., def. A fourth part of manor of West Tylbery, a fourth part of 300 a. ar., 60 a. mw., 130 a. pa., 18 a. wd., 300 a. marsh & 60s. rt. in West Tylbery, East Tylbery, Chawdwell, Lyttle Thurocke, Grayes Thurocke & Orsett, a fourth part of the ferry or passage of West Tylbery, & a fourth part of the advowson of the church of West Tylbery. Def. quitclaimed to pl. & the heirs of Rd. £160.

20. Wm. Bendlowes, serjeant at law, pl. *Jn.* Lawe, Margt. Pollard, wid., late the w. of Edw. Pollard, decd., & Wm. Pollard, def. 1 mess., 3 gdns., 1 orchard, 20 a. ar., 2 a. mw. & 6 a. pa. in Berdefeld Salyng. 100 mks.

21. Hil. & Eas. Rd. Tyterell, pl. Roch *alias* Rok Grene, esq., & w. Eleanor, def. 8 a. ar. in Little Sampforde. £20.

22. Wm. Bendlowes, serjeant at law, pl. *Hy.* Walter, gent., & w. Anne, def. 1 mess., 1 barn, 2 gdns., 1 orchard, 50 a. ar., 3 a. mw. & 7 a. pa. in Berdefeld Salyng, Great Salyng *alias* Old Salyng & Stebbyng. 160 mks.

23. Edm. Markaunt, gent., pl. Jerome Balborowe, gent., def. 2 mess., 4 gdns., 1 a. ar. & 1 a. mw. in the parish of St. Giles by Colchester, Colchester & West Donyland. £40.

24. Tho. Gyver & Jn. Halles, pl. *Tho.* Moore of the city of London, 'mercer', & w. Eliz., def. 1 mess., 1 barn, 1 gdn., 27 a. ar., & 1 a. pa. in Thaxsted. Def. quitclaimed to pl. & the heirs of Tho. £40.

25. Tho. Farnyll & w. Anne, pl. *Jas.* Morley & w. Anne, def. 4 mess., 4 tofts, 3 gdns., 1,000 a. ar., 100 a. mw., 100 a. pa., 100 a. furze & heath & 100 a. marsh in Graies Thorock, West Thorock, Graies Strope, Little Thorock, Styfford and Chaldwell. Def. quitclaimed to pl. & the heirs of Tho. 220 mks.

26. Wm. Algor & Wm. Brett, pl. *Wm.* Kyng & w. Agnes & Jn. Turnor & w. Joan, def. 6 mess., 1 cott., 1 barn, 8 gdns., 2 orchards, 1 a. ar. & 1 a. mw., in Great Berdfeld & Panfeld. Def. quitclaimed to pl. & the heirs of Wm. Alfor. £40.

27. Hil. & Eas. Wm. Walkelyn, pl. Jn. Hunter & w. *Ellen,* A third part of 2 mess., 1 barn, 2 gdns., 40 a. ar., 2 a. mw. & 40 a. pa. in Shalford. £40.

28. Wm. Deynes, pl. Tho. Barbour, esq., *Tho.* Shaa, esq., & Wm. Poley, esq., & w. Alice, def. Manors of Barrowe Hall, Hulberds *alias* Hulberdes Hall, Parrys, Arden Hall, & Hornedon & 40 mess., 2,000 a ar., 500 a. mw., 2,000 a. pa., 1,000 a. marsh, 1,000 a. wd. & £20 rent in Great Wakeryng, Little Wakeryng, Tundersley, Harlowe, Theydon Garnon, Shepyng, Hornedon 'at the Hill', Southchurche, Copersalls, Eppyng, Latton, Estwoode, Great Sutton, Little Sutton, Northwood, Cannouden, Hockley, Canvey & Pryttelwell. And for this pl. gtd. the same to Wm. & Alice & the heirs of her body to

hold of the chief lords, with successive remainders to Tho. Shaa & Robt. Shaa & the heirs male of their bodies & the right heirs of Jn. Shaa, kt.

29. Hil. & Eas. Wm. Symsonne & w. Joan, one of the daus. & heirs of Rd. Swallowe sen., p. Tho. Whyte & w. Margt., one of the daus. & heirs of the said Rd., & Rd. Ram & w. *Margery*, another of the daus. & heirs, def. Two parts of 3 mess., 3 gdns., 1 orchard, 2 a. ar., 1½ a. pa. & 8d. rt. in Bockyng, which Juliana Whyte, wid., mother of Margt. & Margery, holds for life. Pl. & the heirs of their bodies to hold the remainder of the chief lords, with reaminder to the right heirs of Joan. £40.

30. Wm. Martyn, pl. *Tho.* Bragge & w. Margt., def. 1 mess., 1 barn, 1 gdn., 1 orchard & 7 a. ar., in Halsted. £40.

31. Hil. & Eas. Francis Jobson, kt., pl. *Roger* Grace & w. Margt., def. 2 mess., 3 tofts, 1 barn, 2 gdns., 1 orchard, 60 a. ar., 20 a. mw., 40 a. pa. & 2 a. wd. in Peldon & Little Wygborough. 220 mks.

32. Jn. Clerk, pl. Jn. Waytt & w. *Agnes*, def. 1 mess., 1 gdn. & 1 a. ar. in Lammershe. 50 mks.

CP25(2)/259/Easter 2 Eliz.   DIVERS COUNTIES

9. Anth. Huse, Tho. Huse, Wm. Thorold & Jn. Alcocke, pl. Hy., earl of Rutland, def. Manor of Waltham Stowe Tony & 100 mess., 1 mill, 1,500 a. ar., 500 a. mw., 2,000 a. pa., 200 a. wd. & £20 rt. in Waltham Stowe, co. Essex, & property in other counties. Def. quitclaimed to pl. & the heirs of Tho. £6,400. — Lincoln, Leics., Notts., Yorks., Essex.

CP25(2)/126/1611   TRINITY, 2 ELIZABETH   1560

1. Wm. Cordell, kt., master of the rolls of Chancery, pl. *Tho.* Barnabe, gent., & w. Margery, def. Manor of Olyvers & 2 mess., 2 cotts., 2 gdns., 100 a. ar., 20 a. mw., 100 a. pa., 14 a. wd. & 40 a. furze & heath in Stanway. £200.

CP25(2)/126/1612   MICHAELMAS, 2 AND 3 ELIZABETH   1560

1. Eas. & Mich. Wm. Harvye, pl. *Jn.* Trapps sen., & w. Agnes, def. 1 mess., 1 gdn., 1 orchard, 4 a. ar., & 8 a. pa. in Theydon Garnon & Theydon Boyes. £40.

2. Robt. Newman, gent., pl. Edm. West, esq., & w. *Joan*, dau. & heir of Margt. Colleynne, wid., decd., def. 22 a. ar., 2 a. mw., 15 a. pa. & 4 a. wd. in Broxhed. 100 mks.

3. Tho. Harryson, pl. Wm. Ablet & w. *Joan*, def. 1 mess., 1 gdn., 3 a. ar. & 3 a. pa. in Rocheford. £40.

4. Eas. & Mich. Rd. Sparke, gent., pl. Jn. Lowe & w. *Margery*, def. 3 a. ar. & 1½ a. pa. in Wydyngton *alias* Wydyton. £40.

5. Tho. Frenche, pl. *Jas.* Bedell, gent., & w. Eliz., def. Manor of Pytley & 60 a. ar., 30 a. mw., 50 a. pa., 30 a. marsh & rt. in Great Bardefeelde & Little Bardefeelde. £140.

6. Jn. Chapman & Wm. Russell, pl. Jn. Andrewe & w. *Petronilla*, def. 1 mess., 1 quay & 1 gdn. in Harwiche. £40.

7. Eas. & Mich. Chris. Sumner, pl. Tho. Kelloge & w. *Marion*, def. 1 mess., 1 curtilage, 20 a. ar., 10 a. mw. & 16 a. pa. in Ulting, Hatfeld Peverell & Boreham. £80.

8. Robt. Hyrst, gent., pl. *Tho.* Gooddaye & w. Joan, def. 80 a. ar., 3 a. mw., 6 a. pa. & 6 a. wd. in Shering. 130 mks.

9. Rd. Bulle, pl. *Tho.* Frenche & w. Eliz., def. 1 mess., 1 orchard, 4 a. ar., 2 a. mw. & 4 a. pa. in Manewden. £40.

10. Wm. Smyth, pl. Edm. Salyng & w. *Margery*, def. A moiety of 2 mess., 20 a. ar., 12 a. mw. & 8 a. pa. in Barkyng. £40.

11. Nich. Hunte, gent., & Hy. Reynold, pl. Jn. Forde, gent., & w. *Kath.*, def. Manor of Woodhouse & 2 mess., 80 a. ar., 100 a. pa. & 60 a. wd. in Horkesley & Bulmer. Def. quitclaimed to pl. & the heirs of Nich. And for this pl. gtd. the same to def. to hold of the chief lords for their lives without impeachment of waste, with remainder to Eleanor Forde, their dau., & her heirs.

12. Roland Hill, kt., Tho. Whyte, kt., & Jn. Lyon, kt., pl. *Robt.* Hogeson, gent., & w. Eliz., def. 6½ a. land in Wyldemarshe in Westham. Def. quitclaimed to pl. & the heirs of Roland. £40.

13. Tho. Wyseman, gent., pl. *Wm.* Badcock & w. Rose, def. 1 mess., 1 barn, 1 gdn., 1 orchard, 12 a. ar., 7 a. mw. & 11 a. pa. in Great Waltham. £40.

14. Eas. & Mich. Wm. Beryff & Jn. Sterlyng, pl. Jn. Grymesdyche, gent., & w. *Eliz.*, sis. & heir of Tho. Palmer, gent., def. 12 mess., 6 tofts, 12 gdns. & 10 a. ar. in Colchester. Def. quitclaimed to pl. & the heirs of Wm. £80.

15. Eas. & Mich. And. Grey, pl. Wm. Barlee, esq., def. A moiety of manors of Leyer Barley *alias* Breteyne & Moulsham, a moiety of 20 mess., 12 cotts., 12 tofts, 10 dovecotes, 30 gardens, 10 orchards, 1,000 a. ar., 100 a. mw., 400 a. pa., 100 a. wd., 100 a. furze & heath & £6 rt. in Leer Barlee *alias* Bretten, Molsham, Salcotte Wigborough & Leermarnev, 13s. 4d. rt. from the manor of Barstable Haule, the advowson of the church of Tollshunt, & a moiety of the advowson of the church of Salcotte. And for this pl. gtd. the same to def. to hold of the chief lords without impeachment of waste, with remainder to Tho. Leventhorp, gent., & w. Dorothy & the heirs of their bodies, the heirs of the body of Tho. & the right heirs of Dorothy.

16. Wm. Wheler, pl. Wm. Hale & w. *Eliz.*, def. 1 mess. called 'Londons', 1 barn, 1 gdn., 1 orchard, 20 a. ar., 6 a. mw., 20 a. pa. & 6s. rt. in Burnam. And for this pl. gtd. the same to def. & the heirs of their bodies to hold of the chief lords, with remainder to the right heirs of Eliz.

17. Jn. Pole sen., pl. *Ralph* Alleyn, gent., Roger Manwood esq., & w. Dorothy, def. 1 mess., 1 gdn., 1 orchard, 32 a. ar., 4 a. mw. & 16 a. pa. in Thaxstede. 200 mks.

18. Rd. Hobson, pl. *Geo.* Monoux, gent., & w. Eliz., def. 2 mess., 2 gdns., 1 a. mw. & 18 a. pa. in Chynkeford *alias* Chyngford *alias* Chynkford Hatche. £105.

19. Eas. & Mich. Hy. Barrington & Tho. Sammes, pl. Rd. Rye *alias* Raye & w. *Joan*, def. 1 mess., 1 gdn., 1 orchard, 20 a. ar., 4 a. mw., 16 a. pa & 9 a. wd. in Woodham Mortimer & Woodham Water. Def. quitclaimed to pl. & the heirs of Hy. 100 mks.

20. Trin. & Mich. Rose Trott, wid., pl. *Geo.* Brewster & w. Joan, def. 1 mess., 1 cott., 30 a. ar., 24 a. mw., 4 a. pa. & 5 a. wood in Nasynge, common of pasture for 17 animals in Nasyng Mershe in Nasyng, a several fishery or sewer in Nasyng, & a third part of manor of Langrige. £200.

21. Edw. Laurence, pl. Tho. Mall & w. *Denise*, def. 7 a. pa. in Shenfeld. £40.

22. Jn. Salmon, pl. Tho. Phillippes & w. *Joan*, def. 1 barn, 1 gdn., 8 a. ar. & 2 a. mw. in Chelmysford & Spryngefeld. £40.

23. Jn. Kynge, pl. *Edw.* Scotte & w. Kath., def. 3 a. pa. in Little Wakeryng. £40.

24. Margt. Pole, wid., & Jn. Pole jun., pl. *Jn.* Pole sen., & w. Ellen, def. 1 mess., 1 gdn., 1 orchard, 12 a. ar., 2 a. mw. & 10 a. pa. in Toppesfeld. Def. quitclaimed to pl. & the heirs of Jn. 100 mks.

25. Eas. & Mich. Jn. Brocke, esq., pl. *Jn.* Hayward & w. Juliana, def. 4 mess., 3 cotts., 4 gdns., 200 a ar., 20 a. mw., 40 a. pa., 6 a. wd., 20 a. furze & heath, 40 a. fresh marsh & 20 a. salt marsh in Ramsey, Great Ocle, Austeyns, Tolkelones & Harwyche. £266.

26. Wm. Savage, pl. Rd. Archer & w. Anne, def. 1 mess., 2 tofts & 1 gdn. in Brentwood. £33.

27. And. Byatt, pl. Wm. Ellys, def. 1 mess., 2 barns, 2 tofts, 2 gdns., 2 orchards, 100 a. ar., 10 a. mw., 80 a. pa., 30 a. wd., 30 a. furze & heath & 10s. rt. in Great Henney, Little Henney, Bulmer, Twynsted & Midleton. £220.

28. Rd. Skynner, 'clothyer', pl. *Jn.* Cooke, citizen and 'haberdasser' of London, & w. Joan, def. 1 mess., 1 cott., 1 gdn. & ½ a. ar., in Branktre & Bockyng. £40.

29. Robt. Folkes, pl. Geo. Bacon, gent., & w. *Margt.*, def. 1 mess., 1 a. mw. & 18 a. pa. in Layer Bretten. £40.

30. Francis Walsyngham, esq., pl. Tho. Lyttyll, esq., & w. *Eliz.*, one of the daus. & heirs of Robt. Lytton, kit., decd., def. A third part of manor of Hopebrydgehall *alias* Hubbridge Hall & a third part of 2 mess., 10 tofts, 1 dovecote, 3 gdns., 100 a. ar., 20 a. mw., 61 a. pa., 32 a. wd. & £3 rt. in Great Okeley & Little Okeley. £86.

31   Trin. & Mich. Robt. Plome, pl. Wm. Walpole, esq., def. 4 a. ar. & 1 a. mw. in Great Gelham *alias* Great Yeldham. £23.

32.   Trin. & Mich. Wm. Cracherod, gent., pl. Wm. Walpole, esq., def. 4 a. ar., 1 a. mw. & 3 a. pa. in Great Gelham *alias* Great Yeldham & Toppesfeld. £30.

33.   Trin. & Mich. Robt. Legh, gent., & Tho. Harradyne, pl. Geo. Whyte, def. Manor of Runewell & 400 a. ar., 200 a. mw., 500 a. pa., 500 a. wd. & £12 rt. in Runwell & Retyngdon. Def. quitclaimed to pl. & the heirs of Robt. £750.

34.   Geoff. Lorchyn, pl. Humphrey Whyte, def. 1 mess., 1 gdn., 20 a. ar., 3 a. mw., 16 a. pa. & 6 a. wd. in Mountnes Gyng *alias* Gyng Mountnes. Def. quitclaimed to pl. & his heirs, with warranties against himself, Margt. his mother, & Geo. Whyte his brother, & their heirs. £80.

35.   Rd. Hasylwood, pl. Robt. Leeke & w. *Anne*, def. 1 mess., 1 curtilage & 1 gdn. in Ballidon by Sudbury. £40.

36.   Chris. Hyll, pl. Roger Marten, gent., def. 2 a. ar. & 1 windmill in Waterbelcham. And for this pl. gtd. to def. & his heirs a yearly rt. of 6s. 8d. from the same, payable at Michaelmas, with power of distraint.

37.   Eas. & Mich. Nich. Awgar & w. Agnes, pl. *Hugh* Apparrys & w. Jane, def. 1 mess., 1 curtilage, 1 gdn., 6 a. mw. & 10 a. pa. in Westham. Def. quitclaimed to pl. & the heirs of Nich. £80.

38.   Tho. Whitebred sen., pl. Jn. Yeldham *alias* Gelham & w. *Joan* & Rd. Yeldham *alias* Gelham & w. *Kath.*, def. 1 mess., 3 tofts, 4 gdns., 1 orchard, 2 a. mw. & 16 a. pa. in White Notley & Black Notley. £40.

39.   Trin. & Mich. Wm. Collen, pl. Chris. Larke & w. *Margt.* & Margery Ballerd, daus. & heirs of Tho. Ballerd, def. 6 a. ar. & 6 a. pa. in Brychanger. £40.

40.   Eas. 3 & 4 Philip & Mary & Mich. 2 Elizabeth. Francis Goldsmythe, esq., pl. Jn. Aleyn, esq., & w. *Eliz.* & *Jn.* Bowgham & w. Eliz., def. 1 mess., 1 barn, 1 dovecote, 100 a. ar., 6 a. mw. & 8 a. pa. in Ultynge & Hatfeld Peverell, the patronage of the advowson, church & rectory of Ultynge & the advowson of the vicarage of Ultynge. £150.

41.   Robt. Mordaunt, esq., pl. *Edm.* Mordaunt, esq., & w. Agnes, def. 20 a. mw. & 34 a. pa. in Wymbysshe & Thunderley. £140.

41A.   Rd. Denvolde & w. Eliz., pl. *Tho.* Ive, gent., & w. Rose, def. 1 mess., 20 a. ar., 10 a. mw., 40 a. pa. & 40 a. wd. in Reyleyghe & Thundersley. Def. quitclaimed to pl. & the heirs of Rd. £200.

42.   Wm. Tooke, esq., & Jn. Kettell, gent., pl. Wm. Barlee, def. Manor of Elsynham *alias* Elsingham & 40 mess., 20 tofts, 2 water-mills, 2 dovecotes, 40 gdns., 600 a. ar., 100 a. mw., 400 a. pa., 100 a. wd., 40 a. moor, 60 a. marsh & £6 rt. in Elsynham *alias* Elsingham, Stansted, Henham & Broxsted. Def. quitclaimed to pl. & the heirs of Wm. And for this pl. gtd. the same to def. to hold of the chief lords for life without impeachment of waste, with remainder to Rd. Barlee, esq., & Anne Barlee, one of the daus. & heirs apt. of def. & the heirs of their bodies, the heirs of the body of Anne, & the right heirs of Rd.

(43.)   (Rd. Weston, one of the justices of the Bench, & w. Margt., pl. *Jn.* Higham, esq., & w. Martha, def. Manor of Netteswell, 30 mess., 40 cotts., 1 water-mill, 40 gdns., 40 orchards, 1,000 a. ar., 120 a. mw., 600 a. pa., 60 a. wd., 300 a. furze & heath, 60 a. marsh, common of pasture & £20. rt. in Netteswell, Great Parndon, Little Parndon, Latton & Harlowe, & the advowson of the church of Netteswell. Def. quitclaimed to pl. & the heirs of Rd. £518.)

(Taken from the Note, the Foot being missing.)

CP25(2)/259/Mich. 2-3 Eliz.   DIVERS COUNTIES

6.   Trin. & Mich. Jn. Chauncy & Wm. Chauncy, gentlemen, pl. Tho. Raymond, gent., def. 2 mess., 200 a. ar., 30 a. mw., 30 a. pa. & 16 a. wd. in Hatfelde Brodoke & Little Holyngbury, co. Essex, & prop. in Herts., which Bridget Raymond, wid., holds for life. Pl. & the heirs of Jn. to hold the reversion of the chief lords. £240. — Essex, Herts.

7.   Trin. & Mich. Jn. Beverley, esq., & Chris. Twyselton, esqs., pl. Brian Stapilton, esq., son & heir apt. of Rd. Stapilton, kt., & w. *Eliz.*, def. 30 mess., 10 cotts., 20 tofts, 40 gdns., 30 orchards, 600 a. ar., 200 a. mw., 200 a. pa., 100 a. wd., 100 a. furze & heath

& 30s. rt. in Barkyng & Dagnam, co. Essex, and prop. in London. Def. quitclaimed to pl. & the heirs of Jn. And for this pl. gtd. the prop. in Essex to Brian & Eliz. & the heirs of Brian to hold of the chief lords. — Essex, London.

11. Jn. Goodey, pl. *Wm.* Goodwyn, citizen & mercer of London, & w. Margt., def. Prop. in Herts. & 16 a. ar. in Farneham, co. Essex. £200. — Herts., Essex.

12. Wm. Tooke, esq., & And. Graye, gent., pl. Rd. Barlee, esq., def. Prop. in Herts., & the manors of Sowthouse & Sparrowhawkesey *alias* Sparrowhawkesfee & 6 mess., 4 tofts, 1 dovecote, 10 gdns., 200 a. ar., 60 a. mw., 100 a. pa., 40 a. wd. & 40s. rt. in Great Waltham & Little Waltham, co. Essex. Def. quitclaimed to pl. & the heirs of Wm. And for this pl. gtd. the Essex prop. (the dovecote & gdns. not mentioned) to def. to hold for one week, with remainder to himself & w. Anne & his heirs, to hold of the chief lords. — Herts., Essex.

CP25(2)/126/1613   HILARY, 3 ELIZABETH   1561

1. Mich. & Hil. Wm. Harrys, pl. *Tho.* Jeffrey & w. Margery, def. 1 mess., 1 gdn. & 6 a. ar. in Spryngefelde. £40.

2. Mich. & Hil. Tho. Argall, esq., & w. Margt., pl. Ralph Sadler, kt., def. Manor of Walcombstowe Fraunces *alias* Lowhall & 40 mess., 20 tofts, 4 dovecotes, 60 gdns., 1,000 a. ar., 300 a. mw., 1,000 a. pa., 20 a. wd., 200 a. marsh, 100 a. furze & heath, £5 rt. & a free fishery in Walcombstowe with appurtenances in Walcombstowe Fraunces *alias* Lowhall. Def. quitclaimed to pl. & the heirs of Tho. £1,602.

3. Jn. Maye, pl. Roger Cowper, def. 1 mess. called 'a salt howse' in Harwich. £20.

4. Hy. Paynell, esq., & Wm. Methold, gent., pl. Francis Downes, esq., def. 1 mess., 1 toft, 5 a. ar., 2. a. mw., 10 a. pa., 140 a. wd. & 30 a. furze & heath called 'Kyrtons' in Stanwey & Berechurche. Def. quitclaimed to pl. & the heirs of Hy. £40.

5. Mich. & Hil. Jn. Webbe sen., pl. Jn. Yeldham *alias* Gelham & w. *Joan* & Rd. Yeldham *alias* Gellam & w. *Kath.*, def. 1 cott., 1 gdn., 10 a. ar. & 17 d. rt. in Bokkyng. £40.

6. Jn. Savage & Rd. Savage, pl. *Hy.* Denny, esq., & w. Honora, def. Manors of Claverhambury & Hallyfelde & 80 mess., 100 cotts., 20 tofts, 200 gdns., 200 orchards, 10 dovecotes, 80 barns, 5,000 a. ar., 3,000 a. mw., 6,000 a. pa., 2,000 a. wd., 5 a. furze & heath & £40 rt. in Waltham Holy Cross, Nasynge & Eppynge. Def. quitclaimed to pl. & the heirs of Jn. £1,360.

7. Eas. & Hil. Rd. Hubberd, gent., pl. Tho. Reymond, gent., def. 1 mess., 40 a. ar., 10 a. mw., 20 a. pa. & 10 a. wd. in Berchehanger & Stansted Mountychett, which Bridget Reymond, wid., holds for life. Pl. & his heirs to hold the reversion of the chief lords. 70 mks.

8. Jn. Tamworthe, esq., pl. *Edw.* Madyson, gent., & w. Dorothy, def. 1 mess., 1 orchard, 1 gdn., 2½ a. ar., 2 a. mw. & 12. a. pa. in Sandon. 100 mks.

9. Mich. & Hil. Francis Ram, pl. Tho. Lyncoln, def. 20 a. ar., & 4. a. mw. in Nevestocke. £40.

10. Mich. & Hil. Hugh Raven, pl. Jn. Thomas & w. *Joan*, def. 1 mess. & 1 gdn. in Cressyng. £20.

11. Mich. & Hil. Tho. Unwyn *alias* Onyon & Tho. Parke, pl. Alice Aleyn, wid., late the w. of Robt. Smyth *alias* Anneys, decd., def. 2 mess., 2 barns, 2 gdns., 2 orchards, 40 a. ar. & 12 a. pa. in Fynchyngfeld, Bumpsted at the Steeple *alias* Steple Bumpsted, Stamborn & Redeswell. Def. quitclaimed to pl. & the heirs of Tho. Unwyn. And for this pl. gtd. 1 mess., 1 barn, 1 gdn., 1 orchard & all the said tenements in Fynchyngfeld, Stamborn & Redeswell to def. to hold for 1 month with remainder to Robt. Smyth *alias* Anneys, her son & heir apt., & his heirs, to hold of the chief lords; & 1 mess., 1 barn, 1 gdn., 1 orchard & all the said tenements in Bumpsted at the Steeple to def. for 1 month with remainder to Jn. Smyth *alias* Anneys jun., one of her sons, & his heirs, to hold of the chief lords.

12. Mich. & Hil. Tho. Havers, pl. *Tho.* Baltrop *alias* Baltrippe & w. Anne, def. 1 orchard, 10 a. ar. & 1 a. mw. in the hamlet of Pledgden in the parish of Henham. £40.

13. Mich. & Hil. Wm. Browne, pl. *Wm.* Chysshull, esq., & w. Eliz. & Giles Chysshull, gent., def. 1 mess., 1 barn, 1 toft, 2 gdns., 2 orchards, 43 a. ar., 1 a. mw. & 1 a. pa. in

Little Berdefeld. And for this pl. gtd. to Wm. Chysshull & his heirs a yearly rt. of 41s. from the same, payable at the Annunciation & Michaelmas, with power of distraint.

14. Jn. Tamworthe, esq. pl. *Jn.* Dodyngton, gent., & Jn. Jackeson, def. 40 a. ar., 24 a. mw., 60 a. pa. & 12 a. wd. in Waltham Holycrose & Halyfeld. £180.

15. Mich. & Hil. Jn. Cryppes, pl. Jn. Garrard & w. *Christina* & Rd. Hewett & w. *Agnes*, def. 1 mess., 1 gdn. & 6 a. ar. in Salcote Wigbarowe & Tolson Knyghts. £20.

16. Jn. Hodge, pl. Tho. Perryn, def. 5 a. ar. in Crykkyshethe. £40.

17. Jn. Lytle & Anth. Jebbe, pl. Jas. Lytle & w. *Ellen*, def. 5 mess., 5 gdns., 40 a. ar., 20 a. mw. & 10 a. wd. in Barkyng & Daggenham. Def. quitclaimed to pl. & the heirs of Jn. And for this pl. gtd. the same to def. to hold of the chief lords for their lives, with remainder to the heirs of the body of Ellen by Jas. & the right heirs of Jas.

18. Mich. & Hil. Jn. Thurgood, pl. *Rd.* Kynge & w. Mary, def. 1 mess., 1 gdn., 60 a. ar., 20 a. pa. & 4 a. wd. in Mawdelyn Laver. £80.

19. Mich. & Hil. Edw. Solme, pl. *Edw.* Madyson & w. Dorothy, def. 1 mess., 1 gdn. & 7 a. ar. in Sandon. £40.

20. Wm. Nele, pl. Edw. Barrett, esq., def. 18 a. ar., 4 a. mw. & 6 a. pa. in Willinghale Spayne, which Isabel Cooke, wid., holds for life. Pl. & his heirs to hold the reversion of the chief lords. £40.

21. Robt. Thorpe, gent., & Hy. Skynner, pl. Wm. Clopton, esq., def. Manor of Newenham Hall *alias* Newnam Hall & 20 mess., 20 cotts., 20 gdns., 400 a. ar., 70 a. mw., 400 a. pa., 60 a. wd., 60 a. furze & heath & 100s. rt. in Asshedown *alias* Asshedon & Barklowe. Def. quitclaimed to pl. & the heirs of Robt. £600.

22. Mich. & Hil. Robt. Poynyerd, gent., pl. Wm. Rutter, gent., & w. Philippa & *Wm.* Barlee, gent., son & heir of Jn. Barlee, gent., decd., def. 40 a. ar. & 4 a. pa. in Claveryng. £85.

23. Mich. & Hil. Hy. Standyshe, pl. *Wm.* Haryson & w. Lettice, def. 1 mess., & 1 orchard in Waltham Holy Cross. £40.

24. Mich. & Hil. Wm. Holgate, pl. Wm. Rutter, gent., & w. Phillippa & *Wm.* Barlee, gent., son & heir of Jn. Barlee, gent., decd., def. 13 a. ar. & 1 a. pa. in Claveryng & Langley. £40.

CP25(2)/259/Hilary 3 Eliz.   DIVERS COUNTIES

6. Mich. & Hil. Jn. Throkmerton, esq., & Wm. Underehyll, gent., pl. Tho. Smyth, esq., *Jn.* Smyth & Hy. Smyth, gentlemen, def. A fourth part of the manor of West Tylburye & 6 mess., 2 cotts., 2 tofts, 1 windmill, 1 dovecote, 10 gdns., 300 a. ar., 100 a. mw., 300 a. pa., 40 a. wd., 400 a. furze & heath & £10. rt. in West Tylburye, & a fourth part of a ferry or passage across the river Thames called 'Tylburye Fery', co. Essex; & prop. in Gloucestershire. Def. quitclaimed to pl. & the heirs of Jn. And for this pl. gtd. the Essex prop. to Tho. to hold for life of the chief lords without impeachment of waste, with successive remainders to Jn. Smyth, Hy. Smyth & Grisogone Smyth & the heirs of their bodies & the right heirs of Tho. — Essex, Glos.

7. Wm. Cordell, kt., master of the rolls of Chancery, & Rd. Allyngton, esq., pl. *Jn.* Yorke, kt., & w. Anne, def. 1 mess., 2 gdns., 100 a. ar., 80 a. mw., 60 a. pa., 160 a. marsh & 30 a. furze & heath in Barkynge & Westham, co. Essex, & similar prop. in Wollwiche, co. Kent. Def. quitclaimed to pl. & the heirs of Wm. £1,700. — Essex, Kent.

259/Hilary 3 Eliz.   1561

13. Humphrey Radcliff, kt., & Jn. Radcliff, kt., pl. Hy. Radcliff, kt., & w. *Honora*, def. Prop. in co. Southampton, & the manor of Wyckford & 20 mess., 10 cotts., 30 gdns., 30 orchards, 20 barns, 4 dovecotes, 200 a. ar., 100 a. mw., 200 a. pa., 100 a. marsh, 200 a. wd. & 40s. rt. in Wyckford, co. Essex. Def. quitclaimed to pl. & the heirs of their bodies, to hold of the chief lords, with remainder to the heirs of the body of Honora & the heirs of Hy. — Southampton, Essex.

1. Rd. Barkar, pl. Rd. Hansharte & w. *Frances*, def. 1 mess., 40 a. ar., 40 a. mw., 40 a. pa. & 15d. rt. in Wormyngford. £80.

2. Wm. Cotton, esq., pl. *Wm.* Dawson & w. Joan & Jane Purcas, def. 7 a. ar. & 3 a. pa. in Shalforde. £20.

3. Hil. & Eas. Wm. Humfrey & Nich. Humfrey, pl. Nich. Fanne, def. 1 barn, 20 a. ar., 10 a. mw. & 3 a. pa. in Thaxsted. Def. quitclaimed to pl. & the heirs of Wm. £100.

4. Eliz. Ponder, wid., pl. *Wm.* Aylett & w. Margt., def. Two sevenths of 3 mess., 100 a. ar., 20 a. mw., 20 a. pa., 10 a. wd. & 10s. rt. in Little Waltham, Great Leghes & Wytham. £40.

5. Robt. Kyng, pl. *Jn.* Colyn & w. *Joan*, def. 24 a. ar. in High Laver. 20 mks.

6. Rd. Archer, pl. *Walter* Garson & w. Eliz., def. 8 a. ar. & 4 a. mw. in Theydon Garnon. £40.

7. Jn. Bonar, pl. *Wm.* Norman & w. Joan, def. 7 a. ar., 3 a. mw., & 1 a. wd. in Legh. £40.

8. Jn. Pole jun., pl. Robt. Pole & w. *Margery*, def. 2 mess., 2 gdns., 2 orchards, 50 a. ar., 4. a. mw., 10 a. pa. & 12s. rt. in Thaxstede & Hennham. And for this pl. gtd. the same to def. & the heirs of Robt., to hold of the chief lords.

9. Jn. Dowced, pl. *Jn.* Colyn & w. Joan, def. 25 a. ar. & ½ a. pa. in High Laver. £40.

10. Hil. & Eas. Wm. Aylett, pl. Edm. Heygate, gent., & w. *Dorothy*, def. 80 a. fresh marsh & 10 a. salt marsh & two weirs in the island of Walletts in the parishes of Estwood & Pryklewell *alias* Prytwell. £200.

11. Edw. Madyson, pl. *Jn.* Tamworthe, esq., & w. *Cristina*, def. 5 a. mw. & 19 a. pa. in Sandon. £40.

12. Hil. & Eas. Rd. Palmer, pl. Rd. Huberd, gent., def. 13 a. ar. & 5 a. pa. in Stanstede Montfychett. £40.

13. Tho. Aylott, pl. Wm. Lyndesell, def. 1 mess., 1 gdn., 5 a. ar. & 2 a. wd. in Macchyn. £40.

14. Hy. Tayler, pl. Jn. Boner & w. *Margt.*, def. 7 a. pa. & 1 a. wd. in South Hannyngfelde. £15.

15. Wm. Levett, pl. *Jas.* Parker & w. Margery, def. A moiety of 1 mess., 1 gdn., 15 a. ar., 14 a. pa. & 3s. 6d. rt. in Althorne, Maylande & Southmynster. £40.

16. Tho. Byrley, pl. *Jas.* Turpyn & w. Eliz., def. 2 mess. & 2 gdns. in Walden. £20.

17. Edw. Elryngton, pl. *Rd.* Cutts, gent., Francis Knyghton, gent., & w. Kath., def. Manor of Bonehawte & 20 mess., 20 cotts., 20 gdns., 200 a. ar., 40 a. mw., 100 a. pa., 40 a. wd., 40 a. furze & heath & 10s. rt. in Wycken. £200.

18. Mich. & Eas. Wm. Grygges sen., pl. Geo. Felton, esq., def. 3½ a. mw. in Pentlowe. £40.

19. Jn. Franke sen., pl. *Wm.* Aylett & w. Margt., & Jn. Francke jun. & w. Thomasina, def. Two sevenths of 3 mess., 100 a. ar., 20 a. mw., 20 a. pa., 10 a. wd. & 10s. rt. in Little Waltham, Great Leghes & Wytham. £40.

20. Jn. Quedwell, pl. *Robt.* Haywarck & w. Anne, def. 1 mess., 40 a. ar., 6 a. pa. & 4 a. wd. in Twynsted. £40.

21. Jn. Pannell, pl. *Jn.* Smyth, esq., & Jn. Barton & w. Alice, def. 1 mess., 20 a. ar., 10 a. mw., 17 a. pa., 4 a. wd. & 19d. (rt.) in Foxherd. £80.

22. Tho. Adams, pl. Jn. Burneham & w. *Agnes*, def. 1 mess., 1 barn & 1 gdn. in Stratford Langethorne in the parish of Westham. £40.

23. Wm. Rutter & Wm. Haywood, pl. Tho. Hawlyn & w. *Joan*, def. A moiety of 10 a. ar. & 5 a. pa. in Herverd Stocke. Def. quitclaimed to pl. & the heirs of Wm. Rutter. And for this pl. gtd. the same to Tho. for one month with remainder to Joan now the w. of Wm. Tybbolde, to hold of the chief lords.

24. Hil. & Eas. Ralph Pyke, pl. Geo. Manfeld, def. 14 a. ar., 4 a. fresh marsh & 9s. 7½d. rt. in Little Shoebery *alias* North Shoebery & Great Wakeryng. £53.

25. Martin Bowes, esq., pl. *Jn.* Barnardiston, esq., & w. Joan, def. Manor of Passelows & 60 a. ar., 40 a. mw., 100 a. pa., 10 a. wd., £4 rt. & a rt. of 2 cocks, 6 hens, 4 capons, 100 apples (*volemorum*) & 2 red roses in Dagenham & Barkyng. £420.

26. Rd. Lucye, gent., & Tho. Parke, pl. *Jn.* Mordaunte, kt., & w. Joan, def. Manor of Wautons *alias* Waltons & 2 mess., 2 barns, 4 gdns., 1 orchard, 300 a. ar., 55 a. mw. & 200 a. pa. in Bumpsted at the Steeple *alias* Bumpsted, Byrdebroke & Sturmere. Def. quitclaimed to pl. & the heirs of Rd. £440.

27. Rd. Bankes, pl. Wm. Lawrence & w. *Margt.*, def. 1 mess., 1 gdn. & 1 orchard in Terlyng. 20 mks.

28. Tho. Hare, pl. Augustine Hall & w. *Agnes*, def. 1 mess. & 1 gdn. in Legh, which Wm. Morant & w. Clara hold for her life. Pl. & his heirs to hold the reversion of the chief lords. £40.

29. Hil. & Eas. Mathias Bradbury, esq., pl. Wm Barlee, esq., & *Tho.* Leventhorp, esq., & w. Dorothy, def. Manor of Wyckyn *alias* Wyckyn Bonant & 8 mess., 10 cotts., 8 tofts, 4 dovecotes, 10 gdns., 10 orchards, 500 a. ar., 100 a. mw., 200 a. pa., 40 a. wd., 100 a. furze & heath & 8s. rt. in Wyckyn *alias* Wyckyn Bonant, & the advowson of the church of Wyckyn. And for this pl. gtd. a yearly rt. of £24 from the same, payable at the Annunciation & Michaelmas, to Wm. for life, with a penalty of 40s. whenever it may be 40 days in arrear, with power of distraint; & after the death of Wm. a similar rt. of £22 to Tho. & his heirs, with penalty as above.

30. Tho. Cock, pl. *Wm.* Harres, esq., & w. Joan, def. 4 mess., 4 gdns., 160 a. ar., 24 a. mw., 160 a. pa., 20 a. wd. & 200 a. marsh in Great Horkeley, Maldon, Fulnes, Great Wakeryng, Little Wakeryng, Stowe, Norton & Purley. And for this pl. gtd. the same to def. & the heirs of bodies, to hold of the chief lords, with remainder to the heirs of the body of Wm., the heirs of the body of Joan, & the right heirs of Wm.

31. Tho. Luter, pl. Jn. Paschall & *Wm.* Paschall, gent., & Anne w. of the said Wm., def. 1 mess., 40 a. ar., 12 a. mw. & 100 a. pa. in the parishes of Fange, Pytsey, Newingdon & Bartelesdon. £100.

32. Hil. & Eas. Jn. Garrard, pl. Jn. Gelham *alias* Yeldham and w. *Joan* & Rd. Gelham *alias* Yeldham & w. *Kath.*, def. 1 mess., 1 barn, 2 gdns., 2 orchards & 30 s. ar. in Cressyng. 100 mks.

33. Arthur Harrys, pl. Hy. Radclyff, kt., & w. *Honora*, def. Manor of Wyckford & 20 mess., 10 cotts., 30 gdns., 30 orchards, 20 barns, 4 dovecotes, 200 a. ar., 100 a. mw., 200 a. pa., 100 a. marsh, 200 a. wd. & 40s. rt. in Wykeford. £280.

34. Tho. Pullyver, pl. *Robt.* Stepneth, gent., & w. Joan, def. 6 a. ar. in Westham. £40.

35. Hil. & Eas. Edw. Jackman, pl. *Tho.* Powle, esq., & w. Jane & Agatha Rychards, wid., def. Manor of Hackford *alias* Hacton & 3 mess., 1 dovecote, 2 gdns., 1 orchard, 50 a. ar., 20 a. mw., 80 a. pa., 20 a. wd., 10 a. marsh & 10s. rt. in Dagnam, Hornechurche & Upmyster. £340.

36. Robt. Barnard, pl. Nich. Dallan, def. 1 mess., 100 a. ar., 20 a. mw., 20 a. pa., 40 a. wd. & 20s. rt. in Braynktrye & Bockyng. 260 mks.

37. Tho. Stamer, pl. Robt. Wheeler & w. *Joan*, def. 1 mess., 1 gdn. & 2 a. ar. in Wodham Ferys. £12.

38. Wm. Eve, pl. Rd. Benson, gent., def. 1 mess., 160 a. ar., 20 a. mw., 20 a. pa. & 6 a. wd. in Writle, Roxwell, Seint Jeames Chycknall, Seynt Mary Chickenall, Trentewell *alias* Smaly Chyckenall. £40.

39. Wm., marquess of Winchester, treasurer of England. Rd. Sackevyle, kt., under treasurer of the court of Exchequer, & Walter Myldemay, kt., chancellor of the said court, pl. Jn., lord Darcy, def. Manors of Wigborowe, Lee Wyke & Wyers Hall *alias* Aula Guidonis & 20 mess., 20 gdns., 1,000 a. ar., 100 a. mw. & 300 a. pa. in Wigborowe, Lee Wyke & Wyers Hall *alias* Aula Guidonis. Def. quitclaimed to pl. & the heirs of the marquess. £600.

40. Jn. Hewttt *alias* Lewter, pl. *Jn.* Colyn & w. Joan, def. 1 mess., 1 barn, 1 cott., 1 orchard, 1 gdn., 70 a. ar., 5 a. mw. & 5 a. pa. in Litell Laver. £40.

41. Hil. & Eas. Launcellet Spere, Rd. Barker, Edw. Holton, Tho. Harryson, Rd. Walter, Wm. Colman, Robt. Colman, Jn. Gente, Tho. Lorkyn, Jas. Malle, Robt. Malle, Rd. Webbe, Jn. Webbe, Jn. Barker, Tho. Barker, Geo. Holton, Jn. Holton, Tho. Holton jun., Jas. Smyth & Jn. Gararde, pl. *Tho.* Holton sen. & Jn. Malle, def. 1 mess., 2 gdns., 10 a. ar., 4 a. mw. & 6 a. pa. in Peldon. Def. quitclaimed to pl. & the heirs of Launcellet. £40.

42. Hil. & Eas. Jas. Bacon, citizen & 'ffysshemonger' of London, & Bart. Kempe, gent., pl. *Tho.* Hales & w. Eliz., def. Manor of le Lyon & 1 mess., 40 a. ar., 30 a. mw., 70 a. pa., 20 a. wd. & 53. 4d. rt. in Hornechurch. Def. quitclaimed to pl. & the heirs of Jas. £220.

43. Edw. Bell, gent., pl. Jn. Raynberd & w. *Eliz.* & Wm. Haywood & w. Joan, def. 1 mess., 1 gdn. & 2 a. ar. in Harvard Stock. £33.

44. Hil. & Eas. Jn. Ingrame & w. Eliz., pl. *Jn.* Hylton, gent., & w. Mary, def. 4 mess., 4 tofts, 4 gdns., 10 a. ar., 10 a. mw. & 20 a. pa. in Stratford Langhorne & Westham. Def. quitclaimed to pl. & the heirs of Jn. £100.

45. Robt. Stephneth, gent., pl. *Steph.* Tyrrell, gent., & w. Anne, def. 1 mess., 1 barn, 1 stable, 1 gdn., 1 orchard, 40 a. ar., 20 a. pa. & 6 a. wd. in Eastham. £80.

46. Rd. Cock, pl. *Wm.* Harrys, esq., & w. Joan, def. 10 a. ar., 4 a. mw. & 20 a. pa. in Prytwell. £40.

47. Hilary Johnson, pl. *Wm.* Berye & w. Margt., one of the daus. & co-heirs of Alice Squyer, decd., dau. & heir of Jn. Strogyll jun., decd., def. A fourth part of 1 mess. & 1 gdn. in Coggeshale. 10 mks.

48. Robt. Salmond, pl. *Robt.* Sayer & w. Margt., def. 1 mess. & 1 gdn. in Legh. £40.

49. Mich. & Eas. Rd. Pikering & Wm. Russer, gent., pl. Hy. Britton, def. 1 mess., 1 gdn., 100 a. ar., 20 a. mw., 200 a. pa. & 30 a. wd. in Great Walden, Little Walden, Ashedon & Bartloe. Def. quitclaimed to pl. & the heirs of Rd. 400 mks.

CP25(2)/259/Easter 3 Eliz.   DIVERS COUNTIES

9. Robt. Fylmer, gent., pl. Hamnet Bressye & w. Etheldreda & Tho. Rede & w. *Dorothy*, def. 1 mess. called 'Tychemarshe', 1 gdn., 20 a. ar., 20 a. mw., 40 a. pa. & 10 a. wd. in Chygwell, co. Essex, & prop. in Surr. And for this pl. gtd. the same to Hamnet & Etheldreda to hold of the chief lords for their lives, with remainder to Nich. Symson, son of Etheldreda, & his heirs. — Essex, Surr.

17. Hil. & Eas. Augustine Sadler, pl. Hy. Wyner & w. *Mary*, one of the daus. & heirs of Robt. Long, decd., Wm. Meredeth & w. *Martha*, another of the daus. & heirs, & Roger Sadler & w. *Magdalen*, another of the daus. & heirs, def. 9 mess., 8 cotts., 1 dovecote, 1 windmill, 8 gdns., 8 orchards, 701 a. ar., 200 a. mw., 100 a. pa., 109 a. wd., 357 a. marsh, 60 a. furze & heath & £8 13s. rt. in Westurrocke, Duddynghurste, Harmyrys, Orsed, Styfford, Graces, Aulflye & Goorys, & the ferry or passage of Purfleit in Purfleit, co. Essex; & prop. in Salop & Surr. And for this pl. gtd. 4 mess., 4 cotts., 1 windmill, 4 gdns., 4 orchards, 353 a. ar., 100 a. mw., 50 a. pa., 54 a. wd., 173 a. marsh, 30 a. furze & heath, £4 8s. 4d. rt. and a moiety of 1 mess. in the said towns, parcel of the Essex prop. & parcel of the manor of Westhurrocke *alias* Westhall in Westhurrocke *alias* le Vyneyard, co. Essex, to Wm. & Martha & the heirs of their bodies, to hold of the chief lords, with remainder to the right heirs of Martha; & 4 mess., 4 cotts., 1 dovecote, 4 gdns., 4 orchards, 348 a. ar., 100 a. mw., 50 a. pa., 54 a. wd., 184 a. marsh, 30 a. furze & heath, £4 4s. 8d. rt. & a moiety of 1 mess., residue of the same, & the ferry to Roger & Magdalen & the heirs of their bodies, to hold of the chief lords, with remainder to the right heirs of Magdalen; & the prop. in Salop & Surr. to Hy. & Mary & the heirs of their bodies, with remainder to the right heirs of Mary. — Salop, Essex, Surr.

CP25(2)/126/1615   TRINITY, 3 ELIZABETH   1561

1. Jn. Master, pl. *Hy.* Northey of London, gent., & w. Eliz., def. 2 mess., 60 a. ar., 40 a. mw., 60 a. pa., 10 a. wd. & 20s. rt. in Ginge Mounteney & Toby. £38.

2. Rd. Gyver, pl. Geo. Roper & w. *Agnes*, one of the daus. & co-heirs of Jn. Fytche jun., decd., def. 12 a. ar. in Little Sampford. 40 mks.

3.   Rd. Stowers, pl. *Francis* Jobson, kt., & w. Eliz., def. 2 mess., 3 tofts, 2 gdns., 8 a. ar., 7 a. mw., 6 a. pa. & 5 a. moor in Lexden. £40.

4.   Geo. Crymble, pl. *Tho.* Frebarne & w. Eliz., def. 1 mess., 1 gdn., 20 a. ar., 3 a. mw., 10 a. pa. & 15 a. salt marsh in Great Stambridge. £100.

5.   Jn. Josselyn, gent., pl. Tho. Josselyn, esq., & w. *Frances*, def. Manor of Faytes & Wades & 6 mess., 6 gdns., 300 a. ar., 40 a. mw., 100 a. pa., 40 a. wd. & 30s. rt. in Lawford, Dedham, Great Ardley & Myle End *alias* Myland by Colchester. And for this pl. gtd. the same to Tho. & his heirs, to hold of the chief lords.

6.   Tho. Frenche, pl. *Tho.* Josselyn, kt., & w. Dorothy, def. 1 mess., 1 gdn., 1 orchard, 160 a. ar., 20 a. mw., 40 a. pa. & 20 a. wd. in Hatfeld Regis *alias* Hatfeld Brodeoke & Great Canfeld. £200.

7.   Wm. Fytche, gent., pl. Tho. Wyseman, gent., & w. Anne & *Robt.* Wyseman, gent., & w. Mary, def. 1 mess. & 260 a. ar. called 'Moche Canfeld Parke' in Great Canfeld, Takeley, Little Canfeld & Hatfeld Regis. £200.

8.   Jn. Farewell & Roger Gysse, pl. *Jasper* Warner, gent., & w. Antonia, def. 6 mess., 6 tofts, 8 gdns., 10 orchards, 6 barns, 1 dovecote, 80 a. ar., 15 a. mw., 200 a. pa. & 50 a. wd. in North Wokynton *alias* Northukkynton, Suth Wokynton & Upmynster. Def. quitclaimed to pl. & the heirs of Jn. And for this pl. gtd. the same to def & the heirs male of the body of Jasper, with remainder to Roger Coyse, gent., & w. Joan, sis. of Jasper, & the heirs male of her body, & the right heirs of Joan, to hold of the chief lords.

9.   Hy. Baker, pl. *Jn.* Bacheler & w. Agnes, def. 2 mess., 2 gdn., 2 orchards, 10 a. ar., 10 a. mw., 80 a. pa., 2 a. wd., 5 a. fresh marsh & 3s. rt. in Canoudon. £100.

CP25(2)/126/1616   MICHAELMAS, 3 AND 4 ELIZABETH   1561

1.   Hy. Barker, pl. Wm. Kyng & w. *Clemencia*, def. 1 mess., 1 gdn. & 1 orchard in Great Dunmowe. £20.

2.   Rd. Weston, one of the justices of the Bench, & w. Margt., pl. *Jn.* Higham, & w. Martha, def. Manor of Netteswell & 30 mess., 40 cotts., 1 watermill, 40 gdns., 40 orchards, 1,000 a. ar., 120 a. mw., 600 a. pa., 60 a. wd., 300 a. furze & heath, 60 a. marsh, common of pasture & £20 rt. in Netteswell, Great Parndon, Little Parndon, Latton & Harlowe, & the advowson of the church of Netteswell. Def. quitclaimed to pl. & the heirs of Rd. £518.

3.   Hy. Warde & w. Mary, pl. Tho. Byrde & w. *Dorothy*, def. 1 mess., 1 gdn., 1 orchard, 80 a. ar., 2 a. mw. & 12 a. pa. in Claveryng. Def. quitclaimed to pl. & the heirs of Mary. £40.

4.   Eas. & Mich. Jn. Coker, pl. *Wm.* Harres, esq., & w. Joan, def. 1 mess., 70 a. ar. & 4 a. mw. in Stowe Marres, Canudon & Southchurche. 160 mks.

5.   Tho. Sampford, pl. Rd. Burbage, gent., & w. *Anne*, def. A moiety of 1 mess., 70 a. ar., 6 a. mw., 6 a. pa., & 2 a. wd. in Willingale Doo, Shellowe Bowells & Barnars Rothing. 80 mks.

6.   Tho. Sampford, pl. Tho. Bradlaw *alias* Jacobb & w. *Margery*, def. A moiety of 1 mess., 1 gdn., 140 a. ar., 10 a. mw., 20 a. pa., 2 a. wd. & 10s. rt. in Willingall Spayne & Willingall Doo. £80.

7.   Jas. Pargeter, gent., pl. *Jn.* Gosnall & w. Anne, def. A moiety of 1 mess. called 'Farnehall', & 30 a. ar., 8 a. mw., 7 a. pa., 3 a. wd. & 12d. rt. in Barkyng in Argilla. 130 mks.

8.   Kenelm Throckmerton, esq., & Jn. Pavyatt, pl. *Rd.* Weston, one of the justices of the Bench, & w. Margt., def. Manor of Garnetts *alias* Garmets & Markis in Highester *alias* High Easter, High Rothing *alias* High Roding & Great Dunmowe, which Mary Gate, wid., holds for life. Pl. & the heirs of Kenelm to hold the reversion of the chief lords. £483.

9.   Wm. Pascall, gent., & w. Anne, pl. *Robt.* Smyth, esq., & w. Joan, def. Manor of Prestons & 3 mess., 4 tofts, 2 barns, 1 windmill, 1 dovecote, 4 gdns., 4 orchards, 300 a. ar., 30 a. mw., 200 a. pa., 20 a. wd., 100 a. furze & heath & 21s. rt. in Sowthannynge-felde, Westhannyngefelde & Harvardstoke. Def. quitclaimed to pl. & the heirs of Wm. 400 mks.

10. Trin. & Mich. Jn. Cooke, gent., pl. *Rd.* Geslyng, gent., & w. Anne, def. 3 mess., 3 gdns., 1 orchard, 5 a. ar. & 8 a. pa. in Rayleygh. £40.

11. Trin. & Mich. Jn. Cooke, gent., pl. Rd. Gilbart & w. *Dorothy*, def. 2 mess., 1 curtilage, 1 barn, 2 gdns., 10 a. ar., 4 a. mw. & 6 a. pa. in Raylegh. £40.

12. Walter Newman, pl. *Wm.* Gaseley & w. Etheldreda *alias* Awdrea, def. 1 mess. & 1 gdn. in Walden. £80.

13. Edw. Benton, pl. Anne Newton, wid., def. A moiety of 1 mess., 1 barn, 1 gdn., 22 a. ar. & 3 a. mw. in Harlow. £40.

14. Leonard Sandell, gent., pl. *And.* Corbett, kt., & w. Jane, def. Manor of Woodham Mortymer & 10 mess., 6 cotts., 1 dovecote, 500 a. ar., 100 a. mw., 500 a. pa., 200 a. furze & heath, 300 a. wd. & 12s. rt. in Woodham Mortymer, Woodham Water, Purleigh, Halesleigh *alias* Haseley, Studleigh Grene, Ronsell, Danburye, Bykenaker, Boreham & Little Badowe, & the advowson of the church of Woodham Mortymer. £220.

15. Tho. Stamer, pl. Rd. Peycock & w. *Grace*, def. A moiety of 1 mess., 1 barn, 4 a. ar. & 20d. rt. in Reylegh. £40.

16. Eas. & Mich. Jn. Ryvett, pl. Wm. Wood & w. *Joan*, def. 2½ a. ar. in Thoryngton. £20.

17. Jn. Pyke, pl. Tho. Kellogge *alias* Kellocke & w. *Marion*, def. 2 mess., 2 barns, 2 stables, 2 gdns. & 2 orchards in Malden. £40.

18. Rd. Weston, esq., & w. Margt., pl. Kenelm Throkmerton, esq., def. 80 a. pa. called 'Dunmowe' *alias* 'Mutche Donmowe Parke' in Great Donmowe. Def. quitclaimed to pl. & the heirs of Rd. £60.

19. Hil. & Mich. Robt. Mylborn, pl. *Robt.* Skelton & w. Margt., def. 1 mess., 1 curtilage & 1 gdn. in Brentwood. £40.

20. Trin. & Mich. Law Cookson, pl. *Barnard* Hampton, esq., & w. Kath., def. Manor of Grynsted & 2 a. ar., 100 a. mw., 4 mess., 300 a. pa., 60 a. wd. & 100s. rt. in Grynsted, Colchester & Pentryce. And for this pl. gtd. to def. & the heirs of Barnard a yearly rt. of £70 from the same, payable at Michaelmas & the Annunciation, with power of distraint.

21. Hy. Aylett, pl. *Jn.* Aylett & w. Agnes, def. 12 a. ar. & 2 a. mw. in Whyte Rothyng. £10.

22. Robt. Turner, pl. *Rd.* Lincoln & Wm. Mawter & w. Agnes, def. 1 mess. & 1 gdn. in Brentwood. £40.

23. Bart. Averell, gent., pl. *Robt.* Wade & w. Margt., def. 20 a. ar. & 20 a. pa. in Southmynster. £40.

24. Wm. Peter, kt., pl. *Jas.* Nuttyng & w. Agnes, def. 1 mess., 1 curtilage, 1 barn, 1 gdn., 1 orchard, 10 a. ar. & 10 a. pa. in Mountnesyng *alias* Gyngemountney. £40.

25. Jn. Johnson, pl. *Jn.* Patryck & w. Jane, def. Manor of Hethe Place *alias* Amors & 1 gdn., 80 a. ar., 2 a. mw., 40 a. pa., 4 a. wd., 60 a. furze & heath & 20s. rt. in Orsed & Chaldwell. 160 mks.

26. Tho. Kent, pl. Tho. Freman & w. *Agnes*, Tho. Peyke & w. *Joan*, def. 50 a. ar. in Westylbery. £40.

27. Wm. Walker, gent., pl. Wm. Fylde & w. *Kath.*, def 8 a. ar. & 6 a. pa. in Langenho & Westmersey. £40.

28. Robt. Wryght, pl. Jn. Kempe & w. *Agnes*, def. 1 mess., 1 gdn. & 2 a. mw. in Navestoke. £40.

29. Robt. Spryng & w. Joan, pl. Jn. Kent, def. 1 mess., 2 barns, 2 gdns., 56 a. ar., 10 a. mw. & 10 a. pa. in Tylburye by Redeswell, Beauchamp Sancti Pauli, Great Gelham *alias* Great Yeldham & Little Gelham *alias* Little Yeldham. Def. quitclaimed to pl. & the heirs of Robt. 100 mks.

30. Jn. Lawoodd, pl. *Justinian* Johnson & w. Anne, def. 30 a. ar. & 30 a. pa. in Styfford. £40.

CP25(2)/259/Mich. 3–4 Eliz.   DIVERS COUNTIES

4.   Robt. Gurdon sen., esq., & Robt. Gurdon jun., gent., pl. *Wm.* Smythe, gent., & w. Alice, def. 3 mess., 60 a. ar., 10 a. mw., 40 a. pa. & 6 a. wd. in Langham, Ardeley & Dedham, co. Essex; & prop. in Suff. Def. quitclaimed to pl. & the heirs of Robt. jun. £80. – Essex. Suff.

6.   Trin. & Mich. Lewis Stucley, esq., pl. *Tho.* Stucley, esq., & w. Anne, def. 2 mess., 1 barn, 3 gdns., 2 orchards, 50 a. ar., 8 a. mw. & 10 a. pa. in Waltehampstowe & Highambenstede, co. Essex; & prop. in London & Mdx. £1,486. – London, Essex. Mdx.

CP25(2)/126/1617   HILARY, 4 ELIZABETH   1562

1.   Mich. & Hil. Tho. Hare & Robt. Cuttell, pl. Jn. Fowle, def. 2 mess., 2 gdns., 1 orchard, 10 a. ar., 3 a. mw. & 7 a. pa. in Lygh. Def. quitclaimed to pl. & the heirs of Tho. 100 mks.

2.   Jn. Salmon, pl. Tho. Phillipes & w. *Joan*, def. 2 mess. & 2 gdns. in Chelmysford. £40.

3.   Nich. Dryver, pl. Anth. Alleyn & w. *Eliz.*, def. 3 mess., 1 barn, 1 orchard, 12 a. ar. & 8 a. pa. in Henham. £60.

4.   Mich. & Hil. Jn. Dodyngton, gent., & Wm. Nele, gent., pl. *Hy.* Denney, esq., & w. Honora, def. 3 mess., 10 cotts., 5 dovecotes, 1,200 a. ar., 540 a. mw., 2,000 a. pa., 300 a. wd. & £6 rt. in Nasyng, Waltham Holy Cross, Upshere, Halyfelde, Eppyng, Sewardyston & Roydon. Def. quitclaimed to pl. & the heirs of Jn. £3,360.

5.   Mich. & Hil. Geo. Gates, pl. *Tho.* Scott & w. Eliz., def. 8 a. a. in Estwood. £40.

6.   Mich. & Hil. Jn. Goodwyn, esq., pl. *Chris.* Edmonds, esq., & w. Dorothy, def. A fourth part of the manors of Manytree, Shedynghoo *alias* Chedynghoo, Oldhall *alias* Oldehall, Newhall & Abbottes *alias* Edlynges, a fourth part of 60 mess., 20 cotts., 10 tofts, 4 water-mills, 1,000 a. ar., 200 a. mw., 1,000 a. pa., 400 a. wd., 600 a. furze & heath & £20 rt. in Manytree, Shedyngho *alias* Chedynghoo, Oldhall *alias* Oldehall, Newhall, Abbottes *alias* Edlynges, Mystley, Bradfeld, Colchestre, Stanwaye, Wrabney, Wykes & 'Our Lady in the Otes', a fourth part of the rectory & church of Bradfeld & tithes of Bradfeld, & a fourth part of the advowsons of the church of Mystley & vicarage of Bradfeld. £230.

7.   Wm. Lynne, pl. Wm. Waldegrave, esq., def. 2 mess., 2 barns, 2 tofts, 2 curtilages, 2 gdns., 60 a. ar., 12 a. mw., 18 a. pa. & 1 a. wd. in Whethermondford, Bures St. Mary, Bures at the Mount, Great Teye & Chapell Parishe. And for this pl. gtd. to def. & his heirs a yearly rt. of £4 18s. from the same, payable at Easter & Michaelmas, with power of distraint.

8.   Mich. & Hil. Geo. Nicholls, esq., & Nich. Ereswell, pl. Jn. Batemen & w. *Joan*, def. 1 mess. in Walden. Def. quitclaimed to pl. & the heirs of Geo. £20.

9.   Law. Porter, pl. *Tho.* Sampforde & w. Agnes, def. 1 mess., 1 barn, 1 gdn., 1 orchard & 90. a. ar. in Willyngale Dooe. £60.

10.   Wm. Clarke, pl. *Wm.* Morrell & w. Lucy, def. 1 mess., 1 orchard, 1 gdn. & 2 a. pa. in Matchyng. £40.

11.   Mich. & Hil. Wm. Marche, pl. Hy. Smythe, def. 1 mess., 1 gdn., 4 a. ar., 2 a. mw. & 4 a. pa. in Pouls Belcham. £40.

12.   Mich. & Hil. Rd. Sparke, pl. Percival Sheale & w. *Joan*, def. A moiety of 1 rood ar. & 1 a. mw. in Newport Ponde & Wydyngton. £40.

13.   Rd. Ryche, kt., lord Ryche, & Robt. Ryche, kt., pl. *Wm.* Harres, esq., & w. Joan, def. Manors of Westwykehall, Estwyke & Baynards & 6 mess., 200 a. ar., 100 a. mw., 200 a. pa., 40 a. wd, 1,000 a. marsh & £6 13s. 4d. rt. in Burneham. Def. quitclaimed to pl. & the heirs of Robt. £856.

14.   Mich. & Hil. Jn. Bateman, pl. Tho. Boyton & w. *Agnes*, def. 1 mess. in Walden. £40.

15.   Eas. 2 Eliz. & Hil. 4 Eliz. Steph. Craske, citizen & vintner of London, pl. *Rd.* Crompton, gent., & w. Anne, def. 2 mess., 2 gdns. & 4 a. pa. called 'Horse Crofte' in Colchester & Myleende. 130 mks.

16. Mich. & Hil. Robt. More, pl. Jn. Crowche, def. 1 mess. in Walden, which Geo. Whyte & w. Alice hold for her life. Pl. & his heirs to hold the reversion of the chief lords. £80.

17. Wm. Stonerd, pl. Rd. Benson, gent., def. 20 a. ar., 3 a. mw. & 2 a. wd. in Chycknall St. James, Chycknall St. Mary (and) Chycknall Trenchefoyle *alias* Smelie. £40.

18. Mich. & Hil. Jn. Evans, pl. *Wm.* Waldegrave, esq., & Wm. Sidey jun., gent., def. 100 a. ar., 10 a. mw., 40 a. pa., 10 a. alder & 10 a. wd. in Tendryng. And for this pl. gtd. the same to Wm. Sidey to hold from Michaelmas last for 40 years, at a yearly rt. of £4 payable at the Annunciation & Michaelmas, with power of distraint; & the reversion to Wm. Waldegrave & his heirs to hold of the chief lords.

19. Trin. & Hil. Wm. Androwes *alias* Pyers, pl. Wm. Ellys, def. 1 mess., 1 gdn., 1 orchard, 4 a. ar. & 3 a. pa. in Chawreth *alias* Chawrey Strete. £40.

20. Tho. Lorkyn & Rumbold Taverner, pl. *Robt.* Smyth, esq., & w. Joan, def. 6 mess., 3 cotts., 50½ a. ar., 8 a. mw. & 60 a. pa. in Harvardstock & Buttysbury. Def. quitclaimed to pl. & the heirs of Tho. £240.

21. Robt. Mountford, pl. Roger Hopper & w. *Fina*, late the w. of Leonard Monke, decd., def. 1 mess., 1 toft, 1 gdn. & ½ rood ar. in Great Dunmowe. £30.

22. Joan Laxton, wid., pl. *Geo.* Hawkyns, gent. *Geo.* Myddelton & w. Alice, def. 4 mess., 20 a. ar., 4 a. mw., 10 a. pa. & 5s. rt. in Westham. £80.

CP25(2)/259/Hil. 4 Eliz.   DIVERS COUNTIES

10. Mich. & Hil. Nich. Bacon, kt., keeper of the great seal, Francis, earl of Bedford, Wm. Cecyll, kt., Robt. Catlyn, kt., Tho. Cornwallys, kt., & Osbert Moundford, esq., pl. Anne Butts, wid., one of the daus. & heirs of Hy. Bewers, esq., def. A fourth part of the manors of Foxherd & Brokehall & of 80 mess., 30 tofts, 2 mills, 2 dovecotes, 80 gdns., 700 a. ar., 300 a. mw., 1,000 a. pa., 300 a. wd., 500 a. furze & heath, 80 a. marsh & £20 rt. in Foxherd & Brokehall, co. Essex, & prop. in Suff. Def. quitclaimed to pl. & the heirs of Nich. £1,200. — Suff., Essex.

11. Mich. & Hil. The same pl. Tho. Butts, esq., & w. *Bridget*, one of the daus. & heirs of Hy. Bewers, esq., def. A fourth part of the same. Def. quitclaimed to pl. & the heirs of Nich. £1,200. — Suff., Essex.

12. Mich. & Hil. The same pl. Wm. Butts, kt., & w. *Jane*, one of the daus. & heirs of Hy. Bewers, esq., def. A fourth part of the same. Def. quitclaimed to pl. & the heirs of Nich. £1,200. — Suff., Essex.

CP25(2)/126/1618   EASTER, 4 ELIZABETH   1562

1. Tho. Raynolds, pl. *Rd.* Pease & w. Alice, def. 1 mess., 1 curtilages, 1 orchard & 1 gdn. in Chelmesford. £40.

2. Tho. Haryson, pl. Jn. Staveley & w. *Margt.*, def. 1 mess. & 2 gdns. in Rocheford. £40.

3. Hil. & Eas. Edw. Wildon, pl. *Wm.* Wylford, esq., & w. Agnes & Wm. Sydey sen., gent., def. Manor of Hannams *alias* Boleynes & 2 mess., 6 gdns., 300 a. ar., 12 a. mw., 60 a. pa., 12 a. wd. & 10s. rt. in Tendryng. And for this pl. gtd. the same to Wm. Sydey to hold from Michaelmas last for 30 years, rendering £21 yearly to pl. & the heirs, payable at the Annunciation & Michaelmas, with power of distraint; & the reversion to Wm. Wilford & Agnes & the heirs of the body of Wm., to hold of the chief lords, with remainder to the right heirs of Agnes.

4. Mich. & Eas. Wm. Sidey sen., gent., pl. Wm. Waldegrave, esq., def. 15 a. ar., 5 a. mw. & 3 a. pa. in Bures St. Mary. And for this pl. gtd. to def. & his heirs a yearly rt. of 18s. from the same, payable at the Annunciation & Michaelmas, with power of distraint.

5. Hil. & Eas. Tho. Sampford, pl. *Rd.* Sampford & w. Ellen, def. A moiety of 1 mess., 70 a. ar., 6 a. mw., 6 a. pa., 2 a. wd. & 2s. rt. in Willynghale Doo, Shellowe Bowells & Barners Rothing. £80.

6. Hil. & Eas. Jn. Collye, pl. *Edw.* Hales & w. Jane, def. Manor of Gylles & 1 mess., 1 gdn., 1 orchard, 80 a. ar., 18 a. mw., 60 a. pa., 40 a. wd. & 10 a. furze & heath in Eppyng. £400.

7. Hil. & Eas. Matthew Gosnold, gent., pl. *Tho.* Hall & w. Anne, def. 1 mess., 20 a. ar., 10 a. mw., 40 a. pa., 20 a. wd. & common of pasture in Stondon & Duddyngherst. £100.

8. Hil. & Eas. Geo. Basford, pl. Hy. Sharyngton, esq., & w. Anne, def. 20 a. mw. in Waltham Stowe & Leyghton. £40.

9. Nich. Man, pl. Jn. Baron & w. *Maud*, def. 1 mess., 1 cott., 1 gdn., 1 orchard & 1 a. mw. in Wydforde. £40.

10. Rd. Gardener, pl. *Jn.* Thake & w. Eliz., def. 1 mess., 1 gdn., 13 a. ar. & 4 a. pa. in Claveryng. Def. quitclaimed to pl. & his heirs, with warranty against the heirs of Jn. & of Wm. Thake his brother. £26.

11. Rd. Marchall, pl. *Robt.* Wood, gent., brother & heir of Leonard Wood, decd., & w. Joan, def. 1 mess., 1 cott., 1 gdn., 8 a. ar. & 1 a. pa. in Bromefeld. £40.

12. Simon Burton, pl. Rd. Plomer, def. 1 mess., 1 gdn. & 1 barn in Walden. £40.

13. Jn. Wells & w. Alice, pl. Wm. Hodge & w. *Joan*, def. 13 a. ar. in Tolleshunt Knyghts. Def. quitclaimed to pl. & the heirs of Alice. £40.

14. Jn. Bowland, pl. Steph. Spakman, def. 1 mess., 12 a. mw. & 30 a. pa. in Abridge. £60.

15. Jn. Herman, clk., pl. Wm. Hodge & w. *Joan* & Jn. Welles & w. Alice, def. 1 mess. in Goldanger. And for this pl. gtd. the same to Jn. Welles & his heirs, to hold of the chief lords.

16. Mich. & Eas. Nich. Coote, pl. Robt. Wryght, def. 2 mess., 2 cotts., 3 gdns., 2 orchards, 4 a. ar. & 1 a. mw. in Depden, two parts of the greater feodal tithes from the manor of Depden *alias* Depden Hall, two parts of the greater tithes from a field called 'Hochinden' containing 101 a. ar., parcel of the manor of Wolbarnes, & two parts of the greater tithes from a field called 'Alderbury' containing 45 a. ar. in Depden. And for this pl. gtd. the same to def. to hold for one month, with remainder to Agnes Wryght his w. for life & def. & his heirs, to hold of the chief lords.

17. Jn. Browning, pl. Rd. Kent, def. 1 mess., 1 gdn., 1 orchard, 12 a. ar., 4 a. mw. & 10 a. pa. in Ramesden Crayes. £80.

18. Tho. Hyckmans, pl. Jn. Haywarde, def. 1 mess., 3 barns, 1 gdn., 1 orchard, 3 a. ar., 10 a. mw. & 6 a. pa. in Westhamme. 160 mks.

19. Jn. Mershe, esq., & w. Alice, pl. Tho. Harvye, esq., & w. *Margt.*, def. 1 mess., 1 toft, 1 gdn., 1 orchard, 60 a. ar., 10 a. mw., 10 a. pa., 1 a. wd. & 100 a. furze & heath in Dagenham. Def. quitclaimed to pl. & the heirs of Jn. £80.

20. Hil. & Eas. Rd. Josua, pl. Robt. Barker & w. *Eliz.*, def. 1 mess. & 1 gdn. in the parish of All Saints, Maldon. £30.

21. Hil. and Eas. Tho. Franke, esq., & w. Mary, pl. *Rd.* Bowland & w. Agnes, def. 1 mess., 1 gdn. & 20 a. ar. in Hatfeld Regis. Def. quitclaimed to pl. & the heirs of Tho. £40.

22. Hil. & Eas. Jn. Waylett, pl. *Steph.* Sampford & w. Margery & Rd. Sampford, def. Rectory impropriate of Barnes Rodyng, 1 mess., 1 orchard, 1 gdn., 80 a. ar., 20 a. mw., 10 a. pa. & tithes of corn, grain & hay in Barnes Rodyng & Margarett Rodyng, & the advowson of the vicarage of Barnes Rodyng. Def. quitclaimed to pl. & his heirs with warranty for themselves & the heirs of Steph. against themselves & the heirs of Rd. £36.

23. Hil. & Eas. Tho. Frytton, pl. *Geo.* Robertes & w. Joan, def. 1 mess., 1 gdn., 1 orchard & 2 a. ar. in Hatfeld Peverell. £40.

24. Hil. & Eas. Leonard Barker, gent., pl. Jn. Lumpkyn & w. *Joan*, def. 1 mess., 1 gdn., 1 orchard & ½ a. ar. in Barkyng. £40.

25. Tho. Parke & Jn. Hamond, pl. Tho. Algor, Jn. Browne & w. *Agnes*, Jn. Sybthorpe, Rd. Algor, Rd. Serle & w. Anne, def. 2 mess., 1 cott., 4 barns, 4 gdns., 4 orchards, 123 a. ar. 10 a. mw., 20 a. pa. & 10 a. wd. in Great Berdefeld, Little Berdefeld & Berdefeld Salyng *alias* Lytle Salyng. Def. quitclaimed to pl. & the heirs of Tho. £200.

26. Jn. Wright, pl. Wm. Raynolds, gent., def. 1 mess. & 1 gdn. in Chelmysford. £40.

27. Hy. Fanshawe, gent., pl. Martin Bowes, esq., & w. Frances, def. 16 a. mw. in Barking. Def. quitclaimed to pl. & his heirs, with warranty against themselves & the heirs of Martin & Jn. Barnardiston *alias* Barmiston, esq., & his heirs. 160 mks.

28. Wm. Pye, pl. Jn. Harry & w. *Anne*, def. 18 a. ar. in Lytle Holland. £80.

29. Rd. Hubbert, gent., & Avery Barlee, gent., pl. Tho. Reymond, gent., son & heir of Jn. Reymond, gent., decd., def. 2 mess., 2 gdns., 2 orchards, 200 a. ar., 10 a. mw., 60 a. pa. & 20 a. wd. in Hatfylde Regis, Hatfyld Brodeoke & Hallingbury Bourgchier. Def. quitclaimed to pl. & the heirs of Rd. £180.

30. Jn. Brett, pl. *Rd.* Welles & w. Maud, Jn. Welles sen., Jn. Welles jun. & Tho. Welles, def. 2 mess., 2 barns, 2 gdns., 2 tofts, 40 a. ar., 6 a. mw., 12 a. pa. & 2 a. wd. in Tolshunt Darcy, Tolshunt Maior, Goldaunger & Little Tottham. 200 mks.

31. Jn. Somersham, pl. *Robt.* Cooke *alias* Barker & Geo. Cooke *alias* Barker, his son and heir, def. 1 mess. in Keldon. £40.

32. Tho. Wayght, pl. Hy. Luggs & w. *Alice*, def. 1 mess. & 1 gdn. in Hatfelde Brodoke. £40.

33. Matthew Barnarde, pl. *Tho.* Aylett & w. Kath., def. 1 mess., 4 cotts., 1 barn, 1 gdn., 1 orchard, 35 a. ar., 5 a. mw. & 5 a. pa. in Eytheroppe Rothinge. £40.

34. Tho. Pullyver, pl. *Tho.* Baker & w. Dorothy, def. 4 a. marsh in Estham. 80 mks.

35. Jn. London & w. Maud, pl. *Robt.* Watts & w. Agnes, def. 1 mess., 1 gdn & 1 a. mw. in Shenfeld. Def. quitclaimed to pl. & the heirs of Jn. £40.

36. Jn. Steven, pl. Wm. Sone, def. 1 cott., 8 a. ar. & 5 a. pa in Althorne, £40.

37. Wm. Norman & Jn. Staveley, pl. Jn. Wood & w. *Agnes*, def. 1 mess. & 1 gdn. in Leighe. Def. quitclaimed to pl. & the heirs of Wm. £40.

38. Jn. Barnabe, gent., pl. Rd. Wheler & w. *Eliz.*, dau. & heir of Jn. Grove, def. 1 mess. & 1 gdn. in Wytham. £40.

39. Hamnet Bressye & w. Etheldreda & Nich. Sympson jun., pl. Hy. Stevenson & w. *Isabel*, def. 1 mess., 1 gdn., 20 a. ar., 20 a. mw., 40 a. pa. & 10 a. wd. in Chigwell. Def. quitclaimed to pl. & the heirs of Nich. £80.

40. Wm. Veysey & Robt. Veysey & w. Joan, pl. *Edw.* Gylbert & w. Alice, def. Manor of Whykes Abbey & 20 mess., 20 cotts., 20 tofts, 10 dovecotes, 20 gdns., 20 orchards, 1,000 a. ar., 100 a. mw., 500 a. pa., 200 a. wd., 300 a. marsh, 1,000 a. furze & heath & 56s. 8d. rt. in Wykis, Tendryng, Fratyng, Myseley, Bradfild, Wrabnes & Great Okeley. Def. quitclaimed to pl. & the heirs of Wm. £600.

CP25(2)/259/Eas. 4 Eliz.   DIVERS COUNTIES

4. Tho. Seckford, esq., pl. Robt. Wyngfeld, esq., def. The manors of Netherhall and Overhall & 400 mess., 300 tofts, 1 water-mill, 3 dovecotes, 400 gdns., 400 orchards, 2,000 a. ar., 400 a. mw., 600 a. pa., 400 a. wd., 3,000 a. furze & heath, 200 a. moor, 100 a. marsh, 100 a. alder, £40 rt. & a free fishery in Dedham, co. Essex; & property in Suffolk. £800. — Essex, Suff..

CP25(2)/126/1619   TRINITY, 4 ELIZABETH   1562

1. Eleanor Lambert wid., & Wm. Lambert her son, pl. Tho. Ussher & w. *Joan*, def. 1 mess., 1 gdn. & 1½ a. ar. in Shalford. Def. quitclaimed to pl. & the heirs of Eleanor. £15.

2. Rd. Tytterell, Tho. Stock sen., Hy. Badcock & Wm. Holmested sen., pl. Jn. Badcock & w. Joan, Wm. Tanner & w. *Eliz.*, Nich. Badcock & w. *Rose* & Simon Bregge & w. *Joan*, def. 1 mess., 2 barns., 3 gdns., 3 orchards, 53 a. ar., 5 a. mw. & 10 a. pa. in Little Berdefeld & Great Berdefeld. Def. quitclaimed to pl. & the heirs of Rd. £100.

3. Robt. Ingland, pl. *Wm.* Lambe & w. Joan, def. 1 mess., 1 gdn., & 1 a. ar. in Grayes Thurrocke. £20.

4. Jn. Freman, pl. Tho. Berden & w. *Joan*, one of the daus. of Robt. Gyne, decd., def. 1 toft & 16 a. ar. in Great Waltham & Little Waltham. £20.

5. Tho. Powncett, gent., & w. Eliz., pl. *Tho.* Powle, esq., & w. Jane, def. 1 mess., 1 barn, 2 gdns., 1 orchard, 1 dovecote, 200 a. ar., 40 a. mw., 100 a. pa., 20 a. wd. & furze & heath in Barkyng. Def. quitclaimed to pl. & the heirs of Tho. 380 mks.

6. Tho. Baker, & Chris. Alleyn, pl. Margt. Broke, wid., def. 1 mess., 1 curtilage, 12 a. ar., 4 a. mw. & 24 a. pa. in Great Totham, Little Totham & Wickham. Def. quitclaimed to pl. & the heirs of Tho. And for this pl. gtd. the same to def. & her heirs, to hold of the chief lords.

7. Wm. Foster & Tho. Foster jun., pl. Edw. Bugg sen., gent., def. Manor of Morehall & 2 mess., 200 a. ar., 20 a. mw., 100 a. pa. & 20 a. wd. in Harlowe, Latton & Northweld. Def. quitclaimed to pl. & the heirs of Wm. £400.

8. Jn. Cole, gent., pl. *Jn.* Markeshall, gent., & w. Maud, def. Manor of Markeshalle & 2 mess., 4 cotts., 3 tofts, 4 gdns., 2 orchards, 140 a. ar., 40 a. mw., 140 a. pa., 30 a. wd., 40 a. marsh & 15s. rt. in Markeshalle, Ferynge & Earls Colne, & the advowson of the church of Markeshalle. £220.

9. Tho. Parker, pl. *Jn.* Sterlyng and w. Cristiana, def. 1 mess., 30 a. ar. & 1½ a. mw. in Ardeleigh. £40.

10. Eas. & Trin. Rd. Ryche, kt., lord Ryche, & Robt. Ryche, kt., pl. *Geo.* Covert, esq., & Jn. Bolney, esq., def. A third part of manor of Sutton, a third part of 1 mess., 1 barn, 1 gdn., 1 orchard, 100 a. ar., 100 a. mw., 100 a. pa., 40 a. wd., 100 a. furze & heath & 10s. rt. in Great Sutton, Sutton, Estwoodd, & Prytwell, & a third part of the advowson of the church of Great Sutton. Def. quitclaimed to pl. & the heirs of Robt. £100.

11. Tho. Farnyll, pl. *Tho.* Broke, gent., & w. Anne & Margt. Strelly *alias* Styrley, wid., def. 3 mess., 4 cotts., 4 tofts, 5 gdns., 3 orchards, 3 barns, 100 a. ar., 20 a. mw., 30 a. pa., 40 a. salt marsh & 8s. rt. in Thurrock Grey *alias* Greyes Thurrock. 200 mks.

CP25(2)/259/Trin. 4 Eliz.   DIVERS COUNTIES

5. Tho. Allen, pl. Hamnet Bressey & w. Etheldreda & *Nich.* Sympson, 'yoman', son of Rd. Sympson, def. 1 mess., 1 gdn., 20 a. ar., 20 a. mw., 40 a. pa. & 10 a. wd. in Chigwell, co. Essex; & prop. in Surr.. And for this pl. gtd. the same to Hamnet & Etheldreda, to hold of the chief lords for their lives, without impeachment of waste, with remainder to Nich. Sympson, son of the said Etheldreda, & his heirs. – Essex, Surrey.

CP25(2)/126/1620   MICHAELMAS, 4 AND 5 ELIZABETH   1562

1. Jn. Saring, pl. *Tho.* Kyng & w. Margery, def. 1 mess., 1 gdn., 1 orchard & 10 a. ar. in Magdaleyn Lawfer. £40.

2. Wm. Stedman, pl. Rd. Stapleton, kt., & Brian Stapleton, his son & heir apt., & w. Eliz., def. 1 mess. called 'Mugges', 1 toft, 1 gdn., 1 orchard, 60 a. ar., 60 a. mw., 40 a. pa. & 40 a. marsh in Barkyng & Dagenham. £220.

3. Trin. & Mich. Edw. Lytelton, kt., & Matthew Cradocke, pl. Francis Cokayn & w. *Mary*, def. 3 mess., 3 gdns., 3 orchards, 1,000 a ar., 100 a. mw., 1,000 a. pa., 200 a. wd., & 100 a. furze & heath in Little Bromley, Great Bromley, Bramehall, Badley Hall, Little Bentley, Mysteley, Ardeley, Lawford, Okeley & Kyrby. Def. quitclaimed to pl. & the heirs of Edw. And for this pl. gtd. the same to def. & the heirs of the body of Francis by Mary, to hold of the chief lords, with remainder to Tho. Cokayn, kt., for three days, the heirs of the body of Mary, & the right heirs of Francis.

4. Tho. Barbar, gent., & Clement Gymlett, pl. Barnard Busshe & w. *Joan* & Steph. Spylman & w. *Clemencia*, def. 1 mess., 1 barn, 2 gdns., 20 a. ar., 5 a. mw. & 6 a. pa. in Great Lighes & Little Lighes. Def. quitclaimed to pl. & the heirs of Tho. 130 mks.

5. Jn. Turnor, gent., pl. Wm. Woodhouse, kt., & w. *Eliz.*, def. Manors of Bacons & Floreis & 10 mess., 10 gdns., 10 orchards, 300 a. ar., 30 a. mw., 100 a. pa., 60 a. wd., 40 a. furzw & heath, 20 a. fresh marsh & £3 6s. 8d. rt. in Great Tey, Pontysbright, Erlescoln, Mattyshall & Ferynge. And for this pl. gtd. to def. & the heirs of Eliz. a yearly rt. of £13 5s. 10d. from the same, payable at the Annunciation & Michaelmas, with power of distraint.

6. Rd. Weston, one of the justices of the Bench, & Rd. Lee, pl. Rd. Cupper, esq., *Rd.* Love, gent., & w. Anne, def. 1 mess., 20 a. ar., 6 a. mw., 84 a. pa. & 12 a. wd. in Wyckford, Ronwell, Downham & Sowthannyngfeld. Def. quitclaimed to pl. & the heirs of Rd. Weston. £160.

7. Trin. & Mich. Wm. Allyn, citizen & alderman of London, pl. Edw. Jenyn, def. 2 mess., 1 barn, 2 gdns., 30 a. ar., 5 a. mw., 40 a. pa. & 20 a. wd. in Rayleygh, Thundersleigh, Northbemflete & Crawlese. 220 mks.

8. Tho. Eden, esq., pl. Tho. Cracbone, def. A moiety of the manor of Ryes & a moiety of 1 mess., 1 gdn., 200 a. ar., 20 a. mw., 100 a. pa., 40 a. wd., 30 a. reedbed, 20 a. marsh & 20s. rt. in Little Henney. 100 mks.

9. Trin. & Mich. Hy. Fuller, pl. *Tho.* Potter & w. Margt., def. 4 a. ar., & 4 a. mw. in Chygwell. £40.

10. Tho. Newman, gent., pl. *Rd.* Cutt, esq., & w. Mary, def. Manor of Rykelyng & 10 mess., 20 tofts, 10 gdns., 1,000 a ar., 60 a. mw., 500 a. pa., 500 a. wd. & £10 rt. in Rykelyng, Bereden, Ugley & Bolyngton, & common of pasture for 600 sheep in Rykelyng, Ugley & Bolyngton. £360.

11. Wm. Rogers, pl. *Jn.* Sudburye & w. Kath., def. 2 mess., 2 gdns., 1½ a mw. & 10 a. pa. in Runwell. £40.

12. Wm. Muschamp, gent., pl. Wimond Cary, esq., & *Edw.* Cary, gent., def. Manor of Benedic Otes *alias* Benet Otes & 2 mess., 2 gdns., 100 a. ar., 10 a. mw., 20 a. pa., 10 a. wd. & 42s. rt. in Wrytle, Bromefeld, Chygenhale St. James, Chygenhale St. Mary & Chelmsford. 220 mks.

13. Philip Bird, pl. *Hy.* Davy & w. Alice, def. 1 mess., 20 a. ar., 4 a. mw. & 10 a. pa. in Depden. 40 mks.

14. Wm. Raynolds, pl. *Tho.* Malbroke & w. Helen, def. 1 mess., 4 gdns., 13 a. ar., 4 a. mw., 10 a. pa. & 2 a. wd. in Mountendsynge. £40.

15. Trin. & Mich. Rd. Hobson, pl. Tho. Monoux, gent., def. 2 mess., 2 gdns., 2 orchards, 18 a. pa. & 1 a. mw. in Chyngford *alias* Chynkford Hacche. 160 mks.

16. Trin. & Mich. Robt. Cristmas & Jn. Turner, pl. *Geo.* Cristmas, esq., & w. Bridget & Jn. Broke, def. Manor of Downehall, & 400 a. ar., 20 a. mw., 300 a. pa., 40 a. wd., 400 a. marsh & 40s. rt. in Bradwell by the Sea. Def. quitclaimed to pl. & the heirs of Robt. £800.

17. Robt. Sudburye, pl. Tho. Jeffrey & w. *Margery*, def. A third part of 8 a. pa. in Great Stanbridge. £10.

18. The warden and scholars of the college of St. Mary Winton' in Oxford, pl. Geo. Cristmas, esq., def. 200 a salt marsh called 'Shelmershe' in Bradwell by the Sea & two weirs in the water of Pounte in Bradwell by the Sea. Def. quitclaimed to pl. & their successors. £60.

19. Jn. Croell, pl. Lancelot Taylour & w. *Anne*, def. 2 mess. & 1 gdn. in Maldon. £40.

20. Tho. Bennett, pl. *Nich.* Smyth, gent., & w. Grace, def. Manor of Leynshams & 200 a. ar., 20 a. mw., 40 a. pa., 40 a. wd. & 40s. rt. in Revenhall, Cressyng, Stysted, Bockking & Bradwell by Coggeshall. And for this pl. gtd. the same to def. & the heirs of Nich., to hold of the chief lords.

21. Geoff. Fynche, pl. *Jn.* Lytle & w. Joan, def. 1 mess., 1 gdn., 20 a. ar., 4 a. mw. & 8 a. pa. in Chadwell & Barkyng. £40.

22. Rd. Grene, pl. Rd. Carter, def. 2 mess., 2 gdns. & 1 a. ar. in Great Maplestede. £40.

23. Jn. Southcott, serjeant at law, & Tho. Bromley, esq., pl. *Jn.* Braunche, gent., & w. Helen, Francis Mychell, gent., & w. Jane, def. Manor of Garnonshall *alias* Garnyshall

& 2 mess., 4 barns, 2 gdns., 2 orchards, 200 a. ar., 100 a. mw., 200 a. pa., 100 a. wd. & £12 rt. in Theydon Garnon, Theydon Boys & Theydon at the Mount, & view of frank pledge in the Theydon Garnon. Def. quitclaimed to pl. & heirs of Jn. £400.

24. Rd. Brown, Jn. Humfrey & Wm. Brownynge, pl. *Jn.* Tyll & w. Margt., def. 2 mess. in Coggyshall. Def. quitclaimed to pl. & the heirs of Wm. £40.

25. Rd. Fryth, pl. *Jasper* Warren, gent., & w. Antonia, def. 1 mess., 1 gdn, 40 a. ar., 4 a. mw., 20 a. pa., 2 a. wd. & 3 a. furze & heath in Upmyster. 160 mks.

26. Hn. Johnson, pl. Tho. Pyke & w. *Joan* & Tho. Freman & w. *Agnes*, def. 1 mess., 16 a. ar. & 4 a. mw., in Horndon on the Hill. £40.

27. Jn. Parke, pl. *Jn.* Deane & w. Joan & Robt. Walsshe jun. & w. Eliz., def. 1 mess., 1 gdn., 8 a. ar. & £6 rt. in Little Maplested, Great Maplested & Halsted. £40.

28. Wm. Strachye jun., pl. *Wm.* Strachye sen. & w. Annabilla, def. 6 a. ar., 30 a. mw. & 3 a. pa. in Walden & Wymbyshe. 100 mks.

29. Gregory Bretton, pl. *Tho.* Rede, one of the sons of Robt. Rede, decd., & w. Alice, def. 1 mess., 1 gdn., 8 a. ar. & 2 a. pa. in Wethersfeld. 80 mks.

30. Rd. Stane sen. & Rd. Stane jun., his son, pl. Rd. Ryche, kt., lord Ryche, def. Manor of Folyatt *alias* Folyatts Hall & 4 mess., 4 tofts, 4 barns, 5 gdns., 5 orchards, 240 a. ar., 20 a. mw., 10 a. pa., 10 a. wd. & 40s. 5d. rt. in High Ongar & Norton. Def. quitclaimed to pl. & the heirs of Rd. jun. 200 mks.

31. Tho. Parke & Tho. Stock sen., pl. Wm. Tanner & w. *Eliz.* and Simon Bregge & w. *Joan*, def. 17 a. ar. in Great Berdefeld & Little Berdefeld. Def. quitclaimed to pl. & the heirs of Tho. Parke. 80 mks.

32. Jn. Sheregate, pl. Robt. Yonge & w. *Alice*, def. 1 mess. in High Roodyng. £40.

33. Joan Laxton of London, wid., pl. *Jn.* Dymok, citizen & 'draper' of London, & w. Mary, def. 10 a. mw. in Westham. £120.

34. Wm. Bysshoppe *alias* Perryn, pl. Jn. Parker *alias* Lawnes, def. 2 a. ar. in Elmedon. £20.

35. Anth. Broun, one of the justices of the Bench, & Anth. Jebbe, pl. Jn. More, gent., & w. *Alice*, dau. & heir of Jn. Goldan of Southwelde, def. 1 mess., 1 curtilage, 1 gdn., 1 orchard & 3 a. ar. called 'Tyngs' *alias* 'Pelhams' in Navestock. Def. quitclaimed to pl. & the heirs of Anth. Broun. £40.

36. Wm. Markaunt, gent., pl. Rd. Rodes, def. 1 mess., 1 gdn., 1 orchard & 1 a. ar. in Kelvedon *alias* Keldon. And for this pl. gtd. the same to def. & his heirs, to hold of the chief lords.

37. Pet. Walker, pl. Tho. Harryson & w. *Agnes*, def. 1 mess. & 1 gdn. in Rocheford. £40.

38. Rd. Riche, kt., lord Riche, pl. *Matthew* Smyth, esq., & *Jerome* Songer, gent., def. 36 a. mw. in Wymbyshe. £60.

39. Francis Archer, pl. Jn. Dygby & w. *Joan*, def. 1 mess., 1 gdn., 1 orchard & ½ a. mw. in Bokkyng. £30.

40. Robt. Paschall, pl. Jn. Symon sen., & w. Anne, *Tho.* Burle & w. Joan, def. 40 a. pa. in Great Badowe & Sandon. £40.

41. Tho. Nevyll & Tho. Crakebone, pl. Jn. Smyth, esq., son & heir of Clement Smyth, kt., def. Manor of Archiers & Hellonsfeldes & 8 mess., 6 cotts., 10 tofts, 1 dove-cote, 6 orchards, 8 gdns, 260 a. ar., 20 a. mw., 80 a. pa., 60 a.wd. & £4 rt. in Revenhale *alias* Rewenhale, Cressing, Falkeborne, Wyttham, Bradwell & Great Braxsted. Def. quitclaimed to pl. & the heirs of Tho. Nevyll. £360.

42. Jn. Faunce, son & heir apt. of Eliz. Roys, pl. Walter Roys & w. *Eliz.*, def. 1 mess., 1 gdn., 10 a. ar. & 1 a. mw. in Purleighe & Woodham Mortimer. And for this pl. gtd. the same to def. & the heirs of Walter, to hold of the chief lords.

43. Wm. Strong, pl. *Jn.* Frauncys *alias* Puckley & w. Anne, def. 1 mess. & 1 gdn. in Henyngham Syble. £40.

44. Tho. Hookley & w. Eliz., pl. *Jn.* Gardener, citizen & goldsmith of London, & w. Mary, def. 1 mess., 1 barn, 1 gdn. & 1 orchard in Walden. Def. quitclaimed to pl. & the heirs of Tho. £40.

45. Geo. Callys, pl. Rd. Pasfylde & w. *Joan* & Tho. Radley & w. Joan, def. 3 a. ar. in Hyghe Onger. £40.

46. Jn. Jyppes, pl. *Edm.* West, esq., & w. Jane, def. 1 mess., 2 a. mw. & 1 a. pa. in Depden. £40.

47. Wm. Howson, pl. Tho. Bowtell *alias* Bover & w. *Helen*, Jn. Gyldard, clerk, & w. *Joan*, def. 2 mess., 2 gdns., 2 orchards, 20 a. ar., 4 a. mw., & 16 a. pa. in Thaxsted. £120.

48. Wm. Warryson, pl. Edw. Stower, def. 1 mess., 1 gdn., 1 orchard, 1 barn, 1 a. ar., 1 a. mw., 6 a pa. & 2 a. wd. in Brewers St. Mary. £40.

49. Hy. Archer, gent., pl. *Hy.* Clarke & w. Joan, def. 12 a. ar., 3 a. pa., & 7 a. wd. in Theydon Garnon *alias* Cowpersale. £40.

50. Hy. Clarke, pl. *Hy.* Archer, gent., & w. Anne, def. 1 mess., 5 a. ar., 6 a. mw., 5 a. pa. & 3 a. wd. in Theydon Garnon *alias* Cowpersale. £40.

51. Martin Lee & w. Alice, pl. Wm. Man, gent., & *Tho.* Man, def. 2 mess., 2 gdns. & 1 orchard in Balydon in Sudbury. Def. quitclaimed to pl. & the heirs of Martin. £40.

52. Wm. Ayllette, pl. *Wm.* Davenaunte, gent., son & heir of Wm. Davenaunte of Sybell Hennygham, & Jn. Davenaunte, son & heir of Ralph Davenaunte, def. 1 mess., 1 curtilage, 2 gdns., 2 orchards, 60 a. ar., 10 a. mw., 40 a. pa., 4 a. wd., 4 a. moor & 5s. rt. in Stysted, Halsted & Bockynge, which Joan Perpes, wid., holds for life. Pl. & his heirs to hold the remainder of the chief lords. 200 mks.

53. Jn. Sawnder, pl. Wm. Sawnder, def. 2 mess. & 2 gdns. in Coggeshall. £40.

54. Matthew Steven, pl. *Tho.* Lodge, citizen & alderman of London, & w. Anne, def. 2 mess., 2 gdns., 3 tofts, 1 water-mill, 100 a ar., 8 a. mw., 60 a. pa. & 20 a. marsh in Colchester & common of pasture for 140 sheep in Colchester. 230 mks.

55. Jas. Altham, esq., & w. Mary, pl. *Hy.* Parker, kt., lord Morley, & w . Eliz., def. Manor of Markehall & 20 mess., 20 cotts., 20 tofts, 10 barns, 5 dovecotes, 3 mills, 30 gdns., 20 orchards, 300 a. ar., 200 a. mw., 200 a. pa., 100 a. wd., 100 a. moor, 100 a. marsh, 200 a. furzw & heath & £10 rt. in Markehall, Latton & Harlowe. Def. quitclaimed to pl. & the heirs of Jas. £400.

56. Wm. Luckyn, pl. *Robt.* Kynge, gent., & w. Lettice, def. Manor of Sir Hues *alias* Hughes & 3 mess., 200 a. ar., 30 a. mw., 300 a. pa., 40 a. wd. & £7 rt. in Great Badowe, Esthannyngefeld, Westhannyngfeld & Sandon. £500.

57. Tho. Hale, gent., pl. *Tho.* Heron, gent., & w. Cicily, def. 34 a. ar. & 22 a. pa. in Walthamstowe. £40.

CP25(2)/259/Mich. 4-5 Eliz.　　　DIVERS COUNTIES

10. Leonard Sandell, Rd. Heywood, gent., & Jn. Mannyng, pl. Jn. Gessham, gent., and w. Isabel & *Rd.* Cooke, gent., & w. Eliz., def. 20 mess., 10 tofts, 2 dovecotes, 20 gdns., 20 orchards, 500 a. ar., 100 a. mw., 200 a. pa., 100 a. wd., 100 a. heath, 40 a. moor & 100s. rt. in Barkyng, Ileford & Woodford, co. Essex; & property in London. Def. quitclaimed to pl. & the heirs of Leonard. £420. — Essex, London.

CP25(2)/126/1621　　　HILARY, 5 ELIZABETH　　　1563

1. Gabriel Bushe, pl. Jn. Seryche sen., def. 1 mess., 50 a. ar., 10 a. mw., 30 a. pa. & 10 a. wd. in Wymbyshe. 160 mks.

2. Tho. Wilson, pl. Wm. Harrys, esq., def. 18 a. pa. in Mondon. £40.

3. Jn. Ponder, pl. Geo. Reymond & w. *Eliz.*, def. 2 mess., 1 cott., 1 gdn. & 7 a. ar. in Branketre & Bokkyng. £80.

4. Rd. Purcas & Jn. Browne, pl. Wm. Walpole, esq., def. 1 mess., 1 gdn., 26 a. ar., 5 a. mw. & 10 a. pa. in Great Gelham *alias* Great Yeldham, Toppesfeld, Hengham at the Castle *alias* Hennyngham Castell & Hengham Syble *alias* Hennyngham Syble. Def. quitclaimed to pl. & the heirs of Rd. £140.

5. Robt. Bradbury, esq., Wm. Rutter, gent., & Wm. Barley, gent., pl. *Wm.* Howson & w. Rose, def. 2 mess., 2 gdns., 2 orchards, 20 a. ar., 4 a. mw. & 16 a. pa. in Thaxstede. Def. quitclaimed to pl. & the heirs of Robt. £100.

6. Tho. Franke, pl. Robt. Ryche, kt., & w. Eliz., def. A third part of a moiety of the manor of Shopland Hall, a third part of a moiety of 3 mess., 3 gdns., 3 orchards, 100 a. ar., 30 a. mw., 40 a. pa., 20 a. wd., 10 a. furze & heath & 40s. rt. in Shopland, Butlers, Leighe, Hadleight, Sowbery, Raileighe, Rocheford, Hackwell, Great Wakeryng, Cricksy, Sutton & Prytwell, a third part of the manor of Butlers, & a third part of 7 mess., 1 dovecote, 7 gdns., 7 orchards, 200 a. ar., 40 a. mw., 60 a. pa., 30 a. wd., 20 a. furze & heath & £5 rt. in Butlers, Shopland, Leighe, Hadleighe, Sowberye, Raileighe, Rocheford, Hackwell, Great Wakeringe, Cricksye, Sutton & Prytwell. And for this pl. granted the same to def. & the heirs of their bodies, to hold of the chief lords, with remainder to the right heirs of Eliz.

7. Robt. Harte, pl. Jn. Woddwarde & w. *Joan*, def. 1 mess. in Harwyche. £40.

8. Jn. Collyn & Tho. Collyn, pl. Rd. Ryche, kt., lord Ryche, def. Manor of Enfylds & 2 mess., 260 a. ar., 20 a. mw., 80 a. pa., 40 a. wd. & 40s. rt. in Enfylds, Little Laver, High Laver, Fyssehyde, Matchynge & Bechams Rodynge. Def. quitclaimed to pl. & the heirs of Jn. £220.

9. Wm. Howlande, Wm. Smyth, Jn. Cole & Jn. Howlande jun., pl. Roland Elryngton, gent., son & heir of Grace Elryngton, late the w. of Edw. Elryngton, esq., def. 8 a. ar., ½ a. mw. & ½ a. pa. in Wycken *alias* Wycken Bonant. Def. quitclaimed to pl. & the heirs of Wm. Smyth. £40.

10. Jn. Clement, pl. *Wm.* Clement & w. Eliz., def. 21 a. ar. in Dodynghurst. £40.

11. Rd. Stonley *alias* Stanley, esq., pl. *Nich.* Fuljamb & w. Agnes, def. 2 mess., 100 a. ar., 50 a. mw., 100 a. pa., 20 a. wd. & 12d. rt. in Theydon Garnon & Theydon 'at Mounte' and common for 12 pigs and common of pasture for 100 sheep in Theydon 'at Mounte'. Def. quitclaimed to pl. & his heirs, with warranty against Geo. Fabian, son & heir of Anth. Fabyan, decd., & his heirs. £320.

12. Jn. Waylet, pl. Rd. Ryche, kt., lord Ryche, def. Manors of Blackhall & Neworks Norton & 6 mess., 6 gdns., 600 a. ar., 100 a. mw., 200 a. pa., 40 a. wd. & £3 132. 4d. rt. in Bobbyngworth, Morton, High Ongar, Norton, Wyllyngale Spayne & Wyllyngale Doo. £340.

13. Jn. Wallys, pl. *Tho.* Phannynge & w. Margt., def. 2 a. meadow in Little Canfelde. £10.

14. Jn. Lucas, gent., pl. Rd. Sands, gent., & w. Kath., def. Manor of Dembolds & 12 mess., 6 tofts, 140 a. ar., 20 a. mw., 160 pa., 26 a. wd. & 20s. rt. in Wrabnesse, Wyttham, Revenhall & Cressyng, which def. hold for the life of Kath. with reversion to Mary w. of Jn. Lucas & her heirs. Def. quitclaimed whatever they have to pl. for the life of Kath. 230 mks.

15. Edw. Some, pl. *Jn.* Drywood & w. Eliz., def. 14 a. ar. in Pritelwell. £40.

16. Tho. Gent, gent., & w. Eliz., pl. Edw. Palmer, gent., & w. *Margt.*, def. 4 a. mw. in Bockyng. Def. quitclaimed to pl. & the heirs of Tho. £40.

17. Wm. Bendlowes, serjeant at law, pl. Robt. Scrafeld, son of Wm. Scrafeld, decd., & brother & heirs of Walter Scrafeld, decd., def. 1 mess., 1 barn, 2 gdns, 42 a. ar., 2 a. mw., 5 a. pa. & 3 a. wd. in Bromefeld, Chykenhale St. James & Wryttell. £140.

18. Tho. Parke & Tho. Stock sen., pl. Robt. Corney & w. Blanche & Jn. Browne & w. *Agnes*, def. 1 mess., 1 cott., 1 gdn., 1 orchard & 2 a. ar. in Great Berdefeld. Def. quitclaimed to pl & the heirs of Tho. Parke. And for this pl. gtd. the mess., cott., gdn. & orchard, parcel of the same, to Robt. & Blanche & her heirs, to hold of the chief lords.

19. Tho. Gylbert, pl. Jn. Gelham *alias* Yeldham & w. *Joan* & Rd. Gelham *alias* Yeldham & w. *Kath.*, def. 3 mess. & 3 gdns. in Bokkyng. £30.

20. Wm. Ayloff, esq., Roc Grene, esq., Wm. Ayloff, gent., & Wm. Maxey, gent., pl. Anth. Maxey, esq., & w. *Dorothy*, def. Manors of Salynghall *alias* Olde Salyng & Pygotts & 6 mess., 6 gdns., 200 a. ar., 30 a. mw., 300 a. pa. & 40 a. wd. in Little Salyng, Stebbyng, Shalford & Bradwell by Coggeshall. Def. quitclaimed to pl. & the heirs of Wm. Ayloff, esq. £480.

21. Edm. Felton, esq., pl. *Edw.* Wyndesore, kt., lord Wyndesore, & w. Kath., def. A moiety of the manor of Maplested & of 4 mess., 6 tofts, 3 mills, 2 dovecotes, 4 gdns., 600 a. ar., 200 a. mw., 300 a. pa., 100 a. wd., 100 a. furze & heath & 100s. rt. in Maplested. £360.

22. Joan Simon, wid., pl. Tho. Parker, gent., & w. *Eliz.*, def. 1 mess. & 1 toft in Brentwood. £40.

23. Tho. Wyseman, gent., pl. *Tho.* Barryngton, esq., & w. Wenefrida, def. Manor of Barryntons in Chygwell & 20 mess., 20 tofts, 20 barns, 10 cotts., 20 gdns., 20 orchards, 200 a. ar., 100 a. mw., 240 a. pa., 50 a. wd., £6 13s. 4d. rt. & common of pasture for all beasts in the forest of Waltham Holy Crosse in Chygwell, Woodforde & Lowton. £300.

24. Clement Tusser, gent., pl. *Tho.* Essex, esq., son & heir of Wm. Essex, kt., son & heir of Eliz. Swylyngton, wid., & Jane his w., def. Manor of Hohall *alias* Holehall *alias* Martells in Rewenhall & 4 mess., 4 tofts, 1 water-mill, 1 windmill, 400 a. ar., 40 a. mw., 100 a. pa., 100 a. wd., 20 a. moor & £10 rt. in Rewenhall *alias* Revynhall, Falkeborne, Fobbyng, Fayersted, Cressyng, Bradwell by Coggyshall, Coggyshall, Kelwedon, Great Braxsted, Little Braxsted, Feryng, Inford, Messyng, Wykham & Terlyng. £220.

25. Rd. Cutts, esq., pl. Tho., duke of Norfolk, & w. *Margt.*, dau. & heir of Tho. Awdeley, kt., def. Manors of Arkesden & Mynchions & 6 mess., 10 cotts., 1 dovecote, 10 gardens, 10 orchards, 400 a. ar., 40 a. mw., 100 a. pa., 20 a. wd. & 20s. rt. in Arkesden, Elmedon, Langley, Cristeshall & Wenden Loughts, the rectory of Arkesden & all tithes, obventions, profits & emoluments belonging to it in those places except tithes of grain and hay in the manors of Mynchions & Peverells, & the advowson of the vicarage of Arkesden. £480.

26. Mich. & Hil. Jn. Symonde & Wm. Reve, pl. Tho. Smythe, esq., def. Manor of Blakamore *alias* Blakemore & 35 mess., 3 dovecotes, 35 gdns., 35 orchards, 200 a. ar., 50 a. mw., 250 a. pa., 60 a. wd. & £6 rt. in Blakamore *alias* Blakemore, Shellowe, Norton, Shenfeld & Stondon. Def. quitclaimed to pl. & the heirs of Jn. £400.

27. Mich. & Hil. Jn. Lytle, pl. *Anth.* Broun, one of the justices of the Bench, & w. Joan, def. 9 a. ar., 10 a. pa. & 37½ a. marsh in Daggenham. £90.

28. Mich. & Hil. Mathias Bradbury, esq., pl. Tho. Leventhorp, esq., def. £22 rt. in Wyckyn *alias* Wyckyn Bonant. £440.

29. Mich. & Hil. Wm. Horne, pl. Robt. Ewyn & w. *Agnes*, def. 1 mess. & 1 gdn. in Halsted. £40.

30. Mich. & Hil. Rd. Hobson, pl. Geo. Standon, def. 5 a. pa. in Chynkford. £40.

31. Mich. & Hil. Tho. Wyseman, pl. Hy. Songar & w. *Eliz.*, def. 3 a. ar. & 2 a. wd. in Great Waltham. £40.

32. Mich. & Hil. Rd. Emery, gent., pl. *Robt.* Came & w. Alice, def. 1 mess., 1 gdn., 1 orchard, 4 a. mw. & 9 a. pa. in Thaxsted £40.

33. Mich. & Hil. Geo. Bretten, pl. Lau. Walker & w. *Margaret*, def. A moiety of 2 mess., 2 barns, 1 gdn. & ½ a. ar. in Waltham Holy Cross. £40.

34. Mich. & Hil. Rd. Teabold, pl. *Jn.* Kyrkby, gent., & w. Eliz., def. 1 mess., 10 a. ar., 2 a. mw. & 3 a. pa. in Hengham at the Castle *alias* Castell Hennyngham. Def. quitclaimed to pl. & his heirs, with warranty against Francis Glenham, gent., & w. Lettice. £100.

35. Mich. & Hil. Jn. Grene, pl. Jn. Wybarde & w. Alice & *Rd.* Archer, def. 1 mess., 1 cott., 1 toft & 1 garden in Brentwood. £40.

36. Mich. & Hil. Tho. Blackwell, gent., pl. Jn. Smythe, esq., def. Manor of Terlyng *alias* Terlynge Haulle *alias* Tarlynge *alias* Tarlynge Haule *alias* Margeres & 3 mess., 3 gdns., 60 a. ar., 20 a. mw., 40 a. pa. & 20 a. wd. in Terlyng, Fayrested, Boreham, Springefelde, Great Leiga & Hatfelde Peverell. £200.

CP25(2)/127/1622   EASTER, 5 ELIZABETH   1563

1. Tho. Rayner, Edw. Robynson, Robt. Barker & Robt. Louett, pl. *Jn.* Goldynge sen. & w. Joan, Jn. Goldyng his son & w. Alice, def. 5 mess., 5 gdns., 5 orchards, 6½ a. ar. & 2 a. mw. in Thaxsted. Def. quitclaimed to pl. & the heirs of Tho. £80.

2. Edm. Markaunt, gent., pl. *Tho.* Audeley, gent., & w. Beatrice, def. 90 a. ar., 4 a. mw. & 6 a. pa. in Colchester, Myleende & Lexden. 130 mks.

3. Anth. Broun, one of the justices of the Common Bench, & w. Joan, pl. Nich. Tychborne & w. *Thamasina*, late Thamasina Niccolls, wid., def. Manor of Gylles & 1 mess., 300 a. ar., 24 a. mw., 40 a. pa., 36 a. wd & 15s. rt. in Eppynge. Def. quitclaimed to pl. & the heirs of Anth. £260.

4. Hil. & Eas. Edw. Baesshe, esq., pl. *Robt.* Webbe, gent., & w. Jane, def. Manor of Barlands & 7 mess., 200 a. ar., 100 a. mw., 200 a. pa., 40 a. wd. & 20s. rt. in Pryttelwell, Chopland & Sutton. £300.

5. Wm. Edwards & Wm. Braynwodd, pl. Jn. Bonner & w.*Mary*, def. 4 mess., 2 gdns., 2 cotts., 20 a. ar., 20 a. mw. & 1 a. wd. in Rayley. Def. quitclaimed to pl. & the heirs of Wm. Edwards. £120.

6. Hil. & Eas. Wm. Hamond, gent., pl. Jn. Tyrrell, esq., def. 2 mess., 2 gdns., 2 barns, 1 dovecote, 250 a. ar., 40 a. mw., 140 a. pa., 12 a. wd. & 40 a. furze & heath in Fobbyng, Dunton & Langdon on the Hill. £400.

7. Tho. Frenche & Tho. Parke, pl. Robt. Herde, def. 1 mess., 2 gdns., 5 a. ar. & ½ a. mw. in Great Berdefeld. Def. quitclaimed to pl. & the heirs of Tho. Parke, with warranty against the heirs of Jn. Barker, decd., & Matthew Barker *alias* Prentyse, decd. £40.

8. Tho. Brownyng, pl. *Jn.* Tyll & w. Margt. & Jn. Humfrey & w. Joan, def. 1 mess. in Coggeshall. £40.

9. Tho. Patteshale, gent., & Tho. Foster, gent., pl. Wm. Bendlowes, serjeant at law, and Rd. Elyott, gent., def. Manor of Berwykes & 1 mess., 200 a. ar., 20 a. mw., 40 a. pa., 20 a. wd. & 10s. rt. in Stanford Ryvers. Def. quitclaimed to pl. & the heirs of Tho. Patteshale. And for this pl. gtd. the same to Rd. & his heirs, to hold of the chief lords.

10. Morrow of All Souls, 3, & Eas. 5 Eliz. Tho. Franke, esq., & w. Mary, pl. Giles House *alias* Howes, gent., def. Manor of Bollyngtons & 12 mess., 8 curtilages, 6 tofts, 4 barns, 1 dovecote, 12 gdns., 9 orchards, 180 a. ar., 50 a. mw., 160 a. pa. & 40s. rt. in Hatfeld Regis *alias* Hatfeld Brodoke & Canfeld. Def. quitclaimed to pl. & the heirs of Tho., with warranty against Hy. Howes, brother of def. & his heirs. £200.

11. Rd. Aberforde, gent., pl. Hy. Bretton, gent., def. 1 mess., 1 cott. & 1 gdn. in Colchester. £40.

12. Jn. Eliott & Rd. Pylson, gentlemen, pl. Edw. Eliott, gent., & w. *Jane*, def. A third part of the manors of Newland Hall, Wares & Heyrons, & a third part of 8 mess., 6 cotts., 660 a. ar., 140 a. mw., 500 a. pa., 60 a. wd. & £3 6s. rt. in Gyngmergaret, Wydford, Writtle, Chelmesford, Wyllyngale Doe, Wyllyngale Rokkell, Willyngale Spayne, Goodester, Highester, Roxwell, Lutwood, Plesshey, Masshebery, Shellowe Bowells & Great Badowe. Def. quitclaimed one moiety of the above to pl. & the heirs of Jn., & gtd. to the same the reversion of the other moiety, which Robt. Wiseman & w. Mary hold for her life, to hold of the chief lords. £200.

13. Hil. & Eas. Rd. Ryche, kt., lord Ryche, Robt. Tyche, kt., his son & heir apt., & Tho. Wrothe, kt., pl. *Edm.* Mordaunte, esq., & w. Agnes & Hy. Mordaunte, his son & heir apt., def. Manor of Thunderley & 6 mess., 6 gdns., 6 orchards, 200 a. ar., 60 a. mw., 200 a. pa., 100 a. wd. & 10s. rt. in Thunderley & Wymbyshe. Def. quitclaimed to pl. & the heirs of Rd. And for this pl. gtd. to Hy. & his heirs a yearly rt. of £20 from the same, payable at the Annunciation & Michaelmas, with power of distraint, provided that this shall not be a charge on the persons of pl. but only on the prop.; & also gtd. the prop. to Edm. to hold for life of the chief lords without impeachment of waste, with remainder to Agnes for life, the heirs of the body of Edm., & his right heirs.

14. Wm. Colyn, pl. *Wm.* Clarke & w. Florence, def. 3 mess., 3 gdns., 18 a. ar., 4 a. mw. & 4 a. pa. in Takeley & Hatfeld Regis. £120.

15. Jn. Benton, pl. *Hy.* Parker, kt., lord Morley, & w. Eliz., def. Manor of Shyngyll Hall & 160 a ar., 20 a. mw., 60 a. pa., 10 a. wd. & 50s. rt. in Shyngyll Hall, Eppyng & Great Parndon. £120.

16. Hil. & Eas. Leonard Barrett & Pet. Rosewell, pl. Tho. Heyrde & w. *Margt.*, def. A moiety of a fifth part of 20 mess., 10 cotts., 20 gdns., 20 orchards, 300 a. ar., 200 a. pa., 60 a. mw., 40 a. wd. & £10 rt. in Chygwell. Def. quitclaimed to pl. & the heirs of Leonard. And for this pl gtd. the same to def. & the heirs of Tho., to hold of the chief lords.

17. Simon Rewse, pl. *Rd.* Rcson & w. Margt., def. 3 mess., 40 a. ar., 10 a. mw., 30 a. pa., 1 a. wd. & 10 a. moor in Haverell *alias* Haverhyll, Sturmer, Kedyngton & Bumpsted at the Steeple. £80.

18. Geo. Willowes, pl. *Jn.* Rande & w. Margt., def. 2 a. pa. & 2 a. wd. in Hadstock. £30.

19. Hil. & Eas. Anth. Buggs, gent., pl. Edw. Buggs sen., gent., & *Hy.* Buggs, gent., def. Manors of Brent Hall & Kytchyn Hall & 10 mess., 10 cotts., 10 gdns., 400 a. ar., 60 a. mw., 100 a. pa., 100 a. wd. & 20s. rt. in Harlowe. £600.

20. Hil. & Eas. Rd. Flacke jun., pl. Edm. Roberts & w. *Margt.*, Tho. Trundye & w. *Joan*, Tho. Edwards & w. *Eliz.*, & Robt. Overall & w. *Alice*, daus. & co-heirs of Jn. Perlevyn, decd., def. 1 toft, 2 gdns., 8 a. ar., 3 a. mw. & 2 a. pa. in Radwynter. £40.

21. Hil. & Eas. Jn. Cock, pl. *Rd.* Archer & w. Anne, def. 1 mess., 2 tofts & 1 gdn. in Brentwood. £40.

22. Tho. Bedell, gent., pl. Edw. Elyott, gent., & w. *Jane*, def. A third part of 3 mess., 160 a. ar., 20 a. mw., 60 a. pa., 20 a. wd. & 5s. rt. in Wryttle, Roxwell & Margaretynge. Def. quitclaimed one moiety to pl. & his heirs, & gtd. to the same the reversion of the other moiety, which Robt. Wyseman & w. Mary hold for her life, to hold of the chief lords. £60.

23. Tho. Fuller, pl. Francis Vaughan, esq., def. 1 mess., 1 cott., 1 dovecote, 6 a. mw. & 30 a. pa. in Chygwell & Lamborne. £40.

24. Jn. Thruston, pl. *Jn.* Holland & w. Margt., def. 1 mess., 1 barn, 1 dovecote, 2 gdns., 1 orchard & 16 a. ar. in Great Clacton. £40.

25. Jn. Fryer sen., pl. *Wm.* Barker & w. Alice, def. A third part of the manor of Garnans, a third part of 4 mess., 4 gdns., 4 orchards, 100 a. ar., 20 a. mw., 40 a. pa., 40 a. wd. & £5 rt. & a third part of a moiety of 1 mess., 1 gdn., 1 orchard, 40 a. ar., 6 a. mw., 50 a. pa., 10 a. wd. & 10s. rt. in Great Salyng, Rayne & Stebyng. £70.

26. Wm. Hewman *alias* Rutter, gent., pl. Wm. Barlee, gent., son & heir of Jn. Barlee, gent., decd., def. 1 mess. & 9 a. ar. in Clavering. 50 mks.

27. Eliz. Cocke, wid., pl. Jn. Chamberleyn, def. A moiety of 1 mess., 1 cott., 1 gdn. & 2 a. ar. in Brentwood. £400.

28. Tho. Myldemaye, esq., pl. Tho., duke of Norfolk, earl marshal of England, & w. *Margt.*, dau. & heir of tho., late lord Audeley, def. Manors of Terlyng, Leighes & Moche Leighes, 400 mess., 200 cotts., 200 tofts., 4 water-mills, 4 dovecotes, 300 orchards, 400 gdns., 3,000 a. ar., 500 a. mw., 3,000 a. pa., 1,000 a. wd., 200 a. furze & heath & £60 rt. in Terling, Moche Leighes, Little Leighes, Fayerstede, Little Waltham, Hatfelde Peverell, Wytham, Fawborne, Lamborne, Hatfelde Brodocke, Boreham, Spryngfelde, White Notley, Black Notley, Cressing, Reyne, Bragintree & Purleighe, the rectory of Terling & a portion of tithes in White Notley, Wytham & Reyne, the advowson of the church of Moche Leighes, & the advowson of the vicarage of the church of Terlyng. £1,700.

CP25(2)/127/1623   TRINITY, 5 ELIZABETH   1563

1. Tho. Colshill, esq., pl. Wm. Legge, def. A fifth part of the manor of Appletons, & a fifth part of 8 mess., 100 a. ar., 160 a. mw., 160 a. pa. & 100 a. wd. in Chigwell. 130 mks.

2. Eas. & Trin. Tho. Wyseman, esq., & w. Jane, pl. *Ralph* Wyseman, gent., & w. Eliz., def. Manor of Yardeley Hall & 2 mess., 2 cotts., 2 orchards, 2 gdns., 140 a. ar., 10 a. mw., 40 a. pa. & 20s. rt. in Thaxstede, Wymbysshe & Depden. Def. quitclaimed to pl. & the heirs of Tho. £200.

3. Nich. Bacon, kt., keeper of the great seal of England, pl. *Jn.* Mershe & w. Alice, def. 1 mess., 1 toft, 1 gdn. 1 orchard, 60 a. ar., 10 a. mw., 10 a. pa., 1 a. wd. & 100 a. furze & heath in Dagenham. £100.

4. Geo. Stondon & w. Margt., pl. *Robt.* Fynche & w. Grace, def. 2 mess., 2 tofts, 2 gdns., 40 a. ar., 7 a. mw.. & 15 a. pa. in Beachamp Roodyng & Shelley. Def. quitclaimed to pl. & the heirs of Margt. £80.

5. Robt. Fynche, pl. Geo. Stondon & w. *Margt.*, def. 1 mess., 1 toft, 1 cott., 1 gdn., 1 orchard, 26 a. ar. & 5 a. mw. in Shelley, Heigh Onger & Chippyng Onger. £80.

6. Rd. Weston, one of the justices of the Common Bench, & w. Margt., pl. Edw. Leygh, esq., def. A fourth part of the manor of West Tylbery, a fourth part of 300 a. ar., 60 a. mw., 130 a. pa., 18 a. wd., 300 a. marsh & 60s. rt. in West Tylbery, East Tylbery, Chawdwell, Lytle Thurrocke, Greyes Thurrocke & Orset, a fourth part of the ferry or passage of West Tylbery, & a fourth part of the advowson of the church of West Tylbery. Def. quitclaimed to pl. & the heirs of Rd. £160.

7. Tho. Rolffe, pl. *Jas.* Bragg & w. Alice, def. 20 a. ar., 2 a. mw. & 1 a. wd. in Wyxe. £40.

8. Francis Sympson, pl. Hy. Butler, gent., & w. *Agnes*, def. 4 a. ar., & 4 a. pa. in Little Wakeryng. £40.

9. Robt. Ryche, kt., & w. Eliz., pl. Dunstan Felton & w. Mary & Jn. Litle, def. 4 a. ar., 47 a. pa. & 3 a. wd. in Henyngham Syble. Def. quitclaimed to pl. & the heirs of Eliz. And for this pl. gtd. the same to Jn. to hold from Michaelmas last for 500 years without impeachment of waste, rendering 12d. yearly to Eliz. & her heirs, payable at the Annunciation & Michaelmas, with power of distraint for Robt. & Eliz. & her heirs.

10. Edm. Wyllyamson, pl. *Lau.* Alyston & w. Joan, def. 1 mess. & 2 gdns. in Hengham at the Castle *alias* Hennyngham Castell. £40.

11. Wm. Ayllett, pl. Wm. Marler, gent., def. 10 a. ar., 4 a. 3 roods mw. & 12 a. pa. in Keldon. 140 mks.

12. Ralph Solme, pl. *Edw.* Madyson & w. Dorothy, def. 8 a. ar. & 12 a. mw. in Sandon. 130 mks.

13. Ralph Wyseman, gent., & w. Eliz., pl. *Tho.* Wyseman, esq., & w. Jane, def. Manor of Belstedhall & 2 mess., 2 orchards, 2 gdns., 160 a. ar., 8 a. mw., 60 a. pa. & 14s. rt. in Bromfylde & Spryngfyld. Def. quitclaimed to pl. & the heirs of Ralph. £200.

14. Jn. Bacheler & w. Agnes, pl. *Tho.* Kempe *alias* Whythe & w. Agnes, def. 1 mess., 1 curtilage, 1 gdn. & 1 orchard in Chelmesford. Def. quitclaimed to pl. & the heirs of Jn. 130 mks.

15. Rd. Pillesdon & Tho. Wryght, pl. Ralph Wryght & w. *Alice*, def. 6 mess., 240 a. ar., 60 a. mw., 120 a. pa. & 60 a. wd. in Wethersfeld, Shawford, Great Salyng, Rayne & Felsted. Def. quitclaimed to pl. & the heirs of Rd. And for this pl. gtd. the same to def. & the heirs of *Alice*, to hold of the chief lords, with remainder to the right heirs of Ralph.

16. Geoff. Lorkyn, pl. Tho. Ryggs & w. Joan, *Jn.* Ryggs & w. Mary, def. 1 mess., 1 cott., 1 gdn., 5 a. ar. & 2 a. mw. in Buttesbury & Stock. £40.

17. Jn. Joselyn, gent., & Tho. Bartelet, gent., pl. Hy. Joselyn, gent., & w. *Anne*, def. 2 mess., 1 dovecote, 2 gardens, 4 orchards, 200 a. ar., 60 a. mw., 200 a. pa., 80 a. wd. & 300 a. marsh in West Thorocke. Def. quitclaimed to pl. & the heirs of Jn. £400.

18. Eas. & Trin. Jn. Northe, pl. Wm. Tyllyarde & w. *Agnes*, def. 1 mess., 1 gdn., 1 orchard & ½ a. ar. in Stocke. £40.

19. Geo. Hadley, esq., & Tho. Graye, gent., pl. Wm. Barlee, gent., def. Manors of Thurroks & Powcynes *alias* Pownces & 10 mess., 2 gdns., 200 a. ar., 60 a. mw., 100 a. pa., 20 a. wd. & £7 rt. in Clavering, Langley, Berden & Arkesden. Def. quitclaimed to pl. & the heirs of Geo. 400 mks.

20. Wm. Bendlowes, serjeant at law, pl. Eliz. Songer, wid., Jerome Songer, gent., & w. Mary, *Robt.* Songer, gent., & Robt. Pecock & w. Jane, def. 2 mess., 1 cott., 1 barn, 6 gdns., 70 a. ar. & 2 a. wd. in Great Berdefeld, Terlyng, Hatfeld Peverell & Wytham. Def. quitclaimed to pl. & his heirs, with warranty against the heirs of Rd. Songer, gent., decd., & warranty for the heirs of Jerome for the tenements in Terlyng, Hatfeld Peverell & Wytham. £200.

21. Wm. Lynn, pl. *Wm.* Amys, gent., & w. Joan, def. 2 mess., 3 barns, 4 cotts., 2 gdns., 2 orchards, 100 a. ar., 12 a. mw., 40 a. pa. & 8 a. wd. in Great Okeley, Tendrynge & Wykes. £140.

22. Robt. Ryche, kt., & w. Eliz., pl. Dunstan Felton & w. Mary, def. Manor of Hawkewoods & 5 mess., 5 gdns., 5 orchards, 70 a. ar., 20 a. mw., 60 a. pa., 5 a. wd.,

10 a. furze & heath & 40s. rt. in Henyngham at the Castle, Hengham Sybyll, Maplested, Halsted & Gosfeld. Def. quitclaimed to pl & the heirs of Eliz. £200.

23. Wm. Hurrell & Wm. Stronge, pl. Robt. Ryche, kt., & w. *Eliz.*, def. Manor of Hawkewoods etc. (as in last). Def. quitclaimed to pl. & the heirs of Wm. Hurrell. £200.

24. Wm. Petre, kt., & Jn. Petre, esq., his son & heir apt., pl. *Tho.* Barker, esq., & w. Dorothy & Margt. Barker, wid., def. Manor of Chingenhall *alias* Chiggenhall *alias* Chignall *alias* Chignall St. James & 10 mess., 10 cotts., 10 tofts, 2 mills, 2 dovecotes, 20 gdns., 10 orchards, 400 a. ar., 200 a. mw., 400 a. pa., 100 wd., 200 a. furze & heath, 100 a. moor, £6 rt. & free warren & view of frank pledge in Chingenhall *alias* Chiggenhall *alias* Chignall *alias* Chignall St. James, Chignall Zoyn, Bromfeld & Wryttle, & the advowson of the church of Chingenhall *alias* Chiggenhall. Def. quitclaimed to pl. & the heirs of Wm. £280.

25. Eas. & Trin. Jn. Broke, pl. *Jn.* Pascall, gent., & w. Mary, def. 1 orchard & 7 a. ar. in Great Badowe & tithes of sheaves & grain pertaining to the rectory of Great Badowe. £20.

26. Eas. & Trin. Jn. Newporte *alias* Dryver, pl. *Wm.* Newporte *alias* Dryver & w. Agnes, def. 6 a. ar., & 2 a. pa. in Little Stambrydge. £40.

27. Rd. Crymble, pl. *Jn.* Meller *alias* Sawman & w. Alice, def. 1 mess., 1 gdn., 2 a. ar. & 2 a. pa. in Pakelsham. £40.

28. Jn. Bedyll, pl. Jn. Elcock, gent., & w. Joan, det. 1 mess. & 1 gdn. in Brancktre. £40.

CP25(2)/259/ Trin. 5 Eliz.   DIVERS COUNTIES

1. Hy. Capell, Tho. Leventhorp, Rd. Cutt, esquires, Giles Capell & Alexander Scroggs, gentlemen, pl. Wistan Browne, esq., def. Manor of Colvyle Hall *alias* Brownes Manor *alias* Knyghts & 6 mess., 160 a. ar., 40 a. mw., 120 a. pa., 30 a. wd. & 100s. rt. in White Rodynge, Aithorpe Rodynge, Matchynge & Hatfelde Regis, co. Essex; & property in Wilts. Def. quitclaimed to pl. & the heirs of Hy. £860. — Essex, Wilts.

(No fines for Michaelmas term, 5 and 6 Elizabeth, are known. The court adjourned on account of the plague.)

CP25(2)/127/1624   HILARY, 6 ELIZABETH   1564

(Fines for this term were levied at Hertford Castle, the court having adjourned there on account of the plague.)

1. Trin. & Hil. Jn. Fytche, pl. Hy. Aylett & w. *Anne*, def. 1 mess. & 1 gdn. in Hatfeld Regis *alias* Brodcock. £40.

2. Wm. Londe & Jn. Kent, pl. Tho. Bendyshe, gent., & w. *Eleanor*, def. Manor of Woodhowses & 2 mess., 80 a. ar., 100 a. pa., 60 a. wd. & 5s. rt. in Great Horkesley & Bulmer. Def. quitclaimed to pl. & the heirs of Wm. And for this pl. gtd. the same to Tho. and his heirs, to hold of the chief lords.

3. Hy. Fanshawe, esq., pl. *Jn.* Bennyngham *alias* Bedingham & w. Margery, def. 1 mess., 1 dovecote, 1 gdn. & 2 a. ar. in Barking. £40.

4. Jn. Lytle, pl. Wm. Bridge & w. *Alice*, def. A moiety of 1 mess., 1 gdn., 1 orchard & 2 a. ar. in Dagenham & Barkynge. £20.

5. Tho Payne, pl. Jn. Chaundeler & w. *Joan*, def. 2 a. ar. in Southwelde. £40.

6. Jn. Ware, pl. *Wm.* Clarke & w. Joan, def. 5 a. ar. in Chelmesford. £40.

7. Hy. Harrington, pl. Robt. Cotton, gent., & w. *Lettice* and Jn. Chappleyn & w. *Agnes*, def. 1 mess., 1 gdn., 60 a. ar., 2 a. mw., 20 a. pa. & 6 a. wd. in Wycham St. Paul *alias* Wykham Paule & Gestyngthorpe. £140.

8. Tho. Stane, pl. *Tho.* Cubitte & w. Alice, def. 1 mess., 1 curtilage, 1 gdn., 1 orchard, 18 a. ar., 3 a. mw., 4 a. pa. & 2 a. wd. in Fyfehyde *alias* Fyffeld. 50 mks.

9. Tho. Leame, pl. Hy. Drury, esq., & w. *Eliz.*, def. 1 mess. & 5 a. pa. in Bradwell by the Sea. £40.

10. Rd. Horrell sen., pl. Wm. Feld & w. *Kath.*, def. 2 mess., 1 curtilage, 2 gdns., 10 a. ar., 14 a. pa. & ½ a. wd. in Langnoo *alias* Langenho & Westmersey. £40.

11. Robt. Burrowe, pl. *Robt.* Frythe & w. Mary, def. 1 mess., 1 orchard & 1 gdn. in Brokewalden. £40.

12. Reg. Somner, pl. *Jn.* Fyfelde *alias* Fyfhyde & w. Eliz., *Tho.* Sampforde & w. Agnes, def. 1 mess., 1 gdn., 20 a. ar., 6 a. mw., 4 a. pa., 1 a. wd. & 2s. rt. in Fyfelde *alias* Fyfhyde. £40.

13. Wm. Luckyn, pl. Jn. Glasscocke, gent., def. 2 mess., 2 tofts, 2 gdns., 2 orchards, 30 a. ar., 4 a. mw., 20 a. pa. & a moiety of the manor of Dyves Hall *alias* Chygnall Hall *alias* Chygnall Trenchefoyle & a moiety of 3 mess., 3 gdns., 3 orchards, 200 a. ar., 30 a. mw., 60 a. pa., 20 a. wd. & £4 rt. in Smele Chygnall, Saynt James Chignall, Great Waltham. Bromefylde, Wrytle & Masshebery, & a moiety of the advowson of the rectory of the parish church of Smely Chygnall, which Grace Glascock, wid., holds of life. Pl. & his heirs to hold the reversion of the chief lords. 200 mks.

14. Trin. & Hil. Tho. Porter, pl. *Tho.* Hall & w. Anne, def. 1 mess., 2 cotts., 1 gdn., 30 a. ar. & 6 a. mw. in Blakmore & Stonden. Def. quitclaimed to pl. & his heirs, with warranty against the heirs of Rd. Hall. £30.

15. Tho. Stokes, pl. *Wm.* Harrys & w. Agnes, def. 1 mess., 1 gdn., 8 a. ar., 1 a. mw. & 1 a. pa. in Spryngefylde. £40.

16. Trin. & Hil. Jn. Browne, pl. Hy. Hodson & w. Alice, Ralph Taverner & w. Joan & Alice Spurgean, wid., def. 1 mess., 1 gdn., 1 orchard & 2 a. mw. in Hengham at the Castle *alias* Hennyngham Castell. Def. quitclaimed to pl. & his heirs, with warranty of the messuage, gdn., orchard & ½ a. mw., against Hy. & Alice & the heirs of Ralph & Joan & the heirs of Ralph. £50.

17. Wm. Gryggle *alias* Gryges, pl. *Edm.* Hunt & w. Felicia & Hy. Pynell & w. Agnes, def. 1 mess., 1 barn, 3 cotts., 1 gdn., 1 orchard, 60 a. ar., 3 a. mw., 40 a. pa. & 2 a. wd. in Great Bardefeld, Bardefeld Salyng & Great Salyng. £100.

18. Tho. Blakwell, gent., pl. *Hy.* Jernegan *alias* Jernyngham, kt., & w. Frances, def. 2 mess., 1 cott., 3 gdns., 3 orchards, 60 a. ar., 16 a. mw., 20 a. pa. & 10 a. wd. in Layghton *alias* Layton *alias* Layton Stone & Walkanstowe *alias* Waltamstowe. £40.

19. Tho. Haddon, gent., pl. *Hy.* Jernegan *alias* Jerningham, kt., & w. Frances & *Tho.* Blakwell, gent., def. 1 mess., 1 dovecote, 1 gdn., 1 orchard, 4 a. mw. & 20 a. pa. in Layghton *alias* Layton *alias* Layton Stone. £40.

20. Trin. & Hil. Barnard Wytham, pl. Wm. Lame, def. 1 mess., 3 gdns. & 36 a. ar. in Sudmynster *alias* Southmynster. £80.

21. Edw. Jackman, citizen & alderman of London, pl. *Wm.* Legatte, gent., & w. Jane, def. 6 a. pa. & ½ a. wd. in Upmynyster *alias* Upmynster *alias* Upmester. £40.

22. Wm. Somner, pl. Tho. Lytman & w. *Joan,* def. 13 a. ar., & 2 a. mw. in Harlowe. £40.

23. Rd. Pettye, pl. *Geo.* Marden, son of Geo. Marden sen., & w. Joan, def. 8 a. ar. & 4 a. pa. in Kelveden *alias* Keldon. £40.

24. Wm. Dellowe, pl. *Jn.* Meade & w. Mary, def. 10 a. ar. & 7 a. pa. in Claveryng. £40.

25. Rd. Tyrrell, esq., pl. Lewis Mordaunt, esq., def. Manor of Wautons *alias* Waltons & 6 mess., 4 cotts., 1 toft, 7 barns, 1 dovecote, 5 gdns., 8 orchards, 360 a. ar., 70 a. mw., 300 a. pa., 60 a. wd. & 100s. rent in Bumpsted at the Steeple, Haverell, Sturmere & Whixo. £160.

26. Trin. & Hil. Rd. Flack sen. & Wm. Flack, pl. *Robt.* Mordaunt, esq., & w. Barbara, Tho. Cracheroode, gent., & w. Anne, & Jn. Cleydon & w. Anne, def. 1 mess., 1 gdn., 15 a. ar. & 2 a. pa. in Wymbysshe. Def. quitclaimed to pl. & the heirs of Wm. 70 mks.

27. Trin. & Hil. Rd. Flack sen. & Gilbert Flak, pl. The same def. 1 mess., 1 gdn., 12 a. ar. & 3 a. pa. in Wymbysshe. Def. quitclaimed to pl. & the heirs of Gilbert. 40 mks.

28. Wm. Petre, kt., Hy. Tyrrell, kt., Jn. Talbott, Tho. Lucas, Edm. Tyrrell, Geo. Whyte, Tho. Nicolls & Tho. Bromley, esq., pl. *Jn.* Mordaunt, kt., lord Mordaunt, & w. Dame Joan & Lewis Mordaunt, esq., def. Manors of Westhorndon, Ameys, Gyngrauff, Craneham, Feldehouse, Nokehall, Great Bromeford & Typtofts & 200 mess., 2 windmills, 40 gdns., 40 orchards, 4,000 a. ar., 500 a. mw., 2,000 a. pa., 300 a. wd., 2,000 a.

furze & heath, 300 a. moor, 200 a. reedbed, 200 a. marsh & £30 rt. in Westhorndon, Esthorndon, Gyngrauff, Craneham, Chilterdiche *alias* Chilterndyche, Brentwood, Sowthwelde, Great Warley *alias* Warley Walletts, Little Warley, Dunton, Langedon, Hutton, Great Saling, Bulvan, Lyendon, Bartilesden, Ravensden Crey, Great Burstede, Little Burstede, Alvley *alias* Alveley, Bishop's Wokyngdon, South Wokyngdon, Nevenden, Debden, Wygforde, Wymbysshe, Radwynter, Hempstede, Thackstede, Parlecheden, Redeswell & Stifford, & the advowsons of the churches of Westhorndon, Gyngrauff, Craneham & Nevendon. Def. quitclaimed to pl. & the heirs of Wm. £1,600.

29. Trin. & Hil. Rowland Heyward & Jn. Lacye, pl. *Tho.*, duke of Norfolk, & w. Margt., def. Manor of Chalvedowne & 20 mess., 20 cotts., 10 tofts, 1 dovecote, 20 orchards, 20 gdns., 500 a. ar., 300 a. mw., 500 a. pa., 200 a. wd., 300 a. furze & heath & £5 rt. in Pytchesey, Canvey, Hornedowne & Southbenfleet. Def. quitclaimed to pl. & the heirs of Rowland. £760.

30. Wm. Bye, pl. Mich. Sawyer & w. *Eliz.*, Gilbert Motte & w. *Joan*, def. 1 mess. & 1 gdn. in Chepyngwalden. £40.

31. Jn. Reve, pl. Wm. Rede & w. Joan & *Wm.* Eve, def. 6 a. ar. & 5 a. pa. in Great Dunmowe, Highester & Barneston. £40.

32. Jn. Broke, pl. Jn. Richemonde & w. *Agnes*, def. 3 a. mw. in Woodham Mortymer. £20.

33. Wm. Glascock, pl. Rd. Ryche, kt., lord Ryche, def. 84 a. ar. in Fyfelde. £40.

34. Jn. Waylott, pl. Rd. Ryche, kt., lord Ryche, def. Manor of Lampytts & 2 gdns., 1 orchard, 280 a. ar., 20 a. mw., 60 a. pa., 4 a. wd., 20 a. furze & heath & 20s. rt. in Fyfelde, Moreton, Little Laver & Shelley. £200.

35. Tho. Unwyn *alias* Onnyon & Tho. French, pl. Edw. Ryche *alias* Kylhogg & w. *Cecily* & Jn. Cornell & w. Judith, def. 1 mess., 1 toft, 1 gdn., 10 a. ar. & 2 a. mw. in Great Sampford & Byrdebroke. Def. quitclaimed to pl. & the heirs of Tho. Unwyn. £40.

36. Hy. Pynell, pl. Wm. Sone, def. 1 mess. & 1 gdn. in Maldon in the parish of St. Peter. £40.

37. Rd. Style Woman, pl. *Jn.* Stile Woman & w. Bridget, def. 8 a. pa. in Coldenorton. £40.

38. Jn. Sybthorpe, pl. *Wm.* Stokes & w. Margt., def. 8½ a. ½ rood ar. in Great Berdfeld. £20.

39. Rd. Fytche, gent., pl. *Tho.* Sprynge & w. Margt., def. 1 mess. & 1 gdn. in Great Berdefelde. £40.

40. Simon Ruse, pl. *Rd.* Tyrrell, esq., & w. Grace & *Lewis* Mordaunt, esq., def. 1 mess., 1 toft, 1 gdn., 60 a. ar., 8 a. mw., 50 a. pa. & 20 a. wd. in Burdebroke & Redgewell. £80.

41. Jn. Glascock, pl. *Jn.* Waylett & w. Eliz., def. Manor of Blackhall & 10 mess., 200 a. ar., 100 a. mw., 200 a. pa., 100 a. wd. & 10s. rt. in Blackehall & Bobymor *alias* Bobyngeworth. £160.

42. Wm. Bigge, pl. *Tho.* Webbe, son & heir of Rd. Webbe, & w. Alice, def. 1 mess., 1 barn, 1 gdn., 18 a. ar. & 7 a. pa. in Toppesfilde & Hennyngham Sible *alias* Hengham Syble. £60.

43. Tho. Salmon, pl. *Wm.* Wyllande & w. Margt., def. 2 mess. & 1 gdn. in Chippyngongar. £40.

CP25(2)/259/Hil. 6 Eliz.   **DIVERS COUNTIES**

4. Trin. & Hil. Rd. Tyrrell, esq., pl. *Jn.* Mordaunt, kt., lord Mordaunt, & w. Joan, def. Manor of Wautons *alias* Waltons & 8 mess., 4 cotts., 4 tofts, 1 dovecote, 8 barns, 8 gdns., 8 orchards, 500 a. ar., 100 a. mw., 400 a. pa., 100 a. wd. & 100s. rt. in Bumpsted at the Steeple *alias* Steple Bumpsted, Byrdebroke, Reddeswell, Haverell, Sturmere & Wyxho, co. Essex; & 7 a. pa. in Wyxho, co. Suffolk. Def. quitclaimed to pl. & his heirs, with warranty against the heirs of Rd. Fytz Lowes, kt., decd. £660. — Essex, Suff..

5. Wm. Kyng, pl. *Rd.* Tyrrell, esq., & w. Grace & *Lewis* Mordaunt, esq., def. 1 mess., 2 tofts, 1 barn, 2 gdns., 80 a. ar., 18 a. mw., 50 a. pa. & 20 a. wd. in Burdebroke, co. Essex; & 8 a. mw. in Whixo, co. Suff.. £180. — Essex, Suff..

12. Rd. Sakevyle, kt., Tho. Sakevyle, Jn. Sakevyle, esquires, Anth. Bridges & Edw. Barnard, gentlemen, pl. Philip Fynes, gent., def. Manor of Nasshall & 3 mess., 3 cotts., 600 a. ar., 100 a. mw., 200 a. pa., 20 a. wd., 30 a. fresh marsh, 50 a. furze & heath & 20s. rt. in Nasshall, & the advowson of the church of Nasshall, co. Essex; & prop. in other counties. Def. quitclaimed to pl. & the heirs of Rd. £12,660. — Suss., Kent, Essex, London, Suff., Norf., Lincoln, Southampton, Northampton, Berks., Wilts., Dorset, Nottingham, Derby, York, N'humb..

(There are no Essex Fines for Easter & Trinity terms, 6 Elizabeth (1564).)

CP25(2)/127/1625   MICHAELMAS, 6–7 ELIZABETH

1. Mich. Wm. Hammond, gent., & w. Eliz., pl. *Justinian* Champenyes, gent., & w. Elena, def. 1 mess., 100 a. mw., 100 a. pa., 120 a. fresh marsh & 100 a. salt marsh in Fobbyng & a free fishpond in Fobbyng water. Def. quitclaimed to pl. & the heirs of Wm. £400.

2. Mich. Edm. Markaunt, gent., pl. *Tho.* Audeley, gent., & w. Beatrice, def. 12 a. mw. called 'Chene Medue *alias* Horsse Medue' in Lexden. 130 mks.

3. Mich. Wm. Chapman, pl. *Pet.* Girdeley & w. Agnes, def. 1 mess., 2 gdns, 12 a. ar., 6 a. mw. & 12 a. pa. in Redeswell & Tylbury. £40.

4. Mich. Wm. Beryff, gent., pl. *Jn.* Beryff, gent., & w. Dorothy, def. 6 mess., 3 tofts, 6 gdns. & 4 a. ar. in Colchester. £40.

5. Mich. Geo. Blacklock, pl. *Jn.* Estfyld & w. Joan, def. 1 mess., 1 gdn., 1 orchard, 12 a. ar. & 1 a. mw. in Westbergholt *alias* Bergholt Sakevyle. £40.

6. Mich. Joan Awger & Robt. Wodeward, pl. Joan (*recte* John) Uptigrave & w. *Agnes*, Jn. Saverye & w. Joan def. 1 mess. & 1 gdn. in Salcott Wigborough. Def. quitclaimed to pl. & the heirs of Joan Awger. £20.

7. Mich. Francis Eglesfeld, gent., pl. Jn. Byer, esq., & w. *Joan*, def. 8 a. marsh in Estham. £40.

8. Mich. Rd. Ryche, kt., lord Ryche, & Robt. Ryche, kt., his brother & heir apt., pl. *Tho.* Shaa, gent., & w. Anne, def. 2 mess., 600 a. fresh marsh & 200 a. salt marsh on the island of Foulenes, Little Wakeringe, Shaplande & Sutton. Def. quitclaimed to pl. & the heirs of Robt. Ryche. £412.

9. Mich. Jn. Allen, pl. *Tho.* Rychemond & w. Cecily, def. 2 tofts, 10 a. ar. & 24 a. fresh marsh in Dovercourte. 130 mks.

10. Mich. Hy. Marsshe, pl. *Jn.* Rigbye, gent., & w. Anne, def. 1 mess., 1 toft, 1 barn, 1 gdn. & 21s. rt. in Waltham Holy Cross. £40.

11. Mich. Wm. Watson, gent., pl. *Tho.* Awdeley of Stanwaye, gent., & w. Beatrice, def. 3 mess., 2 barns, 3 gdns., 1 orchard & 8 a. pa. in Colchester. £80.

12. Mich. Ralph Turner, pl. *Jn.* Gace & w. Joan, def. 1 mess., 1 barn, 1 gdn., 14 a. ar., 4 a. mw. & 5 a. pa. in Thaxsted. £40.

13. Mich. Steph. Borde, pl. Jn. Denbye, def. 1 mess., 1 barn, 1 gdn, 30 a. pa. & 5 a. wd. in Tendring. £40.

14. Mich. Hy. Mounke, pl. *Rd.* Eve, Jn. Berde & w. Alice, Jn. Ilbye & w. Agnes, def. 1 mess., 1 gdn., 1 orchard, 10 a. ar., 3 a. mw. & 3 a. pa. in Wrytle & Roxwell. £40.

15. Mich. Geo. Nicolls, esq., & Gabriel Busshe, pl. Alexander Raye & w. *Eliz.*, def. 4 mess., 2 barns, 2 gdns., 1 orchard & 45 a. ar. in Walden. Def. quitclaimed to pl. & the heirs of Geo. Nicolls. £240.

16. Trin. & Mich. Jn. Grene sen., pl. Jerome Balborowe, gent., def. 2 mess., 2 gdns., 15 a. ar., 8 a. mw., 8 a. pa. & 5 a. wd. in Barkynge & Dagenham. £160.

17. Mich. Wm. Jaye, gent., & Jn. Kent, pl. Tho. Freman, def. 2 mess. & 2 gdns. in Halsted & Hennyngham Syble *alias* Hengham Syble. Def. quitclaimed to pl. & the heirs Wm. Pl. regranted to def. & his heirs to hold of the chief lords.

18. Trin. & Mich. Roland Harwood, pl. *Alan* Mannynge & w. Bridget, def. 1 mess., 2 cotts., 3 gdns., 2 barns, 2 orchards & 2 a. ar. in Walden. £40.

19. Trin. & Mich. Wm. Cordell, kt., master of the rolls, Jn. Wentworth, kt., Wm. Ayloff, esq., & Jn. Turner, gent., pl. Robt. Waldegrave, esq., & w. *Mary*, def. A moiety of the manor of Little Byrche, & a moiety of 1 water-mill, 400 a. ar., 40 a. mw., 200 a. pa., 60 a. wd., 300 a. furze & heath & 20s. rt. in Little Byrche, Great Byrche, Copford, Stanwaye & Layer delahay, & a moiety of the advowson of Little Byrche church. Def. quitclaimed to pl. & the heirs of Wm. Cordell. £620.

20. Mich. Rd. Josua, gent., pl. *Jn.* Churche, gent., & w. Margt., def. 1 mess., 1 barn, 1 dovecote, 4 cotts., 2 gdns., 1 orchard, 2 a. mw. & 10 a. pa. in Malden within the parish of Blessed Mary. Def. quitclaimed to pl. & the heirs of Rd. Josua. 100 mks.

21. Mich. Jn. Howe, gent., & Edw. Orwell, pl. Jn. Shepperd & w. *Anne*, sis. & heir of Owen Cloune of London, draper, decd., def. Manor of Lostehall *alias* Losthall, & 6 cotts., 6 gdns., 200 a. ar., 100 a. mw., 200 a. pa., 20 a. wd., 100 a. furze & heath & 40s. rt. in Orsett & Hornedon. Def. quitclaimed to pl. & the heirs of Jn. Howe. £140.

22. Mich. Wm. Nayler & Arthur Yong, pl. *Chris.* Borham & w. Kath., def. 1 mess., 20 a. ar., 2 a. mw., 4 a. pa. & 2 a. wd. in Macchyng & Sheryng. Def. quitclaimed to pl. & the heirs of Wm. Nayler. Pl. regranted to def. & heirs of Chris. Borham to hold of the chief lords.

23. Mich. Jn. Thrustle & w. Joan, pl. *Edw.* Coker, gent., & w. Joan, def. 2 mess., 2 barns, 1 cott., 2 tofts, 2 curtilages, 2 gdns., 2 orchards, 12 a. ar., 4 a. mw., 7 a. pa. & 2 a. wd. in Purleygh. Def. quitclaimed to pl. & the heirs of Jn. Thrustle. £40.

24. Mich. Wm. Ayllette, pl. *Francis* Cookucke & w. Kath., def. 1 mess., 1 gdn., 1 orchard, 16 a. ar., 3 a. mw. & 6 a. pa. in Ryvenhall. £80.

25. Mich. Lau. Rochell, pl. *Robt.* Wood, gent., & w. Joan, def. 10 a. ar., 3 a. mw. & 8 a. pa. in Spryngefeld & Little Waltham. £40.

26. Mich. Geo. Hancocks & w. Grace, pl. *Hy.* Johnson & w. Effa, def. 1 mess. & 1 gdn. in Waltham Holy Cross. Def. quitclaimed to pl. & the heirs of Grace Hancocks. £40.

27. Mich. Alban Leverett, gent., pl. Jn. Byer, esq., & w. Joan & *Jn.* Eglesfeld, gent., def. 11 a. fresh marsh in Estham. £80.

28. Mich. Wm. Strachey, pl. *Nich.* Ersewell & w. Joan, def. 1 toft, 1 gdn., 7 a. ar., 7 a. mw., & 1 a. wd. in Walden & Wymbysshe. £80.

29. Mich. Jn. Motham, pl. *Wm.* Lethynge & w. Ellen, def. 4 a. ar. & 2 a. wd. in Pontesbright. £40.

30. Mich. Wm. Hill, gent., pl. Francis Barners, esq., def. 1 mess., 1 gdn., 120 a. ar., 3 a. mw., 12 a. pa. & 4 a. wd. in Fynchingfelde. £220.

31. Mich. Tho. Stocke, sen., & Wm. Browne, pl. Wm. Chisshull, esq., & w. Eliz., Giles Chisshull, gent., & w. Alice, Robt. Corney & w. Blanche, def. 1 mess., 1 cott., 2 gdns. 20 a. ar., 4 a. mw., 3 a. pa. & 45s. rt. in Great Berdefeld, Little Berdefeld, Little Sampford & Great Sampford. Def. quitclaimed to pl. & the heirs of Tho. Stocke. Warranty by *Robt.* & Blanche Corney for the mess., cott., gdns. & 5 a. ar.; by *Wm.* & Eliz. Chisshull & Giles & Alice Chisshull for 15 a. ar., 4 a. mw., 3 a. pa. & 45s. 5d. rt. £200.

32. Mich. Wm. Stronge, pl. Kath. Davenante, wid., & *Wm.* Davenante, gent., her son & heir apt., def. 1 mess. & 1 a. pa. in Henyngham Sible. £40.

33. Morrow of Trin. & Mich. Jn. Medowe *alias* Mede, jun., pl. Giles Thrussell & w. *Joan*, def. A moiety of 1 mess., 1 barn, 2 cotts., 1 gdn., 2 orchards, 16 a. ar. & 4 a. pa. in Great Waltham, in reversion after the dec. of Agnes Glascock, wid., 50 mks.

34. Mich. Humphrey Hastler, pl. *Jn.* Churche, gent., & w. Margt., def. 1 mess., 1 barn, 1 gdn., 12 a. ar., 4 a. mw., 12 a. pa., 3 a. wd., 2 a. moor (*mora*) & common pa. in Great Totham. £100.

35. Morrow of Trin. & Mich. Edw. Some, pl. *Edw.* Madyson & w. Dorothy, def. 1 mess., 1 gdn., 1 orchard, 16 a. ar., 6 a. mw., 26 a. pa & 3 a. wd. in Sondon. £60.

36. Mich. Tho. Chappeleyn, Robt. Harte & Jn. Bedlowe, pl. Jn. Colyn & w. Mary, Wm. Parker & w. Alice, def. 3 mess., 3 gdns., 1 barn, 5 a. ar. & 1 a. mw., in Great Berdefeld, Hempsted & Fynchyngfeld. Def. quitclaimed to pl. & the heirs of Tho. Chappeleyn.

Warranty by *Jn.* & Mary Colyn for 2 a. ar. & ½ a. mw. against themselves & their heirs, Hy. Colyn & his heirs, Wm. Colyn & his heirs, Mich. Colyn & his heirs & heirs of Nich. Colyn, decd.; warranty by *Wm.* & Alice Parker for remainder of prop.. £40.

37. Mich. Rd. Dyer, pl. Jn. Skynner, & w. *Margt.*, def. 1 mess., 1 orchard & 4 a. pa. in Rettyngdon. £40.

38. Mich. Jn. Haukyne, pl. *Tho.* Lawsell & w. Joan, def. A moiety of 1 mess., 1 barn, 2 gdns., 1 orchard & 16 a. ar. in Great Waltham. £40.

39. Mich. Jn. Harryes & Wm. Isaack, pl. *Jn.* Parmanter & Lora, def. 2 mess., 2 gdns., 30 a. ar., 2 a. mw. & 5 a. pa. in Lammershe, Alphamston & Bures St. Mary. Def. quitclaimed to pl. & the heirs of Wm. Isaack. 110 mks.

40. Mich. Wm. Rochester, pl. *Jn.* Churche, gent., & w. Margt., def. 1½ mess., 200 a. ar. 200 a. pa. & 200 a. marsh in the parish of St. Mary Virgin in Maldon & on the islands of Northey & Southey. £80.

41. Mich. Rd. Grene, pl. Hy. Kent & w. Joan, *Jn.* Clench, gent., & w. Kath., def. 1 mess., 1 barn, 1 gdn., 40 a. ar. & 4 a. pa. in Great Maplested, Little Maplested & Halsted. £60.

42. Mich. Hy. Maclwilliam (*sic*), esq., pl. Edw. Mackwilliam, gent., def. Manor of Essex, 1 mess., 1 barn, 1 gdn, 100 a. ar., 20 a. mw., 100 a. pa. & 20 a. wd. in Reddeswell, Stamborne, Tylberye, Toppesfeld & Yeldam. £160.

43. Mich. Jn. Broke of Great Badowe, pl. Jn. Broke of Bradwell-by-the-Sea, *Wm.* Broke, & w. Bridget & Hugh Broke, def. 6 a. ar., 4 a. mw., 4 a. pa. & 6 a. salt marsh in Pakelesham. Warranty by def. against themselves, heirs of Wm. Broke & heirs of Robt. Broke. £40.

44. Mich. Tho. Lawsell & Tho. Laurence, pl. Jn. Kynge & w. Margt., & *Wm.* Kynge, def. 1 gdn., 1 a. ar. & 3 a. pa. in Bockynge. Def. quitclaimed to pl. & the heirs of Tho. Lawsell. £20.

45. Mich. Geo. Trigge, pl. Tho. Greye, gent., & w. *Alice*, Wm. Barlee, gent., & w. *Eliz.*, def. 3 mess., 3 tofts, 1 dovecote, 100 a. ar., 6 a. mw., 20 a. pa. & 4 a. wd. in Elmedon, Wendon Loughts, Arkesden & Crissall *alias* Chrishall. 100 mks.

46. Mich. Alexander Osborne, pl. Tho. Browne & w. *Eliz.*, def. 1 mess., 1 gdn. & 1 orchard in Waltham. £8.

47. Mich. Jn. Broke & Geo. Saunder, pl. *Edw.* Hedge, sen., & w. Kath., def. 1 mess., 1 cott., 2 gdns., 20 a. ar., 4 a. mw. & 12 a. pa. in Woodhamferrers. Def. quitclaimed to pl. & the heirs of Jn. Broke. £40.

48. Mich. Jn. Baron, gent., pl. *Jn.* Thrustle & w. Joan, def. 1 mess., 1 cott., 1 gdn., 1 orchard, 6 a. ar., 2 a. mw., 7 a. pa. & 2 a. wd. in Layerbreton. £50.

49. Mich. Robt. Samson *alias* Sansom, pl. *Wm.* Goodwyn & w. Agnes, def. One fifth of 7 mess. & 10 gdns. in Bockynge & Branktre. £40.

50. Mich. Jn. Howe, gent., pl. Wm. Holstock & w. *Agnes*, def. 3 mess., 3 cotts., 3 tofts, 3 barns, 3 orchards, 3 gdns., 40 a. ar., 10 a. mw., 40 a. pa. & 10 a. wd. in Southokingdon *alias* Southwookingdon. Warranty against def. & heirs of Agnes Holstock, Francis Higham & w. Jane, & the heirs of Jane. £40.

51. Mich. Robt. Dawe, pl. Jn. Pygryme, def. 4 mess., 4 gdns, 100 a. ar., 20 a. mw., 40 a. pa., 20 a. wd. & 10s. rt. in Stysted & Bockyng. 80. mks.

52. Mich. Anne Hayes, wid., pl. *Rd.* Browne & w. Eleanor, def. 1 mess., 1 gdn., 1 orchard, 1½ a. ar. & 1½ a. mw. in Ramesdon Bellowes. £40.

53. Mich. Jn. Quarles, pl. *Tho.* Lodge, kt., & w. Anne, def. 6 mess., 3 barns, 1 dovecote, 3 orchards, 3 gdns., 30 a. ar., 10 a. mw. & 24 a. marsh in Westham & Estham £140.

54. Mich. Hugh Baker, pl. *Hy.* Pease & w. Joan, def. 1 mess., 20 a. ar., 3 a. mw. & 10 a. pa. in Little Badowe & Woodham Water. £40.

55. Mich. Tho. Holmes & Tho. Lawrence, pl. *Wm.* Reve & w. Rose, def. 1 mess., 1 barn, 1 gdn., 40 a. ar. & 20 a. wood in Ardeleigh. Def. quitclaimed to pl. & the heirs of Tho. Holmes. £40.

56. Mich. Ralph Chamberlayne, kt., pl. Wm. Man, gent., def. 1 mess., 1 gdn., 14 a. ar., 1 a. mw. & 6 a. pa. in Bulmer. £40.

57. Law. Porter, pl. *Jn.* Porter & w. Joan, def. 1 mess., 1 gdn., 1 orchard, 12 a. ar., 1 a. mw. & 2 a. pa. in Chignall St. James. £20.

58. Mich. Jn. Goodday, pl. Jn. Tamworthe, esq., & w. Christina, & Chris. Tamworthe, gent., def. Manor of Sandon *alias* Sandon Hall, 4 mess., 4 tofts, 6 gdns., 300 a. ar., 30 a. mw., 200 a. pa., 60 a. wd. & 60s. rt. in Sandon, Great Baddowe, Little Baddowe, Mulsham, Spryngfeld, Danburye, Boreham, Purley, Pryttelwell & Sudmynster. £840.

59. Mich. Jn. Broke of Bradwell-by-the-Sea, pl. Jn. Broke of Great Badowe, *Robt.* Broke & w. Alice, def. 1 mess., 1 cott., 1 gdn., 12 a. ar., 6 a. mw., 15 a. pa. & 2 a. wd. in Barlyng, Great Wakeryng & Little Wakeryng. Warranty by def. against Robt. Broke & his heirs & Steph. Broke, Robt.'s brother, & his heirs. £40.

60. Mich. Jn. Rochell, pl. *Tho.* Arkysden *alias* Axden & w. Joan, def. 1 barn, 8 a. ar. mw. & 4 a. pa. in Little Stambrydge. £40.

61. Mich. Edm. Tyrrell, esq., pl. *Robt.* Slynge & w. Eliz., def. 10 a. ar. & 50 a. pa. in Hockeleye & Rawrye. £100.

62. Mich. Tho. Rampston, gent., pl. Francis Thymbylthorp, def. 1 mess. called Monks in Manyngtre. £20.

63. Morrow of Trin. & Mich. Tho. Fytche & Jn. Howland, pl. *Wm.* Fytche, gent., & w. Anne & Rochus Grene, esq., *alias* Rokus Grene, esq., def. Manor of Little Canfeld, 5 mess., 400 a. ar., 62 a. mw., 140 a. pa., 37 a. wd. & £6 rt. in Little Canfeld, Great Canfeld, Eystances-on-the-Hill, Takeley, Thaxsted & Great Donmowe. Def. quitclaimed to pl. & the heirs of Tho. Fytche. Pl. gtd. to Wm. Fytche & his heirs for life of Wm. & 6 years more the manor, 4 mess., 300 a. ar., 60 a. mw., 100 a. pa., 36 a. wd. & £6 rt., with remainder on expiry of term to Rochus Grene & his heirs by Alianore, lately his w., failing whom to right heirs of Wm. Fytche. Pl. also gtd. to Wm. & his heirs the 1 mess., 100 a. ar., 2 a. mw., 40 a. pa. & 1 a. wd. remaining for his life & one year more, with successive remainders as before.

CP25(2)/259/ 6-7 Eliz. Mich. DIVERS COUNTIES

5. Morrow of Trin. & Mich. Hy. Goldyng, esq., pl. Robt. Waldegrave, esq., & w. *Mary,* def. A moiety of the manors of Esthorpe & Great Byrche, & a moiety of 12 mess., 10 tofts, 1 mill, 800 a. ar., 100 a. mw., 500 a. pa., 120 a. wd., 600 a. furze & heath & £8 rt. in Esthorp, Great Byrche, Little Byrche, Copford, Stanwav, Layer delahay, Layer Breton & Messyng, & a moiety of annual rt. without pension of 5 mks. from the rectory of Great Byrche, & a moiety of the advowson of Esthorpe church in co. Essex; a quarter of the manors of Harsted *alias* Harkested & Clymston, & a quarter of 5 mess., 4 tofts, 100 a. ar., 20 a. mw., 80 a. pa., 40 a. wd. & heath & £4 rt. in Harsted *alias* Harkested, Clymston. Aswarton. Holbrook & Chelmondeston, & a quarter of the advowson of the church of Harsted *alias* Harkested in co. Suff. £520. — Essex, Suff.

6. Mich. Tho. Duncombe, pl. Geo. Poste & w. *Eliz.,* dau. & heir of Wm. Boone, decd., dau. *(sic)* & heir of Jn. Boone decd., brother & heir of Nich. Boone decd., def. 1 mess., 1 gdn., 20 a. ar., 20 a. mw., 40 a. pa. & 10 a. wd. in Chigwell. co. Essex, & 1 mess. & 1 gdn. in the parish of St. Olave in Southwarke, co. Surr. £160. — Essex, Surr.

12. Hil. & Mich. Geo. Yeo, gent., pl. *Jn.* Broke, gent., & w. Kath., def. 2 mess., 2 gdns., 2 orchards, 30 a. ar., 6 a. mw., 16 a. pa., 4 a. wd. & 10 a. furze & heath in Enveld, co. Mdx., & 2 mess., 2 gdns., 2 orchards, 20 a. ar., 4 a. mw., 18 a. pa., 6 a. wd. & 10 a. furze & heath & heath in Seynt Lawrance de Waltham, co. Essex. £40. — Mdx., Essex.

CP26(1)/122, part II HILARY, 7 ELIZABETH 1565

247. Hil. Alban Leverett, gent., pl. *Robt.* Pytman & w. Margt., def. 1 mess., 1 gdn. & 1 orchard in Harwich. £40.

248. Hil. Jn. Fuller, pl. Jn. Tompson & w. *Margt.*, def. 1 mess. & 1 gdn. in Southebemfflete. £40.

249. Hil. Rd. Lee, gent., & Wm. Lovedaie, pl. *Tho.* Shaa, gent., & w. Anne, def. Manor of Seynt Laurence Hall, & 2 mess., 2 gdns., 1 dovecote, 100 a. ar., 20 a. mw., 100 a. pa., 20 a. wd., 20 a. salt marsh, 20 a. fresh marsh & 10s. rt. in Seynt Laurence & Bradwell. Def. quitclaimed to pl. & the heirs of Rd. 310 mks.

250. Hil. Geo. Wylmer, pl. *And.* Fuller & w. Joan, def. 4 a. mw., & 5 a. fresh marsh in Barkyng. £40.

251. Hil. Ranulph Thetkyns, pl. *Tho.* Pounsett, gent., & w. Eliz. & Geo. Pounsett, gent., def. 1 mess., 1 toft, 2 gdns. & 1 orchard in Barkyng. £40.

252. Hil. Jn. Swallowe, Pl. *Tho.* Erswell & w. Margt., def. 1 mess. in Walden. £40.

CP26(1)/123, part 12

253. Hil. Ranulph Thetkyns, pl. *Wm.* Bexwell & w. Joan, def. 2 cotts., & 2 gdns. in Barkyng. £40.

254. Hil. Geo. Onyon, pl. Jn. Mylsent, esq., def. 1 dovecote, 14 a. pa. & 1 a. wd. in Hadstock. £40.

255. Hil. Jn. Chessey, pl. *Wm.* Fytche, esq., & w. Anne, def. 1 mess., 5 a. ar., 6 a. pa. & 1 a. wd. in Little Canfelde. £40.

256. Hil. Wm. Bonar, sen., pl. Jn. Aylyf, esq., def. 1 mess., 1 gdn., 1 orchard. & 4 a. ar. in Legh. £40.

257. Hil. Jn. Corrall *alias* Hunt, pl. Geoff Gybson & w. *Joan,* def. 1 rod of ar. in Brentwood. £3.

258 Hil. Wm. Paschall, pl. *Jn.* Dyer & w. Joan, def. 1 mess., 1 gdn., 1 orchard, 100 a. ar., 10 a. mw., 20 a. pa. & 2 a. wd. in Fyfhyde, Rothing Beauchampe & Willinghall Doo. £40.

259. Hil. Tho. Rowe, citizen & alderman of London, & Wm. Rowe, his son, pl. *Jn.* Goodwyn, esq., & w. Eliz., def. 40 a. ar. & marsh in Westham. Def. quitclaimed to pl. & the heirs of Wm. Rowe. £400 (*sic*).

260. Hil. Robt. Lambert, pl. *Rd.* Godfrey & w. Alice, def. 3 mess., 3 tofts, 2 gdns., 1 orchard & 2 a. pa. in the parish of St. Leonard in the town of *Colcestr'.* £40.

261. Hil. Anth. Maxey, esq., pl. *Ralph* Wryght & w. Alice, def. 3 mess., 3 tofts, 6 gdns., 140 a. ar., 20 a. mw., 140 a. pa. & 20 a. wd. in Great Salyng, Felstede, Little Rayne, Shallforde & Wethersfeld. 230 mks.

262. Hil. Jn. Kynge, pl. Wm. Trayforde & *Tho.* Trayforde, def. 1 mess., 2 gdns., 16 a. ar., 4 a. mw., 6 a. pa. & 2 a. wd. in Althorne & Maylande. £40.

263. Hil. Wm. Vernon, gent., pl. *Tho.* Frytton & w. Agnes, def. 20 a. ar., & 10 a. pa. in Boreham *alias* Boram. £80.

264. Hil. Hy. Fanshawe, esq., pl. *Rd.* Cooke, gent., & w. Eliz., def. 4 a. mw. in Tareswell & Barkinge. £40.

265. Hil. Nich. Wylbore, pl. *Jn.* Shipman & w. Margery, def. 1 gdn. & 10 a. ar. in Stebbynge. £40.

266. Hil. Wm. Brewer, pl. Tho. Bygner & w, *Joan,* def. 1 (mess.?), 1 gdn. & 1 orchard in Takeley. £20.

267. Hil. Rd. Twyddy *alias* Twytty, gent., pl. Tho. Perssey, gent., def. 2 mess., 2 gdns., 2 orchards, 1 a. ar. & 3 a. pa. in Boram & Hatfeld Peverell. £40.

268. (*Beds. & Bucks.*)

269. Hil. Rd. Lee & Wm. Lovedaye, gentlemen, pl. Wm. Byckner, & w. Margt. & *Tho.* (—le), def. 1 mess., 1 gdn., 1 orchard & 10 a. ar., in Bardfelde Salynge. Def. quitclaimed to pl. & the heirs of Rd. Lee. Pl. gtd. property to Nich. & Margt. Byckner to hold of the chief lords for life of both & survivor, with apparent, & the heirs of his body, failing whom to (the heirs) of Margt. Byckner.

270. Hil. Nich. Brodewater, pl. *Rd.* Ivatt & w. *Joan,* def. 1 mess. & 1 gdn. in Rayleigh. £40.

271. Hil. Robt. Rampston, gent., pl. *Tho.* Rampston, gent., & w. Joan, def. Manor of Fennis, & 6 mess., 6 gdns., 300 a. ar., 120 a. mw., 300 a. pa., 100 a. wd. & £4 rt. in Bockyng, Brayntre, Shylds Canfeld *alias* Litell Canfeld, Great Dunmowe, Little Dunmowe, Panefeld, Shalford & Rayne. Pl. gtd. prop. to def. to hold of chief lords for the life of both & survivor, with reversion to pl. & his heirs.

272. (*Derbyshire*).

273. Wm. Barlee & Yves Grey, gentlemen, pl. Robt. Colte, def. 1 mess., 1 gdn., 1 orchard, 1 dovecote & 20 a. ar. in Heydon, Cristishall *alias* Crisshall & Great Chishull. Def. quitclaimed to pl. & the heirs of Wm. Barlee. Pl. gtd. prop. to def. for 1 month, with remainder to def. & Sybil his w. for the life of both & survivor, with remainder to right heirs of def.

274. Hil. Jn. Proctoure & Jn. Webb, pl. Robt. Peyton, esq., def. 2 mess., 1 gdn., 1 dovecote, 300 a. ar., 30 a. mw., 200 a. pa. & 100 a. wd. in Little Chesterforde & Lyttel-burys, held for life by Frances Peyton, wid., mother of def. Def. granted reversion to pl. & the heirs of Jn. Proctoure. £220.

275. Hil. Jn.(- - - - -) & Tho. Hills, pl. Wm. Kyng, & w. *Kath.* and Simon Smyth, def. A third part of (1) messuage, 1 barn, 1 gdn., 30 a. ar., 2 a. mw. & 3 a. pa. in Layer (- - - - -) & Great Wygborough. Def. quitclaimed to pl. & the heirs of Jn. (- - - - -). Pl. gtd. prop. to Simon Smyth & his assigns for 20 years starting from Michaelmas or Annunciation first after the death of Eliz. Turner, wid. of Rd. Cannock, decd., & now w. of Wm. Turner, at rt. of 12d. a year, with reversion to Wm. & Kath. Kyng to hold of chief lords.

276. Hil. Ralph Turner, pl. Jn. Davye & w. *Agnes*, def. 1 mess., 1 barn, 60 a. ar., 16 a. mw., 30 a. pa. & 10 a. wd. in Thaxsted. £40.

1565   COUNTY OF ESSEX

CP26(1)/123 (two original files, arranged by county, without numeration.)

1. Eas. Rd. Rede, pl. Wm. Corneysshe, def. 2 a. land in Mashebury. £5.

2. Eas. Tho. Mylles, pl. Oliver Warbeck *alias* Clerke, def. 5 a. ar. in Waltham Holy-crosse. £40.

3. Eas. Jn. Glascok, gent., & w. Kath., pl. *Jerome* Songer, gent., & w. Mary, def. 30 a. ar. in Wytham. Def. quitclaimed to pl. & the heirs of Jn. Glascok. £20.

4. Eas. Tho. Hockley, pl. Mich. Sawyer & w. *Eliz.*, def. 1 a. pa. in Broke Walden. £10.

5. Eas. Chris. Curteis & w. Joan, pl. Rd. Fest, son & heir of Wm. Fest, decd., def. 1 mess., 1 barn, 1 gdn., 1 orchard & 1 a. ar. in Branketre. Def. quitclaimed to pl. & the heirs of Chris. Curteis. £30.

6. Eas. Wm. Blakwell, esq., & Tho. Blakwell, gent., pl. Tho. Halmer, gent., & w. Margt., def. Manor of Chambers in Eppyng, 200 a. ar., 40 a. mw., 40 a. pa., 40 a. wd. & 40s. rt. in Chambers & Eppyng. Def. quitclaimed to pl. & the heirs of Tho. Blakwell. £280.

7. Hil. & Eas. Anne Fold, w. of Jn. Fold, pl. Reg. Smythe & w. Kath., def. 2 mess., 2 cotts., 2 orchards, 120 a. ar., 50 a. mw., 100 a. pa., 40 a. wd., 100 a. furze & heath & 3s. 4d. rt. in Lytlebury, Elmedon, Stretehall, Great Chestover, & Little Chestover, & common pa. for 200 sheep in the same. 220 mks.

8. Eas. Edw. Walgrave, esq., pl. *Jn.* Bowyer, gent., & w. Eliz., def. 10 a. pa. & 140 a. wd. in Boxstede, Langham, Mileend, Colchester, Dedham & Great Horkesley. 130 mks.

9. Eas. Rd. Ryche, kt., lord Ryche, pl. *Jn.* Goodheye *alias* Gooddaye & w. Mary, def. 1 mess., 1 barn, 15 a. ar., 6 a. mw., 20 a. pa. & 5s. rt. in Branktre, the rectory of the parish church of Branktre & the advowson of the vicarage & church of Branktre. £186.

10. Eas. Jn. Drane, pl. Ralph Hill, & w. *Margt.* & Robt. Lynne, def. A moiety of 1 mess., 40 a. ar., 20 a. mw., 20 a. pa. & 3 a. wd. in Fayrestede & Great Lighes *alias* Moche Lighes. £40.

11. Eas. Tho. Homes, pl. *Wm.* Reve & w. Rose, def. 1 mess. & 3 cotts. in the parish of St. Nicholas of the town of *Colcestr'*. £40.

12. Eas. Nich. Hills, pl. *Nich.* Fuliam & w. Eliz., def. 1 mess. & 16 a. pa. in Chygwell. £80.

13. Eas. Wm. Colyn, pl. *Wm.* Pygotte, Geo. Pygott & w. Philippa, def. 1 mess., 1 barn, 1 dovecote, 1 gdn., 1 orchard, 60 a. ar., 10 a. mw., 20 a. pa. & 6 a. wd. in Thaxsted. 230 mks.

14. Eas. Tho. Clerke & Jas. Goddyng, pl. Tho. Keye, def. 1 mess., 60 a. ar., 12 a. mw., 60 a. pa. & 24 a. wd. in Thaxsted. Def. quitclaimed to pl. & the heirs of Tho. Clarke. £40.

15. Eas. Tho. Wyseman, gent., & w. Dorothy, pl. Jn. White, def. 3 mess., 3 barns, 3 cotts., 3 gdns., 3 orchards, 40 a. ar., 10 a. mw., 20 a. pa., 6 a. wd., 20 a. marsh & 2s. rt. in Upmynster, Est Tylburye, West Tylburye & Muckyng. Def. quitclaimed to pl. & the heirs of Tho. Wyseman. £100.

16. Eas. Tho. Clarke jun., pl. Jn. Goodwyn, def. 8 mess., 8 gdns., 40 a. ar., 20 a. mw., 20 a. pa. & 10 a. wd. in Stansted, Halsted & Little Coggeshall. £220.

17. Eas. Geo. Seyer, pl. *Geo.* Christmas, esq., & w. Bridget, def. 1 water-mill, 8 a. ar. & 4 a. mw. in Westbargholt *alias* Bargholt Sackevyle. £40.

18. Eas. Edw. Waldegrave, esq., & w. Joan, pl. *Robt.* Forthe, esq., & w. Frances, def. 1 mess., 6 tofts, 1 barn, 1 garden, 1 orchard, 100 a. ar., 16 a. mw., 40 a. salt marsh in Lalford *alias* Laleford. Def. quitclaimed to pl. & the heirs of Edw. Waldegrave. £100.

19. Eas. Robt. Thorpe, gent., pl. Nich. Notyngham & w. *Alice*, def. 4 mess., 4 gdns. & 1 barn in Manytree in Mystley parish. £40.

20. Eas. Edw. Waldegrave, esq., & w. Joan, pl. *Wm.* Waldegrave, esq., & w. Eliz., def. 6 tofts, 1 cott., 2 barns, 200 a. ar., 20 a. mw., 100 a. pa., 50 a. wd., 30 a. alder & 5s. rt. in Ardeleigh, Great Bromeley, Little Bromeley, Lalford & Dedham. Def. quitclaimed to pl. & the heirs of Edw. Waldegrave. £200.

21. Eas. Wm. Mortymer & w. Joan, pl. *Hy.* Paynell & w. *Thomasina*, def. 19 a. ar. in Toppisfeld. Def. quitclaimed to pl. & the heirs of Wm. Mortymer. £40.

22. Eas. Robt. Maydestone, pl. Tho. Duke & w. *Margt.*, def. 1 mess., 1 gdn., 1 barn, 1 orchard, 16 a. ar., 1 a. mw. & 3 a. pa. in Boxsted. £40.

23. Eas. Ralph Starlyng, pl. *Robt.* Forke, esq., & w. Frances, def. 1 mess., 6 tofts, 1 barn, 1 gdn., 80 a. ar., 6 a. mw., 20 a. pa. & 4s. rt. in Ardeleigh & Dedham. £100.

24. Hil. & Eas. Wm. Grigell *alias* Griggs & w. Alice, pl. *Tho.* Forde & w. Eliz., def. 2 a. mw. & 6 a. wd. in Berdfeld Salyng *alias* Little Salyng & Great Salyng. Def. quitclaimed to pl. & the heirs of Wm. Grigell. £40.

25. Eas. Wm. Petre, kt., pl. *Rd.* Radley & w. Agnes, def. 16 a. ar. & 7 a. mw. in Ramsden Bellowes. £40.

26. Eas. Robt. Nowell, attorney-general of the Court of Wards, Wm. Lovelace & Edw. Cooke, esquires, pl. *Nich.* Bacon, kt., lord keeper of the great seal, & w. Anne, Nich. Bacon, esq., Jas. Bacon, citizen of London, Augustus Courteys & Bart. Kempe, gentlemen, def. Manor of Marks & Redlyon, 20 mess., 20 tofts, 2 mills, 2 dovecotes, 20 gdns., 10 orchards, 500 a. ar., 200 a. mw., 500 a. pa., 100 a. wd., 200 a. furze & heath & £10 rt. in Romeford, Dagnam, Hornechurche & Haveringe at Bower. Def. quitclaimed to pl. & the heirs of Edw. Cooke. £500.

27. Eas. And. Presteney & w. Eliz., pl. *Hy.* Rydesdale & w. Joan, def. 1 mess., 1 gdn., 1 orchard, 100 a. ar., 15 a. mw., 60 a. pa., 6 a. wd. & 12 a. alder in Little Horkesley & Wormyngford. Def. quitclaimed to pl. & the heirs of And. 130 mks.

28. Eas. Edm. Felton, esq., pl. *Edw.* Wyndesore, kt., lord Wyndesore & w. Kath., def. A moiety of the manors of Dynes, Hosedons & Caxtons, 4 mess., 6 tofts, 3 mills, 2 dovecotes, 4 gdns., 600 a. ar., 200 a. mw., 300 a. pa., 100 a. wd., 100 a. furze & heath & 100s. rt. in Dynes, Hosedons, Caxtons, Great Maplested, Little Maplested, Hennyngham Syble, Hennyngton at the Castle & Gestyngthorpe. 400 mks.

29. Eas. Robt. Drywood, pl. *Jas.* Spender & w. Eliz., def. 1 mess., 1 gdn., 1 curtilage, 10 a. ar., 6 a. mw., 10 a. pa. & 1 a. wd. in Westhannyngfeld. £100.

30. Hil. & Eas. Jn. Pynchon, gent., pl. *Edw.* Elyott, gent., & w. Jane, Chris. Harrys, gent., & w. Mary & Tho. Bedell, gent., def. 4 a. ar. in Wrytle. £20.

31. Hil. & Eas. Rd. Bright, pl. *Edw.* Elyott, gent., & w. Jane, Chris. Harrys, gent., & w. Mary & Tho. Bedell, gent., def. 1 mess., 1 gdn., 1 orchard, 12 a. ar., 6 a. mw. & 12 a. pa. in Wrytle & Roxwell. £20.

113

1565   DIVERS COUNTIES

CP26(1)/123 Scattered at the end of two original files.

(1.) Hil. & Eas. Jn. Brockett, esq., Edw. Brockett, esq., Wm. Baldwyn, gent., & Anth. Grene, gent., pl. Edm. Twynyho, esq., & w. Eliz., def. Manor of Derbolts, 10 mess., 2 dovecotes, 8 gdns., 5 orchards, 140 a. ar., 15 a. mw., 160 a. pa., 10 a. wd., 12 a. furze & heath & 5s. rt. in Erlestonham, Cretynge Holy Mary, Cretynge All Saints, Cretynge St. Olave & Little Stonham, co. Suff.: 1 mess., 1 gdn., 1 orchard, 200 a. ar., 30 a. mw., 200 a. pa. & 60 a. wd. in Great Ocley, Little Ocley, Bradfeld & Asshedon, co. Essex. Def. gtd. prop. to pl. & the heirs of Jn. Brockett for the life of Eliz. Twynyho. Pl. gtd. def. an annual rt. of £20 from the property for the life of Eliz. — Suff., Essex.

(2. *loose.*) Eas. Wm. Burlace & Jn. Hackston, pl. Jn. Burlace, esq., & w. Anne, def. (The manor of - - - - -) *alias* Broxborne, 2 mess., 100 a. ar., 10 a. mw., - - - s. rt. in Stevenage, co. Hertford; a third part of the manors of - - - Bunewalles, Derbolts, Beverleys, Normans, Waylands & Fycketts, - - -, 20 gdns., 2,000 a. ar., 300 a. mw., 2,000 a. pa., - - - of furze & heath & £3 rt. in Barham, Codnam, Hemmyng - - - (Cretyng) St. Mary, Cretyng All Saints, Cretyng St. Olave, Aspolestonham, Pette - - - - Bramforde, Floughton, Great Blacknam, Little Blacknam, Ipswyche, - - - Bafforde Stoke near Ipswyche & Newton, co. Suff.; - - - 40 a. ar., 12 a. mw., 200 a. pa. - - - in Bradfeilde, Asshedon, Great Okeley & Little Okeley, co. Essex. Def. quitclaimed to pl. & the heirs of Jn. Hackston. Pl. gtd. Suff. prop. to (def.) for life of Anne Burlace to hold of chief lords, with remainder to the heirs of the body of Anne. — Herts., Suff., Essex. (*Severely mutilated on right-hand side.*)

(3, *loose*). Eas. Jn. (- - - - - -) & Tho. Hulme, pl. *Jasper* Waren, gent., & w. Antonia, Roger (- - - - -), gent., & w. Joan, def. - - mess., 4 tofts, 6 gdns., 8 orchards, . . . a. ar., 20 a. (mw.), . . . pa., 60 a. wd., 40 a. furze (and heath) . . . rt. in North Wokingdon, South Wokingdon & Upmynster, co. Essex; 10 - - - - -, . . . gdns., 12 orchards, 10 barns, 2 dovecotes, 100 a. ar., 10 a. (mw.), . . . a. pa., 10 a. wd., 150 a. salt marsh & 20 a. furze (& heath) - - - (Alha)llowes *alias* Alhallous, Saynt Maries & Stoke, co. Kent. Def. quitclaimed to pl. & the heirs of Jn. (- - - -). Pl. gtd. prop. to Roger(- - - - — & his heirs to hold of chief lords. — Essex, Kent. (*Severely mutilated.*)

4(*fragment*). (Wm. Cordell, master) of the rolls, pl. Robt. (- - - -), (and w.) Eliz., & Wm. Kaye, son & heir of Geo. Kaye, def. - - - - -Holforde in co. Suff., & 1 a. - - - - - (in co. Essex). £11.

(*Note. The nomination of counties at foot of this reads: (Su)ff. (Esse)x.*)

1564   COUNTY OF ESSEX

CP26(1)/124 (one very large original file, arranged under county, no numeration.)

1. Mich. Tho. Ryvers & w. Etheldreda, pl. Jn. Norell & w. *Joan*, def. 1 mess. & 1 a. ar. in Terlinge. Def. quitclaimed to pl. & the heirs of Tho. £20.

2. Mich. Wm. Longe, gent., pl. Wm. Meredeth & w. *Martha*, dau. & heir of Robt. Longe, decd., Roger Sadeler & w. *Magdalene*, another dau. & heir of Robt. Longe, def. 8 mess., 8 cotts., 1 windmill, 1 dovecote, 8 gdns., 8 orchards, 710 a. ar., 200 a. mw., 100 a. pa., 110 a. wd., 60 a. furze & heath, 360 a. marsh & £9 9s. 4d. rt. in West Thurrocke, Dodinghurst, Harmyrys, Orsed, Styfford, Grace, Aulflye, Purflett & Goris, & passage without a ferry in Purflett. Pl. gtd. to Wm. & Martha Meredeth 4 mess., 4 cotts., 1 windmill, 4 gdns., 4 orchards, 355 a. ar., 100 a. mw., 50 a. pa., 55 a. wd., 30 a. furze & heath, 180 a. marsh & £4 14s. 8d. rt., with remainder to the right heirs of Martha. Pl. gtd. remainder of prop. to Roger & Magdalene Sadeler & the heirs of Magdalene's body, with remainder to the right heirs of Magdalene.

3. Morrow of Trin. & Mich. Wm. Yonge, pl. Geo. Standen & w. *Margt.*, def. 4 mess., 3 gdns., 60 a. ar., 40 a. mw., 60 a. pa. & 20 a. wd. in Belcham Rodings, Shelley, Theydenmunte & Theydengarnishe. Pl. gtd. the prop. to Geo. Standen & his heirs to hold of the chief lords.

4. Mich. Agnes Browne, wid., & Jn. Browne, pl. Jn. Wardley & w. Eliz., def. 1 mess. & 1 gdn. in Rayleygh. Def. quitclaimed to pl. & the heirs of Agnes. £40.

5. Mich. Francis Barnam & w. Alice, pl. Jerome Songer, gent., & w. Mary, def. 3 mess., 1 dovecote, 1 barn, 1 gdn., 1 orchard, 300 a. ar., 80 a. mw., 200 a. pa. & 40 a. wd. in Wytham. Def. quitclaimed to pl. & the heirs of Francis. Pl. gtd. prop. to def. for life of both & survivor at a peppercorn rt.

6. Mich. Wm. Rogers & Roger Gysse, pl. Wm. Harrys, def. 1 mess., 1 gdn., 1 orchard & 2 a. pa. in Newport Pond. Def. quitclaimed to pl. & the heirs of Wm. Rogers. Pl. gtd. prop. to def. & his heirs to hold of the chief lords.

7. Mich. Reg. Mede & Tho. Pamplyn, pl. Tho. Trigge & w. *Marcia*, def. 1 mess., 1 gdn., 1 orchard & 2 a. pa. in Cryssall *alias* Christeshall. Def. quitclaimed to pl. & the heirs of Reg. £40.

8. Mich. Jn. Reynoldes & Wm. Tusser, gent., pl. Clement Tusser, gent., def. 2 mess., 2 tofts, 2 barns, 2 gdns., 150 a. ar., 10 a. mw., 50 a. pa. & 100 a. wd. in Ryvenhall, Wyttham, Cressyng & Falborne. Def. quitclaimed to pl. & the heirs of Jn. £140.

9. Mich. Edm. Shether, pl. *Wm.* Shether & w. Anne, def. 100 a. ar., 20 a. pa. & 10 a. wd. in Branktrey. £160.

10. Mich. Hy. Fanshawe, esq., & w. Dorothy, pl. *Hy.* Stapleton, gent., & w. Eliz., def. 30 a. mw. in Barkynge. Def. quitclaimed to pl. & the heirs of Hy. Fanshawe. £50.

11. Mich. Edw. Hunt, pl. *Wm.* Shether, & w. Anne & Edm. Shether, def. 1 mess., 30 a. ar., 2 a. mw. & 10 a. pa. in Great Waltham. £140.

12. Mich. Jn. Barrett, pl. *Jn.* Coker & w. Margt., def. 12 a. ar., 3 a. mw. & 15 a. pa. in Canewdon. £40.

13. Mich. Nich. Manne, pl. Hy. Grene & w. *Joan*, def, 2 mess., 1 barn, 2 gdns., & 2 a. ar. in Braynktre. £40.

14. Mich. Tho. Gynes, gent., & w. Faith, pl. *Robt.* Gynes, & w. Ursula, def. 1 mess., 1 gdn., 40 a. ar., 6 a. mw., 30 a. pa., 10 a. wd. & 5s. rt. in Great Waltham & Little Waltham. Def. quitclaimed to pl. & the heirs of Tho. £40.

15. Mich. Chris. Sumpner, pl. *Nich.* Collyn & w. Marion, def. 1 mess., 1 gdn., 1 orchard, 30 a. ar., 10 a. mw. & 10 a. pa. in Stebbyng. £80.

16. Trin. & Mich. Edw. Barrett, esq., pl. Jerome Grene, gent., & w. Jane, def. 1 mess., 1 toft, 2 gdns., 60 a. ar., 12 a. mw., 50 a. pa. & 8 a. wd. in Sowthwokyndon. 200 mks.

17. Mich. Rd. Durant & Nich. Durant, pl. *Jn.* Kyng & w. Margt., def. 20 a. ar., 20 a. pa., 20 a. marsh & 2 'lez weeres' without fishing rights in Goldhanger, Great Totham & Little Totham. Def. quitclaimed to pl. & the heirs of Rd. £150.

18. Mich. Tho. Pullyver, pl. *Hy.* Pullyver & w. Agnes, def. 1 mess., 1 gdn., 1 orchard, 6 a. ar., 4 a. mw., 4 a. pa. & 3 a. wd. in Albrugh Hatche & Barkynge. £40.

19. Mich. Tho. Carter, pl. *Jn.* Holland & w. Margt., def. 1 mess., 1 gdn., 1 barn, 34 a. ar. & 4 a. wd. in Great Holland. £40.

20. Mich. Rd. Reve, pl. Jn. Lewgor, def. 2 mess., 2 gdns., 2 orchards, 20 a. ar., 3 a. mw. & 20 a. pa. in Bromefeld & Chelmesforde. £100.

21. Trin. & Mich. Jn. Kennett, pl. *Edw.* Elyott, gent., & w. Jane, Chris. Harrys, gent., & w. Mary, def. 12 a. ar. in High Easter. Pl. to pay Edw. & Jane Elyott & Edw.'s heirs 4d. a year & to owe suit of court at Edw.'s manor of Herons in Essex.

22. Mich. Roger Marten sen., esq., pl. *Wm.* Clopton sen., esq., & Wm. Clopton, gent., his son & heir apt., def. 6½ a. mw. in Lyston. £40.

23. Mich. Wm. Grigge, pl. *Jn.* Hawkeshale & w. Agnes, def. 1 mess., 1 gdn., 1 orchard & 7 a. pa. in Pentlowe. £40.

24. Mich. Benj. Clere, gent., pl. Robt. Steven, son & heir of Jn. Steven, def. 1 mess. called 'The Crowne', 1 gdn., 2 orchards, 1 dovecote & 2½ a. ar. in the parish of St. Leonard *in Novahitha ville Colcestr'*. £40.

25. Mich. Steph. Wyseman, gent., pl. Tho. Wyseman, gent., & w. Dorothy, & *Jn.* Whyte, def. 3 mess., 3 cotts., 3 gdns., 2 a. ar., 2 a. mw. & 2 a. pa. in Upmynster, A(u)velecy & Hornechurche. Pl. gtd. prop. to Jn. Whyte & his heirs to hold of the chief lords.

26. Mich. Wm. Loveday & Edw. Fransham, pl. Jn. Clark & w. *Joan, Wm.* Clark, Robt. Cranwyse & w. *Margery*, Bart. Wayte & w. *Margt.*, Tho. Dennys & w. *Alice*, def. 1 mess. & 1 gdn. in Great Donmowe. Def. quitclaimed to pl. & the heirs of Wm. Loveday. Pl. gtd. prop. to Robt. & Mary Cranwyse & the heirs of Robt. to hold of the chief lords.

27. Mich. Wm. Petre, kt., pl. *Tho.* Smythe, esq., & w. Margt., def. 1 mess., 1 gdn., 1 orchard, 150 a. ar., 20 a. mw., 120 a. pa., 40 a. wd. & 30 a. furze & heath in Gynge Atstone *alias* Gynge ad Petram. Warranty by def. against themselves, the heirs of Tho. & the heirs of Jn. Smythe, esq., his father. 160 mks.

28. Mich. Wm. Frauncis, pl. Jn. Cole & w. *Margt.*, def. 1 mess. & 1 a. 3 rods pa. in Wyvenho. £10.

29. Mich. Jn. Clyffe, gent., pl. Tho. Twede & w. *Agnes*, def. 2 mess., 2 cotts., 1 curtilage, 2 barns, 2 gdns., 2 orchards, 10 a. ar., 12 a. md., 12 a. pa., 2 a. wd. & common pa. in Hartfordstock & Butesberye. £80.

30. Mich. Jerome Grene, pl. Jn. Lucas & w. *Mary*, Rd. Sands & w. Kath., def. 1 mess., 1 barn, 1 gdn. & 7 a. ar. in Wyttham. £40.

31. Mich. Rd. Goldyng, gent., pl. Hugh Barker, clk., Jn. Barker & Tho. Barker, def. 15½ a. ar. & 1 a. pa. in Great Henny & Twynsted. Warranty by each def. against pl. & his heirs. Pl. gtd. Jn. Barker & his heirs an annuity of 3s. 4d. from the prop.

32. Mich. Jn. Waylotte, pl. *Nich.* Collyn & w. Marion, def. 1 mess., 1 gdn., 1 orchard, 60 a. ar., 7 a. mw., 20 a. pa. & 12d. rt. called 'Hodgekyns' in Willingale Doo & Willingale Spayne. £160.

33. Mich. Jn. Wright of Brokestreat, pl. *Jn.* Wylson & w. Joan, def. 1 mess., 1 toft, 1 barn, 1 gdn., 1 orchard & 4 a. ar. in Brokestreat. £40.

34. Mich. Robt. Helmer *alias* Tyler, pl. Jn. Ambrose & w. *Margt.*, def. 1 mess., 1 cott. & 1 gdn. in Bockyng. £40.

35. Mich. Wm. Cordell, master of the rolls, & Jane Alyngton, wid., pl. *Tho.* Goldynge, kt., & w. Eliz., Jn. Harrison, citizen & goldsmith of London, & w. Alice, def. Manor of Blamsters, 4 mess., 6 tofts, 1 dovecote, 6 gdns., 6 orchards, 200 a. ar., 20 a. mw., 200 a. pa., 20 a. wd. & 20s. rt. in Hawstede & Stysted. Def. quitclaimed to pl. & the heirs of Wm. £200.

36. Mich. Geo. Crymbyll, pl. *Tho.* Edmonds, gent., & w. Emma, def. 1 mess., 10 a. ar., 10 a. mw. & 40 a. pa. in Great Stambridge. 130 mks.

37. Morrow of Trin. & Mich. Wm. Hamlyn, pl. *Jn.* Gaunt, sen., & Jn. Gaunt, his son & heir apt., def. 1 mess., 1 barn, 1 gdn., 1 orchard & 28 a. ar. in Tyllingham & Dauncye *alias* De[ngie]e, 199 mks.

38. Mich. Robt. Fyppe, pl. Jn. Heigham, gent., & w. *Eliz.*, Rd. Clover & w. Dorothy & Joan Rawlyns, def. 30 a. ar., 4 a mw., 20 a. pa. & 6 a. wd. in Corryngham, Fobbyng & Est Tylbery. £80.

39. Mich. Wm. Bendlowes, serjeant at law, pl. *Jn.* Collyn & w. Mary & Mich. Collyn, def. Manor of Brenthall, 200 a. mw., 60 a. pa., 20 a. wd. & 20s. rt. in Fynchyngfelde, Stamborne, Great Sampford, Great Berdefelde & Little Berdefelde. Warranty by def. against Jn. & Mary Collyn, Jn.'s heirs, Hy. Collyn, his heirs, Wm. Collyn, his heirs, & the heirs of Mich. Collyn, decd. £140.

40. Mich. Geo. White, Robt. Bradburie & Wm. Rutter, esquires, pl. *Edm.* Ryrrell, esq., & Hy. Tyrrell, kt., def. Manor of Beaches, 4 mess., 100 a. ar., 50 a. mw., 500 a. pa., 200 a. wd., 250 a. fresh marsh, 300 a. salt marsh & £10 rt. in Rawrithe, Raylye, Hockeley, Caneudon, Ligh, Southechurche & Thorpe. Def. quitclaimed to pl. & the heirs of Geo. £600.

41. Mich. Jn. Buttolff & Jn. Kent, pl. Anth. Evered & w. *Eliz.*, def 2 cotts. & 2 gdns. in Great Berdefeld. Def. quitclaimed to pl. & the heirs of Jn. Buttolff. £20.

42. Mich. Wm. Adams *alias* Bocher, pl. *Wm.* Stubbynge & w. Margt., def. Manor of Gaynsfordes, 1 mess., 1 barn, 1 gdn., 200 a. ar., 10 a. mw., 6 a. pa., 2 a. wd. & 6d. rt. in Toppesfeld & Fynchingfelde. £140.

43. Mich. Robt. Sprynge, pl. Tho. Downynge, def. 28 a. ar., 2 a. mw. & 2 a. wd. in Belcham St. Paul. £40.

44. Mich. Joan Laxton, wid., pl. *Tho.* Barker, gent., & w. Dorothy, def. Manor of Mammons *alias* Memmons *alias* Malmeons, 1 mess., 1 gdn., 1 orchard, 100 a. ar., 100 a. mw., 40 a. pa., 80 a. marsh & 20s. rt. in Barkynge, Dagenham & Malemaynes. £280.

45. Mich. Nich. Humfrey *alias* Umfrey, pl. Robt. Pennyngton *alias* Petyton, & w. *Margt.*, 'Averius' Barley, gent., & w. Thomasina, def. 3 a. ar. & 1 a. pa. in Takeley. £40.

46. Mich. Jn. Claydon & Tho. Fuller, pl. Launcelot Warde, def. 1 mess., 3 barns, 1 gdn., 1 orchard, 100 a. ar., 14 a. mw., 100 a. pa. & 12 a. wd. in Wethersfielde. Def. quitclaimed to pl. & the heirs of Jn. £40.

47. Mich. Tho. Parke & Jn. Kent, pl. Rd. Ennewe & w. *Eliz.*, def. 1 mess., 1 barn, 1 gdn. & 16 a. ar. in Stebbynge. Def. quitclaimed to pl. & the heirs of Tho. Pl. gtd. prop. to def. & the heirs of their bodies to hold of the chief lords, with remainder to the heirs of Eliz.'s body, failing whom to the right heirs of Rd.

48. Mich. Geo. Nicolson, pl. Wm. Hurrell, Wm. Stronge & Tho. Sadlyngton, def. 12 a. ar. & 1 a. mw. in Hennyngham Syble, Hennyngham & Hennyngham Castle. Warranty by def. against themselves, the heirs of Wm. Hurrell, Robt. Ryche, kt., & w. Eliz. & the heirs of Eliz. £40.

49. Mich. Edm. Whytte, pl. Jn. Barnarde & w. *Thomasina*, def. 1 mess., 1 toft & 1 gdn. in Chelmesford. £40.

50. Mich. Rd. Mershall, pl. *Wm.* Spryngeffeld & w. Alice, def. 1 mess., 1 gdn. & 1 cott. in Chelmesford. £40.

51. Mich. Edw. Dixon, pl. Jn. Stacye & w. *Eliz.*, def. 1 mess., 1 cotts., 1 gdn., 1 orchard, 7 a. ar., 7 a. mw. & 7 a. pa. in Leighton. £40.

52. Mich. Tho. Flemynge sen., & w. Jocosa & Tho. Flemyng, his son, pl. *Jn.* Clerke & w. Kath., def. 7 a. ar. & 1 a. wd. in Broxhed. Def. quitclaimed to pl. & the heirs of Tho. Flemyng jun. £40.

53. Mich. Miles Lakyn, gent., pl. *Jn.* Cole, gent., & w. Margt., def. 1 mess., 1 barn, 1 gdn., 1 orchard, 24 a. pa. & 2 a. wd. in Ardley *alias* Ardleighe. £40.

54. Mich. Rd. Becke, pl. Jn. Barnard & w. *Margery*, Edw. Everard & w. *Bridget*, def. 30 a. pa. in Sudmynster *alias* Southmynster & Burnham. £80.

55. Mich. Tho. Hanchett, esq., Tho. Meade, esq., & Wm. Tyffyn, gent., pl. *Jn.* Bendyshe, esq., & w. Margery, def. Manors of Bendyshe *alias* Olde Haule & Bower Haule, 15 mess., 1 mill, 2 dovecotes, 15 gdns., 1,000 a. ar., 100 a. mw., 400 a. pa., 100 a. wd. & 66s. 8d. rt. in Bumpstead at the Steeple. Def. quitclaimed to pl. & the heirs of Tho. Hanchett. £640.

56. Mich. Wm. Watson, gent., pl. *Wm.* Wilford, esq., & w. Agnes, def. Manor of Whelers, 2 mess., 3 tofts, 1 barn, 1 dovecote, 3 gdns., 100 a. ar., 20 a. mw., 60 a. pa., 30 a. wd. & 2s. rt. in Great Bentley, Fratynge & Thorington. 190 mks.

57. Mich. Hy. Wayte, pl. Roger Wayte, def. 5 a. ar. in Water Belchampe. £20.

58. Mich. Wm. Watson, gent., pl. *Jn.* Frelove & w. Mary, def. 1 mess., 3 tofts, 1 barn, 2 gdns., 3 orchards, 100 a. ar., 30 a. mw., 70 a. pa., 12 a. wd., 30 a. furze & heath, 10 a. moor, 12 a. marsh & 10 a. alder in Horewoode, Little Bromley & Great Bromley. 130 mks.

59. Mich. Jn. Wright, pl. *Tho.* Laurence & w. Margt., def. 2 mess., 3 tofts, 1 dovecote, 2 gdns., 40 a. ar., 10 a. mw. & 6 a. pa. in Sedfordbroke & Southweld. £100.

60. Mich. Wm. Watson, pl. *Francis* Jobson, kt., & w. Eliz., def. 4 mess., 6 tofts, 1 dovecote, 4 gdns., 70 a. ar., 20 a. mw., 60 a. pa. & 10 a. wd. in Colchester, Harvies, Petehall, Little Wigborough & Wigborough. 200 mks.

61. Mich. Nich. Collyn, pl. *Jn.* Waylotte & w. Eliz., def. Manor of Lampytts, 1 mess., 200 a. ar., 20 a. mw., 60 a. pa., 4 a. moor & 8s. rt. in Fyffeld, Morton & Shelley. £160.

62. Mich. Wm. Tusser, gent., & Charles Belfield, pl. Wm. Bradborne, esq., & w. *Frances*, def. Manors of Cameys Hall, Myles Hall & Boys Hall, 20 mess., 20 gdns., 2,000 a. ar., 100 a. mw., 100 a. pa., 120 a. wd. & £10 rt. in Cameys Hall, Myles Hall, Boys Hall, Heighe Roodinge, Whyte Ro(od)inge, Eithroppe Roodinge, Hatfeild Bradoke, Keldon, Stondon, Navestoke, Chelmesford & Spryngfeld. Def. quitclaimed to pl. & the heirs of

FEET OF FINES FOR ESSEX

Wm. Tusser. Pl. gtd. an annual rt. of £90 from these props. to def. & the legitimate heirs of their bodies.

63. Mich. Tho. Parke & Jn. Kent, pl. *Tho*. Mylkesoppe *alias* Melsoppe, & w. Mary & Tho. Godsalff, def. Manor of Bulmer *alias* Butlers, 1 mess., 1 dovecote, 2 gdns., 200 a. ar., 20 a. mw., 60 a. pa., 50 a. wd. & 20s. rt. in Bulmer & Gestingthrop. Def. quitclaimed to pl. & the heirs of Tho. Parke. Pl. gtd. Mary Mylkesoppe an annual rt. of £10 from the prop. for life; pl. also gtd. the prop. to Tho. Godsalff for 30 years at peppercorn rt. for first five years, at rt. of 40s. a year for the next 16 years, with reversion to Tho. Milkesoppe & his heirs to hold of the chief lords.

1565-66   8 ELIZABETH

CP26(1)/125 (an orginal file)

1. Mich. & Hil. Wm. Ayloff, esq., Jn. Clenche & Wm. Deynes, gentlemen, pl. Hy. Goldyng, esq., & w. *Alice*, Robt. Waldegrave, esq., & w. *Mary*, Hy. Peryent, gent., & w. *Jane*, def. 4 mess., 3 cotts., 5 tofts, 7 gdns., 300 a. ar., 20 a. mw., 240 a. pa. & 40 a. wd. in Little Byrche, Great Byrche, Stanway, Layer Delahay & Copford. Def. quitclaimed to pl. & the heirs of Wm. Ayloff. £600.

2. Hil. Rd. Tirell, esq., pl. Geo. Tyrell, esq., & w. Joan, def. Manor of Fobbinge, 200 a. ar., 40 a. mw., 200 a. pa., 10 a. wd., 200 a. furze & heath, 300 a. fresh marsh, 100 a. salt marsh & 60s. rt. in Fobbinge, Stanford le Hope, Leyndon, Langdon, Estylbury & Westylbury, which def. holds for the life of both & survivor, with remainder to Robt. Tyrell, son of Geo., for his life, with further remainder to Queen Elizabeth, her heirs & successors. Def. gtd. pl. the prop. for the life of def. & survivor. £630.

3. Hil. Steph. Sonde *alias* Butterman & Robt. Scotte, pl. Hy. Welde, def. 1 mess., 15 a. ar., 20 a. pa. & 30 a. wd. in Yngmargarette. Def. quitclaimed to pl. & the heirs of Steph. £60.

4. Hil. Roger Gysse & Rd. Crowche, pl. Pet. Hatche & w. *Alice*, def. 3 mess., 3 cotts., 1 dovecote, 100 a. ar., 20 a. mw., 100 a. pa. & 20 a. wd. in Orsett & Little Thorocke, which Eliz. Banester, wid., holds for her life, with reversion to def. & the heirs of Alice Hatche. Def. gtd. remainder of prop., on death of Eliz. Banester, to pl. & the heirs of Rd. Crowche to hold of the chief lords.

5. Mich. & Trin. Tho. Myldmay, esq., pl. Jn. Tornor, def. 4 mess., 4 gdns., 10 a. ar., 20 a. pa., 4 a. wd. & 20s. rt. in Chelmesforde. 100 mks.

6. Hil. Hy. Wyett, pl. Wm. Cannon & w. *Joan*, & Jn. Tele, def. 1 mess., & 1 gdn. called 'Shorehouse' in Salcott. £40.

7. Hil. Wm. Younge, pl. *Rd*. Haryote, gent., & w. Joan, & Wm. Fyethe, def. 3 mess., 3 tofts, 6 a. ar., 4 a. mw., 3 a. pa. & 3 a. wd. in Stapleford Tawney & Chyngford. £40.

8. Hil. Hy. Goldyng, esq., & w. Alice, pl. Hy. Peryent, gent., & w. *Jane*, def. A moiety of the manor of Little Byrche, a moiety of 1 water-mill, 300 a. ar., 30 a. mw., 100 a. pa., 40 a. wd., 200 a. furze & heath & 20s. rt. in Little Byrche, Copford, Stanwey & Layer Delahey & a moiety of the advowson of Little Byrche church. Def. quitclaimed to pl. & the heirs Hy. Goldyng. Pl. gtd. an annuity of £16 from the prop. to def. & the heirs of Jane Peryent.

9. Hil. Wm. Turnar & w. Joan, pl. Jn. Gooddaye, def. 2 mess., & 2 gdns. & Coggeshall. Def. quitclaimed to pl. the heirs of Joan Turnar. £40.

10. Hil. Dame (*domina*) Mary Gates, wid., pl. *Wm*. Luckyn & w. Thomasina, def. 100 a. ar., 20 a. mw., 60 a. pa. & 20 a. wd. in Great Badowe & Westhanyngfeld. £200.

11. Hil. Francis Barneham & w. Alice, pl. *Anth*. Hall & w. Jane, def. 1 mess., 1 toft, 1 gdn., 1 orchard, 30 a. ar., 10 a. mw., 40 a. pa., 6 a. wd. & 40 a. furze & heath in Owltyng, Hatfeild Peaveyrell & Mawdon. Def. quitclaimed to pl. & the heirs of Francis. 100 mks.

12. Hil. Raymond Kyng, pl. *Jn*. Brocke, esq., & w. Anne, def. 3 mess. & 1 gdn. in Harwyche. 100 mks.

13. Hil. Dame (*domina*) Mary Gates, wid., pl. *Wm*. Luckyn & w. Elianor, def. 60 a. ar., 10 a. mw., 60 a. pa. & 10 a. wd. in Great Badowe. £140.

14. Mich. & Hil. Robt. Boyes, pl. *Tho.* Goldyng, kt., & w. Eliz., def. 2 mess., 2 gdns., 15 a. ar., 2 a. mw. & 2 a. pa. in Halsted. £40.

15. Hil. Anth. Banester, gent., pl. Tho. Bawle, def. 1 mess. & 1 gdn. in the parish of St. Giles in the suburbs of Colchester. Pl. gtd. prop. to def. & his heirs to hold of the chief lords.

16. Hil. Rd. Cock & Jn. Cock, pl. Rd. Storye & w. *Eliz.*, def. 6 a. ar. in Horndon. Def. quitclaimed to pl. & the heirs of Jn. £40.

17. Mich. & Hil. Edm. Harrington, pl. *Wm.* Hurrell & w. Margt., def. 1 mess., 1 gdn., 14 a. ar., 5 a. mw. & 5 a. pa. in Hengham Sible *alias* Hennyngham Syble. Warranty by def. against all men, save for 4 a. mw. warranted against Robt. Rych, kt., & w. Eliz., & the heirs of Eliz. £80.

18. Hil. Tho. Unwyn *alias* Onyon, pl. *Wm.* Cordell, kt., master of the rolls, & w. Mary, *Francis* Barneham & w. Alice, def. 40 a. mw. & 120 a. pa. in Hempsted. £100.

19. Hil. Tho. Hobson, pl. Jn. Hamond, gent., def. 2 mess., 35 a. ar. & 10 a. pa. in Little Sutton, Great Sutton & Pritwell. 130 mks.

20. Hil. Jas Cole, pl. Jn. Dorman, def. ½ a. ar. in Walden. £40.

21. Hil. Hy. Hall, pl. *Robt.* Wood, gent., & w. Joan & Tho. Hunwick, def. 1 mess. called 'Butlers Place', 1 curtilage, 1 gdn., 1 orchard, 30 a. ar., 8 a. mw. & 40 a. pa. in Bromeffeld. Pl. gtd. prop. to Tho. Hunwick for 21 years at annual rt. of 4d. with reversion to Robt. & Joan Wood & the heirs of Robt. to hold of the chief lords.

22. Hil. Wm. Thomson, pl. *Robt.* Pery & w. Joan, def. 2 mess. & 2 gdns. in Thaxstede. £40.

23. Hil. Tho. Barryngton, esq., pl. Robt. Noke, gent., def. Manor of Hatfylde Priorye *alias* Brodoke *alias* Le Priorye de Hatfylde Brodoke *alias* Kyngs Hatfylde, 100 mess., 100 tofts, 40 gdns., 40 orchards, 2 dovecotes, 600 a. ar., 200 a. mw., 300 a. pa., 100 a. wd., 1,000 a. furze & heath & £10 rt. in Hatfylde Brodoke *alias* Kyngs Hatfylde, Tackeleye, Sherynge, Matchinge & Stansted Monfychett. £260.

24. Hil. Wm. Stubbynge, pl. *Wm.* Cordell, kt., master of the rolls, & w. Mary, *Francis* Barnham & w. Alice, def. Manor of Bobulo *alias* Boblowe, 2 mess., 10 tofts, 4 gdns., 100 a. ar., 30 a. mw., 60 a. pa., 10 a. wd. & 40s. rt. in Bumpsted Helion, Bumpsted at the Steeple, Great Sampforde, Little Sampforde, Sturmere, Haverell, Radwynter & Hempsted. £100.

25. Mich. & Hil. Wm. Hyll, gent., pl. Francis Barners, esq., & Arthur Barners, gent., def. 1 mess., 1 gdn., 60 a. ar. & 2 a. mw. in Fynchyngfeld. £80.

CP26(1)/125   DIVERS COUNTIES

(8) Hil. Roger Frythe, clk., & Hy. Charleton, pl. *Tho.* Walsyngham, esq., & w. Dorothy, def. Manors & lands in Kent; & the advowson of Bubbynger church, co. Essex. Def. quitclaimed to pl. & the heirs of Roger. £640.

CP25(2)/127/1626   EASTER, 8 ELIZABETH   1566

1. Eas. Hy. Fortescue, esq., pl. Jn. Garrade & w. *Margery*, def. 1 mess., 1 gdn. & 1 a. 1 rod pa. in Wittham. £40.

2. Eas. Robt. Motte & Jaques Tompson, pl. Wm. Welbecke, def. 1 mess., 1 gdn. & 1 a. ar. in Colchester. Def. quitclaimed to pl. & the heirs of Robt. £40.

3. Eas. Wm. Bull, pl. *Tho.* Newman, gent., & w. Anne, def. 1 mess., 1 barn, 1 gdn., 1 orchard, 25 a. ar., 9 a. mw. & 8 a. pa. in Takeley. 200 mks.

4. Hil. & Eas. Rd. Manne, pl. *Tho.* Goodaye & w. Rose, def. 1 mess. & 2 gdns. in Brayntree. £40.

5. Eas. Jn. Kyllycke, pl. Tho. Kyllycke & w. *Alice*, def. One sixth part of 1 mess., 6 a. ar. & 5 a. pa. in Great Wakeryng & Little Wakeryng. £40.

6. Eas. Wm. Woodde, gent., pl. Geo. Ingram & w. Alice. *Tho.* Salynge & w. Joan, def. 2 mess., 16 a. ar., 6 a. mw. & 10 a. pa. in High Onger. (*Damaged*: ?£40.)

7. Eas. Hy. Harvy, doctor of laws, pl. *Alexander* Ray & w. Eliz., def. 3 mess., 3 tofts, 2 barns, 3 gdns., 100 a. ar., 20 a. mw., 100 a. pa., 40 a. wd. the liberty & course of 1 faldage & common pa. for 300 sheep in Christhall *alias* Cristhall *alias* Cursall. £200.

8. Hil. & Eas. Rd. Metyns, pl. Wm. Combers, def. 1 mess., 1 gdn. & 1 orchard in Navestocke. £40.

9. Eas. Wm. Watson, gent., pl. *Lau.* Betryche & w. Agnes, def. 1 mess., 30 a. ar., 6 a. mw., 20 a. pa., 10 a. wd. & 4s. rt. in Thorington. £30.

10. Eas. Tho. Armiger, gent., pl. Robt. Studde & w. *Eliz.*, def. Manor of Canedon *alias* Canewndon *alias* Canewdon, 4 mess., 100 a. ar., 10 a. mw., 100 a. pa. & 40s. rt. in Canedon (*alias as above*), Assheden, Hakwell, Pakylsham, Little Stambridge, Hokeley & Rocheford. £200.

11. Hil. & Eas. Rd. Herde, citizen & butcher of London, pl. Francis Southwell, gent., son of Robt. Southwell, kt., decd., def. Manors of Lawnders & Lenthroppes, 5 mess., 5 barns, 5 gdns., 5 orchards, 200 a. ar., 50 a. mw., 100 a. pa., 30 a. wd, 40 a. marsh & 20s. rt. in Rayneham & Wynnyngton. £520.

12. Eas. Roger Carewe, esq., Jn. Peterson *alias* Derickson & Hy. Meakes *alias* Pope, pl. Reg. Hollyngworth, esq., def. Site of the former free chapel of St. Nicholas of Stanfordlehoope, 5 mess., 5 tofts, 5 gdns., 5 orchards, 20 a. ar., 4 a. mw. & 8 a. pa. in Stanfordlehoope & Barkynge. Def. quitclaimed to pl. & the heirs of Roger. £80.

13. Eas. Wm. Clarke, pl. Geo. Meade & w. *Margt.*, def. 12 a. ar. in Takeley. £30.

14. Eas. Edw. Thirsbye, esq., pl. Tho. Gent, gent., & w. *Eliz.*, def. 1 mess., 1 gdn. & 8 a. ar. in Bockynge. £40.

15. Eas. Rd. Fryth, pl. *Geo.* Redman *alias* Sunnyff, gent., & w. Christiana, def. 1 barn, 1 gdn., 20 a. ar., 4 a. mw., 10 a. pa., 10 a. wd. & 10 a. furze & heath in Upmynster. £20.

16. Eas. Edw. Alston, pl. Jn. Gent, sen., *Jn.* Gent, jun., & w. Eliz., def. 1 mess., 1 gdn. & 12 a. ar. in Great Horkesleigh *alias* Great Horseley. £40.

17. Eas. Jn. Collyn, pl. *Robt.* Barker & w. Alice, def. 1 toft, 8 a. ar. & ½ a. pa. in Wymbishe. £20.

18. Eas. Jn. Inde, pl. *Wm.* Cocke, gent., & w. Margt., def. 1 mess., 1 gdn., 20 a. ar., 2 a. mw., 12 a. pa. & 2 a. wd. in Bumpsted Helyon. £80.

19. Eas. Tho. Goldyng, kt., pl. *Anth.* Harrolde & w. Marion, def. 2 cotts., 38 a. ar., 2 a. mw., 14 a. pa. & 1 a. wd. in Belcham St. Paul. £80.

20. Hil. & Eas. Jn. Cooke, gent., pl. Jn. Argent, def. 1 mess., 1 barn, 1 dovecote, 2 gdns., 7 a mw. & 5s. rt. in Rocheford *alias* Rocheforth, held by Giles Colford *alias* Calverley & w. Joan for the life of Joan. Def. gtd. reversion to pl. & his heirs. £40.

21. Eas. Jn. Hale, pl. Tho. Mylkesoppe *alias* Melsoppe & w. Mary & *Tho.* Myller, def. 1 mess., 1 gdn. & 6 a. ar. in Wickham St. Paul. £40.

22. Hil. & Eas. Tho. Franke, esq., pl. Jn. Evance & w. *Sibyl*, def. Manors of Ries, Morses, Howses, Thomas by the Wood & La Lee *alias* the Lee Hall, 24 mess., 8 cotts., 4 dovecotes, 12 barns, 24 gdns., 700 a. ar., 120 a. mw., 700 a. pa., 90 a. wd. & £8 rt. in Hatfelde Regis, Halyngbery Bourchyer, Matchynge & Sherynge. £440.

23. Eas. Jn. Craythorne, pl. *Wimundus* Carye, esq., *Rd.* Marten & w. Dorcas (*Dorcacia*), def. 1 mess., 1 gdn., 1 orchard, 60 a. ar., 10 a. mw., 30 a. pa. & 10 a. wd. in Byrchanger, Stortforde & Stansted Monfychet. Warranty by def. against themselves, heirs of Wimundus Carye & Jn. Carye, kt., & his heirs, & Tho. Bemyshe & his heirs. £120.

24. Eas. Joan Petit, wid., pl. Anth. Kytson & w. *Margt.*, def. 2 mess., 2 barns, 1 dovecote, 2 orchards, 2 gdns., 40 a. ar., 12 a. mw., 40 a. pa., 3 a. wd. & common pa. for all his livestock in Grynsted, Stanforde Ryvers & Onger. £40.

25. Eas. Jn. Kent & Wm. Sare, pl. Wm. Bye & w. *Margt.*, def. 1 mess. in Walden. Def. quitclaimed to pl. & the heirs of Jn. Pl. gtd. mess. to Wm. Bye & his heirs to hold of the chief lords.

26. Eas. Tho. Colbye, esq., pl. *Jn.* Zouche, kt., & w. Eleanor, def. Manor of Thurrock Grays *alias* Grays Thurrocke, 30 mess., 30 tofts, 30 gdns., 2,000 a. ar., 200 a. mw.,

1,000 a. pa., 600 a. marsh, 200 a. wd., 100 a. furze & heath & 100s. rt. in Thurrocke *alias* Grays Thurrocke & Styfford *alias* Stifford Cleys, free fishery in the water of Thames & free passage with a boat (*cimba*) on the same water called Greys Ferrye. £1,600.

27. Eas. Jn. Peke, pl. Jn. Burton & w. Jane, Jn. Dyggolett & w. Eliz., Nich. Leache & w. Agnes, def. 1 mess. & 4 a. ar. in Burnham. £40.

28. Eas. Robt. Kempe, esq., pl. *And.* Young, gent., & w. Margery, def. A moiety of the manor of Hovells & a moiety of 1 mess., 1 gdn., 200 a. ar., 40 a. mw., 60 a. pa., 20 a. wd. & 20s. rt. in Fychyngfeld & Shalford. 200 mks.

29. Eas. Jn. Tirrell, kt., Edw. Dymock, kt., Wm. Skypwith, kt., Edm. Hall, esq., Jn. Harryngton, esq., & Francis Harryngton, gent., pl. Ralph Chamberleyn, kt., def. The site of the manor of Pounts *alias* Benetts, 3 mess., 3 cotts., 6 gdns., 3 orchards, 120 a. ar., 30 a. mw., 80 a. pa. & 10 a. wd. in Bulmeare, Henney & Twynsted. Def. quitclaimed to pl. & the heirs of Jn. Tirrell. £400.

30. Eas. Hy. Horseman, pl. Robt. Glascok, gent., & w. Frances, *Rd.* Kelton, gent., & Wm. Walshe, def. 1 mess., 10 a. ar., 6 a. mw., 16 a. pa. & 6 a. wd. in Mylend near Colchester. Pl. gtd. prop. to Robt. Glascok & Wm. Walshe & to the heirs of Robt. to hold of the chief lords.

31. Hil. & Eas. Tho. Gent, gent., Jn. Chapleyn & w. Agnes, pl. *Rd.* Tyrrell, esq., & w. Grace, Jn. Chapman & w. Christina, def. 1 mess., 1 gdn., 2½ a. ar., 1½ a. mw., 22 a. pa. & 2 a. wd. in Bumpsted at the Steeple. Def. quitclaimed to pl. & the heirs of Jn. Chapleyn. Warranty by Rd. & Grace Tyrrell for 1½ a. mw., 22 a. pa. & 2 a. wd. against themselves, the heirs of Rd., Jn. Mordaunt, kt., lord Mordaunt & his heirs, Ludowick Mordaunt, esq., & his heirs, & heirs of Rd. Fitzlewes, kt., decd.; warranty by Jn. & Agnes Chapleyn for remaining mess., gdn. & 2½ a. ar. against themselves & the heirs of Jn. £40.

32. Hil. & Eas. Roger Gysse & Tho. Webbe, pl. *Edw.* Barker & w. Frances, Edm. Smyth & w. Agnes, def. 1 mess., 1 gdn., 1 orchard & 3 a. mw. in Barkynge & Wansted. Def. quitclaimed to pl. & the heirs of Roger Gysse. Pl. gtd. 1 mess., 1 gdn. & 1 orchard in Wansted to Edm. & Agnes Smyth & the legitimate heirs of their bodies to hold of the chief lords, with remainder to Fabian Postolet, son of Agnes Smyth, & his heirs. Pl. also gtd. to Edm. & Agnes Smyth the remaining 3 a. mw. in Barkynge to hold of the chief lords for term of their lives & life of survivor, with remainder to Paul Smythe, son of Edm. & the legitimate heirs of his body, failing whom to Eliz. Smythe, dau. of Edm., & the legitimate heirs of her body, failing whom to Fabian & his heirs.

33. Eas. Wm. Woode, pl. *Jn.* Pratt & w. Mary, def. 1 gdn., 18 a. ar. & 6 a. pa. in Stebbynge. ( ) mks.

34. Eas. Edw. Poole & Edw. Archer, gentlemen, pl. Wm Fabyan & Geo. Hungerford, gentlemen, def. Manor of Pygotts in Patteswycke, 5 mess., 4 tofts, 1 water-mill, 2 dovecotes, 5 gdns., 500 a. ar., 500 a. mw., 500 a. pa., 400 a. wd., 100 a. marsh, 200 a. furze & heath & £6 rt. in Patteswyke, Coggeshall, Feringe, Stysted & Bockynge. Def. quitclaimed to pl. & the heirs of Edw. Poole. £290.

35. Hil. & Eas. Tho. Bedell & Tho. Hantchett, esq., pl. Tho. Barryngton, esq., & w. Wenefrida, def. Manors of Barryngton Hall, Brenthall & Matching Barnes, the former Priory of Hatfeld Regis, (30 mess., 12 cotts., 1) water-mill, 2 dovecotes, 30 gdns., 12 orchards, (740) a. ar., 60 a. mw., 200 a. pa., 8 (*recte* 80) a. wd. & £4 10s. rt. in Hatfeld Regis, (Hatfeld Brodoke, Matchyng, Whyte Rodyng), Takeley, Stansted Mountfytchett & Abbes Rodyng. Def. quitclaimed to pl. & the heirs of Tho. Bedell. Pl. gtd. manor of Barryngton Hall, 6 mess., 1 mill, 1 (dovecote), 6 gdns., 6 orchards, 160 a. ar., 20 a. mw., 40 a. pa., 40 a. (wd.) & £4 10s. rt. in Hatfeld, Stansted Mountfytchett & Takeley, to def. & the heirs male of Tho. Barryngton to hold of the chief lords, with remainder to legitimate heirs of Wenefrida, failing whom Kath., countess of Huntyngdon, lately w. of Francis earl of Huntyngdon, & her legitimate heirs, failing whom to heirs of Margt., countess of (Salisbury), failing whom Queen Elizabeth & her successors. Pl. to pay def. annual rt. of £78 8s. 7¼d. issuing from manors of Brenthall & Matching Barnes, former Priory of Hatfeld Regis, 24 mess., 12 cotts., 1 dovecote, 24 gdns., 6 orchards, 580 a. ar., 40 a. mw., 160 a. pa. & 40 a. wd. in Hatfeld (- - - - -), Hatfeld Brodock, Matching, Rodyng & Abbes Rodyng, with the same successive remainders. Pl. gtd. also remaining prop. to Tho. Barryngton & the legitimate heirs of his body, with successive remainders to the legitimate heirs of the body of Jn. Barryngton, esq., decd., father of Tho., to the legitimate heirs of the body of Nich. Barryngton, kt., decd., grandfather of Tho., to the legitimate

heirs of the body of Kath., countess of Huntingdon, to the legitimate heirs of the body of Margt., countess of Salisbury, & to Queen Elizabeth & her successors.

CP25(2)/127/1627   TRINITY, 8 ELIZABETH   1566

1. Morrow of Trin. Wm. Turnar & w. Joan, pl. Tho. Colman, def. 1 mess. & 1 gdn. in Coggeshall. Def. quitclaimed to pl. & the heirs of Joan. £40.

2. Morrow of Trin. Rd. Kyng, pl. Rd. Frenche & w. *Eliz.*, def. 1 mess. & 1 gdn. in Harwyche. £40.

3. Morrow of Trin. Hy. Grene, pl. Pet. Grene, def. 2 a. ar., 1 a. mw. & 1 a. pa. in Great Sampforde. £40.

4. Morrow of Trin. Edm. West, esq., pl. *Jn.* Jyppes & w. Alice, def. 1 mess., 2 a. mw. & 1 a. pa. in Depden. £40.

5. Morrow of Trin. Robt. Lambart, pl. Wm. Welbecke, gent., def. 1 mess., 1 toft, 1 cott. & 1 gdn. in the parish of St. Leonard's *nove hithe*, Colchester. £40.

6. Eas. & Morrow of Trin. Jn. Abell, esq., pl. Wm. Fabyan, gent., def. Manor of Howolds, 1 mess., 1 gdn., 1 orchard, 160 a. ar., 40 a. mw., 100 a. pa. & 20 a. wd. in Pattesyke, Coggeshall, Bradwell next Coggeshall & Matteshall. £160.

7. Morrow of Trin. Robt. Batsford, pl. *Hy.* Archer & w. Anne, def. 4½a. ar. & 1½ a. mw. in Takeley. £40.

8. Morrow of Trin. Robt. Bedyngfeld, gent., pl. Wm. Turnor & w. Eliz., def. 1 mess., 1 gdn., 1 orchard, 30 a. ar., 10 a. mw., 46 a. pa. & 4 a. wd. in Bockyng. £100.

9. Morrow of Trin. Jn. Smyth, pl. *Wm.* Goodwyn & w. Anne, def. 1 mess., 1 gdn. & 1 orchard in Bockynge. £20.

10. Morrow of Trin. Wm. Smythe, pl. Jn. Bowdon, def. 1 mess., 1 gdn., 10 a. ar., 6 a. mw. & 12 a. pa. in Prytwell. £40.

11. Eas. & Morrow of Trin. Wm. Raynolds & Francis Stacye, gentlemen, pl. *Tho.* Sutton, gent., & Edw. Hollye, def. 1 mess., 2 gdns., 1 orchard & 2 a. pa. in Waltham Holy Cross. Def. quitclaimed to pl. & the heirs of Wm. 130 mks.

12. Morrow of Trin. Francis Barneham, pl. Wm. Fabyan, gent., def. Manor of Jenkyns, 1 mess., 3 tofts, 1 water-mill, 2 dovecotes, 2 gdns., 2 orchards, 200 a. ar., 60 a. mw., 200 a. pa., 20 a. wd., 20 a. moor, 40 a. marsh & 20s. rt. in Bockynge & Stysted. £320.

13. Morrow of Trin. Jn. Yeldham, pl. Rd. Yeldham & w. *Kath.*, a dau. & co-heir of Jn. Swallowe, decd., def. A moiety of 3 mess., 2 gdns., 2 orchards, 2 barns, 60 a. ar., 6 a. mw., 30 a. pa., 20 a. wd. & 9s. 1d. & 2 capons rt. in Bockyn & Fynchyngfeld. £40.

14. Morrow of Trin. Francis Clopton, esq., pl. *Jn.* Odell & w. Joan, def. 3 mess., 2 tofts, 3 gdns., 2 orchards, 140 a. ar., 10 a. mw., 40 a. pa. & 6 a. wd. in Ashedon. Warranty by def. against themselves, heirs of Jn. Odell, & Tho. Whitehand & his heirs. £120.

15. Morrow of Trin. Jn. Humfre, pl. Wm. Baldwyn & w. *Joan*, def. 1 mess., 1 toft, 1 gdn., 1 orchard, 5 a. ar., 12 a. mw. & ½ a. wd. in Brendwood & Shenfyld. £120.

16. Eas. & Morrow of Trin. Tho. Tuke, pl. Wm. Brooke & w. *Margt.*, def. 1 mess., in Roydon. £40.

17. Eas. & Morrow of Trin. Edw. Ryche, esq., pl. Wm. Eatton, *Eugenius* Eatton & w. Eliz. & Alexander Eatton, def. 1 mess. & 3 gdns. & two thirds of 6 mess., 4 tofts, 6 gdns., 60 a. ar., 20 a. mw., 80 a. pa., 10 a. wd., 30 a. marsh & 2 wharves in Staunford le Hope. 130 mks.

18. Morrow of Trin. Francis Archer, pl. *Wm.* Goodwyn, son & heir of Anne Goodwyn, a sis. & heir of Wm. Cowman, jun., Anne the w. of Wm. Goodwyn, Pet. Brett & w. *Margt.*, dau. & heir of Joan Lovedaye, another sis. & heir of Wm. Cowman, def. 4 mess., 3 gdns., 1 orchard, 30 a. ar., 10 a. pa. & 7 a. wd. in Bockynge. £80.

19. Eas. & Morrow of Trin. Jn. Boddy, gent., pl. Jn. Latham, esq., & w. Ellen, def. 1 mess., 1 gdn., 1 orchard, 20 a. ar., 6 a. mw., 20 a. pa. & 10 a. wd. in Purleigh *alias* Purley, Woodham Mortymer & Haselyth *alias* Haseley. 100 mks.

20. Eas. & Morrow of Trin. Rd. Raynesford, gent., pl. *Anth.* Browne, a justice of Common Pleas, & w. Joan, def. Manor of Gylles, 1 mess., 300 a. ar., 24 a. mw., 40 a. pa., 36 a. wd. & 15s. rt. in Eppynge. £240.

21. Morrow of Trin. Jn. Pathe & w. Agnes, pl. *Tho.* Awborowe & w. Anne, def. 1 mess. & 3 a. ar. in Great Badowe. Def. quitclaimed to pl. & the heirs of Jn. £40.

22. Eas. & Morrow of Trin. Chris. Harrys, esq., pl. *Arthur* Harrys, esq., & w. Dorothy, def. Manor of Wyckford, 20 mess., 10 cotts., 4 dovecote, 20 barns, 30 gdns., 30 orchards, 200 a. ar., 100 a. mw., 200 a. pa., 200 a. wd., 100 a. marsh & 40s. rt. in Wyckford. £280.

23. Morrow of Trin. Wm. Strachey, pl. Robt. Daines & w. *Margt.,* Rd. Bell & w. *Joan,* def. 1 mess. in Safferon Walden *alias* Chepyng Walden. £40.

24. Morrow of Trin. Tho. Ive & Jn. Overed, pl. *Jn.* Tyrell, esq., & w. Agnes, def. Manor of Estwarley *alias* Estwarle Semell, 6 mess., 1 dovecote, 1,300 a. ar., 100 a. mw., 200 a. pa., 50 a. wd., 1,000 a. furze & heath, 150 a. marsh & £6 rt. in Little Warley, Great Warley, Estwarley Semell, Childerdiche, Chaldewell, Little Thurrock, Orsett & West Tilberye. Def. quitclaimed to pl. & heirs of Tho. £400.

25. Morrow of Trin. Jn. Tyler & w. Thomasina, pl. Wm. Braystar & w. *Margt.,* Wm. Lystney & w. *Robrigia,* Robt. Grose & w. *Thomasina,* def. 1 mess., 7½ a. ar., 7½ a. pa. & 4 a. fresh marsh in Chaldwell & Lyttle Thurrocke. Def. quitclaimed to pl. & the heirs of Jn. £40.

26. Morrow of Trin. Ralph Typpynge & Rd. Mason, pl. Jn. Bales, Jervase Symons & w. *Anne,* def. 2 mess., 1 barn, 2 gdns., 1 orchard, 10 a. ar., 6 a. mw. & 6 a. pa. in Westham. Def. quitclaimed to pl. & the heirs of Ralph. Pl. gtd. prop. to Jn. Bales & his heirs to hold of the chief lords.

27. Eas. & Morrow of Trin. Hy. Sherman, pl. Tho. Rochester, clk., & w. *Dorothy,* Hy. Broke, clk., & w. Barbara, def. 1 mess., 1 orchard, 1 gdn. & 1 rod of ar. in Dedham. £40.

28. Morrow of Trin. Arthur Harrys, esq., pl. *Chris.* Harrys, esq., & w. Mary & Vincent Harrys, esq., def. Manor of Crycksey *alias* Cryckseth, 10 mess., 6 cotts., 16 gdns., 16 orchards, 300 a. ar., 40 a. mw., 260 a. pa., 50 a. wd., 200 a. furze & heath, 200 a. marsh & £8 rt. in Crycksey *alias* Crickseth, Althorn *alias* Aldern & Burnham, & the advowson of the church of Crycksey *alias* Cryckseth. 400 mks.

29. Eas. & Morrow of Trin. Anth. Broun, a justice of (Common) Pleas, pl. Tho. Hales, gent., def. Manor of Gylles, 1 mess., 300 a. ar., 24 a. mw., 40 a. pa., 36 a. wd. & 15s. rt. in Eppynge. £240.

30. Morrow of Trin. Francis Stacye, pl. *Tho.* Sutton & w. Eliz., def. 1 mess., 1 gdn., 4 a. mw. & 4 a. pa. in Waltham Holy Cross. £80.

31. Morrow of Trin. Tho. Wylson, pl. Rd. Ennewe & w. *Eliz.,* def. 1 mess., 1 barn, 1 gdn. & 20 a. ar. in Stebbynge. £40.

32. Eas. & Morrow of Trin. Rd. Mason & Jn. Osborne, pl. Rd. Durant, gent., & w. Kath. & *Gabriel* Shakelady, def. 2 mess., 6 cotts., 3 tofts, 6 gdns., 3 orchards, 40 a. ar., 12 a. mw., 20 a. pa., 16 a. wd. & 18d. rt. in Warley Waylett *alias* Warley Abbisse *alias* Great Warley. Def. quitclaimed to pl. & the heirs of Rd. Mason. Pl. gtd. prop. to Rd. & Kath. Durant for life of Kath., with remainder to Rd. Durant & his heirs, to hold of the chief lords.

CP25(2)/259/8 Eliz., Trin.   DIVERS COUNTIES

3. Morrow of Trin. Tho. Rowe, citizen & alderman of London, pl. *Tho.* Heron, gent., & w. Cecily, Edm. Heron, gent., Chris. Heron, gent., Hy. Heron, gent., & Jn. Heron, gent., def. Manor of Higham Bemsted *alias* Higham Bempstede *alias* Higham Hall, 2 mess., 2 cotts., 4 tofts, 1 dovecote, 4 gdns., 20 a. ar., 50 a. mw., 30 a. pa. & 5s. rt. in Waltham Stowe & Chynkeforde, co. Essex, & 30 a. mw. in Hackney & Tottenham, co. Mdx. £600.

4. Eas. & Morrow of Trin. Arthur Harrys, esq., & Geo. Higham, gent., pl. *Edw.* Waldegrave, esq., & w. Joan, def. Manor of Lalford Hall *alias* Lalford Sayes *alias* Lawford Hall *alias* Lawford Sayes, 40 mess., 20 tofts, 3 dovecotes, 40 gdns., 30 orchards, 1,000 a. ar., 200 a. mw., 800 a. pa., 300 a. wd., 500 a. furze & heath, 200 a. fresh marsh, 300 a. salt marsh & £20 rt. in Lalford, Ardeleygh, Colchester, Myleende, Boxsted, Dedham,

Moche Bromeley & Lytle Bromeley, & the rectory of Boxsted with tithes of grain, sheaves, hay & wood in Boxsted, & the advowson of the vicarage of Boxsted church, co. Essex, £20 rt. issuing from manors of Moneweden & Solyards, 30 mess., 30 tofts, 30 gdns., 1,000 a. ar., 200 a. mw., 1,000 a. pa. & 300 a. furze & heath in Moneweden, Cretingham, Brandeston, Howe, Erles Some, Framesden, Oteley & Starnefeld, co. Suff. Def. quitclaimed to pl. & the heirs of Arthur. 2,110 mks.

CP25(2)/127/1628   MICHAELMAS, 8–9 ELIZABETH   1566

1. Mich. Jn. Josselyn, pl. Wm. Walter, esq., def. 24 a. ar. & 14 a. pa. in Shellowe Bowells & Wyllyngdale Doe. £40.

2. Mich. Jn. Lynnett, pl. *Hy.* Archer, gent., & w. Anne, def. 1 mess., 1 gdn., 18 a. ar. & 2 a. pa. in Takeley. £40.

3. Mich. Tho. Cole, doctor of sacred theology, pl. *Jerome* Grene & w. Jane, def. 1 mess., 1 gdn., 50 a. ar., 10 a. mw., 40 a. pa., 10 a. wd. & 10 a. furze & heath in Southokynden *alias* Southwokyndon. £140.

4. Mich. Tho. Gynes & w. Faith (*Fides*) pl. *Chris.* Sorrell & w. Alice, def. 12 a. ar., 4 a. pa. & 4 a. wd. in Great Waltham. Def. quitclaimed to pl. & the heirs of Tho. £40.

5. Trin. & Mich. Wm. Carly & Jn. Carter, pl. Jas. Parker, def. 17 a. ar., 9 a. mw. & 20 a. pa. in Buttesbury, Billerica & Great Bursted. Def. quitclaimed to pl. & the heirs of Wm. £100.

6. Mich. Wm. Shether, pl. Jn. Wallenger, def. 3 mess., 2 gdns. & 2 orchards in Chelmesford. £40.

7. Mich. Tho. Clements & Jn. Garbett, pl. Rd. Ellyott, gent., & w. *Kath.*, def. 5 mess., 5 barns, 5 gdns., 5 orchards, 60 a. ar., 12 a. mw., 60 a. pa. & 3 a. wd. in Waltham Holy Cross *alias* Waltham Hollycrosse, Suson *alias* Susen & Upshere. Def. quitclaimed to pl. & the heirs of Tho. £(300) (- - - *scentas libras*).

8. Mich. Jas. Altham, esq., & w. Mary, pl. *Rd.* Westwood & w. Margery, def. 8 mess., 3 cotts., 4 tofts, 10 gdns., 10 orchards, 150 a. ar., 30 a. mw., 40 a. pa. & 20 a. wd. in Latton & Harlowe. Def. quitclaimed to pl. & the heirs of Jas. £200.

9. Morrow of Trin. & Mich. Jn. Luter *alias* Hewett, pl. Chris. Welshe, esq., def. 80 a. pa. in Waltham Holy Cross. £140.

10. Mich. Rd. Drane & w. Margery, pl. Jn. Bowsey & w. *Joan* def. 2 mess., 2 barns, 2 gdns. & 48 a. ar. in Great Waltham & Bromefeld. Def. quitclaimed to pl. & the heirs of Margery. £80.

11. Mich. Rd. Emery, gent., pl. Tho. Hamonde & w. *Eliz.*, a dau. & co-heir of Tho. Cowper *alias* Wheler & w. Alice, dau. of Wm. Spylman, def. A moiety of 1 mess., 1 barn, 4 a. mw. & 4 a. pa. in Thaxstede. £40.

12. Mich. Hy. Fanshawe, esq., pl. Jn. Gaysham, gent., def. 1 mess., 2 gdns., 1 orchard, 20 a. ar., 4 a. mw., 20 a. pa. & 20 a. wd. in Barkyng. £40.

13. Mich. Wm. Rede, pl. *Robt.* Mylborne, Robt. Bysshoppe & w. Joan, def. 50 a. ar., 10 a. mw. & 60 a. pa. in Wyckforde & Rawrethe. Warranty by Robt. Mylborne & his heirs. £80.

14. Mich. Wm. Evered, pl. *Ralph* Wyseman, gent., & w. Eliz., def. 1 mess., 80 a. ar., 6 a. mw. & 10 a. pa. in Bromefylde. Warranty by def. against themselves, the heirs of Ralph, Tho. Wyseman, esq., & his heirs, & heirs of Jn. Wyseman, esq., father of Tho. & Ralph. £140.

15. Mich. Ralph Wiseman, pl. Rd. Wiseman of London, gent., def. 1 mess., 90 a. ar., 12 a. mw., 30 a. pa. & 10 a. wd. in Thaxstede & Tyltie. £40.

16. Mich. Nich. Harwarde, pl. *Jn.* Mylles & w. Margt., def. 1 mess., 1 barn, 1 gdn., 1 orchard, 16 a. ar. & 3 a. wd. in Dagenham. £40.

17. Mich. Rd. Cocke, pl. *Jn.* Barrett & w. Anne, def. 1 mess., & 3 a. mw. in Canewdon. £40.

18. Mich. Tho. Sampforthe, pl. Hy. Josselyn, esq., & w. *Anne*, def. 4 a. wd. in Willingale Dooe. £40.

19. Mich. Wm. Vesey & Robt. Veysey, son & heir apt. to Wm., pl. Hy. Wentworth & w. *Jane*, def. One third of the manors of Brets Hall & Little Hollande, & one third of 20 mess., 20 tofts, 20 gdns., 20 orchards, 60 a. ar., 100 a. mw., 500 a. pa., 200 a. wd., 100 a. furze & heath, 200 a. marsh & £6 rt. in Tendring, Whyley, Little Holland, Little Holland, Little Bentley, Great Claston & Great Bentley. Def. quitclaimed to pl. & heirs of Wm. £320.

20. Mich. Rd. Everard, gent., pl. *Wm.* Shether & w. Anne, def. 12 a. ar. in Great Waltham & Southend. £40.

21. Mich. Arthur Harrys, gent., pl. *Edw.* Madyson & w. Dorothy, def. 1 mess., 1 curtilage, 1 barn, 1 stable, 1 gdn., 1 orchard, 30 a. ar., 5 a. mw. & 5 a. wd. in Purleygh. 100 mks.

22. Mich. Jn. Rycheman, pl. *Jn.* Locke & w. Joan, def. 1 mess. & 13 a. ar. in Althorne. £40.

23. Mich. Wm. Petre, kt., & Jn. Petre, esq., son & heir apt. of Wm., pl. *Geoff.* Scotte, gent., & w. Joan, def. 2 mess., 2 gdns. & 3½ a. mw. in Chelmysforde & Springeffelde. Def. quitclaimed to pl. & the heirs of Wm. £200.

24. Mich. Wm. Tryplowe, pl. *Jn.* Whyte & w. Margery, def. 1 mess., 1 gdn. & 1 orchard in Upmynster. £40.

25. Mich. Wm. Petre, kt., & Jn. Petre, esq., pl. Tho. Bett & w. *Joan*, def. 10 a. ar. & 5 a. pa. in Harverdstock & Buttysbury. Def. quitclaimed to pl. & the heirs of Wm. £40.

26. Mich. Robt. Lukyn, pl. *Hy.* Archer, gent., & w. Anne, def. 6 a. ar. & 2 a. pa. in Takeley. £40.

27. Mich. Rd. Mason & Jn. Norrell, pl. Tho. Burges & w. *Agnes*, def. 1 mess., 20 a. ar., 12 a. mw., 20 a. pa. & 2 a. wd. in Westhaningfeld. Def. quitclaimed to pl. & the heirs of Tho. Burges to hold of chief lords.

28. Morrow of Trin. & Mich. Edw. Watkynson, clk., pl. Tho. Fekeman & w. *Alice*, Wm. Maygate & w. *Eliz.*, def. 1 toft, 10 a. ar. & 2 a. mw. in Ramesden Belhowse. £40.

29. Mich. Tho. Crackebone, pl. *Ralph* Wyseman, gent., & w. Eliz., def. Manor of Takeley *alias* Takeley Graunge, 5 mess., 2 cotts., 3 barns, 7 gdns., 40 a. ar., 6 a. mw., 50 a. pa., 6 a. wd. & 21s. rt. in Takeley, Broxstede, Manuden, Stansted Mountfytchett & Hatfylde Brodocke. Warranty by def. against themselves & the heirs of Ralph Wyseman, Geo. Wyseman, gent., & his heirs, & the heirs of Jn. Wyseman, esq., father of Ralph & Geo. 130 mks.

30. Morrow of Trin. & Mich. Jn. Clarke, pl. *Robt.* Albery & w. Margt., def. 1 mess. in Walden. £40.

31. Mich. Rd. Sampeforde, pl. Jn. Cowlande, def. A fourth part of 1 mess., 1 curtilage, 1 gdn., 1 orchard, 120 a. ar., 18 a. mw., 40 a. pa., 16 a. wd. & 1d. rt. in Aythroppe Rodinge, which Joan, wid. of Tho. More, holds for her life. Def. quitclaimed reversion to pl. & his heirs to hold of the chief lords. £40.

32. Morrow of Trin. & Mich. Tho. Gent, gent., & Geoff. Whiffyn, pl. Jn. Londe, def. 1 mess., 1 gdn., 20 a. ar., 4 a. mw., 16 a. pa. & 1 a. wd. in Bumpsted at the Steeple. Def. quitclaimed to pl. & the heirs of Tho. 100 mks.

33. Mich. Wm. Waldegrave esq., & Jn. Heigham, esq., pl. *Wm.* Harrys, esq., & w. Joan, def. 10 mess., 20 tofts, 4 dovecotes, 10 gdns., 600 a. ar., 200 a. mw., 2,000 a. pa., 500 a. wd., 100 a. furze & heath, 200 a. moor, 400 a. marsh & 20s. rt. in Great Wakeryng, Little Wakeryng, Great Hocklye, Maldon, Fulnes, Stow, Norton & Purley. Def. quitclaimed to pl. & the heirs of Wm. Waldegrave. £880.

34. Morrow of Trin. Mich. Rd. Barnarde & Jn. Barnarde of Thaxsted, pl. *Robt.* Wright and w. Agnes, def. Manor of Deynes *alias* Deanes House, 5 mess., 4 gdns., 3 barns, 160 a. ar., 16 a. mw., 20 a. pa., 4 a. wd. & 10s. rt. in Depden. Def. quitclaimed to pl. & the heirs of Jn. £100.

35. Mich. Jn. Kent, pl. Jn. Thymble & w. *Eliz.*, Jn. George & w. *Kath.*, def. 1 toft, 10 a. ar. & 1 a. mw. in Langenho. £40.

36. Mich. Jn. Cooke, gent., pl. Giles Colford & w. *Joan*, def. 1 mess., 1 barn, 2 gdns. & 7 a. ar. in Rocheford. £40.

37. Mich. Matthew Barnerde, pl. Rd. Sampeforde, def. A fourth part of 1 mess., 1 curtilage, 1 gdn., 1 orchard, 120 a. ar., 18 a. mw., 40 a. pa., 16 a. wd. & 1d. rt. in Aythroppe Rodinge, which Joan, wid. of Tho. More, holds for her life. Def. quitclaimed reversion to pl. & his heirs to hold of the chief lords. £40.

38. Mich. Wm. Herde, pl. Edw. Barrett, esq., def. 5 a. marsh in Raynham. £40.

39. Morrow of Trin. & Mich. Tho. London, pl. *Robt.* Frith & w. Mary, *Jn.* Gardiner & w. Mary, def. 2 mess. in Brokewalden. £40.

40. Mich. Wm. Glascocke, gent., pl. *Wimond* Cary, esq., & Jn. Pavyatt, def. Manor of Thremhall *alias* Threumhall, the site of the priory of Thremhall *alias* Threumhall, 12 mess., 12 tofts, 12 gdns., 6 orchards, 120 a. ar., 20 a. mw., 30 a. pa., 20 a. wd. & 60s. rt. in Stansted Montfytchett, Takeley, Byerden, Hatfylde Brodoke, Hallingbury Morley, Bylchanger, Gelson, Manueden, Sabridgeforth & Sterforth. Warranty by Wimond & Edw. Cary against themselves & their heirs, Jn. Cary, kt., & his heirs, Jocosa Cary, w. of Jn., & her heirs; & warranty by Jn. Pavyatt against himself & his heirs. £200.

41. Morrow of Trin. & Mich. Jas. Clovell, pl. *Wymond* Cary, esq., & Jn. Craythorne, def. 26 a. ar., in Byrchanger, Stortforde & Stansted Montfychett. Pl. gtd. to Jn. Craythorne 11 a. ar. in Byrchanger & Stortforde for 1,000 years at peppercorn rt., & 15 a. ar. in Stansted Montfychett for (*mutilated*) years at peppercorn rt. Def. grtd. reversion to Wymund Carye & his heirs to hold of the chief lords.

42. Mich. Wm. Waldegrave, esq., pl. Wm., marquess of Northampton, def. Manors of Stansted, Halsted, Hennyngham, Hennyngham Sybell, Abell, Claveryngs, Lucas & Pychards, 300 mess., 200 cotts., 6 water-mills, 5 dovecotes, 100 gdns., 2,000 a. ar., 100 a. mw., 3,000 a. pa., 1,000 a. wd., 200 a. furze & heath, 400 a. marsh, 2,000 a. ar. covered with water, £30 rt., rts. of 1 pair of gilt spurs, 1 ploughshare (*vomer*'), 3 lb. pepper, 1 *nisi* 3 cocks, 2 hens, 10 capons & 2 red roses, & common pasture for all animals in Halsted, Stansted, Hennyngham, Hennyngham Sybell, Stysted, Gosfeld, Toppesfeld, Foxerde, Twynsted, Pebmershe, Bulmere, Middleton, Colne Engayn *alias* Gaynes Colne, Alphampston, Great Henny, Little Henny, Maplested, Markeshall, Aldham, Patteswyke, Belcham Otton & Gestingthorp, the free warren of Halsted & Stansted, the liberty of the fairs & markets of Halsted & the advowson of the church of Hennyngham Sybell. £1,000.

43. Morrow of Trin. & Mich. Robt. Potter, pl. Tho. Rolfe & w. *Joan*, Tho. Sadiller & w. *Margery*, Wm. Joye & w. *Margt.*, def. A fourth part of 4 mess., 1 toft, 1 dovecote, 8 gdns., 2 orchards, 120 a. ar., 16 a. mw. & 50 a. pa. in Withermondford *alias* Wormyngford & Fordham. Nich. Steward holds for his life a fourth part of 3 mess., 1 dovecote, 1 toft, 6 gdns., 1 orchard, 90 a. ar., 12 a. mw. & 40 a. pa. in Withermondford *alias* Wormyngford & Fordham, & Eliz. Badcok, wid., holds for her life the remainder of the inheritance of Joan, Margery & Margt. Def. quitclaimed reversion to pl. & his heirs to hold of the chief lords. £80.

44. Morrow of Trin. & Mich. Jn. (------), pl. Jane Tusser, wid., def. Manor of Howehall, (30 a.) pa., 20 a. wd. & 20 a. moor in Revenhall ------, inherited from Jane's late husband, Clement Tusser. Annual rt. of £20 to be paid. (*Very severely stained and mutilated.*)

45. Mich. Tho. Eve, pl. *Wm.* Sandes, gent., & w. Anne & Jn. Levett, def. 1 mess., 1 barn, 1 (toft), 200 a. ar., 30 a. mw. & 70 a. pa. in Woodham Ferres & Stowe Maries. Pl. gtd. prop. to Jn. Levett for 20 years from Michaelmas 15 - - at rt. of £13 6s. 8d. with reversion to Wm. & Anne Sandes to hold of the chief lords. (*Damaged at right hand edge.*)

46. Mich. Tho. Eve, pl. *Tho.* Armiger, gent., & w. Jane & Jn. Barrett, def. 50 a. ar. in Cane(wdon). Pl. gtd. prop. to Jn. Barrett for 21 years from Michaelmas 1570 at rt. of 12d. with reversion to Tho. & Jane Armiger to hold of the chief lords.

47. Morrow of Trin. & Mich. Roger Covert & Jn. Kent, pl. *Tho.* Coverte, gent., & w. Margt. & Rd. Collett *alias* Devenyshe, def. Manor of Porters *alias* Myllers, 1 mess., 1 dovecote, 1 gdn., 78 a. ar., 4 a. mw., 6 a. pa. & 9s. rt. in High Rothinge *alias* Alta Rothinge & Great Dunmowe. Def. quitclaimed to pl. & the heirs of Roger. Pl. gtd. prop. to Rd. Collett for 41 years at rt. of £5 6s. 8d. to be paid at the back door (*anterius ostium*) of Tho. Coverte's house in Histleworth, co. Mdx., with reversion to Tho. & Margt. Coverte, to hold of the chief lords.

48. Mich. Tho. Eve, pl. *Tho.* Armiger, gent., & w. Jane & Robt. Robiant, def. 1 mess., 1 windmill & 4 a. ar. in Canewdon. Pl. gtd. prop. to Robt. Robiant for 21 years from Michaelmas 1570 at rt. of £3., with reversion to Tho. & Jane Armiger to hold of the chief lords.

CP25(2)/127/1629   HILARY, 9 ELIZABETH   1567

1. Tho. Darcy, esq., pl. Brian Darcy, gent., def. 2 mess., 1 barn, 2 gdns., 20 a. ar. & 80 a. pa. in Tolshunt Tregoos *alias* Tolshunt Darcy. 260 mks.

2. Robt. Wood, gent., pl. *Wm.* Bretton & w. Joan, def. 2 mess., 60 a. ar. & 4 a. mw. in Bromesfeld. 200 mks.

3. Mich. & Hil. Wm. Adam, pl. *Jn.* Totnam & w. Margery, def. 1 mess. & 1 barn in Walden. £20.

4. Wm. Rawlen, pl. *Jn.* Morsse & w. Eliz., def. 1 mess. & 1 gdn. in Legh. £40.

5. Geo. Whytte, Robt. Bradburye & Hy. Apleton, esquires, pl. Edm. Tyrrell, esq., def. 1 mess., 1 gdn., 1 orchard, 10 a. mw. & 60 a. pa. called 'Scotts' & 'Cooks Lande' in Hockeley & Rayleye. Def. quitclaimed to pl. & the heirs of Geo. £200.

6. Tho. Fawnce, pl. Jn. Cames & w. *Margt.*, def. 17 a. ar. & 5 a. marsh in Esttylbery. £80.

7. Tho. Parker, pl. Tho. Rochester & w. *Dorothy*, Hy. Brooke & w. *Barbara*, def. 1 mess., 1 toft, 1 gdn., 4 a. ar., 1 a. mw., 5 a. pa. & 3 a. wd. in Ardley*alias* Ardleygh. £40.

8. Nich. Cotton, pl. *Wm.* Armested & w. Margt., def. 8 a. fresh marsh in Dagenham. £40.

9. Pet. Grene, pl. *Rd.* Grene & w. Joan, def. 2 mess., 1 cott., 2 gdns., 2 orchards, 14 a. ar., 4 a. mw. & 10 a. pa. in Great Maplestede. £40.

10. Mich. & Hil. Francis Salperwycke *alias* Gyllam & w. Joan, pl. *Tho.* Myller & w. Eleanor, def. 1 mess., 1 toft, 50 a. ar., 16 a. mw. & 16 a. pa. in Takeley. Def. quitclaimed to pl. & the heirs of Francis. £50.

11. Mich. & Hil. Jn. Bowsye & w. Joan, pl. Rd. Drane & w. *Margery*, def. 1 mess., 1 gdn. & 48 a. ar. in Bromefeld. Def. quitclaimed to pl. & the heirs of Joan. £80.

12. Mich. & Hil. Rd. Gelham *alias* Yeldham & w. Kath., pl. Jn. Gelham*alias* Yeldham & w. *Joan*, def. A moiety of 4 a. ar. & 8½ a. pa. in Fynchingfelde & Toppesfelde. Def. quitclaimed to pl. & the heirs of Kath. £40.

13. Tho. Andrewes & Edm. Wyseman, gentlemen, pl. *Jas.* Lytle & w. Agnes, def. 2 mess., 2 gdns., 2 orchards, 16 a. ar. 8 a. mw., 8½ a. pa. & 3½ a. wd. in Dagenham & Barkinge. Def. quitclaimed to pl. & the heirs of Tho. £160.

14. Tho. Wylson, gent., pl. *Tho.* Flyngant, gent., & w. Emma, def. 20 a. ar. & 20 a. marsh in West Marsey. £40.

15. Mich. & Hil. Wm. Rame, pl. Francis Rame, def. 2 mess., 2 gdns. & 4½d. rt. in Colcestre & Pleacy. £40.

16. Mich. & Hil. Edw. Neale, pl. Jn. Foster, def. 3 a. pa. in Willingale Spayne. £40.

17. Mich. and Hil. Nich. Wilbore, pl. Wm. Tyffyn, gent., def. 1 mess., 1 gdn., 16 a. ar., 6 a. mw. & 12 a. pa. in Hedyngham at the Castle, Hedyngham Sybley & Great Maplested. £100.

18. Mich. & Hil. Edw. Glascocke, gent., pl. Anth. Horrold, gent., def. 1 mess., 1 gdn., 58 a. ar., 14 a. mw., 20 a. pa. & 10 a. wd. in Belchamp St. Paul. £140.

19. Mich. & Hil. Tho. Parker, pl. Silvester Papworthe & w. *Agnes*, def. 1 mess., 1 gdn., 4½ a. ar. & 1 a. pa. in Cryshall *alias* Crystyshall. £40.

20. Mich. & Hil. Jn. Craythorne, pl. *Wm.* Kyng & w. Thomasina, def. 1 mess., 1 gdn., 1 orchard & 2 a. mw. in Great Bursted. £40.

21. Mich. & Hil. Tho. Chapleyn, pl. *Robt.* Maskall, son & heir of Jn. Maskall, & w. Kath., & *Hy.* Brockehole & w. Eliz., def. 1 mess., 2 gdns., & 5 a. ar. in Fynchingfelde. £30.

22. Tho. Gage, pl. Wm. Kynge & w. *Kath.*, def. A moiety of 1 mess., 1 barn, 1 gdn., 30 a. ar., 2 a. mw. & 3 a. pa. in Layer Marney & Great Wigbarowe, which Eliz. the w. of Wm. Turner holds for life. Pl. & his heirs to hold the reversion of the chief lords. £60.

23. Wm. Daye & w. Agnes, pl. *Tho.* Jeppes & w. Agnes, def. 1 mess., 1 gdn, 1 orchard, 12 a. ar., 4 a. mw., 6 a. pa. & 2 a. wd. in Arkesden. Def. quitclaimed to pl. & the heirs of Wm. £40.

24. Mich. & Hil. Jn. Browne, Robt. Plome & Tho. Purcas, pl. *Wm.* Walpole, esq., & w. Anne, def. Manors of Spaynes & Butlers & 3 mess., 200 a. ar., 20 a. mw., 100 a. pa., 20 a. wd., 24s. rt. & a rt. of 3 capons in Great Gelham *alias* Nether Yeldham, Toppesfeld, Hengham Syble *alias* Hennyngham Syble, Hengham at the Castle *alias* Hennyngham Castell & Little Yeldham. Def. quitclaimed to pl. & the heir of Jn., with warranty against the heirs of Wm. Walpole, esq., father of Wm. £480.

25. Nich. Wylbore, pl. *Jn.* Pryor & w. Mary, def. 1 mess., 1 barn, 1 gdn., 1 orchard, 20 a. ar., 8 a. mw., 20 a. pa. & 3 a. wd. in Stysted & Bockyng. £100.

26. Joan Laxton, wid., pl. Jn. Quarles & w. Dorothy, *Tho.* Lodge, kt., & w. Anne, def. 6 mess., 3 barns, 1 dovecote, 3 orchards, 3 gardens, 30 a. ar., 10 a. mw. & 24 a. marsh in Westham & Eastham. £200.

27. Mich. & Hil. Sn. Stevyn, pl. Geo. Haukyn, gent., Edw. Everarde & w. *Bridget*, Jn. Barnarde & w. Margery, def. 1 mess., 1 toft, 1 gdn., 1 orchard, 20 a. ar. & 20 a. pa. in Althorne. £140.

28. Tho. Knightlay, gent., pl. *Jn.* Zouche, kt., & w. Eleanor def. Manor of Torock *alias* Thorock Gray *alias* Greys Thorock & 10 mess., 10 tofts, 10 cotts., 1 mill, 2 dovecotes, 30 gdns., 30 orchards, 1,000 a. ar., 300 a. mw., 1,000 a. pa., 200 a. wd., 200 a. furze & heath, 500 a. marsh, 100 a. alder & £10 rt. in Torock *alias* Thorock Grey *alias* Greyes Thorock & Styfforde, the ferry of Greys, & the advowsons of the churches of Greys & Styfforde. 690 mks.

29. Mich. & Hil. Jn. Kent & Jn. Skyngle, pl. Jn. Gelham *alias* Yeldham & w. *Joan* & Pet. Lyndsell, def. 11 a. ar. in Fynchingfelde. Def. quitclaimed to pl. & the heirs of Jn. Kent. And for this pl. gtd. ½ a. ar., parcel of the same, by Peter's meadow called 'Borleys', to Pet. & his heirs to hold of the chief lords; & 10½ a. ar., the residue, to Pet. to hold from Michaelmas last for 8 years, rendering 2d. yearly to pl. & the heirs of Jn. Kent, with power of distraint, with remainder to def. & the heirs of Jn., to hold of the chief lords.

CP26(1)/131   **EASTER, 9 ELIZABETH**   1567

1. Jerome Songar & Wm. Cownsley, pl. Jn. Lytman & w. *Helen*, def. 10 a. ar., 3 a. mw., 2 a. wd. & 1 a. fresh marsh in Wyckham. Def. quitclaimed to pl. & the heirs of Jerome. And for this pl gtd. the same to def. & the heirs of Jn., to hold of the chief lords.

2. Wm. Vernon, gent., pl. Tho. Eve & w. *Juliana*, def. 1 mess., 1 barn, 20 a. ar., 5 a. mw., 20 a. pa. & 2 a. wd. in Maldon. 100 mks.

3. Jn. Dawson, pl. Jn. Lytman & w. *Helen*, def. 1 mess., 1 gdn., 1 orchard & 3 a. pa. in Wytham. £40.

4. Jn. Watson & Wm. Weldon, pl. *Tho.* Colshill, esq., & *Tho.* Fuller, *Jn.* Maltes, Jn. Jolly & w. *Joan* and *Margery* Hayward, wid., def. 6 mess., 1 cott., 6 gdns., 2 orchards, 200 a. ar., 50 a. mw., 200 (a.) pa., 40 a. wd. & 5s. rt. in Chigwell. Def. quitclaimed to pl. & the heirs of Jn. Watson. £400.

5. Jn. Southcot, one of the justices of pleas before the Queen, & w. Eliz., pl. *Francis* Barneham & w. Alice, def. 3 mess., 1 dovecote, 1 barn, 1 gdn., 1 orchard, 300 a. ar., 80 a. mw., 200 a. pa. & 40 a. wd. in Wytham. £40.

6. Nich. Bacon, kt., lord keeper of the great seal, & Tho. Andrewes, gent., pl. Geoff. Snagges & *Jn.* Snagges & w. Eliz., def. 1 mess., 1 curtilage, 1 orchard, 50 a. ar., 12 a. mw., 20 a. pa. & 30 a. wd. in Barking & Dagenham. Def. quitclaimed to pl. & the heirs of Nich. £200.

7. Humphrey Shelton & Rd. Pykeryng, gentlemen, pl. Hy. Breton, gent., def. Manor of Mychells & 8 mess., 8 tofts, 1 dovecote, 8 gdns., 200 a. ar., 60 a. mw., 600 a. pa., 100 a. wd., 200 a. furze & heath & 16s. rt. in Little Walden, Haddlestock, Assheton *alias* Ashedune, Bartlowe *alias* Barkelowe, Layer Breton, Salcott Vyrley & Muche Byrche. Def. quitclaimed to pl. & the heirs of Rd. £400.

8. Geo. Sayer sen., gent., & Geo. Sayer jun., gent., his son & heir apt., pl. *Jn.* Hardekyn, gent., & w. Eliz., def. Manor of Odwell & 6 mess., 6 cotts., 1 dovecote, 6 gdns., 4 orchards, 300 a. ar., 20 a. mw., 200 a. pa., 30 a. wd., 20 a. alder & 12s. rt. in Gestingthorpe, Maplestede, Odwell & Colchester. Def. quitclaimed to pl. & the heirs of Geo. sen. £140.

9. Tho. Bussard & w. Alice, pl. *Jn.* Holland & w. Margt., def. 1 mess. called 'Est-woode', 2 tofts, 40 a. ar., 30 a. pa., 50 a wd. & 3s. 4d. rt. in Great Bromeleigh, Little Bromeleigh & Little Bentleigh. Def. quitclaimed to pl. & the heirs of Tho. £100.

10. Rd. Cordell, son of Wm. Cordell, decd., & Alice Cordell, wid., pl. Rd. Foster, gent., def. 6 a. ar., 1 a. mw., 6 a. pa. & 2 a. wd. in Chingford. Def. quitclaimed to pl. & the heirs of Rd. £40.

11. Tho. Meade, esq., pl. Nich. Felsted sen. & *Nich.* Felsted jun., def. 1 mess., 1 gdn., 20 a. ar. & 2 a. pa. in Lyttelbury. £40.

12. Rd. Westwood, pl. *Tho.* Baron *alias* Bernes & w. Anne, def. 1 mess., 1 gdn., 12 a. ar., 10 a. pa. & 8 a. wd. in Barkynge. £80.

13. Tho. Somner & Hy. Archer, pl. Reg. Somner, def. 1 mess., 20 a. ar., 5 a. mw., 10 a. pa. & 4 a. wd. in Eppynge & Great Paryngdon. Def. quitclaimed to pl. & the heirs of Tho. And for this pl. granted the same to def. & his heirs, to hold of the chief lords.

14. Tho. Hamond, pl. *Geo.* Smyth, gent., & w. Emma, def. 1 mess., 1 curtilage, 2 gdns., 60 a. ar., 10 a. mw., 40 a. pa., 5 a. wd. & 4s. rt. in Pentlowe & Belchampe St. Paul. 200 mks.

15. Wm. Grigges, pl. *Geo.* Smyth, gent., & w. Emma, def. 1 mess., 2 gdns., 70 a. ar., 13 a. mw., 80 a. pa. & 30 a. wd. in Pentlowe & Belchampe St. Paul. 200 mks.

16. Francis Wyott, esq., pl. Hy. Drury, esq., & w. *Eliz.*, dau. & heir of Tho. Isaak, gent., def. 4 a. ar., & 4 a. marsh called 'Mathewes Hooke' in Tyllyngham. £40.

17. Tho. Stokes, pl. *Tho.* Wale & w. Alice, Tho. Wyseman of Wymbysshe, esq., & w. Joan, def. 1 mess., 2 barns, 2 gardens, 1 orchard, 36 a. ar., 4 a. mw. & 20 a. pa. in Thaxsted & Wymbysshe. £100.

18. Jn. Tye, pl. Robt. Wordyssworth & w. *Joan*, def. 1 mess., 1 gdn., 1 orchard & 12 a. ar. in Great Byrche. £60.

19. Wm. Walshe & Jn. Tye, pl. Robt. Wordyssworth & w. *Joan*, def. 3 mess., 3 gdns., 3 orchards, 120 a. ar., 10 a. mw. & 40 a. pa. in Great Byrch, Little Byrch, Copforth, Esthorpe & Stanwaye. Def. quitclaimed to pl. & the heirs of Wm. And for this pl. gtd. the same to de. & the heirs of Robt., to hold of the chief lords.

20. Hil. & Eas. Jn. Kente & Robt. Frythe, pl. Geo. Lawe & w. *Anne*, def. 1 mess. & 1 gdn. in Walden. Def. quitclaimed to pl. & the heirs of Jn. And for this pl. gtd. the same to def. & the heirs of Robt., to hold of the chief lords.

21. Hil. & Eas. Roger Manwood, esq., Robt. Gynes, gent., Robt. Bogas, gent., & Robt. Dyckeley, gent., pl. Jn. Lucas, gent., & w. *Mary*, def. Manor of Roydon Hall & 10 mess., 600 a. ar., 100 a. mw., 600 a. pa., 50 a. wd. 100 a. marsh, 200 a. furze & heath & £3 rt. in Ramesey, Wrabnes & Wyttam *alias* Wytham. Def. quitclaimed to pl & the heirs of Roger. £320.

22. Tho. Yale, doctor of laws, & w. Joan, pl. *Tho.* Baron, esq., & w. Anne, def. 1 mess., 1 gdn., 1 orchard, 100 a. ar., 40 a. mw., 60 a. pa., 40 a. wd. & common of pa. in Barkynge. Def. quitclaimed to pl. & the heirs of Tho. 400 mks.

23. Robt. Kempe, esq., pl. Jn. Barmbye, gent., def. A moiety of the manor of Hovells & a moiety of 1 mess., 1 gdn., 200 a. ar., 40 a. mw., 60 a. pa., 20 a. wd. & 20s. rt. in Fynchyngfeld & Shalford. 200 mks.

24. Edm. Hurte, pl. *Pet.* Hatche & w. Alice, def. 6 a. ar in Orsett. £40.

25. Wm. Jaxson, pl. *Rd.* Tyler & w. Lucy, def. 4 a. ar., 4 a. pa. & 2 a. wd. in Hawke-well. £40.

26. Tho. Eve, pl. *Rd.* Tyler & w. Lucy, def. 1 mess., 1 barn, 1 gdn., 10 a. ar., 4 a. mw. & 8 a. pa. in Hawkewell. £80.

27. Robt. Golston, pl. Humphrey Kynwelmarshe & w. *Mary*, def. A moiety of 1 mess., 1 barn, 1 gdn. & 5½ a. ar. in Westham. £20.

28. Edw. Lee, pl. *Tho.* Lewson & w. Ursula, def. 12 a. ar. & 12 a. pa. called 'Dewland' in Black Notley. And for this pl. gtd to Tho. & his heirs a yearly rt. of 20s. from the same, payable at the Annunciation & Michaelmas, with power of distraint.

29. Tho. Hobson, pl. *Rd.* Hamond & w. Eliz., def. 1 mess., 1 barn, 1 gdn., 10 a. ar., 4 a. mw. 10 a. pa. in Smethes & Turtell in the parishes of Prytwell *alias* Pryttlewell, Great Sutton & Little Sutton. £80.

30. Robt. Andrewes, pl. Rd. Hawes & w. *Petronilla*, def. 2 mess., 2 tofts, 1 barn, 1 quay, 2 gdns., 2 orchards, 8 a. ar., 8 a. pa., 2 a. wd. & 6s. rt. in Harwyche & Ramsey. £80.

31. Hil. & Eas. Robt. Grene jun., pl. Tho. Tey, gent., & w. *Eleanor, Jn.* Spenser & w. Joan, def. 1 mess., 20 a. ar., 2 a. mw. & 8 a. pa. in Henyngham Sible *alias* Hengham Sible. £40.

32. Tho. Gylbert, pl. Jn. Gelham *alias* Yeldham & w. Joan, def. 1 mess., 1 gdn., 1 orchard & 1 barn in Bockynge. Def. quitclaimed to pl. & his heirs, with warranty of one moiety for the heirs of Joan & the other moiety for the heirs of Jn. £40.

33. Hil. & Eas. Tho. Walworth *alias* Walforde, pl. *Jn.* Pamphelon *alias* Pamflon & w. Eliz., def. 1 mess., 1 barn, 1 gdn. & 2½ a. ar. in Shalforde. £20.

34. Jn. Chapman & w. Mary, pl. *Edw.* Bynder & w. Frances, def. 1 mess., 1 gdn. & 5 a. ar. in Danberye. Def. quitclaimed to pl. & the heirs of Jn. £30.

35. Hil. & Eas. Francis Saunders, esq., & Wm. Walter sen., pl. Jn. Goodwyn, esq., Hy. Josselyn, esq., & w. Anne, & Jn. Lucas, gent., & w. *Mary*, def. Manors of Manytre, Schidynghoo *alias* Chedynghoo, Oldhall *alias* Oldehall, Newhall & Abbottes *alias* Edlynges & 60 mess., 20 cotts., 10 tofts, 4 water-mills, 1,000 a ar., 200 a. mw., 1,000 a. pa., 400 a. wd., 600 a. furze & heath & £20 rt. in Manytre, Scidynghoo *alias* Chedynghoo, Oldhall *alias* Oldehall, Newhall, Abbottes *alias* Edlynges, Mistleigh *alias* Mysteley, Bradfeld, Colchester, Stanwaye, Wrabne *alias* Wrabnes, Wikes, Little Badowe, Lawforde, Little Bromeleigh, Ardleigh, 'and Our Ladye in the Otes', view of frank pledge, free warren, liberties & franchises in Misteleigh & Manytre, the rectory & church of Bradfeld & tithes of Bradfeld, & the advowsons of the church of Misteleigh *alias* Misteley & the vicarage of Bradfeld. Def. quitclaimed to pl. & the heirs of Francis. And for this pl. gtd. one moiety of the same to Jn. Goodwyn & his heirs, & the other moiety to Hy. & Anne & the heirs of Anne, to hold of the chief lords.

CP26(1)/131   DIVERS COUNTIES

4. Hil. & Eas. Tho. Godfrey, pl. *Hy*. Calton & w. Eliz. & Anth. Calton & w. Anne, def. 1 mess., 4 cotts., 3 barns, 1 dovecote, 1 gdn, 50 a. ar., 20 a. mw., 30 a. pa. & 10 a. wd. in Walden, co. Essex; & property in Stortford, co. Herts. £420. — Essex, Herts.

CP25(2)/127/1630   TRINITY, 9 ELIZABETH   1567

1. Robt. Lukyn, pl. Wimund Carye, esq., def. 1 mess., 1 gdn., 40 a. ar., 4 a. mw. & 14 a. pa. in Takeley. £40.

2. Tho. Spakeman, pl. *Tho.* Potter & w. Margt., def. 1 mess., 2 barns, 1 gdn., 1 orchard, 12 a. ar., 4 a. mw., 4 a. pa. & 6 a. wd. in Chigwell £40.

3. Tho. Gynes, gent., & w. Faith, pl. Hy. Mildmay, gent., def. 5 mess., 4 tofts, 4 gdns., 100 a. ar., 6 a. mw., 30 a. pa. & 4 a. wd. in Great Leighes & Boreham. Def. quitclaimed to pl. & the heirs of Tho. £100.

4. Tho. Spakeman, pl. *Nich.* Hyll & w. Joan, def. 1 mess., 2 barns, 1 gdn., 1 orchard, 12 a. ar., 4 a. mw., 4 a. pa. & 6 a. wd. in Chigwell £40.

5. Eas. & Trin. Jas. Baker, esq., pl. Tho. Pike, gent., def. 2 mess., 1 cott., 1 gdn., 200 a. ar., 40 a. mw., 200 a. pa. & 20 a. marsh in Southshubery & Cannyngdon *alias* Canwaydon. £200.

6. R. Bucke, pl. *Rouland* Elryngton & Jn. Curtes, def. 3 a. mw. in Wyddington. £40.

7. Eas. & Trin. Tho. Pike, gent., pl. *Jas.* Baker, esq., & w. Mary, def. 10 a. ar., 2 a. mw., 10 a. pa. & 10 a. marsh in Southshubery. £30.

8. Tho. Goddyshalff, pl. Alice Aliston, wid., *Valentine* Tyler & w. Agnes, def. 1 mess., 2 gdns., & 19 a. ar. in Hengham Syble *alias* Hennyngham Sybbell. 100 mks.

9. Eas. & Trin. Jn. Fytche, pl. Wm. Fytche & w. *Margt.*, def. 3 mess., 3 gdns., 3 or-chards, 40 a. ar., 8 a. mw., 10 a. pa., 4 a. wd. & 3s. rt. in Yeldham, Toppesfyld, Stamborn & Reddeswell. £100.

10. Eas. & Trin. Tho. Parke & Wm. Browne, pl. Wm. Sturton *alias* Strutton & w. *Margt.*, def. 10 a. ar. in Great Berdefelde. Def. quitclaimed to pl. & the heirs of Tho. £30.

11. Hy. Goldinge, esq., pl. Hy. Peryent & w. *Jane*, def. A moiety of 4 mess., 4 tofts, 100 a. ar., 30 a. mw., 80 a. pa., 40 a. wd. & 20s. furze & heath in Little Byrche, Layer Delahey & Stanwey. 230 mks.

12. Jn. Violett, citizen & fishmonger of London, pl. *Rd.* Knyght & w. Anne, def. 1 mess., 1 gdn., 6 a. ar., 6 a. mw., 40 a. pa. & 6 a. wd. in Lowhall Walkehamstowe, Walke-hamstowe Towney, Walkehamstowe Fraunces, Higham Bensted & Hygham Hylls. £120.

13. Edw. Mulleynes, pl. *Jn.* Hubberd & w. Margt., def. 1 mess., 1 gdn., 3½ a. ar. & 1 a. mw. in Halsted. £40.

14. Eas. & Trin. Tho. Wood, pl. Wm. White, def. 1 mess., 1 barn & 24 a. ar. in Barmeston, Dunmowe & Bisshoppwood. £40.

15. Jn. Garrarde, pl. *Francis* Barnham & w. Alice, def. 1 mess., 1 toft, 1 gdn., 1 orchard, 30 a. ar., 10 a. mw. 40 a. pa., 6 a. wd. & 40 a. furze & heath in Owltyng, Hat-feyld Peaveyrell, Woodham Water & Mawdon. 130 mks.

16. Rd. Pickeringe, gent., & Geo. Archer, pl. *Jn.* Elyott & w. Eleanor, Hy. Isham & w. Joan, def. Manor of Holehall *alias* Howhall *alias* Martylls & 4 mess., 4 tofts, 4 gdns., 300 a. ar., 50 a. mw., 100 a. pa., 100 a. wd., 20 a. marsh & £5 rt. in Revenhall, Falborne, Wytham, Little Braxsted, Great Braxsted, Cressynge, Esterford & Coggeshall. Def. quit-claimed to pl. & the heirs of Rd. £200.

17. Hy. Peryent & w. Jane, pl. Hy. Golding, esq., def. A moiety of 4 mess., 4 tofts, 100 a. ar., 16 a. mw., 80 a. pa., 40 a. wd. & 20 a. furze & heath in Great Byrche, Little Byrche, Copforde & Esthorpp. Def. quitclaimed to pl. & the heirs of Jane. 150 mks.

18. Eas. & Trin. Robt. Woodwarde, pl. *Robt.* Crafte & w. Margery, def. 1 mess., 1 gdn., 10 a. ar. & 1 a. mw. in Thaxsted & Wymbyshe. £40.

19. Eas. & Trin. Rd. Grene, pl. *Tho.* Golding, kt., & w. Eliz., def. The rectory of Great Mapplested & 40 a. ar., 8 a. mw., 10 a. pa., 15 a. wd. & 20s. rt. in Great Maplested, & all tithes, portions, oblations, obventions & emoluments belonging to the rectory in Great Maplested, Little Maplested, Gestingthorpe & Wickham St. Paul, & the advowson of the vicarage of the church of Great Maplested. 100 mks.

20. Eas. & Trin. Tho. Wallinger, gent., & Jn. Williams, pl. Jn. Watson & w. *Bridget*, def. 2 mess., 2 gdns., 2 orchards, 25 a. ar. & 6 a. mw. in Navestocke, which Jn. Burton holds for life. Pl. & the heirs of Tho. to hold the reversion of the chief lords. £80.

21. Rd. Marten, esq., & Roger Marten, gent., pl. *Wm.* Cordell, kt., master of the rolls of Chancery, & w. Mary, def. Manor of Smeton *alias* Smeton Halle & 10 mess., 200 a. ar., 100 a. mw., 100 a. pa., 60 a. wd. & 100s. rt. in Bulmer, Walter Belchampe, Willm Belchamp, Borley, Brondon & Little Henny. Def. quitclaimed to pl. & the heirs of Roger. £400.

22. Eas. & Trin. Rd. Pylston, gent., & Robt. Boyton, pl. Wm. Gylson & w. *Margt.*, Rd. Parker & w. *Jane*, def. 2 mess., 2 gdns., 10½ a. ar. & 1 a. mw. in Farneham. Def. quitclaimed to pl. & the heirs of Rd. £40.

23. Jn. Godday sen., pl. *Jn.* Sawyn, gent., & w. Eliz., def. 1 mess., 3 tofts, 3 gdns., 60 a. ar., 6 a. mw., 30 a. pa. & 4 a. wd. in Great Lyghes, Little Lyghes, Fayrested & Little Waltham. £300.

24. Eas. & Trin. Tho. Wylson, pl. *Tho.* Flyngante & w. Emma, def. 1 mess., 1 barn, 1 stable, 1 gdn. & 3 a. ar. in Colchester & a third part of 4 mess., 4 gdns. & 3 a. ar. in Colchester & Grenested. £40.

25. Tho. Phylypson & w. Bridget, pl. *Jn.* Heyward & w. Alice, def. A moiety of 1 mess. & 1 gdn. in Boreham. Def. quitclaimed to pl. & the heirs of Tho. £10.

26. Jn. Cooke, gent., pl. Tho. Lyttell & w. *Eliz.*, def. 6 a. wd. in Thundersleighe. £20.

27. Eas. & Trin. Tho. Wallinger, gent., pl. Jn. Watson & w. *Bridget*, & Jn. Williams, def. 2 mess., 2 gdns., 2 orchards, 25 a. ar. & 6 a. mw. in Navestocke, which Jn. Burton

holds for life. Pl. & his heirs to hold the reversion of the chief lords. And for this pl. gtd. the same to Jn. Williams to hold after the decease of Jn. Burton for 21 years, rendering £4 yearly to pl. & his heirs, at the Annunciation & Michaelmas, with power of distraint, with remainder to Jn. Watson & Bridget & the heirs of Jn., to hold of the chief lords.

CP25(2)/259   DIVERS COUNTIES

6. Wm. Cordell, ktd., master of the rolls of Chancery, pl. *Rd.* Marten, esq., & Roger Marten, gent., his son & heir apt. def. Prop. in Suff.; & 1 a. ar. in Lyston, co. Essex. 910 mks. — Suff., Essex.

CP25(2)/127/1631   MICHAELMAS, 9–10 ELIZABETH   1567

1. Nich. Dryver & Tho. Well, pl. Wm. Sulman, def. 1 mess., 1 barn, 1 gdn., 20 a. ar., 3 a. mw. & 10 a. pa. in Great Sampforde & Little Sampforde. Def. quitclaimed to pl. & the heirs of Nich. And for this pl. gtd. the same to def. & his heirs, to hold of the chief lords.

2. Wm. Freman, pl. *Jn.* Cottyce & w. Joan, def. 3 mess., 1 gdn., 8 a. ar. & 2 a. pa. in Bromefeld. £40.

3. Rd. Rede, kt., pl. *Wm.* Johnson, gent., & Wm. Barland & w. Agnes, def. 1 mess., 3 tofts, 1 barn, 1 dovecote, 3 gdns., 50 a. ar., 20 a. mw. & 40 a. pa. in Wryttell, Rockeswell, Wyllynghale Doo & Wyllynghale Spayne. £140.

4. Wm. Wyllowes, pl. *Wm.* Lestriche *alias* Bocher & w. Eliz., def. 1 mess., 1 gdn., 16 a. ar., 8 a. mw., 6 a. pa. & 7 a. wd. in Asshedon. £40.

5. Mich. Kendall, pl. *Jn.* Wyberde & w. Alice, def. 1 mess., 1 gdn., 1 orchard, 12 a. ar., 8 a. mw., 10 a. pa. & 14d. rt. in Thaydon Garnon. £100.

6. Jn. Bullock & Edm. Morrant, gentlemen, pl. *Hy.* Fanshawe, esq., & w. Dorothy, def. 1 mess., 20 a. ar., 30 a. mw. & 60 a. pa. in Barkinge. Def. quitclaimed to pl. & the heirs of Jn. £70.

7. Tho. Westbrome sen., pl. *Tho.* Westbrome jun. & w. Joan, def. 2 tofts, 40 a. ar., 1 a. mw. & 3 a. marsh in Little Clacton. £100.

8. Clement Bucke, pl. *Jn.* Holte & w. Joan, def. 1 mess., 1 barn, 1 gdn., 1 orchard, 40 a. ar., 10 a. mw., 10 a. pa. & 2 a. wd. in Debden & Wedington. £40.

9. Jas. Drylond, gent., pl. Ralph Nalynghurst *alias* Naylynghurst, gent., def. 2 mess., 2 tofts, 2 curtilages, 1 barn, 2 gdns. & 1 orchard in Badowe *alias* Great Badowe. £40.

10. Joan Lee, Francis Michell & Jn. Brignell, pl. *Humphrey* Whyte & w. Dorothy, def. Manor of Chyngeford St. Paul *alias* Chyngeford Pawle & 4 mess., 4 tofts, 1 mill, 1 dovecote, 4 gdns., 400 a. ar., 40 a. mw., 200 a. pa., 200 a. wd., 30 a. furze & heath, 20 a. moor, 20 a. reedbed, 12 a. marsh, 20 a. alder & £6 rt. in Chyngeford. Def. quitclaimed to pl. & the heirs of Joan, with warranty against Geo. Whyte & Jn. Whyte & their heirs. £500.

11. Tho. Francke, esq., pl. Wimond Carye, esq., def. 40 a. ar., 20 a. mw., & 10 a. pa. in Takele. Def. quitclaimed to pl. & his heirs, with warranty against Jn. Carye, kt., & Edw. Carye, esq., & their heirs. £60.

12. Trin. & Mich. Wm., marquess of Winchester, treasurer of England, & Walter Myldmay, kt., pl. Jn. Darcy, kt., lord Darcy of Chyche, def. Manors of Wygborowe, Lee Wyke & Wyers Hall *alias* Aula Guidonis & 20 mess., 20 gdns., 1,000 a. ar., 100 a. mw. & 300 a. pa. in Wygborowe, Lee Wyke & Wyers Hall *alias* Aula Guidonis. Def. quitclaimed to pl. & the heirs of the marquess. £40.

13. Hy. Lyvynge, pl. Tho. Kynge & w. *Alice* & Agnes Hills, def. 2 mess., 2 gdns. & 1 orchard in Reyleigh. £40.

14. Tho. Wallinger, gent., pl. *Wm.* Eyer & w. Alice, def. 1 mess., 1 gdn., 1 orchard, 80 a. ar., 3 a. mw., 30 a. pa. & 12 a. wd. in Bromesfeld. £60.

15. Jn. Tyler, pl. *Rd.* Barlee, esq., & w. Anne, def. Manors of Sowthowse & Sperhawkesey *alias* Sparowhawkesfee & 6 mess., 4 tofts, 2 dovecotes, 10 gdns., 10 orchards, 300 a. ar., 60 a. mw., 300 a. pa., 40 a. wd. & 40s. rt. in Great Waltham & Little Waltham. And for this pl. gtd. the same to def & the heirs of Rd., to hold of the chief lords.

16. Pet. Gage, pl. Wm. Quodwell & w. *Eliz.*, def. A moiety of 1 mess., 1 gdn. & 1½ a. mw. in Patteswyke. £40.

17. Jn. Godday sen. & Geoff. Caldwall, pl. *Steph.* Craske & w. Margt. & Jn. Hales, gent., def. 5 mess., 6 tofts, 3 barns, 8 gdns., 4 orchards, 30 a. ar., 20 a. mw., 15 a. pa., 6 3 roods mw. & 5 a. pa. in Witham *alias* Wittam. £40.

18. Trin. & Mich. Jn. Ive, gent., pl. Francis Eglesfyld, gent., def. 1 mess., 1 gdn., 1 orchard, 30 a. ar., 10 a. mw., 40 a. pa., 6 a. wd. & 18d. rt. in Chelmesford, Wryttell & Wydford. £140.

19. Rd. Grene & Jn. Kent, pl. *Jn.* Holmsted, gent., & w. Alice, def. Manor of Hypworthe *alias* Hypworth Hall & 1 mess., 100 a. ar., 12 a. mw., 20 a. pa., 20 a. moor & 47s. 5d. rt. in Halsted, Hengham Syble, Little Maplested & Great Maplested. Def. quitclaimed to pl. & the heirs of Rd. £200.

20. Rd. Welles, pl. Jn. Poole & w. *Joan*, Jn. Holman & w. Agnes, Hy. Lodge & w. Margt., Wm. Claye & w. Eliz., def. 1 mess., 7 a. ar. & 1 a. mw. in Fyfhyde *alias* Fyfyld. £60.

21. Trin. & Mich. Edw. Randyll, pl. Vincent Randyll & Rd. Cooke, gentlemen, def. Manor of Wilfealdes & 10 mess., 6 tofts, 1 mill, 1 dovecote, 10 gdns., 300 a. ar., 40 a. mw., 200 a. pa., 10 a. wd., 6 a. furze & heath, 10 a. marsh, 6 a. alder & 100s. rt. in Barkyng. £326.

22. Jn. Sherecroft, pl. *Julian* Waldegrave & w. Cecily, def. Manor of Leden Rodyng & 14 mess., 6 gdns., 400 a. ar., 200 a. mw., 200 a. pa., 60 a. wd. & £8 rt. in Leden Rodyng, Hye Esturne, Whyte Rodyng, Abbes Rodyng & Artrop Rodyng. £260.

23. Tho. Clarke jun. & w. Anne, pl. *Robt.* Noke, gent., & w. Dorothy, def. 3 mess., 1 dovecote, 3 barns, 3 gdns., 3 orchards, 20 a. ar., 10 a. mw., 80 a. pa. & 3 a. wd. in Great Coggeshall, Little Coggeshall, Halstede & Feringe. Def. quitclaimed to pl. & the heirs of Tho. And for this pl. gtd. the same to def. & the heirs of their bodies to hold of the chief lords, with remainder to the right heirs of Robt.

24. Wm. Berlee, gent., & Eliz. Asplond, wid., pl. Wm. Ayloff, gent., def. Manor of Little Chyshull & 30 mess., 10 cotts., 1 wind-mill, 1 dovecote, 500 a. ar., 20 a. mw., 160 a. pa., 160 a. wd. & £12 rt. in Little Chyshull, Great Chyshull, Heydon, Crishall *alias* Cristyshall & Langley, & the advowson of the church of Little Chyshull. Def. quitclaimed to pl. & the heirs of Wm. £380.

25. Rd. Twedy, esq., pl. *Wm.* Kent & w. Susan, Tho. Feakman & w. *Alice*, & Wm. Maygate & w. *Eliz.*, def. 2 mess., 2 gdns., 3 a. ar., 3 a. mw., 3 a. pa. & 1 a. wd. in Hertfordestocke. £40.

26. Edw. Hamnare, pl. Tho. Taye, esq., & w. *Eleanor*, def. 2 mess., 6 tofts, 100 a. ar., 10 a. mw., 40 a. pa., 10 a. wd. & 50 a. marsh in Goldhanger, Great Totham, Little Totham, Tolshunt Maior & Tolshunt Darceye. And for this pl. gtd. the same to def. & the heirs of the body of Eleanor by Tho., to hold of the chief lords, with remainder to her right heirs.

27. Hy. Fanshawe, esq., & w. Dorothy, pl. *Martin* Bowes sen., esq., & Martin Bowes jun., gent., def. Manor of Jenkyns *alias* Dagenham *alias* Dagenhames *alias* Dagenhames Place & 3 mess., 1 dovecote, 2 gdns., 2 orchards, 140 a. ar., 20 a. mw., 40 a. pa., 12 a. wd., 40 a. marsh & 40s. rt. in Barking & Dagenham *alias* Dakenham. Def. quitclaimed to pl. & the heirs of Hy. 400 mks.

28. Jn. Glascocke & Rd. Emerye, gentlemen, pl.*Jn.* Collyn & w. Joan, Hy. Josselyne, esq., & w. Anne, def. 1 mess., 2 curtilages, 2 barns, 4 gdns., 3 orchards, 120 a. ar., 20 a. mw., 60 a. pa., 10 a. wd. & 3s. rt. in Willingale Doe, Willingale Spayne, Norton & High Ongre. Def. quitclaimed to pl. & the heirs of Jn. And for this pl. gtd. the same to Hy. & Anne & the heirs of their bodies, to hold of the chief lords, with remainder to the right heirs of Anne.

29. Eas. & Mich. Jn. Kent & Humphrey Clarke, pl. *Jn.* Scudamore, esq., & Jn. Holmested, gent., def. A moiety of 10 mess., 10 gdns., 400 a. ar., 40 a. mw., 100 a. pa., 60 a. wd., 20 a. furze & heath & £6 rt. in Great Maplested, Little Maplested, Hengham Sible *alias* Hennyngham Syble, Hengham Castell *alias* Hennyngham at the Castle & Gestingthorpe. Def. quitclaimed to pl. & the heirs of Jn. And for this pl. gtd. the same to Jn. Holmested to hold from Michaelmas last for 60 years without impeachment of waste,

rendering £25 yearly to pl. & the heirs of Jn. Kent at the Annunciation & Michaelmas at the greater western door of the Cathedral church of St. Paul, London, with power of distraint; with remainder to Jn. Scudamore & his heirs, to hold of the chief lords.

30. Tho. Meade, serjeant at law, pl. Rd. Cutte, esq., def. 70 a. ar., 7 a. mw. & 40 a. pa. in Elmeden, Arkeisden, Laingley & Wenden Loofthes. And for this pl. gtd. to def. & his heirs a yearly rt. of 10s. from the same, payable at Michaelmas & the Annunciation, with power of distraint.

31. Tho. Bowen, pl. *Wm.* Marler & w. Margt., def. 1 toft, 60 a. ar., 20 a. pa. & 20 a. wd. in Esterford *alias* Kelvedon. £20.

32. Nich. Steven & Jn. Robertson, pl. Matthew Steven, def. 140 a. wd. in Stanweye. Def. quitclaimed to pl. & the heirs of Nich. £100.

33. Jn. Stubbes, pl. Philip Cawstoune, gent., & w. *Joan*, kinswoman & heir of Wm. Gardener, decd., def. 1 mess., 16 a. ar. & 1 a. wd. in Clacktoune. £40.

34. Rd. Manne, pl. *Tho.* Pygrome & w. Anne, def. 1 mess., 1 gdn. & 6 a. ar. in Rayne, Felsted & Bockynge. £40.

35. Rd. Bradley & w. Agnes, pl. *Jn.* Bancks & w. Eliz., def. 1 mess., 1 croft, 1 gdn. & 1 a. ar. in Great Wenden. Def. quitclaimed to pl. & the heirs of Rd. £40.

36. Rd. Wyllis, pl. *Jn.* Cooke, gent., & w. Mary, def. 2 mess., 2 gdns., 1 orchard, 5 a. ar. & 8 a. pa. in Rayleigh. £114.

37. Jn. Tanner, pl. *Jas.* Cressye, Edm. Cressye & Martha Cressye, def. 2 mess., 2 cotts., 3 gdns., 2 orchards & 3 roods pa. in Waltham Holy Cross. £40.

38. Rd. Flack sen. & Rd. Flack jun., pl. *Jn.* Norffolke & w. Anne, def. 1 mess., 1 gdn., 1 orchard, 8 a. ar., 1 a. mw. & 1 a. pa. in Radwynter. Def. quitclaimed to pl. & the heirs of Rd. jun. £40.

39. Jn. Watson, gent., & w. Eliz., pl. *Tho.* Potter & w. Margt., def. Manor of Sargeaunts *alias* Stoctons & 60 a. ar., 15 a. mw., 10 a. wd. & 11d. rt. in Chygwell *alias* Chyckwell. Def. quitclaimed to pl. & the heirs of Jn. 200 mks.

40. Trin. & Mich. Rd. Hubbert, gent., pl. Jn. Castell & w. *Margery*, def. A moiety of 10 a. ar. & 2 a. mw. in Byrchanger. £40.

41. Nich. Collyn, pl. Hy. Josselyn & w. *Anne*, def. 1 a. mw. in Becham Rodinge. £40.

42. Jn. Thymble, pl. Simon Fawce & w. *Joan*, one of the daus. & heirs of Jn. Harvye, def. A fifth part of 1 mess., 2 tofts, 2 gdns., 1 orchard, 24 a. ar & 1 a. mw. in Aburton, Fingringho & Layer de Lahey. £40.

43. Hugh Lancaster, gent., pl. *Jn.* Everard, gent., & w. Eliz., def. 1 mess., 2 gdns., 20 a. ar., 6 a. mw., 40 a. pa. & 20d. rt. in Bumpsted at the Steeple *alias* Steple Bumpsted. 200 mks.

44. Jn. Boode of Rocheford, pl. *Hy.* Baker & w. Anne, def. 2 mess., 2 gdns., 1 curtilage, 20 a. ar., 4 a. mw. & 6 a. pa. in Hadlegh at the Castle & Woodham Ferrys. £140.

45. Wm. Reve *alias* Saunder, pl. *Tho.* Choppyn & w. Eliz., def. 5 a. ar. in Bromefylde. £40.

46. Trin. & Mich. Tho. Lyndesell, pl. Margery Aburforde *alias* Aburforthe, wid., & Wm. Aburforde *alias* Aburforthe, def. 13 a. ar., 3 a. mw. & 10d. rt. in Thaxsted. £40.

47. Walter Fysshe, pl. *Nich.* Haukyn & w. Eliz., def. 1 mess., 1 dovecote, 1 gdn., 1 orchard, 40 a. ar., 20 a. mw., 30 a. pa., 10 a. wd. & 40 a. furze & heath in Leighton & Waltham Stowe. 400 mks.

48. Francis Archer, pl. *Tho.* Brookman & w. Anne, def. 5 mess., 5 gdns., 1 orchard & 1 watercourse in Bockinge. £80.

49. Wm. Brooke, pl. *Jn.* Brooke of Bradwell by the Sea & Hugh Brooke, def. 1 mess., 1 gdn., 12 a. pa. & 1 a. wd. in Pakelsam. £60.

50. Jn. Glascock, pl. Edw. Denny & w. *Alice*, def. 1 mess., 1 curtilage & 1 orchard in Chepyng Onger. £40.

51. Jn. Vavasour, pl. *Cornelius* Avenand *alias* Avenon & w. Eliz., def. 1 mess., 1 gdn., 6 a. ar., 6 a. mw., 6 a. pa., 1 a. wd. & 4 a. furze & heath in Stratford Langthorne in Westham. £80.

52. Trin. & Mich. Jn. Mylborne, pl. *Jn.* Phillippe *alias* Saunder & w. Joan, def. 1 mess., 1 toft, 1 cott., 1 curtilage, 1 barn, 2 gdns., 1 orchard, 10 a. ar., 2 a. mw. & 1 a. pa. in Great Donmowe. £40.

53. Edw. Meade, pl. *Rd.* Meade & w. Joan, def. 1 mess., 1 gdn., 1 orchard, 16 a. ar., 3 a. mw. & 6 a. pa. in Berden. £40.

54. Hy. Fanshawe, esq., pl. *Tho.* Hennage, esq., & w. Anne, def. 60 a. mw. in Colchester Hithe & Newehithe. £40.

55. Simon Bredge, pl. *Jn.* Meade & w. Mary, def. 10 a. ar. & 1 a. pa. in Stebbinge & Felsted. £30.

56. Jn. Whytlocke, pl. *Jn.* Sone & w. Agnes, def. 3½ a. ar. in Goldanger. £40.

57. Trin. & Mich. Jn. Cooke, gent., pl. Jn. Watson & w. *Bridget*, def. 2 mess., 2 gdns., 20 a. ar., 12 a. mw. & 10 a. pa. in Rayleigh, Westham, Estham & Stratford Langthorne. £140.

58. Wm. Quedwell *alias* Codwell, & w. Helen, pl. *Launcelet* Warde & w. Joan, def. 1 mess., 3 barns, 1 gdn., 2 orchards, 200 a. ar., 10 a. mw., 20 a. pa., 12 a. wd. & 10s. rt. in Wethersfelde, Gosfelde & Shalforde. Def. quitclaimed to pl. & the heirs of Helen. £200.

59. Wm. Petre, kt., pl. Jn. Lunsford, esq., def. 4 tofts, 4 gdns., 4 orchards, 100 a. ar., 10 a. mw., 60 a. pa., 16 a. wd. & 6s. rt. in Ramsden Bellhowse, Ramsden Crase *alias* Ramsden Cray & Downeham. £320.

CP25(2)/127/1632   HILARY, 10 ELIZABETH   1568

1. Tho. Gynes, gent., & w. Faith, pl. *Jn.* Lylly & w. Mary, def. 1 mess., 1 gdn., 4 a. ar., 2 a. mw. & 1 a. pa. in Great Leighes. Def. quitclaimed to pl. & the heirs of Tho. £40.

2. Tho. Pullyver, pl. *Tho.* Hickmans & w. Margt., def. 2 mess., 3 barns, 1 gdn., 1 orchard, 3 a. ar., 10 a. mw. & 6 a. pa. in Westhamme. £120.

3. Reg. Meade, gent., pl. Robt. Broke, gent., & w. *Eliz.*, def. 3 a. wd. in Crishale. £40.

4. Mich. & Hil. Wm. Hagar, citizen & 'salter' of London, pl. *Nich.* Clere sen. & w. Alice, def. 1 mess., 2 cotts., 1 gdn. & 2 a. ar. in Colchester. 200 mks.

5. Tho. Smyth, gent., pl. *Anth.* Horrolde & w. Marion, def. Manor of Gawgers & 2 mess., 2 gdns., 60 a. ar., 16 a. mw., 30 a. pa., 14 a. wd. & 20s. rt. in Belchamp St. Paul, Belchamp Otten, Ovyington & Tylbury. £200.

6. Mich. & Hil. Jn. Williams, pl. Jn. Watson & w. *Bridget*, def. 2 mess., 2 gdns., 2 orchards, 25 a. ar. & 6 a. mw. in Navestocke, which Jn. Burton holds for life. Pl. & his heirs to hold the reversion of the chief lords. £80.

7. Jn. Clere, pl. Robt. Spynke, def. 1 mess. & 2 gdns. in Colchester. 10 mks.

8. Mich. & Hil. Jn. Tyler & Wm. Haukyn, pl. Jn. Dawbye & w. *Agnes*, Tho. Childe & w. Kath., Alice Chamberlayne & Bridget Chamberlayne, def. 2 mess. & 2 curtilages, in Brentwood. Def. quitclaimed to pl. & the heirs of Jn. £40.

9. Jn. Raven, pl. Clement Roberts, gent., def. 1 mess., 1 gdn., 1 orchard, 20 a. ar., 3 roods mw. & 5 a. pa. in Witham *alias* Wittam. £40.

10. Mich. & Hil. Tho. Colshill, esq., & w. Mary, pl. *Robt.* Thomas & w. Eliz., def. 1 mess., 1 cott., 1 gdn., 1 orchard, 20 a. ar., 20 a. mw., 20 a. pa. & 20 a. wd. in Chigwell. Def. quitclaimed to pl. & the heirs of Tho. 100 mks.

11. Benjamin Gunson, esq., & w. Ursula, pl. *Robt.* Kynge, gent., & w. Lettice, Jn. Bridges & w. Anne, def. 1 mess., 2 curtilages, 1 barn, 1 dovecote, 2 gdns., 1 orchard, 20 a. ar., 8 a. mw., 37 a. pa. & 7 a. wd. called 'Sabrightes' in Great Badowe. Def. quitclaimed to pl. & the heirs of Benjamin. £200.

12. Trin. & Hil. Robt. Walforde, pl. Ralph Wryghte & w. *Alice*, def. 6 a. ar., 10 a. pa. & 3 a. wd. in Wethersfield & Shalford. £40.

13. Mich. & Hil. Robt. Halle & Wm. James, pl. *Hy.* Denny, esq., & w. Honora, def. Manor of Woodrydden & 2 mess., 2 tofts, 2 gdns., 1 barn, 4 a. ar., 480 a. pa. & 20 a. wd. in Waltham Hollycrosse. Def. quitclaimed to pl. & the heirs of Robt. £220.

14. Mich. & Hil. Francis Kightley & Wm. Holland, pl. *Jn.* Skott & w. Joan, def. 1 mess. cott., 1 barn, 1 gdn., 6 a. ar., 4 a. mw. & 5 a. pa. in Pritewell. Def. quitclaimed to pl. & the he of Francis. £40.

15. Joan Laxton, wid., pl.*Clement* Syseley, esq., & w. Anne & *Agnes* Kyddermynster, wi def. Manor of Barrowe & 2 mess., 200 a. ar., 200 a. mw., 100 a. pa., 50 a. wd., 200 a. marsh £6 rt. in Little Therock & Chadewell. £840.

16. Mich. & Hil. Rd. Drane, pl. *Giles* Osborne, & w. Cecily, def. 5 a. ar., & 2 a. mw. in Gre Leighes. 50 mks.

17. Mich. & Hil. Wm. Strutt, pl. *Tho.* Mylkesoppe *alias* Melsoppe & Jn. Kent, def. 1 mes 1 gdn., 6 a. ar., 9 a. pa. & 11 a. wd. in Walden, Bulmer & Twynsted. Def. quitclaimed to pl. his heirs; Tho. warranting the pa. & wd., & Jn. the mess., gdn. & ar. And for pl. gtd. the mes gdn. & ar. to Jn. & his heirs, to hold of the chief lords.

CP26(1)/135   EASTER, 10 ELIZABETH   15

1. Launcelet Warde, pl. Wm. Quedwell *alias* Codwell & w. *Helen*, def. 1 mess., 3 bar, 1 gdn., 2 orchards, 180 a. ar., 10 a. mw., 20 a. pa., 12 a. wd. & 10s. rt. in Wethersfelde, Gosfel & Shalforde. 200 mks.

2. Jn. Wentworth & Wm. Grabyn, pl. Rd. Burbage & w. *Anne*, def. A moiety of 1 mes 1 dovecote, 2 gdns., 80 a. ar., 20 a. mw., 80 a. pa., 3 a. wd. & 5s. rt. in Wyllynghale Do Wyllynghale Spayne & Wyllynghale Rokell. Det. quitclaimed to pl. & the heirs of Jn. 130 ml

3. Wm. Tyffyn, gent., pl. *Wm.* Fyssher & Jn. Elyston & w. *Margaret*, def. 2 mess., gdns., 2 orchards, 3 a. ar., 1 rood marsh & 6d. rt. in Myddylton & Great Henny. £40.

4. Tho. Leper & Tho. Craneforde, pl. *Rd.* Walforde, Wm. Hyll & w. Beatrice, def. 2 me & 16 a. ar. in Bockinge. Def. quitclaimed to pl. & the heirs of Tho. Leper. And for this pl. g to Rd. & his heirs a yearly rt. of 53s. 4d. from the same from Michaelmas last for 33 years, pa able on the sixth day after the Annunciation & the sixth day after Michaelmas in the nor porch of the parish church of Wethersfeld between the second & fourth hours after noon, wi power of distraint; & also gtd. the tenements to Wm. & Beatrice & the heirs of their bodi to hold of the chief lords, with remainder to Wm. & his heirs.

5. Hil. & Eas. Arthur Breame, esq., pl. Dorothy Dalton, wid., def. Manor of Esteham 100 mess., 100 cotts., 40 barns, 4 dovecotes, 60 gdns., 60 orchards, 1,000 a. ar., 1,000 a. m 1,000 a. pa., 100 a. wd, 2,000 a furze & heath & £20 rt. in Esteham, Westham & Little Ilfor & the advowson of the church of Esteham. £800.

6. Alexander Walforde, pl. *Hy.* Welde & w. Marion, def. 1 mess. & 1 gdn. in Shalforde. £1

7. Jn. Grene, pl. Wm. Cuckowe & w. *Helen*, dau. & heir of Jn. Chamber, decd., def. mess. & 2 gdns. in Halsted. £20.

8. Hil. & Eas. Jn. Spencer & Tho. Palmer, knights, Edw. Gryffyn, Edm. Huddelston, Th Revett, Rd. Carell, And. Joynour & Edw. Carell, esquires, pl. *Jn.* Cotton, kt., & w. Isabel, d Manors of Little Wygborough & Coppydhall & 20 mess., 20 gdns., 20 orchards, 400 a. ar., a. mw., 500 a. pa., 10 a. wd., 100 a. fresh marsh, 400 a. salt marsh & £6 rt. in Little Wygboroug Coppydhall, Great Wygborough, Salcott & Pelden, & the advowson of the church of Litt Wygborough. Def. quitclaimed to pl. & the heirs of Jn. Spencer. 800 mks.

9. Geo. Deane, pl. *Nich.* Palgrave & w. Eliz., def. 3 mess., 3 gdns., 3 orchards & 6 a. ar. Great Dunmowe. £40.

10. Rd. Yeldham & Hy. Snelhauke, pl. *Tho.* Mylsopp *alias* Mylkesoppe & w. Mary, def. mess., 1 barn, 1 gdn., 1 orchard, 38 a. ar. & 2 a. mw. in Redeswell & Redeswell Norton. De quitclaimed to pl. & the heirs of Rd. £40.

11. Rd. Dygbye, Tho. Stewarde & Robt. Walford, pl. Wm. Quedwell *alias* Codwell & Helen, def. 20 a. 1 rood ar. in Wethersfelde. Def. quitclaimed to pl. & the heirs of Rd. £4

12. Hil. & Eas. Hy. Josselyn, esq., & w. Helen, pl. *Anth.* Browne, kt. of the Garter, viscou Mountague, & w. Magdalen, def. The prebend & rectory of Westhurrock & 2 curtilages, 2 toft 2 barns, 1 dovecote, 2 gdns., 2 orchards, 30 a. ar., 20 a. mw., 30 a. pa., 10 a. wd., 40 a. fre marsh, 40 a. salt marsh & 53s. 4d. rt. in Westhurrock, tithes of sheaves, grain & hay in Wes hurrock, & the advowson of the vicarage of the church of Westhurrock. Def. quitclaimed to & the heirs of Hy. £400.

13. Tho. Sayer & Wm. Palmer, pl. Jn. Forde, gent., def. A moiety of the manor of Dangewell *alias* Dangewell Hall & a moiety of 2 mess., 3 tofts, 3 barns, 3 gdns., 2 orchards, 300 a. ar., 20 a. mw., 200 a. pa., 40 a. wd., 20 a. furze & heath & 20s. rt. in Great Okele, Herewyche & Wykes. Def. quitclaimed to pl. & the heirs of Tho. And for this pl. gtd. the same to def. & his heirs, to hold of the chief lords.

14. Hil. & Eas. Jn. Kent & Wm. Choppyne, pl. Wm. Selye & w. *Mary*, def. 2 mess., 1 gdn. & 1 orchard in Bockynge. Def. quitclaimed to pl. & the heirs of Jn. 50 mks.

15. Hil. & Eas. Robt. Hawle, esq., pl. Rd. Martyn *alias* Wignall & w. *Alice*, def. 1 mess., 60 a. ar., 10 a. mw., 20 a. pa. & 10 a. wd. in Hallyfelde & Waltham Holycrosse. £40.

16. Lau. Goff & w. Frances, pl. Jn. Turnor, def. 1 mess., 1 gdn., 1 orchard, 10 a. ar., 10 a. pa. & 2s. 6d. rt. in Harlowe & High Laver. Def. quitclaimed to pl. & the heirs of Lau. £40.

17. Wm. Whyte, pl. *Rd.* Pease & w. Joan, def. 1 mess., 12 a. ar. & 16 a. pa. in Springfyld. £80.

18. Hil. & Eas. Francis Wyott, esq., pl. *Francis* Archer & w. Joan, def. 33 a. ar., 3 a. mw., 18 a. pa. & 4 a. wd. in Theydon Garnon. 50 mks.

19. Hil. & Eas. Jn. Goldynge sen., pl. *Alexander* Sawarde & w. Joan & *Robt.* Barker & w. Agnes, def. 1 mess., 1 gdn., 1 orchard & 7 a. ar. in Thaxsted. £40.

20. Hil. & Eas. Jn. Holmested, gent., pl. *Rd.* Grene & w. Joan & *Pet.* Grene, def. 3 mess., 3 gdns., 3 orchards, 16 a. ar., 2 a. mw. & 2 a. pa. in Great Maplested. £80.

21. Hil. & Eas. Jn. Holmested, gent., & w. Dorothy, pl. *Rd.* Grene & w. Joan, def. 1 mess., 40 a. ar., 8 a. mw., 10 a. pa., 15 a. wd. & 20s. rt. in Great Maplested, Little Maplested, Gestingthorpe & Wickham St. Paul, the rectory of the church of Great Maplested & all tithes, portions, oblations, obventions & emoluments in Great Maplested, Little Maplested, Gestingthorpe & Wickham St. Paul, & the advowson of the vicarage of the church of Great Maplested. Def. quitclaimed to pl. & the heirs of Jn. 100 mks.

22. Hil. & Eas. *Robt.* Lawson *alias* Edmondes & Wm. Lawson *alias* Edmondes, pl. Robt. Riche, kt., lord Riche, & w. Eliz., def. Manor of Soutchurche *alias* Southchurche Hall & 10 mess., 2 dovecotes, 2 gdns., 600 a. ar., 700 a. pa., 60 a. wd., 200 a. marsh & £8 rt. in Southchurche, Lee, Pryttellwell & Hadley. Def. quitclaimed to pl. & the heirs of Robt. And for this pl. gtd. the same to def. & the heirs of Robt. to hold of the chief lords.

23. Wm. Averey, citizen & 'inholder' of London, pl. *Jn.* Stonerd, esq., & w. Anne, def. 48 a. marsh & 1 stank in Barking *alias* Berking. 130 mks.

24. Jn. Harford & Robt. Gracebye, pl. Robt. Heton, gent., & w. *Margt.*, & Arthur Gardyner, def. A third part of the manors of Bretts Hall, Little Holland, Tendringhall & Garnons, a third part of 30 mess., 30 tofts, 30 gdns., 30 orchards, 1,000 a. ar., 300 a. mw., 1,000 a. pa., 300 a. wd., 200 a. furze & heath, 300 a. marsh & £8 rt. in Tendring, Whyley, Little Holland, Little Bentley, Great Clafton, Little Clafton & Great Bentley, & a third part of the advowson of the church of Tendring. Def. quitclaimed to pl. & the heirs of Jn. And for this pl. gtd. the same to def. for one week, with remainder to Robt. Heton & Arthur & the heirs of Robt., to hold of the chief lords.

25. Hamond Carter, pl. *Tho.* Fuller & w. Joan, def. 1 mess., 1 gdn. & 1 orchard in Walden. £40.

26. Matthew Stephen, pl. Wm. May, def. 1 mess., 1 gdn., 20 a. ar., 4 a. mw., 40 a. pa. & 4 a. wd. in Markeshall, Erlescolne & Feringe. 70 mks.

27. Hil. & Eas. Wm. Chycken & w. Eliz., pl. *Wm.* Thorogood & w. Agnes, def. 1 mess., 1 gdn., 45 a. ar., 5 a. mw., 10 a. pa. & 4 a. wd. in Great Parrydon & Roydon. Def. quitclaimed to pl. & the heirs of Wm. 200 mks.

28. Lau. Browne & w. Margt., pl. *Anth.* Duke & w. Margt., def. 1 mess., & 1 gdn. in Wyvenho. Def. quitclaimed to pl. & the heirs of Lau. £40.

29. Hil. & Eas. Jn. Tyler & w. Thomasina, pl. *Jn.* Mordaunt, kt., lord Mordaunt, & w. Joan, def. 2 mess., 50 a. ar., 20 a. mw., 5 a. pa., 6 a. wd. & 4 a. furze & heath in Gingeraffe. Def. quitclaimed to pl. & the heirs of Thomasina. £200.

30. Edw. Throwgood, pl. *Gabriel* Busshe & w. Margery, def. 8 a. ar. in Walden. £40.

31. Wm. Ayleward, pl. *Tho.* Byrde sen. & w. Beatrice, *Jn.* Byrde jun. & w. Alice,

def. 1 mess., & 11½ a. ar. in Walden. 130 mks.

32. Jn. Parker, pl. *Tho.* Pullyver & w. Alice, def. 5 a. marsh in Barkyng. £40.

33. Jas. Lytle, pl. *Edw.* Frythe & w. Agnes, def. 1 mess., 1 gdn., 1 orchard, 40 a. ar., 4 a. mw., 4 a. pa. & 2 a. wd. in Craneham. 100 mks.

34. Jn. Norres jun., pl. Hy. Ellys & w. *Joan*, def. 4 a. ar. in Great Bursted. £40.

35. Hil. & Eas. Jn. Legate, gent., pl. Jn. Estbroke, def. 1 mess., 1 toft, 1 gdn., 1 orchard, 40 a. ar., 12 a. mw., 12 a. pa., 2 a. wd. & 10 a. marsh in Barkyng & Dagenham. £200.

36. Rd. Wyllys, pl. Francis Clopton, esq., def. 16 a. pa. in Raleyghe. £53.

37. Hy. Billingsley, pl. Pet. Poulton & w. *Eliz.*, def. Two thirds of the manors of Franckes *alias* Warleigh Francks, & two thirds of 20 mess., 20 gdns., 200 a. ar., 50 a. mw., 300 a. pa., 40 a. wd., 200 a. furze & heath & 10s. rt. in Abbesse Warley & Raynham. £132.

38. Jn. Owers, pl. Jn. Lambarde & w. Emma & *Roger* Owers, def. 1 mess., 1 toft, 1 orchard, 1 gdn., 30 a. ar., 7 a. mw., 18 a. pa., 3 a. moor & 3 a. fresh marsh in Wethersfeld & Gosfylde. £80.

39. Lau. Clarke *alias* Cooke, pl. Rd. Cutts, esq., & Hy. Cutts, gent., def. 1 mess., 1 gdn., 1 orchard, 60 a. ar., 10 a. mw. & 40 a. pa. in Matching. Def. quitclaimed to pl. & his heirs, each warranting a moiety. And for this pl. gtd. to Hy. & his heirs a yearly rt. of £3 8s. 4d. from a moiety of the same, payable at the Annunciation & Michaelmas, with power of distraint.

40. Geo. Sayer sen., gent., & Geo. Sayer jun., gent., his son & heir apt., pl. *Edm.* Moone, gent., Tho. Davye & Steph. Davye, def. 2 mess., 3 tofts, 2 gdns., 1 orchard, 100 a. ar., 20 a. mw. & 3 a. wd. in Purleighe & Mundon. Def. quitclaimed to pl. & the heirs of Geo. sen. £140.

41. Arthur Harrys, esq., pl. Hy. Browne, esq., & w. Alice, def. 2 mess., 4 tofts, 2 gdns., 2 orchards, 200 a. ar., 100 a. mw., 200 a. pa., 20 a. furze & heath, 100 a. moor, 200 a. marsh & 40s. rt. in Burneham & Southmynster. 400 mks.

42. Jn. Wastell, son & heir of Wm. Wastell, decd., pl. Robt. Stubbynge & w. Margt., def. A third part of 1 mess., 40 a. ar. & 10 a. pa. in Byrdebroke & Hempsted. £40.

43. Tho. Wood, pl. Jn. Perrys *alias* Purye, def. 1 mess., 13 a. ar. & 3 a. mw. in Farneham. £30.

44. Jn. Povy, pl. Edw. Turner, gent., & w. *Martha*, def. 16 a. ar., 16 a. mw., & 42 a. pa. in Great Parnden. £200.

45. Tho. Phillipson & w. Bridget, pl. *Jn.* Cooke, gent., & w. Mary, def. 1 mess., 1 barn & 2 gdns. in Rayleghe. Def. quitclaimed to pl. & the heirs of Tho. £40.

46. Mich. & Eas. Yvo Grey, gent., pl. Francis Glenam & w. *Lettice*, def. 1 mess., 1 dovecote, 1 gdn., 1 orchard, 20 a. ar. & 2 a. pa. in Hengham at the Castle. And for this pl. gtd. the same to def. to hold for their lives of the chief lords, with remainder to the right heirs of Francis.

47. Hil. & Eas. Wm. Ayloff, gent., pl. *Jn.* Brownyng & w. Bridget, def. 1 mess., 1 gdn., 1 orchard, 12 a. ar., 4 a. mw. & 10 a. pa. in Ramsdon Crayes. £80.

48. Hil. & Eas. Robt. Adams, pl. *Anth.* Bugges & w. Anne, Jn. Adams & w. Joan, def. 1 mess., 1 gdn., 40 a. ar., 8 a. pa. & 3 a. wd. in Little Laver, Matchinge, High Laver & Abbas Roothinge. £40.

49. Hil. & Eas. Barnabas Claydon, pl. *Jn.* Freman & w. Jane, def. 1 mess., 1 gdn., 1 orchard, 32 a. ar., 4 a. mw., 12 a. pa., 4 a. wd. & 8s. rt. in Stevyngton, Barkelowe, Bendysshe & Asshedon. £80.

50. Wm. Ayllette, pl. Jn. Goodeve & w. *Joan*, def. 10 a. ar. in Great Lighes. £40.

51. Wm. Beale, pl. Tho. Rande & w. *Agnes*, def. 1 mess., 1 toft & 1 gdn. in Ballidon. £40.

52. Wm. Thorneton, esq., pl. Tho. Goldinghame, esq., def. A moiety of the manor of Goldinghame Hall *alias* Goldynghams, & a moiety of 30 mess., 6 tofts, 3 dovecotes, 30 gdns., 600 a. ar., 60 a. mw., 100 a. pa., 50 a. wd., 40 a. heath, 50 a. marsh & £20 rt. in Bulmer, Geysthrope & Belcham. £300.

FEET OF FINES FOR ESSEX

53. Tho. Wyseman, esq., pl. Jn. Whyte, def. 1 mess., 1 cott., 1 gdn. & 8 a. fresh marsh in Rayneham, & the ferry of Rayneham. £40.

54. Robt. Roote, pl. Hugh Nevell & w. *Eliz.*, def. 1 mess., 1 curtilage, 1 barn, 1 gdn., 1 orchard, 2 a. mw. & 16 a. pa. in Leigh. £60.

55. Wm. Loveday, pl. *Tho.* Symon & w. Agnes, def. 1 mess., 1 toft, 1 cott., 1 barn, 3 gdns., 1 orchard, 30 a. ar., 10 a. mw., 30 a. pa., 4 a. wd. & 20s. rt. in Shenfelde. And for this pl. gtd. the same to def. to hold for their lives of the chief lords, with remainder to Jn. Pynchon, esq., & his heirs.

CP26(1)/135   DIVERS COUNTIES

(12) Rouland Hayward & Tho. Wilbraham, pl. *Martin* Bowes & w. Frances, def. Manor of Passelowes & 10 mess., 1 dovecote, 10 gdns., 2 orchards, 100 a. ar., 20 a. mw., 50 a. pa., 3 a. wd. & 40s. rt. in Dagenham, Barkynge & Upney, co. Essex; & prop. in Surr. Def. quitclaimed to pl. & the heirs of Rouland. £600. — Essex, Surr..

CP25(2)/127/1633   TRINITY, 10 ELIZABETH   1568

1. Wm. Elyott, pl. Francis Eglesfeilde, gent., def. 10 a. ar., 10 a. mw. & 14 a. pa. in Westhannyngfelde. 100 mks.

2. Wm. Strangman, esq., pl. Geoff. Woodde & w. *Mary*, dau. & heir of Jn. Thomson, def. 1 mess. & 1 gdn. in Hadley at the Castle *alias* Hadley Castell. £40.

3. Wm. Stedman, pl. *Tho.* Powle, esq., & w. Jane, def. 20 a. marsh called 'Fronton Acre' in Barking. £220.

4. Rd. Cannon, gent., pl. Francis Eglesfeilde, gent., def. 20 a. pa. in Westhannyngfeld. £40.

5. Tho. French & Rd. Bull, pl. *Wm.* Bull & w. Joan, def. 1 mess., 1 barn, 1 gdn., 1 orchard, 25 a. ar., 9 a. mw. & 8 a. pa. in Takeley. Def. quitclaimed to pl. & the heirs of Tho. £140.

6. Eas. & Trin. Jn. Pinchon, esq., pl. Hy. Drury, esq., & w. *Eliz.*, def. 2 mess., 3 cotts., 7 a. ar., 2 a. pa., ½ a. wd. & 2 a. marsh in Bradwell by the Sea. 130 mks.

7. Tho. Golding, pl. *Anth.* Horrolde & w. Marion, def. 3 a. land, 2 a. mw. & 4 a. pa. in Bealchamp St. Paul. £40.

8. Tho. Wyseman, esq., pl. *Jn.* Poole jun. & w. Joan & Margt. Poole, wid., def. 1 mess., 1 gdn., 50 a. ar., 6 a. mw., 40 a. pa. & 12 a. wd. in Wymbysshe. Def. quitclaimed to pl. & his heirs, with warranty against the heirs of Robt. Poole, decd., father of Jn. £80.

9. Tho. Browne, pl. *Tho.* Trigge & w. Mary, def. 2 mess., 2 tofts, 2 gdns., 90 a. ar. & 12 a. pa. in Elmedon. £140.

10. Chris. Byrde, pl. *Wm.* Pumfrytt & w. Clemencia & Jn. Harvye & w. Margt., def. 1 mess., 1 gdn., 1 orchard, 1 dovecote & 4 a. ar. in Walden. £40.

11. Eas. & Trin. Tho. Barnarde & w. Joan, pl. *Jn.* Jervys, son & heir of Wm. Jervys, & Wm. Wolmer jun., def. 1 mess., 1 barn & 1 gdn. in Chelmysforde. Def. quitclaimed to pl. & the heirs of Tho. £40.

CP25(2)/128/1634   MICHAELMAS, 10-10 ELIZABETH   1568

1. Tho. Barrington, esq., pl. Edw. Armiger & w. *Eliz.*, def. 1 mess., 1 gdn. & 1 orchard in Hatfyeld Regis *alias* Hatfyeld Brodeoke. £40.

2. Hy. Tyng & Edw. Tyng, pl. Wm. Tyng, def. 1 mess., 20 a. ar., 10 a. mw. & 10 a. pa. in Stanforde Ryvers. Def. quitclaimed to pl. & the heirs of Hy. £160.

3. Jn. Motte, pl. *Tho.* Brokeman, gent., & w. Anne, def. 1 mess., 2 cotts., 1 barn, 40 a. ar., 10 a. mw., 40 a. pa. & 30s. rt. in Bockynge. £200.

4. Wm. Marten, pl. *Tho.* Coo & w. Anne, def. 1 mess., 1 cott., 1 gdn., 1 orchard & 30 a. ar. in Halsted. £60.

5. Robt. Bredgeman, pl. Robt. Bredge & w. *Eliz.*, def. 1 mess., 1 gdn., 2 a. ar. & 1 a. pa. in Great Burche. £40.

139

6. Edw. Some, pl. *Edw.* Madyson, gent., & w. Dorothy, def. 6 a. mw. in Sandon. £40.

7. Jn. Ive, gent., pl. *Edw.* Eliott, gent., & w. Jane, def. 40 a. ar., 40 a. pa. & 20 a. wd. in Wrytle *alias* Wryttell. Def. quitclaimed to pl. & his heirs, with warranty against the heirs of Jas. Gedge, decd. £40.

8. Tho. Wyseman, gent., pl. *Geoff.* Blower & w. Alice, def. 1 mess., 1 barn, 1 gdn., 30 a. ar. & 10 a. wd. in High Ester & Barneston. £80.

9. Tho. Burgeaunte, gent., pl. Alexander Raye & w. *Eliz.*, def. 4 a. mw. in Walden. £40.

10. Trin. & Mich. Jn. Lytle, pl. Tho. Sampson, def. 1 mess., 1 toft, 2 gdns., 20 a. ar., 3 a. mw., 4 a. pa. & 2 a. wd. in Halsted, Stansted & Colne Engayne. £40.

11. Edm. Markaunt, gent., pl. Nich. Hancok & w. *Eliz.*, def. 1 mess. & 1 gdn. called 'les Tabard' in Harwich. And for this pl. gtd. the same to def & the heirs of Nich., to hold of the chief lords.

12. Rd. Reede, pl. *Jn.* Pathe & w. Agnes, def. 1 mess. & 4 a. pa. in Great Baddowe. £40.

13. Rd. Rodes, pl. *Tho.* Smyth & w. Eleanor, def. 1 mess. & 1 gdn. in Kelvedon. £40.

14. Trin. & Mich. Tho. Webbe & Humphrey Wylkes, pl. Robt. Broke & w. *Eliz.*, def. 1 mess., 2 cotts., 120 a. ar., 3 a. mw. & 20 a. pa. in Cressall *alias* Cristishall, Heydon & Duxworth. Def. quitclaimed to pl. & the heirs of Humphrey. And for this pl. gtd. the same to def. & the heirs of Eliz., to hold of the chief lords.

15. Roger James, pl. Charles Nuttall & w. *Felicia* def. 5 mess., 5 cotts. & 4 gdns. in Alvythley. £140.

16. Rd. Kytchyn, clk., pl. And. Cowland & w. *Eliz.*, def. 1 mess., 1 barn, 1 gdn., 20 a. ar. & 12 a. pa. in Stysted. £80.

17. Tho. Franke, esq., pl. Tho. Dynes & w. *Agnes*, def. A moiety of 1 mess., 1 gdn. & 30 a. ar. in Hatfeld Regis *alias* Brodeoke & Great Hallyngburye. £40.

18. Trin. & Mich. Wm. Stubbyng, pl. *Jn.* Whitley & w. Joan, def. 1 mess., 1 barn, 1 gdn. & 1 a. pa. in Bumpsted Helyon. £30.

19. Robt. Aylett, pl. Geo. Hawkyns & w. *Margery*, def. 2 a. mw. & 13 a. pa. in Great Dunmo. £40.

20. Nich. Bacon, kt., keeper of the great seal of England, pl. *Jn.* Traves & w. Eliz., def. 1 mess., 1 gdn., 8 a. mw., 40 a. pa., 3 a. wd. & 5s. rt. in Dagenham & Barkinge. £160.

21. Robt. Hasyll, pl. *Rd.* Bridges & w. Kath., *Wm.* Osborne & w. Cristina, def. 1 mess., 1 toft, 1 gdn., 3 a. ar. & 1 a. mw. in Berkyng *alias* Barkyng. £20.

22. Trin. & Mich. Jas Gybbes & w. Joan, pl. *Rd.* Bellamy & w. Kath., def. 1 mess., 1 gdn., 1 orchard, 1 a. ar. & 6 a. marsh in Raynham. Def. quitclaimed to pl. & the heirs of Jas. £40.

23. Hugh Halsall & Jn. Todgyll, pl. Hy. Todgyll & w. *Anne*, def. 1 orchard & 4 a. pa. in Hornedon on the Hill. Def. quitclaimed to pl. & the heirs of Hugh. And for this pl. gtd. the same to def. & the heirs of Hy., to hold of the chief lords.

24. Tho. Phillippson, pl. Wm. Whyghte & w. Joan, def. 1 mess. & 1 gdn. in Raylegh. £40.

25. Jn. Garrard, pl. *Rd.* Wasselynge & w. Mary, def. 1 mess., 1 barn, 1 gdn., 1 orchard, 26 a. ar., 5 a. mw. & 1 a. wd. in Over Yaldham *alias* Little Yaldham. £40.

26. Trin. & Mich. Rd. Blagge, pl. Tho. Gylberte & w. Joan, *Rd.* Ellys & w. Mary, def. 2 mess. & 2 gdns. in Bockynge. £30.

27. Wm. Ramsey, pl. Jn. Hyll & w. Maud, def. 1 mess., 6 a. ar., 1 a. mw. & 2 a. pa. in North Weald Bassett. £40.

28. Joan Sowthoe *alias* Sowth, wid., pl. *Jn.* Malyn & w. Jane, def. 1 mess., 1 gdn., 1 orchard, 3 a. ar. & 3 a. mw. in Westmersey. £40.

29. Edw. Randyll, pl. *Rd.* Cooke, gent., & w. Eliz., def. Manor of Wifealdes & 10 mess., 6 tofts, 1 mill, 1 dovecote, 10 gdns., 300 a. ar., 40 a. mw., 200 a. pa., 10 a. wd.,

6 a. furze & heath, 10 a. marsh, 6 a. alder & 100s. rt. in Barking. £340.

30. Wm. Cosyn & Robt. Kyng, pl. Jn. Prestney & w. *Cristiana*, def. 1 mess., 1 gdn., 1 orchard, 10 a. ar. & 4 a. wd. in Bysshops Wyckham. Def. quitclaimed to pl. & the heirs of Wm. £40.

31. Wm. Stedman, pl. *Brian* Staplyton, esq., & w. Eliz., def. 20 a. mw. in Riple in the parish of Barkyng. Def. to pl. & his heirs, with warranty against the heirs of Robt. Dundas, decd., & all claiming by them. £80.

32. Trin. & Mich. Edw. Turner, pl. *Jn.* Grene & w. Kath., def. 1 mess. & 1 gdn. in Halsted. £40.

33. Robt. Kempe, esq., pl. Robt. Newman, def. A moiety of 1 mess., 1 gdn., 40 a. ar., 10 a. mw. & 20 a. pa. in Fynchingfeld & Redgwell. £40.

34. Tho. Knotte, gent., pl. Edw. Some & w. *Alice*, def. 1 mess., 1 cott., 1 gdn., 1 orchard, 30 a. ar., 12 a. mw., 10 a. pa., 2 a. wd. & 3 a. marsh in White Rothinge & Prytewell. And for this pl. gtd. the same to def. & the heirs of their bodies, to hold of the chief lords, with remainder to the right heirs of Edw.

35. Jas. Moryce, esq., & w. Eliz., pl. Tho. Salman & w. Joan, def. 1 mess. & 1 gdn. in Chepyng Onger *alias* Onger at the Castle. Pl. & the heirs of the body of Jas. to hold of the chief lords, with remainder to his right heirs. £40.

36. Trin. & Mich. John Hull, wid., pl. Jn. Grymewade & w. *Alice*, Jn. Buckerfeld & w. *Ethelreda*, def. 3 mess., 3 gdns., 4 a. ar. & 1 a. mw. in Stebbyng. £35.

37. Hy. Pynchen & Jn. Pynchen, pl. Geo. Lylle & w. *Joan*, def. A third part of 6 mess., 6 gdns., 50 a. ar., 19 a. mw. & 55 a. pa. in Danburye, Sandon, Purley, Little Badowe, Boreham & Chelmesford. Def. quitclaimed to pl. & the heirs of Hy. £80.

38. Jn. Kynge, pl. Tho. Kynge, def. 1 mess., 2 gdns., 2 orchards, 30 a. ar. & 3 a. pa. in Hatfelde Brodoeke *alias* Kynges Hatfelde. £120.

39. Jn. Waterhouse & Jn. Slighe, pl. Edm. Weste, esq., & w. *Joan*, def. 2 mess., 2 gdns., 2 orchards, 20 a. ar., 20 a. mw., 40 a. pa. & 100 a. furze & heath in Broxhedd & Wyddington. Def. quitclaimed to pl. & the heirs of Jn. Waterhouse. And for this pl. gtd. the same to def. & the heirs of the body of Edm., to hold of the chief lords, with successive remainders to the heirs of the body of Joan & the right heirs of Edm.

40. Wm. Tyffyn, gent., pl. *Humphrey* Cornewall, gent., & w. Anne, def. The rectory of Stebbynge & 4 mess., 1 dovecote, 4 gdns., 4 orchards, 200 a. ar., 30 a. mw., 30 a. pa., 10 a. wd., 20s. rt. & rts. of 1 lb. of wax & 1 lb. of pepper & tithes of sheaves, grain & hay in Stebbynge, & the advowson of the vicarage of the church of Stebbynge. £200.

41. Wm. Pratyman, pl. *Wm.* Armigerd *alias* Armiger & *Tho.* Armigerd *alias* Armiger, gentlemen, & Robt. Studde & w. Eliz., def. 1 mess. called 'Cokkys', 40 a. ar., 20 a. mw., 100 a. pa., 8 a. wd. & 6s. 8d. rt. in Little Clakton. 130 mks.

42. Jn. Gyver jun., pl. Tho. Byrde & w. Beatrice, Jn. Byrde & w. Alice, Geo. White & w. Alice, Rd. Stokbridge & w. Eliz. & Jn. Gyver sen. & w. Alice, def. 9 a. ar. in Walden. Def. quitclaimed to pl. & his heirs, with warranty of 5 a. against Tho. & Beatrice, Jn. Byrde & Alice & the heirs of Tho., 1 a. against Geo. & Alice & her heirs, 1½ a. against Rd. & Eliz. & her heirs, & 1½ a. against Jn. Gyver sen. & Alice & her heirs. £40.

43. Tho. Jenyn, gent., pl. *Robt.* Ryche, kt., lord Ryche, & w. Eliz. & Tho. Gooche, def. Manors of Passelowes, Fawconers, Borrowes *alias* Bowres, & 3 mess., 20 barns, 1 dovecote, 20 gdns., 500 a. ar., 50 a. mw., 100 a. pa., 15 a. wd. & £20 rt. in Goodester & Norton Maundevyle. Def. quitclaimed to pl. & his heirs. And for this pl. gtd. the same to Tho. Gooche from Michaelmas for 40 years, rendering £27 6s. 8d. yearly to pl. & his heirs, at the Annunciation & Michaelmas, with power of distraint; with reversion to Robt. & Eliz. & the heirs of Robt., to hold of the chief lords.

44. The same pl. Robt. & Eliz. Ryche & Tho. Eve sen., def. Manors of Newarks & Newelande Fee & 30 mess., 20 barns, 3 dovecotes, 30 gdns., 200 a. ar., 60 a. mw., 200 a. pa., 10 a. wd. & 40s. rt. in Goodester, Margaret Rothinge, Newlandfee & Writtell, & all tithes in Newlandfee, Passelowes, Imberds, Fawconers, Borrowes *alias* Bowres & Wryttell. Similar quitclaim & grt. to Tho. Eve for 40 years at a yearly rt. of £17 with power of distraint; with similar reversion.

141

45. Wm. Prowe & Wm. Shether, pl. *Robt.* Wood, gent., & w. Joan & Tho. Gregells, def. 32 a. pa. in Bromesfeld & Little Walteham. Def. quitclaimed to pl. & his heirs of Wm. Prowe. And for this pl. gtd. the same to Tho. to hold from Michaelmas, 1569, for 21 years, rendering yearly 1d. at Michaelmas to pl. & the heirs of Wm. Prowe, with power of distraint; with reversion to Robt. & Joan & the heirs of Robt., to hold of the chief lords.

46. Wm. Ayleworde, pl. Tho. Raye & w. *Eliz.*, def. 6 a. ar. in Walden. £40.

47. Wm. Ayllette, pl. *Robt.* Noxe, gent., & w. Dorothy, def. 1 mess., 2 gdns., 10 a. ar., 6 a. mw. & 20 a. pa. in Stansted & Halsted. £140.

48. Tho. Turner, pl. Tho. Raye & w. *Eliz.*, def. 1 mess. & 1 toft in Walden. Similar quitclaim. £40.

49. Edw. Frank, pl. Robt. Rychold, def. 2 mess., 2 gdns., 2 orchards & 2 a. pa. in Newland within the parish of Wytham *alias* Wyttam. And for this pl. gtd. the same to def. & Alice his w. & his heirs, to hold of the chief lords.

50. Edw. Frank, pl. *Jn.* Glascock, gent., & w. Kath., def. 4 a. pa. in Terlyng. 20 mks.

51. Wm. Petree, kt., & Jn. Petree, esq., his son & heir apt., pl. *Wm.* Barlee, gent., & w. Eliz., def. Manors of Thurrockes & Powrynges *alias* Pownces & 6 mess., 6 cotts., 10 tofts, 6 gdns., 4 orchards, 200 a. ar., 60 a. mw., 60 a. pa., 16 a. wd. & £7 rt. in Claveringe, Langley, Berden & Arkesden. Def. quitclaimed to pl. & the heirs of Wm. 6 cotts., 20 a. ar., 4 a. mw., 12 a. pa. & £7 rt., parcel of the above; & gtd. to the same the reversion of the residue, which Philippa Newman *alias* Rutter, wid., holds for life, to hold of the chief lords. £400.

CP25(2)/259   MICHAELMAS, 10-11 ELIZABETH   1568

5. Eas. & Mich. Jn. Chawncy & w. Eliz., pl. Hy. Pole, esq., & w. *Eliz.*, def. Manor of Overhall & 4 mess., 4 cotts., 4 tofts, 8 barns, 1 dovecote, 8 gdns., 8 orchards, 400 a. ar., 40 a. mw., 200 a. pa., 60 a. wd., 30 a. furze & heath, 20 a. moor, 20 a. alder, 12 a. reed & 10s. rt. in Gedleston, co. Essex (*sic*); & prop. in Kent. Def. quitclaimed to pl. & the heirs of Jn. 770 mks. — Essex, Kent.

11. Trin. & Mich. The Queen, pl. *Tho.* Hennage, esq., & w. Anne, def. 4 mess., 100 a. mw. & 100 a. pa. in Canewden *alias* Canouden, co. Essex; & prop. in other counties. Def. quitclaimed to pl. & her heirs & successors. £800. — York, Essex, Suff., Norf.

CP25(2)/128/1635   HILARY, 11 ELIZABETH   1569

1. Tho. Peycock, pl. Tho. Colman, def. 1 mess., 1 gdn. & 1 a. ar. in Coggeshall. 40 mks.

2. Tho. Pullyver, pl. Robt. Stepney & w. *Joan*, def. 7 a. ar. in Eastham. 140 mks.

3. Rd. Nicholls, pl. Robt. Goodwyn & w. *Ellen*, def. A moiety of 1 mess., 1 cott. & 1 gdn. in Chelmesford. £20.

4. Tho. Peycock, pl. Jn. Felyxe, def. 2 mess. & 2 gdns. in Coggeshall. £24.

5. Jn. Seman, pl. *Wm.* Browninge & w. Rose, def. 1 mess., 1 cott., 1 curtilage & 1 gdn. in Chelmesforde. £40.

6. Edw. Evererd, pl. Robt. Prowe, def. 1 mess., 1 orchard, 7 a. ar., 2 a. mw. & 10 a. pa. in Little Waltham & Bromeffeld. £40.

7. Walter Hare & Jas. Hompsted, pl. *Tho.* Gynes, gent., & w. Faith, def. 6 mess., 5 tofts, 5 gdns., 5 orchards, 150 a. ar., 16 a. mw., 80 a. pa. & 10 a. wd. in Great Leighes, Borham, Little Leighes & Faiersted. Def. quitclaimed to pl. & the heirs of Walter. £80.

8. Wm. Lucas, pl. *Robt.* Skelton & w. Alice, def. 1 mess., 1 gdn. & 1 orchard in Brentwood. £40.

9. Jn. More *alias* Taylor, pl. Wm. More *alias* Taylor, son & heir of Jn. More *alias* Taylor, son & heir of Wm. More *alias* Taylor, def. 7 a. pa. in Thaxsted. £40.

10. Jn. Chaplen, pl. Wm. Wylford, esq., & w. Agnes, def. 40 a. wd. in Fynchingfeld. Pl. & his heirs to hold of the chief lords whatever def. have for their lives. £40.

11. Robt. Woode & Tho. Wood, pl. *Tho.* Reynolds & w. Bridget, def. 1 mess., 1 curtilage, 1 gdn. & 1 orchard in Chelmesford. Def. quitclaimed to pl. & the heirs of Robt. £40.

12. Mich. & Hil. Jn. Parker, pl. *Tho.* Bregge & w. Kath. & Jn. Reve & w. Alice, def. 2 a. ar., 2 a. mw., 7 a. pa. & 9 a. wd. in Hennyngham Sible & Wethersfeld. 50 mks.

13. Tho. Peycock, pl. *Wm.* Fabian, gent., & w. Anne, def. 4 mess., 1 dovecote, 4 gdns., 4 orchards, 10 a. ar., 4 a. mw., 20 a. pa. & 5 a. wd. in Coggeshall. 80 mks.

14. Steph. Warner, pl. Robt. Allen & w. *Joan,* def. 1 toft, 4 a. ar. & 6 a. pa. called 'Randolls' in Stondon & High Onger. £40.

15. Jn. Tyler, pl. Rd. Marden, def. 1 mess., 2 gdns., 10 a. ar., 10 a. mw., 10 a. pa. & 8 a. wd. in Dodynghurste. £80.

16. Geoff. Reynolds, pl. *Tho.* Reynolde & w. Bridget, def. 1 mess., 1 gdn. & 1 orchard in Chelmesford. £40.

17. Rd. Smyth *alias* Baly, pl. *Nich.* Pomfrett & w. Alice, def. 1 mess., 5 a. ar., 2 a. mw. & 4 a. pa. in Thaxsted. £40.

18. Mich. & Hil. Anth. Maxey, esq., pl. *Wm.* Fabyan, esq., & w. Anne, def. 2 mess., 1 water-mill, 1 fulling mill, 2 gdns., 2 orchards, 10 a. ar., 8 a. mw. & 12 a. pa. in Stisted & Bockinge. £80.

19. Wm. Carewe & Rd. Bydell, gentlemen, pl. *Hy.* Denny, esq., & w. Honora, def. 1 mess., 4 cotts., 6 tofts, 1 croft called 'Seignors Doune', 6 gdns., 6 orchards, 100 a. ar., 100 a. mw., 200 a. pa., 20 a. wd. & 100 a. marsh in Waltham Holycrosse, Nasinge & Eppynge. Def. quitclaimed to pl. & the heirs of Wm. £300.

20. Mich. & Hil. Jn. Goodaye, pl. *Edm.* Byeston & w. Denise, def. 2 mess., 2 curtilages, 1 dovecote & 1 gdn. in Coggeshall. £40.

21. Mich. & Hil. Wm. Westley & w. Anne, pl. Wm. Woodwarde & w. *Agnes,* def. 1 mess., 1 gdn. & 3 a. pa. in Thaxsted. Def. quitclaimed to pl. & the heirs of Wm. 50 mks.

22. Mich. & Hil. Jn. Thurgood sen. & Jn. Thurgood jun., pl. *Jn.* Warner sen. & w. Alice & Jn. Warner jun., his son & heir apt., def. 2 mess., 2 barns, 1 dovecote, 2 gdns., 130 a. ar., 10 a. mw., 18 a. pa. & 4 a. wd. in Manewden & Farneham. Def. quitclaimed to pl. & the heirs of Jn. sen. £200.

CP25(2)/1636   EASTER, 11 ELIZABETH   1569

1. Wm. Collyn, pl. Walter Wolbarte, gent., def. 3 a. ar. & 8 a. mw. in Takeley. £40.

2. Tho. Rattell, pl. *Jn.* Glover & w. Jane, def. 1 mess., 1 cott., 1 gdn., 1 orchard & 1 a. ar. in Hornedon on the Hill. £40.

3. Tho. Spakeman & w. Joan, pl. *Robt.* Fennor & w. Dorothy, def. 1 mess., 1 barn, 1 gdn., 1 orchard & 1 a. mw. in Halstede. Def. quitclaimed to pl. & the heirs of Tho. £40.

4. Jn. Graveley, pl. Wm. Baynbrygge, def. 7 a. mw. in Kelwedon. £40.

5. Geo. Harrison, pl. Wm. Stubbyng, def. 1 mess., 1 toft, 1 barn, 1 gdn., 24 a. ar., 2 a. mw. & 34 a. pa. in Bumpstede Helyon. £80.

6. Wm. Skipwith, esq., pl. *Francis* Rogers, gent., & w. Helen, def. 16 a. marsh in Wannyngton *alias* Wallyngton. Def. quitclaimed to pl. & his heirs, with warranty against Robt. Chapman, Tho. Harman & Jn. Rogers & their heirs. £80.

7. Rd. Crymble, pl. Rd. Kynge, def. 2 mess., 2 gdns. & 1 orchard in Bockyng. £40.

8. Arthur Harrys, esq., pl. Edw. Harrys, gent., def. Manor of Cricksey *alias* Crickseth & 10 mess., 6 cotts., 16 gdns., 16 orchards, 300 a. ar., 40 a. mw., 260 a. pa., 50 a. wd., 200 a. furze & heath, 200 a. marsh & £8 rt. in Cricksey *alias* Crycketh & Burnham, & the advowson of the church of Crycksey *alias* Crickseth. 400 mks.

9. Agnes Wigleswood, wid., pl. *Robt.* Platte & w. Joan, def. 3 mess. & 2 gdns. in Chelmesford. £80.

10. Edw. Tyrrell, esq., pl. *Jn.* Cornwell & w. Margt., def. 80 a. ar., 12 a. mw., 60 a. pa. & 8 a. wd. in Asshedon & Bartlowe. £120.

11. Wm. Bendlowes, serjeant at law, pl. *Jn.* Ferrour & w. Margaret, def. 1 mess., 1 barn, 1 gdn., 16 a. ar., 3 a. mw., 2 a. pa. & 2 a. wd. in Finchingfeld. 100 mks.

12. Wm. Curteys, pl. *Jn.* Danyell & w. Grace, def. 1 mess., 1 toft, 1 gdn., 8 a. ar., 2 a. mw. & 4 a. pa. in Danbury, Woodham Walter & Woodham Mortemer. £40.

13. Edw. Watkynson, clk., pl. *Rd.* Brody & w. Cecily, def. 8 a. ar. in Blakamore.£40.

14. Pet. Johnson, gent., & w. Mary, pl. Edw. Dixon & w. *Kath.*, def. 1 mess., 1 cott., 1 gdn., 1 orchard, 7 a. ar., 7 a. mw. & 7 a. pa. in Leighton & Walthamstowe. Def. quitclaimed to pl. & the heirs of Pet. £40.

15. Wm. Ayllette, pl. *Geo.* Tuke, esq., & w. Margt., def. 1 mess., 1 barn, 1 orchard, 50 a. ar., 5 a. mw., 100 a. pa. & 1d. rt. in Great Totteham, Little Totteham & Hebredge. £200.

16. Jn. Argent, pl. *Jn.* Danyell & w. Grace, def. 1 toft, 1 gdn., 8 a. ar. & 2 a. pa. in Danburye. £40.

17. Jn. Reve, pl. Rd. Sampeford, de. 3 a. ar. in Willingale Spayne. £40.

18. Tho. Hale, pl. *Geo.* Cely, gent., & w. Grace, def. 7 a. mw. in Navestock. £40.

19. Mich. & Eas. Jn. Cooke, gent., pl. Rd. Tyler, def. 1 mess., 1 gdn. & 7 a. ar. in Rocheford & Hawkewell, which Jn. Awger & w. Margt. hold for her life. Pl. & her heirs to hold the reversion of the chief lords. £40.

20. Jn. Knyffe, pl. *Tho.* Kyngesman & w. Margt., def. 1 mess., 1 gdn. & 1 a. ar. in Burnham. £40.

21. Tho. Sayer, pl. *Jn.* Danyell & w. Grace, def. 1 mess., 1 toft, 2 gdns., 20 a. ar., 6 a. mw., 10 a. pa. & 2s. rt. in Danbury. £80.

22. Hil. & Eas. Geo. Abbot, pl. *Robt.* Wade *alias* Warde & w. Eliz. & Rd. Wade *alias* Warde & w. Alice, def. 1 mess., 1 gdn. & 12 a. marsh in Esttylburye. £72.

23. Jn. Ultinge & Jn. Sache, pl. Tho. Pannell, def. 1 mess., 1 cott., 2 tofts., 1 gdn., 1 orchard, 20 a. ar., 12 a. pa., 2 a. wd. & 6 a. moor in Stebbinge. Def. quitclaimed to pl. & the heirs of Jn. Sache. £80.

24. Tho. Convers *alias* Combars & Tho. Hale, pl. *Geo.* Cely & w. Grace, def. Manor of Albyns *alias* Allynes & 5 mess., 240 a. ar., 40 a. mw., 140 a. pa., 10 a. wd., 40 a. furze & heath & 40s. rt. in Stapleford Abbott & Navestocke. Def. quitclaimed to pl. & the heirs of Tho. £270.

25. Hil. & Eas. Chris. Eton, clk., pl. *Rd.* Wade *alias* Warde & w. Alice, def. 1 mess., 1 gdn. & 1 rood ar. in Esttylbury. £20.

26. Rd. Lorkyn, pl. Jn. Fysshe, def. 1 mess. & 4 a. ar. in Westhanyngfeld. £40.

27. Chris. Camberlyn & w. Mary, pl. Jn. Byer & w. *Joan*, def. 30 a. fresh marsh in Estham. Def. quitclaimed to pl. & the heirs of Chris. And for this pl. gtd. the same to def. to hold for their lives of the chief lords without impeachment of waste.

28. Wm. Thurgood, pl. Rd. Cole & w. *Agnes*, def. A third part of 3 mess., 100 a. ar., 20 a. mw. & 40 a. pa. in Great Wenden, Little Wenden, Arkysden & Little Burye. £80.

29. Jas. Tawke & Rd. Betensone, pl. Jn. Pynchyon & w. Jane & *Rd.* Osborne, def. Manor of Tyledhall & 4 mess., 4 tofts, 1 barn, 4 gdns., 4 orchards, 400 a. ar., 100 a. mw., 100 a. pa., 40 a. marsh & 10s. rt. in Lachyngdene. Def. quitclaimed to pl. & the heirs of Rd. 400 mks.

30. Hil. & Eas. Tho. Bartlet, pl. Ewgenius Gatton, gent., & w. *Eliz.*, def. A sixth part of the manors of Copfold Hall *alias* Coldhall & Peverells, & a sixth part of 1 mess., 1 barn, 1 gdn., 60 a. ar., 40 a. mw., 100 a. pa., 20 a. wd. & 13s. 4d. rt. in Gyng Margaret *alias* Margaret Yng & West Hannyngfeld. And for this pl. gtd. the same to Ewgenius & his heirs, to hold of the chief lords.

31. Hil. & Eas. Edw. Glascocke, gent., pl. *Wm.* Hurrell & w. Margt., def. Manor of Hawkewoods & 4 mess., 4 gdns., 4 orchards, 300 a. ar., 40 a. mw., 60 a. pa., 10 a. wd. & £3 rt. in Hennynggam Syble, Hennynggam 'at the Castle', Maplestede, Hawstede & Gosfeld. Def. quitclaimed to pl. & his heirs, with warranty against Robt. Ryche, kt., lord Ryche, & w. Eliz. & her heirs. 160 mks.

32. Jn. Egleston & Tho. Ratle, pl. Wm. Raynolde & w. *Joan* & Wm. Elyotte & w. Eliz., def. 2 mess., 3½ a. ar., 1 a. fresh marsh & 1 a. salt marsh in Fobbinge & Tilberye. Def. quitclaimed to pl. & the heirs of Jn. £40.

33. Hil. & Eas. Wm. Bendlowes jun., gent., & Jn. West, pl. Jn. Smyth, gent., & w. *Anne*, def. 3 mess., 3 gdns., 3 orchards, 200 a. ar., 40 a. mw., 160 a. pa. & 10 a. wd. in Chelmesforde, Mulsham, Wyllingale Doo *alias* Wyllinghale Rokell, Wyllingale Spayne, Wryttle & Margaret Yng. Def. quitclaimed to pl. & the heirs of Wm. And for this pl. gtd. the same to Jn. Smyth & his heirs, to hold of the chief lords.

34. Jn. Kent & Rd. Byggen, pl. Jn. Dygbye, def. 2 mess., 60 a. ar., 6 a. mw. & 50 a. pa. in Halsted, Gosfeld & Hengham Sible. Def. quitclaimed to pl. & the heirs of Jn. And for this pl. gtd. the same to def. & his heirs, to hold of the chief lords.

35. Hil. & Eas. Wm. Claye & w. Margery, pl. *Lau.* Goff & w. Frances, Robt. Downsley & w. *Joan* & *Jn.* Ingoll, def. 1 mess., 1 gdn., 1 orchard, 20 a. ar., 2 a. mw., 3 a. pa. & 2s. rt. in High Laver & Harlowe. Def. quitclaimed to pl. & the heirs of Wm. £60.

36. Wm. Saunders & Tho. Everarde, pl. *Wm.* Everarde & w. Margt., def. 3 mess., 3 gdns., 3 orchards, 90 a. ar., 20 a. mw., 60 a. pa., 10 a. wd. & 10s. rt. in Massheberye, Goodester, Chicknall Smely *alias* Chicknall Trenchefoyle & Radwynter. Def. quitclaimed to pl. & the heirs of Wm., with warranty of the prop. in Massheberye, Goodester & Chicknall against the heirs of Wm. & of the prop. in Radwynter against the heirs of Margt. And for this pl. gtd. the first prop. to def. & the heirs of Wm., to hold of the chief lords; & the second prop. to def. & the heirs of Margt. of the bodies of Wm. & herself to hold of the chief lords, with remainder to the heirs of her body & her right heirs.

37. Tho. Parke & Jn. Kent, pl. *Wm.* Chisshull, esq., *Giles* Chisshull, gent., & w. Alice & Wm. Stocke, def. 1 mess., 1 water-mill, 20 a. ar., 5 a. mw. & 8 a. pa. in Great Berdefelde & Little Berdefelde. Def. quitclaimed to pl. & the heirs of Tho. And for this pl. gtd. the same to Wm. Stocke to hold from Michaelmas, 1572, for 21 years, rendering £8 yearly to pl. & the heirs of Tho., at the Annunciation & Michaelmas, with power of distraint; & the reversion to Giles & Alice & the heirs of their bodies, to hold of the chief lords, with remainder to Wm. Chisshull & his heirs.

CP25(2)/128/1637   TRINITY, 11 ELIZABETH   1569

1. Geo. Nicolls, esq., pl. Margery Busshe, wid., def. 2 mess., 2 barns, 1 gdn., 1 orchard & 8½ a. ar. in Walden *alias* Cheping Walden. £40.

2. Edw. Hubbert, gent., pl. Tho. Patche, def. 15 a. ar., 5 a. pa. & 1 a. wd. in Byrchanger. £40.

3. Tho. Jenyn, gent., pl. Rd. Kyng & w. *Margt.*, def. 1 mess., 1 barn, 1 gdn. & 1 a. ar. in Ardeley. £40.

4. Jn. Cooke, gent., pl. *Rd.* Tyler & w. Lucy, def. 1 mess., 1 gdn. & 10 a. ar. in Rocheford. £40.

5. Wm. Hawke, pl. Jn. Hawke, def. 5 a. ar. & 1 a. mw. in Navestoke. £40.

6. Eas. & Trin. Hy. Wallys, pl. *Rd.* Knyght & w. Anne, def. 1 mess., 1 gdn., 6 a. ar., 6 a. mw., 40 a. pa. & 6 a. wd. in Lowhall Walkehamstowe, Walkehamstowe Toney, Walkehamstowe Frauncis, Higham Bensted & Higham Hylls. £80.

7. Wm. Smythe, pl. Walter Ellett & w. Mary, def. 10 a. pa. in Dengye & Tillingham. £40.

8. Eas. & Trin. Robt. Gale, pl. Roger Cowper & w. *Margt.*, def. 20 a. ar., 10 a. pa. & 3 a. salt marsh in Woodham Ferres. £120.

9. Jn. Pomfrett, pl. Geo. Lawe & w. *Agnes*, def. 1 mess. & 1 gdn. in Walden. £40.

10. Jn. Glascocke, gent., pl. Jn. Wrighte & w. *Judith*, def. 2 mess., 2 gdns., 2 orchards, 40 a. ar., 10 a. mw., 30 a. pa. & 3 a. wd. in Writtle, Roxwell, Matchinge, High Laver, Little Laver, Great Waltham, Little Waltham, Springefeild & Bromfeild. 130 mks.

11. Adrian Smarte, pl. *Bart.* Permanter & w. Alice, def. 20 a. ar., 4 a. pa., 4 a. wd. & 4d. rt. in Berdfeld Saling *alias* Little Saling. £80.

12. Jn. Baker, gent., pl. Tho. Baker, gent., def. 4 mess., 2 cotts., 1 gdn., 2 orchards, 100 a. ar., 3 a. mw. & 4 a. pa. in Great Chesterforde & Littelbury. £80.

13. Geo. Dyve & Tho. Bedells, gentlemen, pl. *Jn.* Mordaunt, kt., lord Mordaunt, & w. Joan, def. 2 mess., 2 tofts, 2 gdns., 46 a. mw., 140 a. pa. & 20 a. wd. in Westhornedon, Esthornedon, Gyngraff & Bulfan. Def. quitclaimed to pl. & the heirs of Geo. £200.

14. Eas. & Trin. Robt. Turner, pl. Geo. Hawkins & w. *Margery*, def. 1 mess., 1 cott., 4 gdns., 1 orchard, 20 a. ar., 10 a. mw. & 6 a. pa. in Muche Donmowe. £40.

15. Jn. Spencer, citizen & grocer of London, pl. *Wm.* Kynge, & w. Thomasina, def. 2 mess., 1 gdn., 30 a. ar., 5 a. mw., 20 a. pa., 2 a. wd., 40 a. salt marsh & common of pasture for 100 sheep in Sandford le Hope *alias* Stanford le Hope & Curryngham *alias* Coryngham. £140.

16. Eas. & Trin. Tho. Wallinger, gent., pl. *Robt.* Reynolds & w. Bridget, def. 1 mess., 1 gdn., 1 orchard, 40 a. ar., 12 a. mw. & 60 a. pa. in Harwardestoke *alias* Harvardestocke & Buttesburye, which Wm. Reynolds hold for life. Pl. & his heirs to hold the reversion of the chief lords. 200 mks.

17. Wm. Whetley, esq., pl. Jn. Glascok, esq., & w. *Kath.*, def. Manor of the Little Wytham *alias* Wittham *alias* Powers Hall & 6 mess., 6 tofts, 4 curtilages, 1 dovecote, 2 gdns., 2 orchards, 500 a. ar., 30 a. mw., 200 a. pa., 20 a. wd. & 40s. rt. in Little Wytham *alias* Wyttham, Fairsted, Falkebourne, Hatfeld Peverell, Terlyng & Wyckham. Def. quit-claimed to pl. & his heirs, with warranty against Hy. Fortescue of Falkeborne, esq., & Tho. Clark of Wytham, 'clothyer', & their heirs. £600.

18. Eas. & Trin. Tho. Hobson, pl. *Chris.* Harrys, esq., & w. Mary, def. 30 a. ar. in Prytwell. Def. quitclaimed to pl. & his heirs, with warranty against the heirs of Wm. Harrys, esq., father of Chris. £40.

19. Wm. Docker, pl. Tho. Bonham, def. A moiety of the major of Stanwaye; & 2 mess., 6 tofts, 1 barn, 1 dovecote, 2 orchards, 100 a. ar., 30 a. mw., 100 a. pa., 6 a. wd. & 40s. rt. in Stanwaye & Copford, & the advowson of the church of Stanwaye. And for this pl. gtd. the same to def. & the heirs male of his body, to hold of the chief lords, with remainder to Frances Bocking, w. of Edm. Bocking, mother of def.

20. Eas. & Trin. Tho. Tendryng & w. Cecily, pl. Jn. Hillar & w. Eliz., Jn. Wylkynson & w. *Beatrice*, def. 2 mess., 1 cott., 2 gdns., 20 a. ar., 6 a. mw. & 16 a. pa. in Boreham, Def. quitclaimed to pl. & the heirs of Tho. £100.

21. Tho. Jenyn, gent., pl. *Wm.* Andrews *alias* Pyers & w. Kath. & Rd. Barnard, def. 1 mess., 1 barn, 1 gdn. & 9 a. ar. in Chawreth. And for this pl. gtd. the same to Wm. & Kath. to hold for their lives, rendering £3 yearly to pl. & his heirs at the Annunciation & Michaelmas, with power of distraint; & the reversion to Rd. & his heirs, to hold of the chief lords.

(No fines for Michaelmas term are known. The court adjourned.)

CP25(2)/128/1639   HILARY, 12 ELIZABETH   1570

1. Wm. Maynerd, pl. Tho. Gent, esq., & w. Eliz., def. 2 mess., 1 gdn., 15 a. ar., 10 a. pa. & 1 a. wd. in Bockyng & Stysted. £40.

2. Jn. Hunwycke, pl. Geo. Byston, def. 1 mess., 1 curtilage, 2 gdns., 1 orchard, 5 a. ar. & 3 a. pa. in Earls Colne *alias* Erles Colne. £40.

3. Rd. Buckfold, pl. *Robt.* Cobb & Steph. Cobb, def. 12 a. mw. & 10 a. pa. in Leighton & Westham. £80.

4. Robt. Gurdon, esq., pl. Jn. Clarke, def. 2 mess., 2 gdns., 100 a. ar., 10 a. mw., 100 a. pa. & 6 a. wd. in Southminster *alias* Sudmester, Asheldam, Mayland, Burnham & Crixsith. £200.

5. Hy. Chauncy, esq., pl. Jn. Phylyp, def. 1 mess., 6 a. ar., 2 a. mw. & 4 a. pa. in Fernham. £40.

6. Hy. Guldeford, esq., pl. *Tho.* Walsingham, esq., & w. Dorothy, def. 2 mess., 2 gdns., 60 a. ar., 20 a. mw., 28 a. pa. & 2 a. wd. in Highe Laver & Magdalene Laver. And for this pl. gtd. the same to def. & the heirs of the body of Tho., to hold of the chief lords, with remainder to the right heirs of Tho.

7. Tho. Goodman, gent., pl. Francis Burye, gent., & w. *Anne*, def. 1 mess., 2 tofts, 2 curtilages, 1 barn, 1 gdn., 1 orchard, 30 a. ar., 6 a. mw. & 20 a. pa. in Danbury & Sandon. £40.

8. Jn. Hecforde, pl. *Wm.* Samwell & w. Alice, def. 1 mess., 1 gdn. & 10 a. ar. in Messinge. £40.

FEET OF FINES FOR ESSEX

9. Geo. Crymbyll, pl. Rd. Asser & w. *Alice*, def. 1 mess., 1 barn, 1 gdn. & 1 a. mw. in Chelmesford. £40.

10. Tho. Grigges, pl. Wm. Clopton, esq., def. Manor of Bradfeildes & 1 mess., 1 gdns., 1 orchard, 80 a. ar., 20 a. mw., 100 a. pa. & 40 a. wd. in Pentlowe, Lyston, Foxherth, Belchamp Otton & Belchamp St. Paul. £160.

11. Robt. Springe, pl. *Tho.* Downynge, gent., & w. Joan, def. 10 a. ar. & 1 a. pa. in Beauchampe St. Paul. £20.

12. Trin. & Hil. Wm. Sompner, pl. *Jn.* Choppyng, gent., & Geo. Choppyn, his son & heir apt., def. 100 a. ar., 10 a. mw., 23 a. pa. & 4 a. wd. in Wyggebarowe, Salcott Virley & Layer Bretton. £140.

13. Mich. Willyams, pl. Tho. Taylour & w. *Joan* & Tho. Warren & w. *Eleanor*, def. 6 a. ar. in Broxhed. £20.

14. Geoff. Porter, pl. Edw. Denny & w. *Alice*, def. 1 a. ar. in High Ongar. £2.

15. Nich. Whale, pl. Jn. Carver & w. *Agnes*, def. 1 mess. & 1 curtilage in Great Dounmowe. £10.

16. Hy. Woode, pl. Wm. Crokes & w. *Barbara*, def. A moiety of 1 mess. & 1 gdn. in Prytwell. £40.

17. Robt. Ball, pl. *Tho.* Carter & w. Mary, def. 1 mess., 1 cott., 1 barn, 1 gdn., 34 a. ar. & 4 a. wd. in Great Holland. £100.

18. Jn. Osborne & w. Kath., pl. Geo. Love & w. *Joan*, def. 6 a. ar. in Lytle Horseley. Def. quitclaimed to pl. & the heirs of Jn. £40.

19. Wm. Hurrell, pl. Tho. Pynde & w. *Anne*, def. 1 mess., 2 gdns. & 1 orchard in Hennyngham Syble. £15.

20. Jas. Anderkyn, pl. *Jn.* Mackyn & w. Mary, def. 1 mess., 1 barn, 1 gdn. & 10 a. ar. in Crixhethe. £40.

21. Geo. Wyseman, gent., & w. Marthe, pl. *Geo.* Celye, gent., & w. Grace, def. Manor of Albyns *alias* Albynes & 5 mess., 240 a. ar., 40 a. mw., 140 a. pa., 10 a. wd., 40 a. furze & heath & 40s. rt. in Navestocke & Staplforthe Abbott. Def. quitclaimed to pl. & the heirs of Geo. 400 mks.

22. Jn. Ive, gent., pl. Wm. Pawne, esq., def. 2 mess., 20 a. ar., 6 a. mw., 10 a. pa. & 6 a. wd. in Wryttle *alias* Wryttell & Wydford. £20.

23. Rd. Purcas, pl. Jn. Freer, gent., def. 1 mess., 2 gdns., 28 a. ar., 5 a. mw., 7 a. pa. & 4d. rt. in Great Gelham *alias* Great Yeldham & Toppesfylde. Def. quitclaimed to pl. & his heirs, with warranty against Wm. Freer & his heirs & the heirs of Joan Freer, decd. £40.

24. Trin. & Hil. Rd. Holborough, pl. Tho. Haveryng & w. *Margt.*, def. 1 mess., 2 gdns., 60 a. ar., 4 a. mw. & 90 a. pa. in Bulmer & Beauchamp William *alias* Water Beauchamp. £80.

25. Mary Gates, wid., pl. Jn. Sampforthe, def. 1 mess., 1 barn, 1 toft, 1 gdn., 1 orchard, 60 a. ar., 20 a. mw., 40 a. pa. & 6 a. wd. in Roxwell & Wrytle. 130 mks.

26. Trin. & Hil. Wm. Cooke & Nich. Ogle, pl. Wm Badbye, def. 2 mess., 50 a. mw., 200 a. pa. & 300 a. marsh in Coringe *alias* Coringham, which Tho. Smyth, esq., holds for life. Pl. & the heirs of Wm. to hold the reversion of the chief lords. £320.

27. Matthew Steven, pl. Jn. Garlynge & w. *Frances*, def. 3 a. wd. in Stanwaye. £20.

28. Jn. Howe, pl. Robt. Lowght & w. *Joan*, Robt. Turner & w. *Mary*, *Margt.* Baker & *Kath.* Baker, def. 2 mess., 2 gdns., 2 orchards, 50 a. ar., 2 a. mw. & 6 a. pa. in Mallendyne. £80.

29. Francis Eglysfyld, esq., pl. *Tho.* Pullyver & w. Alice, def. 12 a. fresh marsh in Estham. £100.

30. Trin. & Hil. Gabriel Poyntz, esq., pl. Geo. Hearde & w. *Eliz.*, def. A moiety of 12 mess., 1 dovecote, 12 gdns., 10 orchards, 202 a. ar., 62 a. mw., 210 a. pa., 102 a. wd. & 40s. rt. in Northwokendon, Cranham, Little Thurrok, Chaldwell & Styfford. 400 mks.

31. Tho. Gynes, gent., & w. Faith, pl. *Jn.* Lyllye & w. Mary, def. 8 a. ar. & 10 a. pa. in Great Leighes. Def. quitclaimed to pl. & the heirs of Tho. £40.

32. Tho. Wylson, pl. *Wm.* Fabyan, esq., & w. Anne, def. Manor of Jenckyns *alias* Bockyngs & 30 mess., 3 cotts., 1 water-mill, 1 dovecote, 3 gdns., 2 orchards, 200 a. ar., 200 a. mw., 200 a. pa., 40 a. wood, 60 a. furze & heath & 60s. rt. in Bockinge, Braintre, Stysted & Feringe. £40.

33. Tho. Barnarde, pl. *Robt.* Barnarde & w. Mary, def. 10 a. ar., 2 a. mw. & 2 a. pa. in Margettrodynge. £40.

34. Wm. Campe, pl. *Hy.* Archer & w. Anne, def. 6 a. ar. in Thoydon Garnon. £40.

35. Hy. Watsone & w. Joan, pl. *Jn.* Glascocke, gent., & w. Anne, def. 1 mess., 1 gdn., 1 orchard, 15 a. ar., 2 a. mw. & 8 a. pa. in Matchynge, High Laver & Little Laver. Def. quitclaimed to pl. & the heirs of Hy., with warranty against Jn. Wright & w. Judith & her heirs. £40.

36. Trin. & Hil. Edm. Pyrton & Geo. Knightley, esquires, pl. Hy. Wentworth esq., & w. *Jane*, def. Manors of Garnons & Tendrynghall & 10 mess., 4 tofts, 10 gdns., 400 a. ar., 20 a. mw., 40 a. pa., 60 a. wd., 12 a. furze & heath, 6 a. moor, £6 rt. & a free fishery in Tendringe, & the advowson of the church of Tendringe. Def. quitclaimed to pl. & the heirs of Edm. £240.

37. Lau. Rochell, pl. *Ralph* Madyson & w. Margt., *Tho.* Sampford & w. Agnes, def. 1 mess., 1 gdn., 1 orchard & 24 a. ar. in Shellowe Bowells. £40.

38. Wm. Barlee & Robt. Fryth, pl. Wm. Wilford, esq., & w. Agnes & *Jn.* Wentworth, esq., def. Manor of Cheswykhall *alias* Flaundens with Cheswyck & 30 mess., 30 tofts, 30 gdns., 10 orchards, 500 a. ar., 20 a. mw., 100 a. pa., 200 a. wd., £12 rt. & liberty of fold-age for 400 sheep in Creshall *alias* Christishall *alias* Crissall, Elmedon, Lowtes, Over-chissall *alias* Over Chissull, Nether Chissell *alias* Nether Chissull & Langeley. Def. quitclaimed to pl. & the heirs of Robt. £240.

39. Wm. Waldegrave, esq., pl. *Tho.* Cotton, esq., pl. *Tho.* Cotton, gent., & w. Joan, def. The rectory of Great Wendon *alias* Wendon & 1 toft, 1 barn, 1 orchard, 40 a. ar., 10 a. mw., 10 a. pa. & 40s. rt. in Great Wendon, Little Wendon & Newport Ponde & all tithes of sheaves, grain & hay in Great Wendon, Little Wendon & Newport Pond, & the advowson of the vicarage of the church of Great Wendon. £120.

40. Trin. & Hil. Wm. Wymond & Jn. Fraunces, pl. *Jn.* Goldynge sen. & w. Joan, Rd. Purcas & w. Kath. & Robt. Almond & w. Joan, def. 1 mess., 1 gdn., 9 a. ar. & 2 a. mw. in Thaxsted. Def. quitclaimed to pl. & the heirs of Wm., with warranty of the land & meadow by Jn. & Joan for themselves & the heirs of Jn. & of the mess. & gdn. by Robt. & Joan for themselves & the heirs of Joan. £40.

41. Hy. Collyn, pl. Tho. Taylour & w. Joan, Tho. Warren & w. Eleanor, Jn. Willyams, Jn. Chapman & Jn. Jenyn *alias* Jenyngs, def. 1 mess., 1 gdn., 16 a. ar., 1 a. mw., 2 a. pa. & 2 a. wd. in Chickney. Def. quitclaimed to pl. & the heirs, with warranty by Tho. & Joan of one moiety against themselves & the heirs of Joan & the heirs of Maud late the w. of Jn. Clarck, by Tho. & Eleanor of the other moiety against themselves & the heirs of Eleanor & the heirs of the said Maud, & by Jn., Jn. & Jn. of the whole against themselves & the heirs of Jn. Willyams. £40.

42. Jn. Frank sen. & Alexander Warner, pl. Rd. Hare & w. *Marian*, def. 1 mess., 1 gdn. & 3 a. ar. in Great Leyghs. Def. quitclaimed to pl. & the heirs of Jn. And for this pl. gtd. the same to def. to hold for their lives of the chief lords, with remainder to Jn. Frank jun., son & heir apt. of the same Jn. Frank sen., & Margery Burle *alias* Sponer, dau. of Marian, & the heir of their bodies & the right heirs of Marian.

43. Trin. & Hil. Jn. Thomson, esq., pl. *Jn.* Brocke, esq., & w. Anne, late the w. of Edm. Sheffeld, kt., lord Sheffeld, def. Manor of Arnoldes *alias* Arnoldes Hall & 4 mess., 4 cotts., 4 tofts, 2 mills, 2 dovecotes, 4 gdns., 4 orchards, 200 a. ar., 120 a. mw., 400 a. pa., 120 a. wd., 100 a. furze & heath, 100 a. moor, 100 a. marsh, 40s. rt. & free warren & several fisheries in Yngmountney *alias* Gingmountney *alias* Mountneysinge *alias* Monesinge & Arnoldes *alias* Arnoldes Hall. £700. (*See also* CP25(2)/128/1641, *no.* 21.)

CP25(2)/259

8. Wm. Cecill, knight, principal secretary of the Queen, pl. Anne, dame marchioness of Northampton, *alias* Anne Burchier, & Lovayne, dau. & heir of Hy., lord Burchier & Lovayne, earl of Essex & Ewe, & w. Mary, one of the daus. & heirs of Wm. Saye, kt., decd., def. Prop. in Herts; & 40 a. ar., 20 a. mw. & a free fishery in the water of Lee in Nasyng & Waltham Holy Cross, co. Essex. £840. – Herts., Essex.

21. Jas. Lord & Wm. Tiffin, pl. Francis Harvye & w. *Mary*, def. Prop. in Yorks.; & 1 mess., 1 cott., 1 barn, 60 a. ar., 60 a. mw. & 60 a. pa. in Mundon & Purlewe, co. Essex. Def. quitclaimed to pl. & the heirs of Jas. And for this pl. gtd. the same to def. to hold for their lives of the chief lords, with remainder to the right heirs of Mary. – York, Essex.

CP25(2)/128/1640

1. Hil. & Eas. Francis Archer, pl. Tho. Goodwyn, gent., def. 4 mess., 4 gdns., 16 a. ar. & 4 a. wd. in Bocking. £40.

2. Jn. Marshall, pl. Tho. Peke, def. 1 mess., 1 gdn. & 7 a. ar. in Little Shoberye *alias* North Shoberye. £40.

3. Jn. Dowe, pl. *Tho.* Fuller & w. Alice, def. 1 mess., 1 gdn. & 1 orchard in Bockinge. £80.

4. Jn. Collman, pl. Jn. Wentworth, esq., def. 60 a. ar., 10 a. pa. & 3 a. wd. in Cressall *alias* Cryshall & Wendon Loofthes. £40.

5. Edw. Halys, clk., pl. Jn. Lucas & w. *Mary*, def. 2 mess., 1 barn, 3 gdns., 1 orchard, 6 a. ar., 4 a. pa. & 2 a. furze & heath in Wytham. Def. quitclaimed to pl. & his heirs, with warranty against Rd. Sandes & w. Kat. £20.

6. Tho. Spakemane & w. Joan, pl. Jn. Stonarde, esq., & w. Anne & *Jn.* Gosnall & w. Eliz., def. 1 mess., 1 cott., 1 gdn., 1 orchard, 4 a. ar. & 6 a. mw. in Chigwell. £40.

7. Wm. Sidey, gent., pl. *Wm.* Wilford, esq., & w. Agnes & Jn. Wilford, his son & heir apt., def. Manor of Hannams *alias* Boleynes & 2 mess., 6 gdns., 300 a. ar., 12 a. mw., 60 a. pa., 12 a. wd. & 10s. rt. in Tendryng. £420.

8. Arthur Armiger & Wm. Frevell, pl. *Jn.* Cutte, esq., & w. Anne, def. 3 mess., 2 gdns., 130 a. ar., 20 a. mw., 60 a. pa. & 6 a. wd. in Thaxsted. Def. quitclaimed to pl. & the heirs of Arthur. £372.

9. Edm. Hurte & Robt. Drywoode, pl. Tho. Maull & w. *Denise*, def. 14 a. pa. & 6 a. wd. in Shendfeld. Def. quitclaimed to pl. & the heirs of Robt. £40.

10. Wm. Soan, pl. Jn. Cawston *alias* Cawson, gent., def. 1 mess., 1 barn, 1 gdn, 40 a. ar., 10 a. mw. & 30 a. pa. in Seynt Lawrence. 130 mks.

11. Tho. Fanshawe, esq., & w. Mary, pl. *Brian* Stapleton, esq., & w. Eliz., def. 1 mess., 1 gdn., 1 orchard, 100 a. ar., 20 a. mw., 100 a. pa., 100 a. wd., 20 a. marsh, 40s. rt. & free warren in Barkynge, Longebridge & Dagenham. Def. quitclaimed to pl. & the heirs of Tho. 230 mks.

12. Geo. Lillye, pl. Walter Davies & s. *Susan*, def. A moiety of 1 mess., 1 gdn., 1 orchard, 17 a. ar., 4 a. mw. & 10 a. pa. in Fayersted. £10.

13. Wm. Aylett, pl. *Wm.* Fabyan, esq., & w. Anne, def. 1 mess., 2 barns, 1 dovecote, 1 gdn., 100 a. ar., 40 a. mw., 40 a. pa. & 20 a. wd. in Patteswicke, Coxall & Bradwell. £80.

14. Tho. Clarke jun., pl. *Robt.* Noke & w. Dorothy, def. 5 mess., 2 barns, 1 dovecote, 3 gdns., 3 orchards, 20 a. ar., 10 a. mw., 70 a. pa. & 3 a. wd. in Great Coggeshall, Little Coggeshall & Ferynge. £140.

15. Wm. Reve *alias* Saunder, pl. Tho. Trapps, def. 3 a. ar. in Spyngffeld. £40.

16. Tho. Sadler, pl. *Robt.* Mannynge & w. Agnes, def. 3 mess., 3 gdns., 3 orchards, 30 a. ar. & 10 a. pa. in Langham. £40.

17. Jn. Newton & w. Margt., pl. Tho. Stane & w. *Bridget*, def. 1 mess., 1 cott., 1 barn, 1 gdn. & 1 a. ar. in Writtle. Def. quitclaimed to pl. & the heirs of Jn. 40 mks.

18. Robt. Broke, pl. *Geoff.* Bowtell & w. Alice, def. 1 mess., 1 toft, 2 gdns., 1 orchard, 7 a. ar., 3 a. mw. & 6 a. pa. in Danburye. £40.

19. Francis Egglesfeild & w. Joan, pl. *Tho.* Pullyver jun. & w. Alice, def. 8 a. marsh, 1 a. reed (*arundinis*) & a free fishery in Eastham & Westham. Def. quitclaimed to pl. & the heirs of Francis, with warranty against Tho. Pullyver sen., father of Tho., & his heirs. £40.

20. Lewis Dollocke, pl. Jn. Wentworth, esq., def. 1 mess., 9 a. ar., 1 a. mw., 2 a. pa. & ½ a. wd. in Wendon Lofthes & Cressall *alias* Cryshall. £35.

21. Tho. Hopper, pl. Jn. Wentworth, esq., def. 8 a. ar. & 4 a. wd. in Cressall *alias* Crishall. £20.

22. Hil. & Eas. Jn. Collyn, pl. Edw. Sullyarde, esq., A moiety of the manor of Otes. £280.

23. Tho. Lond & Tho. Fytch, pl. Tho. Gent, esq., & w. Eliz., *Jn.* Alen jun. & w. Eliz., def. 2 mess., 2 gdns., 2 orchards, 17 a. ar. & 16 a. pa. in Bumpsted at the Steeple. Def. quitclaimed to pl. & the heirs of Tho. Lond. £40.

24. Tho. Burle, pl. *Jn.* Harrye *alias* Harrys & w. Agnes, def. 1 mess., 1 gdn., 1 orchard, 10 a. ar., 8 a. mw. & 10 a. pa. in Little Badowe. £120.

25. Rd. Long, pl. *Geoff.* Smyth & w. Alice, def. 2 mess., 1 gdn., 10 a. ar. & 2 a. pa. in Esse *alias* Asshen. £40.

26. Hil. & Eas. Ralph Wade, pl. Rd. Becke, def. 1 mess. & 20 a. pa. in Southmynster. £40.

27. Tho. Wyseman, esq., pl. Jn. Constable, def. 1 mess., 1 gdn., 8 a. ar., 2 a. pa. & 1 a. wd. in Wymbysshe. £40.

28. Hil. & Eas. Rd. Becke, pl. Ralph Wade, def. 1 mess. & 20 a. pa. in Burneham. £40.

29. Wm. Stronge, pl. Robt. Tyffyn & w. *Judith*, def. 1 mess. & 1 gdn. in Heningham Syble. Def. quitclaimed to pl. & his heirs, with warranty against Jn. Adam, decd., & his heirs. £30.

30. Jn. Butler, pl. *Jn.* Webbe & w. Agnes, def. 1 mess., 1 cott., 1 toft, 1 barn, 1 gdn. & 1 orchard in Bockynge. £20.

31. Hil. & Eas. Nich. Ingram, pl. Jn. Thorn & w. *Joan*, def. A moiety of 1 mess. & 1 a. ar. in Great Byrche. £40.

32. Hil. & Eas. Jn. Wendon, pl. *Wm.* Beryff, gent., & w. Kath. & Tho. Twede & w. Agnes, def. 1 mess., 1 gdn., 1 orchard & 4 a. ar. in Aldham. £40.

33. Matthew Cracherode & Wm. Cracherode, gentlemen, pl. *Tho.* Hunt & w. Eliz., def. 10 a. ar., 6 a. pa. & 4 a. wd. in Bockyng & Stysted. Def. quitclaimed to pl. & the heirs of Matthew. And for this pl. gtd. the same to def. & the heirs of Eliz., to hold of the chief lords.

34. Rd. Stoneley, esq., pl. *Hy.* Goldinge, esq., & w. Alice, def. Manor of Engayneshall & 2 mess., 4 tofts, 1 dovecote, 4 gdns., 4 orchards, 300 a. ar., 40 a. mw., 100 a. pa., 40 a. wd., 60 a. furze & heath & 40s. rt. in Tenderinge, Great Clackton, Little Clackton, Wellye & Thorpe. £120.

35. Hil. & Eas. Geo. Bayne, pl. Jn. Bawde, esq., def. 20 mess., 20 gdns., 20 orchards & 160 a. pa. in Coryngham. And for this pl. gtd. the same to def. & his heirs, to hold of the chief lords.

36. Edm. Tyrrell, esq., pl. *Edw.* Hedge & w. Priscilla, Seth Ivatte & w. Eliz., def. 1 mess., 1 cott., 2 gdns., 20 a. ar., 4 a. mw. & 12 a. pa. in Woodham Ferrers. £200.

37. Tho. Spencer, Lewis Colle & Jn. Tayler, pl. *Geo.* Smyth, esq., & w. Emma, def. 2 a. ar., 6½ a. mw. & 2 a. pa. in Haveryll. Def. quitclaimed to pl. & the heirs of Jn. £40.

38. Hil. & Eas. Edw. Stanhope & Jas Moryce, esq., pl. Anth. Cooke, kt., def. Manors of Mawdelyn Laver & Mascalls Bery & 1,000 a. ar., 500 a. mw., 1,000 a. pa., 200 a. wd., 100 a. furze & heath & £30 rt. in Chigwell, Lamborne, Whyghtroodynge & Mawdelyne Lavor. Def. quitclaimed to pl. & the heirs of Edw. And for this pl. gtd. the same to def. & his heirs, to hold of the chief lords.

39. Hil. & Eas. Francis Stonard, gent., pl. Jn. Stonard, esq., & *Rd.* Stonard, gent., def. 1 mess., 1 barn, 1 gdn., 10 a. ar., 7 a. mw., 10 a. pa. & 2 a. wd. in Lamborne. £70.

40. Rd. Pettye, pl. Jn. Tyler & w. Thomasina, *Jn.* Fynche & w. Margt., def. 2 mess., 2 gdns., 20 a. ar., 4 a. mw., 4 a. pa. & 2 a. wd. in Duddyngherst & Kelwedon. 140 mks.

41. Hil. & Eas. Rd. Northey, pl. Wm. Thurstone, def. 1 mess., 1 gdn., 3 a. ar. & 9 a. pa. in Colcester & Myleend. £40.

42. Jn. Gylbarn, citizen & draper of London, pl. *Ambrose* Nicholas, citizen & alderman of London, & w. Eliz. & Rd. Nixon & w. Cristiana, def. 1 mess., 2 gdns. & 1 orchard in Alvethley *alias* Alveley. £40.

43. Tho. Clarke, pl. *Jn.* Clarke & w. Prisca, def. 1 mess., 1 toft, 1 gdn., 40 a. ar. & 30 a. pa. in Dansey *alias* Dengey. £40.

44. Jn. Everley, pl. Jn. Prentyce & w. *Maud*, def. A moiety of 1 mess., 1 barn & 1 gdn. in Great Badowe. £40.

45. Hil. & Eas. Rd. Rastell, gent., pl. *Tho.* Wyseman, esq., & w. Jane, def. 1 mess., 1 gdn., 40 a. ar., 10 a. mw., 20 a. pa., 2 a. wd., 20 a. fresh marsh & 10 a. salt marsh in Greyes Thurrock & Little Thurrock. £80.

46. Hil. & Eas. Jn. Lyon, pl. Tho. Barnabye, gent., def. 3 mess., 3 gdns., 3 orchards, 20 a. ar., 3 a. mw. & 4 a. pa. in Colchester & Inworth, the rectory of Tolshunt Darcy & all tithes of sheaves, grain & hay in Tolshunt Darcy, & the advowson of the church of Tolshunt Darcy. £140.

47. Hil. & Eas. Geoff. Maydstone, pl. *Tho.* Keeler & w. Agnes, Robt. Keeler & Chris. Keeler, def. 1 mess., 2 gdns. & 2 a. mw. in Marks Taye *alias* Tey Maundevyle & Great Tey. £40.

48. Jn. Lee, pl. *Jn.* Pratt & w. Etheldreda, def. 1 mess., 1 gdn., 1 orchard, 20 a. ar. & 4 a. pa. in Great Chishull & Little Chishull. £40.

49. Hil. & Eas. Jn. Serle, pl. *Chris.* Welshe, esq., & w. Anne, def. Manor of Pyenest & 2 mess., 1 dovecote, 1 gdn., 1 orchard, 50 a. ar., 16 a. mw., 50 a. pa. & 3 a. wd. in Waltham Holy Cross. £220.

50. Rok Grene, esq., pl. *Hy.* Tyrrell, kt., & Tho. Tyrrell, esq., his son & heir apt., def. A moiety of the manor of Olde Sampford & a moiety of 20 mess., 20 tofts, 20 cotts., 12 barns, 1 dovecote, 20 gdns., 16 orchards, 1,000 a. ar., 500 a. mw., 2,000 a. pa., 300 a. wd. & £10 13s. 4d. rt. in Great Sampford, Little Sampford, Thaxsted, Radwynter, Bumsteed & Fynchingfilde. £508.

51. Jn. Mordaunt, kt., lord Mordaunt, pl. *Lewis* Mordaunt, kt., & w. Eliz., def. Manor of Typtofts & 6 mess., 4 tofts, 6 gdns., 1 dovecote, 1,000 a. ar., 60 a. mw., 100 a. pa., 40 a. wd., 100 a. furze & heath, 40s. rt. & a liberty of one fold in Wymbyshe, Debden, Radwynter, Thunderley, Thaxsted, Hempsted & Walden. 400 mks.

52. Jn. Brumley & Jn. Poole, pl. Clement Syslye, esq., & w. *Anne*, def. 1 mess., 1 gdn., 40 a. ar., 10 a. mw. & 30 a. marsh in Barkeinge. Def. quitclaimed to pl. & the heirs of Jn. Brumley. And for this pl. gtd. the same to Clement & his heirs, to hold of the chief lords.

53. Rd. Cornewall, gent., Tho. Pechie & Jn. Burton pl. *Geo.* Smyth, esq., & w. Emma, def. 12 a. ar. & 17½ a. pa. in Haveryll & Bumpsted Hellyn. Def. quitclaimed to pl. & the heirs of Jn. £40.

CP25(2)/259   DIVERS COUNTIES

6. Hil. & Eas. Barnard Whitteston, gent., pl. Wm. Thorneff, gent., & w. *Anne*, def. A third part of the manor of Wodeford & a third part of 40 mess., 40 gdns., 40 orchards, 400 a. ar., 100 a. mw., 500 a. pa., 400 a. wd. & 200 a. furze & heath in Wodeford, co. Essex; & prop. in London. £280. – Essex, London.

CP25(2)/128/1641   TRINITY, 12 ELIZABETH   1570

1. Jn. Howlande, pl. *Jn.* Holt & w. Joan, def. 4 a. ar. in Widdington. £20.

2. Eas. & Trin. Wm. Avery, pl. *Tho.* Powle, esq., & w. Jane, def. 25 a. fresh marsh in Barkyng. £50.

3. Eas. & Trin. Wm. Maynard, pl. *Wm.* Fabyan, esq., & w. Anne, def. 10 a. ar., 3 a. mw. & 6 a. pa. in Stysted. £40.

4. Eas. & Trin. Roger Martyn, esq., pl. Wm. Clopton, esq., def. 1 mess., 5 a. ar., 8 a. mw. 4 a. pa. & 2s. 6d. rt. in Lyston & Foxherde. £80.

5. Hy. Turner, pl. *Tho.* Laurence jun. & w. Kath., def. 1 mess. & 2 gdns. in Bockinge. £40.

6. Eas. & Trin. Jn. Garrarde, pl. Jn. Lucas & w. *Mary* & Rd. Aburforthe, gent., def. 1 mess., 1 gdn., 1 orchard, 15 a. ar., 10 a. mw., 5 a. pa. & 5 a. wd. in Wytham, Cressinge & Ryvenhall. £40.

7. Tho. Powle, esq., pl. Robt. Lukyn, def. 3 a. mw. & 1 a. pa. in Barkyng. £40.

8. Raimond Kyng, pl. *Jn.* Brocke, esq., & w. Anne, def. 4 mess., 3 tofts, 4 gdns., 200 a. ar., 20 a. mw., 40 a. pa., 6 a. wd., 20 a. furze & heath, 40 a. fresh marsh & 30 a. salt marsh in Ramsey & Great Ocle. 230 mks.

9. Eas. & Trin. Rd. Watwood, pl. Geo. Monynges, gent., & w. *Anne* & Geo. Pumfrett, def. 2 mess., 2 orchards, 100 a. ar., 40 a. mw., 60 a. pa. & 10 a. wd. in Littleburie, Elmeden, Great Chestover & Little Chestouer. £40.

10. Hy. Whood, pl. Jn. Meeke & w. *Alice*, def. 1 cott. & 1 a. ar. in Wickford, Downam, Runwell & Sowth Hannyngfeld. £40.

11. Tho. Averye, gent., & Rd. Cuttes, gent., pl. Edw. Elryngton, esq., def. 6 mess., 6 gdns., 6 orchards, 104 a. ar., 87 a. mw., 200 a. pa. & 35 a. wd. in Theydon Boyes & Lowton. Def. quitclaimed to pl. & the heirs of Tho. £400.

12. Edw. Maplesden, pl. Wm. Roche & w. *Joan* & Wm. Norman & w. Margery, def. 1 mess., 1 gdn. & 1 orchard in Waltham Holy Cross. £40.

13. Eas. & Trin. Rd. Stoneley, esq., pl. *Wm.* Armestronge *alias* Armested & w. Margt., def. 1 mess., 1 barn, 1 gdn. & 1 orchard in Dagenham. £80.

14. Rd. Archer, pl. *Jn.* Grave & w. Margt., def. 1 mess., 1 gdn. (*horto*), 1 orchard, 20 a. ar., 20 a. mw. & 20 a. pa. in Theydon at the Mount & Theydon Garnon. £40.

15. Tho. Browne, pl. Geoff. Sewster, def. 5 a. ar. & 11 a. pa. in Elmedon. £40.

16. Eas. & Trin. Wm. Holstok, pl. Tho. Tendrynge, gent., & w. *Cecily*, def. 1 mess., 1 gdn., 20 a. ar., 5 a. mw., 6 a. pa. & 4 a. wd. in Orset. £40.

17. Edw. Isaacke, esq., & Jn. Statham, gent., pl. *Wm.* Sandes, gent., & w. Anne, def. Manor of Edwards & 6 mess., 6 gdns., 6 orchards, 300 a. ar., 40 a. mw., 100 a. pa., 100 a. wd. & 40s. rt. in Woddam Ferrys, Norton & Stowe. Def. quitclaimed to pl. & the heirs of Edw. £280.

18. Geo. Clyfford, esq., & Jn. Philipps, gent., pl. Jn. Lucas jun., & w. *Mary*, def. 1 mess., 1 gdn., 40 a. ar., 50 a. mw., 60 a. pa., 10 a. wd., 30 a. furze & heath & 20s. rt. in Mysteley. Def. quitclaimed to pl. & the heirs of Geo. £80.

19. Jn. Bacon, gent., pl. Robt. Springe, esq., & w. *Jane*, def. A moiety of the manor of Esthorppe & a moiety of 2 mess., 2 cotts., 2 gdns., 343 a. ar., 26 a. mw., 34 a. pa., 20 a. wd., 10 a. moor & £4 8s. rt. in Esthorppe, Great Byrche, Little Byrche, Messinge, Teye, Copford, Stanweye & Fordham, & a moiety of the advowson of the church of Esthorppe. £200.

20. Eas. & Trin. Tho. Franke, esq., pl. *Rd.* Core, gent., & w. Margery & *Jn.* Rawlyns & w. Joan, def. 1 mess., 2 gdns., 100 a. ar., 20 a. mw., 30 a. pa., 6 a. wd. & 100 a. furze & heath in Hatfeild Brodecke *alias* Hatfeild Regis. £240.

21. Jn. Peers & w. Alice, pl. *Jn.* Thomson, esq., & w. Dorothy, def. Manor of Arnoldes *alias* Arnoldes Hall (etc. as in CP25(2)/128/1639, *no.* 43). £600.

22. Eas. & Trin. Oliver, lord Saint John, Tho. Barington, Tho. Sadler, Hy. Capell, Wistan Browne, Hy. Josselyn, Jn. Gyll, Oliver Saint John, esquires, & Tho. Grymesdyche, gent., pl. Tho. Leventhorpe, esq., & w. *Dorothy*, def. Manors of Leyer Barley *alias* Leyer Breton & Mulsham *alias* Moulsham & 20 mess., 12 cotts., 12 tofts, 2 dovecotes, 30 gdns., 10 orchards, 1,000 a. ar., 100 a. mw., 400 a. pa., 30 a. wd., 50 a. furze & heath & £6 rt. in Leyer Barley *alias* Leyer Breton, Mulsham *alias* Moulsham, Salcote Virley, Great Wigborowe, Leyer Marney, Bastable & Leyer de la Hey, & the advowsons of the churches of Leyer Barley *alias* Leyer Breton, Salcote Virley & Tolleshunt Knights. Def. quitclaimed to pl. & the pl. & the heirs of Oliver, lord Saint John. £200.

3. Tho. Osborne, pl. *Robt*. Bogas, gent., & w. Anne, def. 2 mess., 1 dovecote, 2 gdns., 1 orchard, 26 a. ar., 10 a. mw., 20 a. pa. & 2 a. wd. in Boxsted, co. Essex; & prop. in Suff. 190 mks. — Essex. Suff.

CP25(2)/128/1642   MICHAELMAS, 12-13 ELIZABETH   1570

1. Rd. Everard, gent., pl. Jn. Mund *alias* Freman & w. Agnes & *Nich*. Richards & w. Rose, def. 1 toft, 10 a. ar. & 8 a. pa. in Great Waltham & Little Waltham. £40.

2. Trin. & Mich. Wm. Rayner, pl. *Edm*. Essex & W. Alice, def. 1 mess. & 2 gdns. in Thaxsted. £30.

3. Trin. & Mich. Jn. Edwardes, pl. *Wm*. Mortymer & w. Joan, def. 5 a. ar. in Toppesfeld. £20.

4. Trin. & Mich. Tho. Yeldham, pl. *Jn*. Yeldham & w. Joan, def. 2 mess. & 4 gdns. in Fynchingfeld. £30.

5. Jn. Thorogood, pl. Geoff. Crabbe, def. 2 mess., 2 gdns., 2 orchards, 60 a. ar., 6 a. mw., 15 a. pa. & 2 a. wd. in Farneham, Busshopp Stortford, Stansted Mownfizett & Byrchanger. 230 mks.

6. Baldwin Stamer, pl. Tho. Bellyngham & w. Joan & *Robt*. Palmer, def. 1 mess., 1 gdn., 8 a. ar. & 1 rood mw. in Harvardstocke. £20.

7. Nich. Rookes, pl. Tho. Cecyll, gent., & w. Margt., def. 2½ a. mw. in Wedyton. 40 mks.

8. Jn. Poole, pl. *Robt*. Poole & w. Margery, def. 1 mess., 1 gdn., 1 orchard, 36 a. ar., 4 a. mw. & 16 a. pa. in Thaxsted. £100.

9. Trin. & Mich. Jn. Tyler & w. Thomasina, pl. Rd. Jeffrey, def. 1 mess., 1 gdn., 1 orchard , 10 a. ar., 7 a. mw., 8 a. pa. & 2 a. wd. in Sowthweld & Shenfeild. Def. quitclaimed to pl. & the heirs of Jn. £140.

10. Wm. Spycer, pl. *Hy*. Jhonson & w. Dorothy, def. 1 mess., 1 gdn., 1 orchard, 5 a. ar., 3 a. mw., 3 a. pa. & 1½ a. wd. in Chigwell. £80.

11. Rd. Shorte, pl. Rachel Shorte, def. A third part of 1 mess., 1 gdn., 30 a. ar., 10 a. mw., 40 a. pa., 100 a. fresh marsh & 26 a. salt marsh in the parish of St. Osithe *alias* Chyche. £80.

12. Jn. Staple, pl. Jn. Justyce, def. 1 mess., 1 gdn. & 3 a. ar. in Northe Shoberye *alias* Little Shobery. £40.

13. Wm. Nevell, pl. *Nich*. Brodewater & w. Margery, def. 1 mess. & 1 gdn. in Rayleigh. £40.

14. Trin & Mich. Agnes Barnerd, wid., Jn. Ridesdale *alias* Loker & Tho. Boyes, pl. *Wm*. Waldegrave, esq., & w. Eliz., def. 10 a. ar., 3 a. mw. & 5 a. pa. in Halsted. Def. quitclaimed to pl. & the heirs Agnes. £40.

15. Robt. Camme & Jn. Broke, gentlemen, pl. Tho. Hopkyns, gent., & w. *Eliz*., Tho. Flowerdewe, gent., & w. *Anne, Mary* Fanne & *Susan* Fanne, def. 10 mess., 200 a. ar., 20 a. mw., 40 a. pa. & 20 a. wd. in Thaxsted, Broxhead, Tyltey, Chickney & Elsnam. Def. quitclaimed to pl. & the heirs of Robt. £400.

16. Bart. Pertridge, pl. Edw. Poole & w. *Joan*, def. A moiety of 1 mess., 1 gdn., 1 orchard, 2 a. ar. & 1 a. mw. in Navestocke. £40.

17. Edw. Glascock, gent., pl. *Tho*. Edmondes, gent., & w. Emma, def. 40 a. pa. in Sowthmynstre. £80.

18. Tho. Darcye, esq., pl. *Tho*. Barnabye, gent., & w. Isabel, def. The rectory of Tolshunt Darcy & all tithes of sheaves of grain & hay in Tolshunt Darcye, & the advowson of the church of Tolshunt Darcye. £80.

19. Wm. Page, pl. Wm. Brawdshawe & w. *Etheldreda*, pl. A third part of 1 mess., 1 gdn., 1 orchard, 4 a. ar., 3 a. mw., 3 a. pa. & common of pa. for all animals in Hornedon on the Hill. £20.

20. Tho. Wyseman, gent., pl. *Tho.* Wyseman, esq., & w. Jane, def. The manor of Mockynghall & 19 mess., 19 tofts, 2 dovecotes, 19 gdns., 200 a. ar., 50 a. mw., 300 a. pa., 10 a. wd., 100 a. furze & heath, 100 a. salt marsh & £20 rt. in Barlyng, Great Stanbrigge, Great Wakerynge, Little Wakerynge, Leigh, Shopland, Rocheford, Pryttelwell, Bemflete, Fowlnes, Althorne, Thundersley & Hadley. 800 mks.

21. Tho. Hackett, pl. *Wm.* Skipwith, esq., & w. Frances, *Hy.* Stoer & w. Jane, def. 12 a. mw. & 10 a. marsh in Wannington *alias* Wallington. £40.

22. Trin. & Mich. Tho. Nasshe, pl. Rd. Dygbye & w. *Millicent*, Bart. Browne & w. *Alice*, Rd. Walforde & w. *Jane & Thomasina* Reed *alias* Davy, def. 1 mess., 1 gdn. & 2½ a. ar. in Wethersfeld. £30.

23. Robt. Camme, Jn. Boughtell, Tho. Sebroke, Geo. Pygotte & Robt. Barker, pl. Tho. Hopkyns, gent., & other def. & prop. as in C25(2)/128/1642, *no.* 15. Similar quitclaim. £400.

24. Trin. & Mich. Tho. Eve, gent., & Tho. Jenyn, gent., pl. Wm. Shether & w. *Anne*, def. A moiety of the manor of Groves & a moiety of 6 mess., 1 dovecote, 6 barns, 6 gdns., 2 orchards, 300 a. ar., 60 a. mw., 80 a. pa., 80 a. wd. & 10s. rt. in North Wokyndon, Craneham, Little Thurrock, Chadwell & Styfford, which Gabriel Poyntz, esq., & w. Etheldreda hold for her life. Pl. & the heirs of Tho. Eve to hold the reversion of the chief lords. £400.

25. Hy. Swallowe, pl. Jn. Moodye & w. *Agnes*, Hy. Grymward & w. Joan, Wm. Fyner & w. Isabel, Wm. Warde & w. Eliz., Robt. Keler & w. Edith, Robt. Locke & w. Margt., def. 1 mess., 1 gdn., 1 orchard, 16 a. ar., 2 a mw., 10 a. pa. & 2 a. wd. in Great Bentley. £100.

26. Tho. Frenche & Tho. Hasteler, pl. *Tho.* Bendysshe, gent., & w. Eleanor, Jn. Cornell *alias* Cornewell & w. *Judith*, Tho. Hancocke & w. *Agnes*, def. 2 mess., 1 gdn., 18 a. ar., 9 a. pa. & 2 a. wd. in Fynchingfeld & Bumpsted at the Steeple. Def. quitclaimed to pl. & the heirs of Tho. Frenche. £66.

27. Jn. Preston & Geo. Smyth, pl. *Wm.* Woodlande *alias* Egham & Wm. Breeche, def. 8 mess., 1 barn, 8 gdns., 2 orchards, 20 a. ar., 10 a. pa., 3 a. wd. & 3 a. marsh in Barkynge & Dagenham. Def. quitclaimed to pl. & the heirs of Jn. And for this pl. gtd. 1 mess. called 'Smythes Forge', 1 barn, 1 gdn., 1 orchard & 2½ a. ar. in Barkynge, parcel of the same, to Wm. Breeche to hold from Michaelmas last for 21 years, rendering 12d. yearly, at the Purification & Michaelmas, with power of distraint; & the reversion of these & the residue to Wm. Woodlande & his heirs, to hold of the chief lords.

28. Jn. Overed & Wm. Ive, pl. *Jn.* Ultynge & w. Eliz., def. 1 mess., 1 barn, 1 gdn., 1 orchard, 20 a. ar., 2 a. mw., 40 a. pa., 10 a. wd. & 24s. rt. in Danbury & Woodham. Def. quitclaimed to pl. & the heirs of Jn. And for this pl. gtd. the same to def. & the heirs of their bodies, to hold of the chief lords, with remainder to Emma Stelewoman w. of Hy. Stelewoman & Eliz. Cannon w. of Wm. Cannon, sisters of Jn., & the heirs of their bodies, & the right heirs of Jn.

29. Robt. Alleyn, pl. Jn. Hauki . & w. Agnes & *Jn.* Buckford, def. 1 mess., 2 gdns. & 7 a. ar. in Branktre & Bockynge. And for this pl. gtd. to Jn. Haukyn & Agnes for her life an annuity of £4 from the same, at Christmas, the Annunciation, Midsummer & Michaelmas, with power of distraint.

30. Jn. Turner & Jn. Walton, pl. *Tho.* Sackevile, kt., lord Buckherst, & w. Cecily, def. The manor of Barholt Sackvile & 26 mess., 26 cotts., 26 tofts, 2 mills, 2 dovecotes, 26 gdns., 26 orchards, 500 a. ar., 80 a. mw., 500 a. pa., 400 a. wd. & 700 a. furze & heath in Barholte Sackvile & Fordeham *alias* Fordam. Def. quitclaimed to pl. & the heirs of Jn. Turner. And for this pl. gtd. the same to Tho. & his heirs, to hold of the chief lords.

31. Jn. Maxey, gent., & Rd. Emery, gent., pl. Anth. Maxey, esq., & w. *Dorothy*, def. The manor of Bradwell *alias* Bradwell Hall by Coggeshall & 4 mess., 2 water-mills, 200 a. ar., 40 a. mw., 100 a. pa., 40 a. wd., a free fishery in the water of Blackwater & 20s. rt. in Bradwell *alias* Bradwell by Coggeshall, Patteswyke, Coggeshall, Cressyng, Revenall, Stystede, Branketree, Bockyng & Shalforde, & the advowson of the church of Bradwell by Coggeshall. Def. quitclaimed to pl. & the heirs male of Dorothy by Anth., with remainder to her right heirs.

32. Tho. Parke & Simon Ruse, pl. Jn. Heron, gent., & w. *Eliz.*, def. The manor of Hersteds *alias* Hersted Hall & 10 mess., 4 tofts, 10 gdns., 10 orchards, 300 a. ar., 100 a. mw., 200 a. pa., 80 a. wd. & £7 rt. & a moiety of 1 mess., 3 tofts, 1 gdn., 1 orchard, 100

a. ar., 40 a. mw., 60 a. pa., 10 a. wd. & 10 a. moor in Fynchingfeld, Byrdbrooke, Bumpsted, Hempsted, Great Eyston, Little Eyston, Thaxsted & Tyltey. Def. quitclaimed to pl. & the heirs of Tho. £200.

33. Trin. & Mich. Robt. Aston, pl. *Pet.* Wentworthe, esq., & w. Eliz., def. The manor of Westhall & 20 mess., 20 gdns., 300 a. ar., 40 a. mw., 100 a. pa., 10 a. wd. & 20 a. furze & heath in Northe Shoberye *alias* Little Shoberye, Southe Shoberye, Moche Wakeryng, Hadley, Rayley & Thundersleighe. 640 mks.

34. Jn. Warren, pl. Robt. Upcher, def. 6 a. ar. & 6 a. pa. in Bures at the Mount, which Eliz. Upcher, wid., holds for life. Pl. & his heirs to hold the reversion of the chief lords. £40.

35. Trin. & Mich. Arthur Chapleyn, pl. *Jn.* Constable & w. Isabel, def. 1 mess., 1 gdn., 20 a. ar., 2 a. mw. & 5 a. pa. in Radwynter. £40.

36. Robt. Ryche, kt., lord Ryche, pl. Jas Clarke, gent., & w. *Mary*, def. The manor of Gubbyns *alias* Gubions & 6 mess., 3 barns, 6 gdns., 100 a. ar., 10 a. mw., 60 a. pa., 50 a. wd. & 40s. rt. in Great Leighes, Little Leighes, Felsted, Fayrested & Blacknotley. 400 mks.

37. Wm. Sorrell, pl. *Anth.* Maxey, esq., & w. Dorothy, def. 2 mess., 2 gdns., 2 orchards, 80 a. ar., 1 a. mw., 16 a. pa. & 4 a. wd. in Stebbing & Great Salyng *alias* Old Salyng. £140.

38. Geo. Bull, pl. Jn. Archer, def. 2 mess., 2 gdns., 8 a. ar., 3 a. mw. & 2 a. wd. in Great Peringdon *alias* Perndon, Harlowe & Latton *alias* Latten. £80.

39. Wm. Watson, gent., pl. Tho. Myldemay, kt., def. 1 mess., 1 cott., 7 tofts, 3 barns, 2 gdns., 1 orchard, 1 a. ar. & 2 a. mw. in Moulsham & Chelmesford. £80.

40. Tho. Cooke, pl. *Wm.* Parker & w. Joan & Tho. Rawlynson & w. Joan, def. 1 mess., 1 gdn., 1 orchard, 3 a. ar., 2 a. mw. & 2 a. pa. in Great Chissull & Little Chissull. £40.

41. Tho. Bekingham, pl. *Jn.* Fynkell & w. Margt. & Wm. Carter & w. Agnes, def. A moiety of 2 mess., 3 tofts, 3 cotts., 2 curtilages, 4 gdns., 3 orchards, 40 a. ar., 10 a. mw., 20 a. pa. & 5 a. wd. in Great Totham, Little Tctham, Goldanger & Tolleshunt Major. £40.

42. Jn. Lommeys, pl. *Rd.* Stapleton & w. Joan, def. 1 mess., 1 cott., 1 gdn. & 1 rood of land in Branktre. £40.

43. Tho. Sparowe, pl. Rd. Horne & w. *Eleanor*, def. 1 mess. & 1 gdn. in Styesteid. £40.

44. Trin. & Mich. Jn. Dowsett, pl. *Jn.* Warde & w. Agnes, def. 1 mess., 1 gdn., 3 a. ar. & 3 a. pa. in Halingberye Bowcher *alias* Little Halingberye. £40.

45. Wm. Tendering pl. Wm. Bretten & w. *Joan*, def. 15 a. ar. called 'Old Tabors' in Boreham. And for this pl. gtd. the same to def. to hold of the chief lords for the life of Joan.

46. Geo. Varnham, pl. *Walter* Graygose & w. Kath., def. 1 mess., 4 a. ar., 1 a. mw. & 6 a. pa. in Eppinge. £40.

47. Tho. Tyll, pl. Jn. Gregory & w. *Joan*, def. A moiety of 1 mess. & 1 gdn. in Coggeshall. £40.

48. Trin. & Mich. Jn. Coxall & Robt. Swattock, pl. *Wm.* Waldegrave, esq., & w. Eliz., def. 1 mess., 2 tofts, 1 gdn., 62 a. ar., 18 a. mw., 39 a. pa., 5 a. wd. & 19 a. alder in Stansted & Halsted. Def. quitclaimed to pl. & the heirs of Jn. £40.

49. Jn. Rogers, pl. Geo. Bawde, gent., def. 22 a. pa. in Curryngham. £40.

50. Jn. Scofylde, pl. Jn. Mone & *Gilbert* Mone, def. 1 mess., 1 gdn., 10 a. ar., 4½ a. wd. & 6d. rt. in Ardeley. £40.

51. Hy. Archer, pl. Edw. Archer, def. 1 mess., 1 orchard & 3½ a. pa. in Theydon Garnon. £40.

(52) (Robt. Poole, pl. *Nich.* Fanne & w. Mary, def. 1 mess., 1 toft, 10 a. ar. & 4 a. pa. in Thaxsted. £80.)
(*Taken from the Note, the Foot being missing.*)

FEET OF FINES FOR ESSEX

DIVERS COUNTIES

CP25(2)/259   MICHAELMAS, 12–13 ELIZABETH

10. Robt. Hogeson & w. Eliz., pl. *Rd*. Barnes & w. Mary, def. 1 mess., 1 barn, 1 dove-cote, 2 gdns., 30 a. ar., 6 a. mw., 20 a. pa., 2 a. wd. & 4 a. ar. covered with water in Stondon, co. Essex; & prop. in Surr. Def. quitclaimed to pl. & the heirs of Robt. £120. — Essex. Surr.

14. Wm. Sands, gent., & Tho. Maynard, pl. Geo. Cotton, esq., def. The manor of Hempstede & 20 mess., 20 cotts., 500 a. ar., 200 a. mw., 600 a. pa., 200 a. wd. & £10 rt. in Hempsted, co. Essex; & prop. in Suff. Def. quitclaimed to pl. & the heirs of Wm. £740. — Essex. Suff.

CP25(2)/128/1643   HILARY, 13 ELIZABETH   1571

1. Tho. Woode, pl. Jn. Ryvett, def. 1 mess., 1 toft, 1 gdn., 100 a. ar., 20 a. mw., 40 a. pa., 3 a. wd. & 6s. 8d. rt. in Moose, Great Okeley & Beamond. £100.

2. Lau. Chisshull, gent., pl. Jn. Amory, def. 1 mess., 1 gdn., & 1 a. ar. in Great Berdefeld & Little Berdefeld. £20.

3. Wm. Lucas, pl. *Jn*. Drywood & w. Anne, def. 1 mess. & 1 toft in Brentwood. £40.

4. Mich. & Hil. W. Auger, pl. *Rd*. Busbye & w. Kath., def. 1 mess., 1 cott. & 1 gdn. in Maningtre. £40.

5. Jn. Buttolff, pl. *Giles* Chisshull, esq., & w. Alice, def. 1 mess., 50 a. ar., 8 a. mw., 20 a. pa. & 3 a. wd. in Great Berdefeld & Little Berdefeld. £120.

6. Tho. Hurrell, pl. *Rd*. Hardynge, gent., & w. Joan, def. 1 mess., 1 gdn., 4 a. ar., 2 a. mw. & 6 a. pa. in Henyngham Syble. £40.

7. Jn. Motte, pl. Jn. Saunder & w. *Agnes*, dau. & heir of Robt. Haynes, def. 1 mess., 2 cotts., 2 tofts, & 1 gdn. in Branktre. £80.

8. Jn. Andrewe & Tho. Pygrom, pl. *Robt*. Alleyn & w. Beatrice & *Wm*. Adam & w. Agnes, def. 2 mess., 2 cotts. & 2 gdns. in Branktre. Def. quitclaimed to the heirs of Jn. £40.

9. Clement Sysley, esq., pl. *Jas*. Altham, esq., & w. Mary, def. 2 mess., 3 cotts., 3 gdns., 2 orchards, 40 a. ar., 20 a. mw., 60 a. pa. & 12 a. wd. in Barkynge & Dagnam & common of pa. in the forest of Waltham in Barkinge & Dagnam. £60.

10. Wm. White, pl. Tho. Trapps, def. 1 mess., 1 gdn., 3 a. ar., 3 a. mw. & 6 a. pa. in Spryngeffeld. 100 mks.

11. Robt. Hatcheman, pl. Wm. Standishe & w. Eliz., def. A moiety of 1 mess., 1 gdn., 14 a. ar. & 2 a. mw. in Gyngmergarett. £40.

12. Jn. Ponder, pl. *Robt*. Alleyn & w. Beatrice & *Wm*. Adam & w. Agnes, def. 2 mess., 1 cott. & 2 gdns. in Branktre. £40.

13. Rd. Spryngeffeld, pl. *Jn*. Burton sen. & w. Margt. & Jn. Burton jun., def. 6 a. ar. in Buttesberye. £40.

14. Wm. Gowge, pl. *Hy*. Billingesley & w. Eliz., def. 6½ a. ar. in Westham. £40.

15. Trin. & Hil. Anth. Bysshoppe, gent., pl. Wm. Taylor & w. *Eliz*., def. The manor of Abelswyke & 1 mess., 1 gdn., 1 orchard, 40 a. ar., 40 a. mw., 60 a. pa., 40 a. moor, 40 a. wd. & 6s. 4d. rt. in Ardeley. £120.

16. Mich. & Hil. Wm. Fytche, esq., pl. Francis Mannock, esq., def. 1 mess., 1 gdn., 40 a. ar., 6 a. mw., 20 a. pa., 3 a. wd. & 20s. rt. in Lyndesell, the rectory of Lyndesell & tithes of all grain, sheaves & hay & another portion of tithes of Lyndesell, & the advowson of the vicarage of the church of Lyndesell. Def. quitclaimed to pl. & his heirs, with warranty against the heirs of the bodies of def. & Mary his late w. £200.

17. Mich. & Hil. Wm. Smalwood & Jn. Raynolds, pl. Robt. Eton, gent., & w. Joan, def. 2 mess., 2 gdns., 2 orchards, 10 a. ar. & 2 a. mw. in Chelmesford & Spryngfilde. Def. quitclaimed to pl. & the heirs of Wm. And for this pl. gtd. the same to def. & the heirs of Robt., to hold of the chief lords.

156

18. Tho. Fanshawe, gent., pl. Geo. Tyrrell, esq., & w. Joan & Robt. Tyrrell, their son & heir apt., def. The manor of Fobbynge & 100 mess., 100 gdns., 100 a. ar., 100 a. mw., 100 a. pa., 200 a. salt marsh & £10 rt. in Fobynge, Stanford le Hope, Estetylbery, West-etylbery, Orsed, Leynden, Langdon, Bulvan, Nevyndon, Buttysbery, Downeham, Wyck-ford, Runwell, Shenfeld, Byllerica, Downton & Muckynge. Def. quitclaimed whatever they had for their lives to pl. 800 mks.

19. Mich. & Hil. Jn. Coo, pl. Jn. Swayne *alias* Cowper, def. 1 mess., 1 toft, 1 gdn., 1 orchard & 2 a. pa. in Tylbury by Clere. £20.

20. Jn. Dister, gent., pl. *Tho.* Sackvyle, kt., lord Buckherst, & w. Cecily, def. The manors of Barholt Sackvyle & Bures at the Mount *alias* Mount Bures & 36 mess., 36 cotts., 36 tofts, 3 mills, 3 dovecotes, 36 gdns., 46 orchards, 800 a. ar., 120 a. mw., 800 a. pa., 600 a. wd., 1,000 a. furze & heath & 40s. rt. in Barholt Sackvyle, Westbarholt, Bures at the Mount *alias* Mountt Bures & Fordeham, & the advowsons of the churches of Bures at the Mount *alias* Mount Bures & Barholt Sackvyle *alias* West Barholt. £1,880.

21. Jn. Bonar & w. Joan, pl. Wm. Spurgyn & w. *Margt.*, def. 4 a. wd. in Estwood. Def. quitclaimed to pl. & the heirs of Joan. £40.

22. Fardinand Darys, esq., pl. Roland Master, gent., & w. Anne, def. A yearly rt. of £16 13s. 4d. from 300 a. pa. called 'Walden Parke' in Walden, payable at Christmas & Midsummer, which def. hold for the life of Anne. Pl. to hold for the life of Anne, with power of distraint. 500 mks.

23. Trin. & Hil. Jn. Darcy, kt., lord Darcy of Chyche, pl. Hy. Wyndham, esq., def. The manor of Cannehall *alias* Canons Hall & 12 mess., 2 tofts, 12 gdns., 200 a. ar., 40 a. mw., 100 a. pa., 30 a. wd., 20 a. marsh & 5s. rt. in Great Clacton, Little Clacton & Little Holland, the rectories of Great Clacton, Little Clacton & Little Holland & all tithes of sheaves of grain, hay, wool, lambs, calves & sucklings (*lacticiniorum*) & other small tithes belonging to the rectories in Great Clacton, Little Clacton & Little Holland, & a pension of 13s. 4d. from the church & rectory of Great Clacton. £760.

24. Trin. & Hil. Griffin Willams, pl. *Tho.* Beckyngham, esq., & w. Mary & Jn. Kynge, def. 1 mess., 1 gdn., 1 orchard, 60 a. ar., 6 a. mw., 40 a. pa., 10 a. moor & 100 a. marsh in Goldanger, Tolshunt Maior & Tolshunt Darcy. And for this pl. gtd. the same to Jn. to hold from Michaelmas last for 500 years, rendering 20s. yearly to pl. & his heirs at the Annunciation & Michaelmas, with power of distraint; & the reversion to Tho. & his heirs, to hold of the chief lords.

CP25(2)/259   DIVERS COUNTIES

4. Gilbert Gerrard, esq., attorney general of the Q, Tho. Bromley, esq., solicitor general of the Q, Tho. Wilbram, esq., recorder of the city of London, & Edm. Anderson of the Inner Temple within the bars of the city of London, esq., pl. Francis, earl of Bed-ford, & w. Bridget, & Edw., earl of Rutland, def. The manor of Walthamstow Tony *alias* Walcamstowe Tony & 100 mess., 1 mill, 1,500 a. ar., 500 a. mw., 2,000 a. pa., 200 a. wd. & £20 rt. in Walthamstow & Walcamstowe Tony, co. Essex: & prop. in Leics. Def. quit-claimed to pl. & the heirs of Gilbert, with warranty by the earl of Bedford & countess for her life and by the earl of Rutland for himself & his heirs. 1,840 mks. — Essex, Leicester.

CP25(2)/128/1644   EASTER, 13 ELIZABETH   1571

1. Jn. Prentyce sen., pl. Geo. Hassett *alias* Harssett & w. *Alice*, def. 7 a. ar. in Colne Engayne. £20.

2. Robt. Sydley, gent., pl. Martin Sydley, gent., def. 1 mess., 1 barn, 2 gdns., 2 or-chards, 20 a. ar., 6 a. mw., 20 a. pa. & 120 a. salt marsh in Thundersley, Southbemflyte, Hadlowe & the island of Canveye. 130 mks.

3. Robt. Payne & Wm. Payne, pl. Jn. Payne & w. *Eliz.*, def. 6 mess., 6 cotts., 6 gdns., 6 orchards, 60 a. ar., 20 a. mw., 20 a. pa. & 6 a. wd. in Dagenham. Def. quitclaimed to pl. & the heirs of Robt. 200 mks.

4. Jn. Broke, pl. *Jn.* Lewgar & w. Eliz., def. 12 a. ar. & 1 a mw. in Barlyng & Great Wakeryng. £40.

5. Wm. Takeley, pl. *Tho*. Norres & w. Anne, Wm. Wytham & w. Joan, def. 4 a. ar., in Buttesbury, £40.

6. Rd. Stanes & Jn. Maynerd, pl. Hy. Maynerd sen., def. 2 mess., 1 barn, 2 gdns., 30 a. ar., 15 a. mw., 10 a. pa. & 2 a. wd. in Theidon Garnon, Theidon Boyes & Great Paringdon. Def. quitclaimed to pl. & the heirs of Rd. £140.

7. Rok Grene, esq., pl. Giles Chissell, esq., def. 3 a. pa. & 60s. rt. in Little Sampford, Great Sampford & Fynchingfeld, & the advowson of the church of Little Sampford. £60.

8. Jn. Abell, esq., & Jn. Sawen, gent., pl. Hy. Wentworth, gent., def. The manor of Tenderinge Hall & 10 mess., 10 gdns., 10 orchards, 200 a. ar., 100 a. mw., 200 a. pa., 30 a. wd. & 40s. rt. in Tenderinge, & the advowson of the church of Tenderinge. Def. quitclaimed to pl. & the heirs of Jn. Abell. 100 mks.

9. Alex. Raye, gent., & w. Eliz., pl. Jn. Revell & w. *Joan*, def. 2 a. ar., 2 a. pa. & 1 a. wd. in Chypping Walden, Broke Walden & Debden. Def. quitclaimed to pl. & the heirs of Alex. £20.

10. Jn. Drewry & Geo. Agar, gentlemen, pl. Hy. Wentworth, gent., & w. *Jane*, def. A third of the manors of Little Holland & Bretts Hall & a third part of 30 mess., 30 gdns., 30 orchards, 500 a. ar., 200 a. mw., 400 a. pa., 300 a. wd., 500 a. fresh marsh, 500 a. furze & heath & £10 rt. in Little Holland, Great Holland, Bretts Hall, Tenderinge, Little Clofton, Great Clofton, Thorpe, Bentley & Wely. Def. quitclaimed to pl. & the heirs of Jn. £200.

11. Tho. Bewley, clk., & Tho. Mulcaster, gent., pl. Rd. Crymbill, def. 4 mess., 2 tofts, 4 gdns., 30 a. ar., 2 a. mw., 10 a. pa., 1 a. wd. & 1d. rt. in Rocheford & Hackwell. Def. quitclaim to pl. & the heirs of Tho. Bewley. £100.

12. Wm. Humfrey, pl. *Jn*. Busshe & Tho. Busshe, def. 1 mess., 1 gdn., 1 orchard, 40 a. ar., 10 a. mw., 10 a. pa., 3 a. wd. & 20 a. salt marsh in Fange *alias* Vange & Bassilden *alias* Barssilden. £160.

13. Jn. Woode, pl. *Ralph* Smythe & w. Eva, def. 1 mess., 1 gdn., 1 orchard & 2 a. mw. in Little Rayne. £40.

14. Tho. Farrour *alias* Wallenger & Rd. Ponde, pl. Jn. Armour & w. *Isabel*, def. 1 mess., 1 gdn., 5 a. ar. & 2 a. mw. in Great Waltham. Def. quitclaimed to pl. & the heirs of Tho. £40.

15. Wm. Brocke, pl. *Jn*. Garrerd & w. Joan, def. 1 mess., 1 gdn., 1 orchard, 60 a. ar., 7 a. mw., 20 a. pa. & 12d. rt. called 'Hodgekyns' in Willingale Doo & Wyllyngale Spayn. £160.

16. Wm. Lytleberye, gent., pl. *Wm*. Waldegrave, esq., & w. Eliz., def. The manor of Netherhall & 2 mess., 2 gdns., 200 a. ar., 30 a. mw., 200 a. pa., 80 a. wd., 100 a. furze & heath & 90 a. moor in Bradfeld, Manyngtre & Wrabnes. £760.

17. Hil. & Eas. Rd. Stoneley, esq., pl. *Wm*. Armestrong *alias* Armested & w. Margt., def. 1 mess. & 40 a. ar. in Barkyng & Daggenham. £200.

18. Tho. Wylson, pl. Wm. Harrys, esq., & w. *Joan*, def. 1 mess., 1 toft, 1 orchard, 40 a. ar., 20 a. mw., 40 as pa. & 5 a. wd. in Purley, Norton & Stowe. £80.

19. Wm. Adams, pl. Ralph Wrighte & w. *Alice*, def. 1 mess. & 1 gdn. in Branktrey. £40.

20. Robts Aylett, pl. Robt. Ryche, kt., lord Ryche, def. 30 a. ar., 16 a. mw. & 6 a. pa. in Willingale Doo & Shellow Bowells. £40.

21. Jn. Scott. gent., & w. Anne, pl. Jn. Wentworth, esq., def. 8 a. ar. in Cressall. Def. quitclaimed to pl. & the heirs of Anne. £40.

22. Wm. Sammes, pl. *Tho*. Flingant & w. Emma, def. 1 mess., 1 gdn., 3 a. ar., 1 a. mw. & 1 a. pa. in Aldham. £40.

23. Lewis Bell, pl. Tho. Cowle sen. & *Tho*. Cowle jun., his son & heir apt., def. 5 a. pa. in Bumpsted Hellyon. £20.

24. Jn. Ive *alias* Sparhawke, pl. *Hy*. Maynard & w. Dorothy, def. 4 a. ar. in Shalforde. £40.

25. Phil. Tyrrell, gent., pl. Jn. Felton, gent., def. 20 a. ar. in Pentlow. £80.

26. Tho. Franck, pl. Wimund Cary, esq., def. 3 mess., 3 gdns., 140 a. ar., 40 a. mw., 80 a. pa. & 6 a. wd. in Takeley, Staunsted Mountfychett & Elnesham *alias* Elsnam. Def. quitclaimed to pl. & his heirs, with warranty against Edw. Cary & his heirs. £160.

27. Rd. Dun & w. Joan, pl. *Jn*. Geste & w. Dorothy & Jn. Pratte, def. 1 mess. in Chelmesford. Def. quitclaimed to pl. & the heirs of Rd. £40.

28. Wm. Leke & Jn. Brattoffe, pl. Robt. Atkynson, def. 1 mess., 1 gdn., 1 orchard, 20 a. ar., 10 a. mw., 18 a. pa. & 12 a. wd. in Albrugh Hatche & Barkynge. Def. quitclaimed to pl. & the heirs of Wm. £140.

29. Jn. Ive *alias* Sparhauke, pl. *Jn*. Skynner sen. & Jn. Skynner jun., def. 2 mess., 2 cotts., 2 tofts, 1 barn, 3 gdns., 16 a. ar., 4 a. pa., 1 a. wd. & 2 a. alder in Shalforde. 100 mks.

30. Wm. Laste & Alex. Larkyn, pl. Tho. Callys & w. *Eliz*. & Jn. Beale, def. 2 a. ar. & 10 a. pa. in Shalforde. Def. quitclaimed to pl. & the heirs of Wm. £40.

31. Wm. Franckland, esq., & Rd. Gourney, pl. *Tho*. Wentworthe, kt., lord Wentworthe, & w. Anne, def. The manor of Little Stambridge & 10 mess., 3 barns, 1 dovecote, 10 gdns., 400 a. ar., 300 a. mw., 400 a. pa., 100 a. wd., 60 a. fresh marsh, 60 a. salt marsh, 500 a. furze & heath & 100s. rt. in Little Stambridge, Great Stambridge, Canewdon, Rocheford, Hawkewell & Hockley. Def. quitclaimed to pl. & the heirs of Wm. £600.

32. Charles Bonham, gent., & w. Jane, pl. Anth. Maxey, esq., & w. *Dorothy*, def. The manor of Chessull *alias* Chessell & 6 mess., 600 a. ar., 30 a. mw., 100 a. pa., 100 a. wd. & £3 rt. in Over Chessull, Nether Chessull, Heydon & Shepon. Def. quitclaimed to pl. & the heirs of Charles. 830 mks.

33. Tho. Emery, pl. *Wm*. Aylett & w. Margt., def. A moiety of 160 a. fresh marsh & 20 a. salt marsh called 'Alfletnes' *alias* 'Alfletnasse' *alias* 'Alfordenasse marshe' & 2 weirs within the island of Wallets in the parishes of Estwoode & Prykelwell *alias* Prytwell. £200.

34. Tho. Shonke, pl. Humphrey Frythe & w. *Joan*, def. 1 mess., 1 gdn., 1 orchard & 3 a. ar. in Northe Okyndon. £40.

35. Jn. Holmested, pl. *Tho*. Holmested & w. Joan, def. A third part of 30 a. ar. & 20s. rt. in Gyng at Stone *alias* Ingerstone *alias* Fryernynge. £40.

36. Ja. Harvye, pl. *Clement* Sysley, esq., & w. Anne, def. 2 mess., 3 cotts., 3 gdns., 2 orchards, 40 a. ar., 20 a. mw., 60 a. pa. & 12 a. wd. in Barkynge & Dagnam, & common of pa. in the forest of Waltham. £40.

37. Tho. Cockerell, pl. Anth. Maxey, esq., & w. *Dorothy*, def. 4 a. pa. in Bradwell by Cogeshall. £40.

38. Ralph Wyseman, gent., pl. *Robt*. Woode, gent., & w. Joan, def. 1 mess., 2 barns, 1 dovecote, 1 gdn., 1 orchard, 100 a. ar., 10 a. mw., 50 a. pa. & 2 a. wd. in Bromefield & Little Waltham. £80.

39. Robt. Jegons, pl. *Charles* Bonham, gent., & w. Jane, Anth. Maxey, esq., & w. Jane, Anth. Maxey, esq., & w. Dorothy, def. 1 mess., 1 gdn., 1 orchard, 20 a. ar., 6 a. mw. & 6 a. pa. in Coxall *alias* Cogeshall. £100.

40. Wm. Strachie, pl. *Edm*. Pounsibie & w. Eliz., def. 2 mess. in Walden. £20.

41. Tho. Gale & Wm. Gale, pl. *Wm*. Waldegrave, esq., & w. Eliz., def. 50 a. ar., 70 a. pa. 10 a. wd. & 30s. rt. in Ramsey & Wrabnes. Def. quitclaimed to pl. & the heirs of Tho. 200 mks.

42. Jn. Rowe, pl. *Jn*. Garrerd & w. Joan, def. 1 mess., 1 gdn., 1 orchard, 40 a. ar., 6 a. mw., 40 a. pa. & 3 a. wd. in Owltynge, Hatfeld Peverell, Woodham Water & Mawlden. £140.

43. Mich. & Eas. Jn. Champneys & Hy. Welde, pl. Hy. Baxster & w. *Margt*., def. 1 mess., 1 gdn., 1 orchard & 4 a. mw. in Dagenham. Def. quitclaimed to pl. & the heirs of Jn. £30.

44. Jn. Lagden, pl. *Wm*. Raynolde sen., 'draper', & w. Alice, & *Jn*. Goodday sen. & w. Mary, def. 1 mess., 1 cott., 1 barn, 1 dovecote, 2 gdns., 80 a. ar., 12 a. mw., 40 a. pa., 10 a. wd. & 6d. rt. in Great Leighes, Terlyng, Hatfelde Peverell, Boreham & Little Badowe. £260.

45. Wm. Loveday, pl. *Tho*. Glascock & Jn. Glascock jun., his son, def. 1 mess. called 'Hubbardes', 1 cott., 1 barn, 1 gdn., 1 orchard, 12 a. ar., 2 a. mw. & 6 a. pa. in Chicknall Smelye & Great Waltham. And for this pl. gtd. the same to Tho. to hold of the chief lords for life, with remainder to Jn. & his heirs.

46. Hil. & Eas. Jn. Popham & Geo. Wynter, esquires, pl. *Wm*. Fabyan, esq., & w. Anne, def. The manor of Pygotts & 2 mess., 1 dovecote, 2 gdns., 400 a. ar., 30 a. mw., 300 a. pa., 10 a. wd. & 20s. rt. in Pateswycke, Stysted, Feryng & Cogeshall. Def. quitclaimed to pl. & the heirs of Jn. £300.

47. Hy. Medley & Tho. Bedle, esquires, & Edw. Elyott, gent., pl. Vincent Harrys, Arthur Harrys & *Edw*. Harrys, esquires, def. The manor of Cage & 20 mess., 20 cotts., 1,000 a. ar., 300 a. mw., 700 a. pa., 200 a. wd., 300 a. marsh & £13 rt. in Southmynster. Def. quitclaimed to pl. & the heirs of Hy. £400.

48. Tho. Fanshawe, esq., & w. Mary, pl. *Arthur* Breame, esq., & w. Thomasina, def. The manor of Westbury & 1 mess., 2 tofts, 1 dovecote, 600 a. ar., 200 a. mw., 300 a. pa., 10 a. wd., 200 a. furze & heath, 100 a. marsh, £10 rt. in tithes of sheaves of grain & hay in Barkinge. Def. quitclaimed to pl. & the heirs of Tho. £400.

49. Jn. Pygott, gent., & Jn. Ellys, pl. *Robt*. Ryche, kt., lord Ryche, & w. Eliz., & Wm. Lowen *alias* Lewen, gent., def. The manor of Imber & 15 mess., 10 barns, 1 dovecote, 15 gdns., 100 a. ar., 20 a. mw., 80 a. pa. & £8 rt. in Goodester & Norton Mawndevile. Def. quitclaimed to pl. & the heirs of Jn. Pygott. And for this pl. gtd. the same to Wm. to hold from Michaelmas last for 40 years, rendering £12 yearly at the Annunciation & Michaelmas, with power of distraint; & the reversion to def. & the heirs of Robt., to hold of the chief lords.

50. Rd. Lee & Wm. Loveday, pl. Wm. Clopton, esq., def. The site of the manor of Carbonells & 1 mess., 1 dovecote, 1 gdn., 1 orchard, 80 a. ar., 10 a. mw. & 30 a. pa. in Foxherth. Def. quitclaimed to pl. & the heirs of Rd. And for this pl. gtd. the same to def. for one week, with remainder to Wm. Lowther to hold for 120 years, rendering £6 6s. 8d. yearly at the Annunciation & Michaelmas, with power of distraint; & the reversion to def. & his heirs, to hold of the chief lords.

CP25(2)/128/1645   TRINITY, 13 ELIZABETH   1571

1. Wm. Raine & Miles Lakyn, pl. *Rd*. Valentyne & Jn. Clyff, def. 1 mess., 1 gdn., 35 a. ar., 6 a. mw., 16 a. pa. & 5 a. wd. in Ynghospitall *alias* Freyrn Inge. Def. quitclaimed to pl. & the heirs of Wm. £120.

2. Eas. & Trin. Jn. Pavyet, pl. *Tho*. Warde & w. Kath., def. 1 mess., 1 barn & 1 gdn. in Bocking. £40.

3. Eas. & Trin. Tho. Browne, pl. Robt. Brooke & w. Eliz., def. 2 mess., 2 gdns., 20 a. ar. & 2 a. pa. in Crishall. £20.

4. Eas. & Trin. Robt. Aylett, pl. Rd. Sampford, def. 1 mess., 1 gdn., 2 orchards, 9 a. ar., 2 a. mw., 1 a. pa. & ½ a. wd. in Shellow Bowells. £40.

5. Robt. Woode, pl. *Jn*. Clerke & w. Prisca, def. 2 mess., 2 tofts, 2 gdns., 40 a. ar., 10 a. mw. & 20 a. pa. in Dansey *alias* Dengeye. £80.

6. Tho. Kightlay, gent., pl. *Jn*. Ive sen. & Jn. Ive jun. & w. Anne, def. 1 mess., 1 barn, 10 a. ar. & 15 a. marsh in Little Thorock & Greys Thorock. 160 mks.

7. Tho. Nevyll, pl. Hy. Canon & w. *Eliz*., def. 1 gdn., 3 a. ar. & 4 a. pa. in Little Leighes. 40 mks.

8. Robt. Holden & Jn. Ive, pl. Hy. Sowthwell, gent., def. 1 mess., 1 gdn., 1 orchard, 23 a. ar., 8 a. mw. & 5 a. marsh in Rayneham, which Humphrey Nevell holds for life. Pl. & the heirs of Jn. to hold the reversion of the chief lords. £40.

9. Wm. Edmonds, gent., pl. *Robt*. Shonke & w. Joan, def. 1 mess., 1 gdn., 10 a. ar., 20 a. mw. & 10 a. pa. in Navestock. £120.

10. Robt. Lawson *alias* Edmonds & Wm. Lawson *alias* Edmonds, pl. Robt. Ryche, kt., lord Ryche, def. 1 mess., 1 gdn., 12 a. ar. & 3 a. wd. in Estwoode. Def. quitclaimed to pl. & the heirs of Wm. £40.

11. Mich. & Trin. Jn. Marshall, pl. *Wm*. Bawden *alias* Bawdwyn & w. Joan, def. 1 mess., 1 barn, 1 gdn. & 1 orchard in Orsette. £40.

12. Eas. & Trin. Hy. Graye, esq., & w. Anne, pl. *Rd*. Core, gent., & w. Margery, def. 1 mess., 3 gdns., 100 a. ar., 40 a. mw., 100 a. pa., 20 a. wd., 40 a. furze & heath & 10s. rt. in Hatfyeld Brodooke *alias* Hatfyeld Regis. Def. quitclaimed to pl. & the heirs of Hy. £240.

13. Edw. Stallyn, pl. Bart. Hockett, def. 6 a. ar. & 3 a. pa. in Lyston & Foxyearde *alias* Foxherth. £40.

14. Jn. Milborne, pl. *Jn*. Kennett & w. Alice, def. 14 a. ar. in Highe Ester. £40.

15. Tho. Pope, citizen & merchant tailor of London, pl. Oswald Fitche, gent., def. 1 mess., 1 dovecote, 1 gdn., 1 orchard, 40 a. ar., 20 a. mw., 40 a. pa., 3 a. wd. & common of pa. for all beasts in Coggeshall. 160 mks.

16. Jn. Rowe, pl. Wm. Maynolds, gent., & w. Alice, & *Jn*. Raynolds, gent., & w. Mary, def. 1 mess., 1 gdn., 1 orchard, 40 a. ar., 10 a. mw., 30 a. pa. & 6 a. wd. in Boreham, Little Waltham, Little Badowe & Hatefilde Peverell. £40.

17. Jn. Ive, pl. Hy. Sowthwell, gent., def. 1 mess., 1 gdn., 1 orchard, 40 a. ar., 14 a. mw. & 4 a. marsh in Wennyngton, which Wm. Roydenhurst holds for life. Pl. & his heirs to hold the reversion of the chief lords. £100.

18. Jn. Gratay, pl. Roger Bancks & w. Agnes, & Jn. Sturton & w. Abra, def. 1 mess., 1 barn & 1 gdn. in Thacksted. £40.

19. Eas. & Trin. Humphrey Tabor, pl. Emma Gytton, wid., def. 10 a. ar., 3 a. mw., 8 a. pa. & 4 a. wd. & a fourth part of 4 tofts, 20 a. ar., 8 a. mw., 20 a. pa. & 6 a. wd. in Margaretyng *alias* Gyngemargaret. £40.

20. Jn. Hunwycke, pl. *Wm*. Welbeck & w. Susan, def. 2 mess., 2 gdns, 2 orchards, 40 a. ar., 40 a. mw., 160 a. pa., 6 a. wd. & 100 a. marsh in Bradwell by the Sea, Tillyngham, Seynt Lawrence & Seynt Lawrence & Seynt Peters in Bradwell. £240.

21. Eas. & Trin. Jn. Southcot, one of the justices to hold pleas before the Q, & w. Eliz., pl. Geo. Scott, gent., def. The manor of Rookehaule & 8 mess., 3 cotts., 8 gdns., 200 a. ar., 40 a. mw., 100 a. pa., 20 a. wd. & 10s. rt. & a moiety of 1 mess. called 'Fowches' in Great Totteham & Little Totteham. Def. quitclaimed to pl. & the heirs of Jn. £140.

22. Jn. Searle, pl. Edw. Archar, def. 2 mess., 2 cotts., 2 gdns., 2 orchards, 40 a. ar., 30 a. mw. & 50 a. pa. in North Weald Bassett & Thaydon Garnon. £160.

23. Hy. Jarrarde & Wm. Wilson, pl. Tho. Horne & w. *Joan*, def. 6 a. ar., 2 a. mw. & 4 a. pa. in Dagnam. £40.

24. Wm. Latham & w. Anne, pl. Geo. Wyseman, def. The manor of Upmynster in Upmynster. Def. quitclaimed to pl. & the heirs of Wm. And for this pl. gtd. the manor, except 50 a. pa. called 'Le crouchefeld', 60 a. pa. called 'Eche crouchefeld', wds. & underwoods, courts & views of frank-pledge, fines, amercements, profits of courts, escheats, heriots, strays, reliefs & goods waived, to def. & his assigns to hold from Michaelmas, 1576, for 61 years, rendering £40 yearly at the Annunciation & Michaelmas, with power of distraint.

25. Eas. & Trin. Jn. Sidey, pl. *Tho*. Bendyshe, gent., & w. Eleanor, def. The manor of Woodehowse & 2 mess., 2 gdns., 60 a. ar., 10 a. mw., 60 a. pa., 20 a. wd., 200 a. furze & heath & 10s. rt. in Great Horkesleighe. And for this pl. gtd. to def. & the heirs of Tho. a yearly rt. of £8 from the same at the Annunciation & Michaelmas, with power of distraint, & a penalty of 5s. when it is a month in arrears.

26. Wm. Barlee & Tho. Burnell, gentlemen, pl. Nich. Stephens, gent., & w. *Agnes*, Edw. Bell & Rd. Hardinge, gentlemen, def. The manor of Hydehall & 10 mess., 20 tofts, 20 gdns., 10 orchards, 200 a. ar., 40 a. mw., 200 a. pa., 40 a. wd. & 100s. rt. in Rettendon, High Easter, Great Donmowe & Little Donmowe. Def. quitclaimed to pl. & the heirs of Wm. And for this pl. gtd. the manor & 2 mess., 2 gdns., 1 orchard, 100 a. ar., 40 a. mw., 140 a. pa. & £4 rt. in Rettendon, parcel of the same, to Edw. to hold from Michaelmas next for 13 years, rendering £14 13s. 4d. yearly at Michaelmas & the Annunciation, with power of distraint; & the residue & the reversion of the above to Nich. & Rd. & the heirs of Nich., to hold of the chief lords.

1. Wm. Stapler, pl. Hy. Blewit & w. *Joan*, def. A moiety of 1 mess. called 'Durants' *alias* 'Almans', 1 gdn., 1 orchard, 16 a. ar., 4 a. mw., 30 a. pa. & 2 a. wd. in Ging Margarett. £40.

2. Jn. Pokyns, clk., pl. *Nich*. Reynolde *alias* Chaundler & w. Eliz., def. 1 mess. & 3 a. ar. in Oresett. £20.

3. Geo. Howe, pl. Jn. Felton, gent., def. 1 water-mill, 2 gdns., 2 a. mw. & 1 a. pa. in Pentlowe. £140.

4. Geo. Fen, Tho. Fen & Clement Fen, pl. Jn. Felton, gent., def. 2 mess., 1 toft, 4 gdns., 12 a. ar., 2 a. mw., 4 a. pa., 1 a. wd. & 2 a. marsh in Pentlowe & Foxearth. Def. quitclaimed to pl. & the heirs of Geo. £40.

5. Ralph Sheldon, esq., & Wm. Walter, gent., pl. Tho. Throckmerton, esq., & w. *Margt*., def. The manor of Cockfeldes & 200 a. ar., 30 a. mw., 200 a. pa., 30 a. wd. & 10s. rt. in Fynchyngfelde. Def. quitclaimed to pl. & the heirs of Ralph. £120.

6. Reg. Meade, gent., pl. *Rd*. Cutts, esq., & w. Mary, def. A moiety of the manors of Mountnes & Dagworthes & a moiety of 8 mess., 400 a. ar., 7 a. mw., 50 a. pa., 50 a. wd. & 40s. rt. in Elmedon, Wenden Loofthes, Crishall, Strettall & Arcksden. £80.

7. Hy. Lyvynge, pl. Jn. Bonar & w. *Mary*, def. 1 mess. & 1 gdn. in Rayleygh. £40.

8. Jn. Freman & Robt. Freman, pl. *Jn*. Claydon & w. Margt., def. 2 a. ar., 3 a. 3½ roods mw. & 4 a. pa. in Asshedon. Def. quitclaimed to pl. & the heirs of Jn. £40.

9. Jn. Love sen., pl. Rd. Sherman & w. Alice & *Jn*. Bonar def. 3 mess., 3 gdns., 4 a. ar. & 1 a. wd. in Rayleigh & Thundersleigh. £80.

10. Robt. Lawson *alias* Edmonds, pl. *Tho*. Stonham & Eustace Bristowe, def. 1 mess., barn, 1 gdn., 6 a. ar. & 5 a. pa. in Great Wakeryng & Little Wakeryng. £40.

11. Nich. Umfrey. Rd. Skotte, Wm. Skotte & w. Agnes, pl. *Jn*. Gase & w. Joan, def. 14 a. ar. & 4 a. pa. in Thaxsted. Def. quitclaimed to pl. & the heirs of Nich. £40.

12. Trin. & Mich. Nich. Bacon, kt., lord keeper of the great seal of England, pl. *Tho*. Carowe & w. Mary, def. 1 mess. & 10 a. ar. in Dagenham. 80 mks.

13. Jn. Noke, son & heir apt. of Robt. Noke, pl. The same Robt. Noke, def. 3 mess., 1 dovecote, 3 gdns., 66 a. ar., 9 a. mw., 20 a. pa., 10 a. wd. & 12d. rt. in Great Halyngbury, Great Leighes & Black Notley. 200 mks.

14. Wm. Grave, pl. Jn. Welde sen. & w. *Joan*, dau. & heir of Joan Smythes, wid., def. 1 mess., 1 gdn. & 1 a. ar. in Buttesbery. £20.

15. Jn. Disley, gent., pl. *Walter* Morgan, gent., & w. Jane, def. 5 a. wd. called 'Holywell Grove' in Laightonston. £40.

16. Robt. Poole, pl. *Nich*. Fanne & w. Mary, def. 1 mess., 1 toft, 10 a. ar. & 4 a. pa. in Thaxstede. £80.

17. Jn. Meade, pl. Wm. Ferneley & w. *Bridget*, Jn. Ferneley & w. *Martha*, Hy. Walker & w. *Judith* & Robt. Blome & w. *Rebecca*, def. 1 mess., 160 a. ar., 10 a. mw., 20 a. pa. & 3 a. wd. in Claveringe. 130 mks.

18. Rd. Champyon, gent., pl. Jn. Shonk & w. *Alice*, def. 3 a. pa. in Horndon on the Hill. £40.

19. Jn. Olmested, pl. Robt. Marshall & w. *Anne*, def. 1 a. mw. in Fryeringe *alias* Ingerstone. £40.

20. Rd. Wyndell, pl. *Hy*. Sparowe & w. Helen, def. 2 mess., 2 gdns. & 1 a. pa. in Brockynge. £40.

21. Tho. Cropley, pl. *Jn*. Froste & w. Joan, def. 15 a. ar., 1 a. mw. & 16 a. pa. in Asheden. £80.

22. Tho. Rede, pl. Edw. Sulyard, esq., def. 20 a. ar., 5 a. mw., 6 a. pa. & 2 a. wd. in Highe Laver & Matchinge. £20.

23. Tho. Joce, pl. Edw. Harrys & w. *Anne*, def. A moiety of 1 mess., 1 gdn., 1 orchard, 3 a. mw. & 7 a. pa. in Ingrauf. £40.

24. Tho. Bussard, pl. *Wm*. Waldegrave, esq., & w. Eliz., def. The manor of Grovehowse & 1 mess., 1 dovecote, 2 gdns., 3 orchards, 100 a. ar., 10 a. mw., 80 a. pa., 10 a. wd. & 20s. rt. in Kyrkeby & Walton. £200.

25. Wm. Glascocke sen. & Wm. Glascoke jun., pl. *Edw*. Ellyott & w. Jane, def. The manor of Herons & 3 mess., 3 cotts., 3 dovecotes, 3 gdns., 3 orchards, 100 a. ar., 20 a. mw., 50 a. pa., 10 a. wd. & 40s. rt. in Highester, Goodester, Mashbury & Plesshey. Def. quitclaimed to pl. & the heirs of Wm. sen., with warranty against the heirs of Jas. Gedge, esq., £200.

26. Nich. Man. pl. *Tho*. Barnarde & w. Joan, def. 1 mess., 1 barn & 1 gdn. in Chelmesforde. £40.

27. Owin Waller, pl. Roger Tounsend, esq., def. The manor of Manuden *alias* Manewden *alias* Battaylls Hall *alias* Manuden Battells Hall & 20 mess., 20 tofts, 20 gdns., 420 a. ar., 100 a. mw., 278 a. pa., 100 a. wd., 100 a. furze & heath & £9 rt. in Manuden *alias* Manewden, Berden, Ugley *alias* Ougley & Farnham. £420.

28. Wm. Cornell & Jn. Okeman, pl. *Nich*. Ereswell, gent., & w. Joan, def. 6 a. pa. & 1 a. wd. in Walden. Def. quitclaimed to pl. & the heirs of Wm. £40.

29. Arthur Chaplyn & Mich. Petytt, pl. *Tho*. Strachye & w. Marcia, def. 1 mess., 1 gdn., 6 a. ar., 1 a. mw. & 8 a. pa. in Walden. Def. quitclaimed to pl. & the heirs of Arthur. £40.

30. Trin. & Mich. Wm. Kendall & w. Anne, pl. Wm. Crottenden, def. 1 mess. & 1 gdn. in Waltham Hollycrosse. Def. quitclaimed to pl. & the heirs of Wm. £40.

31. Wm. Jennen, pl. Edw. Sulyard, esq., def. 2 mess., 2 cotts., 4 gdns., 100 a. ar., 30 a. mw., 40 a. pa. & 15 a. wd. in Mawdelyn Laver, Highe Laver & Harlow. £108.

32. Tho. Meade, serjeant at law, pl. *Rd*. Cutts, esq., & w. Mary, def. A moiety of the manors of Wigpitts, Cocksolles & Rockelles & a moiety of 30 mess., 1 water-mill, 600 a. ar., 30 a. mw., 200 a. pa., 90 a. wd. & 100s. rt. in Arcksden, Elmedon, Great Wenden, Little Wenden, Wenden Loofthes, Newportt Ponde, Lytlebury & Walden. 400 mks.

33. Jn. Brett, pl. *Rd*. Welles & w. Anne & Jn. Welles, def. 1 toft, 30 a. ar., 10 a. mw., 20 a. pa. & 10 a. wd. in Tolleshunt Darcy. 130 mks.

34. Trin. & Mich. Hugh Gryffyth, esq., & Gilbert Langton, pl. Hy. Mordaunt, gent., def. The manor of Thunderley & 6 mess., 6 gdns., 6 orchards, 200 a. ar., 60 a. mw., 200 a. pa., 100 a. wd. & 10s. rt. in Thunderley & Wymbyshe. Def. quitclaimed to pl. & the heirs of Hugh. £400.

35. Jn. Cock. gent., pl. *Wm*. Frankland, esq., & Edm. Frankland, gent., his son & heir, def. The manor of Little Stambridge & 10 mess., 3 barns, 1 dovecote, 10 gdns, 400 a. ar., 300 a. mw., 400 a. pa., 100 a. wd., 60 a. fresh marsh, 60 a. salt marsh, 500 a. furze & heath & 100s. rt. in Little Stambridge, Great Stambridge, Canewdon, Rocheford, Hawkewell, Hockley & Assyngdon. £600,

36. Tho. Gynes & w. Faith, pl. *Tho*. Edmonds, gent., & w. Emma. def. 2 mess., 2 tofts, 2 gdns., 2 orchards, 60 a. ar., 30 a. mw., 60 a. pa. & 12 a. wd. in Southmynster, Mailand & Steple. 130 mks.

37. Jn. Clenche, gent., pl. Robt. Buxton, def. 2 tofts, 2 gdns., 40 a. ar., 10 a. mw., 60 a. pa. & 4s. & 2 hens rt. in Langenhoo, Fynryngoo, Aberton, Berechyrche, Estdonyland, Westdonyland & Langhoo. Def. quitclaimed 1 toft etc. (half the whole) in Langenhoo, Fynringoo, Aberton, Berechyrche, Estdonyland & Westdonyland to pl. & his heirs; & gtd. to the same the reversion of the residue in Langhoo, which Edw. Strachie & w. Anne hold for her life. to hold of the chief lords. £160.

38. Oswald Fytche, pl. *Tho*. Goodwyn & w. Eliz., *Hy*. Allyson & w. Jane & *Steph*. Coppyng, def. 2 mess., 2 gdns., 2 orchards & 10 a. ar. & a third part of 6 mess. in Bocking & three fifths of 2 mess. in Brancktree. £40.

39. Geo. Hagarthe & Jn. Kyrle, pl. Wm. Mallowes & w. *Margt*., def. A third part of the manors of Bretts Hall, Little Holland, Tendringe Hall & Garnons, a third part of 30 mess., 30 tofts, 30 gdns., 30 orchards, 1,000 a. ar., 300 a. mw., 1,000 a. pa., 300 a. wd., 200 a. furze & heath, 300 a. marsh & £8 rt. in Tendringe, Whyley, Little Holland, Little Bentley, Great Clafton, Little Clafton & Great Bentley, & the advowson of the church of Tendringe. Def. quitclaimed to pl. & the heirs of Geo. And for this pl. gtd. the same

to def. & the heirs of the body of Wm. of the body of Margt., to hold of the chief lords, with remainder to the right heirs of Wm.

40. Robt. Drury, esq., & Edw. Morgan, gent., pl. Pet. Pennant, esq., Tho. Tey, esq., & w. *Eleanor*, def. The manors of Marks Tey *alias* Tey Maundevyll & Moysehall & 40 mess., 10 cotts., 2 water-mills, 4 dovecotes, 40 gdns., 40 orchards, 1,000 a. ar., 400 a. mw., 400 a. pa., 200 a. wd., 100 a. moor, 100 a. furze & heath & 100 s. rt. in Marks Tey *alias* Tey Maundevyll, Palmers in Tey, Little Tey, Aldham & Ardeley. Def. quit-claimed to pl. & the heirs of Robt. And for this pl. gtd. the same to Pet. to hold for life of the chief lords without impeachment of waste, with remainder to Eleanor & the heirs of her body & the right heirs of Tho. Tey, kt., decd.

41. Robt. Drury, esq., & Tho. Cammock, gent., pl. Tho. Tey, esq., & w. *Eleanor*, def. The manors of Marks Tey *alias* Tey Maundevyll, Moysehall, Layer de la Haye & Neverdes & 100 mess., 30 cotts., 20 tofts, 2 water-mills, 4 dovecotes, 100 gdns., 100 orchards, 2,000 a. ar., 1,000 a. mw., 2,000 a. pa., 600 a. wd., 600 a. furze & heath, 250 a. moor, 300 a. marsh, 200 a. alder, a free fishery & £10 rt. in Marks Tey, Little Tey, Aldham, Ardeley, Layer de la Laye, Layer Bretton, Layer Marney, Great Byrche, Little Byrche, Great Wig-borough, Little Wigborough, Copforde, Esthorpe, Messinge, Saltcote Vyrley, Ferynge, Great Totham, Little Totham, Goldanger & Colchester, & the advowson of the church of St. Runwald in Colchester. Def. quitclaimed to pl. & the heirs of Robt. And for this pl. gtd. the manor of Marks Tey & tenements & rents in Marks Tey, Little Tey & Aldham & 3 mess., 3 gdns., 40 a. ar., 4 a. mw. & 6 a. wd., parcel of the said tenements, in Copforde & Marks Tey to def. & the heirs of the body of Eleanor, to hold of the chief lords, with remainder to the said Tho. Tey & his heirs; the manor of Moysehall & tenements & rts. in Ardeley to Eleanor & the heirs of her body, to hold of the chief lords, with remainder to the right heirs of Tho. Tey, kt., decd., her grandfather; the manors of Layer de la Haye & Neverdes, Layer Bretton & Great Birche & 100 a. ar., 10 a. mw., 100 a. pa. & 40 a. wd., another parcel, in Layer de la Haye, Layer Bretton, Great Wigborough & Great Birche to def. & the heirs of Tho., to hold of the chief lords; 16 mess., 400 a. ar., 70 a. mw., 360 a. pa., 100 a. wd., 300 a. furze & heath, 100 a. marsh, 200 a. alder & £5 rt., another parcel, in Copforde, Esthorpe, Feringe, Layer Marney, Layer Bretton, Messinge, Great Birche, Little Birche, Salcote Vyrley, Goldanger, Great Totham, Little Totham & Colchester & the advowson to Eleanor & the heirs of her body, to hold of the chief lords, with remainder to the right heirs of Tho. Tey, kt., decd., her grandfather; & 1 toft & 1 gdn., the residue, in Colchester to Tho. Tey to hold for 16 days, with remainder to Robt. Gynes, esq., & his heirs, to hold of the chief lords.

42. Edm. Thorneton, gent., pl. *Isaac* Wyatt, gent., & w. Eliz. & Tho. Hobson, def. Two thirds of 4 mess., 2 barns, 4 gdns., 2 orchards, 100 a. ar., 40 a. mw., 140 a. pa., 40 a. wd. & 10s. rt. in Great Sutton, Prytwell & Eastwood. And for this pl. gtd. the same to Tho. to hold from Michaelmas next for 41 years, rendering £10 yearly at the Annunciation & Michaelmas, with power of distraint; and the reversion to Isaac & Eliz. & the heirs of Isaac, to hold of the chief lords.

CP25(2)/259   DIVERS COUNTIES

4. Trin. & Mich. Roger Manwood, serjeant at law, Ralph Scrope, esq., & Roger Corham, gent., pl. *Gregory* Fynes *alias* Fenis, lord Dacre, & w. Anne, def. Prop. in Dorset & Kent; & the manor of Nasshe Hall, & 6 mess., 6 tofts, 1 mill, 1dovecote, 6 gdns., 300 a. ar., 40 a. mw., 100 a. pa., 60 a. wd., 100 a. furze & heath, 40 a. marsh & 40s. rt. in Nasshe Hall, & the advowson of the church of Nasshe Hall, co. Essex. Def. quitclaimed to pl. & the heirs of Roger Manwood. 1,690 mks. – Dorset, Kent, Essex.

6. Nich. Bacon. kt., lord keeper of the great seal of England, pl. *Ralph* Maynard, gent., & w. Margery, def. The manors of Abbatts Bury *alias* Rowletts Bury & Mynchinbury & 2 mess., 50 a. ar. & 60s. rt. in Great Chisshull & Little Chisshull, co. Essex; the manor of Abbatts Bury *alias* Rowletts Bury & 2 mess., 30 a. ar., 15 a. mw., 6 a. pa. & 60s. rt. in Harston & Hawston, co. Cambridge; & prop. in Herts. Def. quitclaimed to pl. & the heirs of Ralph. £1,440. – Herts, Essex. Cambridge.

8. Trin.& Mich. Roger Manwod, serjeant at law, Ralph Scrope, esq., & Roger Corham, gent., pl. *Gregory* Fynes *alias* Fenis, lord Dacre, & w. Anne, *Hen.* Norrys, kt., & w.

Margery, & Sampson Lennard, gent., & w. *Margt.*, def. The manor of Nasshe Hall etc. (as above), co. Essex.; & prop. in other counties. Def. quitclaimed to pl. & the heirs of Roger Manwood. £13,000. — Norfolk, Suss., London, Southampton, York, Suff., Lincoln, Northumberland, Berks, Nottingham, Derby, Northampton, Wilts, Dorset, Kent, Essex.

CP25(2)/129/1647   HILARY, 14 ELIZABETH   1572

1. Wm. Fryer jun., gent., pl. *Tho.* Downyng, gent., & w. Joan, def. 9 a. ar., 14 a. pa. & 2 a. wd. in Beauchampe St. Paul. £40.

2. Tho. Jenyn, gent., pl. *Jn.* Pilborowe, gent., & w. Alice, def. 1 mess., 1 gdn., 1 orchard, 40 a. ar., 12 a. mw., 100 a. pa. & 10 a. wd. in Hatfeld Peverell & Boreham. £80.

3. Joan Pakeman, pl. Rd. Grene & w. *Margt.*, Barnabas Challys & w. *Alice*, def. 1 mess. & 2½ a. ar. in Manuden. £20.

4. Robt. Carter, pl. *Chris.* Welshe, esq., & w. Anne, def. 1 mess., 2 gdns., 1 orchard, 30 a. ar., 10 a. mw., 50 a. pa. & 8 a. wd. in Waltham Hollycrosse. £100.

5. Wm. Twedy, gent., pl. Jn. Legge & w. *Joan*, def. 2 mess., 2 gdns., 2 orchards & 2 a. mw. in the parishes of All Saints & St. Peter, Maldon. £40.

6. Jn. Marshall, pl. Tho. Bateman & w. *Agnes*, def. 1 mess., 1 gdn. & 10 a. ar. in Great Wakeringe. £40.

7. Robt. Wade, pl. Esdras Erdeley, def. 1 mess., 50 a. ar., 5 a. mw. & 20 a. pa. in Rawrey. £100.

8. Wm. Samon, pl. *Nich.* Mason, gent., & w. Agnes, def. A third part of 1 mess., 1 barn, 1 gdn., 1 orchard, 4 a. ar., 5 a. mw., 6 a. pa. & 10 a. salt marsh in Stanforthe le Hope, £40.

9. Wm. Skynner, pl. *Wm.* Grene & Rd. Grene, def. 2 mess., 2 cotts., 2 tofts & 2 gdns. in Branktre. £80.

10. Mich. & Hil. Geo. Waller, pl. *Wm.* Barlee & w. Eliz., def. 1 mess., 1 gdn., 1 orchard, 30 a. ar., 2 a. mw. & 4 a. pa. in Claveringe. £80.

11. Arthur Harrys, esq., pl. Tho. Grome, gent., def. The manors of Snorham *alias* Little Lachendon & Hilhouse *alias* Helhouse & 10 mess., 10 cotts., 4 barns, 10 gdns., 6 orchards, 800 a. ar., 50 a. mw., 300 a. pa., 40 a. wd., 120 a. fresh marsh, 20 a. salt marsh & £6 rt. in Lachendon, Lawlinge & Althorne, & the advowson of the church of Snorham *alias* Little Lachendon. £800.

12. Wm. Collyn, pl. Wimond Carye, esq., def. 24 a. ar., 4 a. pa. & 2 a. wd. in Halingbery Morley & Bilchanger. Def. quitclaimed to pl. & his heirs, with warranty against Edw. Carye, gent., prop. of def. & his heirs. £40.

13. Mich. & Hil. Rd. Woodcocke, pl. Leonard Allen & w. *Margt.*, def. A fourth part of 3 mess., 3 cotts., 1 barn & 8 a. pa. in Claverynge. £40.

14. Mich. & Hil. Wm. Noke, pl. Tho. Cocke, def. 1 gdn., 1 a. ar. & 1 a. pa. in Farneham. £40.

15. Mich. & Hil. Wm. Fytche, gent., & w. Anne, pl. *Geo.* Wyseman, gent., & w. Martha, def. The manor of Albyns *alias* Albynes & 1 mess., 1 barn, 1 dovecote, 1 gdn., 100 a. ar., 20 a. mw., 200 a. pa., 20 a. wd., 60s. rt. & free warren in Stapleford Abbott & Navestocke. Def. quitclaimed to pl. & the heirs of Wm. £280.

16. Edw. Riche, esq., pl. *Nich.* Mason, gent., & w. Agnes, def. A third part of 4 mess., 4 cotts., 4 tofts, 4 barns, 4 gdns., 4 orchards, 100 a. ar., 40 a. mw., 100 a. pa., 10 a. wd. & 20 a. furze & heath in Stanford in le Hope. £40.

17. Wm. Sewall, pl. Tho. Sewall, def. 8 a. ar. & 2 a. mw. in Great Maplestede, Little Maplestede & Halstede. £40.

18. Edm. Downinge, gent., pl. *Chris.* Welsh, esq., & w. Anne, def. The manor of Pyenest & 2 mess., 1 dovecote, 2 gdns., 2 orchards, 200 a. ar., 20 a. mw., 200 a. pa. & 10 a. wd. in Waltham Holy Cross. £200.

19. Rd. Yong, pl. *Jn.* Harrington, esq., and w. Anne, *Jn.* Bridgfild *alias* Gansford, gent., & w. Eliz., def. 40 a. ar., 20 a. mw., 40 a. pa. & 50 a. wd. in Westleygh & Langdonhill. £160.

20. Francis Harte, gent., & Wm. Stutvyle, gent., pl. *Eustace* Clovyle, esq., & w. Jane, def. 1 mess., 1 gdn., 50 a. ar., 10 a. mw., 90 a. pa. & 5 a. wd. in Westhannyngfeld. Def. quitclaimed to pl. & the heirs of Francis. And for this pl. gtd. the same to def. & the heirs male of their bodies, to hold of the chief lords, with remainder to the right heirs of Eustace.

21. Alvered Frythe, pl. *Rd*. Grene & w. Joan, def. 1 mess. & 1 gdn. in Brentwood. 80 mks.

22. Francis Wyndham, esq., & Benedict Constance, gent., pl. Wm. Hygham, gent., def. The manor of Bodneck & 2 mess., 1 toft, 3 gdns., 200 a. ar., 20 a. mw., 300 a. pa., 20 a. wd., 10 a. furze & heath & 40s. rt. in Assheldon *alias* Assheden & Seynt Laurence *alias* the parish of St. Laurence. Def. quitclaimed to pl. & the heirs of Francis, with warranty against the heirs of Edm. Bedyngfeld, kt., decd. £480.

23. Mich. & Hil. Robt. Fuller, pl. Jn. Boker & w. *Juliana* def. 1 mess., 1 gdn., 1 orchard & 1½ a. ar. in Stebbinge. £20.

24. Jn. Branche, pl. *Humphrey* White & w. Dorothy, def. The manor of Earl's Chingforde & 30 mess., 20 tofts, 10 cotts., 1 water-mill, 2 dovecotes, 30 gdns., 500 a. ar., 200 a. mw., 500 a. pa., 200 a. wd., 500 a. furze & heath & £15 rt. in Chingforde & a free fishery in the water of Chingforde *alias* 'Mille Streame', and the advowson of the church of Chingforde. £400.

25. Jn. Stocke, Tho. Chote & Wm. Browne, pl. *Giles* Chisshull, esq., & w. Alice, Rd. Chote & w. *Dorothy*, def. 3 mess., 4 gdns., 10 a. ar., 2 a. mw., 2 a. pa. & 21s. rt. in Little Berdefeld, Great Berdefeld, Halsted & Hennyngham Syble *alias* Hengham Sible. Def. quitclaimed to pl. & the heirs of Jn. £80.

CP25(2)/260   DIVERS COUNTIES

5. Wm. Cecill, kt., baron of Burghley, pl. Robt. Savill, esq., & w. *Anne*, Jn. Massingberd, esq., & w. *Dorothy*, *Margt*. Tharold, wid., *Mary* Hall, wid., *Tho*. Horseman, esq., & *Wm*. Clopton, esq., def. Prop. in Herts: & 40 a. ar. & 20 a. mw. & a free fishery in the water of Lee in Nasinge & Waltham, co. Essex. £1,380. – Herts, Essex.

6. Rd. Harker & Geo. Craicall, pl. *Wilfred* Lewtie & w. Margt., & Jn. Blackman & w. Eliz., def. Prop. in Leics.; & 6 mess., 4 cotts., 1 dovecote, 8 gdns., 200 a. ar., 50 a. mw., 60 a. pa., 20 a. wd., 10 a. marsh & 6s. rt. in Alvethley *alias* Alveley, Wenyngton, Westhorock, Stifford & Southwokingdon, co. Essex. Def. quitclaimed to pl. & the heirs of Rd. 400 mks. – Leicester, Essex.

13. Francis Newman & Tho. Wright, pl. Jn. Aylyff, esq., def. Prop. in Wilts; & the rectory of Great Wakeryng & a moiety of 3 mess., 3 cotts., 40 a. ar., 100 a. mw., 120 a. pa. & 200 a. marsh in Burneham, Walletts, Alfernayshe *alias* Alfletnayshe, Pryklewell *alias* Pryttwell & Estwood, co. Essex. Def. quitclaimed to pl. & the heirs of Francis. £440. – Wilts, Essex.

CP26(1)/150   EASTER, 14 ELIZABETH   1572

1. Nathaniel Barnard, pl. Wm. Doryvall, def. 1 mess., 1 gdn. & 6 a. ar. & common of pa. for all beasts in Hawkwell. £40.

2. Tho. Wallinger, pl. And. Potte, def. 20 a. ar. & 10 a. pa. in Barkinge, which Rd. Stapleton, kt., holds for life. Pl. & his heirs to hold the reversion of the chief lords. £80.

3. Jn. Clarke & Wm. Waylett & w. Alice. pl. *Robt*. Benett & w. Eliz., def. 1 mess., 1 barn, 1 gdn., 6 a. ar., 4 a. mw. & 6 a. pa. in Bobynger *alias* Bubyngworth. Def. quitclaimed to pl. & the heirs of Jn. £40.

4. Rd. Ibotson, pl. *Jn*. Stepnethe & w. Anne, def. 3 a. marsh in Westham. £40.

5. Tho. Aylett, pl. *Ralph* Wryght & w. Alice, def. 1 mess., 1 gdn., 1 orchard, 20 a. ar., 4 a. mw. & 4 a. pa. in Maching. £40.

6. Hil. & Eas. Wm. Larke, gent., pl. *Jas*. Pynnocke & w. Eliz., def. 2 mess., 2 gdns., 2 orchards, 4 a. ar., 4 a. mw., 4 a. pa. & 2 a. wd. in Ingraffe. £40.

7. Jn. Saunder, pl. *Geo*. Copsheffe & w. Agnes, def. 2 mess. & 1 gdn. in Coggeshall. £40.

8. Jn. Skynner, gent., & Hy. Coppynger, pl. And. Skynner & w. Kath. & *Pet*. Whyte, def. 3 mess., 3 gdns., 8 a. ar. & 3 a. pa. in Mydleton & Little Hennye. Def. quitclaimed to pl. & the heirs of Hy. £80.

9. Jn. Abell, esq., pl. *Wm*. Fynche & w. Eliz., def. 1 mess., 1 gdn., 1 orchard, 30 a. ar., 20 a. mw., 30 a. pa. & 10 a. wd. in Thorpe & Kyrbye. £80.

10. Hil. & Eas. Margt. Ayloff, wid., pl. Tho. Frebarne & w. Eliz., *Jn*. Towle *alias* Toll & w. Margery, def. 1 mess., 2 cotts., 2 tofts, 1 barn, 2 gdns., 30 a. ar., 3 a. mw. & 10 a. pa. in South Hannyngfeld, Ronwell & Rotyngdon. £60.

11. Rd. Westley, pl. *Robt*. Stubbynge & w. Margt., def. 1 mess., 3 gdns. & 8 a. ar. in Hempsted. £40.

12. Simon Smythe, pl. *Nich*. Thurgoodde & w. Margt., def. 1 mess., 1 gdn., 1 orchard & 3 a. ar. in Elsenham *alias* Elsnam. £40.

13. Jn. Dysberowe & Jn. Clarke, pl. Giles Chisshull, esq., def. 2 mess., 2 barns, 1 windmill, 2 orchards, 100 a. ar., 30 a. mw., 40 a. pa., 20 a. moor & 12d. rt. in Little Berdefelde & Great Berdefelde. Def. quitclaimed to pl. & the heirs of Jn. Dysberowe. £300.

14. Rd. Everarde, gent., pl. *Chris*. Ponde & w. Joan, def. 8 a. ar. in Great Waltham. £40.

15. Jn. Higham, pl. Rd. Barwycke & w. *Eliz*., def. 1 mess., 1 gdn., 1 orchard & 2 a. ar. in Hatfyld Peverell. £20.

16. Wm. Norrys, pl. *Zachary* Fuller & w. Margt., def. 1 mess., 2 barns, 2 gdns., 2 orchards, 10 a. ar., 4 a. mw., 20 a. pa. & 2 a. wd. in Danbury & Purley. £40.

17. Mat. Cracherode, gent., pl. *Jn*. Webbe jun. & w. Emma, def. 1 mess., 1 gdn., & 1 a. ar. in Henyngham Syble. £40.

18. Jn. Foxe, pl. *Jn*. Legatt, gent., & w. Margt., def. 1 mess., 1 toft, 1 gdn., 1 orchard, 40 a. ar., 12 a. mw., 12 a. pa., 2 a. wd. & 10 a. marsh in Barkynge & Dagenham. £200.

19. Giles Buskell, clk., pl. *Tho*. Wood & w. Alice, def. 1 toft called 'Hutchins', 20 a. ar., 3 a. mw., 2 a. wd. & 3 a. marsh in West Tylberye & Little Thurrock. £40.

20. Geo. Neale, pl. Hy. Kyme & w. *Mary*, def. A third part of 1 mess., 1 gdn., 1 orchard, 16 a. ar., 2 a. mw., 2 a. wd. & 6 a. furze & heath in Owting, Hatfeyld Peverell & Langford. £40.

21. Jn. Pynchon, esq., pl. Geo. Maunsfylde & w. *Denise*, def. 1 mess., 1 gdn., 1 orchard, 24 a. ar., 5 a. mw., 12 a. pa., 2 a. wd. & 2s. rt. in Wryttell. £40.

22. Jn. Glascok & w. Kath., pl. *Tho*. Francke, esq., & w. Mary, def. 9 a. ar. in Hatfeld Brodeoke. Def. quitclaimed to pl. & the heirs of Jn. £40.

23. Jn. Mounds *alias* Freman, pl. *Tho*. Edmonds & w. Emma, Tho. Raven & w. Joan, def. 8 a. pa. in Little Waltham. £40.

24. Giles Allen, pl. *Pet*. Whyte & w. Rose, def. 2 mess., 1 gdn., 37 a. ar. & 1 a. mw. in Ardley *alias* Ardleygh. 100 mks.

25. Pet. Reade, pl. Robt. Collyn, def. 6 a. ar., 2 a. pa. & 1 a. wd. in Matchinge. £40.

26. Jn. Harvye, pl. Wm. Bye & w. *Margt*., def. 2 mess., 3 tofts & 2 gdns. in Walden. £40.

27. Hil. & Eas. Wm. Bennold, pl. *Tho*. Ivatt & w. Alice, def. 20 a. ar. in Hockeley. £100.

28. Tho. Parke & Jn. Kent., pl. Wm. Bendlowes, serjeant at law, *Giles* Chisshall, gent., & w. Alice, def. 12 a. ar. & 10 a. mw. in Little Berdefeld. Def. quitclaimed to pl. & the heirs of Tho. And for this pl. gtd the same to Wm. to hold from Michaelmas last for 33 years, with reversion to Giles & Alice & the heirs of Giles of the body of Alice, to hold of the chief lords, & remainder to the right heirs of Giles.

29. Tho. Bowde, pl. Tho. Wynterfludd & w. *Joan* & *Wm*. Sturton, def. 1 mess., 1 barn, 1 gdn. & 1 orchard in Great Donmowe. £40.

30. Wm. Parke, pl. *Jn*. Barnard & w. Bridget, def. 1 toft, 30 a. ar., 30 a. pa. & 4 a. wd. in Gestingthorp & Wickham St. Paul *alias* Wickam Powle. £140.

31. Wm. Sydey, gent., pl. *Wm*. Waldegrave, esq., & w. Eliz., def. 100 a. ar., 10 a. mw., 40 a. pa., 10 a. wd. & 10 a. alder in Tendringe & Mysley. £80.

32. Tho. Mannocke, gent., pl. Rd. London & w. *Agnes*, def. A moiety of 1 mess., 1 gdn., 8 a. ar., 2 a. mw. & 4 a. pa. in Wormyngford. £20.

33. Jn. Harbottell, gent., pl. *Wm*. Walldegrave, esq., & w. Eliz., def. The manor of Bradfyldehall & 6 mess., 3 cotts., 8 tofts, 1 dovecote, 4 gdns., 600 a. ar., 100 a. mw., 400 a. pa., 120 a. wd., 60 a. marsh & 10 a. alder in Bradfyld, Wycks & Mysteley. £800.

34. Wm. Thurgood & w. Kath., pl. Jn. Martyn & w. *Joan*, def. 3 mess., 3 gdns., 3 orchards, 200 a. ar., 20 a. mw. & 40 a. pa. in Great Wenden, Little Wenden, Arkysden, Littlebury, Walden & Newport Ponde. Def. quitclaimed to pl. & the heirs of Wm. And for this pl. gtd. the said tenements in Walden & Newport Ponde to def. & the heirs of the body of Joan, to hold of the chief lords, with remainder to the right heirs of Jn.

35. Jn. Hunwyck, pl. Jn. Colman, def. 1 mess., 1 dovecote, 2 gdns., 40 a. ar., 10 a. mw., 40 a. pa. & 8 a. wd. in Middilton, Great Hennye, Little Hennye & Bulmer, which Alice Alston, wid., holds for life. Pl. & his heirs to hold the reversion of the chief lords. £84.

36. Hil. & Eas. Tho. Eastefeild & Robt. Eastefeild, pl. Jas. Woodcoke, citizen & grocer of London, & w. *Agnes*, def. 6 a. marsh in Westham & Barkynge. Def. quitclaimed to pl. & the heirs of Tho. £80.

37. Nathaniel Barnard, pl. Giles Bawde & w. *Eliz*., def. 2 mess., 1 barn, 2 gdns., 4 a. ar., 3 a. mw., 1 a. wd. & common of pa. for all beasts in Hawkewell Hethe in Hawkewell & Rocheford. And for this pl. gtd. the same to pl. & the heirs of Giles, to hold of the chief lords.

38. Tho. Herde, pl. *Tho*. Wyseman, gent., & w. Dorothy, def. 3 mess., 3 gdns., 1 orchard, 12 a. ar., 3 a. mw. & 6 a. pa. in Upmynster. £100.

39. Ralph Wyseman, gent., pl. *Wm*. Tusser, gent., & w. Eliz. & *Jn*. Tusser, gent., def. 3 mess., 3 gdns., 3 orchards, 100 a. ar., 6 a. mw., 20 a. pa. & 46 a. wd. in Revenhall *alias* Rewenhall, Wyttam, Falborne & Cressyng. 160 mks.

40. Hil. & Eas. Tho. Barnardyston, Tho. Hanchett, And. Grey & And. Maloye, esq., pl. Wm. Clopton, esq., def. The manors of Lyston Overhall, Lyston Weston & Lyston Netherhall & 10 mess., 10 tofts, 10 gdns., 10 orchards, 300 a. ar., 200 a. mw., 200 a. pa. & 40 a. wd. in Lyston, Borley, Foxyerth, Pentlowe & Twynsted, & the advowson of the church of Lyston Netherhall. Def. quitclaimed to pl. & the heirs of Tho. Barnardyston. 400 mks.

41. Jn. Barker, pl. *Wm*. Waldegrave, esq., & w. Eliz., def. The manors of Great Wenden *alias* Wenden & Westbury & 30 mess., 12 tofts, 1 water-mill, 3 dovecotes, 30 gdns., 1,000 a. ar., 100 a. mw., 400 a. pa., 50 a. wd., 40 a. heath, 40 a. marsh, 20 a. alder & £10 rt. in Great Wenden, Little Wenden, Wald(en), Lyttelbury, Neweporte Ponde, Elmeden, Arkesden, Loftes, Wyken & Chesterforde, the rectory of Great Wenden, & the advowson of the church of Little Wenden. £1,000.

DIVERS COUNTIES

Also in CP26(1)/150/unnumbered.

Edw. Waldegrave, esq., pl. *Margt*. Tharolde, wid., Robt. Savell, esq., & w. *Anne*, Jn. Massingberd, esq., & w. *Dorothy*, *Tho*. Horsseman, esq., & *Wm*. Clopton, esq., def. The manor of Lalforde Hall *alias* Lalforde Sayes *alias* Lawforde Hall *alias* Lawforde Sayes & 30 mess., 20 tofts, 2 water-mills, 3 dovecotes, 40 gdns., 30 orchards, 1,000 a. ar., 200 a. mw., 600 a. pa. 40 a. wd., 500 a. furze & heath, 200 a. fresh marsh, 300 a. salt marsh, common of pa., £8 rt. & a free fishery in Lalforde *alias* Lawforde Sayes, Ardeleygh, Colchester, - - - - - - - - - - - - - - -, Great Bromeley, Little Bromeley, Dedham & Mysteleygh, co. Essex; & prop. in Suff. £650. — Essex, Suff.

1. Wm. Raine & Jn. Hunt, pl. Wm. Turnor, def. 1 mess., 2 curtilages, 3 cotts. & 1 gdn. in the parish of St. Leonard within the town of Colchester. Def. quitclaimed to pl. & the heirs of Wm. £40.

2. Rd. Shorte, pl. Jn. Dynes & w. *Agnes*, def. A third part of 1 mess., 1 gdn., 30 a. ar., 10 a. mw., 40 a. pa., 100 a. fresh marsh & 20 a. salt marsh in the parish of St. Osithe *alias* Chyche. £40.

3. Rd. Newman, Tho. Newman jun. & Francis Newman, pl. Agnes Newman, wid., def. 1 mess., 1 orchard, 5 a. ar., 3 a. mw. & 4 a. pa. in Hornechurche. Def. quitclaimed to pl. & the heirs of Rd. £40.

4. Edw. Ryche, esq., pl. *Tho*. Taylor & w. Agnes, def. 1 mess., 1 gdn., 1 orchard, 6 a. ar., 6 a. mw. & 16 a. pa. in Stanford in le Hope. £40.

5. Wm. Bendlowes, serjeant at law, pl. Giles Chisshull, esq., def. 12 a. ar. & 10 a. mw. in Little Berdefeld. £80.

6. Jn. Godday, sen., pl. *Edw*. Isaack, esq., & w. Joyce, def. The manor of Oldholt & 6 mess., 6 tofts, 6 gdns., 2 dovecotes, 600 a. ar., 40 a. mw., 300 a. pa., 20 a. wd. & 25s. rt. in Little Birche, Great Birche, Leyer Marney, Leyer Bretton, Messyng, Copford & Rewenhale. £1,000.

7. And. Noke, pl. Jn. Smythe, gent., def. 1 mess., 1 cott., 1 barn, 1 gdn., 1 orchard, 30 a. ar., 10 a. mw., 30 a. pa. & 3 a. wd. in Willingale Spayne & Willingale Doe. £40.

8. Jn. Ingram, gent., pl. *Edw*. Barker, gent., & w. Frances, def. 6 mess., 2 tofts, 6 gdns., 6 orchards, 10 a. ar., 10 a. mw., 20 a. pa. & 3 a. wd. in Stratforde Langthorne & Westham. £240.

9. Robt. Poole, pl. Jn. Trycker & w. Joan, def. 4 a. ar. in Thaxstede. Def. quit-claimed whatever they had for the life of Joan to pl. & his heirs. £40.

10. Jn. Maye, pl. *Roger* Grave & w. Kath., def. 1 mess. & 1 gdn. in Harwyche. £40.

11. Margery Yeldham & Eliz. Yeldham, pl. Jn. Yeldham & w. *Joan*, def. 1 mess., 1 gdn., 2½ a. mw. & a moiety of 1 mess., 1 barn, 1 gdn., 1 orchard, 40 a. ar., 20 a. mw., 8 a. pa., 4 a. wd., 9s. 1d. rt. & a rt. of 2 capons in Bockinge & Finchingfeld. Def. quit-claimed to pl. & the hiers of Margery. £40.

12. Jn. Layton, pl. Tho. Gent, esq., & w. *Eliz*., & Rd. Emery, def. 1 mess., 1 barn, 1 gdn., 40 a. ar., 10 a. mw., 60 a. pa., 40 a. wd., 10 a. marsh, 10 a. alder & 10 a. furze & heath in Halsted & Gosfylde. And for this pl. gtd. the same to Tho. & Rd. & the heirs of Tho., to hold of the chief lords.

13. Rd. Blakesley, pl. *Tho*. Cocke & w. Prudence, def. 6 a. pa. in Upmynster. £40.

14. Robt. Cammocke, gent., pl. Tho. Badbye, gent., def. 4 mess., 3 cotts., 6 gdns., 6 orchards, 20 a. ar., 20 a. mw., 100 a. pa. & 20 a. wd. in Layermarney, Salcot Vyrley, Great Wygboroughe, Messynge & Great Byrche. £140.

15. Rd. Allen & Roger Searle, pl. Tho. Bagshawe & w. *Joan* & Tho. Popleton, def. 1 mess., 1 gdn., 1 orchard, 20 a. ar., 3 a. mw., 40 a. pa. & 3 a. wd. in Ginge Margarett *alias* Margarett Inge. Def. quitclaimed to pl. & the heirs of Rd. £110.

16. Wm. Latham, pl. Eliz. Barnard, wid., & *Ralph* Sampfurthe, def. 1 mess., 1 gdn., 18 a. ar., 2 a. mw. & 12 a. pa. in Barnes Rothynge. And for this pl. gtd. the same to Eliz., to hold for life of the chief lords, with remainder to Ralph & his heirs.

17. Nich. Metcalf & Edw. Ruste, gentlemen, pl. *Tho*. Sackvyle, kt., lord Buckhurste, & w. Cecily, def. The manor of Bures at the Mount *alias* Mounte Bures & 20 mess., 20 tofts, 2 mills, 2 dovecotes, 20 gdns., 24 orchards, 500 a. ar., 80 a. mw., 500 a. pa., 350 a. wd., 600 a. furze & heath & 30s. rt. in Bures at the mount *alias* Mounte Bures & West Barholte, & the advowsons of the churches of Bures at the Mount *alias* Mounte Bures & West Barholte. Def. quitclaimed to pl. & the hiers of Nich. £1,900.

18. Eas. & Trin. Anth. Maxey, esq., pl. Wm. Wylforde, esq., & w. *Agnes*, & Geo. Nycolls, esq., & Wm. Cardynall, esq., def. The manors of Stowe Marres & Marres in Stowe Marres & Marres in Stowe £: 40 a. mw., 20 a. pa., 24 a. wd., 300 a. marsh, £3 rt. & a rt.

of 13¼ measures (*modiorum*) of salt in Stowe, Wooddham Ferres, Wooddham Witter, Purleygh & Norton, & the advowson of the church of Stowe. And for this pl. gtd. to Geo. & Wm. Cardynall & the heirs of Geo. a yearly rent of £25 from the same payable at Michaelmas & the Annunciation during the life of Agnes at the mansion house of Wm. Wylforde & Agnes at Stepney, co. Mdx., or the Place where it was built, with power of distraint, & a penalty of 40s. when the rt. shall be a month in arrears.

CP25(2)/260   DIVERS COUNTIES

12. Hy. Harpur & Tho. Walmysleye, esquires, pl. *Edw*. Hamonde & w. Margt., def. Prop. in Suff.; & 1 mess., 1 gdn., 40 a. ar., 20 a. mw. & 40 a. pa. in Horkislye, co. Essex. Def. quitclaimed to pl. & the heirs of Hy. £140. — Suff., Essex.

CP25(2)/129/1649   MICHAELMAS, 14-15 ELIZABETH   1572

1. Tho. Bond, pl. *Rd*. Archer & w. Jane, def. 1 mess. in Waltham Holly Crosse. £40.

2. Jn. Broke, pl. *Simon* Josselyn & w. Margt., def. 1 mess., 1 gdn., 1 orchard, 8 a. ar., 2 a. mw. & 14 a. pa. in Great Badowe. £40.

3. Wm. Averye, pl. *Wm*. Stedman & w. Joan, def. 24 a. marsh in Barking. £80.

4. Geo. Heigham, gent., pl. Rd. Osborne, gent., def. 50 a. pa. & 200 a. marsh in Lachingdon & Althorne. 100 mks.

5. Jn. Sharman & Jn. Goldinge, pl. Jn. Ryce, def. 3 mess., 1 toft, 5 gdns., 60 a. ar., 2 a. mw., 10 a. pa. & 5¼d. rt. in Belchamp Otton, Belchamp Water, Middleton, Great Henny & Little Henny. Def. quitclaimed to pl. & the heirs of Jn. Sharman. £100.

6. Tho. Sampford, pl. *Geo*. Tuke, esq., & w. Margt., def. The manor of Gibcraks & 1 mess., 2 curtilages, 3 gdns., 4 orchards, 160 a. ar., 20 a. mw., 80 a. pa., 12 a. wd. & 52s. 10d. rt. in Great Totham, Little Totham, Hebredge & Wickham. 260 mks.

7. Jn. Lambert, pl. *Geo*. Smythe, & w. Emma, def. A moiety of 16 a. ar., 2 a. mw. & 6 a. pa. in Haverell, Sturmer, Bumpsted Helyon & Bardfyld, & a moiety of tithes of sheaves of grain & hay in Haverell. 130 mks.

8. Charles Tyrryll, gent., pl. *Robt*. Wood, gent., & w. Joan, def. 1 mess., 1 curtilage, 1 gdn., 1 orchard, & 2 a mw. in Bromefilde. £40.

9. Law. Rochell, pl. *Tho*. Edmundes & w. Emma, Tho. Ravens & w. Joan, def. 16 a. ar., 1 a. mw. & 12 a. pa. in Little Waltheham. £40.

10. Edw. Turnor, esq., pl. Wm. Campe & w. *Alice*, def. 1 mess., 1 gdn., 10 a. ar., 4 a. mw., 4 a. pa., 2 a. wd. & 4d. rt. in Little Parndon & Great Parndon. £80.

11. Robt. Hatcheman, pl. Geo. Stonerde & w. *Mary*, def. A moiety of 1 mess., 1 gdn., 14 a. ar. & 10 a. mw. in Gyngmergarett. £40.

12. Blaise Salter, pl. *Tho*. Whight & w. Alice, def. 1 mess., 1 water-mill, 8 a. ar. & 10 a. mw. in Great Henney & Twynsted. £120.

13. Jn. Clenche, gent., pl. Edw. Strachye & w. *Anne* & Robt. Buxton, def. 2 tofts, 30 a. ar., 6 a. mw., 40 a. pa. & a rt. of 2 hens in Langenho *alias* Langho, Fynryngho, Aberton, Berechurch, Est Doneland & West Doneland. 130 mks.

14. Edw. Armiger & Edw. Greves, pl. *Jn*. Cutt, kt., & w. Anne, def. 160 a. pa. & 40 a. wd. in Thaxsted. Def. quitclaimed to pl. & the heirs of Edw. Armiger. £20.

15. Trin. & Mich. Geo. Smyth, gent., pl. Jn. Felton, gent., def. The manor of Pentlowe Hall & 6 mess., 6 tofts, 2 dovecotes, 6 gdns., 400 a. ar., 40 a. mw., 100 a. pa., 30 a. wd. & £6 rt. in Pentlowe, Fozearth & Belchampe Saynt Paule, & the advowson of the church of Pentlowe. £200.

16. Hy. Wyngebourne, pl. Chris. Fyneux & w. Eliz., Jn. Harte & w. Anne, Jas. Cryppyn & w. Mary, Edw. Vanwylder & w. Margt. & Kath. Morryce, def. 6 mess., 40 a. ar., 20 a. mw. & 20 a. pa. in Roydon. £40.

17. Trin. & Mich. Tho. Auger, pl. Robt. Polley, def. 2 mess., 1 gdn., 10 a. ar. & 10 a. pa. in Heyghonger. £40.

18. Jn. Drywood, pl. *Robt*. Drywood & w. Alice, def. 1 mess., 30 a. ar. & 10 a. pa. in Southbemflete. £100.

19. Jn. Saunder, pl. *Lancelot* Bromefelde & w. Margt., def. 1 mess., 1 barn, 2 orchards & 6 a. pa. in Highame Hill Bensted in the parish of Walcamstowe. £40.

20. Rd. Betenson, gent., pl. Wm. Osborne, def. 20 a. ar., 16 a. pa. & 16 a. fresh marsh in Lachendon, which Jane Pynchyon holds for life. Pl. & his heirs to hold the reversion of the chief lords. £40.

21. Gabriel Poyntz *alias* Poynes, esq., pl. Geo. Herde *alias* Hearde & w. *Eliz.*, def. A moiety of the manor of Bollingtons & a moiety of 12 mess., 12 tofts, 12 gdns., 100 a. ar., 20 a. mw., 160 a. pa., 10 a. wd., 20 a. marsh & 20s. rt. in Raynham *alias* Raynam, Wenington, Alveley & Wokynden Bishop's. 160 mks.

22. Francis Stacye, gent., pl. Tho. Sutton, gent., def. 1 mess., 1 gdn. & 1 orchard in Waltham Holy Cross. £40.

23. Lau. Glascocke, pl. *Tho*. Choppyn & w. Eliz., def. 1 mess., 3 gdns., 16 a. ar. & 5 a. pa. in Bromeffelde & Chickenhall St. James. £40.

24. Jn. Fuller & w. Kath., pl. *Robt*. Drywood & w. Alice, def. 1 mess., 1 barn, 1 gdn., 20 a. ar. & 4 a. mw. in Hadleigh at the Castle. Def. quitclaimed to pl. & the heirs of Jn. £40.

25. Wm. Cooke, pl. *Tho*. Fawkes & w. Margt., def. 40 a. ar. & 30 a. marsh in Peldon. £100.

26. Rd. Nicolls & w. Alice, pl. *Jn*. Reynolds, gent., & w. Mary, def. 1 mess., 3 cotts., 1 curtilage, 3 a. pa. & 6s. rt. in Chelmesforde. Def. quitclaimed to pl. & the heirs of Rd. 70 mks.

27. Jn. Coker of Purley & Jn. Coker of Cryxheth, pl. Jn. Wright & w. *Joan*, def. 1 mess., 1 barn, 1 gdn., 26 a. ar., 20 a. pa., 60 a. fresh marsh, 6 a. salt marsh & a common ferry (*passagio*) called 'Fambridge Ferrye' in Fambridge & Mundon. Def. quitclaimed to Jn. Coker of Purley & his heirs. £300.

28. Geo. Heigham, gent., pl. Wm. Osborne, def. 50 a. pa. & 200 a. marsh in Lachingdon & Althorne. 100 mks.

29. Rd. Barnard, pl. *Wm*. Piers *alias* Andrewes & w. Kath., def. 1 mess., 1 barn, 1 gdn. & 8 a. ar. in Chawreth. £40.

30. Geo. Smyth, pl. Jn. Felton, gent., def. 1 mess., 1 gdn., 1 orchard, 200 a. ar., 20 a. mw., 100 a. pa. & 20 a. wd. in Pentlowe. £200.

31. Edw. Maplesden, pl. Steph. Hardye & w. *Kath.*, def. 1 mess., 3 shops & 1 gdn. in Waltham Holy Cross. £40.

32. Wm. Gilbourne, pl. *Jn*. Stepneth, gent., & w. Anne, def. 1 mess., 1 gdns., 2 orchards, 60 a. ar., 10 a. mw., 5 a. pa., 20 a moor, 10 a. marsh, common of pa. & 10s. rt. in Westham. £40.

33. Jn. Button, Jn. Halls, Edw. Robynson, Jn. Lorde *alias* Fraunces & Rd. Scott, pl. *Jn*. Gace & w. Joan, def. 2 mess., 4 gdns. & 11 a. ar. in Thaxsted. Def. quitclaimed to pl. & the heirs of Jn. Button. £40.

34. Rd. Stonley, esq., pl. *Wm*. Stedman & w. Joan, def. 1 mess., 1 barn, 1 gdn., 60 a. ar. & 24 a. marsh in Dagenham & Barkyng. 400 mks.

35. Trin. & Mich. Rd. Hyll, pl. *Geo*. Larder & w. Helen, def. 1 mess., 1 gdn. & 2 a. pa. in Northweld Bassett. £40.

36. Wm. Todd, pl. Jn. Marshall, def. 1 mess., 1 barn, 1 gdn., 1 orchard & 2 a. ar. in Horndon on the Hill. £40.

37. Trin. & Mich. Jn. Rawlyns, pl. Wm. Darnell, def. 1 mess. in Mannyngtre. £20.

38. Trin. & Mich. Wm. Roger, pl. *Nich*. Marston & w. Agnes, def. A third part of 1 mess., 1 gdn. & 50 a. salt marsh in Stanford in le Hope. £40.

39. Reg. Hygat, esq., pl. Isaak Wyat, gent., def. 1 mess., 1 gdn., 150 a. ar., 30 a. mw. & 100 a. pa. in Crixsey, Burneham & Althorne, which Tho. Cheveley & w. Jane hold for her life. Pl. & his heirs to hold the reversion of the chief lords. £200.

40. Rd. Short, pl. Barnard Swete & w. *Mary*, def. A third part of 1 mess., 1 gdn., 30

a. ar., 10 a. mw., 40 a. pa., 100 a. fresh marsh & 20 a. salt marsh in the parish of St. Osithe *alias* Chiche. £80.

41. Jn. Lucas, pl. Tho. Eve & w. *Juliana*, def. 1 cott., 1 barn & 2 gdns. in Brentwoode. £20.

42. Jn. Smyth & w. Agnes, pl. Jn. Maykyn & w. *Joan* & Rd. Stone & w. *Eliz.*, def. 6 a. ar. & 2 a. pa. in Pebmersshe. Def. quitclaimed to pl. & the heirs of Jn. £40.

43. Rd. Barker, gent., pl. Geoff. Nyghtyngale, gent., def. 5 mess., 4 cotts., 5 tofts, 6 gdns., 5 orchards, 100 a. ar., 20 a. mw., 40 a. pa. & 5 a. wd. in Newport Pounde, Wydyngton, Debden, Wenden & Wymbyshe. £80.

44. Martin Skyner, pl. *Chris.* Curtis & w. Joan, def. 1 mess., 2 gdns., 3 cotts., 1 barn & 1 a. pa. in Branktre. £40.

45. Jn. Wryght jun., pl. Robt. Wryght jun. & w. *Susan*, def. 1 mess., 1 gdn. & 1 a. ar. in Lyghe. £40.

46. Barnabas Claydon, pl. Tho. Fytche & w. *Alice*, def. 1 mess., 1 gdn., 1 orchard, 32 a. ar., 4 a. mw., 12 a. pa., 4 a. wd. & 8s. rt. in Stevyngton, Barkelowe, Bendyshe & Asshedon. £40.

47. Trin. & Mich. Edw. Heron & Wm. Wyseman, gentlemen, pl. Tho. Curteys & w. *Plesance*, def. A fourth part of 5 mess., 2 tofts, 5 gdns., 160 a. ar., 10 a. mw., 20 a. pa., 20 a. wd. & 10 a. heath in Whyte Notley, Blacke Nottley & Branktree. Def. quitclaimed to pl. & the heirs of Wm. £80.

48. Tho. Tayleford, pl. Wm. Glascock & w. *Mary*, def. 1 mess., 1 gdn., 10 a. ar., 5 a. mw., 3 a. pa. & 1 a. wd. in Boreham *alias* Boram. £40.

49. Jn. Cutt, kt., pl. Hy. Cutt sen., esq., def. 3 mess., 2 gdns., 140 a. ar., 20 a. mw., 60 a. pa. & 6 a. wd. in Thaxsted. £372.

50. Trin. & Mich. Jn. North, pl. *Abel* Smyth & w. Joan, def. 1 mess., 1 gdn., 1 orchard, 4 a. ar. & common of pa. for all beasts in Thunderley. £40.

51. Wm. Yonge, pl. *Incencius* Godman & w. Anne & Anth. Brooke, def. 1 mess., 1 gdn. & 4 a. pa. in Great Ilford. £40.

52. Trin. & Mich. Tho. Gent, esq., pl. Tho. Lyttle & w. *Cristiana*, def. 3 mess., 3 gdns., 20 a. ar., 1 a. mw. & 15 a. pa. in Bumpsted at the Steeple. £40.

53. Jn. Searle, pl. Jn. Halles & w. *Margt.*, def. 1 mess., 2 tofts, 1 gdn., 1 orchard, 100 a. ar., 20 a. mw. & 30 a. pa. in North Weald *alias* North Weald Basset. £40.

54. Steph. Coppyng, pl. Jn. Machell & w. Helen, def. The manor of Boones & 20 mess., 10 tofts, 10 cotts., 10 gdns., 10 orchards, 40 a. wd., 20 a. furze & heath, £5 rt. & a free fishery in Bocking, Branktree, Gosfeld, Wryttle, Felsted, Mundon, Stysted, Halsted, Panfeld, Wydford & Great Badowe. Def. quitclaimed whatever they had for the life of Helen to pl. & his heirs. £280.

55. Francis Newdegate & Tho. Newdegate, esquires, pl. *Rd.* Crayford, esq., & w. Anne, def. The manor of Dovers & 3 mess., 3 tofts, 600 a. ar., 100 a. mw., 500 a. pa., 100 a. wd., 200 a. marsh & £6 rt. in Hornechurche, Bowersgyfford & Haveringe. Def. quitclaimed to pl. & the heirs of Francis. £400.

56. Jn. Southcot, one of the justices to hold pleas before the Q, pl. Francis Fortescue, gent., son & heir apt. of Hy. Fortescue, esq., def. 12 a. mw. & 12 a. pa. in Witham & Falkborne, which Hy. & w. Mary hold for their lives. Pl. & his heirs to hold the reversion of the chief lords. £40.

57. Wm. Bridges, pl. Ralph Courtman & w. *Dorothy*, Eload Fryssell & w. *Joan* & *Helen* Bridges, def. 10 a. ar. & 2 a. pa. in Westhannyngfylde. £40.

58. Wm. Gombersall, pl. Wm. Waldegrave, gent., & w. Dorothy, Ralph Gosylinge & w. *Helen*, def. 1 mess., 1 toft, 2 gdns. & 1 orchard in Barkynge. £40.

59. Tho. Gardyner, gent., pl. Geo. Monynges, gent., & w. Anne & *Geo.* Pumfrett, def. 2 mess., 2 tofts, 2 orchards, 120 a. ar., 40 a. mw., 100 a. pa., 40 a. wd., 100 a. furze & heath, 3s. 4d. rt., a liberty of one foldage & common of pa. for 200 sheep in Lyttelbury, Elmedon, Strethall, Great Chestover & Little Chestover. 200 mks.

60. Em. Enyver, pl. Jn. Heron, esq., & w. *Eliz.* & *Edw.* Heron, gent., def. 80 a. ar.,

10 a. mw. & 10 a. pa. & a moiety of 1 mess., 2 barns, 3 tofts, 1 gdn., 80 a. ar., 20 a. mw., 80 a. pa., 5 a. wd., 20 a. moor & 20 a. alder in Great Eyston *alias* Eystans at the Mount, Little Eyston, Thaxsted & Tyltey. £140.

61. Trin. & Mich. Owin Waller & Jn. Waller, his son & heir apt., pl. Tho. Pulliver & w. Alice, Edw. Pulliver & Alice Pulliver, wid., def. 25 a. marsh in Barkinge & Estham. Def. quitclaimed to pl. & the heirs of Owin, with warranty of 17 a. in Barking & Estham against the heirs of Tho. & 8 a. in Estham against the heirs of Edw. £80.

62. Rd. Coulford & Gabriel Coulford, pl. Robt. Ballard & w. Margery, *Jn.* Hove & w. Joan, Robt. Hove & w. Petronilla, Rd. Hove & w. Alice, Tho. Coulford & w. Joan, & Pet. Hove, def. 50 a. ar., 5 a. mw., 10 a. pa. & 15 a. wd. in Kellowdon *alias* Keldon. Def. quitclaimed to pl. & the heirs of Rd. £140.

63. Jn. Poole of Lyndesell, pl. Jn. Poole sen. & w. *Eleanor* & Jn. Poole jun. & w. *Eliz.*, def. 2 mess., 2 cotts., 2 barns, 2 gdns., 80 a. ar., 10 a. mw., 40 a. pa. & 8 a. wd. in Thaxsted & Lyndesell, & a moiety of 1 mess., 20 a. ar., 10 a. mw., 10 a. wd. & 20 a. alder in Elmested & Fraytyng. 400 mks.

64. Edw. Cokar Jn. Levett & Abel Clarck, pl. Mary Garryngton, wid., def. The manor of Breamsons *alias* Bremsons *alias* Newehall & 2 mess., 2 cotts., 2 barns, 2 gdns., 200 a. ar., 40 a. mw., 60 a. pa., 10 a. wd. & 10s. rt. in Purleighe. Def. quitclaimed to pl. & the heirs of Edw. £200.

65. Jn. Cowland & w. Alice, pl. Robt. Drywood & w. Alice & *Jn.* Nokes & w. Mary, def. 3 mess., 1 barn, 1 gdns., 2 orchards, 12 a. ar., 10 a. mw., 10 a. pa. & 3 a. wd. in Westhannyngfeild & Chelmsford. Def. quitclaimed to pl. & the heirs of Jn.; with warranty of 1 mess., 1 gdn., 1 orchard, 1 barn, 12 a. ar., 10 a. mw., 10 a. pa. & 3 a. wd. in Westhannyngfeild against the heirs of Robt. & 2 mess., 1 gdn. & 1 orchard in Chelmsford against the heirs of Jn. Nokes. £100.

66. Eas. 2 & 3 Philip & Mary, & morrow of All Souls, 14 Eliz. Clement Lyncoln, pl. Jn. Bright, def. 1 mess., 1 gdn., 1 orchard, 28 a. ar., 1 a. mw. & 2 a. pa. in Roxwell & Wryttell, which Robt. Parker & w. Margt. hold for her life. Pl. & his heirs to hold the reversion of the chief lords. £40.

67. Jn. Stock, pl. Jn. Harte sen. & w. *Agnes*, *Jn.* Sewell & w. Eliz., *Wm.* Sorrell & w. Joan, Marion Ynde *alias* Saunder, wid., & Tho. Hunwyck, def. 1 mess., 1 gdn., 1 orchard, 2 a. ar., 2½ a. mw. & 1½ a. pa. in Stebbyng. £40.

CP25(2)/129/1650   **HILARY, 15 ELIZABETH**   1573

1. Mich. & Hil. Edw. Staper, pl. Tho. Hopper, def. 2 mess., 1 gdn. & 1 rood ar. in Coggeshall. And for this pl. gtd. the same to def. & his heirs, to hold of the chief lords.

2. Hil. 13 & Hil. 15. Jn. Braddyll & Paul Dayrell, esquires, pl. Geo. Tyrrell, esq., def. The manor of Southwookenton & 100 mess., 50 cotts., 50 tofts, 1 dovecote, 100 gdns., 100 orchards, 2,000 a. ar., 300 a. mw., 500 a. pa., 200 a. wd., 300 a. furze & heath & £3 rt. in Colecartes, Camberlens, Hamptons, Styfford, Bustes, Bakers, Northcroftes, Gyps, Wrestes, Aveley, Prowdes & Southwookenton, & the advowson of the church of Sowthwookenton. Def. quitclaimed to pl. & the heirs of Jn. 1,520 mks.

3. Nich. Welbore, pl. *Wm.* Grigle *alias* Griggs & w. Alice, def. 2 mess. & 2 gdns. in Brancktre. £40.

4. Lau. Reve, pl. *Wm.* Sorrell & w. Joan, def. 22 a. ar. in High Ester. £40.

5. Wm. Strachie sen., pl. Margt. Smyth, wid., & *Mich.* Smyth, def. 20 a. pa. & 17 a. wd. in Walden, Wymbyshe & Thunderley. £50.

6. Jn. Maye, pl. Jn. Gamon & w. *Eliz.*, def. 1 mess. & 1 cott. in Harwiche. £40.

7. Rd. Brockman, gent., pl. *Robt.* Marshall & Tho. Bett & w. Joan, def. 1 mess., 1 gdn., 1 orchard & 2 a. ar. on Horndon on the Hill. £40.

8. Tho. Wrothe, kt., & Robt. Creswell, pl. Jn. Latham, gent., def. The manor of Lachingdon Barnes *alias* Purley Barnes & 2 mess., 2 gdns., 300 a. ar., 60 a. mw., 200 a. pa., 80 a. fresh marsh & 40 a. salt marsh in Purely & Lachingdon. Def. quitclaimed to pl. & the heirs of Tho. £400.

173

9. Tho. Bendishe, gent., pl. *Geo*. Smyth, esq., & w. Emma, def. A moiety of 16 a. ar., 2 a. mw. & 6 a. pa. in Haverell, Sturmer, Bumpsted Helyon & Bardfilde, & a moiety of all tithes of corn, hay & sheaves in Haverell. £40.

10. Mich. & Hil. Tho. Tyrrell, pl. *Hy*. Fallofelde, gent., & w. Jane, def. 1 mess., 1 curtilage, 1 gdn., 1 orchard & 2 a. mw. in Westham. £40.

11. Geoff. Gamage, pl. *Rd*. Norcot & w. Joan & Joan Willowes, wid., def. 1 mess., 1 barn & 1 gdn. in Walden. £40.

12. Walter Farr & Rd. Farr, pl. *Jn*. Gilberd & w. *Eliz*., def. 6 a. ar. & 3 a. mw. in Little Bursted. Def. quitclaimed to pl. & the heirs of Rd. £40.

13. Wm. Clerk, pl. Tho. Cockley & w. *Joan*, def. 1 mess., 1 shop, 1 gdn. & 1 orchard in Great Dunmowe. £40.

14. Tho. Wyseman, gent., pl. Walter, earl of Essex, def. 1 mess., 1 cott., 1 toft, 1 dovecote, 1 barn, 1 gdn., 1 orchard, 200 a. ar., 100 a. mw., 100 a. pa., 10 a. wd., 10 a. moor, 10 a. reed-bed (*iuncarie*), 200 a. fresh marsh, 100 a. salt marsh, 40 a. ar. covered with water, free fishery & wreck of sea in Great Totham, Goldanger & the island of Ovesey. £200.

15. Nich. Stanton, gent., & w. Eliz., pl. *Edw*. Cole, gent., & w. Agnes & Edm. Cole, gent., def. 1 mess., 1 gdn., 20 a. ar., 6 a. mw., 20 a. pa. & 16 a. wd. in Grensted. Def. quitclaimed to pl. & the heirs of Eliz. And for this pl. gtd. the same to Edw. & Agnes to hold of the chief lords for their lives, without impeachment of waste, rendering a rose at the feast of St. John Baptist to pl. & the heirs of Eliz., with reversion to the same to hold of the chief lords.

16. Rd. Brockman, gent., pl. Geo. Frewen, gent., & w. Agnes, def. 2 mess., 2 cotts., 2 barns, 2 gdns., 2 orchards, 60 a. ar., 14 a. mw. & 40 a. pa. in Stifford. Def. quitclaimed whatever they had for the life of Agnes to pl. & his heirs. And for pl. gtd. a yearly rt. of £6 13s. 4d. from the same to def. for the life of Agnes, payable at the Nativity of St. John Baptist & Christmas, with power of distraint.

CP25(2)/260   DIVERS COUNTIES

3. Chris. Cowper, pl. Wimond Cary, esq., def. 2 mess., 160 a. ar., 10 a. mw., 20 a. pa., 4 a. wd. & 3d. rt. in Farneham, Byrchanger, Stansted Mountfytchett & Takeley, co. Essex; & prop. in Herts. 260 mks. — Essex. Herts.

CP25(2)/129/1651   EASTER, 15 ELIZABETH   1573

1. Wm. Braynwood, pl. Jn. Hare & w. *Margery*, def. 1 mess., 1 gdn., 4 a. ar. & 2 a. pa. in Stow. £40.

2. Jn. Wailett, pl. *Tho*. Bridges & w. Eliz., def. 1 mess., 1 curtilage & 1 gdn. in Wydford. £40.

3. Jn. Harte & Jn. Harvye, 'ropemaker', pl. Robt. Parkyn & w. Agnes & *Jn*. Chapman, def. 1 mess., 1 barn, 1 dovecote, 1 gdn., 1 orchard, 3 a. ar. & 3 a. mw. in Walden. Def quitclaimed to pl. & the heirs of Jn. Harte. £40.

4. Tho. Muffett sen., pl. *Francis* Egglesfelde & w. Joan, def. 6 a. mw. & 3 a. marsh in Eastham. Def. quitclaimed to pl. & his heirs, with warranty against Wm. Mereddeth & w. Magdalen & his heirs. £40.

5. Wm. Marshall, gent., pl. Wm. Pylston & *Geo*. Pylston his son, def. The manors of Fowchings *alias* Fowchins *alias* Howchins & 300 a. ar., 20 a. mw., 200 a. pa., 10 a. wd. & 53s. 4d. rt. in Feringe, Great Tey, Little Tey, Cogeshall & Kelvedon. £200.

6. Jn. Brette, pl. *Wm*. Eyre & w. Alice, Wm. Brownyng & w. Rose, def. 18 a. ar. in Bromeffelde. £40.

7. Wm. Vernon, pl. *Geo*. Wyseman & w. Martha, def. 16 a. mw. & 51 a. pa. in Maldon. Def. quitclaimed to pl. & his heirs, with warranty against the heirs of Jn. Wyseman, decd., father of Geo. £160.

8. Hil. & Eas. Wm. Richardson, pl. Rd. Prowde, def. 1 mess., 1 barn, 1 gdn., 10 a. ar., 10 a. mw., 30 a. pa., 20 a. wd. & 20s. rt. in Southwokyndon. £80.

9. Jn. Brette, pl. Wm. Brownynge & w. Rose, def. 9 a. pa. in Bromeffelde. £40.

10. Rd. Tanner, pl. *Nich.* Jon *alias* Feltwell & w. Edith, def. 2 mess. & 2 a. ar. in Great Wenden. £40.

11. Hil. & Eas. Jn. Jackson, pl. Wm. Wylford, esq., & w. Agnes, def. 6 mess., 2 barns, 2 tofts, 2 gdns., 60 a. ar., 40 a. mw., 140 a. pa. & 30 a. wd. in Mountnessing *alias* Gygmountney. Def. quitclaimed whatever they had for the life of Agnes to pl. & his heirs. 160 mks.

12. Robt. Wythers, pl. *Tho.* Vyncent & w. Alice, def. 10 a. ar., 6 a. mw. & 10 a. pa. in Woodham Mortymer. £40.

13. Wm. Babham, gent., pl. Phil. Browne, gent., def. 2 mess., 2 gdns., 1 orchard, 40 a. ar., 20 a. mw., 40 a. pa. & 10 a. wd. in Westham, Estham & Little Ilford. £200.

14. Jn. Drywood, pl. *Jn.* Gylman & w. Clemencia, def. 1 mess., 1 gdn. & 8 a. ar. in Dunton. £40.

15. Hy. Aylett, pl. *Rd.* Sabbesforde & w. Eliz., def. 1 mess., 1 gdn., 2 a. ar. & 2 a. pa. in White Rodynge. £25.

16. Hugh Picott, pl. *Jn.* Sayer & w. Margery, def. 1 mess., 1 gdn., 1 orchard & 1 a. ar. in Danburie. £40.

17. Edw. Hoye, pl. *Ewgenius* Gatton, gent., & w. Eliz., def. 1 mess., 1 gdn., 50 a. ar., 5 a. mw., 10 a. pa. & 5 a. wd. in Ging Margarett *alias* Margarett Ing. 130 mks.

18. Jn. Potter jun., Jn. Prentyce sen. & Robt. Nicoll, pl. Roger Martyn, esq., def. The manor of Bromptons & 8 mess., 8 tofts, 8 gdns., 100 a. ar., 30 a. mw., 60 a. pa., 30 a. wd., 20 a. marsh, 20 a. alder & 30s. rt. in Colne Engayne *alias* Gaynes Colne & Pedmershe. Def. quitclaimed to pl. & the heirs of Jn. Potter. £140.

19. Jn. Jadwyn, pl. *Jn.* Kent & w. Joan, def. 2 mess., 2 gdns., 8 a. ar. & 6 a. pa. in Hatfeld. £40.

20. Adrian Smarte, pl. Jn. Hardyng & w. *Jane,* def. 1 mess., 1 dovecote, 1 gdn., 1 orchard & 2 a. mw. in Wytham. £40.

21. Jn. Watson, gent., & w. Eliz., pl. Jn. Goodchilde & w. *Agnes,* def. The manor of Sargeaunts *alias* Stoctons & 100 a. ar., 15 a. mw., 10 a. wd. & 11d. rt. in Chygwell *alias* Chyckwell. Def. quitclaimed to pl. & the heirs of Jn. £80.

22. Hil. & Eas. Matthew Barnard, pl. Walter, earl of Essex. def. The manor of Eytroppe Hall *alias* Eytrope Rothinge *alias* Eytroppe Rodynge *alias* Rothinge Aythorp & 30 mess., 30 gdns., 400 a. ar., 60 a. mw., 200 a. pa., 100 a. wd. & £11 rt. in Eytroppe Rothinge *alias* Rodynge Aythroppe *alias* Rothinge Aythorpe, Highe Rothinge *alias* Highe Rodynge, Leaden Rothinge *alias* Leaden Rodynge & Highe Ester, & the advowson of the church of Eytroppe Rothinge *alias* Rothinge Aythorpe. £440.

23. Hil. & Eas. Geo. Whiffyne & Edw. Pasfeld, pl. Tho. Payne & w. *Margt.,* def. A moiety of 1 mess., 1 gdn., 10 a. ar. & 30 a. pa. in Layer Marney, Wigbarowe & Messinge. Def. quitclaimed to pl. & the heirs of Geo. £40.

24. Hil. & Eas. Jn. Claye, pl. Edw. Sulyard, esq., def. 1 mess., 1 gdn., 1 orchard, 12 a. ar., 3 a. mw. & 8 a. pa. in Great Stambridge, which Margt. Sulyard, wid., mother of def., holds for life. Pl. & his heirs to hold the reversion of the chief lords. £40.

25. Hil. & Eas. Wm. Sorrell, pl. Anth. Maxey, esq., def. 2 mess., 2 gdns., 2 orchards, 60 a. ar., 4 a. mw., 16 a. pa. & 4 a. wd. in Old Salyng *alias* Great Salyng & Little Salyng. £80.

26. Tho. Staples sen., pl. *Tho.* Balden *alias* Baldwyn & w. Anne, Jn. Balden *alias* Baldwyn & w. Agnes, def. 8 a. ar. & 2 a. pa. in Westham. £40.

27. Hil. & Eas. Tho. Woode, gent., pl. Anth. Maxey, esq., def. 1 mess., 1 curtilage, 1 gdn., 1 orchard, 60 a. ar., 4 a. mw., 16 a. pa. & 3 a. wd. in Great Salyng & Rayne. £90.

28. Jn. Felton, gent., & Rd. Elyott jun., pl. *Geo.* Howe & w. Margery, def. 1 watermill, 1 gdn., 1 a. mw. & 2 a. pa. in Pentlowe. Def. quitclaimed to pl. & the heirs of Jn. £140.

29. Hil. & Eas. Wm. Burton, pl. *Walter* Bucklande, esq., & w. Barbara, def. 1 mess., 2 gdns., 1 orchard, 5 a. ar., 3 a. mw. & 5 a. pa. in Westham. £40.

30. Hil. & Eas. Edw. Armiger & Jn. Kent., pl. *Jn.* Cutt, kt., & w. Anne, def. 1 mess., 1 gdn., 46 a. ar., 10 a. mw., 10 a. pa. & 4 a. wd. in Thaxsted & Chaureth. Def. quitclaimed to pl. & the heirs of Edw. 85 mks.

31. Hil. & Eas. Robt. Reary, pl. Rd. Bykener, def. 1 mess., 1 curtilage, 1 gdn., 2 a. ar., 1½ a. mw. & 10 a. pa. in Bokkyng, which Humphrey Horsenayle & w. Agnes hold for her life. Pl. & his heirs to hold the reversion of the chief lords. £80.

32. Hy. Graye, esq., & Mary Graye, wid., pl. Wm. Holland & w. *Jane*, def. The manor of Martells *alias* Holehall & 300 a. ar., 50 a. mw., 300 a. pa., 100 a. wd. & 40s. rt. in Ryvenhall. Def. quitclaimed to pl. & the heirs of Hy. £200.

33. Mary Gate, wid., & Geoff. Gate, gent., pl. *Hy.* Josselyn, esq., & w. Anne, def. The prebend & rectory of Westthurrock & 2 curtilages, 2 tofts, 2 barns, 1 dovecote, 2 gdns., 2 orchards, 30 a. ar., 20 a. mw., 30 a. pa., 10 a. wd., 40 a. fresh marsh, 40 a. salt marsh & 53s. 4d. rt. in Westthurrock, tithes of sheaves, grain & hay in Westthurrock, & the advowson of the vicarage of the church of Westthurrock. Def. quitclaimed to pl. & the heirs of Geoff. £400.

34. Tho. Pecocke, pl. *Tho.* Pope & w. Thomasina, *Jasper* Cholmeley, gent., & *Robt.* Colman & w. Barbara, def. 2 mess., 2 cotts., 2 tofts, 1 dovecote, 1 barn, 2 gdns. & 2 orchards in Coggeshall. £40.

35. Tho. Walter, Jn. Glascocke & Tho. Wallynger, gentlemen, pl. *Wm.* Walter, esq., Rd. Bryght, Wm. Prowe & w. *Joan* & Emma Salmon, wid., def. 1 mess., 1 curtilage & 1 gdn. in Chelmesford. Def. quitclaimed to pl. & the heirs of Tho. Walter. And for this pl. gtd. the same to Emma to hold for life of the chief lords, with remainder to Joan for life & Tho. Eton, gent., son & heir of Robt. Eton, gent., decd., & his heirs.

CP25(2)/260   **DIVERS COUNTIES**

5. Rd. Rede, kt., pl. *Francis* Sills & Wm. Cocke, def. 6 mess., 6 tofts, 1 dovecote, 6 gdns., 6 orchards, 200 a. ar., 30 a. mw. & 100 a. pa. in Wryttle, Estham & Westham, co. Essex; & prop. in other counties. £3,620. — Herts, Bedford, Bucks, Berks, Dorset, Essex, Mdx., Southampton, London.

CP25(2)/129/1652   **TRINITY, 15 ELIZABETH**   1573

1. Wm. Strachye, pl. Margt. Smyth, wid., & *Mich.* Smyth, gent., def. 1 mess., 1 dovecote, 1 barn, 1 gdn. & 1 orchard in Walden. £40.

2. Eas. & Trin. Rd. Holborowe, pl. *Wm.* Heyward & w. Alice, def. 1 mess., 1 barn, 1 gdn., 12 a. ar., 6 a. mw. & 8 a. pa. in Bulmere. £40.

3. Rd. Tebold, Jn. Mace *alias* Tyler & Tho. Frebarne, pl. *Jn.* Holmested, gent., & w. Margt., def. 24 a. ar. & 1½ a. mw. in Great Maplested & Little Maplested. Def. quitclaimed to pl. & the heirs of Rd., with warranty against the heirs of Edm. Felton, esq., decd., & against Eliz. late w. of Edm., & against Jn. Scudamore, esq., & their heirs. £40.

4. Tho. Wynyff, gent., & Jn. Baxster, pl. *Tho.* Goldyngham, gent., & w. Dorothy, def. 60 a. ar. & 20 a. pa. in Bulmer. Def. quitclaimed to pl. & the heirs of Tho. £80.

5. Hy. Fynch, pl. *Charles* Bonham, gent., & w. Jane, def. 1 mess., 1 gdn., 20 a. ar., 4 a. mw., 12 a. pa. & 6 a. wd. in Bradwell. Stysted, Ferynge, Coggyshall *alias* Coxsall & Keldon. £80.

6. Robt. Ryche, kt., lord Ryche, pl. Rd. Ryche, esq., def. The manors of Patchinghall & Woodhall & 10 mess., 20 cotts., 10 tofts, 10 barns, 1 dovecote, 20 gdns., 20 orchards, 500 a. ar., 100 a. mw., 300 a. pa., 100 a. wd., 100 a. furze & heath & £8. rt. in Bromefield, Chelmesford & Chicknall Smeley. £310.

7. Rd. Brockman, gent., pl. Jn. Ellett & w. *Margt.* & Jn. Trower & w. *Grace*, def. 1 mess., 1 barn, 1 gdn., 1 orchard & 8 a. ar. in Curryngham & Fobbyng. £40.

8. Eas. & Trin. Tho. Aylett & Hy. Aylett, pl. *Matthew* Barnarde & w. Joan, def. 1

mess., 1 gdn., 60 a. ar., 10 a. mw., 10 a. pa. & 24 a. wd. in Aythropp Rodynge *alias* Rothinge Eythorppe. Def. quitclaimed to pl. & the heirs of Tho. £80.

9. Jn. Cole, pl. *Rd*. Radley & Jn. Radley, def. 1 mess., 1 barn, 1 gdn. & 7 a. ar. in Runsell & Danbury. £40.

10. Jn. Harte, pl. *Robt*. Stepneth, esq., & w. Joan, & *Wm*. Muschampe, esq., & w. Mary, def. 1 barn, 1 toft, 40 a. ar. & 20 a. pa. in Eastham. £100.

11. Nich. Holmsted, pl. Wm. Sponer & w. *Beatrice*, def. 2 mess., 1 toft, 1 gdn. & 1 orchard in Brancktree. £40.

12. Eas. & Trin. Jn. Petre, esq., pl. Eugenius Gatton, gent., & w. *Eliz*., def. 1 gdn., 30 a. ar., 4 a. mw., 20 a. pa. & 7 a. wd. in Gingmargaret *alias* Margaret Ing, Ging Abbissa *alias* Ging ad Petrum & Wryttle. £80.

13. Wm. Barlee, gent., pl. *Jn*. Feltwell *alias* Jon & w. Alice, def. 3 mess., 3 gdns., 1 orchard, 500 a. ar., 4 a. mw. & 2 a. pa. in Little Wenden, Great Wenden, Walden, Littleburie, Newport Pond & Arkesden. 400 mks.

14. Jn. Holland, pl. *Tho*. Taylor & w. Agnes, def. 1 mess., 1 barn, 1 gdn., 1 orchard & 8 a. ar. in Horndon on the Hill. £40.

15. Margt. Harlakenden, wid., pl. *Jn*. Paxton & w. Gertrude, def. 1 mess., 1 barn, 1 gdn., 9 a. ar., 4 a. mw. & 9 a. pa. in Barking & Dagenham. £40.

16. Anth. Parker, pl. *Geo*. Kynge & w. Alice, def. 1 mess. & 3 gdns. in Thaxsted. 40 mks.

17. Jn. Outinge & Leonard Levett, pl. *Jn*. Shypman & w. Margery, def. 2 mess., 2 barns, 2 gdns., 27 a. ar. & 3 a. pa. in Stebbynge. Def. quitclaimed to pl. & the heirs of Jn. £80.

18. Tho. Leaper, pl. Jas. Moryce, gent., & *Hy*. Wyngebourne, gent., & w. Eliz., def. 4 mess., 4 gdns., 4 orchards, 40 a. ar., 20 a. mw. & 20 a. pa. in Roydon. £40.

19. Geo. Grene & Wm. Rayner, pl. *Jn*. Holmested, gent., & w. Margt., def. 52 a. ar., 2 a. mw., 3 a. pa. & 4 a. wd. in Great Maplested, Little Maplested & Halsted. Def. quitclaimed to pl. & the heirs of Geo., with warranty against the heirs of Edm. Felton, esq., decd., & against Eliz. late w. of Edm., & against Jn. Scudamore, esq., & their heirs. £40.

20. Eas. & Trin. Rd. Wyatt, pl. Wm. Loveday, gent., def. 26 a. ar., 10 a. mw., 20 a. pa. & 2 a. wd. in Little Canfylde & Great Canfylde. £40.

21. Eas. & Trin. Wm. Burton, pl. Rd. Cutts, gent., def. 1 mess., 2 gdns., 2 orchards, 10 a. ar., 3 a. mw., 26 a. pa. & 1 a. wd. in Keldon, Ferynge & Coxhall. £40.

22. Jn. Shipman, gent., & Hy. Yonge of Saynt Olyves, gent., pl. Nich. Strelley, gent., & w. *Susan*, def. 1 mess., 1 cott., 2 tofts, 2 water-mills, 1 gdn., 1 orchard & 32 a. mw. in Westham. Def. quitclaimed to pl. & the heirs of Jn. £100.

23. Wm. Evered, pl. Edm. Styleman & w. Marian, Geo. Styleman & w. Eliz., & *Jn*. Styleman, def. 14 a. ar. & 1 a. mw. in Goodeaster & Masheburye *alias* Mascalburrye. £40.

24. Brian Darcye, esq., pl. *Tho*. Babyngton, gent., & w. Helen, def. A third part of the manor of Benyngtons & of 1 mess., 60 a. ar., 10 a. mw., 20 a. pa. & 4 a. wd. in Wikeham, Witham & Hatfeld Peverell. 100 mks.

25. Tho. Samford, pl. Wm. Peverell, Jn. Peverell & Jn. Cofyld, def. 2 mess., 1 curtilage, 1 gdn. & 1 orchard in Colchester. £80.

26. Wm. Mongey *alias* Mountioye, pl. *Geo*. Breton, esq., & w. Anne, def. 4 mess., 4 cotts., 6 tofts, 2 dovecotes, 6 gdns., 100 a. ar., 12 a. mw., 100 a. pa., 6 a. wd. & 200 a. furze & heath in Layer Breton, Salcott Virley, Great Byrche, Copforde & Layer de la Haye. 400 mks.

27. Eas. & Trin. Agnes Browne, wid., & Jn. Browne pl. Francis Eglysfeld, gent., def. 1 mess., 1 barn, 1 gdn., 10 a. ar., 3 a. mw. & 12 a. pa. in Easthannyngfeld, Southehannyngfeld, Ronwell & Rotyngdon. Def. quitclaimed to pl. & the heirs of Jn. £40.

28. Robt. Plome & Tho. Purcas, pl. *Jn*. Browne & w. Agnes, & Tho. Browne & w. Agnes, def. The manor of Spaynes & 1 mess., 1 dovecote, 100 a. ar., 7 a. mw., 15 a. pa. & 32s. rt. in Great Yeldham, Little Yeldham *alias* Over Yeldham, Henyngham Castell, Toppesfeld & Stamborne. Def. quitclaimed to pl. & the heirs of Robt. 200 mks.

29. Rd. Wolgrave *alias* Wollard & w. Joan, pl. Tho. Taylor & w. *Agnes*, & Wm. Todd & w. *Joan*, def. 1 mess., 1 gdn., 1 orchard & 7 a. ar. in Horndon on the Hill. Def. quitclaimed to pl. & the heirs of Rd. £40.

30. Eas. & Trin. Jn. Josselyn, pl. Wm. Walter, gent., def. 1 mess., 1 gdn., 1 orchard, 140 a. ar., 10 a. mw., 10 a. pa. & 10 a. wd. in Roxwell & Newlonde called 'Bolinghatch'. £140.

31. Jn. Kent & Jn. Wryght, pl. Wm. Laste & w. Margt. & Hugh Cornell & w. *Anne*, def. 1 mess. & 1 gdn. & a moiety of 1 mess., 1 barn, 1 gdn., 1 orchard, 40 a. ar., 20 a. mw., 8 a. pa., 4 a. wd., 9s. 1d. rt. & a rt. of 2 capons in Bockynge & Fychingfeld. Def. quitclaimed to pl. & the heirs of Jn. Kent. £40.

32. Tho. Webbe & Wm. Danyell, pl. Rd. Barlee, esq., & w. *Anne*, def. The manor of Elsynham *alias* Elsenham & 40 mess., 20 tofts, 2 water-mills, 2 dovecotes, 40 gdns., 600 a. ar., 100 a. mw., 400 a. pa., 100 a. wd., 40 a. moor & £6 rt. in Elsynham *alias* Elsenham, Stanstede, Hennam & Brockstede. Def. quitclaimed to pl. & the heirs of Tho. And for this pl. gtd. the same to def. & the heirs of Rd., to hold of the chief lords.

33. Jn. Wood & Jas. Morres, pl. Mary Gray, wid., & *Hy*. Gray, esq., def. The manor of Holehall & 1 mess., 1 gdn., 1 orchard, 200 a. ar., 20 a. mw., 100 a. pa., 20 a. wd. & 100 a. moor in Holehall & Ryvenhall. Def. quitclaimed to pl. the heirs of Jn. And for this pl. gtd. the same to Mary to hold for life of the chief lords, with remainder to the heirs male of the body of Jn. Gray, kt., lord Gray, decd., & the Q & her heirs & successors.

34. Eas. & Trin. Wm. Bendlowes, serjeant at law, & Tho. Chapplyn, pl. Tho. Throckmerton, esq., & w. *Margt*. & *Tho*. Whorwood, esq., def. The manor of Cockfeld *alias* Cockfeldes & 1 mess., 1 barn, 200 a. ar., 20 a. mw., 40 a. pa., 20 a. wd. & 10s. rt. in Fynchingfelde. Def. quitclaimed to pl. & the heirs of Wm., with warranty against the heirs of Wm. Whorwood, esq., decd. 200 mks.

CP25(2)260   DIVERS COUNTIES

5. Wm. Gosnolde, gent., pl. Wm. Bramfylde, gent., def. Prop. in London; & 1 mess., 1 gdn., 1 orchard & 12 a. ar. in Little Ilforde, co. Essex. £160. — London, Essex.

CP25(2)/129/1653   MICHAELMAS, 15-16 ELIZABETH   1573

1. Tho. Marchall, pl. Jn. Pomfrett & w. *Ingata*, def. 1 mess., 1 gdn., 1 orchard & 7 a. ar. in South Okendon. £40.

2. Jn. Staunton, gent., pl. Jerome Staunton, gent., def. 1 mess., 2 barns, 1 gdn. & 5 a. ar. in Westham. £80.

3. Robt. Collin, pl. *Jn*. Collin & w. Joan, def. 1 mess., 1 orchard, 30 a. ar., 30 a. pa., 10 a. furze & heath & 2s. rt. in Southchurche & Wyats. £40.

4. Ralph Turner, gent., pl. Jn. Cutt, kt., def. 2 mess., 2 barns, 2 gdns., 2 orchards, 30½ a. ar., 15 a. mw., 15 a. pa. & 1 a. wd. in Thaxsted & Depden. 200 mks.

5. Chris. Kent *alias* Reynold & Jn. Humfrey, pl. *Nich*. Fanne & w. Mary, def. 1 mess., 1 barn, 26 a. ar., 2 a. mw., 2 a. pa. & 2 a. wd. in Thaxsted. Def. quitclaimed to pl. & the heirs of Chris. £120.

6. Jn. Lense, pl. *Tho*. Hubbard & w. Margery, def. 1 mess., 1 cott., 1 barn, 1 gdn., 1 orchard & 60 a. ar. in Ultyng, Langforde & Hatfeild Peverell. £120.

7. Edw. Thedam, pl. Jn. Chaundeler, gent., def. 20 a. ar., 4 a. mw. & 16 a. pa. in Langham. £40.

8. Jn. Wyncoll, gent., pl. *Tho*. Wyllett jun. & w. Mary, def. 1 mess., 1 toft, 1 gdn., 1 orchard, 20 a. ar., 6 a. mw., 10 a. pa., 2 a. wd., 6 a. marsh & 3s. rt. in Alphamston, Twynsted & Great Hennye. £80.

9. Jn. Walker, pl. *Robt*. Lystor & w. Margt., def. 2 mess. & 2 gdns. in Balyngton by Sudburye. £30.

10. Rd. Palmer, pl. Tho. Eve, def. 1 mess., 1 barn, 2 gdns., 1 orchard, 15 a. ar., 3 a. mw. & 6 a. pa. in Stebbinge, Great Dunmowe & Little Dunmowe. £40.

11. Jn. Watson, gent., pl. *Geo*. Flyngant & w. Joan, def. 19 a. ar. & 3 a. mw. in Great Wigboroughe, Little Wigboroughe & Layer de la Haye. £40.

12. Francis Shakerley, gent., pl. *Matthew* Gosnold, gent., & w. Bridget, def. 1 mess., 20 a. ar., 10 a. mw., 40 a. pa., 20 a. wd. & common of pa. in Stondon & Duddyngherst. £100.

13. Jas. Woodland & w. Denise, pl. *Robt*. Golston & w. Agnes, def. 4 a. pa. & 2 a. fresh marsh in Westham. Def. quitclaimed to pl. & the heirs of Denise. £40.

14. Trin. & Mich. Ralph Typpynge, gent., pl. Wm. Burton, def. 2 mess., 40 a. ar., 20 a. mw., 30 a. pa. & 2 a. wd. in Westham. £40.

15. Tho. Gylbart, pl. *Wm*. Laste & w. Margery, def. 1 mess., 1 cott. & 1 gdn. in Bockinge. £40.

16. Jn. Cracknell & Tho. Chote, pl. *Edw*. Heron, gent., & w. Anne, def. 2 mess., 2 gdns., 2 orchards, 10 a. ar., 4 a. mw. & 3 a. pa. in Bumpsted at the Steeple & Fynchingfelde. Def. quitclaimed to pl. & the heirs of Jn. £80.

17. Jn. Enyvere, pl. *Jn*. Jenyns, gent., & w. Jane, def. A moiety of mess., 2 barns, 1 curtilage, 1 gdn., 2 orchards, 60 a. ar., 20 a. mw., 40 a. pa. & 10 a. wd. in Eyston at the Mount, Eyston at the Steeple, Thaxsted & Tyltie. 130 mks.

18. Jn. Parke, pl. Hy. Deane & w. *Joan*, def. 1 mess., 2 gdns. & 1 a. ar. in Little Maplested. £20.

19. Rd. Hamond, pl. Jn. Shedd & w. *Joan*, def. 1 mess., 1 gdn., 1 orchard, 20 a. ar., 2 a. mw., 10 a. pa. & 1 a. wd. in Depden. £80.

20. Robt. Wordysworth, gent., pl. *Jn*. Colvyle & Wm. Colvyle, def. 1 mess., 2 barns, 1 gdn., 1 orchard, 80 a. ar., 21 a. pa. & 4 a. wd. in Copford, Great Burche, Little Burche, Estthorpe & Stanwaye. 160 mks.

21. Jerman Alexander, pl. *Wm*. Wright & w. Anne, def. 20 a. ar., 20 a. pa. & 20 a. salt marsh in Bradwell. £80.

22. Tho. Adams, pl. *Robt*. Jenens & w. Joan, def. 1 mess., 1 curtilage, 1 gdn. & 1 orchard in Harlowe. £40.

23. Jn. Wentworth & Wm. Maxye, gent., pl. *Tho*. Beckingham, esq., & w. Mary, def. The manors of Belhowse & Howes & 10 mess., 6 gdns., 2 orchards, 2 dovecotes, 500 a. ar., 40 a. mw., 500 a. pa., 40 a. wd., 200 a. furze & heath & 10s. rt. in Great Stanwey, Little Stanwey, Copford & Byrche. Def. quitclaimed to pl. & the heirs of Jn. 160 mks.

24. Tho. Herd, pl. *Tho*. Heyward & w. Alice, def. 1 mess., 1 gdn., 1 orchard & 20 a. ar. in Wrabnesse. £40.

25. Rd. Mors & w. Joan, pl. Jas. Waulker & w. Alice, def. A moiety of 1 mess., 1 gdn., 1 orchard, 12 a. ar., 6 a. mw., 20 a. pa. & 2 a. wd. in Duddynghurst, Blakemore & Fyngreth. Def. quitclaimed to pl. & the heirs of Rd. £40.

26. Tho. Phillippson & w. Bridget, pl. Gilbert Branthwaite & w. *Joan*, def. 16 a. pa. in Rayligh. Def. quitclaimed to pl. & the heirs of Tho. £40.

27. Robt. Potter, pl. Hy. Laye & w. *Edith*, def. A fourth part of a third part of 2 mess., 2 tofts, 4 gdns., 2 orchards, 1 dovecote, 100 a. ar., 12 a. mw., 60 a. pa. & 5 a. wd. in Wethermonford *alias* Wormyngford, Fordham & Bures at the Mount. £40.

28. Tho. Gooddaye, pl. *Steph*. Mumford & w. Eliz., & Robt. Turnor & w. Grace, def. 1 toft, 20 a. ar., 5 a. mw., 5 a. pa. & common of pa. in Langford & Owltinge. £80.

29. Geo. Hudson, pl. Jn. Byshopp & w. *Joan*, def. A moiety of 1 mess., 1 gdn., 30 a. ar. & 10 a. wd. in Kirkbye Soca. £80.

30. Jn. Lucas, pl. *Jn*. Pumfrett & w. Ingatta, def. 1 mess., 1 stable & 1 gdn. in Brentwood. £40.

31. Trin. & Mich. Jn. Lennard, esq., pl. Geo. Dacres, esq., def. The manor of Mawneys & 2 mess., 10 tofts, 300 a. ar., 40 a. mw., 200 a. pa., 40 a. wd. & £7 rt. in Mawneys, Hornechurche, Rumford & Haveryng at Bower, & view of frank-pledge in Rumford. £400.

32. Wm. Heckford, pl. *Tho*. Aldust & w. Kath., def. 1 mess., 1 gdn., 1 orchard, 20 a. ar. & 1 a. mw. In Ardeley. £60.

179

33. Jn. Spender, pl. Chris. Bexwell & w. *Alice*. def. 1 mess., 1 gdn., 1 orchard & 1 a. ar. in Fobbyng. £40.

34. Wm. Jennynges, pl. Wm. Haynes & w. *Isabel*, def. 1 mess., 2 cotts., 2 tofts, 4 gdns., 30 a. ar., 6 a. mw., 6 a. pa. & 3 a. wd. in Matchinge & Highe Laver. £40.

35. Wm. Crosse, pl. *Tho*. Crawley, esq., & w. Margt., def. The manor of Chawrethe *alias* Chawreyhall & 100 a. ar., 20 a. mw. & 40 a. pa. in Chawreth *alias* Chawrey, Chyckney & Broxsted. And for this pl. gtd. the same to def. & the heirs of Tho., to hold of the chief lords.

36. Jn. Baron, pl. Robt. Mydleton & *Robt*. Mydleton, his son & heir apt., def. 2 mess., 2 tofts, 2 gdns., 2 orchards, 10 a. mw. & 30 a. pa. in Great Wigborowe, Saltcot Wigborowe, Tolson Knyghts & Saltcot Vyrley. 130 mks.

37. Chris. Franke, pl. *Tho*. Harvie *alias* Hulman & w. Eliz., def. 1 mess., 1 gdn., 1 orchard, 20 a. ar. & 4 a. pa. in Terlinge. £40.

38. Hy. Baker. clk., pl. Tho. Pett, clk., & w. Juliana, Jonas Pett, *Jn*. Maye & w. Susan, def. 1 mess., 10 a. ar., 12 a. pa. & 2 a. wd. in Althorne, Mayland & Purleighe. £40.

39. Jn. Harpham, pl. Ralph Bowtell & w. *Martha*, def. 2 mess., 1 toft, 2 gdns., 10 a. ar., 5 a. mw., 8 a. pa. & 1 a. wd. in Canewden *alias* Canoudon. £40.

40. Francis Stonerde, pl. *Tho*. Edmonds & w. Emma, def. 2 mess., 2 gdns., 2 orchards, 20 a. ar., 10 a. mw. & 20 a. pa. in Steple, Assheldame *alias* Assheldhame & Saynt Laurence. £80.

41. Robt. Campe, pl. *Wm*. Whytnall & w. Edith, *Jn*. Jacobbe & w. Joan, def. 1 mess., 1 barn, 1 gdn., 1 orchard, 15 a. ar. & 5 a. pa. in Roydon. £80.

42. Tho. Parke & Jn. Kent, pl. *Wm*. Hill & w. Beatrice, *Jn*. Butler & Rd. Tebold, def. 2 mess., 2 gdns. & 16 a. ar. in Bockynge. Def. quitclaimed to pl. & the heirs of Tho. £80.

43. Edw. Rawlyn, pl. Jas. Betts & w. Margt., def. 4 mess., 2 tofts, 4 gdns., 30 a. ar., 2 a. mw., 10 a. pa., 1 a. wd. & 1d. rt. in Rocheford & Hackwell. Def. quitclaimed to pl. & his heirs, with warranties of one moiety against the heirs of Jas. & the other against the heirs of Margt. £200.

44. Tho. Ive, gent., & Nich. Sutton, gent., pl. Gilbert Cherche *alias* Churche, def. 2 mess., 2 gdns., 100 a. ar., 10 a. mw., 80 a. pa. & 6 a. wd. in Fyfeld *alias* Fyfeld & Belcham Roodyng. Def. quitclaimed to pl. & the heirs of Tho. And for this pl. gtd. the same to def. & his heirs, to hold of the chief lords.

45. Ralph Bossevile, esq., & Hy. Bossevile, gent., pl. *Clement* Smyth, esq., & w. Dorothy, def. 1 mess., 2 barns., 100 a. ar., 100 a. mw., 200 a. pa. & 20 a. wd. in Langforde. Def. quitclaimed to pl. & the heirs of Ralph. And for this pl. gtd. the same to def. & the heirs of Clement, to hold of the chief lords.

46. Wm. Colshyll, gent., & w. Barbara, pl. *Wm*. Higham of Hasleygh, gent., & w. Eliz., def. 2 mess., 170 a. ar., 20 a. mw., 20 a. pa., 3 a. wd. & 20 a. marsh in Southefambridge & Assingdon. Def. quitclaimed to pl. & the heirs of Barbara. £200.

47. Hy. Wentworth, gent., pl. *Tho*. Fytche & w. Eliz., Wm. Browne & w. Margery, Jn. Walker & w. *Joan*, & Jn. Whyffyn & w. Alice, def. 1 mess., 1 gdn., 1 orchard & 6 a. ar. in Bumpsted at the Steeple *alias* Steple Bumpsted. £40.

48. Jn. Brocke, esq., pl. Edw. Strachye & w. *Anne*, & *Robt*. Buxton *alias* Buckston & w. Priscilla, def. 2 mess., 2 gdns., 2 orchards, 6 a. ar. & 6 a. pa. in Colchester. £80.

49. Jn. Sammes & Edw. Sammes , pl. Wm. Sammes & w. Grace, def. A moiety of 6 mess., 2 tofts, 1 barn, 6 gdns., 130 a. ar., 12 a. mw., 40 a. pa. & 2 a. wd. in Markestey, Peldon, Aldham, Feringe, Little Tey, Great Birche & Esthorpe. Def. quitclaimed a moiety of 2 mess., 1 toft, 1 barn, 2 gdns., 70 a. ar., 8 a. mw., 2 a. pa. & 2 a. wd. in Markestey, Aldham, Feringe, Little Tey, Great Byrche & Esthorpe to pl. & the heirs of Jn., & gtd. to the same the reversion of the remainder in Markestey & Peldon, which Jn. Moteham holds for life, to hold of the chief lords.

50. Trin. & Mich. Jn. Petre, esq., & w. Mary, pl. *Lewis* Mordaunt, kt., lord Mordaunt, & w. Eliz., def. The manors of Westhorndon, Ameys, Ingrave, Gyngrave, Gyngraff, Craneham, Feldehowse, Nokehall & Great Bromeforde & 200 mess., 2 windmills, 60 gdns., 60 orchards, 6,000 a. ar., 500 a. mw., 3,000 a. pa., 500 a. wd., 4,000 a. furze & heath, 300

a. moor, 200 a. reedbed (*juncarie*), 200 a marsh & £40 rt. in Westhorndon, Chilterdyche *alias* Childerdyche, Great Warley *alias* Warley Wallett, Little Warley, Craneham, Alveley, Bishop's Okendon, Northokendon, Southokendon, Bulvan, Salinge, Liendon *alias* Layndon, Donton, Esthorndon, Ingrave *alias* Gynggrave, Brentwood, Southwelde, Shenfeld, Hutton, Great Bursted, Little Bursted, Ravensden Crayes, Ravensden Bellowes, Nevendon & Bartylsden, & the advowsons of the churches of Westhorndon, Gyngrauff, Craneham & Nevenden. Def. quitclaimed to pl. & the heirs of Jn. £3,200.

51. Wm. Peryman, gent., pl. Wm. Peverell, Jn. Peverell & Jn. Colfylde, def. 1 mess., 1 gdn., 100 a. ar., 20 a. mw., 60 a. pa. & 30 a. wd. in Chiche Regis *alias* Chyche St. Osithe & Weleigh. 230 mks.

52. Rd. Goldynge, gent., & Jn. Holmested, gent., pl. *Tho.* Goldyngham, gent., & w. Dorothy, Nich. Bragge & Wm. Bragge, def. 1 mess., 1 dovecote, 1 gdn., 1 orchard, 230 a. ar., 16 a. mw. & 40 a. pa. in Bulmer. Def. quitclaimed to pl. & the heirs of Rd. And for this pl. gtd. the same to Nich. & Wm. to hold from Michaelmas for 21 years, rendering £29 yearly at the Annunciation & Michaelmas, with power of distraint, with remainder to Tho. & Dorothy & the heirs of Tho., to hold of the chief lords.

53. Rd. Saltonstall, pl. *Edw.* Tyrrell, esq., & w. Mary, def. 16 mess., 20 tofts, 2 mills, 2 dovecotes, 40 gdns., 40 orchards, 1,000 a. ar., 500 a. mw., 1,000 a. pa., 100 a. wd., 500 a. furze & heath, 100 a moor, 100 a. marsh & 60s. rt. in Southwokendon *alias* Southokingdon Rockell, Brokestreate, Great Warlye, Little Warley, Alveley, Childerdiche, Styfford, Upmynster, Southwelde, Brendwoode, Northokendon & Rainham, a moiety of the manor of Sowthwokendon in the same places, & the advowson of the church of Sowthokendon *alias* Southokingdon Rockell. £1,260.

54. Jas. Harveye, citizen & alderman of London, pl. *Wm.* Nutbrowne, gent., & w. Anne, def. 3 a. pa. & 16 a. wd. in Dagnaham. £40.

55. Jn. Sams, pl. Jn. Moyne, gent., & w. Margt., def. 2 a. ar. & 16 a. pa. in Great Totham, which def. hold for the life of Margt., with reversion to Wm. Laurence, gent., & his heirs. Def. quitclaimed whatever they had to pl. & his heirs. £40.

56. Jn. Drurye, esq., & Geo. Hagarth, gent., pl. Wm. Scott, gent., & w. *Prudence*, Wm. Mallowes, gent., & w. *Margt.*, def. The manors of Bretts Hall, Little Holland, Tendringe Hall & Garnons & 30 mess., 30 tofts, 30 gdns., 30 orchards, 1,000 a. ar., 300 a. mw., 1,000 a. pa., 300 a. wd., 200 a. furze & heath, 300 a. marsh & £8 rt. in Tendringe, Whyley, Little Holland, Little Bentley, Great Clafton, Little Clafton & Great Bentley, & the advowson of the church of Tendringe. Def. quitclaimed to pl. & the heirs of Jn. 400 mks.

CP25(2)/260   DIVERS COUNTIES

2. Wm. Cecill, kt., lord Burghley, treasurer of England, Walter Myldmay, kt., chancellor of the Exchequer, Gilbert Gerrard, esq., attorney general, & Tho. Bromley, esq., solicitor general, pl. Walter, earl of Essex, def. The manors of Tolleshunt, Tollesbury & Hallingbury Bourghchier & 40 mess., 40 cotts., 40 tofts, 1 water-mill, 60 gdns., 6,000 a. ar., 500 a. mw., 8,000 a. pa., 300 a. wd., 4,000 a. furze & heath & £80 8s. 9d. rt. in Tolleshunt, Tollesbury, Bourghchiers Hall, Old Hall, Hallingbury Bourghchier, Wivenho, Goldanger, Pottinge & Rushley, the parks of Hallingbury & Tollesbury, & the advowson of the church of Hallingbury, co. Essex; & prop. in Bucks. Def. quitclaimed to pl. & the heirs of Wm. £2,200. — Essex. Bucks.

3. Rd. Wyllye, pl. Wm. Pylston & w. Joan, def. 5 a. ar. & 3 a. pa. in Stansted Mowntfichet, co. Essex; & prop. in Herts. Def. quitclaimed whatever they had for the life of Joan to pl. & his heirs. £100. — Essex. Herts.

4. Wm. Atwood & Jn. Wentworth, gentlemen, pl. Francis Bacon, gent., & w. *Mary*, def. The manor of Keldenhall & 150 a. ar., 40 a. mw., 260 a. pa., 100 a. wd. & 13s. rt. in Keldon, Feryng, Messyng, Inworth & Braxsted, co. Essex; & prop. in Suff. Def. quitclaimed to pl. & the heirs of Wm. 2,000 mks. — Essex. Suff.

5. Anth. Crane, esq., pl. Jn. Massingberd, gent., & w. *Dorothy*, def. A twentieth part of the manor of Wykenhamehall & of 20 mess., 20 barns, 7 mills, 6 dovecotes, 20 gdns., 1,000 a. ar., 400 a. mw., 300 a. pa., 100 a. wd., 100 a. furze & heath & 20s. rt. in Farnam, co. Essex; & a twentieth part of the manor of Wikehamehall & of 20 mess. (etc. as above) in Bisshoppe Storford, Litle Hadham & Abrey, co. Herts. £160. — Herts, Essex.

181

1. Mich. & Hil. Jn. Camber, pl. Jn. Pascall, def. 72 a. salt marsh in Fange, South-bemflyte & Canvey. £80.

2. Robt. Fryth, pl. Nich. Erswell, def. 4 a. ar. in Walden. £40.

3. Robt. Alcock & Robt. Watson, pl. Francis Fowler, def. 1 mess., 1 gdn., 1 or-chard, 12 a. ar., 6 a. mw., 10 a. pa. & 1 a. wd. in Gynge Mountney *alias* Mountnesynge. Def. quitclaimed to pl. & the heirs of Robt. Alcock. £30.

4. Tho. Large, pl. *Robt*. Jacobbe & w. Joan, def. 1 cott., 1 gdn. & 20 a. wd. in Twynsted. £40.

5. Mich. & Hil. Tho Bewley, clk., pl. Tho. Shaa, esq., def. 1 mess., 1 gdn., 1 orchard, 60 a. ar., 4 a. mw., 40 a. pa., 30 a. wd. & 7s. rt. in Thundersley, Rayleigh, Hadleigh & Pritwell. £80.

6. Wm. Ayloff, esq., & Tho. Ayloff, gent., pl. Bart. Strangman, gent., def. The manor of Barons & 10 mess., 6 gdns., 400 a. ar., 100 a. mw., 600 a. pa., 400 a. wd., 200 a. marsh, 100 a furze & heath & £10 rt. in Purley, Rayleygh & Rawreth. Def. quitclaimed to pl. & the heirs of Wm. £400.

7. Joan Hawkyn, wid., pl. Humphrey Kervyne & w. *Joan*, def. 4 a. wd. in Hatfyld Peverell. £40.

8. Rd. Brockman, gent., pl. Wm. Burges & w. *Tomasina*, def. 1 mess., 1 gdn. & 1 a. ar. in Coggeshall. £40.

9. Tho. Shypton, clk., pl. Wm. Heynes & w. *Isabel*, def. 1 mess., 2 tofts, 1 gdn., 1 orchard, 26 a. ar., 2 a. mw. & 2 a. pa. in Hygh Laver & Matchyng. £40.

10. Geo. Gascoygne, gent., pl. *Tho*. Wallynger, gent., & w. Avice, def. 1 mess., 1 gdn., 1 orchard, 40 a. ar., 12 a. mw. & 60 a. pa. in Harwardstocke *alias* Harvardstock & Buttes-bury. £80.

11. Tho. Pyper, pl. *Wm*. Ratheby & w. Cicily, def. 1 mess., 20 a. ar., 10 a. mw., 25 a. pa. & 10 a. wd. in Muche Holland. Def. quitclaimed to pl. & the heirs of Wm. 130 mks.

12. Jn. Buttolff, pl. *Jn*. Coo & w. Eliz., def. 1 mess., 1 toft, 2 gdns. & 2 a. ar. in Tylburye. £40.

13. Rd. Northen, pl. *Jn*. Lucas, esq., & w. Mary, def. 1 mess., 1 gdn., 40 a. ar., 50 a. mw., 60 a. pa., 10 a. wd., 30 a. furze & heath & 20s. rt. in Mysteley. 130 mks.

14. Wm. Turnor, pl. *Jn*. Ive *alias* Sparhauke & w. Alice, def. 2 mess. in Brancktre. £40.

15. Joan Strangman, wid., pl. Bart. Strangman, gent., def. The manors of Clements & Westhall in Hackwell *alias* Hakewell, Rocheforde, Pakelsham, Canewden, Great Stam-brigge & Little Stambrigge, & 2 mess., 2 gdns., 100 a. ar., 30 a. mw., 60 a. pa., 20 a. wd., 10s. rt. & common of pa. for all animals in Southe Shuberye & Northe Shuberye. Pl. to hold for her life. £520.

16. Hy. Averell & Jn. Tredgolde sen., pl. Jn. Thurgood, def. 1 mess., 1 toft, 1 gdn., 40 a. ar., 3 a. mw., 20 a. pa. & 2 a. wd. in Matchinge & Heigh Laver. Def. quitclaimed to pl. & the heirs of Hy. £80.

17. Jn. Kynge, pl. *Jn*. Parker & w. Eliz., def. 1 mess., 1 barn, 1 gdn., 22 a. ar. & 12 a. pa. in Elmedon. £80.

18. Wm. Vigorus & Rd. Byggen, pl. *Tho*. Goldyngham, esq., & w. Dorothy, def. The manor of Goldingham Hall & 1 mess., 1 dovecote, 300 a. ar., 20 a. mw., 100 a. pa., 40 a. wd. & £4 rt. in Bulmer & Gestyngthorp. Def. quitclaimed to pl. & the heirs of Wm. £600.

19. Mich. & Hil. Wm. Sorrell, pl. Nich. Lasshe, def. 1 mess., 1 gdn. & 12 a. ar. in Great Salyng *alias* Old Salyng. £40.

20. Joan Dale, wid., & Matthew Dale, pl. Tho. Bellyngeham & w. Joan, def. 1 mess., 1 gdn., 1 orchard, 18 a. ar., 10 a. mw., 18 a. pa. & 4 a. wd. in Harwardestock & common of pa. for all animals in Stocke 'Comen'. Def. quitclaimed to pl. & the heirs of Matthew for the life of Joan, def. 100 mks.

21. Wm. Bateman, pl. *Jn.* Fytche & w. Margt., Wm. Fytche, Tho. Fytche, Rd. Fytche, & Chris. Fytche & w. Joan, def. 20 a. ar., 6 a. mw. & 16 a. pa. in Toppesfelde. £40.

22. Gilbert Branthwayte & w. Joan, pl. *Robt.* Jarvys & w. Agnes, *Giles* Williams & w. Agnes, def. 1 mess., 1 barn. & 1 gdn. in Hennyngham Castell *alias* Hengham at the Castle. Def. quitclaimed to pl. & the heirs of Gilbert. £30.

23. Tho. Churche & Jn. Loveday, gentlemen, pl. *Jn.* Lentall, esq., & w. Frances, def. 1 mess., 2 barns, 40 a. ar., 10 a. mw. & 40 a. pa. in Navestocke, Keldon, Welde & Rumford. Def. quitclaimed to pl. & the heirs of Tho. 130 mks.

24. Jn. Skyll, gent., pl. *Jn.* Joye & Hy. Joye, def. 18 a. ar., 5 a. mw., 16 a. pa. & 1 a. wd. in Rayleigh *alias* Raley. £40.

25. Tho. Myldmaye, kt., pl. Walter, earl of Essex, def. The manors of Legatts, Knypso & Dredgers & 4 mess., 4 cotts., 6 tofts, 2 dovecotes, 4 gdns., 4 orchards, 300 a. ar., 300 a. mw., 1,300 a. pa., 20 a. wd., 20 a. moor, 200 a. marsh & 20s. rt. in Mayland, Tyllingham, Legatts, Knypso & Dredgers. £540.

26. Tho. Crushe, pl. *Tho.* Lyndsell & w. Joan, def. 3 mess., 120 a. ar., 20 a. mw. & 40 a. pa. in Roxwell. £140.

27. Jas. (Harvey), citizen & alderman of London, p. *Jn.* (Thatcher) & (w.) Martha, def. 2 mess., 2 barns, 2 gdns., (50 a. ar.), 10 a. mw., 20 a. pa. & 15 a. (wd. in) Chaldwell & Dagenham. £1. . . .

28. Roger (Banks) & Wm. Samways, pl. Jn. Banks, def. 3 mess., 1 toft, 3 barns, 3 gdns., 40 a. ar., 16 a. mw. & 8 a. pa. in Great Wenden & Little Wenden. Def. quitclaimed to pl. & the heirs of Roger. £80.

29. Barnabas Gaymar, pl. *Jn.* Ive *alias* Sparhauke & Alice (w. def.) 1 mess., 1 cott., 1 gdn., 2 orchards, 20 a. ar., (1 a. mw. & 3) a. pa. in Shalford. £40.

CP25(2)/260   DIVERS COUNTIES

3. Mich. & Hil. Hy. Cocke & Jas. Moryce, esquires, pl. Anne Newman, wid., def. 2 mess., 100 a. ar., 40 a. mw., 100 a. pa. 20 a. wd. & 20 a. marsh in Stortford Bishop's *alias* Bysshoppes Stortforde & Thorley, co. Herts; & the same in Stortforde Bishop's *alias* Bisshoppes Stortforde & Thorley, co. Essex. Def. quitclaimed to pl. & the heirs of Hy. £300. — Herts. Essex.

10. Tho. Touneshend, esq., & Wm. Yaxle, esq., pl. *Hy.* Bedingfeld, kt., & w. Kath., def. The manors of Cottonhall & Tuddenham & 17 mess., 6 tofts, 614 a. ar., 290 a. mw., 750 a. pa., 70 a. wd. & £6 rt. in Kedyngton *alias* Ketton, Barmestone, Great Wrattynge, Haverell, Sturmer, Stoke by Clare, Pentlowe, Charsfelde, Swyllande, Tuddenham, Westerfeld, Wytnesham & Culpho, co. Suff.; & the manor of Cottonhall & 6 mess., 4 tofts, 200 a. ar., 100 a. mw., 300 a. pa., 40 a. wd. & 60s. rt. in Kedyngton *alias* Ketton, Barmeston, Great Wrattynge, Haverell, Sturmer, Stoke by Clare & Pentlowe, co. Essex. Def. quitclaimed to pl. & the heirs of Tho. £1,800. —Suff., Essex.

CP25(2)/129/1655   EASTER, 16 ELIZABETH   1574

1. Nich. Clere, gent., pl. Robt. Luson & w. *Anne*, def. 1 a. ar. & 2 a. wd. in Wyvenhoo. £40.

2. Jn. Locke, pl. Tho. Fylpott & w. *Anne*, def. 1 mess., 1 barn, 1 gdn., 20 a. ar., 4 a. mw. & 8 a. pa. in Canewdon. £140.

3. Nich. Martyn, pl. *Tho.* Carter & w. Mary, def. 1 mess., 1 barn, 1 toft, 1 gdn., 10 a. ar., 3 a. pa. & 2 a. marsh in Little Maplested & Pedmershe. £40.

4. Tho. Darcy, esq., pl. Brian Darcy, esq., def. 1 mess., 4 a. mw. & 20 a. pa. in Tolleshunt Maior *alias* Tollshunt Mauger, Tollshunt Darcye, Great Totnham, Little Totnham & Goldanger. Def. quitclaimed to pl. & his heirs, with warranty against Bridget Darcy, w. of def., & her heirs. 80 mks.

5. Wm. Wylson, pl. Wm. Bretten & w. *Joan*, def. 1 mess., 1 gdns. & 1 rood ar. in Horndon on the Hill. £40.

6. Robt. Potter, pl. Maurice Martyn, def. 10 a. ar. & 10 a. pa. in Fordham. £40.

7. Hy. Cock, esq., & And. Hemerford, esq., pl. Jas. Moryce, esq., def. 1 water-mill, 30 a. ar., 10 a. mw. & 20 a. pa. in Heighe Onger. Def. quitclaimed to pl. & the heirs of Hy. 200 mks.

8. Clement Syseley, esq., pl. Arthur Breame, esq., def. A certain portion of tithes of sheaves, corn & hay in the ward of Ripple & Chaldwell in the parish of Barkynge with lands called Estbury before this demised or occupied in Barkynge. £40.

9. Jn. Crysall, pl. Pet. Garrolde *alias* Butcher, def. 1 mess., 1 gdn., 1 orchard, 2 a. ar. & 14 a. pa. in Ovyngton. £80.

10. Ambrose Germeyne, kt., & Tho. Badbye, esq., pl. *Charles* le Grys, esq., & w. Ester, def. 1 mess., 100 a. ar., 200 a. mw. & 200 a. marsh in Little Thorrock. Def. quit-claimed to pl. & the heirs of Ambrose. £800.

11. Jn. Wood, pl. Tho. Keightley, esq., 1 mess., 1 gdn., 2 orchards, 4 a. ar., ½ a. mw., 3 a. pa. & ½ a. wd. in Styfford. £40.

12. Tho. Pery sen., pl. *Robt.* Flemyng & w. Mary, *Miles* Barker & w. Anne, def. 2 mess., 2 gdns., 1 orchard & 20 a. ar. in Thaxstede. 130 mks.

13. Walter Myldmaye, esq., pl. *Tho.* Myldmaye, kt., & w. Frances, def. The manor of Legates & 1 mess., 50 a. ar., 60 a. pa., 120 a. marsh & 4d. rt. in Tyllingham, Bradwell by the Sea & Denge. £200.

14. Jas. Wilsemer, pl. *Nich.* Ereswell & w. Joan, def. 1 mess., 2 orchards, 10 a. ar., 2 a. mw., 6 a. pa. & 2 a. wd. in Walden. £40.

15. Tho. Cammock, gent., pl. Tho. Tey, esq., & w. *Eleanor*, def. 1 mess., 1 toft, 1 gdn., 1 orchard, 150 a. ar., 10 a. mw., 80 a. pa. & 30 a. wd. in Copford, Layremarney, Great Byrche, Little Byrche, Layrebretton & Salcott Vyrley. £220.

16. Tho. Clarke, pl. *Tho.* Upchere, clk., & w. Joan, def. 1 mess., 1 barn, 1 orchard & 3 gdns. in Bockynge. £40.

17. Marcellinus Owtred, pl. *Jn.* Bateman & w. Agnes, def. 1 mess., 1 gdn., 1 orchard, 28 a. ar., 2 a. mw. & 10 a. pa. in Great Clacton & Little Clacton. £120.

18. Jn. Tyler, pl. Wm. Rogers & w. *Charity*, def. 2 mess. & 6 a. ar. in Tarlyng. £40.

19. Rd. Raynolds, pl. *Wm.* Norrys & w. Alice, def. 2 mess., 2 gdns., 2 orchards, 10 a. ar., 10 a. mw., 18 a. pa. & 8 a. wd. in Purley & Danburye. £40.

20. Wm. Roche, pl. Jn. Wryght & w. *Margery*, def. 1 mess. & 1 orchard in Little Warley. £40.

21. Tho. Mershe, pl. Jn. Skull & w. *Rose*, def. 1 mess., 1 gdn. & 1 orchard in Cressynge. £40.

22. Steph. Cleybrooke, pl. *Robt.* Flemynge & w. Mary, def. 1 mess., 1 gdn., 1 orchard, 80 a. ar., 12 a. mw., 30 a. pa. & 10 a. wd. in Broxhed. 230 mks.

23. Reg. Heygate, esq., pl. Walter, earl of Essex, def. The manor of Messynge *alias* Bourchiers Hall in Messynge & 30 mess., 20 cotts., 10 tofts, 2 dovecotes, 10 gdns., 10 orchards, 400 a. ar., 100 a. mw., 1,000 a. pa., 20 a. wd., 200 a. moor & 20s. rt. in Messynge. Inworth, Ferynge, Esthorpe & Keldon. £240.

24. Wm. Littelburye, gent., pl. Wm. Samuell & w. *Joan*, def. 1 a. ar. in Ardeley. £40.

25. Rd. Brokeman, gent., pl. Jas. Atwood, def. 1 mess., 1 cott., 2 gdns., 1 orchard, 10 a. ar., 6 a. pa. & 7 a. marsh in Little Thorrock. £80.

26. Hil. & Eas. Tho. Sandford, pl. Edm. Docwra, esq., & w. Dorothy, def. 1 mess. & 3 gdns. in Colchester, which def. hold for the life of Dorothy, with remainder to pl. & his heirs. £80.

27. Rd. Champyon, gent., pl. *Robt.* Sedley, esq., & w. Eliz., def. 13 a. ar. in Standford in le Hope. £80.

28. Jn. Lytherland, pl. Garrard Shilbury & w. *Anne*, def. 1 mess. in Coggeshall. £40.

29. Hil. & Eas. Pet. Lynsey, pl. *Walter* Ellyott & Wm. Dove, def. 2 mess., 2 tofts, 2 gdns., 2 orchards, 200 a. ar., 40 a. mw., 60 a. pa. & 10 a. wd. in Westhannyngfeild & Margettyng. £80.

30. Tho. Cotton, gent., & w. Joan, pl. *Rd*. Prowde & w. Alice, & Wm. Rychardson & w. Joan, def. 1 mess., 2 tofts, 1 barn, 2 gdns., 2 orchards, 60 a. ar., 20 a. mw., 40 a. pa., 30 a. wd. & 40s. rt. in South Wokington *alias* South Wokingdon *alias* South Wokington Rokell *alias* South Wokendon Rokell, North Wokendon, Styfforde, Alveley & Horne-churche. Def. quitclaimed to pl. & the heirs of Tho. 130 mks.

(Endorsement: registered in Exchequer, Hilary 17 Elizabeth.)

31. Tho. Atkyn & Rd. Onyon *alias* Unwyn, pl. Tho. Loude & Jn. Hempsted & w. Kath., def. 1 mess., 1 gdn. & 2 a. ar. in Bumpsted at the Steeple. Def. quitclaimed to pl. & the heirs of Tho., with warranties by Tho. Loude of the mess. & gdn. & by him & Jn. of the 2 a. £40.

32. Hil. & Eas. Tho. Cooke, pl. Robt. Hagger, def. 1 mess., 80 a. ar., 5 a. mw., 40 a. pa., 2 a. wd. & 10s. rt. & a rt. of 1 lb. of pepper in Great Chyssull, Little Chyssull & Haidon. £150.

33. Hil. & Eas. Tho. Wallinger, gent., pl. *Rd*. Dun & w. Joan, def. 1 mess. in Chelmes-ford. £40.

34. Hil. & Eas. Alice Pynnocke *alias* Aungell, wid., pl. *Wm*. Kendall & w. Anne, def. 1 mess. & 1 gdn. in Waltham Holy Cross. £40.

35. Jn. Peers, Simon Egerton & Hy. Perte, pl. Jn. Stamer, gent., def. 2 mess., 2 tofts, 1 windmill, 2 gdns., 100 a. ar., 20 a. mw., 120 a. pa., 3 a. wd., 20 a. furze & heath, 10s. rt. & common of pa. for all beasts in Rawreth. Def. quitclaimed to pl. & the heirs of Jn. 200 mks.

36. Hil. & Eas. Edm. West, pl. *Jn*. Cutts, kt., & w. Anne, def. The manor of Amberden Halle & 20 mess., 20 cotts., 20 tofts, 20 gdns., 20 orchards, 400 a. ar., 100 a. mw., 200 a. pa., 300 a. wd., 100 a. furze & heath & £10 rt. in Depden, Amberden & Wyddington. £440.

37. Clement Sysley, esq., pl. *Wm*. Brooke & w. Kath., & Rd. Turke & w. Alice, def. 1 mess., 1 barn, 1 gdn., 1 orchard, 4½ a. ar., 3 a. mw. & 2 a. pa. in Barkinge. £40.

38. Aphabel Partridge, pl. *Jn*. Owtred, gent., & *Jn*. Drywood, gent., & w. Frances, def. 2 mess., 3 cotts., 2 barns, 2 gdns., 2 orchards, 30 a. ar., 20 a. mw., 20 a. pa., 10 a. wd., 10 a. furze & heath & 10 a. marsh in Navestock & Keldon *alias* Kelwedon. 130 mks.

39. Alexander Harrington, Jn. Martyn *alias* Wendon & Hy. Clerke, pl. Tho. Forde & w. Eliz., & Wm. Jolye & w. Anne, def. 2 mess., 1 cott., 2 gdns. & 14 a. 3 roods ar. in Berdefelde Salynge. Def. quitclaimed to Alexander & his heirs, with warranties for the heirs of Tho. of 1 mess., 1 gdn., 1 orchard & 5 a. 3 roods ar. & for the heirs of Anne of the residue. £40.

40. Wm. Chapman, pl. *Wm*. Clerke sen. & w. Eliz. & *Wm*. Clerke jun., def. 2 a. mw. & 12 a. pa. in Esche *alias* Esse *alias* Asshen & Reddyswell *alias* Redgeswell *alias* Redgewell. £40.

41. Tho. Edon, esq., pl. Tho. Robynson & w. Anne, Rd. Turnor *alias* Colyer & Alice Turnor, wid., def. 9 a. ar. & 1 a. mw. in Bulmer & Twynsted. Def. quitclaimed to pl. & his heirs, with warranties for the heirs of Tho. of 7 a. ar. in Bulmer & for the heirs of Rd. of 2 a. ar. & 1 a. mw. in Twynsted. £40.

42. Alice Isbell, wid., pl. Jn. Barker & w. Kath., & Robt. Cornell & w. Sarah, def. 2 mess., 1 gdn. & 1 orchard in Thaxsted & Walden. Def. quitclaimed to pl. & her heirs, with warranties for the heirs of Kath. of 1 mess., 1 gdn. & 1 orchard in Thaxsted & for the heirs of Sarah of 1 mess. in Walden. £40.

43. Hil. & Eas. Tho. Clerke, pl. Rd. Horsepytt, def. 1 mess., 1 gdn., 12 a. ar. & 3 a. salt marsh in Tollesburye, which Margery Pollerd w. of Wm. Pollerd & Cristiana Bennett w. of David Bennet hold for life. Pl. & his heirs to hold the reversion of the chief lords. £40.

44. Jn. Collyn, pl. Edw. Sulyarde, esq., & Eustace Convyld, esq., def. A moiety of the manor of Otes & of 2 mess., 2 cotts., 2 tofts, 1 dovecote, 2 gdns., 2 orchards, 200 a. land, 40 a. mw., 40 a. pa., 20 a. wd. & 80s. rt. in High Laver, Little Laver, Magdalen Laver, & Matchynge. 400 mks.

45. Edw. Jobson, gent., pl. Jn. Jobson, esq., def. A third part of the manors of East-donyland, Westdonyland, Acresflete *alias* Ackesfletemershe & Monkewyck & of 40 mess.,

30 tofts, 6 dovecotes, 50 gdns., 2,000 a. ar., 300 a. mw., 600 a. pa., 500 a. wd., 400 a. furze & heath, 400 a. fresh marsh, 300 a. salt marsh & £6 13s. 4d. rt. in Eastdonyland & Westdonyland, & a third part of the advowson of the church of Eastdonyland & of a portion of tithes within the manor of Westdonyland & within the parishes of Stonwey & Lexden & of tithes called 'Castell Lands', late parcel of the possessions of the late dissolved monastery of St. John Baptist by Colchester, except 1 mess. called 'le George' in Colchester, & 1 mess. called 'le Harte' in Stonwey. £300.

46. Tho. Gilder & w. Joan, pl. *Jn*. Snowe & w. Joan, & *Nich*. Bonye & w. Joan, def. 1 mess., 1 barn, 1 gdn. & 1 orchard in Wytham. Def. quitclaimed to pl. & the heirs of Tho. £40.

47. Wm. Webbe, pl. *Roger* Warren, gent., son & heir apt. of Roger Warren, gent., & w. Mary & Wm. Turnor, def. The manor of le Motehall & 2 mess., 2 cotts., 2 tofts, 3 gdns., 3 orchards, 200 a. ar., 30 a. mw., 40 a. pa., 20 a. wd., 20 a. marsh & 20 a. alder in Alphamston, Lamarshe, Twynsted & Henny. And for this pl. gtd. the same to Wm. Turnor to hold from Michaelmas last for 32 years, rendering £26 6s. 8d. yearly to pl. & his heirs at the Annunciation & Michaelmas, with power of distraint, with remainder to Roger & Mary & the heirs of Roger, to hold of the chief lords.

CP25(2)/260   DIVERS COUNTIES

2. Jn. Clenche, Jn. Skynner & Wm. Hanbery, pl. Wm. Durant, def. 4 mess., 6 cotts., 3 (tofts), 8 gdns., 6 orchards, 130 a. ar., 30 a. mw., 80 a. pa., 20 a. wd., 40 a. furze & heath, 20 a. marsh, 2 'lez weares' & fisheries & £3 18s. rt. in Warley Wayletts *alias* Warley Abbysse *alias* Great Warley, Great Totham, Little Totham & Goldanger, co. Essex; & prop. in London. Def. quitclaimed to pl. & the heirs of Jn. Clenche. £180. – Essex. London.

17. Hil. & Eas. Geo. Nycholdes, esq., Tho. Darcey, esq., Wm. Ayloff, esq., & Steph. Beckyngham, gent., pl. *Tho*. Beckyngham, esq., & w. Mary, def. Prop. in Surr.; & 200 a. ar., 40 a. mw., 150 a. pa., 30 a. wd. & 20 a. furze & heath in Toulshunt Darcye, Toulshunt Maior, Great Tottham Little Tottham & Goldanger, co. Essex. Def. quitclaimed to pl. & the heirs of Geo. £300. – Surr., Essex.

CP25(2)/129/1656   TRINITY, 16 ELIZABETH   1574

1. Tho. Harrys, pl. Geo. Bayforde & w. Eliz., def. 1 barn & 1 a. ar. in Harlowe. £40.

2. Charles Waldegrave, esq., pl. *Geo*. Smyth, gent., & w. Emma, def. 1 mess., 1 gdn., 100 a. ar., 20 a. mw., 60 a. pa. & 20 a. wd. in Pentlowe & Powles Belchampe. £200.

3. Robt. Wells & w. Agnes & Anne Humfrye, pl. *Mark* Hall & w. Joan, def. 1 mess. in Walden. Def. quitclaimed to pl. & the heirs of Anne. £40.

4. Tho. Porter, pl. Wm. Reynolds, gent., def. 3 mess., 3 tofts, 3 gdns., 100 a. ar., 20 a. mw., 40 a. pa. & 10 a. wd. in Gyngmonteneys *alias* Montnesinge, Shenfeilde & Duddinghurste. £320.

5. Robt. Cole jun., pl. *Jn*. Lylley & w. Eliz., def. 1 mess. & 1 gdn. in Manyngtre. 160 mks.

6. Eas. & Trin. Rd. Goldyng, gent., pl. *Wm*. Fyrmyn & w. Anne, def. 1 mess., 1 toft, 2 gdns., 1 orchard, 12 a. ar., 2 a. mw. & 6 a. pa. in Bulmer. £80.

7. Wm. Bendlowes, serjeant at law, pl. *Geo*. Maxey, gent., & w. Margery, def. 2 mess., 3 gdns., 42 a. ar., & 1 a. mw. in Berdefelde Salynge, Great Salynge & Stebbynge, all tithes of hay, calves, cheese, lambs, wool, piglets, ducks & other minute tithes & oblations in Berdefeld Salynge & the chapel of Berdefeld Salynge. £200.

8. Wm. Dowe, pl. Jn. Hapten, def. 2 a. ar. and 1 a. pa. in Westhanyngfeild. £40.

9. And. Clarke, gent., pl. *Jn*. Morrell & w. Rebecca, def. 1 mess., 1 gdn., 100 a. ar., 40 a. mw., 40 a. pa., 10 a. wd. & 2s. rt. in Bockinge. £100.

10. Geo. Savell, pl. *Wm*. Keye and w. Barbara, def. 1 mess., 1 gdn., 1 orchard & 4 a. ar., in Walden. 130 mks.

11. Hy. Baron, pl. *Roger* Martyne & w. Eliz., def. 1 mess., 1 gdn., 20 a. ar. & 2 a. mw. in Halsted. £80.

12. Wm. FitzWilliam, kt., pl. *Hy*. Clarke & w. Joan, def. 1 mess., 1 cott., 1 gdn., 1 orchard, 4 a. mw., 4 a. pa. & 3 a. wd. in Theydon Garnon *alias* Cowpersale. £40.

13. Jn. Hamonde, pl. *Jn*. Hedyche, Jn. Wells & w. Alice., Jn. Gaywood & w. Joan, def. 1 mess., 1 barn, 1 gdn., 20 a. ar. 10 a. mw. & 10 a. pa. in Southmynster & Steple. £160.

14. Jn. Bently, pl. Tho. Warren & w. Margt., Wm. Humfrey & w. *Grace*, & Tho. Morecock & w. *Dorothy*, def. 1 mess., 2 gdns., 1 orchard & 2 a. pa. in Belchamp William *alias* Water Belchamp. 50 mks.

15. Wm. Atwood & Ralf Scryvener, pl. Francis Bacon, esq., & w. *Mary*, def. The manor of Ewell *alias* Ewell Hall & 2 mess., 2 gdns., 2 orchards, 120 a. ar., 6 a. mw., 14 a. pa., 4 a. wd. & 10s. rt. in Keldon, Ferynge & Inworth. Def. quitclaimed to pl. & the heirs of Wm. 400 mks.

16. Robt. Wells & w. Agnes & Jn. Humfrye, pl. *Wm*. Leder & w. Annabel, def. 1 mess. & 1 gdn. in Walden. Def. quitclaimed to pl. & the heirs of Jn. £40.

17. Tho. Tey, esq., pl. *Robt*. Midleton sen. & Robt. Midleton, his son & heir apt., def. 1 mess., 1 toft, 1 gdn., 1 orchard, 10 a. ar., 4 a. mw., 6 a. pa. & 6 a. moor in Layre de la Hay & Peldon. £40.

18. Jn. Stavorde, pl. *Wm*. Howson & w. Rose, Robt. Platt & w. Joan, def. 6 mess., 4 gdns. & 2 orchards in Chelmysforde. £320.

19. Nich. Martyn, pl. Jn. Turnor & w. *Agnes*, def. 1 mess., 1 barn, 1 toft, 1 gdn., 10 a. ar., 3 a. pa. and 2 a. marsh in Little Maplested & Pedmershe. £40.

20. Nich. Conven, pl. Rd. Hovell *alias* Smythe, gent., & w. *Margery*, def. 4 mess., 4 gdns., 2 orchards, 20 a. (ar.), 4 a mw., 20 a. pa. & 6 a. wd. in Bradfeld (& Wyckes). £80.

21. Edw. Capell, kt., & Tho. Leventhorpe, esq., pl. Edm. Huddilston, esq., & w. Dorothy, def. (Two thirds of) the manors of Southwelde, Costehall *alias* Costedhall & Calcote *alias* Caldecote & (200) mess., 100 cott., 60 tofts, 10 barns, 2 mills, 3 dovecotes, 3,000 a. ar.,) 300 a. mw., 1,000 a. pa., 600 a. wd., 600 a. furze & heath, 20 a. marsh, (£10 rt., free warren & free chace) in South Welde, Shenfeld, Dodinghurste, Brentwood, Brokestreate, N(avestock, Kelvedon, Gyngrave, Great Warley,) Little Warley, Upmynster & Haverynge, two thirds of the rectory of the church of South Welde & of the advowson of the vicarage in South Welde, & two thirds of fairs (*nundinarum*) & a market (in Brentwood;) which def. hold for the life of Dorothy. Def. quitclaimed whatever they held for her life to pl. & his heirs. £(880).

(22.) (Jn. Bullock, esq., pl. *Wistan* Browne, esq., & w. Mary, def. The manor of Cockermouth & 10 mess., 10 cotts., 1 barn, 10 tofts, 10 gdns., 200 a. ar., 100 a. mw., 100 a. pa., 3 a. wd., 20 a. furze & heath, 100 a. marsh & 80s. rt. in Dagenham & Barkinge, & the advowson of the vicarage of the church of Dagenham. Def. quitclaimed to pl. & his heirs, with warranty against Anth. Brown, decd. & his heirs. £480.)

(23.) Jn. Petre, esq., & w. Mary, pl. Tho. Kemp, kt., & w. Joan, def. The manors of Westhorndon, Ingrave, Gyngrave *alias* Gyngraff, Craneham, Feldehowse, Great Bromeford & Nevendon & 200 mess., 2 windmills, 60 gdns., 70 orchards, 6,000 a. ar., 500 a. mw., 3,000 a. p., 500 a. wd., 4,000 a. furze & heath, 300 a. moor, 200 a. marsh & £40 rt. in Westhordon, Chilterdiche *alias* Childerdiche, Great Warley *alias* Warley Wallett, Little Warley, Craneham, Alveley, Bishop's Okendon, Northokendon, Sowthokendon, Bulvan, Salynge, Lyendon *alias* Layndon, Donton, Esthorndon, Ingrave *alias* Gyngrave, Brentwood, Sowth Weld, Shenfield, Hutton, Great Bursted, Little Bursted, Ravensden Crayes, Ravensden Bellowes, Nevendon & Bartilsden, & the advowsons of the churches of Westhorndon, Ingrave, Gyngrave *alias* Gyngraff, Craneham & Nevendon; except the manors of Ameys, Nokehall, Wauton *alias* Waltons, Typtofts, Highams, Pyncknes & Warley & 4 mess., 4 cotts., 4 tofts, 4 gdns., 4 orchards, 100 a. ar., 60 a. mw., 100 a. pa., 60 a. wd., 100 a. furze & heath, 40 a. marsh & £10 rt. in Brendwood, Wymbysh, Westhorndon, Esthorndon, Bulvan, Childerdich, Ingrave & Shenfield known & called by the names of Ameys, Nokehall, Stulpes, Wauton *alias* Waltons, Typtoftes, Hygham, Pynckneys & Warleys. Def. quitclaimed to pl. & the heirs of Jn. And for this pl. gtd. a yearly rt. of £200 from the same to Joan for her life, payable at the Annunciation & Michaelmas at the capital mess. in Westhorndon, the first payment at Michaelmas next, & a penalty of £20 whenever it may be 8 weeks in arrears, with power of distraint.

(*These two fines are taken from the Notes, the Feet being missing.*)

CP25(2)/129/1657   MICHAELMAS, 16–17 ELIZABETH   1574

1. Jn. Tyler, pl. Wm. Lorkyn, def. 7 a. ar. & 8 a. pa. in Shenfelde, £40.

2. Jn. Hynde, pl. *Jn.* Lyvynge & w. Maud, def. A moiety of 1 mess. in Chelmesforde. £40.

3. Robt. Bullock & Jn. Perrye, pl. *Jn.* Cutt, kt., & w. Anne, def. 3 mess., 3 barns, 3 gdns., 3 orchards, 50 a. ar., 6 a. mw., 40 a. pa. & 4 a. wood in Thaxsted & Chawreth. Def. quitclaimed to pl. & the heirs of Jn. £73.

4. Edm. Hynde, pl. Francis Bull, def. 2 mess., 2 barns, 2 orchards, 30 a. ar. 3 a. mw., 3 a. pa. & 3 a. wd. in Rycklyng & Quenden. £120.

5. Rd. Blakesley, pl. Francis Staunton, def. 1 mess., 1 gdn., 1 orchard, 20 a. ar., 4 a. mw., 30 a. pa. & 10 a. wd. in Grensted. 130 mks.

6. Tho. Muschampe, pl. *Hy.* Turner & w. Margery, def. 1 mess., 2 gdns. & 2 orchards in Bockinge. £40.

7. Robt. Pannell, pl. Tho. Pannell & w. *Joan*, def. 16 a. ar. in Reddeswell. £40.

8. Phil. Byrde, gent., pl. Simon Flemynge *alias* Saunder, def. 1 mess., 1 barn, 1 gdn., 2 orchards, 34 a. ar., 5 a. mw., 12 a. pa. & 2 a. wd. in Depden. £80.

9. Hy. Siles & Edw. Bryght, pl. *Jn.* Symon & w. Joan, def. 3 a. ar., 2 a. mw. & 2 a. pa. in Stonden. Def. quitclaimed to pl. & the heirs of Hy. £40.

10. Jas. Harvey, citizen & alderman of London, pl. Paul Stevyns, def. 1 mess., 30 a. ar. & 2 a wd. in Dagenham & Barkynge. £40.

11. Edm. Harrington, pl. *Edw.* Glascocke, gent., & w. Joan, def. The manor of Hawke-woods & 1 mess., 1 gdn., 1 orchard, 100 a. ar., 20 a. mw., 70 a. pa., 3 a. wd. & 60s. rt. in Hennyngham Syble, Hennygham at the Castle, Great Maplested, Halsted & Gosfeld. £200.

12. Rd. Sampford, pl. *Edw.* Sampforde & w. Eliz., def. 1 mess., 1 gdn., 1 orchard, 12 a. ar., 5 a. mw. & 6 a. pa. in Shellowe Bowells. £40.

13. Trin. & Mich. Walter Oswolde & Jn. Layton, gentlemen, pl. Tho. Reynolds, gent., def. 1 mess., 1 dovecote, 1 gdn., 1 orchard, 100 a. ar., 16 a. mw., 100 a. pa. & 4 a. wd. in Asshen, Ovyngton & Reddeswell *alias* Rydgewell. Def. quitclaimed to pl. & the heirs of Walter. £140.

14. Rd. Peers, pl. *Jn.* Stamer & w. Joan, def. 4 mess., 3 tofts, 1 windmill, 4 gdns., 140 a. ar., 40 a. mw., 200 p. pa., 20 a. wd., 100 a. furze & heath, 40s. rt. & common of pa. for all beasts in Rawreth, Wyckeford & Rawreth Heeth. And for this pl. gtd. the same to Jn. & his heirs, to hold of the chief lords.

15. Jn. Wade, pl. *Elizeus* Bushe & w. Mary, def. 1 mess., 3 gdns., 12 a. ar., 2 a. mw. & 6 a. pa. in Leire Bretton *alias* Leyre Barley & Great Byrche. £40.

16. Chris. Underwood, pl. Robt. Potter, def. 10 a. ar., 5 a. pa. & 1 a. wd. in Colne Wake & Bures at the Mount. £40.

17. Edm. Hodilowe, gent., pl. *Matthew* Cawston, gent., & w. Joan, def. 20 a. ar., 50 a. pa. & 2 a. wd. in Lachingdon. £200.

18. Alice Boyes, wid., pl. Geo. Olyff & w. *Joan*, def. 1 mess., 1 gdn. & 1 orchard in Halsted. £40.

19. Jn. Overell & Jn. Mesante, pl. *Jn.* Cutt, kt., & w. Anne, def. 1 mess., 1 barn, 1 gdn., 1 orchard, 45 a. ar., 6 a. mw., 45 a. pa. & 4 a. wd. in Thaxsted. Def. quitclaimed to pl. & the heirs of Jn. Overell. £40.

20. Wm. Keye, Jas. Jarvys, Robt. Burton & Edw. Reve, pl. *Jn.* Cutt, kt., & w. Anne, def. 5 mess., 4 barns, 7 gdns., 5 orchards, 108 a. ar., 16 a. mw., 90 a. pa. & 8 a. wd. in Thaxsted, Depden & Chawreth. Def. quitclaimed to pl. & the heirs of Wm. £200.

21. Jn. Collyn sen., pl. *Edw.* Sullyarde, esq., & w. Anne, def. A moiety of the manor of Otes & 1 mess., 1 dovecote, 5 gdns., 600 a. ar., 80 a. mw., 220 a. pa. & £9 rt. in High Laver, Mawdelyn Laver *alias* Magdalen Laver, Little Laver & Matchynge. £220.

22. Jn. Cocke, pl. *Robt.* Cooke & w. Margt., def. 1 mess. in Brentwood & Southweld. £40.

23. Hy. Smyth, pl. *Tho*. Levermer sen. & w. Helen, & Tho. Levermer jun. & w. Clemencia, def. 1 mess., 1 gdn. & 3 a. ar. in Toppesfeld & Great Yeldham *alias* Great Gelham. £40.

24. Tho. Staples, pl. *Jn*. Vavasor & w. Kath., def. 1 mess., 1 gdn., 2 orchards, 6 a. ar. 3 a. mw., 2 a. pa. & 1 a. wd. in Westham & Stratford Langthorne. £40.

25. Wm. Muschamp, gent., pl. *Ralph* Fryth & w. Joan, def. The manor of Bowells *alias* Cokk a Bowels & 1 mess., 1 gdn., 60 a. ar., 30 a. mw., 40 a. pa., 6 a. wd. & 7s. 2d. rt. in Southweld. £60.

26. Jn. Harrington, pl. *Edm*. Harrington & w. Cecily, def. A moiety of 1 mess., 1 toft, 1 gdn., 60 a. ar., 10 a. mw. & 40 a. pa. in Great Maplested & Hennyngham Syble. £80.

27. Abraham Fookes, pl. *Wm*. Cooke & w. Anne, def. 40 a. ar. & 30 a. marsh in Peldon. £100.

28. Agnes Hall, wid., Edw. Robynson, Jn. Salmon & Tho. Thorne, pl. *Jn*. Cutt, kt., & w. Anne, def. 4 mess., 4 barns, 4 gdns., 5 a. ar., 6 a. mw. & 20 a. pa. in Thaxsted. Def. quitclaimed to pl. & the heirs of Edw. £83.

29. Robt. Petre, esq., pl. Francis Salperwycke *alias* Salperwig *alias* Gillam & w. *Joan*, & Tho. Myller & w. Eleanor, def. The manor of Takeley *alias* Waltham Hall & 15 mess., 1 cott., 1 windmill, 1 dovecote, 16 gdns., 160 a. ar., 40 a. mw., 160 a. pa., 40 a. wd., 200 a. furze & heath & £6 rt. in Takeley & Elsnam *alias* Elsenam. £144.

30. Jn. Boughtell, pl. *Robt*. Stubbyng & w. Margt., def. 16 a. pa. in Thaxstede. £40.

31. Geo. Nicolls, esq., & And. Gyver, pl. *Jn*. Cutt, kt., & w. Anne, def. 10 a. ar. & 12 a. pa. in Thaxsted. Def. quitclaimed to pl. & the heirs of And. £40.

32. Jn. Humfrey, pl. *Jn*. Cutt, kt., & w. Anne, def. 1 mess., 1 gdn., 1 orchard, 16 a. ar., 3 a. mw. & 4 a. pa. in Thaxsted. £40.

33. Anselm Beckett, pl. *Rd*. Wilcocks & w. Joyce, Edw. Plomer & w. Eliz., def. 8 a. ar. & 2 a. mw. in Chynkford. £40.

34. Jn. Byrde, pl. *Hy*. Grene & w. Joan, def. 4 a. mw. & 2 a. pa. in Great Hallingbury. £40.

35. Nich. Hauckyn, pl. *Wm*. Newman sen. & w. Eliz., def. A third part of 2 mess., 4 gdns., 2 a. ar., 9 a. mw. & 1 a. pa. in Westham & Stratford Langthorne. £40.

36. Jas Harvey, citizen & alderman of London, pl. *Rd*. Battye and w. Joan, def. 1 mess. & 4 a. ar. in Dagenham. £40.

37. Edw. Randyll, gent., pl. Rd. Cooke, gent., & *Stansfeld* Cooke, gent., & w. Eliz., def. The manor of Wyfealdes & 10 mess., 6 tofts, 1 mill, 1 dovecote, 10 gdns., 300 a. ar., 40 a. mw., 200 a. pa., 10 a. wd., 6 a. furze & heath, 10 a. marsh, 6 a. alder & 100s. rt. in Barkinge. £325.

38. Jn. Kent & Jn. Newman, pl. *Clem*. Smyth, esq., & w. Dorothy, def. 26 a. wd. in Langforde & the advowson of the church of Langforde. Def. quitclaimed to the heirs of Jn. Kent, And for this pl. gtd. the same to def. & the heirs of Clement, to hold of the chief lords.

39. Robt. Commyn, pl. *Tho*. Powle, esq., & w. Jane, def. 12 a. ar., 6 a. mw., 12 a. pa. & 2 a. wd. in Ilford *alias* Great Ileford & Barkynge. £40.

40. Edw. Meade, pl. *Jn*. Cutt, kt., & w. Anne, def. 3 mess., 3 barns, 3 gdns., 3 orchards, 150 a. ar., 10 a. mw., 40 a. pa. & 4 a. wd. in Thaxsted & Great Sampforde. £40.

41. Robt. Mydleton & Edw. Thedam, pl. Jn. Wynter & w. *Anne*, & Christ. Wynter & w. *Emma*, def. 4 mess., 4 gdns., 2 orchards, 20 a. ar. and 10 a. pa. in Keldon *alias* Esterford, Inford & Messynge. Def. quitclaimed to pl. & the heirs of Robt. 130 mks.

42. Edw. Sulyarde, esq., pl. Margt. Newport *alias* Dryver, wid., def. A third part of 1 mess., 1 cott., 1 barn, 1 toft, 1 gdn., 1 orchard, 12 a. ar., 8 a. mw., 12 a. pa. & 3 a. wd. in Runewell & Wickeford. £40.

43. Jn. Glascock, gent., & Hy. Long, pl. Rd. Stylman sen., def. 1 mess., 1 dovecote, 1 gdn., 1 orchard, 70 a. ar., 10 a. mw., 20 a. pa., 6 a. wd. & 6s. rt. in Heighester, Goodester & Pleishey. Def. quitclaimed to pl. & the heirs of Hy. £100.

44. Wm. Dowe, pl. Eustace Clonvyld, esq., & Edw. Sulyard, esq., def. 30 a. ar., 5 a. mw., 10 a. pa. & 2 a. wd. in Westhannyngfeild. £40.

45. Edm. Tyrrell, esq., pl. Walter, earl of Essex, def. The manor of Ramesden *alias* Ramesden Barrington *alias* Barrington Hall & 40 mess., 20 tofts, 2 dovecotes, 40 gdns., 40 orchards, 1,000 a. ar., 200 a. mw., 1,000 a. pa., 200 a. wd., 400 a. furze & heath, £10 rt. & a rt. of 2 pairs of gilt spurs, 1 lb. of cloves (*garophill'*), 1 lb. of pepper, 20 capons, 10 cocks, 20 hens & 10 ducks in Ramesden Bellowes, Ramesden Greys, Bursted, Downeham, Nevindon, Barstable, Lanedone, Basseldon, Duddinghurst, Southweld, Yng, Iyng Jaberd, Harverstocke & Buttesbury, the park of Ramesden, the free warren of Ramesden, & the free chapel of Barrington Hall *alias* the free chapel of Ramesden. £420.

46. Robt. Aylett & Jn. Burre, pl. Matthew Barnard & Tho. Aylett, def. A moiety of the manor of Eythroppe Hall *alias* Eythrope Rothinge & 30 mess., 30 gdns., 400 a. ar., 60 a. mw., 200 a. pa., 100 a. wd. & £11 rt. in Eytroppe Rothinge *alias* Rodinge Aythroppe, *alias* Rothinge Aythroppe, Highe Rothinge *alias* High Rodinge, Leaden Rothinge *alias* Leaden Rodynge & High Ester, & a moiety of the advowson of the church of Eytroppe Rothinge *alias* Rothinge Aythroppe. Def. quitclaimed to pl. & the heirs of Robt., with warranties by Thos. of a moiety of 24 a. wd. & by Matthew of the residue. £(200).

47. Jn. Ryce, pl. *Wm.* Symonde & w. Eliz., def. 5 mess., 3 cotts., 2 tofts, 6 gdns., 7 orchards, 100 a. ar., 20 a. mw., 100 a. pa., 16 a. wd. & 100 a. furze & heath in Thaxsted. Pl. & the heirs male of his body to hold of the chief lords, with remainder to the heirs male of the body of Robt. Ryce, decd., his father, & the right heirs of Jn. Ryce, decd., father of the latter & grandfather of pl. £420.

CP25(2)/260   DIVERS COUNTIES

4. Jn. Braunche, esq., & Wm. Uvedall, gent., pl. Wm. Dawtrey, esq., def. The manor of Ryvershall & 60 mess., 20 cotts., 60 gdns., 60 orchards, 4 water-mills, 3 dovecotes, 500 a. ar., 300 a. mw., 300 a. pa., 300 a. wd., 500 a. furze & heath & £10 rt. in Boxtede & Langham, co. Essex; and prop. in Suss. Def. quitclaimed to pl. & the heirs of Jn. £1,200. — Essex; Suss.

5. Trin. & Mich. Nich. Bacon, kt., lord keeper of the great seal of England, pl. *Hy.* Gooddere, esq., & w. Frances, def. The manors of Abbatts Burye *alias* Rowletts Burye, Minchinburye, Hoores & Apasaburye *alias* Napsaburye & 12 mess., 20 tofts, 2 mills, 3 dovecotes, 20 gdns., 1,000 a. ar., 60 a. mw., 500 a. pa., 300 a. wd., 200 a. furze & heath & £30 rt. in Barley, Barckwaye & the parish of St. Peter by the town of St. Albans, co. Hertford; the manors of Abbatts Burye *alias* Rowletts Burye & Mynchynburye & 2 mess., 50 a. ar. and 60s. rt. in Little Chissell, co. Essex; & the manor of Abbatts Burye *alias* Rowletts Bury & 2 mess., 30 a. ar., 15 a. mw., 6 a. pa. & 60s. rt. in Harston & Hawston, co. Cambs. £960. — Herts., Essex. Cambs.

CP25(2)129/1658   HILARY, 17 ELIZABETH   1575

1. Jas. Morice esq. & Tho. Cheveley gent., pl. Philip Morice gent., def. 1 mess., 1 gdn. & 20 a. pa. in Roydon. Def. quitclaimed to pl. & the heirs of Jas. £40.

2. Clement Cyseley esq., pl. *Wm.* Nutbrowne gent. & w. Anne, def. 6 a. meadow in Eastbury & Barking Marsh. £40.

3. Jn. Benson, pl. Agnes Hutchynson wid., def. 2 mess. & 2 gdns. in Barking. £40.

4. Frs. Rayner, pl. *Jn.* Cutt kt. & w. Anne, def. 1 mess., 3 gdns. & 7 a. ar. in Thaxted. £40.

5. *Jn.* Westley of Boytons & Christopher Byflett, pl. Rich. Westley, def. 1 mess., 1 gdn., 1 orchard, 24 a. ar., 3 a. mw. & 20 a. pa. in Hempstead, Gt. Sampford, Finchingfield & Helions Bumpstead. Def. quitclaimed to pl. & the heirs of Jn. £80.

6. Hil. Robt. Ball, pl. Tho. Carter & w. Mary, def. 18 a. ar. & 1 a. mw. in Great Holland. £40.

7. Hil. 'Incencius' Godman, pl. *Wm.* Standon & w. Agnes, def. 1 mess., 1 gdn. & 3 a. ar. in Barking and Ilford. £40.

8. Mich. & Hil. Francis Archer, pl. *Wm*. Ramsey & w. Joan, def. 2 mess., 2 gdns., 4 a. ar., 2 a. mw. & 2 a. pa. in Northeweld Bassett. £40.

9. Hil. Wm. Bathe & Rd. Parsons, pl. *Jn*. Seynt John, esq., & Nich. Seynt John, gent., def. 1 mess., 500 a. ar., 60 a. mw., 200 a. pa. & 40 a. wd. in Hatfyld Bury *alias* Hatfyld Peverall. Def. quitclaimed to pl. & the heirs of Wm. £360.

10. Hil. Rd. Brockman, gent., pl. Hy. Clarke, def. 3 mess., 3 gdns., 3 orchards, 20 a. ar., 20 a. mw. & 20 a. pa. in Halsted & Witham. 400 mks.

11. Hil. Jn. Dyster, gent., pl. Jn. Pawlett, kt., marquess of Winchester, & w. Wenefrida, def. The manor of Barholte Sackevile, & 20 mess., 20 cotts., 20 tofts, 1 mill, 1 dovecote, 20 gdns., 20 orchards, 400 a. ar., 60 a. mw., 400 a. pa., 300 a. wd., 500 a. furze & heath & 40s. rt. in Barholte Sackevile, West Barholte & Fordeham, held by the marquess & his w. for the life of Wenefrida, with reversion to Tho. Sackevile, kt., lord Buckhurste, & his heirs. Def. granted prop. to pl. for the life of Wenefrid. £1,216.

12. Mich. & Hil. Lewis Reynold, pl. Jn. Price & w. Margery, Ralph Goslyng & w. *Helen* & Eliz. Wylkynson, wid., def. 3 mess., 3 cotts. & 3 gdns. in Barkyng. £40.

13. Mich. & Hil. Wm. Bygge, pl. *Wm*. Fytche, sen., Oswald Fytche, Wm. Fytche, jun., Steph. Fytche, 'Goldingus' Fytche & Tho. Fytche, def. 10 a. ar., 10 a. mw. & 10 a. pa. in Great Yeldham & Toppysfylde. £100.

14. Hol. Rd. Brokeman, gent., pl. Jn. Tyler & w. *Thomasina*, def. 1 mess., 1 gdn., 10 a. ar., 6 a. pa. & 5 a. fresh marsh in Chaldwell & Little Thurrock. £40.

15. Hil. Jn. Oldham, pl. Jn. Hewlett & w. *Martha*, def. 1 mess., 1 gdn., 1 orchard, 20 a. ar., 3 a. mw. & 20 a. pa. in Little Bursst(de). £80.

16. Hil. Thos. Darcye, esq., pl. Brian Darcye, esq., def. 7 a. ar. & 8 a. pa. in Toleshunt Darcye *alias* Toleshunt Tregoos & Tollesbury. £40.

17. Hil. Jn. Smyth, pl. Arthur Dexter, def. 1 mess. & 1 gdn. in Colchester. £40.

18. Hil. Rd. Gourney, pl. *Rd*. Brokeman, gent., & w. Mary, def. 3 mess., 4 cotts., 4 gdns., 3 orchard, 80 a. ar., 12 a. mw. & 60 a. pa. in Stifford. £400.

19. Hil. Vincent Randyll & Edw. Randyll, gentlemen, pl. *Arthur* Breame, esq., & w. Thomasina, def. 1 mess., 3 cotts., 4 gdns., 4 orchards, 100 a. ar., 100 a. mw., 100 a. pa., 100 a. wd., 100 a. furze & heath & 20 a. moor in Barkyng, all tithes of sheaves, grain & hay & all other tithes pertaining to a mess. called 'Gayeshams Hall' in Barkyng. Def. quitclaimed to pl. & the heirs of Edw. (*mutilated*).

20. Hil. Esq. Whytyngham, pl. Hugh Lyte & w. *Helen*, def. A fourth part of 2 mess., 2 gdns., 2 orchards, 130 a. ar. & 10 a. wd. in Whytenotley, Blackenotley & Brancktree. £40.

21. Hil. Tho. Burlinge & Humfrey Parrys, pl. *Hy*. Chauncye, esq., & w. Jane, def. 5 mess., 5 tofts, 5 gdns., 5 orchards, 95 a. ar., 6 a. mw., 12 a. pa. & 5 a. wd. in Farneham. Def. quitclaimed to def. & the heirs of Tho. £80.

22. Hil. Tho. Tyrrell, pl. Wm. Pawne, esq., *Francis* Holte, gent., & w. Alice, def. 2 mess., 2 cotts., 2 gdns., 2 orchards, 80 a. ar., 20 a. mw., 60 a. pa., 20 a. wd. & 20 a. furze & heath in Wryttell, Chelmesford & Ingerston. £80.

23. Hil. Jn. Gaywood, pl. Edw., earl of Oxford, def. 6 a. mw. & 50 a. pa. in Steple & Mayland. £40.

24. Mich. & Hil. Robt. Spencer, esq., pl. *Jn*. Stamer & w. Joan & *Rd*. Peers, def. 2 mess., 2 gdns., 40 a. ar., 10 a. mw., 30 a. pa., 3 a. wd. & common pasture for all livestock in Rawreth, Wyckeford & Rawreth Heathe. £120.

25. Hil. Robt. Petre & Edm. Downynge, pl. Walter Myldmay, kt., def. The manors of Seyntclers & Herons, & 30 mess., 30 cotts., 20 tofts, 30 gdns., 30 orchards, 1,200 a. ar., 300 a. mw., 1,200 a. pa., 300 a. wd., 200 a. marsh, 100 a. alder, 1,000 a. furze & heath & £10 rt. in Danbury, Sandon, Great Badowe & Little Badowe, & the advowson of the church of Danbury. Def. quitclaimed to pl. & the heirs of Robt. Pl. gtd. prop. to def. & his heirs to hold of chief lords.

26. Hil. Greg. Kyne, pl. *Jn*. Lock, Tho. Fylpoott & w. Anne, def. 1 mess., 1 gdn., 10 a. ar., 4 a. mw. & 16 a. pa. in Canonden *alias* Canewdon. £40.

27. Hil. Robt. Sydley, gent., pl. *Rd*. Brokeman, gent., & w. Mary, def. 2 mess., 2 gdns., 2 orchards & 13 a. ar. in Curringham. £80.

28. Mich. & Hil. Hercules Mewtys, esq., & Paul Umpton, gent., pl. *Hy*. Myldmaye, esq., & w. Jane, def. The manors of Great Lyes & Busshops Lyes, & 20 mess., 20 cotts., 10 tofts, 1 water-mill, 4 dovecotes, 50 gdns., 300 a. ar., 100 a. mw., 200 a. pa., 100 a. wd., 100 a. furze & heath & 80s. rt. in Great Lyes, Little Lyes, Terling, Boreham, Fayersted & Little Waltham, & the advowson of the church of Great Lyes. Def. quitclaimed to pl. & the heirs of Hercules. £400.

29. Hil. Rd. Farr, gent., & Ursula More, pl. *Walter* Farr, esq., & w. Fredeswide, def. The manor of Standforde le Hope, 30 mess., 10 barns, 6 tofts, 30 gdns., 4 orchards, 150 a. ar., 60 a. mw., 150 a. pa., 10 a. wd., (. . .) a. fresh marsh, 500 a. salt marsh, common fishing & £6 rt. in Stanford le Hope, Mockynge, Coryngham, Hornedon & Southebemflete. Def. quitclaimed to pl. & the heirs of Rd. (*mutilated*).

(*Walter Farr is misnamed William on his first appearance in the fine.*)

30. Hil. Rd. Warde & Agnes Barthelmewe, wid., pl. *Tho*. Downynge & w. Joan, def. 1 mess., 1½ a. ar. & 4½ a. mw. in Belchampe Seynt Powl *alias* Beauchampe St. Paul. Def. quitclaimed to pl. & the heirs of Rd. £34.

31. Hil. Jn. Collyn & Tho. Wynterflod, pl. *Launcelot* Patrick, *Mich*. Collyn, & w. Marion & *Hy*. Collyn, def. 2 mess., 2 gdns., 2 orchards, 43 a. ar., 10 a. mw., 10 a. pa. & 10 a. wd. in Stysted, Broxhed & Tyltey. Def. quiteclaimed to pl. & the heirs of Jn. Warranty by Launcelot Patrick for 1 mess., 1 gdn., 43 a. ar., 6 a. mw., 10 a. pa. & 10 a. wd. in Stysted; warranty by Mich. & Marion Collyn for 1 mess., 1 gdn., 2 orchards & 4 a. mw. in Broxhed & Tyltey; warranty by Hy. Collyn for these latter props. in Broxhed & Tyltey. £40.

32. Hil. Edw. Turner & Wm. Vigorus, pl. *Tho*. Sampson & w. Jane, Robt. Guye & w. Joan, def. 1 mess., 1 gdn. & 1 orchard in Earles Colne, & a moiety of 1 mess., 1 gdn. & 1 orchard in Halsted. Def. quitclaimed to pl. & the heirs of Edw. Warranty by Tho. & Jane Sampson for the prop.; warranty by Robt. & Joan Guye for the moiety in Halsted only. £40.

33. Hil. Jas. Altham, esq., pl. *Tho*. earl of Suss. & w. Frances, def. The manor of Sherynge *alias* Sherynghall, & 40 mess., 40 cotts., 40 tofts, 1 mill, 4 dovecotes, 40 gdns., 40 orchards, 400 a. ar., 80 a. mw., 100 a. pa., 20 a. wd., 30 a. furze & heath & 40s. rt. in Sherynge, Harlowe, Hatfeild & Sabsford (co. Herts.), & the advowson of the church of Sheringe. 400 mks.

34. Hil. Jn. Watson, gent., pl. *Nich*. Smyth, gent., & w. Grace, def. The manor of Leynehams, & 3 mess., 3 cotts., 3 tofts, 1 dovecote, 3 gdns., 3 orchards, 150 a. ar., 20 a. mw., 150 a. pa., 60 a. wd., 20 a. furze & heath & 40s. rt. in Revenhall *alias* Ruenhall, Cressinge *alias* Kersings, Bockinge, Breyntree, Stysted & Bradwell. £200.

CP25(2)/260   DIVERS COUNTIES

4. Hil. Tho. Byrde, pl. *Tho*. Lodge, kt., & w. Anne, def. 4 mess., 16 a. ar., 16 a. mw. & 16 a. pa. in Great Horseley (in co. Essex), and prop. in Suff. £160. — Essex, Suff.

CP25(2)/129/1659   EASTER, 17 ELIZABETH   1575

1. Eas. Tho. Westbrome, pl. Steph. Cooke, def. 1 mess., 1 gdn., 5 a. ar. & 1 a. mw. in Little Clacton. £40.

2. Eas. Nich. Wall, pl. Wm. Clere, def. 20 a. ar. in Great Halyngburye & Little Halingburye. £40.

3. Eas. Hy. Chotche, pl. Edw. Solme & w. *Alice*, def. 1 mess., 1 barn, 1 gdn., 7 a. ar., 3 a. mw. & 7 a. pa. in Prytwell. £40.

4. Eas. Jn. Watson, gent., pl. *Rd*. Reynolds & w. Mary, def. 4 mess., 4 tofts, 2 gdns., 2 orchards, 6 a. ar. & 2 a. pa. in Chelmesford, Mulsham *alias* Mowssam & Spryngfeilde. 130 mks.

5. Eas. Robt. Aylett, pl. *Jn*. Hoskyn sen., & w. Eliz., def. 1 mess., 1 gdn., 1 orchard, 16 a. ar., 4 a. mw., 2 a. pa. & 2 a. moor in Rothyng Beauchampe *alias* Beauchampe Rodynge. £40.

6. Eas. Jn. Burr, pl. Robt. Damyon, def. 1 mess., 10 a. ar. & 1 a. mw. in Marks Teye *alias* Teye Mandevyle. £40.

7. Eas. Geo. Lucas, pl. *Jn.* Atkynson & w. Helen, def. 4 mess., 4 gdns. & 1 orchard in Brentwood. £103.

8. Eas. Tho. Hulle & Jn. Wallys, pl. *Wm.* Fuller & w. Eliz., def. 2 mess., 3 gdns., 1 orchard & 8 a. ar. in Stebbynge. Def. quitclaimed to pl. & the heirs of Tho. £40.

9. Eas. Rd. Goldyng, gent., pl. Roger Fyrmyn, def. 1 mess., 1 toft, 2 gdns., 1 orchard, 12 a. ar., 2 a. mw. & 6 a. pa. in Bulmer. £80.

10. Eas. Rd. Rogers, pl. Jn. Rogers, def. 1 mess., 1 barn, 1 orchard, 10 a. ar., 19 a. mw. & 19 a. pa. in Thaydon Garnon. £40.

11. Eas. Edm. Stane, pl. *Jn.* Cowland & w. Alice, def. 1 mess., 1 curtilage, 1 gdn., 10 a. ar., 6 a. mw., 10 a. pa. & 1 a. wd. in Westhannyngfeild. 100 mks.

12 Eas. Robt. Rerye, pl. *Wm.* Whyne & w. Agnes, def. 1 mess., 1 gdn., 10 a. ar., & 1 a. mw. in Black Notley. £40.

13. Hil. & Eas. Rd. Redryche *alias* Rice, clk. pl. *Wm.* Knyghtbrydge & w. 'Rabardgia', def. 10 a. pa. in Downeham. Def. quitclaimed to pl. £40.

14. Eas. Wm. Rogers, pl. Nich. Marson, gent., & w. Anne, def. A third part of 2 mess., 1 barns, 1 gdn., 1 orchard, 50 a. ar., 240 a. pa., 3 a. wd., 10s. rt. & common pa. for 60 sheep in Stanford le Hope. £200.

15. Eas. Anne Browne, wid., pl. *Tho.* Page & w. Margt., def. 1 mess., 1 gdn., 5 a. ar., 1 a. mw. & 3 a. pa. in Asshyn *alias* Esse. £40.

16. Eas. Rd. Harrys, pl. *Wm.* Fowle & w. Mary, def. 6 a. ar. in Mylton Shore *alias* Myddelton & Prytwell. £40.

17. Eas. Jn. Wethers & Rd. Grenacres, pl. *Hy.* Mordaunt, gent., & w. Suzanna, def. 20 a. ar., 10 a. mw. & 40 a. pa. in Wymbyshe & Thunderley, Def. quitclaimed to pl. & the heirs of Rd. £60.

18. Eas. Jn. Stock, Wm. Stock & Giles Stock, pl. *Giles* Chysshull, esq., & w. Alice, def. 2 mess., 2 gdns., 50 a. ar., 4 a. mw. & 12 a. pa. in Little Berdefeld & Great Berdefeld. Def. quitclaimed to pl. & the heirs of Jn. £40.

19. Eas. Robt. Raven, sen., pl. Jn. Sparrowe & w. Eliz., def. 1 gdn. & 4 a. ar. in Stystede. £40.

20. Eas. Clement Cyseley, esq., pl. *Wm.* Nutbrowne, gent., & w. Anne, def. 1 mess. & 7 a. ar. in Upton in the parish of Barkyng. £40.

21. Eas. Wm. Grene & w. Helen, pl. *Jn.* Harte & w. Grace, def. 1 mess., 1 gdn. & 1 quay (*kaium*) in Harwico. Def. quitclaimed to pl. & the heirs of Wm. £40.

22. Eas. Tho. Hopper, pl. *Tho.* Parker & w. Mary, Robt. Broke, gent., & w. Eliz., def. 4 a. ar. in Crishall. £40.

23. Eas. Tho. Salmon, pl. *Lau.* Rochell & w. Joan, def. 2 mess., 60 a. ar., 30 a. mw., 20 a. pa. & 10 a. wd. in Ramesdon Belhouse, Ramesdon Crayes & Downeham. £40.

24. Eas. Wm. Lake, pl. Wm. Staunton, gent., *Francis* Staunton, gent., Rd. Offeley & w. Jane, def. 1 mess., 1 gdn., 9 a. ar. & 3 a. mw. in Stanford Ryvers. £60.

25. Eas. Wm. Porter, pl. Jn. Porter, def. 1 barn, 20 a. ar., 6 a. mw. & 30 a. pa. in Great Braxsted. £40.

26. Eas. Wm. Deane, gent., pl. *Jn.* Holmested, gent., & w. Margt., def. The manor of Dynes, Hosedennes & Caxtons, & 2 mess., 3 tofts, 1 mill, 1 dovecote, 4 gdns., 200 a. ar., 40 a. mw., 40 a. pa., 40 a. wd., 20 a. furze & heath & £12 rt. in Great Maplested, Little Maplested, Hengham Syble *alias* Hennyngham Syble, Hengham Castell *alias* Hennyngham ad Castrum & Gestyngthorpe. £1,000.

27. Eas. Jas. Harvey, citizen & alderman of London, pl. *Wm.* Nutbrowne, gent., & w. Anne, def. 40 a. ar., 6 a. mw., 3 a. wd. & 6 a. marsh in Dagenham, & common pa. for all animals in Dagenham. Warranty by def. against Wm. Nutbrowne, his heirs, Martin Bowes, sen., esq., & his heirs. £40.

28. Eas. Wm. Norris, pl. *Steph*. Collyn & w. Helen, def. 1 mess., 1 toft, 1 barn, 1 gdn., 1 orchard, 40 a. ar., 20 a. mw., 30 a. pa. & 6 a. wd. in Great Baddowe. £40.

29. Eas. Edw. Whyttyngham, pl. *Edw*. Heron, gent., & w. Anne, def. A fourth part of 3 mess., 3 gdns., 140 a. ar., 3 a. mw., 10 a. pa. & 20 a. wd. in Whyte Notley, Black Notley & Branktree. £40.

30. Eas. Jn. Pope, pl. *Wm*. Lorkyn & Rd. Lorkyn, def. 1 mess., 1 gdn., 1 orchard, 30 a. ar., 10 a mw. & 20 a. pa. in Shenfeld. £100.

31. Eas. Robt. Hulwood, pl. *Tho*. Pyper & w. Joan, def. 1 mess., 20 a. ar., 10 a. mw., 25 a. pa. & 10 a. wd. in Muche Holland. £80.

32. Eas. Jn. Bowsey, pl. *Jn*. Bretton & w. Eliz., def. 2 mess., 2 cotts., 1 barn, 2 gdns., 5 a. ar. & 3 a. pa. in Chycknall St. James and Wryttell. £40.

33. Eas. Edw. Osborne, citizen & alderman of London, pl. *Wm*. Nutbrown, gent., & w. Anne, def. 6 a. ar. & 5 a. pa. in Barkynge. £40.

34. Eas. Jas. Woodhall & Wm. Byrd, pl. *Tho*. Petyt & w. Cicily, *Wm*. Calton & w. Anne, def. 1 mess., 1 barn, 1 gdn. & 1 orchard in Walden. Def. quitclaimed to pl. & the heirs of Wm. Byrd. £40.

35. Eas. Robt. Sames, pl. *Tho*. Marshall & w. Margt., def. 1 mess., 1 barn, 1 gdn., 1 orchard, 16 a. ar., 3 a. mw., 3 a. pa. & 2 a. wd. in Little Waltham. 100 mks.

36. Eas. Wm. Clark, pl. *Wm*. Byrle & w. Etheldreda, def. 1 mess., 1 toft & 1 rod of ar. in High Laver. £40.

37. Eas. Humfrey Hayes, pl. *Geoff*. Gate, esq., & w. Eliz., def. The prebend & rectory of Westhurrock, & 2 tofts, 1 dovecote, 2 gdns., 30 a. ar., 20 a. mw., 30 a. pa., 10 a. wd., 40 a. fresh marsh, 40 a. salt marsh & 53s. 4d. rt. in Westhurrock, tithes of sheaves, grain & hay in Westhurrock & the advowson of the vicarage of the church in Westhurrock. £400.

38. Eas. Hy. Slyter, pl. Jn. Berd & w. *Philippa*, def. 1 mess., & 2 gdns. in Maldon. £40.

39. Eas. Jn. Aylyff & w. Susanna, pl. *Jn*. Bridges & w. Anne, *Geoff*. Scott & w. Jane, def. 6 mess., 1 curtilage, 1 barn, 7 gdns., 1 orchard, 8 a. mw. & 4 a. pa. in Chelmysford. Def. quitclaimed to pl. & the heirs of Jn. Aylyff. 130 mks.

40 Eas. Jn. Watts & Rd. Sheryff, pl. *Clement* Smyth & w. Dorothy, def. 1 mess., 1 fulling mill, 1 gdn. & 5 a. mw. in Langford. Def. quitclaimed to pl. & the heirs of Jn. Pl. gtd. prop. to def. & the heirs of Clement to hold of the chief lords.

41. Eas. Jn. Barker, Rd. Barker, Hugh Taylor, Tho. Cressall, Robt. Colman, Jn. Osborn, Wm. Kelmache, Rd. Webb, Tho. Haryson, jun., Jas. Mawle, Jn. Mawle, jun., Geo. Mawle, Jn. Barker, jun., And. Pares, Rd. Walter, Jn. Walter & Tho. Howlton, pl. *Jn*. Mawle & Tho. Lorken, def. 1 mess., 2 gdns., 10 a. ar., 4 a. mw. & 6 a. pa. in Layer Bretyn. Def. quitclaimed to pl. & the heirs of Jn. Barker. £80.

42. Hil. & Eas. Tho. Brydgis, gent., pl. *Jn*. Parker & Jne. Sympson, def. 1 mess., 1 gdn., 1 orchard, 40 a. ar., 10 a. mw., 20 a. pa. & 5 a. wd. in Little Waltham. Pl. gtd. prop. to Jn. Sympson for 11 years at rt. of £4 a year; pl. gtd. reversion to Jn. Parker to hold of chief lords.

DIVERS COUNTIES

3. Hil. & Eas. Jn. Peter & Francis Wyndam, esquires, pl. Hy. Chauncy, esq., def. Site of the manor of Hartyshoburye, 2 mess., 1 water-mill, 1 dovecote, 2 gdns., 1 orchard, 300 a. ar., 30 a. mw. & 200 a. pa. in Fernham & Stansted Mountfitchet, so. Essex; & prop. in Hertford. Def. quitclaimed to pl. & the heirs of Jn. 410 mks. — Essex, Herts.

4. Eas. Robt. Baspole & Tho. Bartlett, pl. Tho. Jernegan, gent., & w. *Eliz*., def. Prop. in Herts. and 15 a. ar. in Great Halyngburye, co. Essex. Def. quitclaimed to pl. & the heirs of Robt. £210. — Herts., Essex.

CP25(2)/129/1660   TRINITY, 17 ELIZABETH   1575

1. Morrow of Trin. Jn. Bret, pl. *Edw*. Baber, esq., & w. Kath., def. 1 mess., 1 cott., 1 dovecote, 2 gdns, 1 orchard, 14 a. ar., 2 a. mw. & 15 a. pa. in Little Badowe. £60.

2. Morrow of Trin. Rd. Smyth, pl. Benj. Clere & w. Anne, def. A fourth part of 1 mess., 1 barn, 20 a. ar. & 2. a. wd. in Ardeleigh. £40.

3. Trin. Rd. Peacock, pl. *Jn.* Eckford & w. Denise, def. 1 mess., 2 gdns. & 1 a. ar. in Barlinge. £40.

4. Morrow of Trin. Tho. Cooke, pl. Geo. Warren & w. Joan, Jn. Leffingwell & w. *Alice*, def. A moiety of 1 mess., 1 gdn. & 14 a. ar. in Wickham St. Paul *alias* Wickham Powle. 40 mks.

5. Morrow of Trin. Jn. Botolff, jun., pl. *Wm.* Botolff & w. Cecily, def. 2 mess., 2 gdns., 2 orchards, 40 a. ar., 2 a. mw. & 10 a. pa. in Lyndsell. £40.

6. Morrow of Trin. Jn. Ive, gent., pl. *Tho.* Bedell, esq., & w. Eliz., def. 6 a. ar., 2 a. pa. & 2 a. wd. in Wryttell. £40.

7. Trin. Jn. Dyer, pl. *Nich.* Dyer & w. Joan, def. 15 a. ar., 1 a. mw. & 2 a. pa. in Farnham. £20.

8. Morrow of Trin. Jerome Garrade, pl. Tho. Babyngton & w. *Helen*, def. 3 mess., 1 dovecote, 2 barns, 1 gdn., 1 orchard, 30 a. ar., 20 a. mw., 40 a. pa. & 10 a. wd. in Wytham. £40.

9. Trin. Tho. Powle, esq., pl. *Walter* Morgan, gent., & w. Jane, def. 30 a. mw. & 4 a. pa. in Great Ilford in the parish of Barkynge. £200.

10. Morrow of Trin. Jn. Fenyx, pl. *Tho.* Herde & w. Eliz., def. 1 mill, 5 a. ar. & 1 rod of pa. in Upmynster. £40.

11. Morrow of Trin. Reg. Heigate, esq., pl. *Jn.* Clarke & w. 'Prisca', def. 1 mess., 3 cotts., 3 gdns., 3 orchards, 80 a. ar., 10 a. mw., 40 a. pa. & 20. a. wd. in Southmynster, Burnham & Ashyldam. £200.

12. Trin. Wm. Wilkyns, pl. Tho. Durant, def. 2 mess., 2 gdns., 20 a. ar., 4 a. mw., 20 a. pa. & 3 a. wd. in Lamburne. £40.

13. Morrow of Trin. Tho. Walsyngham, kt., & w. Dorothy, pl. Jn. Rochester, esq., & *Edw.* Rochester, gent., def. 6 mess., 6 barns., 1 windmill, 6 gdns., 106 a. ar., 40 a. mw., 100 a. pa., 26 a. wd. & £4 4s. rt. in Bobyngworthe, Stanford Ryvers & Northweld Basset, & the moiety of the advowson of the church of Bobyngworth. Def. quitclaimed to pl. & the heirs of Tho. £200.

14. Morrow of Trin. Wm. Pawne, esq., pl. *Jn.* Symond & w. Joan, def. 1 mess., 1 gdn., 30 a. ar., 10 a. mw. & 30 a. pa. in Blakamore. £80.

15. Morrow of Trin. Tho. Myldmay, pl. *Robt.* Arthur & w. Margaret, def. 1 mess., 1 orchard, 22 a. ar., 1 a. mw. & 8 a. pa. in Spryngefeld. 100 mks.

16. Morrow of Trin. Wm. Fynche, pl. *Wm.* Fytche, sen., Oswald Fytche & Golding Fytche, def. 1 mess., 1 gdn., 1 orchard & 1 a. mw. in Great Gelham *alias* Great Yeldham. £40.

17. Morrow of Trin. Jn. Churche, gent., pl. *Wm.* Rogers & w. Joan, def. 2 mess., 2 gdns., 1½ a. mw. & 10 a. pa. in Runwell. £40.

18. Trin. Kath. Audeley, wid., pl. Jn. Christmas, esq., def. 4 mess., 1 dovecote, 4 gdns., 4 a. pa. & 10 a. wd. in the town of Colcestr', Grenested & Myleend. £40.

19. Morrow of Trin. Tho. Pullyson, citizen & alderman of London, & Gabriel Colstone, pl. *Walter* Fyshe & w. Eliz. def. 1 mess., 10 a. ar., 10 a. mw., 60 a. pa. & 12 a. wd. in Layghton & Waltham Stoe. Def. quitclaimed to pl. & the heirs of Tho. £220.

20. Morrow of Trin. Rd. Morse, pl. *Edw.* Gylder & w. Anne, def. A moety of 1 mess., 1 barn, 1 orchard, 40 a. ar., 20 a. mw., 6 a. pa. & 4 a. wd. in Duddynghurst & Blackmore. £80.

21. Morrow of Trin. Robt. Tanfeld, gent., son of Francis Tanfeld, esq., & Tho. Smyth, pl. Wm. Tanfeld, esq., & w. *Eliz.*, Jn. Tanfeld, gent., son & heir apt. of Wm., and 'Clovilus' Tanfeld, gent., def. The manor of Coptfoldhall *alias* Coldhall, & 6 mess., 5 cotts., 1 dovecote, 6 gdns., 300 a. ar., 100 a. mw., 200 a. pa., 200 a. wd. & 100s. rt. in Gyngemargerett *alias* Margettinge, Chycknell & Wryttyll. Def. quitclaimed to pl. & the heirs of Robt. £400.

22. Eas. & Morrow of Trin. Rd. Champyon, gent., pl. *Hy*. Todgill & w. Alice, *Rd*. Story & w. Joan, def. 8 a. pa. in Horndon-on-the-Hill. £40.

23. Morrow of Trin. Robt. Folks & Tho. Folks, pl. Geo. Nicolls, esq., def. 20 mess., 20 tofts, 4 dovecotes, 20 gdns., 20 orchards, 300 a. ar., 60 a. mw., 200 a. pa. & 50 a. wd. in Walden, Littlebery, Great Wenden, Ashdon & Wymbishe. Def. quitclaimed to pl. & the heirs of Robt. Pl. gtd. def. prop. for 40 days, with remainder to Joan, w. of def., to hold of the chief lords for her life, with remainder to def. & his heirs to hold of the chief lords.

24. Eas. & Morrow of Trin. Robt. Halle, pl. *Jn*. Hare, Francis Hare, Hy. Osborne & w. Matilda, def. 1 mess., 1 gdn., 10 a. ar., 4 a. mw. & 6 a. pa. in White Notley. Def. quit-claimed to pl. & his heirs. Pl. gtd. prop. to Hy. & Matilda Osborne to hold of the chief lords.

25. Eas. & Morrow of Trin. Tho. Myldmay, kt., pl. *Hy*. Myldmay, esq., & w. Jane, def. The manor of Bysshoppes Leighes, & 20 mess., 10 cotts., 20 tofts, 1 water-mill, 1 dovecote, 20 gdns., 20 orchards, 500 a. ar., 100 a. mw., 500 a. pa. 200 a. wd., 300 a. furze & heath, 20 a. moor, 20 a. marsh & 60s. rt. in Bysshoppes Leighes, Muche Leighes, Terlynge, Fayersted, Lyttell Leighes, Chatley & Boreham. 130 mks.

26. Morrow of Trin. Wm. Cordell, kt., master of the rolls, & Tho. Pledgerd, esq., pl. Arthur Breame, esq., def. The manor of Estham, & 40 mess., 10 barns, 4 dovecotes, 40 gdns., 300 a. ar., 100 a. mw., 200 a. pa., 40 a. wd., 100 a. fresh marsh & £10 rt. in Estham & Westham, the rectory of Estham & the advowson of the vicarage of the church of Estham. Def. quitclaimed to pl. & the heirs of Wm. Pl. gtd. prop. to def. to hold of the chief lords, with remainder to Giles Breame, gent., son & heir apt. of def., & the legitimate heirs of his body, failing whom to the right heirs of def.

27. Eas. & Morrow of Trin. Jn. Barker, pl. *Jn*. Goodwyn, kt., & w. Eliz., def. A moiety of the manors of Maningtree, Shiddinghoo *alias* Shedynghoo, Oldhall *alias* Olde-hall, Newhall & Abbotts *alias* Edlyngs, & a moiety of 600 mess., 20 cotts., 10 tofts, 4 water-mills, 1,000 a. ar., 200 a. mw., 1,000 a. pa., 400 a. wd., 600 a. furze & heath & £20 rt. in Manyngtree *alias* Manytree, Mysteleygh *alias* Mysteley, Bradfeld, Colchester, Stanwaye, Wrabney *alias* Wrabnes, Wyks, Little Badowe, Lawforde, Little Bromley & Ardeleyghe, & a moiety of view of frankpledge, free warren, liberties & franchises in Mysteleygh & Mannyngtree, & a moiety of the rectory & church of Bradfild, the tithes of Bradfild & the advowsons of the church of Mysteleygh *alias* Mysteley & the vicarage of the church of Bradfeld. Warranty by def. against themselves, the heirs of Jn. Goodwyn & the heirs of Jn. Reynsforth, kt., decd. £420.

DIVERS COUNTIES

3. Morrow of Trin. Rd. Coulford, pl. *Wm*. Barley, & w. Dorothy, & Tho. Parvys sen., def. Prop. in London, & 1 mess., 1 gdn., 20 a. ar., 10 a. mw. 20 a. pa., 10 a. wd. & 20 a. furze & heath in Chipping Ongger, Highe Ongger & Shelleye, co. Essex. 190 mks. – London, Essex.

10. Morrow of Trin. Wm. Bridgewater & Robt. Moore, pl. Jn. Borlas, esq., & w. *Anne*, def. Prop. in co. Suff., & the manor of Hoobridge Haule, 2 mess., 2 cotts., 2 tofts, 2 barns, 1 windmill, 1 dovecote, 1 gdn., 1 orchard, 100 a. ar., 30 a. mw., 100 a. pa., 20 a. wd. & 10 a. furze & heath in Great Okeley, Little Okeley, Bradfeilde & Asheden, co. Essex. Def. quitclaimed to pl. & the heirs of Wm. £600. – Suff., Essex.

13. Eas. & Morrow of Trin. Juliana Holcrofte, wid., Tho. Manners, kt., Jn. Manners, esq., Gilbert Gerrard, esq., attorney-general, Tho. Holcrofte, esq., & Robt. Markham, esq., pl. Edw., earl of Rutl., def. Prop. in York, & the manor of Waltomstowe Tonye, & 60 mess., 60 cotts., 30 tofts, 60 gdns., 60 orchards, 1,000 a. a., 500 a. mw., 1,000 a. pa., 200 a. wd., 200 a. furze & heath, 200 a. marsh, 100 a. moor, & 40s. rt. in Waltomstowe Tonye & common pa. there, co. Essex. Def. quitclaimed to pl. & the heirs of Juliana. £1,100. – York, Essex.

CP25(2)/130/1661   MICHAELMAS, 17-18 ELIZABETH   1575

1. Mich. Tho. Popleton & w. Mary, pl. *Jn*. Solme & w. Alice, def. 1 mess., 1 curtilage, 1 gdn. & 6d. rt. in Chelmesford. Def. quitclaimed to pl. & the heirs of Tho. £40.

2. Mich. Wm. Chycken, pl. Tho. Chycken, def. 2 mess., 2 gdns., 2 orchards, 40 a. ar., 5 a. mw., 20 a. pa. & 6 a. wd. in Mutche Perndon & Roydon. £80.

3. Mich. Wm. Bode, gent., pl. *Francis* Stonar, esq., & w. Lucy, def. The manors of Freerne *alias* Freine & Jackeletts, & 1 mess., 1 barn, 1 gdn., 160 a. ar., 60 a. mw. & 80 a. pa. in Purleyghe & Mundon. £600.

4. Mich. Hy. Goldynge, esq., pl. Tho. Waynewright & w. *Dorothy*, def. 1 mess., 1 gdn., 1 orchard, 7 a. ar., 2 a. mw., 7 a. pa. & 1 a. wd. in Great Byrche. £40.

5. Mich. Jn. Phenix, pl. *Tho.* Herd & w. Eliz., def. 1 mess., 1 barn, 1 gdn., 6 a. ar., 1 a. mw. & 6 a. pa. in Upmynster. £80.

6. Mich. Cornelius Browne, a son of Tho. Browne, & Tho. Browne, another son of Tho., pl. Tho. Browne, the father of pl., def. 1 mess., 1 gdn., 1 orchard, 20 a. ar., 10 a. mw., 30 a. pa. & 2 a. wd. in Great Bursted. Def. quitclaimed to Cornelius. £80.

7. Mich. Robt. Potter, pl. Esq. Thedam & w. *Mary*, def. 1 barn, 30 a. ar., 4 a. mw. & 10 a. pa. in Wethermontford *alias* Wormyngforde & Bures-at-the-Hill. 200 mks.

8. Mich. Hy. Archer, gent., pl. Rd. Archer, def. 1 mess., 1 gdn., 1 orchard & 10 a. mw. in Thaydon Garnon. £40.

9. Mich. 'Libertus' Cranvyn & w. Joan, pl. Geo. Flyngant, def. Two-thirds of 3 mess. & 3 gdns. in Colcestria. Def. quitclaimed to pl. & the heirs of 'Libertus'. £40.

10. Mich. Tho. Gyver, pl. *And.* Gyver & w. Joan, def. 1 mess., 1 gdn., 1 orchard, 2 a. ar. & 2 a. pa. in Thaxsted. £40.

11. Mich. Giles Flacke & Robt. Cornell, pl. Wm. Wallys & w. *Agnes*, Tho. Dune *alias* Ellys & w. *Eliz.*, def. 1 mess., 1 barn, 1 gdn., 1 orchard & 6 a. ar. in Walden. Def. quitclaimed to pl. & the heirs of Giles. £40.

12. Mich. Geo. Vawyn *alias* Onion, pl. *Jn.* Bawde & w. Joan, def. 4 a. ar. in Hadstocke. £40.

13. Trin. & Mich. Tho. Lucas, kt., pl. *Jn.* Abell, esq., & w. Mary, def. 3 rods of mw. in Great Fordham. £40.

14. Mich. 'Samicia' Rawlyns, wid., Edw. Pecke & w. Agnes, Margt. Smyth & Joan Smyth, pl. Martin Bowes, gent., def. 15 a. ar. & 15 a. marsh in Dagnam. Def. quitclaimed to 'Samicia' & her heirs. £80.

15. Mich. Ralph Choppyn, pl. Mich. Foxe & w. *Anne*, def. 1 mess., 1 gdn., 1 orchard, 12 a. ar., 6 a. mw. & 12 a. pa. in Stowe Marrys. £80.

16. Mich. Wm. Smyth, gent., pl. Jn. Pye & w. *Rhoda*, def. A moiety of 10 mess., 10 tofts, 4 barns, 10 gdns., 10 orchards, 40 a. ar., 6 a. mw., 40 a. pa. & 6 a. wd. in Bockynge & Brancktre. £40.

17. Mich. Robt. Ryche, kt., Lord Ryche, pl. Tho. Shaa, esq., def. 2 mess., 4 tofts, 2 gdns., 100 a. ar., 60 a. mw., 300 a. pa., 100 a. wd. & £11 rt. in Estwood & Prytwell *alias* Prytewell. £220.

18. Mich. Tho. Colshill, esq., pl. *'Wistanus'* Browne, esq., & w. Mary, def. 3 mess., 1 toft, 3 gdns., 13 a. 3 rods mw. & 12½ a. pa. in Chigwell. Warranty by Wistanus Browne against himself, his heirs & the heirs of Anth. Browne, kt., decd. £80.

19. Mich. Jas. Altam, esq., & w. Mary, pl. *Hy.* Byrkheued, gent., & w. Eliz., def. 1 mess., 60 a. ar., 8 a. mw., 60 a. pa. & 15 a. wd. in Harlowe & Latton. Def. quitclaimed to pl. & the heirs of Jas. £160.

20. Mich. Edw. Hubbert, gent., pl. Robt. Thorowgood, def. 7 a. ar. & 3 a. mw. in Byrchanger. £40.

21. Mich. Wm. Chapman, pl. *Tho.* Stutevile, esq., & w. Anne, def. 7 a. ar. in Haverell. £40.

22. Mich. Robt. Wynche, pl. *Wm.* Hodge & w. Joan, *Jn.* Bolle & w. Suzanna, def. 10 mess., 6 cotts., 10 gdns. & 6 orchards in Waltham Holy Cross. £220.

23. Mich. Jn. Hawkyns, pl. Josias Sampson, def. 6 mess., 6 cotts., 4 gdns. & 7s. 11d. rt. in Branktre. £40.

24. Mich. Tho. Clarke, pl. *Tho.* Gylbert & w. Joan, def. 3 mess. & 3 gdns. in Bockyng. £40.

25. Mich. Joan Strangman, wid., pl. Jn. Wyseman, gent., def. 3 mess., 2 tofts, 4 gdns., 100 a. ar., 10 a. mw., 20 a. pa. 10 a. wd. & 10 a. furze & heath in Thaxsted. Wymbyshe & Debden. 160 mks.

26. Morrow of Trin. & Mich. Wm. Franklyn & Jn. Bonner, pl. Ralph Radclyff & w. *Joan*, def. 2 mess., 2 gdns., 2 orchards, 50 a. ar., 20 a. mw., 20 a. pa., 16 a. wd., 40 a. furze & heath & 40 a. marsh in Fange at Noke. Def. quitclaimed to pl. & the heirs of Wm. £160.

27. Mich. Mary Waspe & Anne Waspe, pl. Rd. Lawsell, def. 1 barn, 14 a. ar. & 1 a. pa. in Hengham Syble *alias* Henyngham Syble. Def. quitclaimed to pl. & the heirs of Mary. £40.

28. Mich. Robt. Wynche, pl. *Robt*. Acatro & w. Eliz., def. 1 mess., 1 stable, 1 gdn. & 1 orchard in Waltham Holy Cross. £40.

29. Mich. Jn. Force, gent., & w. Kath., pl. Wm. Peers, gent., & w. Anne, def. 1 mess., 1 cott. & 2 gdns. in Reyneham. Def. gtd. prop. to pl. for the life of Anne Peers. £20.

30. Mich. Jn. Brooke, pl. Rd. Burrell & w. *Rachel*, Robt. Reynolde & w. *Agnes*, def. 16 a. ar. & 2 a. wd. in Southmynster. £40.

31. Mich. Nich. Reve, pl. Tho. Carter, gent., & w. *Anne*, def. 1 mess. & 1 gdn. in Walden. £40.

32. Mich. Wm. Fuller & Jn. Fuller, pl. *Rd*. Grene & w. Martha, def. The manor of Hypforde *alias* Hypworth Hall, & 1 mess., 80 a. ar., 12 a. mw., 20 a. pa., 20 a. moor & 47s. 5d. rt. in Halsted, Hengham Syble, Little Maplested & Great Maplested. Def. quitclaimed to pl. & the heirs of Jn. £200.

33. Mich. Rd. Stoneley, esq., & Geo. Warner, gent., pl. *Tho*. Terrell & w. Margt., def. 1 mess., 1 barn, 1 dovecote, 40 a. ar., 10 a. mw., 40 a. pa., 16 a. wd., 100 a. furze & heath & common pa. for all livestock in Writtle. Def. quitclaimed to pl. & the heirs of Rd. £160.

34. Mich. Tho. Darcye, esq., pl. Jn. Dawson & w. *Joan*, def. 3 a. pa. in Saltcote *alias* Salcote Wigborough. £40.

35. Mich. Rd. Everard, pl. *Jn*. Freman *alias* Mundes & w. Agnes, def. 1 mess., 4 tofts, 4 gdns., 10 a. ar., 1 a. mw. & 10 a. pa. in Great Waltham & Little Waltham. £40.

36. Mich. Jn. Thymble, pl. Jn. Harrys, def. A fifth part of 1 mess., 2 tofts, 2 gdns., 1 orchard, 24 a. ar., 1 a. mw. & 6 a. pa. in Aburton, Fingringho & Layer Delahey. £40.

37. Mich. Nich. Umfrey, pl. *Jn*. Cutt, kt., & w. Anne, def. 1 mess., 1 barn, 1 gdn., 100 a. ar., 4 a. mw., 30 a. pa. & 2 a. wd. in Thaxsted & Great Sampford. £80.

38. Mich. Matthew Cawston, pl. *Jerome* Cawston & w. Margt., def. 9 a. pa. in Latchingdon. £40.

39. Mich. Tho. Gybbes, pl. *Jn*. Stepney & w. Anne, def. 2 a. ar. in Westham. £40.

40. Mich. Geo. Reynowldes, pl. *Rd*. Mores & w. Joan, def. 4 a. pa. in Blackmore. £40.

41. Mich. Robt. Payne, pl. Wm. Wytham & w. Agnes, *Wm*. Gascoigne, gent., Geo. Gascoigne, gent., & Wm. Lorkyn, def. 20 a. mw., 12 a. pa., 3 a. wd. & 24 a. furze & heath in Mountnesend *alias* Gingmountnay & Shenfeild. £80.

42. Mich. Robt. Paternoster, clk. pl. *Anth*. Carter & w. Anne, def. 1 mess., 1 gdn., 25 a. ar., 7 a. mw. & 10 a. pa. in Pentlowe. £80.

43. Mich. Helen Walles, pl. Wm. Maners & w. *Joseana*, def. A quarter of 6 a. mw. & 12 a. pa. in Bulfane. £40.

44. Mich. Christ. Homan, pl. *Robt*. Murden & w. Agnes, def. 1 mess., 1 barn, 1 gdn. & 1 orchard in Lawford. £40.

45. Trin. & Mich. Jn. Grene, pl. *Francis* Stanton, gent., & w. Emma. def. The manor of Borowes *alias* Burghe, & 6 mess., 120 a. pa., 20 a. wd., 2 a. moor, & 10s. rt. in Stanford Ryvers *alias* Stamford Ryvers. £160.

46. Mich. *Reg*. Busshe & Jn. Wangforde, pl. Edm. Rydnall & w. *Joan*, Rd. Chote & w. *Dorothy*, def. 2 mess., 2 gdns. & 2 orchards in Feringe & Halsted. Def. quitclaimed to pl. & the heirs of Reg. Warranty by Edm. & Joan Rydnall for 1 mess., 1 gdn. & 1 orchard in Ferynge, by Rd. & Dorothy Chote for the remainder in Halsted. £40.

47. Mich. Jn. Spencer, pl. *Jn.* Stamer, gent., & w. Joan, & *Robt.* Stamer, def. 3 mess., 3 tofts, 1 mill, 3 gdns., 200 a. ar., 40 a. mw., 200 a. pa., 6 a. wd., 40 a. furze & heath. 10s. rt. & common pa. for all livestock in Rawreth. £100.

48. Morrow of Trin. & Mich. Jn. Rochester, esq., & Edw. Rochester, gent., pl. *Tho.* Walsyngham, kt., & w. Dorothy, def. 12 mess., 3 barns, 1 dovecote, 12 gdns., 103 a. ar., 40 a. mw., 85 a. pa., 16 a. wd. & £5 13s. 1d. rt. & the rt. of a red rose in Bobingworth, Stanford Ryvers & Northwelde Bassett & a moiety of advowson of the church of Bobingworth. Def. quitclaimed to pl. & the heirs of Jn. £300.

49. Mich. Anth. Martyn, pl. Jn. Parsmyth *alias* Cheyney, jun., & w. Mary, def. The rectory of Manewden, & 1 mess., 1 gdn., 1 orchard, 240 a. ar., 10 a. mw., 20 a. pa. & 40 a. wd. in Manewden & the advowson of the church of Manewden. Def. gtd. prop. to pl. for the life of Mary Cheyney. £320.

50. Mich. Clement Smyth, esq. & Hy. Smyth, gent., pl. Wm. Smyth, gent., & w. *Grace*, def. A moiety of 10 mess., 10 tofts, 4 barns, 10 gdns., 10 orchards, 40 a. ar., 6 a. mw., 40 a. pa. & 6 a. wd. in Bockynge & Brancktre. Def. quitclaimed to pl. & the heirs of Clement. Pl. gtd. prop. to def. for the life of both & the survivor to hold of the chief lords, with remainder to Tho. Smyth, son & heir apt. of Wm. & Grace Smyth.

51. Mich. Jn. Adams, gent., Wm. Andrewes, gent., Jn. Balthropp & Wm. Sharnebroke, pl. Edw. Sharnebroke & w. *Agnes*, Edw. Hynde & w. *Kath.*, def. 1 mess., 1 barn, 1 orchard & 18 a. ar. in Roydon. Def. quitclaimed to pl. & the heirs of Jn. Adams. £40.

52. Trin. & Mich. Robt. Jegon & Jn. Pyreson, pl. *Geo.* Copsschef & w. Anne, def. 3 mess. & 3 gdns. in Coggeshall. Def. quitclaimed to pl. & the heirs of Robt. £60.

53. Mich. Wm. Fytche, esq., pl. *Wm.* Tyffyn, gent., & w. Mary, def. The rectory of Stebbinge, & 4 mess., 1 dovecote, 4 gdns., 4 orchards, 200 a. ar., 30 a. mw., 30 a. pa., 10 a. wd., 20s. rt., rt. of 1 lb. wax & of 1 lb. pepper, tithes of sheaves, grain & hay in Stebbinge & the advowson of the vicarage of the church of Stebbinge. £200.

54. Mich. Jn. Eden. gent., & w. Eliz., pl. Edw. Parker, esq., def. The manor of Pakenho *alias* Pakenhohalle *alias* Pakenhalle *alias* Patenhalle, & 3 mess., 2 cotts., 5 tofts, 10 barns, 10 gdns., 500 a. ar., 60 a. mw., 200 a. pa., 20 a. wd. & 20s. rt. in Manweden *alias* Maneuden *alias* Maunden. Def. quitclaimed to pl. & the heirs of Jn. £160.

55. Mich. Jas. Edwardes, pl. *Tho.* Hurrell & w. Margt., *Tho.* Cracherode & w. Anne, def. 2 mess., 2 gdns., 20 a. ar., 1 a. mw. & 6 a. pa. in Hennyngham Syble *alias* Hengham Syble & Toppesfeld. £40.

56. Mich. Jn. Boughtell, Tho. Sebroke, Wm. Swallowe, Wm. Collyn, Jn. Collyn, Jn. Waylett, Wm. Starlinge, Nich. Adams, Jas. Jarvys, Jn. Jarvys, Jn. Carter, Rd. Emery, Jn. Browne, Alice Fethergyll, Helen Fethergyll & Margt. Prestlande, pl. Jn. Broke & *Ferdinand* Broke, def. 10 mess., 1 windmill, 200 a. ar., 20 a. mw., 40 a. pa. & 20 a. wd. in Thaxsted, Broxheade, Chawreth, Tyltaye, Chyckenay & Elsenham. Def. quitclaimed to pl. & the heirs of Jn. Boughtell. £400.

57. Mich. Geo. Nycolson & Matthew Aliston, pl. *Chris.* Sidey & w. Prudence, Robt. Rand & w. *Benet*, def. 1 mess., 1 gdn., 1 orchard, 20 a. ar., 2 a. mw., 10 a. pa. & 4 a. marsh in Hengham Sible *alias* Heningham Sible. Def. quitclaimed to pl. & the heirs of Geo. Warranty by Robt. & Benet Rand for 1 mess., 1 gdn. & 1 orchard, by Chris. & Prudence Sidey for the remaining prop. £80.

DIVERS COUNTIES

9. Mich. Tho. Meade, gent., pl. Robt. Brooke, gent., & w. *Eliz.*, def. 41 a. ar. & ½ a. pa. in Crishall & Heydon, co. Essex; & prop. in co. Cambs. £120. — Essex, Cambs.

10. Morrow of Trin. & Mich. Kath. Durant, wid., pl. Jn. Clenche, gent., Jn. Skynner, gent, & Wm. Hanbery, def. 6 mess., 6 gdns., 30 a. ar., 12 a. mw. 20 a. pa. & 10 a. wd. in Great Warley, Little Warley, Craneham & Upmynster, co. Essex; & prop. in London. Warranty by each def. in turn against himself, his heirs, Wm. Durant & his heirs. £240. — Essex. London.

11. Mich. Jn. Glascock, gent., & Edm. Gryffyn, gent., pl. Jn. Sawyn, gent., & w. Eliz., & *Edm*. Alleyn, gent., son & heir of Jn. Alleyn, gent., decd., def. The site of the former priory of Hatfyld Peverell, the manor of Hatfyld Peverell, & 20 mess., 10 tofts, 10 curtilages, 10 barns, 4 dovecotes, 20 gdns., 10 orchards, 350 a. ar., 40 a. mw., 250 a. pa., 200 a. wd., 100 a. furze & heath, 20 a. alder & £10 rt. in Hatfyld Peverell, Wytham, Ultinge, Great Totham, Little Totham, Tolleshunt Darcy, Goldhanger, Wodham Mortemer, Wodham Walter, Terlynge, Boreham, Little Badowe, Langford, Little Waltham, Nantwyche, Debden & Blunteshall, the rectory of Hatfyld Peverell, all tithes of sheaves, grain, hay, wool, milk & lambs & all petty tithes in Hatfyld Peverell, all tithes in Nantwyche in Terlynge, an annual rt. of 40s. issuing from the rectory of Little Waltham, two-thirds of all tithes in the demesne of Blunteshall in Wytham & the advowsons of the churches of Hatfyld Peverell & Little Waltham, co. Essex; & prop. in Suff. Def. quitclaimed to pl. & the heirs of Jn. Pl. gtd. prop. to Eliz. Sawyer to hold of the chief lords, with remainder to Edm. Alleyn & his heirs. — Essex. Suff.

15. Trin. & Mich. Nich. Bacon, kt., lord keeper of the great seal, pl. Wm. Skypwyth, esq., def. The manors of Abbotts Burye *alias* Rowletts Burye & Mynchynbury, & 2 mess., 50 a. ar. & 60s. rt. in Great Chysshell & Little (Chysshell), co. Essex; & prop. in Herts. & Cambs. Def. quitclaimed to pl. & his heirs. £1,600. — Herts., Essex. Cambs. (See also Divers Cos., Hil., 18 Eliz., no. 5.)

CP25(2)/130/1662   HILARY, 18 ELIZABETH   1576

1. Hil. And. Grey, esq., pl. Tho. Dorant, def. 1 mess., 1 gdn., 1 orchard, 30 a. ar., 4 a. mw., 30 a. pa., 4 a. wd. & 20s. rt. in Lamborne. £40.

2. Hil. Jn. Lawrence, pl. Rd. Tye & w. *Edith*, Tho. Walden & w. *Alice*, def. 1 mess., 1 gdn. & 10 a. ar. in Great Maplested & Little Maplested. £30.

3. Hil. Wm. Symonde, pl. Tho. Robyns *alias* Robynson & w. *Kath*., def. 1 mess., 1 toft, 1 gdn. & 1 orchard in Thaxsted. £15.

4. Hil. Jn. Gower, pl. 'Wistanus' Davye & w. *Joan*, def. A moiety of 1 mess., 1 gdn., 16 a. ar., 2 a. mw. & 6 a. pa. in Eythroppe Rodynge *alias* Eythroppe Roothinge. £40.

5. Hil. Jn. Spencer, pl. Tho. Forbye & w. *Agnes*, def. 1 mess., 20 a. ar., 20 a. pa., 1 a. wd. & common pa. for all livestock in Rawreth. £40.

6. Hil. Rd. Garnett, pl. *Jn*. Saunder & w. Eliz., def. 1 mess., 1 barn, 2 orchards & 6 a. pa. in Highame Hill, Bensted & Waltamstowe. £40.

7. Hil. Rd. Patten, pl. Robt. Hodge & w. *Margt*., def. 2 mess., 2 gdns. & 2 orchards in Ardley. £40.

8. Hil. Jn. Mathewe, pl. *Tho*. Philipson & w. Bridget, def. 1 mess., 1 gdn. & 1 orchard in Rayleigh. £40.

9. Hil. Jn. Holmested, gent., & w. Margt., pl. *Jn*. Archer & w. Mary, def. 7 a. ar. in Halsted. Def. quitclaimed to pl. & the heirs of Jn. £20.

10. Hil. Rd. Thurston, pl. 'Marcelinus' Owtred, def. 1 mess., 1 gdn., 28 a. ar., 2 a. mw. & 10 a. pa. in Great Clacton & Little Clacton. £120.

11. Hil. Rd. Archer, pl. *Hy*. Archer, gent., & Edw. Archer, def. 1 mess., 1 gdn. & 1 orchard in Theydon Garnon. £40.

12. Hil. Wm. Brewster, gent., pl. Rd. Brewster & Jn. Brewster, def. 1 mess., 1 gdn., 1 orchard, 24 a. ar., 6 a. mw., 4 a. pa. & 6 a. wd. in Great Yeldham & Little Yeldham, held for life by Thomasina Sibley, wid. Def. gtd. reversion to pl. & his heirs to hold of the chief lords. £40.

13. Hil. Jn. Harte, pl. *Jn*. Deacon, gent., & w. Eliz., def. 1 mess., 1 gdn. & 12 a. ar. in Estham. £40.

14. Hil. Rd. Rogers, pl. Hy. Archer, gent., def. 6 a. ar. & 6 a. pa. in Theydon Garnon. £40.

15. Hil. Jn. Southwell, esq., & Wm. - - - he, gent., pl. Geo. Darrell, esq., & w. Bridget & *Jn*. Cristmas, gent., def. 3 mess., 1 dovecote, - - - - - & 4 a. pa. in Colchester. Def. quitclaimed to pl. & the heirs of Jn. £40. (*Mutilated on left-hand side*)

16. Hil. Tho. Sandforde & Rd. Sandforde, his son & heir apt., pl. *Jn*. Christmas, gent., Geo. Darrell, esq., & w. Bridget, def. 12 a. wd. in the parish of St. Michael at Myle Ende in Colcestr'. Def. quitclaimed to pl. & the heirs of Tho. £10.

17. Hil. Jn. Petyt, pl. Tho. Freman, def. 4½ a. ar., 1 a. mw. & ½ a. wd. in Asshedon. £40.

18. Hil. Wm. Reynolde *alias* Kente, pl. Wm. Symonde & w. *Eliz*., def. 1 mess., 14 a. ar. & 1 a. mw. in Gyngemounteney. £80.

19. Hil. Anth. Radclif, pl. *Rd*. Bellamy & w. Kath., def. The manor of Southall, & 2 mess., 2 cotts., 4 gdns., 400 a. ar., 200 a. mw., 200 (a.) pa., 40 a. wd., 300 a. marsh & £6 (rt.) in Reynam, Wennyngton, Alveley, Upmynstre & Okyngton. 800 mks.

20. Hil. Wm. Stubbyng, pl. Tho. Bell, def. 1 mess., 1 barn, 1 gdn., 1 orchard, 5 a. ar., 3 a. mw., 4 a. pa. & 2 a. wd. in Bumsted Helleon. £40.

21. Hil. Rd. Maryon, pl. *Jn*. Reynolde, gent., & w. Mary, def. 1 mess., 1 curtilage, 1 gdn. & 1 orchard in Chelmesford. £40.

22. Mich. & Hil. Jn. Camber, pl. *Jn*. Woodde & w. Mary, def. 20 a. fresh marsh & 20 a. salt (marsh) in Estylbery. £100.

23. Hil. Edm. Rychards & Arthur Forthe, gentelemen, pl. Jn. Col, def. 1 mess., 1 gdn., 3 a. ar. & 3 a. pa. in Asshdon. Def. quitclaimed to pl. & the heirs of Edm. Pl. gtd. prop. to def. to hold of the chief lords.

24. Hil. Chas. Copartwhaite, pl. *Eliz*. Rypton, wid., Tho. Foster & w. *Joan*, def. 1 mess., 1 toft, 1 gdn., 2 curtilages, 9 a. mw., 1 a. wd. & 9 a. fresh marsh in Stratford Langthorne & Westham. £160.

25. Hil. Jn. Searle, pl. Adriana Smyth, wid., *Nich*. Smyth, Nich. Saunderson, & w. Eliz. & Susanna Smyth, def. The manor of Taklees, & 1 mess., 2 tofts., 2 gdns., 1 orchard, 50 a. ar., 12 a. mw., 60 a. pa., 2 a. wd & 10s. rt. in Eppinge *alias* Eppinge Presbiter. £120.

26. Hil. Jn. Thirgood & Rd. Dowsett, pl. Adriana Smyth, wid., *Nich*. Smyth, Nich. Saunderson & w. Eliz. & Susanna Smyth, def. 2 mess., 2 tofts, 2 gdns., 2 orchards, 40 a. ar., 12 a. mw., 40 a. pa. & 2 a. wd. in Northweld Bassett, Highe Honger & Mawdelen Lavar. Def. quitclaimed to pl. & the heirs of Jn. £100.

27. Hil. Oswald Fitch, pl. *Tho*. Goodwyn & w. Eliz., *Anth*. Barber, & w. Margt. & *Nich*. Smyth, def. The manor of Boones, & 20 mess., 10 cotts., 10 tofts, 10 gdns., 10 orchards, 400 a. ar., 20 a. mw., 100 a. pa., 40 a. wd., 20 a. furze & heath, 100s. rt. & free fishery in Bocking, Brancktree, Gosfeld, Felsteed & Writtle. £200.

28. Hil. Wm. Bendlowes, serjeant at law, pl. Robt. Riche, kt., Lord Riche, & w. *Eliz*. & Edm. Thorneton, def. The manor of Butlars, & 4 mess., 3 dovecotes, 20 gdns., 500 a. ar., 50 a. mw., 100 a. pa., 60 a. wd., 100 a. furze & heath & £20 rt. in Shopland, Sutton, Prittelwell, Lighe, Hadleigh, Great Wakeringe, Little Wakeringe, Showberye, Rochedorde, Hackwell, Rawreth & Cryksyhethe, & a moiety of the manor of Shoplande Hall in Shoplande. Pl. gtd. the site of the aforesaid manor, the tenements & moiety to Edm. Thorneton for 21 years from Michaelmas 1576 at rt. of £30 a year, with reversion to Robt. & Eliz. Riche & the heirs of Eliz., to hold of the chief lords.

CP25(2)/260   DIVERS COUNTIES

3. Hil. Jn. Ive, gent., & w. Frances, pl. Wm. Dawtrey jun., gent., def. The manor of Ryvershall, & 40 mess., 20 cotts., 10 tofts, 3 barns, 1 water-mill, 2 dovecotes, 20 gdns., 20 orchards, 280 a. ar., 190 a. mw., 200 a. pa., 60 a. wd., 100 a. furze & heath, 10 a. ar. covered with water, £20 rt., common pa. for all animals & view of frankpledge in Boxsted, Langham, Great Horseley & Myleend & free fishing in the water of Boxsted, co. Essex; & prop. in Suff. Def. quitclaimed to pl. & the heirs of Jn. £840. – Essex, Suff.

5. Hil. Nich. Bacon, kt., keeper of the great seal, pl. Geo. Herde & w. *Eliz*., def. (Prop. in Herts, Essex & Cambs. virtually similar to Divers Counties 17 & 18 Elizabeth Michaelmas, *no*. 15.) £600. – Herts., Essex, Cambs.

CP26(1)/167 (an original file)

1. Eas. Jas. Harvye, citizen & alderman of London, pl. *And*. Fuller & w. Joan, def. 8 a. pa. in Barkynge. £40.

2. Eas. Wm. Cooke & Tho. Brydges, pl. *Tho*. Knotte & w. Kath., def. 2 mess., 2 tofts, 2 gdns., 10 a. ar. & 2a. pa. in Chelmysford & Spryngfyld. Def. quitclaimed to pl. & the heirs of Wm. £60.

3. Eas. Jas. Pyke, pl. Wm. Williamson & w. Joan, Jn. Sallowes & w. *Anne*, def. 1 mess., 1 barn, 1 gdn., 1 orchard, 5 a. ar. & 3 a. pa. in Great Showberye *alias* South Showberye. £40.

4. Eas. Rd. Potto, pl. Wm. Potto, def. 2 mess. & 3 gdns. in Great Berdfeld. £40.

5. Eas. Jn. Byrcheley, gent., & Jn. Tanner, pl. Jas. Parker, def. 2 tofts, 40 a. ar., 30 a. mw., 20 a. pa., 4 a. wd. & 12d. rt. in Great Bursted, Bylleryca & Buttesbury. Def. quitclaimed to pl. & the heirs of Jn. Byrcheley. Pl. gtd. prop. to def. to hold of the chief lords.

6. Eas. Jn. Ingold, pl. *Jn*. Collen & w. Joan, def. 20 a. ar., 4 a. pa. & 2 a. wd. in High Laver. £40.

7. Eas. Reg. Foster, pl. *Jn*. Collen & w. Joan, def. 1 mess. & 18 a. ar. in Matching & High Laver. £40.

8. Hil. & Eas. Kath. Awdeley, wid., pl. *Jn*. Cristmas, esq., Geo. Darrell, esq., & w. Bridget, def. The manor of Barnchams, & 1 mess., 3 gdns., 70 a. ar., 10 a. mw., 100 a. pa., 6 a. wd. & 10s. rt. in Beamond, Wealeigh, Tenderinge & Thorpe. £140.

9. Eas. Jas. Boreham, pl. Edw. Savage & w. *Margt*., def. 1 mess., 1 gdn. & 1 a. ar. in Roydon. £40.

10. Hil. & Eas. Tho. Stokes, pl. Hy. Browne, esq., & w. *Alice*, def. The manor of Fryers Grange, & 6 mess., 6 tofts, 6 cotts., 6 gdns., 6 orchards, 150 a. ar., 20 a. mw., 40 a. pa., 30 a. wd., 10 a. furze & heath & 10s. rt. in Eythrop Roodynge, High Roodynge, High Ester & Leaden Roodinge. Warranty by def. against themselves, the heirs of Alice, Chas., former duke of Suff., Robt. Trappes & Nich. Trappes & their heirs. £140.

11. Eas. Robt. Latham & Geo. Easte, gentlemen, pl. Jn. Cutt, kt., def. 10 a. 1 rood of wd. in Thaxsted. Def. quitclaimed to pl. & the heirs of Robt. £40.

12. Eas. Tho. Meade, serjeant at law, pl. *Tho*. Whetnall, esq., & w. Dorothy, Fulk Cuslowe, esq., & w. Mary, def. The manor of Walburie, & 12 mess., 6 cotts., 2 dovecotes, 600 a. ar., 60 a. mw., 200 a. pa., 80 a. wd. & £10 rt. in Great Halyngburye, Little Halyngburie, Halyngburie Morele & Halyngburie Bowsers. £400.

13. Eas. Wm. Saunder, pl. Tho. Nele & w. *Anne*, Jn. Trundell & w. Joan, def. 1 mess. & 1 gdn. in Great Coggeshall & Little Coggeshall. £40.

14. Eas. Edw. Sulyarde, esq., pl. Wm. Indesor & w. *Margt*., def. A third part of 1 mess., 1 cott., 1 barn, 1 toft, 1 gdn., 1 orchard, 12 a. ar., 8 a. mw., 12 a. pa. & 3 a. wd. in Runwell & Wickeford. £40.

15. Eas. Martin Trott, pl. Robt. Suszen & w. *Eliz*., def. 3 a mw., 1 a. pa. & 1 a. wd. in Waltham Holy Cross. £40.

16. Eas. Jn. Ball, pl. *Edw*. Hamonde, gent., & w. Margt. & Geo. Britten, gent., def. 1 mess., 1 gdn., 40 a. ar., 20 a. mw. & 40 a. pa. in Horkisley. Warranty by Edw. & Margt. Hamonde against themselves, the heirs of Edw., Geo. Brytten, Anne his w. & their heirs. £80.

17. Eas. Tho. Parke, Jn. Kent, Jn. Holmsted & Wm. Deane, pl. Jn. Selong *alias* Selond & w. *Margt*., Edw. Turnor & w. Anne, Robt. Kettle & w. *Agnes*, def. 1 mess., 1 gdn., 7 a. ar. & 2 a. mw. in Fynchingfeld, Halstede & Great Maplested. Def. quitclaimed to pl. & the heirs of Tho. £80.

18. Eas. Barnard Dyckman & w. Alice. pl. Tho. Barker & w. *Agnes*, def. 1 mess., 1 gdn. & 1 orchard in Goldanger. Def. quitclaimed to pl. & the heirs of Barnard. £40.

19. Eas. Wm. Cocke, pl. *Hy*. Byrkydd & w. Margt., def. 3 a. ar. & 2 a. 1 rood of pa. in Southwyld. £40.

20. Eas. Nich. Mann, pl. *Tho.* Spencer & w. Joan, def. 1 mess., 1 cott., 1 curtilage, 1 gdn., 1 orchard, 4 a. ar. & 1 a. wd. in Woodham Mortymer. £40.

21. Eas. Jn. Cooke, gent., & Wm. Wyseman, gent., pl. Wm. Bode, gent., def. 3 mess., 3 tofts, 3 barns, 3 curtilages, 3 gdns., 100 a. ar., 20 a. mw., 40 a. pa., 20 a. wd. & common pa. for all livestock in Leyham Playne, Woodham Ferres, Rayleigh & Hawkewell. Def. quitclaimed to pl. & the heirs of Jn. £300.

22. Eas. Eliz. Martyn, wid., pl. *Tho.* Bartell & w. Elena, def. 3 mess., 3 gdns., 30 a. ar., 12 a. mw. & 12 a. pa. in Estham & Ilford. £80.

23. Eas. Geo. Sayer, jun., gent., & Jn. Spenser, pl. Rd. Sayer & w. *Alice*, def. 6 mess., 1 dovecote, 6 gdns., 6 orchards, 80 a. ar., 12 a. mw. & 80 a. pa. in Markeshall, Erles Colne, Great Tayne, Ferynge, Chelmysforde & Maldon. Def. quitclaimed to pl. & the heirs of Geo. £200.

24. Eas. Wm. Cooke, esq., pl. *Geoff.* Carowe & w. Denise, def. 2 mess., 2 gdns., 2 a. ar., 1 a. mw., 2 a. pa. & 2 a. wd. in Lamborne & Affebridge. £63.

25. Eas. Tho. Emerye, pl. *Jn.* Baron & w. Thomasina, def. 8 a. pa. in Westhannyngfylde. £40.

26. Eas. Wm. Rowe, pl. Etheldreda Smyth, wid., *Nich.* Smyth, gent., Nich. Saunderson, gent., & w. Eliz. & Suzanna Smyth, def. The manor of Hayles, & 3 mess., 1 cott. 2 dovecotes, 3 gdns., 3 orchards, 50 a. ar., 30 a. mw., 100 a. pa., 20 a. wd. & 40s. rt. in Eppynge & Latton. £400.

27. Eas. Jn. Saunder, pl. Tho. Gladwyn & w. *Mary*, def. 1 mess. & 1 curtilage in Coggeshall. £40.

28. Eas. Jn. Hyde & w. Fortuna, pl. Nemrod Eckford, def. 1 mess. & 1 gdn. in Great Stambridge. Def. quitclaimed to pl. & the heirs of Jn. £40.

29. Eas. Tho. Beckyngham, pl. Tho. Tey & w. *Elianor*, def. 14 a. pa. & 20 a. salt marsh in Goldhanger, Tolleshunt Major & Tolleshunt Darcy. £60.

30. Eas. Jn. Cooke, gent., & Wm. Wyseman, gent., pl. Edw. Bode, gent., def. 1 mess., 1 gdn., 40 a. ar., 6 a. mw. & 10 a. pa. in Rayleigh. Def. quitclaimed to pl. & the heirs of Jn. £180.

31. Eas. Tho. Marven, pl. Rd. Jonson, def. 2 mess., 1 gdn., 1 a. ar. & 1 wharf in Harwyche. 160 mks.

32. Eas. Jn. Onyon, pl. *Jn.* Wastell & w. Eliz., def. 1 mess., 4 a. ar., 3 a. mw. & 2 a. pa. in Hempsted. £40.

33. Eas. Edw. Morgan, esq., & Wm. Pennant, gent., pl. Pet. Pennant, esq., def. 1 mess., 1 gdn., 3 orchards, 6 a. ar., 10 a. mw. & 20 a. pa. in Haverynge at Bower. Def. quitclaimed to pl. & the heirs of Edw. 100 mks.

34. Eas. Wm. Morlye, pl. Jn. Fyrlonge & w. *Jane*, def. 2 mess., 2 gdns. & 1 a. ar. in Wyvenhoo. £40.

35. Hil. & Eas. Wm. Nutbrowne, esq., Wm. Cordell, kt., Tho. Fanshawe & Tho. Powle, esquires, pl. *Jn.* Bullock, esq., & w. Eliz., def. The manor of Cockermouth, & 10 mess., 10 cotts., 1 barn, 10 tofts, 10 gdns., 200 a. ar., 100 a. mw., 100 a. pa., 3 a. wd., 20 a. furze & heath, 100 a. marsh & 80s. rt. in Dagenham & Barkyng, & the advowson of the vicarage of the church of Dagenham. Def. quitclaimed to pl. & the heirs of Wm. Nutbrowne. 230 mks.

DIVERS COUNTIES

2. Hil. & Eas. Robt. Tayllor, esq., pl. *Wm.* Dauntesey, esq., & w. Anne, def. Prop. in Mdx. & 20. a ar., 20 a. mw. & 10 a. pa. in Westham, co. Essex. 460 mks. — Mdx., Essex.

CP25(2)/130/1663   TRINITY, 18 ELIZABETH   1576

1. Morrow of Trin. Jn. Fowle, pl. Jn. Parkynson, def. 3 mess., 3 cotts., 3 gdns., & 3 orchards in Barkynge. 130 mks.

2. Trin. Jn. Haukyn, gent., & Tho. Sawen, pl. *Rd.* Betts & w. Alice, def. 8 a. ar. & 8 a. pa. in Spryngfelde & Bromefelde. Def. quitclaimed to pl. & the heirs of Jn. £40.

3. Morrow of Trin. Jn. Barrett, pl. Wm. Sammes & w. *Grace*, def. 2 a. pa. in Earls Colne. £40.

4. Morrow of Trin. Jn. Sharpe, gent., pl. Jn. Lukyn, gent., & w.*Margt.*, def. 4 mess., 1 windmill, 4 gdns., 80 a. ar., 20 a. mw., 60 a. pa. & 10 a. wd. in Great Baddowe, Westhanningfeild & Horndon. £400.

5. Morrow of Trin, Tho. Randall, pl. *Tho.* Barnes & w. Mary, def. 20 a. wd. in Barkynge. £40.

6. Morrow of Trin. Wm. Lytleburye & Elias Wortham, pl. Jn. Lambert & w. *Emma*, def. 2 mess., 2 gdns., 1 a. ar., 2 a. mw. & 3½ a. pa. in White Notley & Great Leighes, Def. quitclaimed to pl. & the heirs of Wm. £40.

7. Morrow of Trin. Robt. Cammocke, gent., pl. *Tho.* Francke, esq., & w. Mary, def. 4 a. mw. & 16 a. pa. in Maldon. £70.

8. Hil, & Morrow of Trin. Jn. Broke, gent., pl. Jn. Christmas, gent., def. 2 mess., 2 cotts., 2 gdns., 200 a. ar., 10 a. mw., 150 a. pa., 20 a. wd., 140 a. fresh marsh & 60 a. salt marsh in Bradwell-by-the-Sea. £400.

9. Morrow of Trin. Wm. Hollawaye, son of Wm. Hollawaie, decd., the brother of Jn. Hollawaye, pl. Jn. Hollawaie, def. 1 mess., 1 gdn., 1 orchard, 8 a. ar., 4 a. mw. & 4 a. pa. in Eppinge. £80.

10. Trin. Wm. Aylett, pl. *Tho.* Luther & w. Philippa, def., 1 mess., 40 a. ar., 12 a. mw. & 100 a. pa. in Fange, Pytsey, Newyngdon & Bartelesdon. £580.

11. Morrow of Trin. Edw. Hubbert, gent., pl. Wm. Beckett *alias* Beckwith, clk., Robt. Peke & w. *Eliz.*, def. 3 mess., 3 tofts, 3 gdns., 1 orchard, 3 a. ar. & 2 a. mw. in Erles Colne. £40.

12. Morrow of Trin. Wm. Ellett, pl. *Jn.* Newport *alias* Driver & w. Joan, def. 6 a. ar. & 2 a. pa. in Little Stambridge. £40.

13. Trin. Jn. Sames, Jn. Locke, Rd. Bacon, Josias Harvye & Jas. Russell, pl. *Clement* Smythe, esq., & w. Dorothy, def. 5 mess., 2 cotts., 4 barns, 2 tofts, 4 gdns., 4 orchards, 200 a. ar., 40 a. mw., 50 a. pa., 4 a. wd., 3 a. moor, & the first crop of ½ a. mw. in Langford & Great Totthill. Def. quitclaimed to pl. & the heirs of Jn. Sames. £240.

14. Eas. & Morrow of Trin. Rd. Saltonstall, pl. Rd. Leighe, gent., & w. Margery, def. 16 mess., 20 tofts, 2 mills, 2 dovecotes, 40 gdns., 40 orchards, 1,00 a. ar., 500 a. mw., 1,000 a. pa., 100 a. wd., 500 a. furze & heath, 100 a. moor, 100 a. marsh & 60s. rt. in Sowthokenden *alias* Sowthokyngdon Rockell, Brockestrete, Great Warley, Little Warley, Aveley, Chylderdych, Styfford, Upmynster, Sowthweld, Brentwood, Northokendon & Raynham, & a moiety of the manor of Sowthwokenden with appurtenances in Sowthwokenden *alias* Sowthwokyngden Rockell, Brockstreat, Great Warley, Little Warley, Alveley, Chylderdych, Styfford, Upmynster, Sowthweld, Brentwood, Northokenden & Raynham & the advowson of the church of Sowthokenden *alias* Sowthokyngdon Rockell. Warranty by def. against themselves. £420.

15. Eas. & Morrow of Trin. Ralph Wyseman, esq., pl. Walter, earl of Essex & Ewe, earl marshal of Ireland, def. The manors of Bourchiers Halle, Merkes & Leylofte *alias* Laylofte *alias* Loftehall, & 20 mess., 10 cotts., 8 tofts, 20 gdns., 10 orchards, 300 a. ar., 40 a. mw., 200 a. pa., 40 a. wd., 100 a. furze & heath & 100s. rt. in Ryvenhall *alias* Ruenhall, Wytham, Cressynge, Kelvedon, Great Barcksted, Little Barcksted, Braynktre, Stysted, Great Totham, Heybridge & Blackwater *alias* Bradwell. 1,000 mks.

16. Morrow of Trin. Rd. Higham & w. Margt., pl. Robt. Gascoyne, gent., & w. Mary, def. 2 mess., 2 gdns., 100 a. ar., 10 a. mw., 40 a. pa., 20 a. furze & heath, 10 a. fresh marsh & 6 a. salt marsh in Hadleigh at the Castle, held by def. for the life of Mary Gascoyne. Def. gtd. prop. to pl. for 21 years from Annunciation 1578 at rt. of £20 a year. Warranty by def. against themselves for the whole term if Mary Gascoyne survives so long. £200.

17. Morrow of Trin. Tho. Turner, pl. *Jn.* Harvye & w. Margt., Jn. Kyrbye & w. *Agnes*, def. 3 mess., 1 dovecote, 1 barn, 2 gdns. & 4 a. 1 rood ar. in Walden. £40.

CP26(1)/167   DIVERS COUNTIES

2. Trin. Tho. Roper & Anth. Roper, esquires, pl. Wm. Dawtrey sen., esq., & w. Margt., def. The manor of Ryvershall, & 40 mess., 20 cotts., 10 tofts, 3 barns, 1 water-mill, 2 dovecotes, 20 gdns., 20 orchards, 300 a. ar., 200 a. mw., 300 a. pa., 60 a. wd., 10 a. ar. covered with water, 500 a. furze & heath & £20 rt. in Boxsted, Langham, Great Horsley, Myleende & Colchester & free fishing in the water of Boxsted, co. Essex; & prop. in Suff. Def. quitclaimed to pl. & the heirs of Tho. £840. — Mdx., Essex.

4. Morrow of Trin. Roger James, pl. *Tho.* Wilson & w. Eliz., def. Prop. in Mdx., & 12 a. marsh in Chingford, co. Essex. £140. — Mdx., Essex.

CP25(2)/130/1664   MICHAELMAS, 18-19 ELIZABETH   1576

1. Mich. Abraham Everson, pl. *Jn.* Justanus & w. Anne, def. 1 mess., 1 gdn. & 1 orchard in Elmestead *alias* Elmested Markett. £40.

2. Mich. Hugh Wilson, pl. *Hy.* Swallowe & w. Helen, def. 1 mess., 1 gdn., 1 orchard, 16 a. ar., 2 a. mw., 10 a. pa. & 2 a. wd. in Great Bentley. £80.

3. Mich. Edw. Rawlyn, pl. Robt. Cobyn & w. Margt., def. A moiety of 1 mess., 1 gdn., 30 a. ar., 16 a. mw., 20 a. pa., 16 a. wd., 10 a. furze & heath & 10 a. marsh in Barlyng. Def. quitclaimed to pl. & his w. 130 mks.

4. Mich. Tho. Parker, gent., pl. *Sam.* Parker, gent., Chas. Newcomen, gent., & w. Joan, def. 1 mess., 1 toft, 1 gdn., 3 a. mw. & 4 a. pa. in Shenfeld. £40.

5. Mich. Jn. Lucas, pl. *Wm.* Lincoln & w. 'Rochella', *Jn.* Lincoln & w. Agnes, def. 2 mess., 2 gdns. & 3½ a. ar. in Southwelde & Brendwood. 130 mks.

6. Mich. Edw. Goldynge, pl. *Jn.* Clearke & w. Alice, def. 1 mess. & ½ a. ar. in Bockyn. £40.

7. Mich. Jn. Oldham, pl. Geo. Copcheff & w. Agnes, def. 1 mess. & 2 cotts. in Coggeshall. 130 mks.

8. Mich. Anth. Broke, pl. *Innocent* Godman & w. Anne, def. 2 mess., 4 gdns., 40 a. ar., 4 a. mw. & 20 a. pa. in Great Ilford. 130 mks.

9. Mich. Tho. Meade, pl. Reg. Meade. gent., Robt. Brooke & w. *Eliz.*, def. 41 a. ar. in Christishall *alias* Chrissall. Warranty by Robt. & Eliz. Brooke alone. £40.

10. Mich. Jn. Tinnholme, clk., pl. *Rd.* Longe & w. Philippa, def. 8 a. ar., in Esse *alias* Asshen. Warranty by def. against themselves, the heirs of Rd. Longe & the heirs of Geoff. Smyth. £40.

11. Mich. Tho. Randall, pl. *Geo.* Mayle & w. Alice, *Jn.* Smyth & w. Agnes, def. 2 mess. & 2 gdns. in Barkynge. £40.

12. Mich. Wm. Lewes & w. Mary, pl. *Jn.* Sympson & w. Kath. & Jn. Parker, def. 1 mess., 1 gdn., 1 orchard, 40 a. ar., 10 a. mw., 20 a. pasture & 5 a. wd. in Little Waltham. Def. quitclaimed to pl. & the heirs of Wm. £140.

13. Mich. Edw. Turnor, pl. *Wm.* Chicken & w. Eliz., def. 2 mess., 2 gdns., 2 orchards, 40 a. ar., 5 a. mw., 30 a. pa. & 5 a. wd. in Great Parndon & Roydon. £80.

14. Mich. Jas. Brydge, Jn. Pechye & w. Joan & Simon Brydge, pl. *Anth.* Maxey, esq., & w. Dorothy, def. 1 mess., 1 gdn., 1 orchard, 30 a. ar., 30 a. pa. & 3 a. wd. in Bardfelde Salyng & Stebbyng. Def. quitclaimed to pl. & the heirs of Jas. £120.

15. Mich. Jas. Turke, pl. *Jn.* Skele & w. Mary, def. 1 mess., 1 gdn., 20 a. ar., 10 a. mw., 5 a. pa. & 80 a. marsh in Fobbinge & Curringham. 230 mks.

16. Mich. Tho. Gryggs & w. Bridget, pl. *Wm.* Gryggs & w. Margt., def. 1 mess., 1 barn, 1 gdn., 1 orchard, 14 a. ar. & 16 a. pa. in Pentlowe. Def. quitclaimed to pl. & the heirs of Tho. £80.

17. Mich. Wm. Samwayes, pl. Reg. Meade, gent., & w. Barbara, Robt. Brooke & w. *Eliz.*, def. 3 mess., 1 barn. 1 dovecote, 2 gdns., 1 orchard, 28 a. ar. & 20. pa. in Christishall *alias* Chrissall. Def. quitclaimed to pl. & his heirs. Warranty by Robt. & Eliz. Brooke only. 130 mks.

18. Mich. Jn. Ligitt, pl. Rd. Waterman & w. *Denise*, Jn. Hurrell & w. *Grace*, def. 1 mess., 1 gdn. & 1 orchard in Wytham. £40.

19. Mich. Wistanus Broun, esq., pl. *Wm.* Bancks, citizen & skinner of London, & w. Helen and Hy. Bancks, clk., son & heir apt. of Wm., def. 3 mess., 2 barns, 2 tofts, 2 gdns., 2 orchards, 42 a. ar., 8 a. mw., 37 a. pa., 40 a. fresh marsh, 20 a. salt marsh & 5s. rt. in Langenhoo. Warranty by def. against themselves, the heirs of Wm. Bancks & the heirs of Hugh Banks, decd. £200.

20. Mich. Rd. Stoneley, esq., pl. Arthur Breame, esq., *Jas.* Platte & w. Bridget, def. 50 a. marsh in Estham & Westham. Warranty by Jas. & Bridget Platte only. £200.

21. Mich. Wm. Marshe & w. Maud, pl. Tho. Rochester & w. *Dorothy*, def. The advowson of the church of Great Ockley *alias* Okeley. Def. quitclaimed to pl. & the heirs of Wm. £23.

22. Mich. Wm. Cecyll, K. G., Lord Burghley, Lord Treasurer, & Wm. Cordell, kt., master of the rolls, pl. *Jn.* Smyth, esq., & w. Mary, def. The manors of Mugdenhall *alias* Muckledenhall & Graces & 30 mess., 30 cotts., 3 mills, 20 barns, 4 dovecotes, 20 gdns., 20 orchards, 2,000 a. ar., 1,000 mw., 1,000 a. pa., 200 a. wd., 500 a. furze & heath, 100 a. moor, 100 a. marsh & £10 rt. in Owtinge, Hatfelde Peverell, Little Badewe, Terlinge, Witham, Great Waltham, Little Waltham, Little Lees, Boreham & Springsfeild *alias* Springfeild. Def. quitclaimed to pl. & the heirs of Wm. Cecill. £2,000.

23. Mich. Hy. Doylye, Roger Woodhowse, Wm. Blenerhassett & Miles Hubbert, esquires, pl. 'Drogo' Drury, esq., & w. *Eliz.*, def. An annual rt. of £13 5s. 10d. from the manors of Bacons & Florres with appurtenances in Muche Tey, Pontesbright, Earlescolne, Matteshall & Ferynge. Def. quitclaimed to pl. & the heirs of Miles. £265.

24. Mich. Edm. Gryffyn, gent., & Ralph John, pl. Rd. Drane & w. *Margery*, def. 2 mess., 2 gdns., 2 orchards & 50 a. ar. in Great Waltham & Bromfeilde. Def. quitclaimed to pl. & the heirs of Edm. Pl. gtd. prop. to def. to hold of the chief lords for the life of both & survivor, with remainder to the right heirs of Rd. Drane.

25. Trin. & Mich. Robt. Bell, esq., & Steph. Thymylbye, esq., pl. Jn. Tuscon, esq., & w. *Cristiana*, Tho. Wylford, esq., & w. *Mary* & *Kath.* Browne, def. The manor of Radley-hall *alias* Radleyhalle, & 20 mess., 30 tofts, 2 dovecotes, 20 gdns., 20 orchards, 500 a. ar., 50 a. mw., 200 a. pa., 100 a. wd., 40 a. moor & £8 rt. in Radleyhall *alias* Radleyhalle, Tyrlinge *alias* Tarlinge, Boreham, Falkborne, Great Lees, Little Lees, Hatfeild Peverell, Great Waltham, Little Waltham, view of frankpledge in Radleyhall *alias*, Radleyhalle. 11 twelfths of the rectory of Manewden of 200 a. ar., 40 a. mw., 100 a. pa. & 20 a. wd. in Manewden & Barden *alias* Berden & the advowson of the vicarage & the church of Manewden. Def. quitclaimed to pl. & the heirs of Robt. £1,460.

26. Mich. Wm. Rochester & Tho. Webbe, pl. Simon Pasfyld & w. *Anne*, def. 2 mess., 1 gdn., 1 orchard & 8 a. ar. in Wytham. Def. quitclaimed to pl. & the heirs of Wm. Pl. gtd. prop. to def. to hold of the chief lords, the 8 a. for the life of Simon Pasfyld, the rest for the life of both survivor, with remainder to Wm. Pasfyld, son & heir apt. of def. & to Margt. Rochester, Wm.'s future w., & their legitimate heirs.

27. Mich. Fulk Gryvell, kt., & Mathew Moreton, esq., pl. Edm. Purton, esq., def. The manors of Little Bentley, Hampstall&Balwyns *alias* Baldens, & 40 mess., 20 cotts., 40 tofts, 40 gdns., 20 orchards, 500 a. ar., 100 a. mw., 500 a. pa., 200 a. wd., 1,000 a. furze & heath & 40s. rt. in Little Bentley, Hampstall, Baldwyns *alias* Baldens, Tendryng, Wyks, Mystley, Bradfeld & Little Bromley. Def. quitclaimed to pl. & the heirs of Fulk. £880.

28. Mich. Mark Goodwyne, pl. *Adrian* Smarte & w. Margery, def. 1 mess., 1 gdn., 1 orchard & 2 a. mw. in Wytham. £40.

29. Mich. Geoff. Warner, pl. *Robt.* Peake & w. Margt., def. A moiety of 1 mess., 1 gdn., 20 a. ar., 6 a. pa. & 2 a. wd. in Langham. £80.

30. Mich. Wm. Deynes, gent., pl. Tho. Cropley, def. 5 a. ar. in Bumpsted Helyon. £40.

31. Mich. Tho. Rande, pl. *Jn.* Garrold *alias* Butcher & w. Jane, def. 1 mess., 1 gdn., 4 a. ar., 3 a. mw. & 6 a. pa. in Little Yeldham. £40.

32. Mich. Tho. Lodge, gent., pl. *Wm.* Strachye & w. Jane, def. 1 mess. in Walden. £40.

33. Mich. Hy. Laye, pl. Jn. Laye, def. 8 a. pa. in Wythermondford. £40.

34. Mich. Wm. Somer, pl. Rd. Frydaye & w. *Joan,* def. 1 mess. & 1 gdn. in Rayleygh. £40.

35. Mich. Tho. Jolye, clk., pl. *Wm.* Robynson & w. Margt., def. 6 a. ar. & 6 a. pa. in Rayleigh. £40.

36. Mich. Jn. Shawarden, gent., pl. *Geo.* Abbott, gent., & w. Susanna, def. 2 mess., 1 barn, 1 orchard, 120 a. ar. & 20 a. mw. in Pentlowe. £340.

37. Mich. Tho. Barrington, kt., pl. Jn. Champnys, def. 1 mess., 1 barn, 1 gdn., 40 a. ar., 5 a. mw., 2 a. pa. & 3 a. wd. in Hatfield Regis *alias* Hatfeild Brodock. £80.

38. Mich. Jn. Fryth, pl. Edw. Peck & w. *Agnes*, def. 4 a. ar. in Barkyng & Dagenham. £40.

39. Mich. Hy. Lane, pl. Chris. Kemys *alias* Morgan & w. *Anne* def. 1 mill & 2 a. ar. in West Tylbery. £40.

40. Morrow of Trin. & Mich. Tho. Cocke, pl. Rd. Spuddle & w. *Susanna*, def. 2 a. marsh in Dagenham. £40.

41. Mich. Mary Turnor, wid., pl. Wm. Tanfelde, esq., & w. *Eliz.* & *Jn.* Tanfelde, gent., def. 1 mess., 1 barn, 1 gdn., 1 orchard, 30 a. pa. & 10 a. salt marsh in Fange *alias* Vange. £140.

42. Mich. Geo. Whyte, esq., & w. Kath., pl. *Edw.* Moone, gent., & w. Benet. def. A moiety of manor of Rawreth *alias* Rawreth Hawll, & a moiety of 12 messuages, 6 tofts, 2 dovecotes, 10 gdns., 300 a. ar., 80 a. mw., 200 a. pa., 10 a. wd. & £4 rt. in Rawreth, Rayleigh, Rocheford & Wyckford. Def. quitclaimed to pl. & the heirs of Geo. £400.

43. Mich. Rd. Gourney, pl. *Ralph* Watts & w. Agnes, def. 12 a. ar. & 3 a. mw. in Styfford. £40.

44. Mich. Tho. Hunt & Tho. Sames, pl. *Wm.* Lawrence, gent., & w. Eliz., def. 20 a. pa. in Great Totham. Def. quitclaimed to pl. & the heirs of Tho. Hunt. £40.

45. Mich. Robt. Towers, clk., & Humphrey Cratford, pl. Hy. Baker, def. 2 mess., 2 tofts, 3 gdns., 2 orchards, 4 a. ar., 4 a. mw., 10 a. pa., 3 a. wd. & 2s. 1d. rt. in Woodham Ferrers *alias* Woodham Ferres. Def. quitclaimed to pl. & the heirs of Robt. £100.

46. Mich. Jn. Vavasour, gent., pl. *Tho.* Lyndon & w. Joan, def. 1 mess., 1 gdn., 1 orchard, 1 toft, 1 croft, 4 a. mw. & 30 a. pa. in Waltham Holy Cross. £120.

47. Mich. Wm. Doggett, gent., pl. *Edw.* Honynge, esq., & w. Ursula, def. 20 a. ar., 10 a. mw. & 20 a. pa. in Westham. £100.

48. Mich. Robt. Stave, pl. Geo. Hatter & w. Dorothy, def. Three-quarters of 1 mess., 1 garden, 1 orchard & 3 a. ar. in Childerdiche. £40.

49. Mich. Wm. Prowe, gent., pl. Robt. Wood, gent., def. 1 mess., 1 dovecote, 2 gdns., 2 orchards, 50 a. ar., 12 a. mw., 16 a. pa., 4 a. wd. & 7d. rt. in Bromefeld & Little Waltham. £200.

50. Mich. Hy. Hayles & Wm. Softley, pl. *Geo.* Copcheff & Agnes, def. 1 mess. & 15 a. ar. in Coggeshall. Def. quitclaimed to pl. & the heirs of Hy. £80.

51. Mich. Jerome Garrard, pl. Wm. Hassellon *alias* Haselom, def. 1 mess., 1 barn, 1 gdn., 1 orchard, 8 a. ar., 2 a. mw. & 10 a. pa. in Black Notley. £40.

52. Mich. 16 Eliz. & Mich. 18 Eliz. Rd. Mund *alias* Ellys, pl. Humphrey Barnes & w. *Joan*, def. 1 mess., 1 gdn. & ½ a. ar. in Barkyng. 20 mks.

53. Mich. Jn. Holmested, gent., pl. *Wm.* Waldegrave, kt., & w. Eliz., def. The site of the manor of Stanstede Hall *alias* Stansted, & 1 mess., 4 gdns., 1 orchard, 100 a. ar., 16 a. mw., 30 a. pa., 80 a. wd. & 10 a. alder in Halsted. £400.

54. Mich. Jn. Southcot, a justice of Q's Bench, pl. *Jn.* Lawrence & Wm. Lawrence, def. 4 a. mw. & 6 a. pa. in Wytham. £40.

55. Mich. Jn. Pye & Tho. Barker, pl. Wm. Cardynall & w. *Joan*, def. 6 mess., 2 mills, 6 gdns., 3 orchards, 10 a. ar., 12 a. mw., 20 a. pa. & 6d. rt. in Colchester & Ardley. Def. quitclaimed to pl. & the heirs of Jn. £270.

DIVERS COUNTIES

5. Mich. Jn. Ive. gent., & w. Frances, pl. Wm. Dawtrey jun., gent., def. The manor of Ryvers Hall, & 60 mess., 20 cotts., 10 tofts, 1 water-mill, 3 barns, 2 dovecotes, 20 gdns., 20 orchards, 300 a. ar., 300 a. nîw., 200 a. pa., 200 a. wd., 10 a. ar. covered with water, 500 a. furze & heath, £20 rt., common pa. for all livestock & view of frankpledge in Boxsted, Langham, Great Horseley, Myleende & Colcester & free fishing in the water of Boxsted, co. Essex; & prop. in Suff. Def. quitclaimed to pl. & the heirs of Jn. £840. — Essex. Suff.

6. Mich. Hugh Travers, gent., pl. *Tho*, Covert, gent., & w. Margt., def. The manor of Porters *alias* Whelers, & 8 mess., 8 tofts, 1 dovecote, 8 gdns., 8 orchards, 100 a. ar., 40 a. mw., 240 a. pa., 40 a. wd., 60 a. furze & heath & 40s. rt. in High Rothynge & Great Dunmowe, co. Essex; & prop. in Suss. £280. — Essex, Suss.

CP25(2)/130/1665   HILARY, 19 ELIZABETH   1577

1. Hil. Rd. Grene, pl. *Tho*. Porter & w. Anne, def. 7 a. ar., 1 a. mw. & 7 a. pa. in Navestocke. £40.

2. Hil. Jn. Halffehide, pl. *Edw*. Hynde & w. Kath., def. 4 a. ar. & 2 a. pa. in Rayden. £40.

3. Hil. Jn. Warner jun., gent., & Wm. Neverd, pl. Hy. Windham, esq., & w. *Bridget*, def. 2 mess., 2 orchards, 100 a. ar., 8 a. mw., 83 a. pa., 5 a. wd. & 14 a. marsh in Bradfeld, Mysleye, Manyngtree & Wrabnes. Def. quitclaimed to pl. & the heirs of Jn. £200.

4. Hil. Rd. Champyon, gent., pl. *Tho*. Taylour & w. Agnes, def. 1 mess., 1 gdn., 1 a. pa. & 1 a. wd. in Hornedon-on-Hill. £40.

5. Hil. Phil. Symonds, pl. *Jn*. Marven & w. Anne, def. 10 a. ar. & 2 a. wd. in Ardeley, Lawford, Great Bromeley & Little Bromeley. £40.

6. Hil. Rd. Stonley, gent., pl. *Tho*. Sackevile, kt., Lord Buckehurst, & w. Cecily, def. 7 a. mw. & 32 a. fresh marsh in Barckyng & Dagnam. £540.

7. Hil. Wm. Judde & Walter Parker, pl. *Jas*. Woodcocke & w. Mary, def. 1 mess., 1 gdn., 1 orchard, 6 a. ar. & 7 a. pa. in Farnham. Def. quitclaimed to pl. & the heirs of Wm. £40.

8. Hil. Jas. Rychardson, pl. *Rd*. Goldynge, gent., & w. Mrgt., def. 1 mess., 1 gdn., 34 a. ar., 4 a. mw. & 6 a. pa. in Pebmershe & Colne Engayne. £140.

9. Hil. Jn. Hubberd, pl. *Wm*. Waldegrave, kt., & w. Eliz., def. 1 mess., 1 gdn., 1 orchard, 70 a. ar., 4 a. mw., 20 a. pa., 2 a. wd. & a. marsh in Halsted. £220.

10. Hil. Jas. Platte, pl. *Arthur* Breame & w. Thomasina. def. 40 a. marsh in Westham. £160.

11. Hil. Aphabellus Partridge, pl. *Bart*. Partridge & w. Petronilla, def. 16 a. ar., in Great Warley. £40.

12. Hil. Tho. Norton & w. Margt., pl. *Jn*. Baker & w. Jane, def. 1 mess., 1 barn, 1 gdn., 1 orchard & 1½ a. mw. in Great Chesterforde & Lytelburye. Def. quitclaimed to pl. & the heirs of Tho. 130 mks.

13. Hil. Jn. Gefferey, pl. *Tho*. Barnes *alias* Baron, gent., & w. Mary, def. 2 mess., 2 barns, 2 gdns., 2 orchards, 100 a. ar., 10 a. mw., 10 a. pa. & common pa. in Barkynge. 400 mks.

14. Hil. Aphabellus Partridge, pl. *Wm*. Arrarde & w. Alice, def. 6 a. mw. & 6 a. marsh in Eastham. £40.

15. Hil. Jn. Seman, pl. Edw. Neale & *Robt*. Neale, def. 1 mess., 1 gdn., 12 a. pa. & 6 a. salt marsh in Stowe Maryshe. Warranty by Robt. Neale alone. £40.

16. Hil. Jn. Fuller, pl. Lau. Stoughton, esq., & w. *Rose*, def. 1 mess., 1 barn, 1 gdn. & 10 a. ar. in Rayleigh. £80.

17. Hil. Edw. Derawgh, esq., pl. *Wm.* Waldegrave, kt., & w. Eliz., def. 1 mess., 1 barn, 1 gdn., 1 orchard, 140 a. ar., 8 a. mw., 80 a. pa., 70 a. wd. & 20 a. marsh in Halsted. 400 mks.

18. Hil. Giles Allen, pl. Tho. Neverd & *Rd.* Tomson, def. 2 mess., 60 a. ar., 6 a. mw., 40 a. pa., 6 a. wd. & 6 a. alder in Ardleigh. Warranty by Rd. Tomson alone. £200.

19. Hil. Jn. Cotton & w. Eliz., pl. *Tho.* Norton & w. Margt., def. 1 mess., 1 barn, 1 gdn., 1 orchard & 1½ a. mw. in Great Chesterforde & Lytelburye. Def. quitclaimed to pl. & the heirs of Jn. 130 mks.

20. Hil. Wm. Cooke & Edw. Fradsham, pl. *Wm.* Glascocke & w. Philippa, def. 1 mess., 1 barn, 1 gdn., 1 orchard, 4 a. ar. & pa. in Great Dunmowe. Def. quitclaimed to pl. & the heirs of Wm. £80.

21. Hil. Tho. Taylford, pl. Jn. Dawtry, def. 2 mess., 2 gdns., 6 a. ar., 2 a. mw. & 8 a. pa. in Little Warley & Childerdiche. £40.

22. Hil. Arthur Breame, gent., pl. *Wm.* Waldegrave, kt., & w. Eliz., def. The Manor of Abells *alias* Halsted, & 8 mess., 8 gdns., 8 orchards, 2 water-mills, 200 a. ar., 17 a. mw., 70 a. pa., 16 a. wd., 10 a. alder, 6 a. marsh, £12 rt., view of frankpledge & fairs, holidays & markets (*nundine, ferie et mercata*) in Halsted, Gosfeld, Toppesfeld, Foxherth & Aldham. £400.

23. Hil. Steph. Sonde & w. Eliz., pl. Hy. Ilforde & w.*Marion*, Wm. Hobbie & w. Mary, def. 1 mess., 1 gdn. & 2 a. ar. in Wyllyngale Spayne. Def. quitclaimed to pl. & the heirs of Steph. £40.

24. Mich. & Hil. Leonard Vyccarye, pl. Jn. Samer, def. 1 mess., 1 gdn., 1 orchard, 40 a. ar., 10 a. mw., 20 a. pa., 10 a. wd. & common pa. in South Hannyngfyld & West Hannyngfyld. £80.

25. Mich. & Hil. Nich. Clere, pl. *Tho.* Willett & w. Alice, def. 5 mess., 6 a. ar., 2 a. mw. & 3 a. pa. in Ballyngdon juxta Sudbury. £80.

26. Hil. Jn. Poole & Rd. Freman, pl. *Eustace* Rolffe & w. Joan, def. 1 mess., 60 a. ar., 4 a. mw., 30 a. pa. & 2 a. wd. in Little Waltham & Bromefeld. Def. quitclaimed to pl. & the heirs of Jn. £200.

27. Hil. Joseph Manne, pl. *Wm.* Waldegrave, kt., & w. Eliz., def. 1 mess., 1 barn, 1 gdn., 1 orchard, 40 a. ar., 6 a. mw., 20 a. pa. & 16 a. wd. in Halsted & Stystede. £40.

28. Hil. Jn. Dygbye & Edw. Chappelyn, pl. *Wm.* Waldegrave, kt., & w. Eliz., def. The manor of Claveryngs Lucas & Pytchardes, & 8 mess., 6 tofts, 10 gdns., 10 orchards, 200 a. ar., 10 a. mw., 80 a. pa., 100 a. wd., 20 a. moor & £3 rt. in Halsted, Stansted, Stysted, Patteswycke & Markeshall. Def. quitclaimed to pl. & the heirs of Jn. £160.

29. Hil. Jn. Bayles, pl. *Arthur* Breame, esq., & w. Thomasina, *Jas.* Platt & w. Bridget, def. The manor of Stonehall & 3 mess., 3 gdns., 3 orchards, 100 a. ar., 40 a. mw., 100 a. pa., 20 a. wd. & 32 a. marsh in Barkinge & Westham. 400 mks.

30. Hil. Robt. Phillipp *alias* Saunder, Hy. Purcas & Simon Bredge, pl. *Jn.* Pechye, & w. Joan & *Jn.* Thurgood, def. 1 mess., 1 gdn. & 8 a. ar. in Little Canfelde & Berdefelde Salinge. Def. quitclaimed to pl. & the heirs of Robt. Warranty by Jn. & Joan Pechye for 8 a. against themselves & the heirs of Jn.; warranty by Jn. Thurgood for the mess. & gdn. against all men. £40.

31. Hil. Charles Arundell, esq., pl. Edw. earl of Oxford, def. The manor of Battyshall *alias* Battylshall, & 2 mess., 2 cotts., 6 tofts, 6 gdns., 6 orchards, 300 a. ar., 40 a. mw., 100 a. pa., 40 a. wd., 300 a. furze & heath, £10 rt. & common pa. in Stapleford Abbott. Pl. gtd. prop. to def. & his heirs to hold of the chief lords.

32. Hil. Tho. Randall, pl. *Robt.* Atkynson & w. Joan, def. 1 mess., 68 a. pa. & 12 a. wd. in Barkynge. £140.

33. Hil. Rd. Tolson, gent., & Wm. Warde, gent., pl. Jn. Dalston, jun., esq., & w. *Anne*, def. 1 cott., 60 a. pa. & 120 a. wd. in Brydebroke. Def. quitclaimed to pl. & the heirs of Rd. Pl. gtd. prop. to def. & the legitimate heirs of their bodies to hold of the chief lords, with remainder to the right heirs of Anne Dalston.

CP25(2)/260/19 Eliz., Hil.   **DIVERS COUNTIES**

8. Hil. Tho. Lodge. kt., & w. Anne, pl. *Tho.* Byrde, gent., & w. Eliz., def. Prop. in Suff.; & 4 mess., 4 gdns., 4 orchards, 30 a. ar., 16 a. mw. & 16 a. pa. in Great Horseley, co. Essex. Def. quitclaimed to pl. & the heirs of Anne. £200. — Suff., Essex.

CP25(2)/130/1666   **EASTER, 19 ELIZABETH**   1577

1. Eas. Robt. Artur, pl. Wm. Luck & w. *Helen*, def. 3 a. mw. in Spryngfeild. £40.

2. Eas. Tho. Wallinger, pl. *Charles* Tyrell, gent., & w. Anne, def. 1 mess., 1 curtilage, 1 gdn., 1 orchard & 2 a. mw. in Bromefyld. £40.

3. Eas. Jn. Francke, pl. *Hy.* Mildmaye, esq., & w. Jane, def. 14 a. ar. & 1 a. pa. in Little Waltham. £40.

4. Eas. Jn. Marshe, pl. *Matthew* Smyth, esq., & w. Jane, def. 1 mess., 1 gdn., 10 a. ar., 1 a. mw. & 6 a. pa. in Pateswycke. £40.

5. Eas. Jn. Chapman, pl. Tho. Bynder, def. 1 mess., 2 cotts., 1 gdn. & 6 a. ar. in Danbery. £40.

6. Eas. Jn. Archer, pl. Edw. Archer, def. 1 mess., 2 barns, 1 gdn., 1 orchard, 20 a. ar., 20 a. mw. & 20 a. pa. in Theydon Garnon. £200.

7. Eas. Jerome Garrard, pl. *Robt.* Rery & w. Margt., def. 1 mess., 1 gdn., 10 a. ar., 1 a. mw. & 10 a. pa. in Nigra Notley *alias* Black Notley. £40.

8. Eas. Oliver Skynner, pl. Geo. Cole & *Jn.* Cole, def. 2 mess., 1 cott., 1 toft, 2 gdns. & 3 a. mw. in Maldon. £40.

9. Eas. Wm. Saunder, pl. *Clement* Gymlett & w. *Margt.*, def. 1 mess. & 1 gdn. in Coggeshall. £40.

10. Eas. Robt. Rookes, pl. Rd. Horsepitt & w. *Grace*, def. 1 gdn. & 2 a. pa. in Erles Colne. £40.

11. Eas. Mark Mott, pl. Jn. Wentworth, esq., def. 1 mess., 2 gdns. & 13 a. ar. in Bockynge, held for life by Jane Webb, wid., with reversion to def. Def. gtd. pl. the reversion of the prop. £40.

12. Eas. Jn. Sharpe, gent., pl. Jn. Pope, def. 1 mess., 1 gdn., 1 curtilage & 3 a. ar. in Leighe. £40.

13. Eas. Tho. Reve, pl. Simon Mumforde & w. *Joan*, def. 1 mess., 1 gdn. & 1 barn in Walden. £80.

14. Eas. Wm. Saunders, pl. *Geo.* Copsheff & w. Agnes, def. 1 mess., 1 dovecote, 3 gdns., 9 a. ar. & 9 a. pa. in Coggeshall. £80.

15. Eas. Jn. Mylbourne, pl. *Edw.* Raymonde, gent., & w. Marcia & Francis Raymonde, Edward's brother, def. 1 barn, 1 toft, 8 a. ar., 2 a. mw., 12 a. pa., 2 a. wd. & 2s. rt. in Great Donmowe. £40.

16. Eas. Rd. Bowlande, esq., pl. *Geo.* Whyte, esq., & w. Kath., def. 2 mess., 200 a. ar., 100 a. mw., 100 a. pa. & 100 a. marsh in Great Hockley & Little Hockley. £140.

17. Eas. Robt. Sorrell, pl. *Hy.* Mildmaye, esq., & w. Mary, def. 1 mess., 1 gdn., 30 a. ar. & 15 a. pa. in Great Leighes. £130.

18. Eas. Edw. Neweman, pl. Tho. Clerke, def. 1 mess., 1 orchard & 5 a. ar. in Alresford. £40.

19. Eas. Alexander Cracknell & Robt. Annys *alias* Smyth, pl. *Edw.* Heron, esq., & w. Anne, def. 14 a. ar., 2 a. mw. & 10 a. pa. in Fynchingfeild. Def. quitclaimed to pl. & the heirs of Alexander. £40.

20. Eas. Mich. Foxe, pl. *Jn.* Seaman & w. Anne, def. 1 mess., 1 gdn., 14 a. ar., 14 a. pa. & 6 a. fresh marsh in Danbery. £140.

21. Eas. Robt. Snellyng, pl. Hy. Clarke, def. 3 mess., 40 a. ar. & 20 a. mw. in Halsted, Witham & Newland. £260.

22. Hil. & Eas. Brian Darcye, esq., pl. *Rd*. Brokeman, gent., & w. Agnes & *Jn*. Seynclere, gent., def. 1 mess., 20 a. ar., 20 a. mw., 20 a. pa., 100 a. wd. & 10 a. furze & heath in Chiche Regis *alias* Sancts Ositha *alias* Saint Osethes. £300.

23. Eas. Tho. Mylles, pl. Steph. Wryght & w. *Joan*, def. 5 a. ar. in Waltham Hollycrosse. £40.

24. Eas. Hy. Whyte, pl. Jn. Battisford & w. *Eliz*., def. 2 mess., 2 gdns. & 2 orchards in Thaxsted. £40.

25. Eas. Edm. West, esq., pl. Tho. Sarynge & w. *Dorothy*, 1 mess., 1 gdn., 1 orchard, 2 a. ar., 2 a. mw. & 1 a. pa. in Depden. £40.

26. Eas. Jn. Sherewysbury, pl. Tho. Browne, def. 2 mess. & 1 gdn. in Rayleyghe. £40.

27. Eas. Wm. Waldegrave, kt., pl. Maurice Marten & w. *Alice*, def. 1 mess., 1 toft, 3 gdns., 16 a. ar., 1 a. mw., 6 a. pa. & 1 a. wd. in Wethermonford *alias* Wormyngforde, Great Fordham & Bures-on-the-Hill. £40.

28. Eas. Wm. Kequick, pl. *Rd*. Hayes & w. Joan, def. 1 mess., 1 gdn., 3 a. mw. & 13 a. pa. in Ramsdon Crayes. £40.

29. Eas. Chris. Elryngton, gent., pl. *Tho*. Sackvile, kt., Lord Buckhurst, & w. Cecily, def. 12 a. marsh in Berkynge. 130 mks.

30. Eas. Leonard Levett, pl. Edw. Sudburye & w. *Margt*., def. 1 mess., 1 gdn., 20 a. ar., 1 a. mw. & 14d. rt. in Stebbyng & Felsted. £40.

31. Eas. Tho. Myller, pl. Jn. Myller, def. 7 a. ar. in Takeley. £40.

32. Eas. Robt. Symon, pl. *Jas*. Turner & w. Agnes, Samuel Turner, Rd. Turner & Tho. Turner, def. 8 a. ar., 2 a. pa. & ½ a. wd. in Ashedon. Warranty by Jas. & Agnes Turner only. £40.

33. Hil. & Eas. Jn. Southcot, a justice of Queen's Bench, pl. *Clement* Roberts, gent., & w. Mary, def. 12 a. ar. in Witham & Ryvenhall. £40.

34. Eas. Geo. Potyer & w. Eliz., pl. *Rd*. Holborowe & w. Cristiana, def. 1 mess., 2 gdns., 15 a. ar. & 11s. 6d. rt. in Earl's Colne. Def. quitclaimed to pl. & the heirs of Eliz. £40.

35. Eas. Geo. Maye, gent., Jn. Watson, gent., & Jn. Norton, pl. Tho. Fremlyn, & w. *Joan*, def. 1 mess., 1 gdn. & 2 a. ar. in St. James parish in the town of Colcestr'. Def. quitclaimed to pl. & the heirs of Geo. £40.

36. Eas. Tho. Felton & Robt. Sharpe, pl. Jn. Watson, Rd. Watson & *Wm*. Pannell, def. 1 mess., 2 gdns., 4 a. ar., 2 a. mw. & 4 a. pa. in Bumpsted-at-the-Steeple & Hempsted. Def. quitclaimed to pl. & the heirs of Tho. Pl. gtd. prop. to Jn. & Rd. Watson & the heirs of Jn. Watson to hold of the chief lords.

37. Hil. & Eas. Edw. Hubberd, gent., pl. Robt. Bevys & Geo. Bevys, def. 1 mess., 1 barn, 1 gdn., 1 orchard, 14 a. ar., 3 a. mw., 3 a. pa. & common pa. in Hastinges Woodd in Northweld Bassett. £80.

38. Eas. Nich. Wall, pl. *Reg*. Highegate, esq., & w. Mary & *Jn*. Daniell, esq., def. 2 mess., 2 gdns., 2 orchards, 30 a. ar., 3 a. mw., 70 a. pa. & 5 a. wd. in Great Byrche, Little Byrche, Stanwey, Copford & Leyer Bretton. Def. quitclaimed to pl. & his heirs. £100.

39. Eas. Tho. Soone & Robt. Letherlond, pl. Robt. Clyat & w. *Mary*, Jn. Patche & w. Margt., Charles Belfeild & w. *Alice*, def. 2 mess., 2 gdns., 3 a. mw. & 10 a. pa. in Salcote Wygborowe, Tolleshunt Knights & Coggeshall. Def. quitclaimed to pl. & the heirs of Tho. Warranty by Charles & Alice Belfeild for 1 mess. & 1 gdn. in Coggeshall; warranty by other def. for remaining prop. in Salcote Wygborowe & Tolleshunt Knights. £40.

40. Eas. Wm. Thymble, pl. *Tho*. Bussard & w. Joan, *Wm*. Whight & w. Eliz., def. The manor of Grovehowse, & 3 mess., 1 dovecote, 4 gdns., 5 orchards, 160 a. ar., 40 a. mw., 150 a. pa., 20 a. wd. & 20s. rt. in Kirkebye, Walton & Bradwell-by-Sea. £400.

41. Eas. Jn. Stelewoman & Robt. Bancks, pl. *Hy*. Saunders, & w. Mary & Edm. Stane, def. 1 mess., 1 cott., 2 barns, 2 tofts, 2 gdns., 2 orchards, 20 a. ar. & 40 a. pa. in Boreham & Hatfeild Peverell. Def. quitclaimed to pl. & the heirs of Jn. Pl. gtd. prop. to Edm. Stane for 10 years from Mich. 1577 at annual rt. of 4d., with remainder on expiry of term to Hy. Saunders & his heirs to hold of the chief lords.

DIVERS COUNTIES

8. Eas. Francis Jermye, esq., & Wm. Jermye, gent., pl. Hy. Palmer, esq., & w. *Jane*, Tho. Appleton, esq., & w. Mary, Jn. Jermye, esq., & w. Margt., def. The manor of Hyghall, & 2 mess., 1 toft, 2 gdns., 2 orchards, 134 a. ar., 12 a. mw., 142 a. pa. & 64 a. wd. in Towlesburye, Towlson Maior, Wytham, Towlson Darsey, Salcott Virley, Great Wigborowe & Layermarney, co. Essex; & prop. in Suff. & Kent. Def. quitclaimed to pl. & the heirs of Francis. 2,530 mks. – Essex. Suff., Kent.

15. Eas. Edm. Asheffeld, gent., & Wm. Atwood, gent., pl. Francis Bacon, esq., & w. *Mary*, def. Prop. in Suff; & the manors of Kelveden Hall *alias* Kelden Hall & Ewell Hall, & 300 a. ar., 60 a. mw., 360 a. pa., 106 a. wd. & 14s. rt. in Braxsted, Kelden, Feringe, Messinge & Inworthe, co. Essex. Def. quitclaimed to pl. & the heirs of Edm. £1,540. – Suff., Essex.

CP25(2)/130/1667   TRINITY, 19 ELIZABETH   1557

1. Morrow of Trin. Jn. Howe, sen., pl. Jn. Garrett & w. *Agnes*, def. 1 mess. & 1 gdn. in Navestocke. £40.

2. Morrow of Trin. Jn. Lorde *alias* Fraunces, pl. Jn. Tricker & w. *Joan*, def. 5 a. ar. in Thaxsted. £40.

3. Morrow of Trin. Mary Fortescue, wid., & Dudley Fortescue, gent., pl. Wm. Tusser, esq., def. 1 toft, 10 a. ar., 6 a. mw. & 20 a. pa. in Ryvenhall. Def. quitclaimed to pl. & the heirs of Dudley. £40.

4. Morrow of Trin. Geo. Reynold, pl. Jn. Marrian & w. *Joan*, def. A fourth part of 1 mess., 1 gdn., 1 orchard, 60 a. ar., 2 a. mw. & 1 a. wd. in Great Chesterford & Littelberie. £40.

5. Morrow of Trin. Jn. Wentworthe of Bockinge, esq., pl. Robt. Ramston, gent., def. 3 a. mw. in Bockyng. £40.

6. Trin. Jn. Duke, pl. Jn. Thurgood, def. 1 mess., 1 gdn., 6 a. ar., 1 a. mw. & 5 a. pa. in Shearinge. Warranty by def. against himself, his heirs, Robt. Thurgood his father, Robert's heirs, Nich. Thurgood, John's grandfather, & Nicholas's heirs. £40.

7. Morrow of Trin. Rd. Grene, pl. Phil. Wyllyams & w. *Etheldreda*, def. A fourth part of 1 mess. & 3 a. pa. in Navestock. £40.

8. Morrow of Trin. Wm. Evans, pl. Jn. Ingram, def. 2 mess., 4 cotts., 6 gdns. & 22 a. pa. in Stratford Langthorne & Westham. 400 mks.

9. Trin. Walter Heyward, pl. Tho. Warner & *Jn*. Warner, def. 1 mess., 2 gdns., 1 orchard, 45 a. ar., 6 a. mw. & 4 a. pa. in Berdon. £80.

10. Morrow of Trin. Hy. Archer, esq., pl. Jas. Ryvers & w. *Eliz*., def. A moiety of 1 mess., 1 toft. 6 a. ar. & 4 a. mw. in Wansted. £40.

11. Morrow of Trin. Geo. Gates, pl. *Wm*. Harryson & w. Thomasina, def. 1 mess., 1 gdn., 1 orchard, 3 a. ar. & 4 a. pa. in Rocheford. £40.

12. Morrow of Trin. Wm. Roche, pl. Mich. London & w. Judith & *Jn*. London, def. 1 mess., 1 gdn., 10 a. ar., 10 a. mw. & 10 a. pa. in Little Warley. £60.

13. Morrow of Trin. Mary Gate, wid., pl. *Edw*. Gylder & w. Agnes, def. 1 mess., 1 barn, 1 gdn. 40 a. ar., 10 a. mw., 30 a. pa. & 6 a. wd. in Shenfeld & Hutton. £160.

14. Morrow of Trin. Tho. Emilye *alias* Emeley, pl. Jn. Dennys, esq., def. The manors of Southouse & Sawyers, & 1 mess., 1 gdn., 30 a. ar., 100 a. mw., 600 a. pa., 20 a. wd., 30 a. furze & heath, 200 a. marsh & 100 a. ar. covered with water in Malden, Munden & Purleigh. £160.

15. Trin. Mich. London, pl. Jn. London, sen., def. 1 mess., 1 toft & 1 gdn. in Brentwood. £40.

16. Eas. & Morrow of Trin. Rd. Lycett, pl. Jn. Chaplyn & w. *Susanna*, def. 1 mess. & 1 a. ar. in Estham. £40.

17. Morrow of Trin. Jn. Fowle, pl. Jn. Parkynson, def. 1 mess., 1 gdn. & 1 orchard in Barkynge. £40.

18. Morrow of Trin. Hy. Baker, sen., pl. Robt. Stammer, def. 1 mess., 1 toft, 2 gdns., 1 orchard, 30 a. ar., 10 a. mw., 30 a. pa. & 5 a. wd. in Rawreth. £80.

19. Morrow of Trin. Tho. Luther *alias* Hewett, pl. Tho. Taverner, def. 1 mess., 40 a. ar., 10 a. mw., 40 a. pa. & 5 a. wd. in Lamborne. £150.

20. Morrow of Trin. Walter Farre, gent., pl. *Wm*. Lorkyn & w. Alice, Jas. Parker & w. Margery, def. 9 a. ar. & 1 a. mw. in Stock & Buttesburye. £40.

21. Morrow of Trin. Jn. Hawtrye, gent., pl. *Rd* Grenacres, gent., & w. Frances, def. 20 a. ar., 10 a. mw., 40 a. pa. & 20 a. wd. in Wymbyshe & Thunderley. £100.

22. Morrow of Trin. Francis Ellyott, pl. Jn. Felton, gent., & w. *Kath.*, def. 1 watermill, 1 gdn., 1 a. mw. & 2 a. pa. in Pentlowe. 200 mks.

23. Morrow of Trin. Susanna Watts, pl. *Tho*. Coo, gent., & w. Kath., def. 1 mess., 1 gdn., 30 a. ar., 6 a. mw., 10 a. pa. & 6 a. wd. in Gestingthorpe & Belchampe Walter *alias* Belchampe William. £200.

24. Morrow of Trin. Wm. Glascock, sen., gent., pl. *Wm*. Glascock, jun., & w. Philippa, def. 1 mess., 1 toft, 1 barn, 2 gdns., 1 orchard, 6 a. ar. & 6 a. pa. in Great Donmowe. £100.

25. Morrow of Trin. Edw. Kympton, pl. *Ralph* Typpynge, gent., & w. Joan, def. 1 mess., 1 gdn., 1 orchard & 8 a. pa. in Westham. £40.

26. Morrow of Trin. Charles Newcombe, gent., & Tho. Parker, gent., pl. Tho. Taverner, gent., def. 5 a. mw. & 6 a. pa. in Lamborne. Def. quitclaimed to pl. & the heirs of Charles. £30.

27. Morrow of Trin. Tho. Eve, pl. Tho. Fraunces & w. *Margt.*, def. 1 cott. in Prytwell. £40.

28. Eas. & Morrow of Trin. Barnard Wyttam, pl. *Geo*. Whyte, esq., & w. Kath., def. 2 mess., 100 a. ar., 100 a. pa. & 100 a. marsh in Tillyngham & Denge. £200.

29. Morrow of Trin. Wm. Cordell, kt., Tho. Fanshawe, esq., & Pet. Palmer, gent., pl. Jn. Wrighte & w. *Eliz.*, def. 1 mess., 1 gdn., 10 a. ar., 10 a. mw. & 10 a. pa. in Barkynge & Dagenham. Def. quitclaimed to pl. & the heirs of Wm. £40.

30. Trin. Tho. Slowman & Geo. Slowman, pl. Robt. Slowman & w. *Joan*, def. A moiety of 1 mess., 2 barns, 1 toft, 1 gdn., 1 orchard, 12 a. ar., 5 a. mw. & 13. a. pa. in Messyng & Inworth. Def. quitclaimed to pl. & the heirs of Tho. £40.

31. Trin. Jn. Browne, gent., pl. *Jn*. Latha(m), gent., & w. Helen, def. 1 mess., 2 cotts., 2 barns, 2 tofts, 1 dovecote, 3 curtilages, 2 gdns., 1 orchard, 60 a. ar., 12 a. mw., 50 a. pa. & 6 a. wd. in Sanden & Great Baddowe. £200.

32. Morrow of Trin. Tho. Collyn, pl. *Edm*. Heygate, gent., & w. Grace, def. 2 mess., 2 gdns., 92 a. ar., 10 a. mw., 20 a. pa., 20 a. wd., 54 a. fresh marsh & 7s rt. in Assyngdon & Southfambrydge. Warranty by def. against themselves, Edmund's heirs, Margt., formerly w. of Tho. Heygate, gent., & her heirs. 400 mks.

33. Morrow of Trin. Edw. Hubberd, gent., pl. *Geo*. Bevys & w. Eliz. & *Robt*. Bevys, def. 3 mess., 2 barns, 3 gdns., 2 orchards, 40 a. ar., 8 a. mw., 30 a. pa. & 5 a. wd. in Great Peringdon & Little Peringdon & common pa. for all animals in Great Peringdon, Little Peringdon & Epping. £240.

34. Morrow of Trin. Tho. Croftes, esq., Jn. Southwell esq., & Charles Croftes, gent., pl. Wm. Fryer, gent., def. The manor of Garnons with appurtenances in Bumsted ad Turrim *alias* Steple Bumsted. Def. quitclaimed to pl. & the heirs of Charles. £160.

35. Trin. Tho. Baxster & Robt. Berney, gent., pl. Wm. Playters, esq., & w. *Thomasina*, def. A fourth part of the manors of Cocksolls, Scottes & Plumborowe *alias* Plumbergh & a fourth part of 5 mess., 5 tofts, 3 dovecotes, 8 gdns., 8 orchards, 600 a. ar., 200 a. mw., 600 a. pa., 150 a. wd., 60 a. furze & heath, 200 a. marsh, 30 a. alder, & £10 rt. in Northbemflete, Sowthbemflete, Wickford, Thundersleye, Newndon, Cannewdon *alias* Canouden, Hockley, Assheldon *alias* Assheldham, Rawreth, Wodonferis, Raileigh *alias* Railie, Basseldon, Langdon, Pitsey, Rocheforde, Stanforde & Hawkewell & a fourth part of the advowson of the church of Northbemflete. Def. quitclaimed to pl. & the heirs of Tho. £300.

CP25(2)/260   DIVERS COUNTIES

1. Morrow of Trin. Robt. Felder & Robt. Dyrlynge, pla. Jn. Rice & w. *Eliz.*, def. 2 mess., 2 gdns., 2 orchards & 10 a. pa. in Waltham & Nazynge, co. Essex; & prop. in Dorset & Kent. Def. quitclaimed to pl. & the heirs of Robt. Felder. £160. — Dorset, Essex, Kent.

CP26(1)/173   MICHAELMAS, 19–20 ELIZABETH   1577

1. Mich. Geo. Neale, pl. *Zacharias* Fuller & w. Margt., def. 1 mess., 1 barn, 1 gdn., 2 orchards, 3 a. mw. & 13 a. pa. in Danbury. £40.

2. Mich. Sigismond Rytcholl, pl. Wm. Larke & w. *Thomasina*, def. 1 mess. & 1 gdn. in Wytham. £40.

3. Mich. Camillus Rusticens & w. Margery, pl. Wm. Drane & w. *Sabiana*, 1 mess., 1 cott., 1 gdn., 1 orchard, & 1. a. mw. in Wydford. Def. quitclaimed to pl. & the heirs of Margery. £40.

4. Mich. Tho. Wyllyams & w. Margery, pl. *Rd.* Lorkyn & Wm. Lorkyn. def. 1 barn, 20 a. ar., 4 a. mw., 20 a. pa., 2 a. moor & 1 a. alder in Shenfeyld. Def. quitclaimed to pl. & the heirs of Margery. 200 mks.

5. Mich. Tho. Bussard, pl. Tho. Gladwyn & w. *Mary*, def. A moiety of 1 mess., 1 toft, 2 gdns., 10 a. ar. & 6 a. mw. in Colchester. £40.

6. Mich. Jn. Harte, pl. *Chris.* Eglisfeilde, gent., & w. Eliz., *Aphabellus* Partriche & w. Denise, def. 20 a. ar., 6 a. mw., 20 a. pa. & 10 a. marsh in Estham. £100.

7. Mich. Jn. Barker, gent., pl. Hy. Josselyn, esq., & w. *Anne*, def. A moiety of the manors of Manyngtre, Shyddynhoo *alias* Shedynghoo, Old Hall *alias* Oldehall, Newhall & Abbottes *alias* Edlynges, & 60 mess., 20 cotts., 10 tofts, 4 water-mills, 1,000 a. ar., 200 a. mw., 1,000 a. pa., 400 a. wd., 600 a. furze & heath & £20 rt. in Manyngtre *alias* Manytree, Mystleigh *alias* Mysteley, Bradfeld, Colchester, Stanwaye, Wrabney *alias* Wrabnes, Wyks, Little Badowe, Lawforde, Little Bromley & Ardleighe, a moiety of view of frankpledge, free warren, liberties & franchises in Mysteleigh & Manyngtree, a moiety of rectory & church of Bradfelde, of all tithes in Mystley, & Bradfeld vicarage. Warranty by def. against themselves, the heirs of Anne, & the heirs of Jn. Raynsforth, kt., decd. £400.

8. Mich. Rd. Kynge, pl. Wm. Follwell *alias* Folly & w. *Margt.*, def. 1 mess., 1 barn, 1 gdn., 5 a. ar. & common pa. for all livestock in Rocheford. £40.

9. Mich. Jn. Andrewe, pl. Robt. Cooke, def. 2 mess. & 2 gdns. in Raileighe. £40.

10. Mich. Jn. Collyn, pl. *Tho.* Wyberde & w. Anne, def. 10 a. ar., 20 a. mw., 10 a. pa. & 30 a. marsh in Westham. £200.

11. Mich. Jn. Hunt & Leonard Aylett, pl. Jn. Page & w. *Eliz.*, David Loge & Emma Caser, def. 1 mess., 1 toft, 1 orchard, 20 a. ar. & 16 a. pa. in Ardeleigh. Def. quitclaimed to pl. & the heirs of Jn. £40.

12. Mich. Tho. earl of Suss., pl. *Tho.* Tenderynge & w. Cicily, def. 1 mess., 1 gdn., 1 orchard, 30 a. ar., 24 a. pa. & 20 a. wd. in Boreham, Little Waltham & Great Leighes. £40.

13. Mich. Tho. earl of Suss., pl. *Tho.* Tyrrell, esq., & w. Margt., def. 20. wd. in Little Waltham & Spryngfeild. £40.

14. Mich. Tho. Clerke, pl. Wm. Pollerd & w. Margery, def. 1 mess., 1 gdn., 12 a. ar. & 3 a. salt marsh in Tollesburye. Def. gtd. & quitclaimed to pl. the prop. for the life of Margery Pollerd. £40.

15. Mich. Joseph Mann, pl. *Tho.* Pawe, Roger Pawe, Geoff. Pawe & Phil. Pawe, def. 1 mess. & 1 gdn. in Branktre. £40.

16. Mich. Steph. Clarke, pl. *Jn.* Peryman & w. Bridget, def. 5 a. ar., in Ginge Mountney *alias* Mountneys Inge. £40.

17. Mich. Hy. Sames & Abraham Fokes, pl. Tho. Westbroome & w. *Eliz.*, Wm. Sames & w. Grace, def. 7 mess., 6 tofts, 1 barn, 2 gdns., 160 a. ar., 20 a. mw., 50 a. pa. & 2 a. wd. in Marks Taye, Aldham, Peldon, Ferynge, Little Taye, Great Byrche, Copforde & Estthorpe. Def. quitclaimed to pl. & the heirs of Hy. Sames 3 mess., 5 tofts, 1 barn, 4 gdns., 100 a. ar., 16 a. mw., 30 a. pa. & 2 a. wd. in Marks Taye, Aldham, Peldon, Feringe, Little Taye, Great Byrche, Copford & Estthorpe; def. gtd. to pl. & the heirs of Hy. the reversion of the remaining 4 mess., 1 toft, 4 gdns., 60 a. ar., 4 a. mw. & 20 a. pa. in Marks Taye & Peldon, held for life by Jn. Moteham, to hold of the chief lords. Warranty by Tho. & Eliz. Westbroome for one moiety of the prop.; by Wm. & Grace Sames for the other. £400.

18. Mich. Simon Passefyld & w. Anne & Tho. Passefyld, their son, pl. *Clement* Roberts, gent., & w. Mary, def. 10 a. ar. in Wytham. Def quitclaimed to pl. & the heirs of Tho. £40.

19. Mich. Olive Gregill *alias* Grigge, wid., pl. *Tho*. Evererd & w. Agnes, def. 20 a. ar. in Chycknale Trenchefoyle. £40.

20. Mich. Jn. Richemond & w. Agnes, pl. *Jn*. Brooke & w. Eliz., def. Two thirds of 1 mess., 7 a. ar., 3 a. marsh & the river-crossing called 'Fambridgeferrye' in Northfambridge. Def. quitclaimed to pl. & the heirs of Jn. £40.

21. Mich. Rd. Elyott, gent., pl. Jn. Rygbye, gent., & w. *Anne*, def. 1 cott., 1 orchard, 15 a. ar. & 10 a. pa. in Upshire & Sywardston. £40.

22. Mich. Nich. Bragge, pl. Robt. Boreham, def. 1 mess., 1 gdn. & 4 a. ar. in Bulmer. £40.

23. Mich. Robt. Noble, pl. *Jn*. Love, sen., & w. Alice, def. 1 gdn., 2 a. ar. & 2 a. wd. in Thundersleygh. £40.

24. Mich. Mary Wells, wid., Jn. Wells & Mary Wells, pl. Wm. Mosse & w. *Mary*, def. 1 cott. & 1 gdn. in Rochford. Def. quitclaimed to pl. & the heirs of Jn. £40.

25. Mich. Geo. Webbe, citizen & scrivener of London, pl. Rd. Hall, def. 1 mess., 1 toft, 1 gdn., 1 orchard, 10 a. ar., 2 a. mw., 20 a. pa. & 2 a. wd. in Stoneden *alias* Stonden. £60.

26. Mich. Wm. Sydaye, gent., pl. *Jn*. Byatt & w. Phebe, def. 1 mess., 2 barns, 2 tofts, 2 gdns., 2 orchards, 100 a. ar., 10 a. mw., 80 a. pa., 30 a. wd., 30 a. furze & heath & 10s. rt. in Great Henney, Little Henney, Bulmer, Twynsted & Midleton. £160.

27. Mich. Geo. Stacye, pl. Jn. Sabyster *alias* Sapister, def. 1 mess., 14 a. ar., 2 a. mw., 3 a. pa. & 2 a. wd. in Hallingberye Morley. £80.

28. Mich. Jn. Kent. gent., & Wm. Case, pl. Jn. Humfrey & w. *Frances*, *Edw*. Whittingham & w. Anne, def. 3 mess., 6

29. Trin. & Mich. Robt. Aylett, pl. Edw. Creswell, gent., & w. *Mary*, def. 2 mess., 2 gdns., 2 orchards, 100 a. ar., 20 a. mw. & 40 a. pa. in Fyfeild, Wyllingale Doe, Betcham & Rodinge *alias* Rowdinge. £200.

30. Mich. Jas. Harryngton & Wm. Laste, pl. Nich. Bothomley & w. *Jane*, def. 1 mess., 1 gdn. & 2 a. pa. in Fynchyngfeld. Def. quitclaimed to pl. & the heirs of Jas. £40.

31. Mich. Wm. Cooke & Tho. Walforde, pl. Jn. Purcas & w. *Margt*. & Tho. Purcas, John's son & heir apt., def. 1 mess., 1 gdn., 10 a. ar., 4 a. mw. & 2 a. pa. in Great Berdefelde & Little Berdefelde. Def. quitclaimed to pl. & the heirs of Wm. £80.

32. Mich. Rd. Boilland, esq., pl. *Reg*. Hiegate, esq., & w. Mary & *Jn*. Danyell, esq., def. 1 mess., 20 a. mw., 100 a. pa. & 40 a. wd. in Althorne, Burneham & Southmynster. £40.

33. Mich. Rd. Boilland, esq., pl. *Reg*. Hiegate, esq., & w. Mary, def. 3 mess., 40 a. mw., 200 a. pa. & 100 a. wd. in Crixsey, Althorne, Burneham & Southmynster. £40.

34. Mich. Esq. Turnor, pl. *Jn*. Archer & w. Mary, def. 1 mess. & 2 gdns. in Halsted. £04.

35. Mich. Wm. Bendlowes, serjeant at law, pl. Robt. Veer, esq., & w. *Barbara*, *Arthur* Barners, gent., *Jn*. Barners, gent., & *Wm*. Barners, gent., def. 1 mess., 1 cott., 2 gdns., 200 a. ar., 10 a. mw., 20 a. pa. & 20 a. wd. in Fynchingfeld & Great Bardefeld. £200.

36. Mich. Jn. Reve, pl. *And.* Clerke, gent., & w. Mary, Edw. Derawgh, esq., & w. Margt., def. 36 a. ar., 2 a. mw., 10 a. pa. & 3 a. wd. in Gosfelde & Bockynge. Warranty by And. & Mary Clerke only. Pl. gtd. annuity of £8 from the prop. to Edw. & Margt. Derawgh for the life of Margt.

37. Mich. Robt. Cocke, pl. *Jn.* Collyn & w. Joan, def. A moiety of the manor of Camys Hall *alias* Camoyse Hall *alias* Camoys Haull & 3 mess., 3 tofts, 1 dovecote, 3 gdns., 300 a. ar., 30 a. mw., 30 a. pa., 10 a. wd. & 21d. rt. in White Rodynge *alias* Morrell Roodynge, Highe Rodinge, Eythroppe Roodynge & Hatfelde. 400 mks.

38. Mich. Jn. Steven, pl. Jn. Bonde, def. 1 mess., 12 a. ar., 3 roods mw. & 3 a. 3 roods wd. in Ardeley & Dedham. £40.

39. Mich. Tho. Eden, esq., pl. *Jn.* Bragg & w. Thomasina, def. 16 a. ar., 3 a. mw., 14 a. pa., 16 a. wd., 3 a. marsh & a moiety of the manor of Little Hennye *alias* Ryes in Bulmer, Little Hennye, Great Hennye & Middleton & a moiety of the advowson of the church of Little Hennye. 200 mks.

40. Mich. Tho. Freman, pl. *Jn.* Trigge & w. Margt., Margt. Trigge, wid., & Hy. Trigge, def. 1 mess., 1 gdn., 1 orchard, 1 barn, 12 a. ar., 1 a. mw. & 3 a. pa. in Elmedon, Wenden Loosthes & Crishall. £80.

41. Mich. Jn. Metcalfe, pl. Jn. Bawde & w. *Joan*, def. 1 mess., 1 barn, 1 gdn. & 1 orchard in Barklowe & Assheton. £40.

42. Mich. Jn. Prentys, jun., pl. Jn. Prentys, sen., def. A third part of 1 mess., 1 barn, 1 gdn. & 21 a. ar. in Great Chishull. £40.

43. Mich. Rd. Cragge, pl. Geo. Bull & w. Joan, Jn. Ruste & w. *Agnes*, Nich. Sewell & w. Margt. & Alice Waren, def. 1 mess. & 1 orchard in Claveringe. £40.

44. Mich. Jas. Pyke, pl. Rd. Osborne & w. *Dorothy*, def. A. moiety of 1 mess., 1 barn, 1 gdn., 1 orchard, 5 a. ar. & 3 a. pa. in Great Showberye *alias* South Showberye. £40.

45. Trin. & Mich. Rd. Brokeman, gent., pl. *Jn.* Mawldon & w. Anne & Jn. Pack, def. 1 mess., 1 gdn., 1 orchard & 2 a. ar. in St. Botolph parish in Colchester. £80.

46. Trin. & Mich. Nich. Wall, pl. *Reg.* Hygate, esq., & w. Mary & *Jn.* Daniell, esq., def. 20 a. pa. & 10 a. wd. in Great Byrche, Layer Marner, Layerbretton, Layer Delaye & Esthorpe. £100.

47. Mich. Tho. Aylett, pl. Jn. Glascocke, def. The manor of Keers, & 16 mess., 16 gdns., 16 orchards, 140 a. ar., 20 a. mw., 40 a. pa., 10 a. wd., 30 a. furze & heath & 80s. rt. in Aytroppe Roodinge. 320 mks.

48. Trin. & Mich. Jn. Gover, pl. Jn. Jennynges, def. 2 mess. & 1 gdn. in Harwyche. £40.

49. Trin. & Mich. Alice Goldynge, wid., pl. *Reg.* Heygate, esq., & w. Mary & *Jn.* Danyell, esq., def. 50 a. ar., 20 a. pa. & 50 a. furze & heath in Great Byrche. 130 mks.

50. Mich. Francis Stacy, gent., pl. Edw. Holley & w. *Eliz.*, def. 1 mess., 2 gdns. & 2 a. pa. in Waltham Holy Cross. £140.

51. Trin. & Mich. Tho. Tirrell, esq., Geo. White, esq., Jn. Glascock, esq., & Tho. Staunton, esq., pl. *Jn.* Latham, gent., & w. Helen, def. The manor of Barnehall *alias* Baronhall, & 6 mess., 1 dovecote, 6 gdns., 200 a. ar., 40 a. mw., 200 a. pa., 40 a. wd., 20 a. furze & heath, 200 a. marsh & 20s. rt. in Downham, Ranwell, Wickford, South Hanfeild, Esthanfeild, Westhanfeild, Southbemfleit & the island of Canvay. Def. quit-claimed to pl. & the heirs of Tho. Tirrell. £280.

52. Mich. Wm. Jermye, gent., pl. *Reg.* Heygate, esq., & w. Mary & Jn. Danyell, esq., def. 1 mess., 1 gdn., 30 a. ar., 20 a. mw., 30 a. pa. & 6 a. wd. in Ponsebright *alias* Pontesbright, Chappell, Great Tey, Mont Bures & Colnewake. £100.

53. Mich. Rochus Ryche, pl. Wm. Starlynge & w. Barbara, *Isaac* Flemynge & w. Lucrecia & *Hy.* Churche, def. 1 mess., 1 barn, 1 gdn., 1 orchard & 5 a. ar. in Thaxstede. £40.

FEET OF FINES FOR ESSEX

CP26(1)/173   DIVERS COUNTIES

11.   Trin. & Mich. Nich. Bacon, kt., lord keeper of the great seal, & Jn. Osborne, gent., pl. *Francis* Egglesfield & w. Joan, def. Prop. in Kent; & 10 a. marsh & free fishery in Eastham, co. Essex. Def. quitclaimed to pl. & the heirs of Nich. £640. — Kent. Essex.

CP25(2)/130/1668   HILARY, 20 ELIZABETH   1578

1.   Hil. Tho. Byrche, Ralph Reynolde & Jn. Reynolde, pl. Abraham Clerke, def. 2 mess., 10 a. ar., 1 a. mw. & 8 a. wd. in Langham. Def. quitclaimed to pl. & the heirs of Tho. £40.

2.   Hil. Ralph Ratclife, esq., & Nich. Clarke, pl. Wm. Lawrence, gent., def. 2 mess., 1 toft, 3 gdns., 2 orchards, 60 a. ar., 10 a. mw., 40 a. pa. & 4 a. wd. in Faulkeborne *alias* Faulkeborne *alias* Falborne, Def. quitclaimed to pl. & the heirs of Nich. £160.

3.   Hil. Tho. Stocke, pl. *Wm.* Strachie & w. Jane, def. 6 a. mw. in Wydington. £80.

4.   Hil. Robt. Alexander, clk., pl. Bart. Jennyngs, & w. Joan & *Tho.* Haywarde, def. 10 a. ar., 4 a. mw., 14 a. pa. & 10 a. marsh in Great Holland. £80.

5.   Hil. Jn. Brewster, gent., pl. Robt. Brewster, gent., def. 2 mess., 2 gdns., 2 orchards, 80 a. ar., 10 a. mw., 10 a. pa. & 6 a. wd. in Gestyngthorpe & Bulmer, held for life by Thomasina Sibley, wid. Def. gtd. reversion of prop. to pl. & heirs to hold of the chief lords. £40.

6.   Hil. Jn. Glascocke, gent., & Jn. Meade, pl. *Tho.* Wyberde & w. Anne, def. 1 curtilage, 20 a. mw., 20 a. pa. & 20 a. fresh marsh in Westham. Def. quitclaimed to pl. & the heirs of Jn. Glascock. £100.

7.   Hil. Pet. Symonds & w. Anne, pl. Edw. Lee sen., def. 4 mess., 4 barns, 1 mill, 2 dovecotes, 200 a. ar., 40 a. mw., 100 a. pa., 40 a. wd. & 20s. rt. in Theydon Garnon. Def quitclaimed to pl. & the heirs of Pet. £400.

8.   Hil. Oliver Skynner, pl. *Hugh* Cole, gent., & w. Eliz., def. 2 mess., 1 cott., 1 toft, 2 gdns. & 3 a. mw. in Maldon. £40.

9.   Hil. Rd. Jeffrey, pl. *Hy.* Randall & w. Agnes, def. 4 mess., 4 gdns., 4 orchards, 40 a. ar., 10 a. mw., 40 a. pa. & 6 a. wd. in Great Bursted & Little Bursted. 160 mks.

10.   Hil. Barnard Beseley, pl. Chris. Wade, def. 2 mess. & 2 gdns. in Coggeshall *alias* Coxall. £90.

11.   Hil. Robt. Balle, pl. *Jn.* Sampson & Josias Sampson, def. The manor of Berthall, & 60. a. ar., 6 a. mw., 30 a. pa. & 8s. rt. in White Colne. £160.

12.   Hil. Lionel Egerton & Robt. Goodwyn, pl. Geo. Kyllyngworth & w. *Jane*, def. 1 mess., 3 a. ar., 1 rood mw. & 3 a. pa. in Laighton. Def. quitclaimed to pl. & the heirs of Lionel. £80.

13.   Hil. Geo. Gascoigne, pl. Tho. Parker, gent., def. 10 a. mw., 20 a. pa. & 5 a. wd. in Shenfeild. £80.

14.   Hil. Jn. Gyver & Tho. Gyver, pl. *Cesar* Tournor & w. Eliz., *Wm.* Tournor & w. Agnes, def. 9 a. mw. & 3 a. pa. in Thaxsted & Walden. Def. quitclaimed to pl. & the heirs of Jn. £80.

15.   Hil. Rd. Brokeman, gent., pl. *Jn.* Pokyns & w. Agnes, def. 1 mess., 4 a. ar. & common pa. for all livestock in Orsett. £40.

16.   Wm. Roche, pl. Jn. Yonge & w. *Anne*, def 1 mess., 1 gdn., 1 orchard, 2 a. ar., 2 a. mw. & 2 a. pa. in Little Warley. £40.

17.   Hil. Edw. Brande, pl. *Vincent* Amcotts & w. Kath., def. A moiety of 1 mess. & 1 gdn. in Stratforde Langthorne. £40.

18.   Hil. Wm. Fludd, gent., & Joan Pratt, pl. *Edw.* Stileman *alias* Stelewman *alias* Stelowman & w. Grace, def. 1 mess., 6 a. ar., 2 a. mw., 6. a. pa. & 2 a. wd. in Woodham Ferrys. Def. quitclaimed to pl. & the heirs of Wm. £80.

217

FEET OF FINES FOR ESSEX

19. Hil. Jas. Rowbotham, pl. *Wm.* Tryplowe & w. Agnes, def. 1 mess., 1 gdn. & 1 orchard in Upmynster. £40.

20. Hil. Wm. Stane, pl. Jn. Bur, gent., def. 2 mess., 1 gdn., 1 orchard, 40 a. ar., 8 a. mw., 18 a. pa. & 4 a. wd. in Norton Mandevile. 310 mks.

21. Hil. Rd. Stanes, jun., pl. *Nich.* Harvy & w. Anne, def. 1 mess., 1 barn, 1 gdn., 2 a. ar., 3 a. mw. & 2 a. pa. in Newporte & Wydington. £80.

22. Hil. Jn. Southcot, a justice of Queen's Bench, pl. Tho. Tey, esq., & w. *Eleanor*, def. An annual rt. of 10s. from 1 mess., 50 a. ar., 10 a. mw., 100 a. pa. & 10 a. wd. in Great Totham & Little Totham. £10.

23. Hil. Roger Banks, pl. Wm. Wallys & w. *Agnes*, Tho. Ellys *alias* Dune & w. *Eliz.*, def. 2 mess., 2 gdns. & 1 orchard in Great Wenden. £40.

24. Hil. Tho. Tyrrell, pl. *Francis* Crompton & w. Eliz. & *Rd.* Shaw, def. 11 a. ar. in Eastham. Warranty by Francis & Eliz. Crompton for 7 a. by Rd. Shawe for 4 a. £40.

25. Mich. & Hil. Jn. Frankeleyn, jun., pl. Anth. Frankeleyn & w. *Susanna*, def. 4 mess., 1 barn, 5 gdns., 15 a. ar., 10 a. mw., 12 a. pa. & 40 a. wd. in Pritwell, Leighe, Hadle, Bures, Thundersley, Rayle, Eastwood & Rochforde. £120.

26. Hil. Jn. Edgeat & Jn. Spencer, pl. Jn. Wreight, def. 2 mess., 2 gdns., 2 orchards, 50 a. ar., 2 a. mw., 20 a. pa., 4 a. wd. & 20 a. furze & heath in Chaldewell & Westilbery. Def. quitclaimed to pl. & the heirs of Jn. Edgeat. £80.

27. Hil. Jn. Camber, pl. *Robt.* Hurte & w. Jane, *Wm.* Hurte & w. Anne, def. 3 mess., 1 barn, 30 a. ar., 5 a. mw., 10 a. pa., 1 a. wd., 30 a. fresh marsh & 5 a. salt marsh in Eastilbery. 460 mks.

28. Hil. Adrian Smarte & Jn. Sparhauke, pl. Jn. Webbe, def. 30 a. ar., 10 a. pa. & 2 a. wd. in Bockinge, held for life by Jane Webbe, wid. Def. gtd. reversion of prop. to pl. & the heirs of Adrian Smarte to hold of the chief lords. £80.

29. Hil. Tho. Lorde, pl. *Wm.* Key & w. Barbara, *Robt.* Bullocke & w. Eliz., def. 1 mess. & 4½ a. ar. in Thaxstede. Warranty by Robt. & Eliz. Bullocke for 1 a ar.; by Wm. & Barbara Key for remaining prop. £40.

30. Mich. & Hil. Wm. Wells, pl. Bart. Freman, def. 5 a. pa. in Maldon. Pl. gtd. prop. to def. for 21 years from Mich. 1578 at rt. of 1d. per annum.

31. Hil. Clement Smyth, esq., pl. Hy. Smyth, gent., def. 60 a. ar., 3 a mw. & 24 a. wd. in Cressyng & Ryvenhall. Pl. gtd. prop. to def. for 50 years from Mich. 1577 at rt. of 26s. 8d. per annum, with right to entry & distraint to pl. & his heirs male in case of default.

32. Hil. Hy. Dyngley & Robt. Holgate, pl. Jn. Danyell, esq., (and w.) *Margt.* & Wm. (- - - - -), def. A fourth part of the (manors of) (- - -)eshall *alias* Northbemflete, Scotts & Plumberoughe *alias* Plumberghe, & a fourth part of 7 mess., 7 cotts., 7 - - - - - - - mw., 500 a. pa., 200 a. wd., 50 a. salt marsh, 80 a. fresh marsh & £10 rt. in Nor(thbemflete), - - - -, Thundersley, Southbemflete, Southechurche, Woodham Ferrers, Rochforde, Eastwoode & Runwell & the advowson of a fourth part of the church of Northbemf(lete). (Def. quitclaimed to) pl. & the heirs of Hy. Dyngley. Pl. gtd. prop. to Wm. (- - - -) for 15 years from Mich. 1577 at rt. of £50 per annum, with reversion to Jn. & Margt. Danyell & their legitimate heirs to hold of the chief lords, with remainder to the legitimate heirs of John's body, failing whom to the right heirs of Margt. (*severely mutilated*).

CP25(2)/130/1669   EASTER, 20 ELIZABETH   1578

1. Eas. Jn. Watson, gent., pl. Arthur Hall & w. *Joan*, def. A moiety of 3 mess., 1 barn, 2 gdns., 2 orchards, 10 a. ar., 6 a. mw., 10 a. pa. & 2 a. wd. in Colchester. £20.

2. Eas. Nich. Taber, pl. Jn. Pathe & w. *Joan*, def. 1 barn & 1 a. ar. in Runwell. £40.

3. Eas. Wm. Goldyng, esq., pl. *Tho.* Downyng, gent., & w. Joan, def. 1 toft, 1 gdn., 8 a. ar. & 1 pond (*stagnum*) in Belchamp St. Paul. £40.

4. Eas. Robt. Poole, pl. Jn. Trycker, & w. Joan & *Jn.* Spylman, def. 5 a. ar. & 5 a. pa. in Thaxsted. £40.

218

5. Eas. And. Sumner, gent., & Chris. Sumner, pl. Wm. Sumner & w. *Thomasina*, Wm. Colt & w. Joan, def. 1 mess., 1 gdn., 12 a. ar., 8 a. mw., 4 a. pa. & 2 a. marsh in Dagenham. Def. quitclaimed to pl. & the heirs of And. £80.

6. Eas. Geo. Fytche, pl. Joseph Mann, def. 1 mess. & 1 gdn. in Branktre *alias* Brayntre. £40.

7. Eas. Geo Martyn, pl. *Jn*. Watson, gent., & w. Frances, def. 1 mess., 3 tofts, 1 barn, 2 gdns., 3 orchards, 100 a. ar., 30 a. mw., 70 a. pa., 12 a. wd., 30 a. furze & heath, 10 a. moor, 12 a. marsh & 10 a. alder in Great Bromley & Little Bromley, Warranty by def. against themselves, & his heirs of Jn. Watson & the heirs of Wm. Watson, decd., John's father. 200 mks.

8. Eas. Vincent Sheffelde & Rd. Wilkinson, pl. Matthew Amcotes, def. A moiety of 7 mess., 10 cotts., 10 gdns., 3 orchards, 4 a. mw. & 4 a. pa. in Stratford Langthorne, Westham & Stebenheth. Def. quitclaimed to pl. & the heirs of Vincent. 130 mks.

9. Eas. Jn. Gaynsford, pl. *Rd*. Younge & w. Joan, def. 4 a. mw., 10 a. pa. & 10 a. wd. in Langdon Hills & Layndon. £40.

10. Eas. Robt. Leyston, pl. *Robt*. Fyppe & w. Alice, def. 1 barn, 20 a. ar. & 3 a. wd. in Eastilberye. 70 mks.

11. Eas. Jn. Pragell, sen., pl. *Jn*. Pragell, jun., & w. Eliz., def. 4 a. fresh marsh in Westham. £40.

12. Eas. Josias Francke, pl. *Tho*. Deere & w. Joan, def. 1 mess. & 1 gdn. in Bockynge. £40.

13. Eas. Wm. Tooke, jun., gent., pl. Jn. Tycheborne, gent., def. 3 mess., 3 gdns., 3 orchards, 2 a. ar. & 3 a. pa. in Roydon. £40.

14. Eas. Edm. Harryngton, pl. Jn. Godsalff & w. Alice, *Wm*. Harvye & w. Eliz., def. 1 mess., 1 gdn., 30 a. ar., 3 a. mw., 10 a. pa. & 10 a. alder in Great Maplested & Hennyngham Sible. £100.

15. Eas. Jn. Southcott, a justice of Queen's Bench, pl. *Alexander* Warner & w. Joan, def. 1 mess., 1 barn, 1 toft, 1 orchard, 30 a. ar., 6 a. mw., 30 a. pa. & 4 a. moor in Wytham. 130 mks.

16. Eas. Jn. Beale, sen., pl. Tho. Lewis & w. Alice, def. 1 mess., 2 gdns., 20 a. ar., 5 a. mw., 20 a. pa. & 2 a. wd. in Wrabnesse. 130 mks.

17. Eas. Tho. Durrant, pl. *Wm*. Platt & w. Margt., def. 3 a. ar. in Chelmsford. £40.

18. Eas. Jn. Harrys, pl. Rd. Goldynge & w. *Joan*, def. 6 a. ar., 1 a. mw. & 5 a. pa. in Great Bentley. £40.

19. Eas. Rd. Brokeman, gent., pl. Jn. Tyrell, esq., def. 2 mess., 1 cott., 2 barns, 3 gdns., 2 orchards, 100 a. ar., 40 a. mw., 60 a. pa., 200 a. fresh marsh & 10 a. salt marsh in Chawdwell, Little Thorrock & Orsett. £480.

20. Hil. & Eas. Jn. Brooke of Bradwell-by-Sea, pl. *Hugh* Cole, gent., & w. Eliz., def. 12 a. ar. & 1 a. wd. in Bradwell-by-Sea. £40.

21. Eas. Hy. Caldam, pl. *Francis* Stacye, gent., & w. Maud, def. 1 mess., 1 barn, 2 gdns. & 1 orchard in Waltham Holy Cross. £40.

22. Eas. Tho. Coke pl. Wm. Totnam & w. *Bassella*, *Wm*. Baker & w. Margt., def. 49 a. ar. in Great Chishull & Little Chishull. Warranty by Wm. & Basella Totnam for 7 a.; by Wm. & Margt. Baker for remaining 42 a. £80.

23. Eas. Hy. Capell, Tho. Leventhorp, Rd. Cutt, Hy. Josselyn & Tho. Burgoyne, esquires, pl. Wistanus Browne, esq., def. The manor of Churche Hall, & 3 mess., 1 barn, 2 tofts, 2 gdns., 2 orchards, 200 a. ar., 40 a. mw., 200 a. pa., 30 a. wd., 40 a. fresh marsh, 30 a. salt marsh & 100s. rt. in Pakelsham & Great Stambridge, & a moiety of 3 mess., 2 barns, 2 tofts, 2 gdns., 2 orchards, 42 a. ar., 8 a. mw., 37 a. pa., 40 a. fresh marsh, 20 a. salt marsh & 5s. rt. in Langenhoo. Def. quitclaimed to pl. & the heirs of Hy. Capell. 830 mks.

24. Eas. Tho. Meade, a justice of Common Pleas, pl. *Tho*. Crawley, esq., & w. Margt., def. The manor of Wendenlowtes *alias* Wendenloosthes, & 3 mess., 1 dovecote, 1 windmill, 3 barns, 3 tofts, 3 gdns., 300 a. ar., 6 a. mw., 140 a. pa., 60 a. wd. & 20s. rt. in Wendlowtes *alias* Wendenloosthes, Elmedon & Christisthall *alias* Crissall. £400.

25. Eas. Jn. Munt, pl. Hy. Evered, def. 1 mess., 1 orchard & 9 a. ar. in Ardeleigh, held by Edw. Lufkyn & w. Joan for the life of Joan. Def. gtd. reversion of prop. to pl. & his heirs to hold of the chief lords. £40.

26. Eas. Wm. Stubbynge, pl. *Arthur* Goldynge, *Geo.* Goldynge, gentlemen, *Chris.* Corey & w. Margt., def. 3 a. ar., 2 a. mw. & 9 a. pa. in Wykes. 130 mks.

27. Eas. And. Pascall, gent., pl. *Jn.* Pascall, esq., & w. Mary, def. The manor of Cuton Hawll *alias* Kewton Hall, & 10 mess., 10 cotts., 6 barns, 10 tofts, 1 dovecote, 10 gdns., 10 orchards, 200 a. ar., 100 a. mw., 200 a. pa., 60 a. wd., 20 a. furze & heath & 30s. rt. in Springfild. £240.

28. Eas. Jn. Maxey, gent., & Tho. Reynolds, pl. Anth. Maxey, esq., & w. *Dorothy*, def. 30 a. ar., 10 a. mw., 55 a. pa. & 3 a. wd. in Little Rayne *alias* Little Reighnes. Def. quitclaimed a pl. & the heirs of Jn. Pl. gtd. prop. to def. & the heirs male of Dorothy's body begotten by Anth. Maxey, to hold of the chief lords, with remainder to the right heirs of Anth.

29. Eas. Jn. Clerke, pl. Robt. Raymewe, & w. *Margt.* & Jn. Newton, def. 1 mess., 1 barn, 1 gdn., 1 orchard, 50 a. ar., 6 a. mw., 40 a. pa., 6 a. wd. & 6 a. marsh in Colne Wake, Colne Ingayne & Mounts, Pl. gtd. to Robt. & Margt. Raymewe for 1 month, with remainder to Jn. Newton to hold of the chief lords.

30. Eas. Wm. Luckyn & Jn. Luckyn, pl. Francis Salperswicke *alias* Gillam, gent., & w. Joan & *Jn.* Salperswicke, def. 1 mess., 1 barn, 1 gdn., 1 orchard, 60 a. ar., 6 a. mw., 20 a. pa. & 2 a. wd. in Little Easton, Great Dunmowe & Easton-on-the-Hill. Def. quitclaimed to pl. & the heirs of Jn. Warranty by def. against themselves, the heirs of Jn. Salperswicke & the heirs of Wm. Salperswicke, the father of Francis. £80.

31. Eas. Geoff. Ricard, pl. *Walter* Harrys, Eliz. Cuckoo, wid., & *Wm.* Cuckoo, def. 1 barn, 1 gdn., ½ a. ar. & 2 a. pa. in Great Bursted. Warranty by Walter Harrys for whole prop.; by Eliz. Cuckoo & Wm. Cuckoo for 2 a. pa. Pl. gtd. prop. to Walter Harrys & his heirs to hold of the chief lords.

32. Eas. Tho. Wallynger & Pet. Rosewell, pl. *Tho.* Tyrell, esq., & w. Margt., def. 1 barn, 1 toft, 70 a. ar., 50 a. mw. & 30 a. pa. in Spryngefylde & a moiety of the advowson of the church of Spryngefylde called Bosvile portion *alias* Boswells portion. Def. quitclaimed to pl. & the heirs of Tho. Pl. gtd. prop. to def. & the heirs of Tho. Tyrell to hold of the chief lords.

33. Eas. Hugh Lancaster, gent., & Tho. Lancaster, gent., pl. *Wm.* Crackroode, gent., pl. *Wm.* Crackroode, gent., & w. Eliz., *Tho.* Crackroode, gent., & w. Anne, *Matthew* Crackroode, gent., & w. Mary, def. 2 mess., 2 gdns., 2 orchards, 60 a. ar., 4 a. mw., 13 a. pa. & 3 a. wd. in Toppesfelde, Great Yeldham & Hennyngham Sible. Def. quitclaimed to pl. & the heirs of Hugh. £200.

CP25(2)/260   DIVERS COUNTIES

11. Eas. Tho. Rede, pl. Innocent Rede, esq., Jn. Rede, gent., & Nich. Rede, gent., def. Prop. in co. Southampton; & 2 (mess.?), 2 barns, 1 dovecote, 2 gdns., 50 a. ar., 10 a. pa. & 1 a. - - - - - in Writtell, Rockeswell, Willinghale Spayne & Willinghale Doo, co. Essex. Each def. gave warranty against himself with his heirs in turn. 190 mks. — Southampton. Essex.

CP25(2)/130/1670   TRINITY, 20 ELIZABETH   1578

1. Trin. Robt. Finche, pl. *Jn.* Stringer & w. Agnes, def. 1 mess., 1 gdn. & 1 orchard in Waltham Holy Cross. £40.

2. Trin. Robt. Benne, pl. Alice Oglander, wid., def. 100 a. fresh marsh & 100 a. salt marsh in Fobbynge. 200 mks.

3. Morrow of Trin. Wm. Earnsbye, pl. Jn. Starlynge, def. 2 mess., 1 toft & 1 gdn. in Colchester. £80.

4. Morrow of Trin. Robt. Cooke & w. Margt., pl. Wm. Webbe & w. *Joan*, def. 2 mess. & 2 gdns. in Rayleigh. Def. quitclaimed to pl. & the heirs of Robt. £40.

5. Morrow of Trin. Jn. Cely, gent., pl. *Tho.* Rattell & w. Judith, def. 1 mess., 1 gdn. & 3 a. ar. in Fobbyng. £40.

6. Morrow of Trin. Jasper Nichols, pl. *Edw.* Maplesden & w. Agnes, def. 1 mess., 3 shops & 2 gdns. in Waltham Holy Cross. £80.

7. Morrow of Trin. And. Byles, pl. *Edw.* Rottour & w. Agnes, Rd. Reddryche & w. Kath., def. 1 mess., 1 gdn., 1 orchard, 12 a. ar., 5 a. mw. & 20 a. pa. in Ramysden Belhous. 160 mks.

8. Trin. Tho. Newman, esq., pl. Tho. Whetenhall, esq., def. The manor of Fange, & 2 mess., 2 cotts., 2 tofts, 2 gdns., 2 orchards, 20 a. ar., 20 a. mw., 40 a. pa. & 10s. rt. in Fange. £160.

9. Morrow of Trin. Rd. Yonge, pl. Jn. Gaynsford, esq., def. 1 cott., 2 tofts, 60 a. ar., 10 a. mw., 50 a. pa. & 80 a. wd. in Langdon, Layndon & Westley. £140.

10. Morrow of Trin. Robt. Grene, pl. *Geoff.* Nightyngale, gent., & w. Kath., def. 32 a. ar., 3 a. mw., 2 a. pa. & 3 a. wd. in Wymbyshe & Thunderley. £80.

11. Morrow of Trin. Tho. Meade, gent., pl. *Jn.* Cosyn & w. Kath., def. 1 mess., 1 barn, 1 gdn., 1 orchard, 30 a. ar. & 1 a. pa. in Heydon, Great Chissell & Christishall *alias* Crissall. £80.

12. Morrow of Trin. Jn. Harrys, pl. Jn. Wolmar & w. *Kath.*, def. A third part of 1 mess. & 2 orchards in Spryngfeld. £40.

13. Morrow of Trin. Jn. Norkot, pl. *Rd.* Birdsall, & w. Agnes & Wm. Birdsall, def. 1 mess. in Walden. £40.

14. Morrow of Trin. Lau. Bingham, gent., pl. *Paul* Pope & w. Kath., def. 2 mess., 2 gdns., 2 orchards, 20 a. ar., 6 a. mw., 30 a. pa. & 2 a. wd. in Danbery. £100.

15. Morrow of Trin. Edw. Camber, pl. Jn. Camber, def. 2 mess., 2 gdns. & 1 orchard in Eastylberye. Pl. gtd. prop. to def. & his heirs to hold of the chief lords.

16. Morrow of Trin. Tho. Gynes, gent., pl. Edm. Thorpp & w. *Joan*, def. 2 mess., 2 cotts., 3 gdns., 2 orchards, 10 a. ar. & 8 a. pa. in Bockinge & Branktree. £40.

17. Morrow of Trin. Tho. Wylson, one of the Queen's principal secretaries, & w. Jane, pl. *Francis* Holte & w. Alice, def. 4 mess., 2 tofts, 1 dovecote, 4 gdns., 4 orchards, 10 a. ar., 2 a. mw. & 10 a. pa. in Writtle *alias* Writtell. Def. quitclaimed to pl. & the heirs of Tho. £40.

18. Morrow of Trin. Hy. Peart, pl. *Jn.* Peers & w. Alice, def. The manor of Arnoldes *alias* Arnoldes Hall, & 4 mess., 4 cotts., 4 tofts, 2 mills, 2 dovecotes, 4 gdns., 4 orchards, 200 a. ar., 120 a. mw., 400 a. pa., 120 a. wd., 100 a. furze & heath, 100 a. moor, 100 a. marsh, 40s. rt., free warren & separate fishing rights (*separalis piscaria*) in Yngmountney *alias* Gyngmountney *alias* Mountnesynge *alias* Monesynge & Arnoldes *alias* Arnoldes Hall. £600.

19. Morrow of Trin. Chris. Robynson, gent., pl. Robt. Kynwelmershe, gent., & w. *Anne*, def. 1 mess., 1 gdn. & 2 a. ar. in Waltham Holy Cross. £80.

20. Morrow of Trin. Edm. Gryffyn, gent., pl. *Jn.* Bentley & w. Kath., def. 1 mess., 1 barn, 1 gdn. & 2 a. ar. in Wytham. £40.

21. Morrow of Trin. Jn. Casse & Tho. Waterman, pl. *Jn.* Shyngton *alias* Lee & w. Joan, def. 1 mess., 1 cott., 1 gdn., 1 orchard, 8 a. ar., 1 a. mw. & 14 a. pa. in Stanford Ryvers. Def. quitclaimed to pl. & the heirs of Jn. £80.

22. Morrow of Trin. Jn. Cotton, esq., pl. *Brian* Darcy, esq., & w. Bridget, def. 3 mess., 2 tofts, 1 dovecote, 2 gdns., 60 a. ar., 40 a. mw., 160 a. pa., 5 a. wd., 10 a. furze & heath & 20s. rt. in Steple, Standesgate, Saynt Lawrance & Assheldon. £280.

23. Morrow of Trin. Wm. Stane, pl. *Jn.* Bur & Rd. Pole, def. 1 mess., 1 gdn., 1 orchard, 10 a. ar., 10 a. mw. & 10 a. pa. in Norton Mandevile. £100.

24. Morrow of Trin. Anth. Rose, pl. Jn. Smyth, def. 1 mess. & 1 gdn. in Rayleigh. Pl. gtd. to def. & his heirs to hold of the chief lords.

25. Trin. Hy. earl of Pembroke, pl. *Jn*. Traves, merchant tailor of London, & w. Anne, def. The manor of Aldresbroke, & 20 mess., 20 cotts., 20 gdns., 100 a. ar., 200 a. mw., 300 a. pa., 20 a. wd., 20 a. furze & heath & 40s. rt. in Great Ilforde, Little Ilforde & Wansted. Warranty by def. against themselves, the heirs of Jn. Traves, & the heirs of Jn. Traves decd., the father of the def. £200.

26. Trin. Jn. Penruddoke, esq., pl. Wm. Chaderton, esq., & w. *Bridget*, def. The manor of Chyvers Hall *alias* Pasfylde Chyvers, & 40 mess., 6 cotts., 10 tofts, 2 dovecotes, 40 orchards, 400 a. ar., 120 a. mw., 300 a. pa., 60 a. wd., 100 a. furze & heath & 60s. rt. in High Ongar, Ongar, Blackemore & Writtle. £400.

27. Morrow of Trin. Tho. Harryson & Jn. Wright, gentlemen, pl. Hy. Cutte, esq., def. A moiety of the manors of Mountnes & Dagworthes *alias* Elmedon Berry, & a moiety of 12 mess., 6 barns, 10 gdns., 10 orchards, 600 a. ar., 12 a. mw., 80 a. pa., 60 a. wd. & the liberty of faldage for 400 sheep in Elmedon, Crissall, Wenden Lostes & Stretall. Def. quitclaimed to pl. & the heirs of Tho. Pl. gtd. prop. to def. & his heirs to hold of the chief lords.

28. Trin. Jn. Chaplyn & Robt. Sharpe, pl. *Tho*. Gent, esq., & w. Eliz., & Walter Oswald, def. 3 mess., 3 gdns., 30 a. ar., 10 a. mw., 30 a. pa. & 21. a. wd. in Bockinge, Bumpsted Steeple & Byrdbroke. Def. quitclaimed to pl. & the heirs of Jn. Pl. gtd. 2 mess., 2 gdns., 10 a. ar., 5 a. mw., 10 a. pa. & 20 a. wd. in Bockinge to Tho. Gent & Walter Oswald & the heirs of Tho. to hold of the chief lords; pl. gtd. the remaining 1 mess., 1 gdn., 20 a. ar., 5 a. mw., 20 a. pa. & 1 a. wd. in Bumpsted Steeple & Byrdbroke to Tho. & Eliz. Gent & the legitimate heirs of their bodies to hold of the chief lords, with remainder to the right heirs of Eliz. Gent.

29. Trin. Anth. Russhe, esq., pl. Charles Cutler, esq., & w. *Suzanna*, def. A moiety of the manor of Ramesden Barrington, & 6 mess., 2 dovecotes, 6 gdns., 600 a. ar., 200 a. mw., 600 a. pa., 200 a. wd., 600 a. furze & heath, 100 a. marsh, 100 a. alder & £10 rt. in Ramesden Barrington & a fourth part of the manors of Cocksalls *alias* Northbemflete, Scottes & Plumborowe *alias* Plumbergh, & 7 mess., 3 dovecotes, 7 tofts, 8 gdns., 600 a. ar., 200 a. mw., 600 a. pa., 150 a. wd., 60 a. furze & heath, 200 a. marsh, 30 a. alder & £10 rt. in Northbemflete, Southbemflete, Wickford *alias* Wickforthe, Thundersley, Newndon, Canneudon *alias* Canouden, Hockley, Assheldon *alias* Assheldain, Rawreth, Woodehamferries, Rayleigh *alias* Raylie, Bassildon, Langdon, Pytsey, Rochford, Estwood, Runwell, Standford & Hawkewell & a fourth part of the advowson of the church of Northbemflete. 560 mks.

CP25(2)/260   DIVERS COUNTIES

5. Morrow of Trin. Alice Dyster, wid., pl. *Tho*. Sackvyle, kt., lord Buckhurst, & w. Cecily, def. The manors of Bures on the Hill *alias* Mount Bures *alias* Mount & Barholt Sackvyle, & 100 mess., 100 tofts, 2 mills, 2 dovecotes, 100 gdns., 100 orchards, 1,000 a. ar., 100 a. mw., 2,000 a. pa., 600 a. wd., 2,000 a. furze & heath & £15 rt. & view of frankpledge in Bures on the Hill (*alias* as above), Pontesbrighte *alias* Chappell, Bures Seynt Marie, Barholt *alias* Westbarholt, Fordeham, Lexton *alias* Lexden, Wormyngforde *alias* Wethermountforde, Earl's Colne, Colne Wake, White Colne, Aldham, Great Horkesley & Little Horkesley, co. Essex; 10 mess., 10 gdns., 100 a. ar., 40 a. mw., 100 a. pa., 40 a. wd. & 20s. rt. in Bures on the Hill (*alias* as above), Bures Saynt Marie & Wormyngforde, co. Suff. £640. — Essex, Suff.

9. Trin. Rd. Betenson & w. Eliz., pl. *Robt*. Tayllor, esq., & w. Rose, def. Prop. in Mdx.; & 20 a. ar., 20 a. mw. & 10 a. pa. in Westham, co. Essex. Def. quitclaimed to pl. & the heirs of Rd. £260. — Mdx., Essex.

CP25(2)/130/1671   MICHAELMAS, 20–21 ELIZABETH   1578

1. Mich. Tho. Wallynger, pl. Tho. Tyrrell, esq., def. 7 a. pa. in Chelmesford. £40.

2. Mich. Jn. Roo, pl. *Tho*. Wyseman, gent., & w. Dorothy, def. 2 mess., 2 tofts, 2 barns, 2 gdns., 2 orchards, 50 a. ar., 4 a. mw., 10 a. pa. & 2 a. wd. in Nevingdon *alias* Nevenden & Northbemflete. 130 mks.

3. Mich. Robt. Benne, pl. Margt. Lyvers, wid., def. 100 a. fresh marsh & 100 a. salt marsh in Fobbinge. 200 mks.

4. Mich. Augustus Ketcher, pl. Hy. Archer, esq., Robt. Kynge, gent., & w. *Anne*, def. 1 mess., 4 a. ar. & 4 a. pa. in Wansted. £40.

5. Mich. Jn. Royden, pl. Rd. Roades, def. 2 mess., 1 cott., 2 gdns., 1 orchard & 2 a. mw. in Kelvedon. £40.

6. Mich. Josias Francke, pl. Jn. Francke, def. 1 mess., 1 gdn., 1 orchard, 100 a. ar., 10 a. mw., 40 a. pa. & 6 a. wd. in Terlynge, Fayrsted, Fawkeborne, Wytham & Hatfyld. £400.

7. Mich. Tho. Clerck, pl. *Wm.* Hutt & w. Alice. def. 1 mess., 2 cotts., 2 gdns. & 1 orchard in Bockynge. £40.

8. Mich. Geo. Wylmer, pl. *Charles* Cutler, esq., w. Susanna, def. A moiety of the manor of Ramesden Barrington, & 6 mess., 2 dovecotes, 6 gdns., 600 a. ar., 200 a. mw., 600 a. pa., 200 a. wd., 600 a. furze & heath, 100 a. marsh, 100 a. alder & £10 rt. in Ramesden Barrington. £60.

9. Mich. Nich. Wilbore, pl. *Robt.* Polly & w. Grace, *Jn.* Buckford & w. Alice, def. 2 mess., 2 gdns., 1 orchard, 15 a. ar. & 4 a. mw. in Branktre & Stysted. £40.

10. Eas. & Mich. Tho. Browne, pl. Jn. Brewster & Jn. Brewster & Rd. Brewster, def. 2 mess., 2 gdns., 2 orchards, 80 a. ar., 10 a. mw., 10 a. pa. & 6 a. wd. in Gestingthorpe & Bulmer, held for life by Thomasina Sibley, wid. Def. gtd. reversion to pl. to hold of the chief lords. Warranty by each of def. against himself & his heirs. £40.

(*Only fines levied on the Morrow of Martin appear in this file. Since Michaelmas is normally the most prolific term for fines, a large number have probably been lost, but may be recoverable from the notes.*)

CP26(1)/177 *Notes checked: there is nothing to add.*

CP25(2)/260   DIVERS COUNTIES

1. Mich. Fulk Grevyle, kt., & Tho. Bromley, esq., pl. *Francis* Willughby, kt., & w. Eliz., def. The manor of Steplehall, & 20 a. mw., 1,000 a. pa. & 5s. rt. in Steplehall, co. Essex; & prop. in Kent, Notts., Lincs., Warws., Leics., Dorset, & Coventry. Def. quit-claimed to pl. & the heirs of Fulk. £10,000 — Kent, Essex, Notts., town of Nottingham, Lincs., Warws., Leics., Dorset, city of Coventry.

CP25(2)/130/1672   HILARY, 21 ELIZABETH   1579

1. Mich. & Hil. Robt. Plampyn, pl. Tho. Letten & w. *Joan*, def. 1 mess. & 1 gdn. in Bulmer. £40.

2. Hil. Chris. Hardye, pl. Esq. Shingey *alias* Shingle & w. *Dorothy*, def. 1 mess. & 1 gdn. in Foxherde *alias* Foxerthe. £40.

3. Hil. Jn. Grene & Geo. Woodye, pl. Rd. Grene, def. 1 gdn., 4 a. ar., 2½ a. mw., 4 a. pa. & 1½ a. marsh in Earl's Colne & Colne Engayne. Def. quitclaimed to pl. & the heirs of Jn. £40.

4. Hil. David Kynge, pl. Tho. Blande & w. *Joan*, def. 1 mess., 1 gdn., 1 orchard, 2 a. ar. & 2 a. pa. in White Notley. Warranty by def. against themselves, the heirs of Joan & the heirs of Robt. Hall decd. £40.

5. Hil. Hy. Snelhauke, gent., pl. Jn. Humfrey & w. *Frances*, def. 1 mess., 2 gdns., 30 a. ar., 2 a. mw., 5 a. pa. & 10 a. wd. in White Notley, Blacke Notley & Brancktree. £80.

6. Hil. Wm. Fordham, pl. Nich. Fordham, def. 1 mess., 1 barn, 1 gdn. & 1 orchard in Great Chissell. £40.

7. Hil. Robt. Blake, pl. *Abel* Clarke & w. Mary, def. 1 mess., 1 gdn., 1 curtilage, 26 a. ar., 10 a. mw., 10 a. pa. & 10 a. wd. in Esthannyngfeld. £100.

8. Hil. Hy. Barnarde, pl. Tho. Allett & w. *Alice*, def. 1 mess., 1 barn, 1 gdn. & 1 orchard in Chepingonger. £40.

9. Mich. & Hil. Edw. Elyott, gent., pl. Wm. Chaderton, esq., & w. *Bridget*, def. 1 mess., 1 gdn., 15 a. ar., 3 a. mw., 6 a. pa. & 5s. rt. in Norton Maundevyle, the rectory of Norton Maundevyle, all tithes of sheaves, grain, hay & lambs and all tithes in Norton Maundevyle & the advowson of the church of Norton Maundevyle. £80.

10. Hil. Edw. Hubberd, gent., pl. Edw. earl of Oxford, def. 3 mess., 3 gdns., 40 a. ar., 20 a. mw., 300 a. pa. & 40 a. wd. in Stansted Mountfitchett *alias* Stansted Mownfizett. £480.

11. Hil. Margt. Frandesham, wid., pl. Wm. Glassecocke, def. 5 mess., 1 toft, 5 gdns., 6 a. ar. & 6 a. pa. in Great Dunmowe. £140.

12. Hil. Jn. Collyn & Nich. Collyn, pl. Abacuck Harman, gent., & w. *Mary*, def. 34 a. mw. & 34 a. marsh in Eastham. Def. quitclaimed to pl. & the heirs of Jn. £200.

13. Mich. & Hil. Rd. Mathew, pl. *Wm*. Day & w. Agnes, def. 1 mess., 1 barn, 1 gdn., 1 orchard, 20 a. ar., 4 a. mw. & 2 a. pa. in Arkesden. £100.

14. Hil. Esq. Bonham, pl. *Jn*. Hunt & w. Mary, def. 1 mess., 1 gdn., 20 a. ar. & 4 a. mw. in Rayleigh. £140.

15. Hil. Edw. Sharnebroke, pl. Edw. Hynde & w. *Kath*., def. A moiety of 1 mess., 1 barn, 1 orchard & 18 a. ar. in Roydon. £40.

16. Hil. Tho. Bearde, pl. Robt. Prowe & w. *Anne*, def. 2 mess., 2 gdns., 2 orchards, 20 a. ar., 5 a. mw. & 10 a. pa. in Writtle. £80.

17. Mich. & Hil. Tho. Cooke, pl. Nich. Fordham, def. 40 a. ar., 3 a. mw., 20 a. pa. & 6 a. wd. in Great Chisshell & Little Chisshell. £80.

18. Mich. & Hil. Robt. Hamond, pl. *Francis* Archer & w. Anne, def. 1 mess., 1 gdn. & 1 rood ar. in Bockynge. £40.

19. Hil. Rd. Grene, pl. Philip Godson & w. *Anne* def. A fourth part of 1 mess. & 6 a. pa. in Navestock. £40.

20. Hil. Jn. Strayte & w. Joan, pl. *Tho*. Wyseman, esq., & w. Jane, def. The manor of Sompners, & 1 mess., 1 gdn., 1 orchard, 40 a. ar., 2 a. mw., 10 a. pa., 2 a. wd. & 7s. rt. in Wethersfeld. Def. quitclaimed to pl. & the heirs of Jn. £80.

21. Hil. Margt. Ayloff, wid., pl. *Hy*. Tyrrell, kt., & Tho. Tyrrell, esq., def., 1 mess., 1 gdn., 1 orchard, 100 a. ar., 10 a. mw., 100 a. pa., 10 a. wd. & rt. of 12 measures (*modii*) salt in Rettinden. £220.

22. Hil. Jn. Solme, pl. *Jn*. Strayte & w. Joan, def. 1 mess., 3 tofts, 2 gdns. & 43 a. ar. in Hatfylde Peverell. £40.

23. Hil. Wm. Waylett, pl. *Jn*. Ayer & w. Joan, def. 1 mess., 1 toft, 1 gdn., 1 orchard, 3½ a. ar. & 8d. rt. in Stansted Mountfitchet. £40.

24. Hil. Jn. Griggs & w. Alice, pl. *Wm*. Penyngton & w. Alice, def. 1 mess., 1 gdn. & 1 orchard in Manitree. Def. quitclaimed to pl. & the heirs of Jn. £40.

25. Hil. Hugh Beiston, gent., & Geoff. Crome, pl. Edw. earl of Oxford, def. 40 a. ar., 40 a. mw., 40 a. pa. & 120 a. salt marsh in Bower Gyfford. Def. quitclaimed to pl. & the heirs of Hugh. £180.

26. Hil. Wm. Garrett, pl. *Jn*. Peryman & w. Bridget, & Steph. Clarke, def. 4 a. ar., 1 a. 1 rood mw. & 2 a. pa. in Gingmountney *alias* Mountneysing. Warranty by Jn. & Bridget Peryman only. Pl. gtd. prop. to Steph. Clarke & his heirs to hold of the chief lords.

27. Mich. & Hil. Jn. Collyn, pl. *Gilbert* Flacke & w. Joan, def. 1 mess., 1 gdn., 1 orchard, 10 a. ar., 4 a. mw. & 4 a. pa. in Wymbysshe. £40.

28. Hil. Jn. Wright, pl. Robt. Wright, *Tho*. Wright & w. Roberga, def. 1 mess., 2 tofts, 10 a. ar., 6 a. mw., 20 a. pa., 2 a. wd. & 20 a. furze & heath in Brokestreat & Sowtheweld. £100.

29. Hil. Jas. Hewyshe, pl. *Philip* Simond & w. Mary & *Geo*. Lewes, def. 14 a. pa. & 6 a. wd. in Ardeley, Lawforde, Great Bromeley & Little Bromeley, 100 mks.

30. Hil. Geo. Harvye, esq., pl. *Tho*. Sackvyle, kt., lord Buckhurst, & w. Cecily, def. 20 mess., 20 tofts, 20 gdns., 40 a. ar., 80 a. mw., 80 a. pa., 10 a. wd. & 80 a. marsh in Barkyng. £400.

31. Hil. Tho. Phicksall *alias* Rogers, pl. *Aphabellus* Partridge & w. Denise, def. 5 a. ar., 3 a. mw., 10 a. pa. & 3 a. wd. in Great Warley. £80.

32 Mich. & Hil. Jn. Benolde, pl. *Jn.* Hollier, gent., & w. Eliz., def. 1 mess., 1 gdn., 4 a. ar., 1 a. mw. & 2 a. pa. in Foxherth. £40.

33. Hil. Robt. earl of Leicester, pl. *Robt.* Riche, kt., lord Riche, & w. Eliz., def. The manor of Wansted, & 40 mess., 2 water-mills, 4 dovecotes, 40 gdns., 500 a. ar., 200 a. mw., 500 a. pa. 300 a. wd., 1,000 a. furze & heath & 100s. rt. in Wansted, Wodford, Waltham Stoe, Layton & Ilford & the advowson of the church of Wansted. £400.

34. Mich. & Hil. Josias Francke & w. Joan, pl. *Jn.* Dyckley & w. Margt., def. The manor of Dyckley, & 4 mess., 4 gdns., 300 a. ar., 20 a. mw., 100 a. pa., 60 a. w. & 10s. rt. in Mystleigh & Little Bromeley. Def. quitclaimed to pl. & the heirs of Josias. £240.

35. Mich. & Hil. Jn. Noke, pl. *Jn.* Bedwell & w. Agnes, def. 1 a. ar. & 6 a. pa. in Great Halingbury. £40.

36. Mich. & Hil. Hy. Archer, esq., pl. Wm. Johnson, def. 1 mess., 1 gdn. & 1 orchard in Theydon Garnon. £40.

37. Hil. Tho. Colshill, esq., pl. Jn. Jollye, sen., & w. *Joan*, def. 1 mess., 1 gdn., 40 a. ar., 20 a. mw., 60 a. pa. & 5s. rt. in Chigwell. £200.

38. Hil. Jn. Bendishe, jun., pl. Jn. Bendishe, sen., esq., def. 1 mess. & 22 a. pa. in Steeple Bumpsted & Stamborne. £40.

39. Hil. Edw. Bullock, pl. Tho. Taye, esq., & w. *Elianor*, def. 4 mess., 1 dovecote, 4 gdns., 4 orchards, 100 a. ar., 30 a. mw., 60 a. pa., 30 a. wd., 12 a. marsh & 20s. rt. in Great Totham, Little Totham, Tolleshunt Maior & Goldanger. £320.

40. Mich. & Hil. Rd. Unwyn *alias* Onyon & Jn. Browne, pl. *Rd.* Eden, gent., & w. Margt., def. 1 mess., 1 gdn., 120 a. ar., 15 a. mw., 50 a. pa. & 30 a. wd. in Little Yeldham & Great Yeldham. Def. quitclaimed to pl. & the heirs of Rd. £400.

41. Mich. & Hil. Denise Mannock, wid., Edm. Mannock, gent., Anth. Mannock, gent., Tho. Mannock, gent., & Edw. Mannock, gent., pl. *Wm.* Waldegrave, kt., & w. Eliz., def. 16 a. ar. & 12 a. pa. in Wynthermonford *alias* Wormyngford. Def. quitclaimed to pl. & the heirs of Denise. £40.

42. Hil. Geo. Harvye, esq., pl. Tho. Sackvyle, kt., lord Buckhurst, def. The site of the former monastery of Barkynge, & 2 dovecotes, 2 gdns., 2 orchards, 60 a. ar., 30 a. mw., 40 a. pa., 20 a. w. & 60 a. marsh in Barkynge, held for life by Wenefrida, marchioness of Winchester. Def. gtd. reversion to pl. & his heirs to hold of the chief lords £720.

43. Mich. & Hil. Jn. Cornell *alias* Cornewell, sen., pl. *Tho.* Wyseman, esq., & w. Jane, Joan Newman, wid., & *Jn.* Hockeley, def. 1 mess., 1 gdn., 1 orchard, 20 a. ar., 2 a. mw., 8 a. pa. & 4 a. wd. in Thaxsted. Warranty by Tho. & Jane Wyseman for 5 a. ar.; by Joan Newman & Jn. Hockeley for the rest of the prop. £80.

44. Mich. & Hil. Jn. Mylborne & Geo. Mylborne, pl. *Robt.* Warde *alias* Bennet & w. Joan, Jn. Kynge & w. Joan, def. 3 mes., 2 gdns., 2 orchards, 1 barn & 1 a. pa. in Great Dunmowe. Def. quitclaimed to pl. & the heirs of Jn. Warranty by Jn. & Joan Kynge for 1 mess., 1 gdn. & 1 orchard; by Robt. & Joan Warde for rest of prop. £60.

45. Mich. & Hil. Wm. Waldegrave, kt., & w. Eliz., pl. *Denise* Mannock, wid., Edm. Mannock, Anth. Mannock, Tho. Mannock, & Edw. Mannock, gentlemen, def. 3 a. mw., 10 a. pa., 18 a. wd. & 1 a. alder in Wythermonford *alias* Wormyngford. Def. quitclaimed to pl. & the heirs of Wm. £40.

46. Hil. Robt. Petre, esq., pl. Anth. Wingfeild, esq., & w. Eliz., *Edw.* Honynge, esq., & w. Ursula, Wm. Honynge & Hy. Honynge, esquires, def. 60 a. mw. & 54 a. pa. in Westham. £100.

47. Mich. & Hil. Wm. Marshall, esq., pl. Matthew Cawston, gent., def. 4 mess., 2 tofts, 2 dovecotes, 2 barns, 2 gdns., 2 orchards, 40 a. ar., 20 a. mw., 100 a. pa. & 4 a. wd. in Latchynden *alias* Latchendon *alias* Latchyngdon. 400 mks.

48. Hil. Jn. Wright, pl. *Lau.* Grene & w. Margt., Edw. Meade & w. Joan, def. 2 mess., 2 cotts., 3 tofts, 3 gdns., 2 orchards, 60 a. ar., 20 a. mw., 30 a. pa., 10 a. wd., 20 a. furze & heath & 5s. rt. in Elsenham, Tackley & Stansted Monfitchett. £100.

FEET OF FINES FOR ESSEX

49. Hil. Osmund Lakes, Sam. Flemyng & Wm. James, gentlemen, pl. *Anth*. Barber & w. Margt., def. 1 mess., 2 gdns., 2 orchards, 60 a. ar., 20 a. mw., 80 a. pa. 20 a. wd., 6 a. marsh & 6 a. alder in Halsted. Def. quitclaimed to pl. & the heirs of Osmund. £240.

50. Mich. & Hil. Simon Roberts & Tho. Clement, pl. *Tho*. Tyrrell, Esq., & w. Margt. & Tho. Munds, def. 1 mess., 1 barn, 2 gdns., 1 orchard, 160 a. ar., 12 a. mw. & 160 a. pa. in Spryngfeild & Boreham. Def. quitclaimed to pl. & the heirs of Simon. £500.

51. Hil. Tho. Harrys, gent., pl. Jn. Stonerd, esq., & w. Anne & *Francis* Stonerd, esq., def. The manor of Steple *alias* Steple Grange, & 3 mess., 3 gdns., 3 orchards, 150 a. ar., 40 a. mw., 500 a. pa. & common pa. for all livestock in Steple, Saynt Laurence & Woodhum. Pl. gtd. prop. to Jn. & Anne Stonerd for the life of both & survivor, with remainder to Francis Stonerd & his heirs to hold of the chief lords.

52. Hil. Robt. Bretten, pl. *Rd*. Brokeman, gent., & w. Agnes, *Wm*. Bretten & w. Joan, def. 2 mess., 2 gdns., 1 orchard, 4 a. ar. & 10 a. pa. in Horndon. £120.

53. Hil. Jn. Bromhall, esq., Rd. Berwise, Geo. Elryngton & Tho. Wheteley, gentlemen, pl. Edw. Penruddocke, esq., & w. *Anne*, def. The manors of Cristehall *alias* Cursall, Fryers & Barnes, & 40 mess., 20 tofts, 40 gdns., 500 a. ar., 200 a. mw., 300 a. pa., 300 a. wd., 60 a. furze & heath & 40s. rt. in Cristeshall *alias* Cursall, Elmedon, Great Chisshull, & Little Chisshull. Def. quitclaimed to pl. & the heirs of Jn. £600.

54. Hil. Rd. Ibotson, Tho. Spaight *alias* Spike & Jn. Rowell, pl. Anth. Wingfeld, esq., & w. Eliz., *Edw*. Honynge, esq., & w. Ursula, Hy. Honynge & Wm. Honynge, gentlemen, def. 2 mess., 2 gdns., 16 a. ar., 7 a. mw. & 7 a. pa. in Westham. Def. quitclaimed to pl. & the heirs of Rd. £100.

55. Hil. Jn. Eden, gent., & w. Eliz., pl. *Edw*. Morley & w. Eliz., & *Anne* Parker, sister of Edw., def. The manor of Pakenho *alias* Pakenhohalle *alias* Pakenhale *alias* Patenhall, & 3 mess., 2 cotts., 5 tofts, 10 barns, 10 gdns., 500 a. ar., 60 a. mw., 200 a. pa., 20 a. wd. & 20s. rt. in Manweden *alias* Maneuden *alias* Manuden. Def. quitclaimed to pl. & the heirs of Jn. £160.

CP25(2)/130/1673   EASTER, 21 ELIZABETH   1579

1. Eas. Nich. Moyne & Geo. Deane, pl. *Wm*. Cocke & w. Anne, Jn. Sawkyn & w. Kath., def. 2 mess., 2 gdns. & 2 orchards in Great Dunmowe. Def. quitclaimed to pl. & the heirs of Geo. £80.

2. Eas. Mary Brett, wid., & Jn. Brett, pl. Tho. Darcye, esq., def. 2 a. ar. & 2 a. pa. in Tolleshunt Darcy. Def. quitclaimed to p. & the heirs of Jn. £40.

3. Eas. Hy. Wood, pl. *Anth*. Norman & w. Joan, Jn. Haynes & w. Mary, def. 1 mess., 1 gdn., 1 orchard, 2 a. mw. & 2 a. pa. in Eppyng. £40.

4. Eas. Edw. Grymston, gent., & Jn. Barker, gent., pl. Hy. Joslyn, gent., & w. *Anne*, def. 60 a. pa., 10 a. wd. & 10 a. furze & heath in Bradfeild, Mesleigh & Wykes. Def. quitclaimed to pl. & the heirs of Edw. £40.

5. Eas. Lau. Rochell, pl. *Wm*. Sawen & Jn. Sawen, gentlemen, def. 1 mess., 1 gdn., 1 orchard, 60 a. ar., 10 a. pa. & 7 a. wd. in Little Waltham & Great Leighes. 130 mks.

6. Eas. Jn. Foster, pl. *Edw*. Bugges, gent., & w. Anne, def. 1 mess., 4 a. ar., 4 a. mw. & 8 a. pa. in Harlowe. £40.

7. Eas. Jn. Danyell, gent., pl. Hugh Cole, gent., def. 1 mess., 1 gdn., 1 orchard, 30 a. ar., 5 a. mw., 40 a. pa. & 10 a. wd. in Woodham Mortimer & Woodham Water. £100.

8. Eas. Tho. Hull, pl. Wm. Androes & w. Kath., def. 1 mess., 1 gdn. & 1 orchard in Stebbynge. Def. quitclaimed to pl. & his heirs for the life of Kath. Androes. £40.

9. Eas. Wm. Strachie, sen., pl. Marcia Strachie, wid., & *Helia* Strachie, def. 10 a. pa. in Walden. £80.

10. Eas. Hy. Thomson, pl. *Jn*. Holmested, gent., & w. Margt., def. 6 a. ar. & 6. a. pa. in Halsted. £40.

11. Eas. Rd. Hall, pl. Tho. Bratley & w. *Suzanna*, def. 4 a. ar. & 2 a. pa. in Ardeleigh. £40.

226

12. Eas. Wm. Sumner, pl. *Jn.* Lukyn & w. Margt., def. 1 mess., 1 gdn., 1 orchard, 30 a. ar., 20 a. mw. & 40 a. pa. in Muche Baddowe & Weste Hannyngfeild *alias* Westhanfeilde. £200.

13. Eas. Jn. Andrewe, pl. Jn. Coker, def. 1 mess. & 1 gdn. in Prytwell. Def. quitclaimed to pl. & his heirs. Pl . gtd. def. prop. to hold of the chief lords.

14. Hil. & Eas. Tho. Myldmay, gent., pl. Wm. Lucke & w. *Helen*, def. 13 a. ar. & 2 a. pa. in Spryngfeilde. £60.

15. Eas. And. Byles, pl. *And.* Rottour & w. Jane, def. 1 mess. & 4 a. pa. in Ramysden Belhous. £40.

16. Hil. & Eas. Tho. Myldmay, gent., pl. Edw. earl of Oxford, def. The manor of Langdon Hylles, & 2 mess., 2 gdns., 300 a. ar., 20 a. mw., 60 a. pa., 40 a. wd. & 10s. rt. in Langdon Hylles, Layndon, Dunton & Hornedon-on-the-Hill. £310.

17. Eas. Salamon Lovedaye, pl. Rd. Peers & w. *Emma*, Jn. Sherston & w. *Hester*, def. 1 mess., 1 gdn., 6 a. ar., 2 a. mw. & 4 a. pa. in Faiersted. £40.

18. Eas. Lau. Rochell, pl. *Tho.* Clerke & w. Agnes, def. 1 mess., 12 a. ar., 8 a. pa. & 3 a. wd. in Langham, Boxested, Dedham & Ardeley, £40.

19. Eas. Jasper Cholmeley, gent., pl. *Matthew* Cawston, gent., & w. Joan, def. 4 mess., 2 tofts, 2 dovecotes, 2 barns, 2 gdns., 2 orchard, 40 a. ar., 20 a. mw., 100 a. pa. & 4 a. wd. in Lachenden *alias* Latchenden *alias* Latchindon. £40.

20. Eas. Geoff. Warner, pl. Edw. Moyese & w. *Joan*, def. 1 mess., 1 barn, 20 a. ar., 4 a. mw., 12 a. pa. & 2 a. wd. in Langham. £100.

21. Eas. Rd. Boilland, esq., pl. *Jn.* Danyell & w. Avice, def. 1 mess., 60 a. ar., 20 a. mw., 80 a. pa. & 20 a. wd. in Althorne, Burnam & Southmynster. £40.

22. Eas. Arthur Harris, esq., pl. *Jn.* Danyell, esq., & w. Avice, def. The manor of Great Briche *alias* Great Birche, & 2 mess., 1 gdn., 1 orchard, 100 a. ar., 20 a. mw., 100 a. pa. & 60s. rt. in Great Birche, Esthorpe, Layer Breton, Copeforde & Stanway. £220.

23. Eas. Jn. Sowthwell, esq., pl. *Tho.* Bonham, gent., & w. Joan, def. The manor of Bovills *alias* Bovildes, & 2 mess., 2 gdns., 100 a. ar., 10 a. mw., 40 a. pa., 20 a. wd. & 20s. rt. in Ardeleighe. £140.

24. Eas. Anth. Hyde, pl. Jn. Lyngwood & w. *Jane*, def. 1 mess. & 1 gdn. in Branktre. £40.

25. Eas. Edm. Gryffyn, gent., & Jn. Bedell, pl. Tho. Tyrrell, esq., def. 1 mess., 80 a. ar., 20 a. mw., 100 a. pa. & 10 a. wd. in Stocke & Buttesburye. Def. quitclaimed to pl. & the heirs of Edm. Pl. gtd. prop. to def. to hold of the chief lords.

26. Hil. & Eas. Robt. earl of Leicester, pl. *Arthur* Breame, esq., Jn. Bayles & Tho. Bayles, def. The manor of Stonehall, & 3 mess., 3 gdns., 300 a. ar., 70 a. mw., 300 a. pa., 40 a. wd. & 30 a. marsh in Barkinge. £67.

27. Hil. & Eas. Simon Campion & Tho. Tyman, pl. Jn. Haynes & w. Mary, *Joan* Somner & Anth. Norman, def. 1 mess., 1 gdn., 1 curtilage, 9 a. ar., 2 a. mw., 4 a. pa. & 1 a. wd. in Eppynge, Theydon Boyes & Theydon Garnans. Def. quitclaimed to pl. & the heirs of Tho. £80.

28. Eas. Robt. Payne, pl. Jn. Sadler, def. 1 cott., 40 a. ar., 20 a. mw., 40 a. pa., 4 a. wd. & 20 a. salt marsh in Styfforde & Westhorocke, held for life by Roger Sadler. Def. gtd. reversion to pl. & his heirs to hold of the chief lords. £220.

29. Eas. Tho. Whitbread, sen., pl. Tho. Hodges & w. *Mary* & Jn. Lambert, jun., def. 1 mess., 1 gdn., 1 a. ar., 2 a. mw. & 3 a. pa. in Little Notley. £40.

30. Eas. Wm. Brooke & w. Clement, pl. *Jn.* Belsted & w. Margery, def. 1 mess., 1 gdn., 1 orchard, 20 a. ar., 6 a. pa. & 3 a. wd. in Little Waltham. Def. quitclaimed to pl. & the heirs of Wm. 160 mks.

31. Eas. Roland Walhed, pl. Tho. Parker, gent., def. 1 mess., 1 gdn., 1 orchard, 40 a. ar., 12 a. mw., 20 a. pa. & 12 a. wd. in Shenfeild. £200.

32. Eas. Hy. Moncke & w. Eliz. & Jn. Rowley, pl. *Jn.* Lukyn & w. Margt., def. 1 mess., 1 windmill, 1 gdn., 1 orchard, 30 a. ar., 10 a. pa. & 6 a. wd. in Great Baddowe. Def. quitclaimed to pl. & the heirs of Hy. 130 mks.

33. Eas. Tho. Danbye, kt., pl. Tho. Teye, esq., & w. *Elianor*, def. The manor of Moysehall, & 10 mess., 20 gdns., 20 orchards, 100 a. ar., 30 a. mw., 100 a. pa., 60 a. wd., 100 a. furze & heath & 10 a. marsh in Moysehall & Ardeley. £300.

34. Eas. Edm. Gryffyn, pl. Philip Browne & w. *Susanna*, def. 1 mess., 1 gdn. & 5 a. pa. in Fobbinge. Pl. gtd. prop. to def. & the heirs of Susanna to hold of the chief lords.

35. Eas. Jn. Chapman & Leonard Levett, pl. Jn. Bedingfeld, gent., & w. *Margt.*, def. 7 mess., 7 gdns., 40 a. ar., 6 a. mw. & 14 a. pa. in Thaxsted, Stebbinge, Berdefeld Salinge, Olde Salinge & Felsted. Def. quitclaimed to pl. & the heirs of Jn. £260.

36. Eas. Jn. Carter, sen., & Jn. Carter, jun., his son, pl. *Rd*. Brokeman, gent., & w. Agnes, def. 5 a. fresh marsh in Little Thurrocke. Def. quitclaimed to pl. & the heirs of Jn. Carter, sen. £40.

37. Eas. Robt. Crushe, pl. *Geoff*. Stane, & w. Joan, Rd. Stane & Tho. Stane, def. 1 mess., 1 barn, 1 orchard, 4 a. ar. & 17. a. pa. in Norton Maundevilde. £40.

38. Eas. Robt. Noble, pl. *Rd*. Brokeman, gent., & w. Agnes, def. 1 mess., 1 gdn., 1 orchard, 4 a. ar. & common pa. for all livestock in Thundersleigh. £40.

39. Eas. Robt. Wordysworth, pl. Kath. Powers & Emma Powers, def. 2 mess., 1 gdn., 40 a. ar., 20 a. mw. & 40 a. pa. in Great Burche, Copford, Stanwaye & Easthorpe. Warranty by Kath. Powers for one moiety of the prop. by Emma for the other. £60.

40. Eas. Helen Carder, wid., & Mary Carder, pl. *Sam*. Hunt & w. Margt., Jas. Wattes & w. *Margt.*, Tho. Hughes & w. *Joan*, Reg. Ricard & w. *Kath.*, Gervase Byrche & w. *Grisilda*, def. 1 mess., 1 gdn., 10 a. ar. & 3 a. pa. in Branketre. Def. quitclaimed to pl. & the heirs of Mary. £60.

41. Hil. & Eas. Rd. Pellett, esq., Jn. Pye, Wm. Raine, gentlemen, & Jn. Turner, pl. Abel Clearke & w. *Mary*, def. The manor of Estnewlande, & 1 mess., 3 barns, 1 gdn., 200 a. ar., 10 a. mw., 150 a. pa., 10 a. wd. & 2s. rt. in Saynte Laurence. Def. quitclaimed to pl. & the heirs of Rd. 400 mks.

42. Eas. Wm. Isaac, Jn. Trolls & Geoff. Sydaye, pl. *Hy*. Syday & w. Anne, *Tho*. Cooke & w. Margt., def. 3 mess., 1 dovecote, 3 gdns., 3 orchards, 43 a. ar., 1 a. mw., 16 a. pa. & 6 a. wd. in Alphamstone, Buers Seynt Mary & Lamarshe. Def. quitclaimed to pl. & the heirs of Wm. £100.

43. Eas. Tho. Crawle *alias* Crawley, pl. Tho. Meade, a justice of Common Pleas, def. A fourth part of the manors of Chawreth Hall, Manewden Hall, Strathall *alias* Strethall, Croweley Berrye & Oldhall, & 300 a. ar., 20 a. mw., 40 a. pa., 20 a. wd., & common pa. for 1,000 sheep in Curringham, Fobbinge, Fange, Est Tylbery, West Tylbery, Manewden, Ugley, Farneham, Standsted Mountfychet, Chawreth, Chikney, Broxsted, Thaxsted, Strathall *alias* Strethall, Wymbisshe, Depden, Thunderlye, Great Chisshull, Great Wenden, Little Wenden, Great Chesterford & Little Chesterford & a fourth part of the rectory of Elmedon, & of the advowson of the vicarage of the church of Strathall *alias* Strethall. £400.

44. Eas. Tho. Webbe & Jn. Reynolds, pl. *Rd*. Kytchyn & w. Anne, *Wilfrid* Lewtye & w. Margt., def. 5 a. mw. in Alveley. Def. quitclaimed to pl. & the heirs of Tho. Warranty by Rd. & Anne Kytchyn for 1. a. by Wilfrid & Margt. Lewtye for the remaining 3½ a. Pl. gtd. these 3½ a. to Wilfrid & Margt. Lewtye & the heirs of Wilfrid to hold of the chief lords: and the 1½ a. to Rd. Kytchyn & his heirs to hold of the chief lords.

45. Hil. & Eas. Tho. Pakeman, pl. *Jn*. Eden, gent., & w. Eliz., def. 42½ a. ar. in Manweden *alias* Maneuden *alias* Maunden *alias* Mauneden. Warranty by def. against themselves, the heirs of Jn. Eden, the heirs of Hy. Parker, lord Morley, decd., Edw. Parker, lord Morley & his heirs. Pl. gtd. def. & the heirs of Jn. Eden an annuity of 11s. 8d. from the prop.

CP25(2)/131/1674   TRINITY, 21 ELIZABETH   1579

1. Morrow of Trin. Tho. Fuller, pl. *Jn*. Bryce & w. Eliz., def. 1 a. 3 roods ar. in Billerikay & Great Bursted. Warranty by def. against themselves, the heirs of Jn. Bryce, Jn. Bryce, jun., Tho. Bryce & their heirs. £40.

2. Morrow of Trin. Jn. Lufkyn, pl. Wm. Welles def. 1 mess., 1 toft & 1 gdn. in Maldon. 80 mks.

3. Trin. Geo. Clarke, pl. Tho. Crymes & w. *Jane*, Hy. Toppesfelde & w. *Susanna*, def. 3 mess., 3 gdns. & 10 a. ar. in Bocking. 130 mks.

4. Eas. & Morrow of Trin. Rd. Abraham, pl. Jn. Lacye & w. *Margery*, def. 1 mess. & 1 gdn. in Bocking. £40.

5. Morrow of Trin. Jn. Mott, pl. Tho. Tenderinge, def. The manor of Boreham, & 20 mess., 20 gdns., 20 orchards, 3 dovecotes, 200 a. ar., 60 a. mw., 200 a. pa., 100 a. wd. & 16s. rt. in Boreham. £140.

6. Morrow of Trin. Geo. Goldyng, gent., & Tho. Whetcroft, gent., pl. Jn. Carter, def. 1 mess., 1 gdn., 1 orchard, 10 a. ar., 1 a. mw. & 5 a. pa. in Gestyngthorpe. Def. quitclaimed to pl. & the heirs of Geo. Pl. gtd. prop. to def. & his heirs to hold of the chief lords.

7. Trin. Hy. Hamond, pl. Robt. Grene & w. *Fredeswida*, def. 2 mess., 2 tofts, 2 gdns., 2 orchards, 48 a. ar., 4 a. mw., 10 a. pa. & 6 a. wd. in Depden, Thunderley & Wynbyshe. £200.

8. Eas. & Morrow of Trin. Geo. Wood, pl. Jn. Lacye & w. *Margery*, def. 1 mess. & 1 gdn. in Bocking. £40.

9. Morrow of Trin. Edw. Bayly, pl. Rd. Pellett, esq., & w. *Mary*, def. 1 mess., 1 gdn., 1 orchard, 10 a. ar., 10 a. mw., 20 a. pa., 3 a. wd. & 10 a. salt marsh in Fange at Noke *alias* Fange *alias* Vange. 220 mks.

10. Eas. & Morrow of Trin. Oswald Fytche, gent., pl. Jn. Lacye & w. *Margery*, Josias Sampson & Robt. Sampson, def. 1 mess., 1 gdn. & 1 a. ar. in Bocking. £80.

11. Trin. Tho. Tyrrell, pl. *Steph*. Bull & w. Joan, def. 4 a. mw. in Westham. 110 mks.

12. Trin. Wm. Ayloff, a justice of Q.'s Bench, pl. Robt. Veer, esq., def. The manors of Wennyngton & Kennyngton, & 6 mess., 6 gdns., 200 a. ar., 20 a. mw., 100. a. pa., 20 a. wd., 100 a. fresh marsh, 200 a. salt marsh, 100s. rt. & several fishery (*separalis piscaria*) in Wennyngton, Alveley *alias* Alvethley & Raynham. £680.

13. Morrow of Trin. Rd. Eve, pl. *Rd*. Thorneton & w. Mary & Margt. Thorneton, wid., def. 1 mess. & 1 gdn. in Rocheford. £40.

14. Morrow of Trin. Tho. Browne, pl. *Tho*. Hoggeken *alias* Hodgisken & w. Mary, def. 1 mess. & 1 gdn. in Walden. £40.

15. Eas. & Morrow of Trin. Jn. Petytt, pl. *Jn*. Claydon & w. Margt., def. 1 mess., 1 gdn., 30 a. ar., 4 a. mw. & 10 a. pa. in Asshedon & Barklowe. £40.

16. Morrow of Trin. Tho. Gent, Esq., pl. Jn. Dalston, jun., esq., & w. *Anne*, def. 2 mess., 2 gdns., 2 orchards, 60 a. ar., 5 a. mw. & 15 a. pa. in Debden & Great Sampford. £80.

17. Morrow of Trin. Tho. Spakeman, pl. *Tho*. Colshill, esq., & w. Mary, def. 2 mess., 2 gdns., 2 orchards & 2 a. mw. in Chigwell. £40.

18. Morrow of Trin. Nich. Walle, pl. *Jn*. Danyell, esq., & w. Avice, def. 2 mess., 2 gdns., 2 orchards, 70 a. ar., 10 a. mw., 70 a. pa. & 20 a. wd. in Great Byrche, Little Byrche, Stanwaye, Layer Marney, Esthorpe, Copforde, Layer Bretton & Layer de la Haye. £100.

19. Morrow of Trin. Jn. Cordall, pl. *Tho*. Stoneden & w. Joan, def. 2 mess., 2 gdns., 2 orchards, 3½ a. ar. & 1½ a. mw. in Chynchford *alias* Chyngelford. £40.

20. Morrow of Trin. Jn. Nicols, pl. *Jn*. Stonarde & w. Rebecca, def. 1 mess., 1 barn, 1 gdn., 1 orchard, 6 a. ar. & 7 a. pa. in Woodhamferrers. £80.

21. Morrow of Trin. Tho. Hone, gent., & Tho. Purcas, pl. Chris. Cutbertson & w. *Agnes*, Wm. Smythe & w. *Mary*, Jn. Scott & w. *Eva*, def. 1 mess., 1 gdn. & 2 a. 1 rood ar. in Thaxstede. Def. quitclaimed to pl. & the heirs of Tho. Hone. Warranty by Jn. & Eva Scott for the land, by the other def. for the mess. & gdn. £40.

22. Morrow of Trin. Wm. Twydie, esq., pl. Edw. earl of Oxford, great chamberlain, def. 2 mess., 1 cott., 1 toft, 2 gdns., 2 orchards, 60 a. ar., 15 a. mw., 100 a. pa. & 12 a. wd. in the parishes of All Saints, St. Peter & St. Mary in the town of Maldon & Woodham Mortymer. £280.

23. Morrow of Trin. Jn. Poole, pl. *Wm*. Stane & w. Mary, Geo. Haull & w. Mary, def. 1 mess., 1 barn, 1 orchard, 7 a. ar., 3 a. mw. & 4 a. pa. in Stondon. £40.

24. Morrow of Trin. Tho. Church & Edm. Thornton, pl. Wm. Rede, def. 3 mess., 3 gdns., 100 a. ar., 30 a. mw. & 100 a. pa. in Wickforde & Rawrithe. Def. quitclaimed to pl. & the heirs of Tho. £140.

25. Trin. Margt. Crackenell, wid., pl. Edw. Heron, esq., & w. *Anne*, def. 1 toft, 6 a. ar., 4 a. 1 rood mw. & 18 a. pa. in Fynchingfelde. £80.

26. Morrow of Trin. Jn. Cheyney, pl. *Ralph* Cheyney & w. Anne, def. 4 a. pa. in Waltham Holy Cross. £40.

27. Morrow of Trin. Ralph Pratt, pl. *Robt.* Aprece, sen., esq., & w. Joan & *Robt.* Aprece, jun., gent., son & heir apt. of Robert sen., def. 4 mess., 2 cotts., 3 barns, 4 tofts, 4 gdns., 4 orchards, 60 a. ar., 40 a. mw., 80 a. pa., 26 a. wd. & 25 a. marsh in Walthamstowe *alias* Walthamstowe Tonye & Leyton. £320.

28. Morrow of Trin. Tho. Chote & Robt. Annys *alias* Smyth, pl. Edw. Heron, esq., & w. *Anne*, def. 1 toft, 26 a. ar., 11 a. mw., 26 a. pa. & 16 a. wd. in Byrdebroke, Steeple Bumpsted & Fynchingfeld. Def. quitclaimed to pl. & the heirs of Tho. £200.

29. Morrow of Trin. Hy. Bosvile, gent., & Rd. Baylye, pl. *Clement* Smyth, esq., & w. Dorothy, def. The manor of Langforde, & 1 mess., 1 water-mill, 2 barns, 2 gdns., 2 orchards, 100 a. ar., 100 a. mw., 200 a. pa. & 40 a. wd. in Langforde, Oultynge, Wytham, Hayebridge, Maldon, Totham & Wickham & the advowson of the church of Langforde. Def. quitclaimed to pl. & the heirs of Hy. Pl. gtd. prop. to def. & the heirs of Clement Smyth to hold of the chief lords.

30. Trin. Jn. Scott & w. Eva, pl. Chris. Cutberson & w. Anne, Wm. Smythe & w. *Mary*, def. 1 mess., 1 gdn., 1 orchard, 20 a. ar., 10 a. mw. & 20 a. pa. in Thaxstede. Def. quitclaimed to pl. & the heirs of Jn. Pl. gtd. prop. to Christ. & Anne Cutberson to hold of the chief lords for the life of both & survivor, with remainder to Agnes Robynson, Susanna Robynson & Margt. Robynson, daus. of Tho. Robynson, decd., & the legitimate heirs of their bodies, failing whom to the right heirs of Anne Cutbertson.

31. Morrow of Trin. Gregory Yonge & w. Suzanna, pl. *Jn.* Penneruddock, esq., & w. Joan, def. 1 mess., 1 barn, 1 gdn., 1 orchard, 30 a. ar., 8 a. mw., 20 a. pa. & 2 a. wd. in Alta Ongar *alias* Hiegh Ongar. Def. quitclaimed to pl. & the heirs of Gregory. Pl. gtd. Jn. Penneruddock & his heirs an annual rt. of 4d. from the prop.

32. Eas. & Morrow of Trin. Tho. Reynolds & Jn. Andrewe, pl. Jas. Dryland, gent., & w. *Alice* & Jn. Lukyn, gent., def. 1 mess., 2 gdns., 22 a. ar. & 12 a. mw. in Great Badowe. Def. quitclaimed to pl. & the heirs of Tho. Pl. gtd. prop. to Jas. & Alice Dryland for the life of both & survivor: after the death of the survivor 1 mess., 2 gdns., 14 a. ar. & 12 a. mw. to remain to Jn. Lukyn & his heirs to hold of the chief lords: the remaining 8 a. ar. to remain to Jn. Lukyn for 15 years after death of Jas. & Alice at rt. of a red rose to pl., with reversion to Alice Dryland & her heirs to hold of the chief lords.

CP25(2)/260   DIVERS COUNTIES

4. Morrow of Trin. Francis, earl of Bedford, & Gilbert Lytleton, esq., pl. Jn. Russell, esq., def. 6 mess., 6 tofts, 6 gdns., 100 a. ar., 50 a. mw. & 20 a. pa. in Rayleigh, Hockley & Thundersley & a moiety of the manors of Easthamburnells, Westhamburnells, Estwestham & Plays, & 200 a. ar., 100 a. mw., 200 a. pa., 16 a. fresh marsh & 20s. rt. in Westham & Estham, co. Essex; & props. in London, Mdx., Kent, Surr. & Cambs. Def. quitclaimed to pl. & the heirs of Earl of Bedford. £1,520. — London, Mdx., Essex, Kent, Surr. Cambs.

CP25(2)/131/1675   MICHAELMAS, 21-22 ELIZABETH   1579

1. Mich. Wm. Egeott, pl. Jn. Samer, def. 1 mess., 1 gdn., 1 orchard, 40 a. ar., 10 a. mw., 20 a. pa., 10 a. wd. & common pa. for all livestock in Sowthannyngefield & Westhannyngefield. £80.

2. Mich. Tho. Sadler, pl. Wm. Acheley, def. 6 a. mw. in Langham. £40.

3. Mich. Wm. Gardener, pl. Wm. Stedman, def. 70 a. fresh marsh in Barkinge. £240.

4. Mich. Hy. Longe & Rd. Stylman, pl. Wm. Clerke, gent., & w. *Isabella*, Tho. Dennys & w. *Alice*, def. 1 mess., 1 gdn., 1 orchard & 2 a. pa. in Great Dunmowe. Def. quitclaimed to pl. & the heirs of Hy. £80.

5. Mich. Tho. Grene, pl. *Pet.* Pett & w. Eliz., def. 1 mess. & 1 gdn. in Harwiche. 130 mks.

6. Mich. Tho. Furnes, pl. Ralph Ayloff, gent., def. 2 mess., 1 gdn., 1 orchard & ½ a. ar. in Malden. £40.

7. Mich. Wm. Burges, pl. Adam Sandford, gent., & w. *Eliz.*, def. 1 mess., 1 gdn., 1 orchard, 10 a. ar., 10 a. mw. & 10 a. pa. in Chygwell. £100.

8. Mich. Jas. Wallinger, gent., pl. Wm. Knight & w. *Grace*, def. 2 mess., 30 a. ar., 100 a. pa. & 10 a. wd. in Navestock & Morton. £160.

9. Trin. & Mich. Wm. Malym, gent., & w. Mary, pl. *Tho.* Fremlyn, gent., & w. Margt., def. 1 mess., 1 gdn. & 2 a. ar. in St. James parish in the town of Colcester. Def. quitclaimed to pl. & the heirs of Wm. £40.

10. Trin. & Mich. Wm. Ayloff, a justice of Q's Bench, & Wm. Ayloff, gent., his son & heir apt., pl. Edw. earl of Oxford, def. 40 a. salt marsh in Raynham, Wennyngton & Alveley *alias* Alvethley. Def. quitclaimed to pl. & the heirs of Wm. Ayloff, jun. £16.

11. Mich. Robt. Sams, pl. Robt. Wood, gent., def. 2 mess., 1 barn, 2 gdns., 24 a. ar., 14 a. mw. & 30 a. pa. in Bromeffeld. £160.

12. Trin. & Mich. Tho. Carowe, gent., pl. *Geoff.* Lorkyn & Edw. Lorkyn, def. 1 mess., 5 gdns., 2 orchards, 100 a. ar., 20 a. mw., 60 a. pa. & 20 a. wd. in Shenfeild & Duddinghurste. £140.

13. Mich. Roger Tasker, pl. *Ralph* Pratte & w. Margt., def. 2 mess., 2 gdns., 2 orchards, 10 a. ar., 20 a. mw. & 20 a. pa. in Walthamstowe *alias* Walthamstowe Tony. £80.

14. Mich. Tho. Claye, pl. *Jn.* Browne & w. Joan, def. 1 mess., 2 gdns., 2 orchards & 5 a. ar. in High Laver. £40.

15. Mich. Wm. Goldyng, esq., pl. *Tho.* Downyng, gent., & w. Joan, def. 8 a. ar., 10 a. pa., 20 a. wd. & 4d. rt. in Belchamp Saint Paul. £80.

16. Mich. Wm. Westley, sen., pl. Tho. Okeman & w. Alice, Rd. Marcham & w. *Eliz.*, def. 4 mess., 2 gdns., 1 orchard & 1 a. mw. in Thaxsted. £40.

17. Trin. & Mich. Wm. Hawkyn, pl. Camillus Rusticens & w. *Margery*, def. 1 mess., 1 cott., 1 gdn., 1 orchard & 1 a. mw. in Wydford. £40.

18. Mich. Rd. Verden, pl. *Jn.* Pasfeild & w. Matilda, def. 2 mess., 1 barn, 2 gdns., 1 orchard & 5 a. ar. in Black Notley. £40.

19. Mich. Daniel Goodinge, pl. *Weston* Andrewe & w. Anne, def. 1 mess., 1 gdn., 1 orchard, 30 a. ar. & 3 a. wd. in Great Okelie. 130 mks.

20. Mich. Gilbert Rolffe, pl. *Simon* Judye & w. Margt., def. 8 a. ar., 8 a. mw. & 8 a. pa. in Lawforde. £40.

21. Mich. Jasper Nicholls, pl. Roger Taylor & w. *Mary*, def. 1 mess., 3 a. mw., 2 a. pa. & 5 a. wd. in Waltham Holy Cross. £40.

22. Mich. Jn. Cele, gent., pl. Tho. Clynton *alias* Fynes, esq., & w. *Mary*, def. 1 mess., 1 toft, 2 cotts., 1 barn, 1 gdn., 1 orchard, 100 a. ar., 8 a. mw., 120 a. pa. & 40 a. wd. in Langdon *alias* Langdon Hills & Hornedon. £480.

23. Mich. Tho. Ive, gent., pl. Tho. Shaa, esq., def. The manor of Great Stambrig *alias* Stanbrige *alias* Stanbrigge, & 100 mess., 400 a. ar., 100 a. mw., 200 a. pa., 100 a. wd., 300 a. marsh & 100s. rt. in Great Stambrige, Little Stambrige, Rochford, Rawreth, Paglesham, Caneudon, South Churche, Prittelwell & Thondersley & the advowson of the church of Great Stambrige. 610 mks.

24. Mich. Tho. Hull, pl. Tho. Brickett & w. *Blandina*, def. A fourth part of 2 mess., 2 gdns. & 8 a. ar. in Stebbynge. £40.

25. Mich. Robt. Jackson & w. Sitha, pl. Jn. Atkinson, def. 1 mess., 1 barn, 1 toft & 1 gdn. in Brentwood. Def. quitclaimed to pl. & the heirs of Robt. £40.

26. Mich. Wm. Thorowgood, gent., & Jn. Ballard, gent., pl. Edm. Harrington, def.

2 mess., 1 barn, 2 gdns., 40 a. ar., 6 a. mw., 20 a. pa. & 1 a. wd. in Stamborne & Reddeswell. Def. quitclaimed to pl. & the heirs of Wm. Pl. gtd. prop. to def. & his heirs to hold of the chief lords.

27. Mich. Wm. Lyvinge & w. Mary, pl. *Steph*. Ritche & w. *Kath*., def. 1 mess., & 12 a. ar. in Peldon. Def. quitclaimed to pl. & the heirs of Wm. 130 mks.

28. Mich. Rd. Tomson, pl. *Rd*. Brokeman, gent., & w. Agnes, def. 1 mess., 1 gdn. & 1 orchard in the town of Colcestr'. 80 mks.

29. Mich. Tho. Foster, pl. *Robt*. Collyn & Nich. Collyn, def. 1 mess., 1 gdn., 1 orchard, 20 a. ar. & 6 a. pa. in Little Laver, High Laver & Matchinge; held for life by Agnes Sumpner, wid. Def. gtd. reversion to pl. & his heirs to hold of the chief lords. £40.

30. Mich. Tho. Cooke & Jn. Wright, pl. Wm. Ayloff, esq., & w. Alice, Wm. Barlee, gent., & w. *Eliz*., Wm. Cooke, gent., & w. Alice., def. 50 a. ar., 2 a. pa. & 12 a. wd. in Great Chissell, Little Chissell, Heydon & Chrissall. Def. quitclaimed to pl. & the heirs of Tho. £80.

31. Mich. Tho. Godfrey & Tho. Herde, pl. *Wm*. Ayloff, a justice of Q's Bench, & w. Jane, def. The manor of Ramsey, & 30 mess., 30 gdns., 30 orchards, 120 a. ar., 60 a. mw., 120 a. pa., 130 a. wd. & £16 6s. rt. in Ramsey, Wrabnes & Bradfeild. Def. quitclaimed to pl. & the heirs of Tho. Godfrey. £600.

32. Mich. Jn. Waylette, pl. *Wm*. Platte & w. Margt., def. 1 mess., 3 gdns & 3 a. ar. in Chelmesford & Wydford. £40.

33. Mich. Hy. Hasell, Jn. Sharpe & Chris. Terrenden, pl. Jn. Preston & w. Margery & *Elias* Saunder, def. 2 a. ar., 30 a. fresh marsh & 10 a. salt marsh in Great Shoberye *alias* Southeshoberye. Pl. gtd. prop. to Jn. & Margery Preston for the life of both & survivor, with remainder to Hy. Hasell & his heirs to hold of the chief lords.

CP25(2)/131/1676   HILARY, 22 ELIZABETH   1580

1. Hil. Jn. Rochell, pl. Anth. Walker & w. *Joan*, def. 6 a. ar., 3 a. mw. & 3 a. pa. in Great Stambridge. £40.

2. Hil. Tho. Tanner, pl. *Jn*. Mynott & w. Wenefrida, def. 1 mess., 1 gdn., 6 a. ar. & 3 a. pa. in Felsted. £40.

3. Hil. Jn. Armond & Nich. Bonye, pl. *Rd*. Burley & w. Kath., def. 1 mess., 1 cott., 1 barn, 1 orchard & 4 a. pa. in Rayne. Def. quitclaimed to pl. & the heirs of Jn. £40.

4. Hil. Jn. Browne, pl. *Wm*. Browne & w. Suzanna, def. 1 mess., 1 gdn., 1 orchard & 4 a. ar. in Great Yeldham *alias* Nether Yeldham. £40.

5. Hil. Roger Marten, pl. *Tho*. Fuller & w. Joan, Roger Bybbye & w. Anne, def. 1 mess. in Walden. £80.

6. Hil. Jn. Poudre, pl. Rd. Wastlyn, def. 2 mess., 2 gdns., 14 a. ar. & 2 a. pa. in Hedingham Sible. £80.

7. Hil. Jn. Frier, jun., gent., pl. *Tho*. Downyng & w. Joan, def. 10 a. ar. in Belchampe St. Paul. £40.

8. Hil. Rd. Stonley, gent., pl. Edw. earl of Oxford, great chamberlain, def. 1 mess., 2 tofts, 2 gdns., 80 a. ar., 20 a. mw., 60 a. pa., 80 a. wd. & 10 a. furze & heath in Dodinghurst. Warranty by def. against himself, his heirs & the heirs of his father, Jn., lately earl of Oxford. 130 mks.

9. Hil. Jn. Birde, pl. *Jn*. Jobson & Edw. Jobson, esquires, def. 1 mess. in Colchester. £40.

10. Hil. Jn. Petre, kt., pl. Edw. earl of Oxford, great chamberlain, def. The manor of Mounteneysing *alias* Gyng Mountney, & 100 mess., 20 cotts., 10 tofts, 100 gdns., 100 orchards, 1,000 a. ar., 200 a. mw., 100 a. pa., 100 a. wd., 90 a. furze & heath. £20 rt. free warren & free fishing in Mounteneysing *alias* Gyng Mountney, Hutton, Greate Bursteade & Buttsbery. £480.

11. Hil. Jn. Ryder & Edw. Ryder, pl. Jn. Questell, def. 1 mess. & 3 gdns. in Cheping-onger. Def. quitclaimed to pl. & the heirs of Edw. £40.

12. Hil. Tho. Wylson, pl. Edw. earl of Oxford, great chamberlain, def. 70 a. ar., 10 a. mw. & 50 a. marsh in Mundon & Purley. 130 mks.

13. Hil. Rd. Brokeman, gent., pl. Jn. Burton & w. *Margt.*, def. 1 mess., 1 gdn., 1 orchard, 10 a. ar., 10 a. mw., 12 a. pa. & common pa. for all livestock in Little Bursted. £80.

14. Hil. Hy. Standyshe, pl. Jn. Alee & w. *Eliz.*, def. 9 a. pa. in Waltham Holy Cross. £60.

15. Hil. Tho. Lamberd, pl. Robt. Cooke, def. 2 mess., 2 gdns. & 1 a. ar. in Halsted. £40.

16. Hil. Hy. Glascocke, pl. *Hy*. Chauncye, *Tho*. Salisburye & w. Maud, def. The manor of Harteshoburye *alias* Hassowburye, & 1 mess., 1 water-mill, 2 orchards, 220 a. ar., 40 a. mw., 80 a. pas., 30 a. wd. & £7 rt. in Farnham & Stansted Mountfitchett. £200.

17. Hil. Wm. Smythe, pl. *Wm*. Hedgeman & w. Joan, def. 1 mess., 1 gdn., 16 a. ar., 4 a. mw. & 6 a. pa. in Orsett. £100.

18. Hil. Pet. Wittham, pl. Daniel Spring, def. 2 tofts, 28 a. ar., 2 a. mw., 12 a. pa., 4 a. wd. & 4s. 2d. rt. in Cressinge. £40.

19. Hil. Wm. Colshyll, gent., & w. Barbara, pl. Wm. Massye, Edw. Over, & w. Denise & *Rd*. Scoffeyld, def. 1 mess., 100 a. ar., 100 a. mw., 100 a. pa. & 100 a. marsh in South-fambridge & Assyngdon. Def. quitclaimed to pl. & the heirs of Barbara. £200.

20. Hil. Jn. Blades & Tho. Ramsey, pl. Wimond Cary, esq., def. The rectory of Stansted Mountfytchat. Def. quitclaimed to pl. & the heirs of Jn. £400.

21. Hil. Rd. Whighte & w. Margt., pl. Simon Eccles *alias* George & w. *Agnes*, def. 1 mess. & 1 gdn. in Willingall Doo. Def. quitclaimed to pl. & the heirs of Rd. £40.

22. Hil. Tho. Cooke, pl. Jn. Dyke & w. *Margt.*, def. 4 a. ar. in Great Chissell & Little Chissell. £40.

23. Hil. Gabriel Poyntz, esq., pl. Wm. Sheather & w. *Anne*, def. A moiety of the manors of Groves & Billingtons, & 12 mess., 12 tofts, 2 dovecotes, 12 gdns., 12 orchards, 300 a. ar., 80 a. mw., 300 a. pa., 100 a. wd., 40 a. marsh & 60s. rt. in Northwokendon, Cranham *alias* Wokendon Episcopi, Little Thurrock, Grayse Thurrock, Chaldewell, Rayn-ham, Wenyngton & Alveley. £520.

24. Hil. Hy. Bradbury, esq., pl. *Wm*. Lasshe & w. Kath., *Nich*. Felsted sen. & w. Alice, Rd. Felsted & w. Eliz., def. 1 mess., 1 gdn., 20 a. ar., 2 a. pa. & the liberty of a fold for 100 sheep in Lyttelbury, Strattall & Walden. £80.

25. Hil. Nich. Stanes & Jn. Clerk, pl. Tho. Clerk, def. 1 mess., & 1 a. pa. in Walden. Def quitclaimed to pl. & the heirs of Jn. 100 mks.

26. Hil. Jn. Godsalve, pl. Jn. Worrall, gent., & w. *Mary*, def. 1 mess., 1 barn, 1 wind-mill, 1 gdn., 13 a. ar. & 1½ a. mw. in Belchame William *alias* Water Belchame. £40.

27. Hil. Edm. Griffyn, gent., pl. Edm. Gibson & w. *Agnes,* def. 1 mess., 1 curtilage, 1 barn, 1 gdn., 1 orchard & 1 a. ar. in Wytham, held for life by Robt. Bastwyk *alias* Bastike. Def. gtd. reversion to pl. & his heirs to hold of the chief lords. £40.

28. Hil. Tho. Randall, pl. *Walter* Morgan, gent., & w. Jane, def. 10 a. ar., 12 a. pa. & 4 a. wd. in Barkynge. £80.

29. Hil. Wm. Garfourth & Tho. Lane, pl. Mathias Lavell & w. *Eliz.*, def. 1 mess., 1 gdn., 1 orchard, 60 a. ar., 10 a. mw., 40 a. pa. & 6 a. wd. in Fyfelde & Bewchampe Rodinge. Def. quitclaimed to pl. & the heirs of Wm. £100.

30. Hil. Edm. Church, gent., pl. Anth. Maxey, esq., & w. *Dorothy* & Charles Bonaham, gent., def. The manor of Stanley Hall, & 4 mess., 2 tofts, 6 gdns., 6 orchards, 200 a. ar., 12 a. mw., 100 a. pa., 50 a. wd. & 100s. rt. in Pedmarshe *alias* Pelmarshe, Colne, Engayne, Twynsted, Halsted, Bulmer, Great Maplested, Little Maplested, & Esse *alias* Asshen, held for life by Margt. Ayloff, wid., with reversion to Dorothy Maxey. Def. gtd. pl. the re-mainder of the prop. after Dorothy's death. £200.

31. Mich. & Hil. Tho. Burle, pl. Edw. Neale & w. Margt., *Robt*. Neale, *Jn*. Seman & w. Anne, def. 1 mess., 1 gdn., 12 a. pa. & 6 a. salt marsh in Stowe Marishe. £40.

32. Mich. & Hil. Jn. Bakere, esq., & Simon Toppesfelde, gent., pl. Tho. Bakere, esq., & w. *Grisilla*, def. 1 mess., 1 barn, 20 a. ar., 10 a. mw., 10 a. pa., 6 a. wd. & 5s. 6d. rt. in Fobbyng & Curryngham. Def. quitclaimed to pl. & the heirs of Jn. 70 mks.

33. Hil. Rd. Todd, pl. *Jn*. Nicolson & w. Margt. & *Robt*. Lytherland, def. 1 mess., 1 gdn., 13 a. ar., 2 a. mw. & 6 a. pa. in Hengham Sible *alias* Henningham Sible & Great Maplested. Warranty by Jn. & Margt. Nicolson for 1 mess., 1 gdn. & 6 a. pa.; by Robt. Lytherland for the remaining 13 a. ar. & 2 a. mw. £40.

34. Hil. Edw. Sulyarde, esq., & w. Anne, pl. *Tho*. Bonham, gent., & w. Joan, def. The manors of Belhowse & Howes, & 20 mess., 2 dovecotes, 20 gdns., 800 a. ar., 100 a. mw., 400 a. pa., 200 a. wd. & 200 a. furze & heath in Muche Stanwey, Little Stanwey, Copforde, Laxton, Great Byrche, Little Byrche & Fordam; & a moiety of the manor of Muche Stanwey, & 800 a. ar., 40 a. mw., 200 a. pa., 100 a. wd., 500 a. furze & heath & 40s. rt. in Muche Stanwey, Little Stanwey, Copforde, Laxton, Great Byrche, Little Byrche & Fordam; & a moiety of the advowson of the church of Muche Stanwey. Def. quitclaimed to pl. & the heirs of Edw. £600.

35. Hil. Robt. Barney, Hy. Cutler & Wm. Tyffyn, pl. *Edm*. Churche, esq., Jn. Daniel, esq., & w. *Margt*., *Wm*. Playters, esq., & w. Mary, Charles Cutler & w. *Susanna*, def. The manors of Northbemflett *alias* Coxalls, Scotts & Plomborowe *alias* Plumburgh, & 10 mess., 8 cotts., 6 dovecotes, 10 gdns., 10 orchards, 1,000 a. ar., 200 a. mw. 1,000 a. pa., 200 a. wd., 400 a. fresh marsh, 100 a. salt marsh, 50 a. moor & £20 rt. in Caneuden *alias* Canewden *alias* Canewden, Rawreth, Raylye *alias* Rayleighe, Thundersley, Wickforde, Hockley *alias* Ockleye, Hawkewell, Woodhamfferres, Northbemflett, Hadley, Runwell, Southbemflett, Newenden, Asheldham, Petsey, Northfambridge & Southchurche, & the advowson of the church of Northbemflett. Def. quitclaimed to pl. & the heirs of Robt. Warranty by all def. save Mary Playters. £1,600.

CP25(2)/260/22   DIVERS COUNTIES

4. Mich. & Hil. Jn. Huband, kt., Jn. Dudley, esq., & Jn. Nuthall, esq., pl. Robt. earl of Leicester, def. The manors of Wansted *alias* Waunsted & Stonehall, & 60 mess., 2 tofts, 1 mill, 3 dovecotes, 60 gdns., 1,000 a. ar., 200 a. mw., 2,000 a. pa., 50 a. wd., 1,000 a. heath & 60s. rt. in Wansted *alias* Waunsted, Stonehall, Woodford, Waltham Stoe, Layton & Ilford & the advowson of the church of Wansted, co. Essex; & props. in Berks, Stafford, Mdx., Warwick, Coventry, Salop. Worcester & Gloucester. Def. quitclaimed to pl. & the heirs of Jn. Huband. £800. — Essex, Berks, Stafford, Mdx., Warwick, city of Coventry, Salop, Worcester, Gloucester.

6. Hil. Wm. Vavasour, esq., Joan Bradshawe, wid., Wm. Atwoode, gent., & Ralph Hatton, pl. Chris. Kenne, esq., & w. *Eliz*., *alias* Eliz. Beckwithe, def. The manors of Esthamburnells, Westhamburnells, Estwestham & Playce, & 30 mess., 20 cotts., 400 a. ar., 400 a. mw., 100 a. pa., 100 a. wd., 400 a. furze & heath, 300 a. moor, 400 a. marsh & £15 rt. in Esthamburnells, Westhamburnells, Estwestham, Plaice, Estham, Westham & Orsett, co. Essex; & props. in Kent, Mdx., Surr. & London. Def. quitclaimed to pl. & the heirs of Wm. Vavasour. £2,020. — Kent, Essex, Mdx., Surr., London.

CP25(2)/131/1677   EASTER, 22 ELIZABETH   1580

1. Eas. Pet. Garrord, pl. Miles Oxboroughe & w. *Margt*., def. 4 a. ar. & 1 rood pa. in Mount Bures. £20.

2. Eas. Robt. Petre, esq., pl. Edw. earl of Oxford, great chamberlain, def. 100 a. wd. in Jepcrake, Purley & Sandon. Warranty by def. against himself, his heirs & the heirs of his father, Jn. late earl of Oxford, decd. £40.

3. Eas. Wm. Twidye, esq., pl. Edw. earl of Oxford, great chamberlain, def. The manor of Maldon, & 3 mess., 2 cotts., 1 stall (*stallum*), 1 gdn., 1 orchard, 1 a. ar. & 60s. rt. in the parishes of All Saints & St. Peter in the town of Maldon. Warranty by def. against himself, his heirs & the heirs of his father. Jn. late earl of Oxford, decd. 130 mks.

4. Eas. Wm. Davenante, gent., pl. *Robt*. Tyffyn & w. Judith, Jn. Potter & w. Alice, def. 1 mess., 1 gdn., 1 orchard, 26 a. ar., 4 a. mw., 10 a. pa. & 3 a. wd. in Waterbelchampe, Gestingthorpe & Little Yeldham. £80.

5. Eas. Anne Legatte, wid., pl. *Hy*. Legatte & w. Kath., def. 6 a. pa. in Theydon Garnon. £40.

6. Eas. Geo. Knightley, esq., pl. Edw. earl of Oxford, great chamberlain, def. The manor of Crustwich *alias* Crustich *alias* Custrichall, & 4 mess., 3 tofts, 2 mills, 1 dovecote, 3 gdns., 200 a. ar., 40 a. mw., 100 a. pa., 40 a. wd. & 20s. rt. in Weleigh, Saynt Osithe, Muche Bentley & Tenderinge. Warranty by def. against himself, his heirs & the heirs of his father, Jn. late earl of Oxford, decd. £220.

7. Eas. Edw. Heron, esq., pl. Robt. Brooke, gent., & w. *Eliz*., def. 20 a. 1 rood ar. in Chryssall *alias* Christishall. £40.

8. Eas. Jn. Kent & Robt. Yonge, pl. Robt. Wood, Tho. Lodge, *Jn*. Chalke & w. Joan, def. 2 mess., 2 gdns., 120 a. ar., 40 a. mw., 60 a. pa. & 10 a. wd. in Wryttle. Def. quit-claimed to pl. & the heirs of Jn. Warranty by Jn. & Joan Chalke only. £200.

9. Eas. Jn. Birde, pl. Edw. earl of Oxford, great chamberlain, def. The manor of Battyshall *alias* Battylshall, & 2 mess., 2 cotts., 6 tofts, 6 gdns., 6 orchards, 500 a. ar., 40 a. mw., 100 a. pa., 160 a. wd., 300 a. furze & heath, £10 rt. & common pa. for all animals in Stapleford Abott. Def. quitclaimed to pl. 400 mks.

10. Hil. & Eas. Arthur Harrys, esq., pl. *Reg*. Heygate, esq., & w. Mary, def. The manor of Great Briche *alias* Great Birche, & 2 mess., 1 gdn., 1 orchard, 100 a. ar., 20 a. mw., 100 a. pa. & 60s. rt. in Great Birche, Estthorpe, Layer Bretton, Copford & Stan-waye. £220.

11. Eas. Edw. Miller & w. Eliz., pl. *Jn*. Hoggekyn & w. Eliz., def. 1 mess., 1 gdn. & 1 orchard in Beachampe Rothinge. Def. quitclaimed to pl. & the heirs of Edw. £40.

12. Eas. Wm. Tymperley, esq., pl. Tho. Darcye, esq., def. 1 mess., 1 dovecote, 1 gdn., 1 orchard, 20 a. mw. & 220 a. pa. in Tolshunt Darcye *alias* Tolshunt Tregoes. £600.

13. Eas. Jn. Francklyn & Rd. Francklyn, pl. *Hy*. earl of Pembrok, & w. Mary, def. 40 a. marsh in Barkinge. Def. quitclaimed to pl. & the heirs of Jn. £200.

14. Eas. Roger Goodday, gent., pl. *Jn*. Shawarden, gent., & w. Anne, def. 2 mess., 1 barn, 1 orchard, 120 a. ar. & 20 a. mw. in Pentlowe. 410 mks.

15. Eas. Geo. Niccolls, esq., pl. Nich. Ereswell, def. 6 a. ar. in Walden. £40.

16. Eas. Tho. Thompson, pl. *Charles* Howarde, K. G., lord Howarde of Effingham, & w. Kath., def. The manor of Shalford, & 30 mess., 10 tofts, 300 a. ar., 30 a. mw., 200 a. pa., 10 a. wd., 20 a. furze & heath & £20 rt. in Shalford, Wetherfeld & Finchfeld & free fishing in Shalford, Wetherfeld & Finchfeld. £200.

17. Eas. Edw. Hubberd, gent., pl. Edw. earl of Oxford, great chamberlain, def. The manor of Bentfeld Burye, & 20 mess., 20 tofts, 1 mill, 2 dovecotes, 20 gdns., 1,000 a. ar., 100 a. mw., 500 a. pa., 200 a. wd. & £20 rt. in Stansted Mowntfitchett, Farneham, Mallendyne, Uggley, Elsenham & Takeley, Warranty by def. against himself, his heirs & the heirs of his father, Jn. late earl of Oxford, decd. £400. (*Note added*: registered in the Treasury, 26 Elizabeth I.)

18. Eas. Steph. Wapoole *alias* Nobbes, pl. *Anth*. Maxey, esq., & w. Dorothy, *Tho*. Forde & w. Eliz., def. 1 mess., 1 gdn., 1 orchard, 36 a. ar. & 4 a. pa. in Little Salyng *alias* Bardfeld Salyng. £100.

19. Eas. Rd. Stonley, esq., pl. Edw. earl of Oxford, great chamberlain, def. The manor of Dodinghurst *alias* Doddinghurst, & 20 mess., 20 gdns., 200 a. ar., 30 a. mw., 200 a. pa., 100 a. wd., 20 a. furze & heath, 100s. rt. & rt. of 1 capon in Dodinghurst *alias* Dodding-hurst, Stondon, Blakamoore, Keldon *alias* Kelvedon, Mountnezing & Bentley, view of frankpledge in Dodinghurst *alias* Doddinghurst & the advowson of the church of Dodding-hurst *alias* Doddinghurst. Warranty by def. against himself, his heirs & the heirs of his father, Jn. late earl of Oxford, decd. £360.

20. Eas. Roger James, pl. *Tho*. Spaighte & w. Coniera, def. 1 mess., 1 barn, 1 toft, 10 a. mw. & 2 a. pa. in Westham & Strotforde Langthorne. £120.

21. Eas. Agnes Upcheir, wid., pl. Hy. Reade & w. *Eliz*., def. 2 mess., 20 a. ar., 3 a. marsh & 6d. rt. in Fordham. £40.

22. Eas. Tho. Godsalff, pl. *Jn.* Holmested, gent., & w. Margt., def. 90 a. ar., 7 a. mw. & 12 a. pa. in Great Maplested & Little Maplested. Warranty by def. against themselves, John's heirs, the heirs of Edm. Felton, esq., decd., against Eliz., his wid., Jn. Scudamore, esq., & his hiers. 400 mks.

23. Eas. Tho. Skynner, pl. Robt. earl of Leicester, def. The manors of Wansted *alias* Waunsted & Stonehall, & 43 mess., 2 mills, 4 dovecotes, 43 gdns., 800 a. ar., 270 a. mw., 800 a. pa., 340 a. wd., 1,000 a. furze & heath, 30 a. marsh & 100s. rt. in Wansted *alias* Waunsted, Barkynge, Stonehall, Woodforde, Waltham Stoe, Layton & Ilford & the advowson of the church of Wansted *alias* Waunsted. £400.

24. Eas. Robt. Rewse & Jn. Garrold *alias* Bocher, pl. *Jn.* Freer, gent., & w. Bridget, def. 2 a. ar., 10 a. pa. & 7 a. wd. in Little Gelham. Def. quitclaimed to pl. & the heirs of Robt. £40.

25. Eas. Tho. Herd, pl. Wm. More, kt., def. 1 mess., 3 tofts, 1 gdn., 1 orchard, 80 a. ar. & 12 a. pa. in Harlowe. Warranty by def. against himself, his heirs & the heirs of Wm. Sworder, decd. £160.

26. Eas. Ja. Rowbothum, pl. *Robt.* Hearde & w. Bertlina, def. 1 mess., 1 cott., 1 gdn., 1 orchard, 40 a. ar. & 20 a. pa. in Upmynster. 200 mks.

27. Eas. Edw. Hunt, gent., pl. *Charles* Howarde, K. G., lord Howarde of Effingham, & w. Kath., def. 1 mess., 1 gdn., 1 orchard, 10 a. ar., 20 a. mw. & 100 a. pa. in Ultinge & Langforde. £160.

28. Eas. Rd. Brooke & Nich. Lambert, pl. Edw. earl of Oxford, great chamberlain, def. 1 mess., 2 cotts., 2 tofts, 1 dovecote, 3 gdns., 80 a. ar., 20 a. mw., 80 a. pa., 60 a. wd., 20 a. furze & heath, 10 a. marsh & common pa. for all animals in Stowes Maris *alias* Stoe *alias* Stoke *alias* Stocke, Purleigh *alias* Purley *alias* Pulye, Mundon *alias* Munden, Woodham Mortymer, Lawlinge, Woodham Ferrys, Danbury *alias* Dandbury *alias* Danbery-on-the-Hill, Norton *alias* Coldenorton, Northffambridge *alias* Northfanbridge, Hulbridge, South annyngfeild, Est Hannyngfeild, Southfambridge, Hockley, Rawreth & Rettindon *alias* Rettinden. Def. quitclaimed to pl. & the heirs of Rd. Warranty by def. against himself, his heirs & the heirs of his father, Jn. late earl of Oxford. dec. 130 mks.

29. Eas. Wm. Rochester, pl. *Francis* Fortescue, esq., & w. Dorothy, def. The manor of Okenden Fee *alias* Owles Hill, & 8 a. ar., ½ a. pa. & 62s. 3d. rt. in Tarlinge. £80.

30. Eas. Robt. Petre, esq., pl. *Charles* Howarde, K. G., lord Howarde of Effingham & w. Kath., def. The manor of Thaxstede *alias* Thaxted, & 10 mess., 20 cotts., 1 dovecote, 10 gdns., 10 orchards, 200 a. ar., 100 a. mw., 200 a. pa., 20 a. wd., 50 a. furze & heath & £6 rt. in Thaxstede *alias* Thaxted, the rectory of Thaxstede *alias* Thaxted *alias* Priors Hall, all tithes whatsoever in Thaxstede *alias* Thaxted & the advowson of the church of Thaxstede *alias* Thaxted. £400.

31. Morrow of Trin. 21 Elizabeth, & Eas. 22 Elizabeth. Edw. Robgent, pl. Jn. Fawkes & w. *Margt.*, def. ½ a. ar. in Stanforde le Hope. £40.

32. Hil. & Eas. Tho. Wrothe, gent., & Wm. Wrothe, gent., pl. Robt. Wrothe, esq., & w. *Susanna*, def. The manor of Luxborowes *alias* Loughborowes, & 4 mess., 4 gdns., 4 orchards, 200 a. ar., 150 a. mw., 160 a. pa., 40 a. wd., 100 a. fresh marsh & 40s. rt. in Chigwell, Barkyng & Dagnam. Def. quitclaimed to pl. & the heirs of Tho. Pl. gtd. prop. to def. to hold of the chief lords for the life of both & survivor, with remainder to the right heirs of Robt. Wrothe to hold of the chief lords.

33. Eas. Jn. Watson, gent., pl. Reg. Smyth, son & heir apt. of Nich. Smyth, gent., def. The manor of Leynehams, & 3 mess., 3 cotts., 3 tofts, 1 dovecote, 3 gdns., 3 orchards, 150 a. ar., 20 a. mw., 150 a. pa., 60 a. wd., 20 a. furze & heath & 40s. rt. in Revenhall *alias* Ruenhall, Cressynge *alias* Kersynge, Bockyng, Breyntree, Stysted & Bradwell. £200.

34. Eas. Edw. Lawrence, gent., pl. Edw. earl of Oxford, great chamberlain, def. The manor of Gubbyons *alias* Gobyons, & 10 mess., 1 dovecote, 10 gdns., 400 a. ar., 100 a. mw., 200 a. pa., 40 a. wd., 20 a. furze & heath, 100 a. rushes (*juncaria*), 400 a. marsh & 100s. rt. in Est Tilbury, West Tylbury & Muckynge & view of frankpledge in Est Tilbury. £600.

35. Eas. Hy. Longe & Tho. Reynolds, pl. *Jn.* Hunwycke & w. Joan, Nich. Moyne & w. *Margt.*, def. 1 mess., 1 gdn. & 4 a. ar. in Stebbynge. Def. quitclaimed to pl. & the heirs of Hy. Pl. gtd. prop. to Nich. & Margt. Moyne & the heirs of Nich. to hold of the chief lords.

36. Eas. Geo. Golding, gent., & w. Mary, pl. Edw. earl of Oxford, great chamberlain, def. The manors of Waltons *alias* Waltuns & Netherhall, & 20 mess., 20 tofts, 4 mills, 12 dovecotes, 100 gdns., 1,000 a. ar., 300 a. mw., 800 a. pa., 400 a. wd., 400 a. furze & heath, 10 a. marsh, £10 rt. & common pa. for all animals in Purleigh *alias* Purley *alias* Purlie, Mundon *alias* Munden, Woodham Mortymer, Lawling, Woodham Ferris, Danbury *alias* Dandbury *alias* Danbery-on-the-Hill, Norton *alias* Colde Norton, Stowe Maris *alias* Stoe *alias* Stoke *alias* Stocke, Northfambridge *alias* Northfanbridge, Gestingthorpe *alias* Gestin- throp *alias* Gesthrop *alias* Gesthorp *alias* Gestrop *alias* Gastlingthrop, Otten Belchamp *alias* Belcham *alias* Otin Belcham Foxhearth, Belcham William *alias* Belchamp William *alias* Water Belcham *alias* Water Belchamp, Belchamp Saynt Pawle *alias* Belcham Saynt Pawle *alias* Powles Belcham, Bulmer, Ovington, Twisted *alias* Twinsted, Stamborne, Til- bery *alias* Tilbury *alias* Tilbery next Clare, Ridgewell *alias* Reddeswell, Little Yeldham *alias* Overyeldham *alias* Little Gelham *alias* Overgelham, Wickham Powle, Codham, Pedmershe, Hulbridge, Southanningfield, Esthanningfield, Southfambridge, Hockeley, Rawreth, Retendon *alias* Retenden, Little Maplested *alias* Little Mapsted, Great Maplested *alias* Great Mapsted, Henningham *alias* Hedingham-at-the-Castle *alias* Castel Henningham *alias* Castel Hedingham, view of frankpledge in Waltons *alias* Waltuns & Netherhall, & the advowson of the church of Gestingthorp *alias* Gestingthrop *alias* Gesthrop. Def. quit- claimed to pl. & the heirs of Geo. Golding. Warranty by def. against himself, his heirs & the heirs of his father, Jn. late earl of Oxford, decd. £320.

CP25(2)/260/22   DIVERS COUNTIES

1. Eas. Rd. Tolson, pl. Jn. Dalston, jun., esq., & w. *Anne*, def. The manor of Bird- broke, & 20 mess., 2 mills, 1 dovecote, 20 gdns., 20 orchards, 1,000 a. ar., 100 a. mw., 300 a. pa., 300 a. wd., 200 a. furze & heath & £10 rt. in Birdbroke, Bumpsted, Stambourne, Fynchingfeild & S- - - - & the advowson of the church of Birdbroke, co. Essex; & prop. in London. Pl. gtd. prop. to def. to hold of the chief lords for the life of both & survivor, with remainder to legitimate heirs of bodies of def., failing whom to the right heirs of Anne Dalston, to hold of the chief lords. — Essex, London.

8. Eas. Wm. Stoughton, gent., & Adrian Stoughton, gent., pl. Lau. Stoughton, esq., & w. *Rose*, def. Prop. in Surr.; & an annual rt. of 40 mks. from the manor of Malgraves, co. Essex. Def. quitclaimed to pl. & the heirs of Wm. 950 mks. — Surr., Essex.

CP25(2)/131/1678   TRINITY, 22 ELIZABETH   1580

1. Morrow of Trin. Jn. Collyn jun., pl. *Jas*. Platt, gent., & w. Bridget, def. 20 a. pa. & 20 a. marsh in Westham. £200.

2. Morrow of Trin. Jn. Collyn, jun., pl. Jn. Mylborne & w. *Joan*, def. 1 mess., 1 gdn. & 1 a. ar. in High Laver. £40.

3. Morrow of Trin. Wm. Stedman, pl. *Jn*. Ownested & w. Avice, def. 1 mess., 1 toft, 1 gdn., 1 orchard & 6 a. pa. in Barkinge. £40.

4. Morrow of Trin. Jn. Barker, pl. *Robt*. Fourthe, esq., & w. Frances, def. 1 mess., 1 gdn., 1 orchard, 50 a. ar., 15 a. mw., 15 a. pa., 6 a. wd. & 4 a. alder in Manyntree, Mystleighe & Lawford. £120.

5. Morrow of Trin. Rd. Brokeman, gent., pl. *Robt*. Williams, clk., & w. Jane, def. 4 mess., 4 gdns. & 1 orchard in Maldon. £80.

6. Morrow of Trin. Rd. Welles, pl. Rd. Samwell, def. 1 mess., 1 barn, 1 curtilage, 1 shop & 2 gdns. in Maldon. £60.

7. Morrow of Trin. Tho. Gent, esq., pl. Edw. Whithed & w. *Agnes*, def. 2 mess., 2 gdns., 2 orchards, 10 a. ar., 4 a. mw. & 10 a. pa. in Bumpsted Steeple & Byrdebroke. £40.

8. Trin. Tho. Bedyngfyld, esq., & Hy. Carvyle, esq., pl. *Jn*. Bernard, gent., & w. Dorothy, Rd. Bernard & Wm. Bernard, def. 2 mess., 2 gdns., 100 a. ar., 12 a. mw. & 20 a. pa. in Halsted. Def. quitclaimed to pl. & the heirs of Tho. £160.

FEET OF FINES FOR ESSEX

9. Morrow of Trin. Miles Lakyn, gent., & Wm. Cosyn, pl. Rd. Stower, def. 1 mess., 1 gdn., 1 orchard, 50 a. ar. & 20 a. pa. in Little Clacton *alias* Little Claston. Def. quitclaimed to pl. & the heirs of Miles. Pl. gtd. prop. to def. & his heirs to hold of the chief lords.

10. Morrow of Trin. Tho. Trotter, pl. *Jn.* Trotter & w. Eliz., def. 1 mess., 1 gdn., 1 orchard & 9 a. ar. in Fyngrythe & Blackmore. £40.

11. Morrow of Trin. Edm. Stane, pl. *Geo* Saunders & w, Margt., Jn. Preston & w. Margery, def. 1 mess., 2 tofts, 2 gdns., 40 a. ar., 10 a. mw., 20 a. pa. & 4 a. wd. in Boreham & Hatfeild Peverell. Warranty by Geo. & Margt. Saunders only. £100.

12. Morrow of Trin. Jn. Josselyn, pl. *Ralph* Turnor & w. Margery, def. 1 mess., 1 barn & 1 gdn. in Brancktrey. £40.

13. Morrow of Trin. Tho. Jollye, clk., pl. *Jn.* Hewson *alias* Parker & w. Mary, def. 1 mess., 1 barn, 1 gdn., 2 orchards, 2 a. ar. & 2 a. pa. in Rayleighe. £40.

14. Trin. Jn. Celye, gent., pl. Philip Broune & w. *Susanna*, Tho. Boyton & w. *Agnes*, def. 1 mess., 1 gdn., 1 curtilage & 4 a. ar. in Fobbyng. £40.

15. Eas. & Morrow of Trin. Jn. Roger, pl. *Edw.* Lawrence, gent., & w. Alice, def. 1 mess., 2 barns, 3 gdns., 80 a. ar., 6 a. mw., 40 a. pa., 7 a. wd. & 15 a. fresh marsh in Westylberye & Muckyng. Warranty by def. against themselves, the heirs of Edw. Lawrence & against Edw. earl of Oxford & his heirs. 220 mks.

16. Trin. Jas. Rychardson, pl. Fitzralph Chamberleyn, esq., def. 40 a. ar., 10 a. mw., 16 a. pa., 2 a. wd. & 4 a. marsh in Lamarshe, Alphamston, Pebmershe & Colne Engayne. £100.

17. Trin. Edw. Benleys, gent., pl. Tho. Powle, esq., def. 1 a. pa. & 33 a. marsh in Barking. £200.

18. Morrow of Trin. Jn. Ball, pl. *Rd.* Hovell *alias* Smythe, gent., & w. Mgy., def. The manor of Woodehowse, & 2 mess., 2 gdns., 60 a. ar., 10 a. mw., 60 a. pa., 20 a. wd., 200 a furze & 10s. rt. in Great Horkesleighe. 130 mks.

19. Eas. & Morrow of Trin. Jn. Celye, gent., pl. *Anne* Lawrence, wid., *Edw.* Lawrence, gent., & w. Alice, def. 1 mess., 1 barn, 3 gdns., 9 a. ar., 5 a. mw., 5 a. pa. & 50 a. fresh marsh in Estylbery. £140.

20. Morrow of Trin. Rd. Branthwaytt, gent., pl. Edw. earl of Oxford, great chamberlain, def. The manor of Fingrith *alias* Fingerith *alias* Fingrith Hall, & 100 mess., 100 gdns., 1,000 a. ar., 400 a. mw., 800 a. pa., 200 a. wd., 200 a. furze & heath & £10 rt. in Fingrith, Blackamore, Dodinghurst, Shenfeild, Thobye, Wryttle, Rockeswell, Frierninge, Ingerston, Kelden, Margettinge, Highehonger, Stondon and Norton Mandevyle, & a fair in Fingrith. Warranty by def. against himself, his heirs & the heirs of his father, Jn. late earl of Oxford, decd. £200.

21. Eas. & Morrow of Trin. Jn. Gurdon, esq., & Tho. Appleton, gent., pl. Isaak Wyncoll, gent., def. The manors of Twynsted & Harvard, & 6 mess., 6 gdns., 220 a. ar., 50 a. mw., 200 a. pa., 100 a. wd., 10 a marsh, 20 a. alder, & 60s. rt. in Twynsted, Great Hennye, Bulmer, Pebmershe, Alphampston, Lammershe, Rayley, Hockley & Rawreth. Def. quitclaimed to pl. & the heirs of Jn. £480.

22. Eas. & Morrow of Trin. Jn. Wyseman, esq., pl. Edw., earl of Oxford, great chamberlain, def. The manor of Great Canfeild, & 100 mess., 20 cotts., 20 tofts, 2 mills, 1 dovecote, 100 gdns., 1,500 a. ar., 260 a. mw., 1,000 a. pa., 100 a. wd., 100 a. furze & heath & 100s. rt. in Great Canfeild, Little Canfeild, Muche Dunmowe, Hatfeild Brodock, High Rodinge, Eythrop Rodinge, Eyston, Brocksted & Takeley, free warren in Great Canfeild & view of frankpledge in Great Canfeild. Warranty by def. against himself, his heirs & the heirs of his father, Jn., late earl of Oxford, decd. 400 mks.

23. Morrow of Trin. Tho., earl of Suss., Hy. Sydney, K. G., & Wm. Fitzwilliams, kt., pl. Tho. Eden, esq., def. The manors of Lacheley & Ryes, & 4 mess., 3 tofts, 3 cotts., 1 dovecote, 4 gdns., 4 orchards, 300 a. ar., 50 a. mw., 200 a. pa., 100 a. wd., 60 a. furze & heath & 60s. rt. in Bumpsted Steeple, Hemsted, Little Henney & Great Henney, & the advowson of the church of Little Henney. Def. quitclaimed to pl. & the heirs of the earl of Suss. £800.

24. Morrow of Trin. Jn. Innewe, pl. Arthur Gilgate, gent., & w. Margery & *Robt.* Vigorus, def. 1 mess., 1 gdn. & 1 orchard in Bockinge. £40.

25. Morrow of Trin. Tho. Frenche & Tho. Anneys *alias* Smythe, pl. Edw. Heron. esq., & w. *Anne*, def. 1 mess., 3 gdns., 70 a. ar., 7 a. mw., 49 a. pa., 22 a. wd., 15d. rt. & rt. of 3 capons in Byrdebroke & Fynchingfelde. Def. quitclaimed to pl. & the heirs of Tho. Frenche. 200 mks.

26. Morrow of Trin. Israel Amyce, gent., & Wm. Tyffyn, gent., pl. Edw., earl of Oxford, great chamberlain, def. The manor of Colnewake *alias* Wakes Colne, & 20 mess., 10 tofts, 1 water-mill, 1 dovecote, 20 gdns., 200 a. ar., 30 a. mw., 200 a. pa., 10 a. wd. & 60s. rt. in Colnewake *alias* Wakes Colne, Erles Colne *alias* Colne Comitis, Colne Engayne *alias* Gaynes Colne, Colne Alba *alias* Whyght Colne, Great Tayne, Little Tayne, Fordham, Pontesbright *alias* Chapell Paryshe & Bures Mount, view of frankpledge in Colne Wake *alias* Wakes Colne & the advowson of the church of Colne Wake *alias* Wakes Colne, Def. quitclaimed to pl. & the heirs of Wm. Warranty by def. against himself. his heirs of Wm. Warranty by def against himself, his heirs, all claimants & the heirs of his father, Jn., late earl of Oxford, decd. 400 mks.

27. Morrow of Trin. Adam (*Adamus*) Trigge, pl. Robt. Broke, gent., & w. *Eliz.*, def. 4 mess., 1 barn, 1 dovecote, 3 gdns., 3 orchards, 14 a. ar. & 18½ a. pa. in Crishall *alias* Cristishall and a fourth part of 1 mess., 1 gdn., 1 orchard, 4 a. ar. & 2 a. pa. in Crishall *alias* Cristishall. £80.

28. Morrow of Trin. Wm. Stubbinge, pl. Edw., earl of Oxford, great chamberlain, def. The manor of Bumpsted Hall, & 20 mess., 20 gdns., 1,000 a. ar., 100 a. mw., 500 a. pa., 40 a. wd. & £6 rt. in Bumpsted Helyon *alias* Earl's Bumpsted, Bumpsted Steeple & Hempsted. Pl. gtd. def. & his heirs an annuity of £30 from the prop.

29. Morrow of Trin. Tho. Spicer, pl. Jas. Harris & w. *Alice*, Walter Harris & w. *Wenefrida*, def. 4 mess., 4 gdns., 4 orchards, 5 a. ar., 2 a. mw. & 10 a. pa. in Southbem-flete & Woodham Ferris. Pl. gtd. 3 mess., 3 gdns. & 3 orchards to Jas. & Alice Harris to hold of the chief lords for life of both & survivor, with remainder to the right heirs of Alice. Pl. gtd. the rest of the prop. to Walter & Wenefrida Harris to hold of the chief lords for life of both & survivor, with remainder to the right heirs of Wenefrida.

30. Trin. Josias Clerke, gent., pl. *Edw*. Hubberd, esq., & w. Jane & Rd. Clerke, def. 24 a. wd. in Stansted Mountfitchett. Pl. gtd. prop. to Rd. Clerke for and his heirs. Pl. gtd. prop. to Rd. Clerke for 2,000 years at rent of 3s. 4d. a year, with reversion to Edw. & Jane Hubberd to hold of the chief lords.

CP25(2)/260/22 Eliz. Trin.   DIVERS COUNTIES

5. Morrow of Trin. Jn. Cheyney, sen., esq., pl. Wm. Rowe, esq., def. The manor of Higham Bensted *alias* Higham Bempstede *alias* Higham Hill, & 2 mess., 2 cotts., 4 tofts, 1 dovecote, 4 gdns., 20 a. ar., 40 a. mw., 30 a. pa. & 5s. rt. in Walthamstewe & Chynkford, co. Essex; & prop. in Mdx. £480. — Essex. Mdx.

CP25(2)/131/1679   MICHAELMAS, 22-23 ELIZABETH   1580

1. Mich. Geo. Cressener, pl. Sibil Reighnolde, wid., def. 1 mess. & 1 gdn. in Colne Comitis *alias* Earles Colne. £40.

2. Mich. Robt. Hearde, pl. *Robt.* Tayler & w. Agnes, def. 2 mess., 2 cotts., 10 a. ar., 6 a. mw. & 40 a. pa. in Upmynster & Southwelde. £140.

3. Mich. Hy. Palmer, pl. *Edw.* Suliarde, esq., & w. Anne, def. The manor of Deweshall, & 4 mess., 2 gdns., 300 a. ar., 50 a. mw., 100 a. pa., 40 a. wd. & 20s. rt. in Lamborne, Theydon Boyse & Abrydge. £200.

4. Mich. Tho. Walford, pl. *Tho*. Anson & w. Mary, def. 1 mess., 1 gdn., 6 a. ar., 2 a. mw. & 4 a. pa. in Wethersfild. Warranty by Tho. Anson only. £40.

5. Mich. Rd. Welles, pl. Rd. Samwell & w. Anne, def. 1 mess. & 2 gdns. in Maldon. £40.

6. Mich. Simon Pasfild, pl. Tho. Hardinge & w. *Joan*, def. 1 mess. & 1 gdn. in Wytham. £20.

7. Mich. Tho. Tey, esq., pl. Jn. Searles & w. *Anne*, def. 1 mess., 10 a. pa. & 3 a. wd. in Layer Delahay. £80.

8. Mich. Walter Myldmay, esq., pl. Jn. Christmas, gent., def. The manor of Downehall, & 2 mess., 2 gdns., 200 a. ar., 12 a. mw., 100 a. pa., 20 a. wd., 300 a. marsh & 30s. rt. in Bradwell-by-the-sea, Tyllyngham & Seynt Lawrence. £360.

9. Mich. Jn. Brett, pl. *Rd.* Raynoldes & w. Mary, def. 1 mess., 1 barn, 1 gdn., 1 orchard, 12 a. ar., 2 a. mw., 4 a. pa. & 2 a. wd. in Purleigh *alias* Purley. £40.

10. Mich. Nich. Hollowaye, pl. *Jn.* Somner & w. Elianor, def. 1 mess., 1 gdn. & 3 a. ar. in Eppyng. £40.

11. Mich. Alexander Feast, pl. Jn. Lacye & w. *Margery*, def. 1 mess. & 1 gdn. in Bockyng. Warranty by def. first for two-fifths, then for the remaining three-fifths of the prop. against all men. £40.

12. Mich. Geo. Willmer, pl. *Tho.* Warner & w. Magdalene, def. 12 a. marsh in Westham. £140.

13. Mich. Geo. Ilett, pl. Tho. Ramsey, def. 1 mess., 1 gdn. & 1 orchard in Byrchanger. £40.

14. Mich. Jn. Camber, pl. *Jn.* Celye, gent., & w. Rachel, def. 1 mess., 1 barn, 3 gdns., 9 a. ar., 5 a. mw., 5 a. pa. & 50 a. fresh marsh in Estylbery. £140.

15. Mich. Arthur Herrys, esq., pl. Wm. Grome, def. A moiety the manor of Ulhams & a moiety of 1 mess., 100 a. ar., 40 a. mw., 100 a. pa., 10 a. wd. & 100 a. marsh in Lachindon, Lawlyng, Purlegh & Colenorton. £400.

16. Mich. Jn. Whyacres, pl. *Rd.* Lyttle & w. Agnes, def. 1 mess., 1 dovecote, 1 barn, 1 gdn., 1 orchard, 2 a. ar., & 20s. rt. in Mannyngtree & Wrabnes & free fishing in Mannyngtree, Wrabnes & Ramzey. £40.

17. Mich. Robt. Salmon, pl. *Hy.* Dore & w. Alice, def. 1 mess., 1 barn, 1 gdn, 1 orchard, 20 a. ar., 4 a. mw. & 18. a. pa. in Nevyngdon. 130 mks.

18. Mich. Geo. Remonde, pl. *Matthew* Raine & w. Eliz., def. 1 mess., 1 gdn., 1 orchard, 20 a. ar., 4 a. mw., 6 a. pa. & 2 a. wd. in Stebinge. £40.

19. Mich. Hy. Holwey, pl. *Walter* Holwey & w. Jocosa, def. 1 mess., 1 gdn. & 2 a. ar. in Eppinge. £40.

20. Mich. Jn. Watson, esq., pl. Jn. Pease & w. *Frances*, def. A fourth part of 3 mess., 6 gdns., 3 orchards, 20 a. ar., 6 a. mw., 18 a. pa. & 6 a. wd. in Ryvenhall *alias* Ruynhall, Cressynge & Braxsted. 130 mks.

21. Mich. Tho. Twydd, pl. *Jn.* Beale & w. Sarah, def. 1 mess. & 1 quay (*kaius*) in Hartwyche. £40.

22. Mich. Geoff. Cokoe & w. Rose, pl. *Robt.* Wordisworthe, gent., & w. Joan, def. 1 mess., 1 toft, 1 gdn., 10 a. ar. & 18 a. pa. in Great Byrche *alias* Muche Byrche. Def. quitclaimed to pl. & the heirs of Geoff. Warranty by def. against themselves, the heirs of Robt. & the heirs of Wm. Poore, decd. £40.

23. Mich. Jn. Quodwell & Ralph Northey, pl. *Wm.* Weet *alias* Turner & w. Alice, def. 28 a. ar. & 1 a. pa. in Pebmershe & Alphamston. Def. quitclaimed to pl. & the heirs of Jn. £100.

24. Mich. Jn. Wakeman, pl. *Edm.* Churche, gent., & w. Dorothy, def. 1 mess., 1 gdn., 1 orchard, 6 a. ar., 3 a. mw., 37 a. pa. & 2 a. wd. in Tyllingham. £80.

25. Mich. Tho. Ive, gent., pl. *Ralph* Wyseman, esq., & w. Eliz., def. 2 mess., 1 toft, 1 dovecote, 2 barns, 2 gdns., 2 orchards, 100 a. ar., 20 a. mw., 60 a. pa., 10 a. wd., 100 a. furze & heath, 20 a. marsh, 20s. rt. & free fishing in Great Totham, Little Totham & Heybridge. £160.

26. Mich. Tho., earl of Suss., pl. *Ralph* Wyseman, esq., & w. Eliz., def. The manor of Belsted Hall, & 1 mess., 1 toft, 1 gdn., 100 a. ar., 10 a. mw., 100 a. pa., 20 a. wd. & 20 a. furze & heath in Bromefeild & Spryngfeild. 200 mks.

27. Mich. Tho. Roper, esq., & Anth. Roper, esq., pl. Tho. Ive, gent., def. 2 mess., 1 toft, 1 dovecote, 2 barns, 2 gdns., 2 orchards, 100 a. ar., 20 a. mw., 60 a. pa., 10 a. wd., 100 a. furze & heath, 20 a. marsh, 20s. rt. & free fishing in Great Totham, Little Totham & Heybridge. £160.

28. Mich. Anne Latten, pl. *Nich.* Adam & w. Margt., def. 1 mess., 1 gdn. & 9 a. ar. in Thaxted. Warranty by def. against themselves. their heirs, Tho. Boughtell, Jn. Boughtell & their heirs & the heirs of Jn. Boughtell, decd., father of the said Jn. £40.

29. Mich. Mathew Dale, esq., pl. Jn. Avery, gent., def. The manor of Colnigayne *alias* Gaynes Colne, & 10 mess., 1 mill, 400 a. ar., 100 a. mw., 100 a. pa., 20 a. wd., 200 a. furze & heath & 40s. rt. in Gaynes Colne, Wakes Colne, Chappell, Fordham & Earles Colne, & the advowson of the church of Gaynes Colne. £400.

30. Mich. Robt. Harryngton, clk., pl. Tho. Reve, gent., & w. *Agnes*, def. All tithes whatsoever in the manors of Graveshall & Bloyes & in 606 a. ar. in Hengham Sible *alias* Henyngham Sibble. Warranty by def. against themselves, the heirs of Agnes & the heirs of Mark Stroude, decd. 160 mks.

31. Mich. Wm. Croxeston, pl. *Jn.* Rewce & w. Frances, def. 1 mess., 4 a. ar., 1 a. mw. & 5 a. pa. in Ramsdon Craies. £40.

32. Mich. Annastacia Hale, pl. Margery Ball, wid., def. A moiety of 2 mess., 2 gdns. & 1 orchard in All Saints parish in the town of Maldon. £40.

33. Mich. Robt. Williams, pl. *Barnard* Wyttam & w. Thomasina, def. 2 mess., 3 tofts, 2 barns, 60 a. ar., 20 a. mw., 60 a. pa., 40 a. fresh marsh & 100 a. salt marsh in Tillingham & Denge *alias* Dengye. £200.

34. Mich. Tho. Ussher & Jn. Nashe, pl. Jn. Reve & w. *Alice*, def. 1 mess., 1 barn, 1 gdn. & 1 orchard in Wethersfield. Def. quitclaimed to pl. & the heirs of Tho. £40.

35. Mich. Anth. Everarde, gent., pl. *Jn.* Lathum, gent., & w. Helen, *Robt.* Gooddaye & w. Joan, def. 3 mess., 3 cotts., 3 barns, 3 gdns., 50 a. ar., 20 a. mw., 40 a. pa., 4 a. wd. & 2s. rt. in Sandon. £100.

36. Mich. Nich. Umfrye & Pet. Purcas, pl. Jn. Goldynge, def. 1 mess., 2 gdns., 2 orchards, 40 a. ar., 6 a. mw. & 10 a. pa. in Thaxsted, Def. quitclaimed to pl. & the heirs of Nich. £80.

37. Mich. Jn. Watson, esq., pl. Arthur Hall & w. *Joan*, def. 3 mess., 2 gdns., 2 orchards, 10 a. ar. & 24 a. pa. in Colchester & Myleend next Colchester. £40.

38. Mich. Tho. Nicolson, pl. *Jn.* Nicolson & w. Margt., def. A moiety of 20 a. ar., 6 a. mw., 10 a. pa. & 6 a. wd. in Halsted & Gosfeild. £40.

39. Mich. Jn. Gallilie *alias* Gallie, gent., & w. Eliz., pl. *Wm.* Bowlinge & w. Rose, def. 6 a. ar., 6 a. mw. & 6 a. pa. in Walden. Def. quitclaimed to pl. & the heirs of Jn. Warranty by def. against themselves, the heirs of Wm. & against Alexander Raye, gent., & w. Eliz. 130 mks.

40. Mich. Jn. Huttyspurre, pl. *Tho.* Luter & w. Philippa, *Rd.* Luter & w. Eliz., def. 2 mess., 3 tofts, 3 gdns., 80 a. ar., 8 a. mw., 10 a. pa. & 2 a. wd. in Highester & Aythorpe Rothynge. Warranty, separately, by Tho. & Rd. Luter only. £200.

41. Mich. Anne Latten, pl. *Alan* Raymond & w. Agnes, def. 9 a. ar., 9 a. pa. & 1 a. wd. in Thaxten. Warranty by def. against themselves, the heirs of Alan, against Tho. Boutell & Jn. Boutell & their heirs, & against the heirs of Jn. Boutell, decd., father of Jn. £40.

42. Mich. Robt. Newdigate, esq., & Tho. Newdigate, gent., pl. *Rd.* Crafforde, esq., & w. Anne, def. The manor of Dovers *alias* Dover *alias* Dovors, & 3 mess., 1 dovecote, 6 gdns., 200 a. ar., 100 a. mw., 300 a. pa., 40 a. wd., 200 a. marsh & £10 rt. in Hornechurche & Bowers Gifford. Def. quitclaimed to pl. & the heirs of Robt. Pl. gtd. prop. to def. & Richard's heirs to hold of the chief lords.

43. Mich. Jas. Wallenger, gent., pl. Wm. Knight & w. *Grace*, def. 2 mess., 2 tofts, 1 dovecote, 2 gdns., 2 orchards, 43 a. ar., 22 a. mw., 52 a. pa., 11 a. wd. & common pa. for all livestock in Navestock *alias* Nastock & Moreton *alias* Moorton. 220 mks.

44. Mich. Wm. Litilberye & w. Joan, pl. *Wm.* Maynard & w. Anne, def. 8 a. ar. & 4 a. pa. in Stysted. Def. quitclaimed to pl. & the heirs of Wm. £40.

45. Mich. Chris. Henworth, gent., & Robt. Boggas, gent., pl. Arthur Barners, esq., def. The manors of Dyves & Peches, & 6 mess., 10 cotts., 4 barns, 1 windmill, 1 dovecote, 200 a. ar., 60 a. mw., 200 a. pa., 40 a. wd., 100 a. furze & heath & £6 13s. 4d. rt. in Fynchingfeld & Wethersfeld. Def. quitclaimed to pl. & the heirs of Chris. £220.

46. Mich. Wm. Lynne, gent., pl. Anth. Crowebrooke & w. *Anne*, Benj. Clerke & w. *Anne*, def. 3 mess., 3 gdns., 3 orchards, 60 a. ar., 3 a. mw., 10 a. wd. & 3 a. reeds (*iuncar'*) in Great Horkesley, Little Horkesley & Wormyngforde. £100.

47. Mich. Chris. Chibborne, esq., Edw. Larence & Geo. Abbott, gent., Tho. Shawarden, citizen & grocer of London, & Jn. Shawarden, gent., pl. *Ralph* Wyseman, esq., & w. Eliz., def. 24 a. pa. in Horndon-on-the-Hill. Def. quitclaimed to pl. & the heirs of Chris. £58.

48. Mich. Jn. Payne jun., & w. Eliz., pl. *Jn.* Payne sen., & w. Eliz., def. 60 a. ar., 10 a. mw., 60 a. pa. & 10 a. wd. in Duddinghurst & Southweald. Def. quitclaimed to pl. & the heirs of Jn. Payne jun. £200.

49. Mich. Jn. Lukyn, gent., & Wm. Brydges, gent., pl. Humfrey Brydges, esq., & Rd. Wyllys, def. 2 mess., 1 barn, 1 gdn., 1 orchard, 40 a. ar., 30 a. mw., 40 a. pa., 20 a. wd. & 10. a. marsh in Rayleigh, Great Mawlden, Little Mawlden, Purleigh, Hadley & Leigh. Def. quitclaimed to pl. & the heirs of Jn. Pl. gtd. prop. to Humfrey Brydges & his heirs to hold of the chief lords.

50. Mich. Tho. Reynolds & Jn. Newman, pl. Wm. Browne & w. Clemencia, def. 2 mess., 1 toft, 4 gdns., 3 orchards, 10 a. ar., 4 a. pa. & 1 a. moor in Stebbynge. Def. quitclaimed to pl. & the heirs of Tho. Pl. gtd. prop. to def. & the heirs of Wm. to hold of the chief lords.

51. Mich. Tho. Walforde, pl. Jn. Sturdyvall & w. *Joan*, Tho. Freston & w. *Eliz*., Tho. Trappes & w. *Alice*, def. 1 mess., 1 gdn., 3 a. ar. & 1 a. mw. in Fynchingfelde. £40.

52. Mich. Jn. Pigot, gent., pl. *Robt.* Riche, kt., lord Riche, & And. Larder, gent., def. 2 mess., 3 tofts, 2 gdns., 200 a. ar., 60 a. mw. & 200 a. pa. in Northweld Bassett. Pl. gtd. prop. to And. Larder for terms of 21 years from Michaelmas 1583 at annual rt. of £10 with reversion to Robt. Riche to hold of the chief lords.

53. Mich. Jn. Lock, gent., pl. *Giles* Brett of Great Braxted, & w. Anne & Giles Brett of Tolleshunt Maior, def. 1 mess., 16 a. ar., 2 a. mw., 12 a. pa. & 20 a. marsh in Goldanger & Little Totham. Pl. gtd. prop. to Giles Brett of Tolleshunt Maior for term of 21 years from Michaelmas 1584 at annual rt., of 40s. with reversion to Giles & Anne Brett of Braxted Magna to hold of the chief lords.

CP25(2)/260   DIVERS COUNTIES

5. Mich. Wm. Cecyll, kt., lord Burghley, treasurer, pl. *Wm*. Franckland & w. Hester & *Hugh* Franckland, def. prop. in Hertford; & 12 a mw. in Roydon, co. Essex. Warranty by def. against themselves, the heirs of Wm. & Hugh Franckland & the heirs of Wm. Franckland, decd., William's father. £80. — Hertford, Essex.

18. Mich. Edw. Byrde, gent., pl. Wm. Byrde, gent., & w. *Alice*, def. A moiety of the manor of Bassingbornes, & 10 mess., 10 cotts., 200 a. ar., 100 a. mw., 200 a. pa., 40 a. wd. & £8 rt. in Takeley, co. Essex; and prop. in Warws., Worcester & Leicester. Pl. gtd. prop. to def. & the legitimate heirs of their bodies to hold of the chief lords, with remainder to heirs of William's body, failing whom all save certain props. in Worcester & Leicester to right heirs of Alice: the excepted prop. to remain to Tho. Umpton, Mary Umpton & Anne Umpton children of Jasper Umpton & the heirs of their bodies, failing whom to right heirs of Tho. Umpton. — Warwick, Worcester, Essex, Leicester.

INDEX OF PLACES

Editorial notes. (1) To help readers identify the parishes in which many strange names of manors occur, these have been cross-referenced in their Calendar forms to their respective parishes. (2) Only major variants in spelling are noted. (3) Names of messuages and streets (but not fields) are indexed. (4) The modern forms of parishes and hamlets are used. (5) Non-Essex parishes/manors are indexed *only* under their counties. (6) Where more than one reference appears on a page, it is denoted by '(2)', etc. (7) 'm' denotes manor, 'adv.' denotes advowson. See also *Abbreviations* at head of *Text*.

Abberton (Aburton), 22, 51(2), 62, 67, 134, 163(2), 170, 198.
Abbatts Bury *alias* Rowletts Bury see Chishall, Gt.
Abbotts *alias* Edlynges m. see Mistley.
Abells m. see Halstead.
Abelswyke m. see Ardleigh.
Abridge see Lambourne.
Acresflete Marsh m. see Canewdon.
Adams see Belchamp St. Paul.
Adyncars see Dagenham.
Affebridge see Lambourne.
Albrugh Hatche see Ilford.
Albynes *alias* Allynes m. see Stapleford. Abbots.
Aldham, 24(2), 37, 39, 48, 126, 150, 158, 164(3), 180(2), 209, 215(2), 222.
Aldorney see Althorne.
Aldresbroke m. see Ilford, Lt., and Wanstead.
Alfernayshe see Wallasea Island.
Algaays m. see Althorne.
'Almans' *alias* 'Durants' see Margaretting.
Alphamstone, 9, 66, 109, 126, 178, 186, 228, 238(2), 240; Motehall m., 186.
Alresford (Allerford), 9, 13, 14, 16, 23, 26, 43, 58(3), 67, 210; m., 58; adv., 58 58; A. Ford, 58.
Althorne (Aldorney), 2, 7, 15, 19, 20, 38, 46, 50(2), 52(2), 61, 64, 86, 94, 111, 123, 125, 128, 154, 165, 170, 171(2), 180, 215(2), 227; Algaays m., 38; Dykers m., 38; Herons *alias* Countys-brydge 61; Lytteryn m., 38; Stockys (Stoke Hall) m., 38.
Alvelegh see Aveley.
Amberden see Debden.
Ameys m. see Horndon, East.
Amours *alias* Heath Place m. see Orsett.
Appletons m. see Bulphan and Chigwell.
Archiers m. see Rivenhall.
Arden Hall m. see Horndon-on-the-Hill.
Ardleigh, 3, 6, 18, 20, 40, 44, 47, 66(2), 68, 69, 76, 89, 91, 95(20), 113(2), 117, 123, 127, 130, 145, 155, 156, 164(3), 167, 168, 179, 184, 195, 196, 200, 208(2), 209, 214(2), 216, 220, 224, 226, 227, 228; Abelswyke m., 66, 156; Badleyhall m., 66, 95; Bovills m., 227; Moysehall m., 164(3), 228.

Ardley see Hornchurch.
Arkesden, 8, 27, 44, 45, 52, 62, 100(2), 103, 109, 127, 134, 142, 144, 162, 163, 168(2), 177, 224; Mynchions (? Mynchinbury) m., 100(2), 164; adv., 100.
Arnoldes Hall m. see Mountnessing.
Arundells Marsh see Foulness.
Ashdon (Asshedowne, Assheton), 2, 5, 14, 37, 44, 45, 46, 59, 76, 85, 88, 114(3), 120, 122, 128, 132, 138, 143, 162(2), 172, 196(3), 201(2), 211, 216, 229; Loundres (or Londess) m., 2; Newenham Hall *alias* Newnam Hall m., 85; Thykkoo m.. 2.
Asheldham (Asheldame, Ashldon), 5, 17, 32, 65, 146, 166, 180, 195, 213, 221, 222, 234; Bodneke m., 65, 166; Newhall m., 91, 130.
Ashen (Atshe, Esse), 5, 63(2), 75, 150, 185, 188, 193, 205, 233; Clarett Hall m., 63.
Ashingdon (Asschyngdon), 5, 10, 15, 39, 63, 77, 163, 180, 213, 233.
Asshewell Hall m. see Finchingfield.
Audleyend see Walden, Saffron.
Aungevynes wd. see Langham *and* Boxted.
Austeyns (unidentified), perhaps Ramsey or Oakley, Gt., 82.
Aveley (Auflye), 2, 9, 13, 18, 19, 37, 62, 66, 75, 88, 106, 114, 115, 140, 151, 166, 171, 173, 181(2), 185, 187, 201, 204(2), 228, 229, 231, 233; Kennyngton m., 9(2), 229; Spaynes Marsh, 75; 'Courts', 75; 'Banks', 75.
Ayshe see Ashen.
Ayston (Aiston, Aston) see Easton, Gt. and Lt.

Babyngworth see Bobbingworth.
Bacons m. see Mountnessing, Tey, Gt. and Chapel (Pontesbright).
Baddow, Gt. (Baddo, Badewe), 1, 2, 5, 18, 21, 24(2), 26, 30(2), 32(2), 33, 34, 49, 58, 74, 97, 98, 101, 104, 109, 110(2), 118(2), 123, 132, 135, 140, 151, 170, 172, 191, 204, 213, 227(2), 230; Sabryghts (Seabrights), 1, 26, 135; Syr Hewghes *alias* Hughes Stisteds m., 18, 33(2), 98.

Benfleet, 46, 154.
Benfleet, North (Northbemflete), 60, 61,
96, 213, 218, 222, 234; Barfilds *alias*
Bardevyles m., 61; Bradfeildes m., 147;
Cocksalls m., 213, 222, 234; adv., 213,
218, 222, 234.
Benfleet, South, 14, 30, 36, 58, 106, 110,
157, 171, 182, 192, 213, 216, 218,
222, 234, 239.
Benningtons or Benyngtons see Witham.
Bensted see Walthamstow.
Bentfyld Bury see Stansted Mountfichet.
Bentley see Weald, South.
Bentley, Gt., 2, 9(2), 14, 15, 45, 72, 117,
125, 137, 154, 163, 181, 205, 219,
235; Whelars m., 117(2).
Bentley, Lt., 9, 15, 66, 95, 125, 129, 137,
163, 181, 206; m., 206.
Bentons *alias* Benyngton m. see Witham.
Beremans m. see Chignall Smealey.
Berden (Byerden, Barden), 10, 67, 68, 96,
103, 126, 135, 142, 163, 206, 212.
Berechurch see West Donyland.
Bergholt, West, 2, 17, 27, 69, 71, 73(2),
107, 113, 154, 157(2), 169(2), 191(2),
222; Ba(e)rholt Sackvile m., 17, 154,
157, 169, 191, 222; Commes *alias*
Combes m., 18; adv., 157.
Berkelowe see Bartlow.
Berkshire, 9, 107, 165, 176, 234.
Berthall m. see Colne, White.
Berwykes m. see Stanford Rivers.
Billericay (Billeryca) see Burstead, Gt.
Billingtons m. see Ockendon, North.
Birch, 179.
Birch, Gt. (Muche Burche), 25(4), 56, 78,
79, 108, 110, 118, 128, 129(2), 131,
139, 150, 152, 164(2), 169(2), 177,
179, 180(2), 184, 188, 197, 211,
215(2), 216(2), 227, 228, 229, 234(2),
235, 240; Birch, Gt. m., 110, 227, 235;
Holts m., 79; Goodwyns, 25; Lucassys,
25; rectory, 113.
Birch, Lt., 25(3), 78, 79, 108, 110, 118(2),
129, 131(2), 152, 164(2), 169, 179,
184, 211, 229, 234(2); adv., 108, 118;
m., 108, 118; Oldholt m., 78, 79, 169.
Birchanger (Bartechanger,
By(l)che(h)anger), 7(2), 43, 44, 52, 83,
84, 120, 126(3), 134, 145, 153, 165,
174, 197, 240; Stanstede Myll, 43.
Birdbrook (Brydebroke, Burdebroke,
Byrbroke), 13, 14, 22, 63, 67, 87,
106(5), 138, 155, 209, 222(2), 230,
237(3), 239; adv., 237; m., 237.
Bishop's Wokyndon see Cranham.
Bisshoppwood see Dunmow, Gt.
Blackhall m. see Bobbingworth.
Blackmore (Blakemore), 9, 12, 67, 100,
105, 144, 179, 195(2), 198, 222, 235,
238(2); m., 100; Fynggerett m., 9(2),
179, 238(2); F. fair, 238.
Blamsters m. see Halstead.
Blonteshaull see Witham.

Bloyes m. see Hedingham Sible.
Blumpsters m. see Easton, Gt.
Blumsall (Blunteshall) m. see Witham.
Bobbingworth (Bobymor, Bobynger,
Bubbynger), 5, 6, 21, 28, 57, 99, 106,
166, 195(2), 199; adv., 119, 195, 199;
Babyngworth m., 28; Blackhall m., 99,
106.
Bobulo m. see Bumpstead, Helion.
Bocking (Bokkyng), 4, 6, 7, 8, 10(3),
13(2), 15, 16, 17(2), 25, 27(2), 28(3),
29, 33(2), 35(2), 37, 42, 49, 54, 57(3),
58(4), 59, 60, 62, 68, 70, 73, 74, 76,
77, 79(3), 81, 82, 84, 87, 96, 97,
98(2), 99(2), 109(3), 111, 116, 120,
121, 122(4), 128, 130, 134(2), 136,
137, 139, 140, 143(2), 146, 148,
149(2), 150(2), 152, 154(2), 160, 162,
163, 169, 172, 176, 178, 179, 180,
184, 186, 188, 192, 197(2), 199, 201,
205, 210, 212(2), 216, 218, 219, 221,
222(2), 223, 224, 229(3), 236, 238,
240; Bartelotts, 58; Boones m., 6, 10,
172, 201; Dorewards m., 57; Fennis
m., 111.
Bodneke m. see Asheldham.
Bollingtons m. see Hatfield Broad Oak and
Ugley.
Bonchawte m. see Wicken Bonhunt.
Boones m. see Bocking.
Boreham, 8, 14, 16, 20, 31, 34, 36, 46,
49, 54(2), 55(2), 62, 64, 66, 70, 71,
72, 81, 90, 100, 102, 110, 111(2), 130,
131, 141, 142, 146, 155, 159, 161,
165, 172, 192, 196, 200, 206(2), 211,
214, 226, 238; m., 229; Trowers, 14.
Borley, 15, 131, 168.
Borndewoode see Brentwood.
Borrowes m. see Easter, Good and
Stanford Rivers.
Botelers m. see Broomfield, Bulmer,
Shopland and Yeldham, Gt.
Bounches see Gosfield.
Bourghchiers (Bowers) Hall m. see
Rivenhall and Tollesbury.
Boveldes m. see Clacton, Lt.
Bovildes, Bovills, m. see Witham.
Bowells *alias* Cokk a Bowel m. see Weald,
South.
Bower Haule m. see Bumpstead, Steeple.
Bowers Gifford (Bures Gyfford), 9(2),
14(2), 58, 172, 224, 241.
Bowres m. see Easter, Good.
Bowsers *alias* Little Laver Hall n. see
Laver, Lt.
Boxted (Boxstid), 12, 40, 46, 65(2), 112,
113, 123, 124, 153(2), 190, 201(3),
205(3), 208(3), 227; adv., 124;
Ryvershall m., 190, 201, 205, 208;
Aungevynes wd., 65.
Boys *alias* Dynes m. see Halstead.
Boys Hall m. see Navestock.
Boytons see Finchingfield.
Bradfeildes m. see Benfleet, North.

Eytheroppe Rothinge see Roding, Aythorpe.

Fairstead (Fayersted), 8, 16, 19, 20, 34, 37, 41, 55, 57, 63, 67, 70, 100(2), 102, 112, 131, 142, 146, 149, 155, 192, 196, 223, 227; Walley Hall m., 63.

Fal(ke)born m. see Faulkbourne.

Fambridge, North, 9, 15, 45, 215, 234, 236, 237; ferry, 171, 215.

Fambridge, South, 39, 180, 213, 233, 236, 237.

Fange see Vange.

Farewood Common see Leighs, Gt.

Farnehall see Barking.

Farnham, 38, 64(2), 71, 84(2), 131, 138, 143, 146, 153, 163, 165, 174, 181(2), 191, 194, 195, 228, 233, 235; Hartshoeburye (Hassobury) m., 194, 233; Wykenhamehall m., 181(2).

Faulkbourne (Falbarne, Fawborne), 4, 16, 32, 38, 42, 54, 55, 57, 63, 67, 70, 97, 100, 102, 115, 131, 146(2), 168, 172, 202, 206, 217, 223; adv., 67; m., 67; Blomsham Hall m., 70.

Fawconers m. see Easter, Good.

Fayersted see Fairsread.

Faytes m. see Lawford.

Feering (Feryng), 1, 6, 7, 41, 49, 67, 77, 95, 96, 100, 121, 133, 137, 148, 149, 160, 164(2), 174, 176, 177, 180(2), 181, 184, 187, 198(2),203, 206, 212, 215(2); Fowchings *alias* Howchyns m., 67, 174.

Feldehouse m. see Horndon, West.

Felsted, 4, 13, 17, 33, 34, 42, 61, 66, 79, 103, 111, 134, 135, 155, 172, 201, 211, 228, 232.

Fennis m. see Bocking.

Feryng see Feering.

Fifhide see Fyfield.

Finchingfield (Finchfeld), 4, 15, 20, 33, 41, 42, 62(2), 67, 69, 71, 75, 76, 78, 84(2), 108(2), 116(2), 119, 121, 122, 127(2), 128, 129, 141, 142, 143, 151, 153, 154, 155, 158, 162, 169, 178(2), 179, 190, 202, 210, 215(2), 230(2), 235(2), 237, 239, 241, 242; Asshewell Hall m., 20; Boytons, 190; Brenthall m., 4, 116; Cockfeldes m., 162, 178; Dyves m., 241; Hovells m., 121, 129; Peches m., 241.

Fingringhoe (Fynrygoo), 51(2), 134, 163(2), 170, 198.

Fingrith m. see Blackmore.

Flaundens *alias* Cheswykhall m. see Chrishall.

Flaunderswyke m. see Purleigh.

Fletehall m. see Sutton.

Fobbing, 1, 5, 39(2), 40, 46, 51, 100, 101, 107, 116, 118, 144, 157, 176, 180, 205, 220, 221, 222, 228(2), 234, 238; m., 118, 157.

Folyatt m. see Ongar, High.

Fordham, Gt. and Lt., 2, 9, 29, 30, 49, 71, 126, 152, 154, 157, 179, 184, 191, 197, 211, 222, 234(2), 235, 239, 241.

Foulness Island (Fowlnes, Fulnes), 12(2), 15, 46, 79, 87, 107, 125, 154; adv., 12; Arundells Marsh m., 12; Bradworth (? = Bourgwerth) m., 79; Estwyke m., 12; Foulnes Hall m., 12; Mounkyngbarne m., 12, 121(2); Nesshwyke m., 12; Newyke m., 12; Pottinge (Potton Island), 181, 208; Rogworth m., 12; Rushley, 181; Shelford m., 79; Southwyke m., 12.

Fowches see Totham, Lt.

Fowchyns *alias* Howchyns m. see Feering.

Foxearth (Foxherd), 65, 69, 82, 92, 147, 152, 160, 161, 162, 168, 170, 202, 223, 225, 237; m., 92(3); Brokehall m., 92(3); Carbonells (Cardinal's) m., 160.

Franckes m. see Warley, Gt.

Frating (Fraytyng), 2, 9, 14, 24, 58, 72, 94, 117, 173.

Fraunces m. see Walthamstow.

Freerne (Freine, Frierne) see Purleigh.

Frewells m. see Goldhanger.

Frieninge see Fryerning.

Frinton, 10, 19, 29, 31, 66(2); m., 29; adv., 29.

Frowyke m. see St. Osyth.

Fryerning (Gynghospytall, Ingberners), 21, 160, 162, 238.

Fryers m. see Chishall, Gt.

Fryers Grange m. see Roding, Althorpe.

Fryth Hall m. see Ongar, High.

Fulchars see Easter, Good.

Fulnes see Foulness.

Fyfield (Fyfhide, Fyssechyde), 6, 32, 46, 73, 76, 99, 104, 105, 106(2), 111, 117, 133, 180, 215, 233; Lampytts m., 106, 117.

Fynggerett m. see Blackmore.

Fyssehyde see Fyfield.

Garnetts m. see Easter, High.

Garnonshall (Garnishall) m. see Theydon Garnon.

Garnons m. see Bumpstead, Steeple, Stebbing and Tendring.

Gawgers m. see Belchamp St. Paul.

Gaynsfordes m. see Toppesfield.

Gayshamhall see Barking.

Gedleston see Gestingthorpe.

Gelham see Yeldham.

Gerpyns m. see Rainham.

Gestingthorpe (Geysthrope, Gaslingthrop, Gedleston), 9(3), 17(2), 74, 104, 113, 118, 126, 128, 131, 133, 137(2), 138, 142, 168, 182, 193, 213, 217, 223, 229, 235, 237; adv., 237; Nether Hall m., 9, 237; Odwell m., 128; Overhall m., 142; Parks (Parkys), 9.

Hampton Barnes m. see Stambridge, Gt.

Hamptons (unidentified), 173.

Hannams *alias* Bulleyns m. see Tendring.

Hanningfield, East (sthanyngton), 16, 45, 77, 98, 177, 216, 223, 236, 237.

Hanningfield, South (Hanfeild), 5(2), 16, 22, 51, 57, 77, 86, 89, 96, 152, 167, 177, 209, 216, 230, 236, 237; Prestons m., 89.

Hanningfield, West (Hanfeld), 1, 16, 18, 33(2), 38, 64, 77, 89, 98, 118, 125, 139(2), 144(2), 166, 172, 173(2), 184, 186, 190, 193, 203, 204, 209, 216, 227, 230; Peverells m., 10, 38, 144.

Harbardys m. see Rayleigh.

Harlow, 6, 11, 17, 28, 31, 34, 43, 50, 55, 71, 80, 83, 89, 90, 95, 98, 102, 105, 124, 137, 145, 155, 157, 163, 179, 186, 192, 197, 226, 236; Brent Hall m., 102; H. Bury m., 43; Hulberds Hall m., 80; Kytchyn Hall m., 102; Morehall m., 95; adv., 43.

Harmyrys see Orsett.

Harkested m. see Bumpstead, Steeple.

Hartyshoburye m. see Farnham.

Harvard m. see Rayleigh.

Harvardstoke see Stock.

Harvies see Peldon.

Harwich (Hartwyche), 9, 10, 16, 19, 37, 41, 44(2), 60, 62, 65, 76, 81, 82, 84, 99, 110, 118, 122, 130, 137, 140, 169, 173, 193, 203, 216, 231, 240; quay, salt and fish houses, 37, 81, 240; 'les Tabard', 140.

Haselyth see Hazeleigh.

Hassingbrooke m. see Stanford-le-Hope.

Hassowburye see Farnham.

Hatfield, 175, 192, 223.

Hatfield Broad Oak (Hatfyeld Brodocke, Bradoke, Kingis, Regis), 9, 19, 25, 31(2), 37, 51(2), 66, 69, 83, 89(2), 93, 94(3), 101(2), 102, 104(2), 117, 119(2), 120, 121(3), 125, 126, 139, 140, 141, 152, 161, 167, 192, 207, 216, 238; Barryngton Hall m., 121(2); Bollyngtons m., 101; Brent Hall m., 121; Hatfylde Priorye *alias* Brodoke m., 119, 121; Howses and Morses m., 120; Lee Hall m., 120; Matching Barnes m., 121; former Priory, 121; Ries m., 120; Thomas by the Wood m., 120.

Hatfield Peverel (Hatfeyld Bury), 8, 11, 16, 25, 28, 34, 35, 36(2), 48, 49, 54, 55, 61, 64, 67, 70, 72, 77, 81, 83, 93, 100, 102, 103(2), 111, 118, 121, 131, 146, 159(2), 161, 165, 167(2), 175, 177, 178, 182, 191, 200(3), 206(2), 211, 216, 224, 238; adv., 70; Peverell m., 70, 200; Mugdenhall *alias* Muckledenhall (Mowden Hall) m., 206; site of former Priory, 70, 200.

Hatfield Regis see Hatfield Broad Oak.

Havengore (Island), Rushley, 181.

Haverhill (Haveryll, the part in Essex), 19, 40, 41, 42, 48, 52(2), 55, 102, 105, 106, 119, 150, 151, 170, 174(2), 183(2), 197; see also Suffolk; Curpayles m., 41.

Havering-atte-Bower, 54, 70, 76, 80, 113, 172, 179, 187, 203.

Haverings m. see Rayne.

Hawkwell (Hakewell, Hackwell), 5, 9, 18(2), 37, 39, 75, 77, 80, 99(2), 120, 129(2), 144, 158, 159, 163, 166, 168, 180, 182, 201, 203, 213, 222, 234; m., 18; Clements m., 182; Swane or Swayne m., 18.

Hawkewoods m. see Hedingham, Sible.

Hawsted see Halstead.

Hayes see Stow Maries.

Hayles m. see Epping.

Hayrons (Herons) see Danbury and Easter, High.

Hazeleigh (Halesleigh, Hayless, Haselyth, Hasylle), 9, 70, 90, 122, 180.

Hebredge see Heybridge.

Hedingham, Castle (Hennyngham ad Castrum, Hengham), 9, 15, 18, 98, 100, 103, 104, 105, 113, 117(2), 127, 128, 133, 138, 144, 177, 183, 188, 193, 237; H. m., 126.

Hedingham, Sible (Sybbelhennyngham), 9(2), 14, 15, 23(2), 34, 36(3), 39, 41, 42, 46, 53, 62, 64, 66, 78, 79, 97, 98, 103, 104, 106, 107, 108, 113, 117, 119, 126(2), 127, 128, 130(2), 133(2), 143, 144, 145, 147, 150, 156, 166, 167, 188, 189, 193, 198(2), 199, 219, 220, 232, 234, 241; adv., 126; Bloyes m., 241; Graveshall m., 241; Hawkewoods m., 103, 104, 144, 188; H. S. m., 126; Peppers (Pevors) m., 9; Prayours m., 9.

Hellonsfeldes m. see Rivenhall.

Hempstead, 9, 20, 24, 31, 66, 67, 106, 108, 119(2), 138, 151, 155, 156(2), 167, 190, 203, 206, 211, 238, 239; m., 156.

Henham, 25, 44, 58, 60, 67, 83, 84, 86, 91, 178; Parlecheden (Plechden, Pledgdon) m., 44, 67(2), 84, 106.

Henny, 186.

Henny, Gt. (Hennay), 2, 9, 49, 77, 82, 116, 126, 136, 168, 170(2), 178, 215, 216, 238(2).

Henny, Lt., 2, 15, 82, 96, 121, 126, 131, 167, 168, 170, 215, 216, 238; adv., 216, 238; Henny, Lt. *alias* Ryes m., 96, 216, 238.

Hennyngham see Hedingham.

Herberds (Harvard) m. see Rayleigh.

Herford Stok see Stock.

Herons *alias* Countysbrydge m. see Althorne.

Herons (Hayrons) m. see Danbury and Easter, High.

Hersted m. see Bumpstead, Steeple.

Hertfordshire, 7, 9, 23, 24(2), 47, 48, 55,

255

84; Hallyfelde, 25, 57, 84, 85, 91,
137; Pyenest m., 151, 165; Saint
Lawrence de Waltham, 110(2);
Sewardston *alias* Suson or Susan, 55,
68(2), 91, 124, 215; Upshire, 22, 57,
60, 91, 124, 215; West Street, 54;
Woodrydden m., 135; Water of Lee,
149, 186.
Waltham, Lt., 12, 17, 27, 40(2), 45, 54,
55, 56(2), 61, 62, 63, 70, 71(2),
84(2), 86(2), 95, 102, 108, 115, 131,
132, 142(2), 145, 153, 156, 159,
161, 167, 170, 192, 194(2), 198,
200(2), 205, 206(2), 207, 209, 210,
214(2), 226, 227; adv., 70, 200;
Sparrowhawkesey m., 71, 84, 132.
Walthamstow, 56, 78(2), 79(3), 81(2),
84, 91, 93, 98, 105, 123, 131(3),
134, 144, 145(3), 157(3), 171, 195,
196, 200, 225, 230, 231, 234, 236,
239; Bensted, 171, 200; Higham
Bensted *alias* Higham Hall (Hills), 79,
91 123, 131, 145, 171, 187, 200,
239; Walcamstowe Tony m., 81, 131,
145, 157, 196; Walcombstowe
Fraunces *alias* Lowhall m., 84, 131,
145.
Walton-le-Soken, 4, 10, 31, 163, 211.
Waltons (Waulton) m. see Bartlow End,
Bumpstead, Steeple, Mucking and
Purleigh.
Wannington see Wennington.
Wanstead (Waunsted), 42, 54, 58, 75,
121, 212, 222, 223, 225, 234, 236;
adv., 225, 234, 236; m., 225, 234,
236; Aldresbroke m., 54, 222.
Warehill in ?, 9.
Wares m. see Easter, Good.
Warley, Gt. (Warlye Abbatisse, W.
Waylett), 8, 78, 106, 123(2), 138,
181(2), 186, 187(2), 199, 204, 208,
225; Warleigh Franckes m., 138.
Warley Lt., 75, 106, 123(2), 181(2), 184,
187(2), 199, 204(2), 209, 212, 217;
Estwarley Semell m., 123.
Warners m. see Waltham, Gt.
Warwickshire, 66, 223, 234, 242.
Water Belcham see Belchamp, Water.
Waterhall m. see Nazeing.
Wautons *alias* Waltons m. see Bumpsted,
Steeple.
Weald Bassett, North (Northwyeld,B.,
Norwelbassett), 4, 5, 6, 12, 14, 28,
53, 36(2), 44, 95, 140, 161, 171,
172, 191, 195, 199, 201, 211, 242;
Marshalls m., 36; Parys m., 80; Weyld
Gullett, 12.
Weald Gullett see Weald Bassett, North.
Weald, South (Southwell), 2, 10(3), 16,
18, 23, 25, 26, 28, 31, 48, 87, 97,
104, 106, 117, 153, 181(2), 183,
187(3), 188, 189, 190, 202, 204(2),
205, 224, 239, 242; m., 187; adv.,
187; Bentley, 235; Bowells *alias*

Cokk *alias* Bowels (Bawd's Hall) m.,
25, 189; Brokestreat, 116(2), 181,
187, 204(2), 224; Caldcote
(Colecartes) m., 173, 187; Costehall
(Costed Hall) m., 187; Sedfordbroke,
117.
Weeley (Weleygh, Wellye, Whyley, Wilie),
8, 27, 40, 44, 45, 47, 51, 125, 150,
158, 163, 181(2), 202, 235;
Crustwick *alias* Custrichall (Guttridge)
m., 9, 45, 235.
Wekes *alias* Wek m. see Tolleshunt Major.
Weldebernes m. see Debden.
Weleghe see Weeley.
Wenden, 8, 45, 172.
Wenden, Gt., 4, 32, 36(2), 52, 134, 144,
148(2), 163, 168(2), 175, 177, 183,
196, 218, 228; adv., 36, 148; rectory,
168; Gt. W. m., 165; Westbury m.,
168.
Wenden, Lt., 36(2), 52, 144, 148, 163,
168(2), 177, 183, 228; adv., 168.
Wenden Lofts (W. Loofthes, W. Lostes,
W. Lowetis), 8, 32, 45, 68, 70, 100,
109, 134, 149, 150, 162, 163, 168,
172, 216, 219, 222; m., 219;
Lowghtes, 8, 148.
Wennington (Wallington, Wannington),
9(2), 18, 37, 120, 143, 154, 161, 166,
171, 201, 229, 231, 233; Lenthroppes
m., 120; m., 229.
Westbury see Barling and Wenden, Gt.
Westdonyland m. see Donyland, West.
Westhall m. see Paglesham, Ramsey and
Thurrock, West.
West Ham see Ham, West.
Westhamburnells see Ham, West.
Westhanyngton see Hanningfield, West.
Westhorndon m. see Horndon, West.
West Horoch see Thorrock, West.
Westleygh (Westley) see Lee Chapel.
Westminster, 68.
West Tylbery m. see Tilbury, West.
Westurroke *alias* Westhall m. see Thurrock
West.
Westwykehall m. see Burnham.
Wethermondford see Wormingford.
Wethersfield, 20(2), 23(2), 41, 42, 79(2),
97, 103, 111, 117, 135(2), 136(2), 138,
143, 154, 224, 235(2), 239, 241(2);
m., 79; Coddham m., 79, 237; Shorne
Hall m., 79?; Sompners m., 224.
Weydington see Widdington.
Whela(e)rs m. see Bentley, Gt. and
Roding, High.
Wheleighe see Weeley.
Whetleygh m. see Rayleigh.
Whykes Abbey m. see Wix.
Whyley see Weeley.
Whytes m. see Burstead, Gt.
Wicken Bonhunt (Wychen Bonant), 68(2),
86, 87(2), 99, 100, 168; W. Bonehawte
m., 68, 86, 87; adv., 68, 87.
Wickford (Wyckforthe) 4, 5(2), 42, 57,

INDEX OF PERSONS

Abbreviations. Ag.-Agnes; Al.-Alice; Amb.-Ambrose; Ant.-Anthony; Ar.-Arthur; Barb.-
Barbara; Benj.-Benjamin; Brt.-Bridget; Cath.-Catherine; Chr.-Christopher; Clem.-
Clement; Dan.-Daniel; Dor.-Dorothy; Edm.-Edmund; Edw.-Edward; Elr.-Eleanor; El.-
Elizabeth; Frs.-Francis; Gab.-Gabriel; Geof.-Geoffrey; Gilb.-Gilbert; Hy.-Henry; Hum.-
Humphrey; Ja.-James; J.-John; Jos.-Joseph; Kath.-Katherine; Lau.-Laurence; Leo.-
Leonard; Let.-Lettice; Mgy.-Margery; Mgt.-Margaret; Mat.-Matthew; Mic.-Michael;
Nic.-Nicholas; Pe.-Peter; Ph.-Philip; Rh.-Ralph; Rd.-Richard; Rt.-Robert; Rog.-Roger;
Si.-Simon; Ste.-Stephen; Theo.-Theodore; Th.-Thomas; Wal.-Walter; W.-William.

Ab(b)ott (Abbatt), Al., 40; George, 144,
207, 242; J., 7; Mgy., 60, 65; Rt., 40;
Susan, 207; W., 60, 65.
Abell, Ag., 44; J., 77, 122, 158, 167, 197;
Mary, 197; W., 13.
Ablet, Joan 81; W., 81.
Abeforde (Aburforth), Anne, 67; J., 10,
67; Mgy., 134; Rd., 65, 152; W., 134.
Abraham, Rd., 229.
Acatro, El., Rt., 198.
Acheley, W., 230.
Ac(k)el(e)ane, J., Mgt., 18, 34.
Adam(s), Ag., 156; Joan, 76, 138; J., 27,
138, 150, 199; Mgt., 62, 241; Nic.,
199, 241; Rt., 138; Th., 31, 86, 179;
W., 43, 65, 127, 156, 158.
Adams *alias* Bocher, W., 116.
Ad(d)yngton, Chr., 43, 54; Ellen, 43; J.,
43, 54; Mgy., 43; Th., 54; Rh., 54;
W., 43.
Albar, Wolvur *alias* see Wolvur.
Albery (Albrough, Awborowe), Anne, 123;
Ant., 57; Mgt., Rt., 125; Th., 23, 74,
123.
Albright, Ag., Rt., 37.
Adcock(e), J., 81; Rt., 182.
Alcock(e), J., 81; Rt., 182.
Alcrofts, Wal., W., 48.
Aldriche, J., 51.
Aldust, Kath., th., 179.
Alee, El., J., 233.
Alexander, Jerman, 179; Rt., 217.
Aleyn (Al(l)e(y)n), Ag., 5, 40; Al., 84;
Ant., 91; Beatrice, 156; Chr., 5, 31, 36,
40, 49, 95; Edm., 200; El., 83, 91, 150;
Giles, 49, 167, 209; Joan, 143; J., 49,
70, 107, 150, 200; Leon., 165; Mgt.,
46, 165; Rh., 82; Rd., 169; Th., 75, 95;
W., 96.
Algor (Auger, A(w)gar), Ag., 83; Al., Anne,
74; Geo., 158; Joan, 107; J., 74, 144;
Mgt., 144; Nic., 83; Rd., 34, 74, 93;
Rt., 74; Th., 16, 74, 93, 170; W., 80,
156.
Alham (Allam) see Athelham.
Aliston (Allyson), Al., 130; Hen., Jane,
163; Joan, Lau., 161; Mat., 199.
Allett, Al., Th., 223.
Alman (Almond, Armond), Geo., 57;
Joan, 148; J., 232; Rt., 26, 148.
Alspo (Ausop), 3; J., 3, 5, 14.

Alston, Edw., 77, 120.
Alt(h)am, Ja., 98, 124, 156, 192, 197;
Mary, 98, 124, 156.
Alyngton (All-), Al., Geo., 55; Jane, 55,
116; J., 28, 55; (Sir) Giles, 42, 55, 79;
Ph., 55; Rd., 55, 85; Ursula, W., 55.
Am(b)ros(e), Joan, 5; J., 116; Mgt., 116;
W., 5.
Amcotes (Amcotts), Hamo, 15, 21; Kath.,
217; Mat., 219; Vincent, 217.
Amory, J., 156.
Amyce (Amys), David, 35; Israel, 239;
Joan, 103; Rog., 49; W., 103.
Anderkyn (-ken), Ja., 5, 17, 20; J., 147;
Mgt., 17, 18, 20; W., 17, 18, 20, 52.
Anderson, Edm., 157.
Andrewe(s) (Androwes), Anne, 22, 231;
El., 8; J., 22, 81, 156, 214, 226, 230;
Kath., 226; Petronilla, 81; Rt., 8, 130;
Th., 127,128; Weston, 231; W., 146,199.
Androwes *alias* Paynter, El., 30, 62; Th.,
62; W., 30.
Androwes *alias* Pyers (Piers), Kath., 146,
171; W., 92, 146, 171.
Anneys, Rt., 59.
Ann(e)ys *alias* Smyth, Al., J., 84; Rt., 84,
210, 230; Th., 239.
Anson, Mary, Th., 239.
Apparys (-rye), Hugh, 69, 83; Jane, 83.
Ap(p)leton (Appulton), Hy., 127; Mary,
212; Rog., 30; Th., 212, 238.
Aprice (Aprece), Edm., 78; Joan, 78, 230;
J., Lewis, 78; Rt., 78, 230-1; W., 78.
Archer, Ag., 40, 67; Anne, 82, 98, 102,
122, 124, 125, 148, 224; Edw., 121,
155, 161, 200, 210; Frs., 31, 73, 97,
122, 134, 137, 149, 191, 224; Geo.,
131; Hy., 50, 66, 73, 98, 122, 124,
125, 129, 155, 197, 200(2), 223, 212,
225; Jane, 170; Joan, 31, 137, 148; J.,
155, 200, 215; Kath., 30; Mary, 200,
215; Rd., 1, 8, 73, 82, 86, 100, 102,
152, 170, 197, 200; Ste., 50; Th., 40,
50, 67; W., 16, 30, 36, 39.
Ardeley, Rt., 43.
Ares myth, Mgt., W., 30.
Argall, Mgt., th., 84.
Argent, J., 120, 144.
Arkysden (Axden), Joan, th., 110.
Armystedde (Armested), Mgt., 127; Winifred, 27, 28; W., 27, 28, 127.

Armestronge *alias* Armested, Mgt., W., 152, 158.

Armiger(d), Ar., 149; Edw., 139, 170, 176; El., 139; Jane, 126; Th., 37, 120, 126, 141; W., 141.

Armond see Alman.

Armour, Isabel, J., 158.

Arnold, Joan, 48; Th., 27, 48.

Arrarde, Al., W., 208.

Art(h)ur, Mgt., 195; Rt., 1, 44, 195, 210.

Arundell, Chas., 209.

Asheffeld, Edm., 212.

Asp(e)lond(e), Ant., 22, 59, 69; El., 59, 133; Rt., 59.

Asshedon, J., 17.

Assheley, Ursula, 66.

Asser, Al., Rd., 147.

Astlett, W., 66.

Aston, Rt., 155.

Athelham (Alham, Allam), Geof., 45, 47, 56, 74; Ja., 41, 45, 47; Joan, 56, 74.

Atkyn, Th., 185.

Atkynson, Helen, 193; Isabel, Ja., 21; Joan, 209; J., 79, 193, 231; Rt., 159, 209; Thomasina, W., 39.

Atwood(e), Ja., 53, 184; Joan, 53; W., 181, 187, 212, 234.

Aud(e)ley (Aw-), Beatrice, 100, 107; Juliana, 23; Kath., 59, 195, 202; Th., 23, 59, 100, 107.

Aulfield, Joan, Rd., 25, 35, 36.

Auncell, Joan, W., 65.

Aungell, Pynnocke *alias* see Pynnocke.

Ausop see Alsop.

Austyn, Juliana, W., 26.

Avenon *alias* Avenon, Cornelius, El., 134.

Averell, Bart., 19, 39, 52, 61, 69, 90; Hy., 182.

Aver(e)y, J., 241; Th., 152; W., 137, 151, 170.

Awborowe see Albery.

Axden see Arkysden.

Ayer (Eyer, Eyre), Al., 46, 69, 132, 174; Joan, J., W., 46, 69, 132, 174.

Ayland, J., 42.

Aylett, Ag., 90; Anne, 104; Hy., 50, 57, 62, 77, 90, 104, 175, 176; J., 19, 90; Kath., 86, 94; Leon., 214; Mgt., 40, 159; Rt., 34, 140, 158, 160, 190, 192, 215; Th., 37, 86, 94, 166, 176, 190, 216; W., 23, 32, 40, 41, 45, 86, 98, 103, 138, 142, 144, 149, 159, 204.

Ayleward (-word, -wood), Ag., 11, 12, 14; J., 62; Th., 11, 12, 14; W., 137, 142.

Ayleff (Aylyff, Ayloff), Al., 232; Anne, 4; Erkenwald, 64; Jane, 232; J., 44, 64, 111, 166, 194; Mgt. 51, 167, 224, 233; Rh., 231; Susan, 64, 194; Th., 182; W., 4, 24, 34, 51, 57, 68, 108, 118, 133, 138, 182, 186, 229, 231, 232.

Aynolff *alias* Ellys, J., 8.

Baber, Edw., Kath., 194.

Babham, W., 175.

Babyngton, Helen, Th., 177, 195.

Bachelor, Ag., J., 89, 103.

Bacon, Frs., 181, 187, 212; Geo., 43, 51, 82; Ja., 60, 70, 88, 113; J., 152; Mgt. 43, 51, 82, 88; Mary, 181; Nic., lord keeper of the great seal, 92, 102, 113, 190, 200, 201, 217; Rd., 204.

Badbye, Th., 169, 184; W., 147.

Badco(c)k, El., 30, 126; Geo., 7, 57; Hy., Joan, 94; J., 15, 94; Nic., 94; Rose, 82, 94; W., 82.

Baesshe, Edw., 76, 101; Thomasina, 76.

Bagsha(we), Ag., Hum., 24, 32, 44, 58; Joan, 169; J., Rt., 58; Th., 169.

Baker, Anne, 134; Dor., 94; Edw., 78; Grisilla, 234; Hy., 4, 16, 43, 134, 180, 207, 213; Hugh, 109; Ja., 14, 36, 130; Jane, 208; J., 32, 53, 57, 145, 208, 234; Kath., 147; Mgt., 147, 219; Mgy., 32, 53; Mary, 36, 78, 130; Rt., 65, 137; Th., 54, 145, 234; W., 16, 219.

Baker, Cooke *alias* see Cooke.

Baker, Richards *alias* see Richards.

Balborowe, Jerome, 48, 80, 107.

Baldok, Ag., Geo., 20.

Baldwin (Balden, Bawdyn), Ag., Anne, 175; Dale, 6; Joan, 122, 161; J., 175; Mgt., 6; Th., 175; W., 114, 122, 161.

Bales, J., 123.

Ball(e) (Bawle), Joan, 67; J., 202, 238; Mgy., 241; Rt., 147, 190, 217; Th., 67, 119; W., 56.

Ballard (-erd), Al., 19; Joan, 7; J., 7, 42, 232; Mgy., 83, 173; Rt., 173; Th., 19, 83.

Balt(h)rop(p) (-ippe), Anne, 84; J., 199; Th., 84.

Bambrough, Th., W., 73.

Banester, Ant., 119; El., 118; Rd., 25; Rt., 65.

Banc(k)(e)s, Ag., 116; El., 134; Helen, Hy., Hugh, 206; J., 134, 183; Rd., 87; Rt., 211; Rog., 116, 183, 218; W., 206.

Bantoft, Wal., 18.

Barber (-our), Ant., 7, 201, 226; Mgt., 201, 226; Th., 80, 95.

Barfote, Th., 50.

Bar(c)ker, Ag., 41, 52, 56, 202; Al., 120; Anne, 184; Dor., 104, 117; Edw., 40, 58, 121, 169; Frances, 40, 169; Frs., 121; Hugh, 116; Isabel, 11; Joan, 56; J., 49, 56, 101, 116, 168, 185, 194, 196, 214, 226, 237; Kath., 185; Mgt., 104; Miles, 184; Rd., 11, 172, 194; Rt., 41, 56, 67, 100, 120, 154; Th., 49, 52, 104, 116–17, 202, 208; W., 102.

Barker *alias* Prentyse, Mat., 101.

Barker, Cooke *alias* see Cooke.

Barland, Ag., W., 132.

Barley (Barlee, Berlee), Anne, 83, 132, 178; Avery, 94, 117; Dor., 196; El., 109, 142, 165, 232; Hy., 43; J., 85; Joyce, 43, 80; Rd., 83, 132, 178; Thomasina, 117; W., 43, 46, 68, 80, 82,

Bramfylde, W., 178.
Bramley, Rd., 73.
Branche (Braunche), Ag., 12; Ellen, 18, 63;
　Helen, 96; J., 12, 18, 63, 96, 166, 190.
Brande, Edw., 217.
Brandon, Charles, duke of Suffolk, 202.
Branthwaite, Gilb., Joan, 179, 183; Rd.,
　238.
Bratley, Susan, Th., 226.
Bratley, Susan, Th., 226.
Braffoffe, J., 159.
Brawdshawe see Bradshawe.
Braynewood, Th., 47; W., 101, 174.
Braystar, Mgt., W., 123.
Breame, Ar., 136, 160, 184, 191, 196, 206,
　208-9, 227; Giles, 196; Thomasina,
　160, 191, 208-9.
Bredge (Bregge) see Bridge.
Bredgeman, Rt., 139.
Bredges see Bridges.
Breeche, W., 154.
Brende, Mgy., 26; Th., 26, 66.
Bressye, Etheldreda, Hamnet, 94, 95.
Bret(te), Ag., 23; Anne, 242; Giles, 7, 242;
　J., 7, 43, 46, 94, 163, 174, 194, 226,
　240; Lettice, 43; Mgt., 122; Mary, 226;
　Pe., 122; Rt., 49; Th., 23; W., 80.
Bret(t)on (-ten, -tyn), Al., 33; Anne, 68,
　177, 202; El., 33, 134; Geo., 100, 177,
　202; Greg., 97; Hy., 31, 88, 101, 128;
　Ja., 68; Joan, 127, 155, 183, 226; J.,
　194; Rt., 12, 226; Thomasina, 33; W.,
　66, 127, 155, 183, 226.
　Brewer, W., 111.
Brewster, Geo., Joan, 82; J., Rd., 200, 217,
　223; W., 200.
Brickett (Bry-), Blandina, 231; Rt., 62;
　Th., 231.
Bridge(s) (Bry-, Bregge), Al., 104; Anne,
　135, 194; Ant., 107; Beatrice, 19; El.,
　139, 174; Geo., 55; Helen, 172; Ja.,
　205; Joan, 94, 97; J., 8, 19, 24, 40, 49,
　135, 194; Kath., 140, 143; Rd., 140;
　Rt., 40, 45, 139; Si., 94, 97, 135, 205,
　209; Th., 143, 174, 192, 202; W., 104,
　172.
Bridges (Bry(d)ges), Hum., 242; W., 242.
Bridgewater, W., 196.
Bridgfild alias Gainsford, El., J., 165.
Bright (Bryght), Edw., 188; Frs., 75; J.,
　173; Rd., 113, 176.
Brignell, J., 132.
Bristowe, Eustace, 162.
Brocke see Brooke.
Brockehole, El., Hy., 127.
Bro(c)kes, J., 11, 76; Ursula, 76; W., 76.
Bro(c)kett, Edw., 42, 43, 58, 69, 114;
　Ellen, 47; J., 114; Zelathiel, 47.
Brockman see Brookman.
Brodewater Mgy., 153; Nic., 28, 111, 153.
Brody, Cecily, 144; Rd., 32, 144.
Broke, Geo., lord Cobham, 5.
Brokes see Brockes.
Brokhoussen, Jasper, 45.

Broman, Ag., And., 19.
Brome, Mgy., Th., 65.
Bromefelde, Lancelot, Mgt., 171.
Bromhall, J., 226.
Bromley (Brum-), J., 151; Th., 96, 157,
　181, 223.
Brooke (Broke, Brocke), Al., 110; Anne,
　95, 118, 148, 152; Ant., 172, 205;
　Barbara, 123, 127; Bridget, 109;
　Clement, 227; El., 135, 140, 160, 199,
　206, 215, 235, 239; Francis, 26; Hy.,
　77, 123, 127; Hugh, 109, 134; J., 11,
　35, 68, 82, 104, 106, 109, 118, 134,
　148, 152, 153, 157, 170, 180, 198,
　199, 204, 215, 219; Kath., 110, 185;
　Mgt., 35, 95, 122; Rd., 236; Rt., 31,
　109, 110, 135, 140, 149, 160, 193,
　199, 206, 235, 239; Ste., 110; Th., 95;
　W., 11, 22, 109, 122, 134, 158, 185,
　227.
Brookman (Brock-, Broke-), Ag., 211,
　226, 228, 232; Anne, 16, 134, 139;
　Ant., 34; J., 16, 20, 31, 34; Mary, 191;
　Rd., 173, 182, 184, 191, 211, 216, 217,
　219, 226, 228, 232, 237; Th., 34, 134,
　139.
Browne (Broun(e)), Ag., 37, 93, 114, 177;
　Al., 154, 138, 202; Anne, 193; Ant., 3,
　10, 12, 16, 18, 25, 45, 50, 56, 70, 123,
　197; Bart., 154; Chas., 70; Clemencia,
　242; Cornelius, 197; Christiana, 14; El.,
　5, 13, 50-1, 72, 109; Elr., 109;
　Etheldreda, 50; Geo., 50-1; Hugh, 2;
　(Sir) Hum., 37; Hy., 33, 72, 138, 202;
　Jasper, 48; Joan, 3, 16, 18, 45, 50, 56,
　197, 231; J., 14, 51, 70, 93, 105, 114,
　128, 177, 199, 213, 225, 231, 232;
　Kath., 206; Lau., 137; Mgt., 137; Mgy.,
　180; Mary, 187, 197; Ph., 158, 228,
　238; Rd., 51, 109; Rt., 5, 13, 17;
　Susan, 228, 235, 238; Th., 72, 109,
　139, 152, 160, 177, 197, 211, 223,
　229; W., 5, 13, 68, 70, 71, 108, 131,
　166, 232, 242; Wistan, 50-1, 104, 152,
　180, 187, 197, 206, 219.
Browne alias Cuckuk, El., Th., 62.
Brown, Darlyng alias see Darlyng.
Browning (-yng), Brt., 138; J., 93, 138;
　Rose, 35, 142, 175; Th., 171; W., 35,
　97, 142, 174, 175.
Brumley see Bromley.
Bryce, El., J., 228; Rd., 42; Th., 228.
Bryggs, Patmere alias see Patmere.
Brysley, Mich., 73.
Buck(e) (Buk(ke)), Clem., 132; J., 10, 27,
　57, 60, 67; Kath., 27; Rd., 130; Ste., 45.
Buckerfield, Etheldreda, J., 141.
Buckford, Al., 223; J., 154, 223.
Buckfold, Rd., 146.
Buckhurst, lord see Sackville.
Bucklande, Barb., Wal., 176.
Buckston see Bux(s)ton.
Bugg(es), Anne, 138, 226; Ant., 102, 138;
　Edw., 95, 102, 226; Hy., 102.

Draper, Joan, Rd., 16; W., 18, 37, 39.
Draper, Sawyer *alias* see Sawyer.
Driver (Dryver), J., 70; Nic., 91, 132.
Driver, Newport *alias* see Newport.
Drury(e) (Drewry), 'Drogo', 206; El.,
104, 129, 139, 206; J., 158, 181; Hy.,
104, 129, 139; Rt., 164.
Dryf(f)eld, Ag., 28; W., 28, 50.
Dryland (Drylond), Al., 230; Ja., 21, 30,
32, 33, 37, 132, 230.
Drywood(e) (Dray-), Al., 58, 171, 173;
Anne, 156; El., 99; Frances, 185; J.,
36, 39, 99, 156, 171, 175, 185; Rt.,
48, 113, 149, 171, 173; W., 14, 58.
Ducke, J., 40.
Duckett, Al., J., 42.
Dudley, Rt., earl of Leicester, 225, 227,
234, 236.
Dudley, J., 234.
Duke, Ant., 137; J., 212; Mgt., 113, 137;
Th., 113.
Dunche, W., 56.
Duncombe, Th., 110.
Dun(e), Al., 58; Joan, 159, 185; J., 58;
Rd., 159, 185.
Dune *alias* Ellys, El., Th., 197, 218.
Dur(r)ant (Dorant), Kath., 65, 123, 199;
Nic., 115; Rd., 35, 65, 78, 115, 123;
Th., 195, 219; W., 186, 199.
Dyck(e)ley, J., Mgt., 225; Rt., 129.
Dyckman, Al., Barnard, 202.
Dyer, Frances, 9; Joan, 111, 195; J., 76,
111, 195; Nic., 195; Rd., 109; Th., 9,
20.
Dygby(e), Joan, 97; J., 34, 97, 209;
Millicent, 154; Rd., 136, 145, 154.
Dyggolett, El., J., 121.
Dyke, J., Mgt., 233.
Dymo(c)k, Sir Edw., 121; J., 71, 97.
Dynes, Ag., 169; J., 169; Th., 140.
Dyngley, Hy., 218.
Dypdale, Joan, J., 15. Dyrlynge, Rt., 214.
Dysberowe, J., 167.
Dyve, Geo., 145.

E(a)rdeley, Brt., 40; Esdras, 165; Th., 40.
Earnsbye, W., 220.
Eason, J., 45.
Easte, Geo., 202.
E(a)stefeild, Joan, J., 107; Rt., Th., 168.
Eatton see Eton, Heton.
Eccles *alias* Geoge, Ag., Si., 233.
Eckford, Denise, J., 195; Nimrod, 203.
Eden (Edon), El., J., 199, 226, 228; Mgt.
Rd., 225; Th., 96, 185, 238.
Edgeat (Egeott), J., 218; W., 230.
Edmond(e)s (Edmundes), Chr., 91; Dor.,
91; Emma, 116, 153, 163, 167, 170,
180; Th., 116, 153, 163, 167, 170, 180;
W., 160.
Edmondes, Lawson *alias* see Lawson.
Edward(e)s, El., 102; Ja., 199; Joan, 53;
J., 153; Th., 102; W., 53, 101.

Egerton, Lionel, 217; Si., 185.
Eg(g)lesf(i)eld, Chr., 214; El., 214; Frs.,
107, 133, 139, 147, 150, 174, 177,
217; Joan, 36, 150, 174, 217; J., 108.
Egham, Woodlande *alias* see Woodlande.
Eglam *alias* Knyght, Mgt., Th., 38.
Egleston, J., 144.
Elcock, Joan, J., 104.
Elesford, J., 23.
Elkyn, Joan, Rd., 18.
El(l)iot(t) (-yot, -ett), Edw., 101, 113, 115,
140, 160, 163, 224; El., 144; Elr., 131;
Frs., 213; Jane, 101, 113, 115, 140,
163; J., 47, 64, 71, 101, 131, 176;
Kath., 124; Mgt., 64, 176; Mary, 145;
Rd., 101, 124, 175, 215; Wal., 184; W.,
139, 144, 204.
Ellys, Hy., 138; Joan, 138; J., 160; Mary,
140; Rd., 29, 140; W., 82, 92.
Ellys, Aynolff *alias* see Aynolff.
Ellys *alias* Dune see Dune.
Ellys, Mund *alias* see Mund.
Elryngton, Chr., 207; Edw., 111, 86, 99,
152; Geo., 226; Grace, 99; J., 136;
Rowland, 99, 130.
Elyston, J., Mgt., 136.
Emerson, W., 48.
Emery(e), Rd., 70, 100, 124, 133, 154,
169, 199; Th., 5, 159, 203.
En(n)ew(e)(s) (Innewe), El., 117, 123; J.,
238; Rd., 24, 71, 117, 123.
Enyver(s), Ag., 62, 71; El., 52–3; J., 52–3,
59, 179; W., 38, 54, 62, 71, 172.
Erdeley see Eardeley.
Er(e)swell (Erys-), Joan, 73–4, 108, 163,
184; Mgt., 23, 74, 111; Nic., 73–4, 91,
108, 163, 182, 184, 235; Th., 23, 28,
39, 74, 111.
Essex, earls of, see Bourchier, Devereux.
Essex, Al., Edm., 153; Jane, Th., Sir W.,
100.
Estbroke, J., 138.
Esterford, Rd., 19.
Estfyld see Easterfeild.
Eton (Eatton, Eyton), Alex, 122; Chr.,
144; El., Eugenius, 122; Joan, 156,
176; Rt., 34, 156; Th., 176; W., 122.
Evans (Evance), J., 92, 120; Sibyl, 120;
W., 212.
Eve, Ellen, 7; J., 3, 34, 50; Juliana, 16, 26,
128, 172; Rd., 49, 107, 229; Th., 3, 7,
15, 16, 26, 74, 126, 128, 129, 141,
154, 172, 178, 213; W., 2, 22, 87, 106.
Everard (-erd), Ag., 15, 215; Ant., 116;
Brt., 117, 128; Cecily, 43; Edw., 117,
128, 142; El., 66, 116, 134; Hy., 5, 15,
220; Joan, 5; J., 5, 66, 134; Mgt., 25,
145; Nic., 43; Rd., 8, 23, 28, 66, 125,
153, 167, 198; Th., 25, 145, 215; W.,
124, 145, 177.
Everley, J., 151.
Everson, Abr., 205.
Eweley, J., 3, 21.
Ewen, Ag., J., 10.

Ewsdon, W., 32.

Ewyn, Ag., Rt., 100.

Eyer (Eyre) see Ayer.

Eyon *alias* Jen., Al., Th., 39, 44. See also Yon.

Eyton see Eton.

Fabian (Fabyan), Anne, 143, 148, 149, 152, 160; Ant., 25, 99; Edw., 41; Geo., 99; Mgt., 42; Thomasina, 25; W., 121, 143, 148, 149, 152, 160.

Fallofelde, Hy., Jane, 174.

Fan(ne), Al., 19; El., 135; J., 19; Mary, 153, 155, 162, 178; Nic., 24, 86, 155, 162, 178; Rd., 10; Rt., 27; Susan, 153.

Fannyng (Ph-), Clemencia, 11, 53; Mgt., 99; Rt., 28, 61; Th., 11, 53, 99.

Fanshawe, Dor., 115, 132, 133; Hy., 68, 94, 104, 111, 115, 124, 132, 133, 135; Mary, 149, 160; Th., 149, 157, 160, 203, 213.

Farewell, J., 89.

Farmer, Frances, Th., 80. See Fermour.

Farnyll, Anne, 80; Th., 80, 95.

Farr(e), Fredeswida, 29, 192; Rd., 174, 192; Wal., 11, 29, 174, 192, 213.

Farrour *alias* Wallenger, Th., 158.

Farthing *alias* Goodewe, Edm., Joan, 50.

Faunce (Faw(n)ce, Fauns, Vaunce), Joan, 134; J., 9, 24; Si., 62, 134; Th., 127.

Fawkes, J., 236; Mgt., 171, 236; Th., 171.

Feakman (Feke-), Al., Th., 125, 133.

Fe(a)st, Alex., 240; Rd., W., 112.

Feld(e) (F(e)yld(ys)), Joan, 4; J., 4, 52; Kath., 104; Rt., 104; Rose, 104; W., 104.

Felder, Rt., 214.

Felsted, Al., El., 233; Nic., 129, 233; Rd., 233.

Felsted, Belcheff *alias* see Belcheff.

Felton, Dunstan, 103; Edm., 99, 113, 176, 177, 236; El., 176, 177, 236; Geo., 86; J., 158, 162, 170–71, 175, 213; Kath., 213; Mary, 103; Th., 211.

Feltwell *alias* Jon, Al., 177; Edith, 175; J., 177; Nic., 175.

Felyxe, J., 142.

Fen, Clem., 4, 162; Geo., 162; Rose, 4; Th., 162.

Fenis, Fynes *alias* see Fiennes.

Fennor, Dor., Rt., 143.

Fensclyff, W., 22.

Fenyx see Phenix.

Fermour, Anne, Rd., 19. See also Farmer.

Ferneley, Brt., J., Martha, W., 162.

Fer(r)ers, Barb., 65; Brt., 52; Edw., 9, 52; Sir Hum., 77; J., 65, 77.

Ferrour, J., Mgt., 143.

Fest see Feast.

Fethergyll, Al., Helen, 199.

Fiennes (Fynes), Gregory, lord Dacre, dame Anne, 164; Ph., 107.

Fiennes de, Clinton, see Clinton.

Finche (Fynche), El., 167; Geo., 96; Grace, 102; Hy., 176; J., 150; Mgt., 68, 150; Rt., 102-3, 220; Th., 68, 69; W., 167, 195.

Fitche (Fytche), Al., 172; Anne, 110-1, 165; Chr., 4, 20, 183; El., 180; Geo., 219; Gober, 15; Golding, 191, 195; Joan, 4, 20, 78, 183; J., 104, 131, 183; Mgt., 30, 131, 183; Mgy., 43, 77; Oswald, 161, 163, 191, 195, 201, 229; Rd., 22, 77, 106, 183; Rog., 14, 42, 43; Ste., 191; Th., 110, 150, 172, 180, 183, 191; Tristram, 30; W., 30, 54, 62, 64, 89, 110–11, 131, 165, 183, 191, 195, 199.

Fitzlewes, Rd., 106, 121.

Fitzwilliam(s), Anne, 36, 39; Sir W., 36, 39, 75, 187, 238.

Fla(c)k(e), Gilb., 105, 224; Giles, 197; Joan, 224; J., 45; Rd., 102, 105, 134; W., 105.

Flemyng(e), Isaac, 216; Jocosa, 117; Lucrecia, 216; Mary, Rt., 184; Sam., 226; Th., 117.

Flemynge *alias* Saunder, Mgt., 61; Si., 188; W., 61.

Fletewood, W., 66.

Flingant(e) (Fly-), Emma, 127, 131, 158; Geo., 179, 197; Joan, 179; Th., 127, 131, 158.

Flower, Mgt., Rd., 73.

Flowerdewe, Anne, Th., 153.

Fludd, W., 217.

Fold, Anne, J., 112.

Folkes (Fo(w)ke(s), Fookes), Abr., 189, 215; Rt., 82, 196; Th., 196; W., 17.

Follwell *alias* Folly, Mgt., W., 214.

Forbye, Ag., Th., 200.

Force, J., Kath., 198.

Ford(e), Elr., 81, 113; El., 185, 235; J., 81, 137; Kath., 81; Th., 39, 41, 113, 185, 235.

Fordham, Nic., 223; W., 223.

Forger, Ag., 48.

Forke, Frances, Rt., 113.

Forker, Ag., Rd., 77.

Fortescue (-cew(e)), Dor., 236; Dudley, 212; El., 2, 17; Frs., 172, 236; Hy., 2, 17, 24, 54, 63, 67, 71, 119, 146, 172; Mary, 212.

Forthe (Fourthe), Ar., 201; Frances, Rt., 113, 237.

Fo(r)ster, Joan, 53, 201; J., 127, 226; Mic., 40; Reg., 202; Rd., 129; Rt., 40; Th., 95, 101, 201, 232; W., 3, 95.

Fowke see Folkes.

Fowle, J., 14, 71, 91, 203, 213; Mgy., 14; Mary, W., 193.

Fowler, Frs., 182.

Fox(e), Anne, 197; J., 167; Mic., 197, 210; Nic., 60; W., 19.

Foxley, Anne, Mgy., Rh., 65.

Foxton, J., 21, 27.

Francis (Fraunces, Frauncys), J., 75, 148; Mgt., 213; Rt., 72; Th., 213; W., 116.

INDEX OF PERSONS

Francis (Frauncys) *alias* Puckley, Anne, J., 97.

Francis, Lorde *alias* J., 171, 212.

Fran(c)k(e), Chr., 180; Edw., 142; Frs., 16, 27; Joan, 40; J., 16, 27, 40, 86, 148, 210, 223, 225; Josias, 219, 223, 225; Mary, 93, 101, 167, 204; Th., 16, 27, 56, 64, 80, 93, 101, 120, 132, 140, 152, 159, 167, 204; Thomasina, 40, 86.

Fran(c)land, Edm., 163; Hester, Hugh, 242; W., 159, 163, 242.

Fran(c)kl(e)yn, Ant., 218; Cecily, Hy., 20; J., 218, 235; Rd., 235; Susan, 218; W., 198.

Fra(nd)esham, Edw., 116, 209; Mgt., 224.

Frauncys see Francis.

Frebarne, El., 89, 167; Th., 89, 167, 176.

Freer see Frier.

Frelove, J., Mary, 117.

Freman, Ag., 90, 97; Al., 7, 29; Bart., 218; Edith, 58, 62; Jane, 138; J., 7, 11, 29, 45, 95, 138, 162; Rh., 58, 62; Rd., 209; Rt., 162; Th., 28, 65, 90, 97; 107, 201, 216; W., 132.

Freman, Mund (Moundes) *alias* see Mund(es).

Fremlyn, Joan, 211; Mgt., 231; Th., 211, 231.

French(e), El., 81, 122; Rd., 122; Th., 81, 89, 101, 106, 139, 154, 239.

Frende, Clem., 4; Rd., 4, 28.

Freston, Th., 242.

Fretton (Frytton), Ag., 111; Th., 15.

Frevell, W., 149.

Frewen, Ag., Geo., 174.

Frier (Fryer, Freer), Brt., 236; Joan, 38, 147; J., 38, 41, 102, 147, 236; W., 147, 165, 213.

Frith(e) (Frythe), Ag., 138; Alvered, 166; Edw., 138; Geo., 12, 27, 159; Hum., 25, 60, 61; Joan, 159, 189; J., 75, 207; Mary, 105, 126; Rh., 189; Rd., 97, 120; Robergia, 25, 60; Rt., 105, 126, 129, 148, 182; Rog., 119; W., 61, 74.

Frohoke (Frohake), Oliver, 27; W., 60.

Froste, Joan, J., 162.

Frydaye, Joan, Rd., 207.

Fryssell see Thrustle.

Frytton see Fretton.

Fuljamb (Fuliam), Ag., 99; El., 112; Nic., 99, 112.

Full, Fredeswida, Hugh, 80.

Fuller, Ag., 1; Al., 149; And., 27, 42, 111, 202; El., 193; Hy., 71, 96; Joan, 137, 202, 232; J., 31, 50, 111, 171, 198, 209; Kath., 171; Mgt., 31, 167, 214; Mgy., 50; Rt., 166; Th., 72, 102, 117, 128, 137, 149, 228, 232; W., 1, 193, 198; Zachary, 167, 214.

Fulnetbye, Bart., Mgt., 57.

Fulston, Ag., W., 78.

Furnes, Th., 231.

Fyethe, W., 118.

Fyfelde *alias* Fyfhyde, El., 105; J., 73, 105.

Fylde see Felde.

Fygge (Fyggys), Joan, 12, 70; Pe., 70; Th., 12.

Fylmer, Rt., 88.

Fylp(o)tt, Anne, Th., 183, 191.

Fyner, Isabel, W., 154.

Fynes see Fiennes.

Fyneux, Chr., El., 170.

Fynkell, J., Mgt., 155; W., 19.

Fyppe see Phypp.

Fyrlonge, Jane, J., 203.

Fyrmyn, Anne, 186; Rog., 193; Th., 69; W., 186.

Fys(s)he, El., 195; J., 144; Wal., 134, 195.

Fyssher, W., 136.

Fytz, J., 49.

FytzWater see Radcliffe.

Gace (Gase), Joan, J., 107, 162, 171.

Gage, Pet., 133; Th., 127.

Gainsford (Gayn-), Cecilia, 41, 42; J., 41, 42, 49, 219, 221.

Gainsford, Bridgfild *alias* El., J., 165.

Gale, Rt., 145; Th., W., 159.

Gall(il)ie, El., J., 241.

Gamage, Geof., 174.

Gamon, El., J., 173.

Garbett, J., 124.

Gardener (-yner), Ar., 137; Brt., 44; Joan, 13; J., 4, 49, 97, 126; Mary, 97, 126; Rd., 93; Rt., 13; Th., 5, 172; W., 134.

Garfourth, W., 233.

Garlynge, Frances, J., 147.

Garner *alias* Gardyner, J., Th., 45.

Garnett, Ag., 23; Rd., 200, 234.

Garra(r)d(e) (-erd, -ord), Christina, 85; Jerome, 195, 207, 210; Joan, 158, 159; J., 34, 35, 60, 85, 87, 119, 131, 140, 152, 158, 159; Mgt., 43; Mgy., 119; Pe. 234; Rd., 28.

Garrett, Ag., J., 212; W., 224.

Garrold(e) *alias* Butcher, Jane, 207; Joan, 77; J., 207, 236; Pe., 184; Th., 77.

Garryngton, Mary, 173.

Garson, El., Wal., 86.

Gascoyne (-oigne), Geo., 198, 217; Mary, Rt., 204; W., 198.

Gase see Gace.

Gas(e)ley, Etheldreda, W., 71, 90.

Gate(s), Ag., 69; Al., 7; El., 194; Geo., 91, 212; Geof., 176, 194; Sir J., 30, 34; J., 11, 69; dame Mary, 118; Mary, 89, 147, 176, 212; Rd., 69; W., 24.

Gatton, El., Ewgenius, 144, 175, 177; Joan, J., 46.

Gaunt, J., 116.

Gawdye, Th., 16.

Gaymar, Barnabas, 183.

Gaysham (Gess(h)am), Isabel, 98; J., 78, 98, 124.

Gaywood, Joan, 187; J., 187, 191.

Gedge, Ja., 140, 163.

Gefferey see Jeffrey.

281

Gelham, Yeldham *alias* see Yeldham.

Genyng see Jennyng.

Gent(e), Ag., 22; El., 99, 120, 146, 150, 169, 222; J., 88; Th., 99, 120, 121, 125, 146, 150, 169, 172, 222, 229, 237; W., 4, 22, 29.

George, Eccles *alias* Ag., Si., 233.

George, J., 73, 125; Kath., 125.

Germeyne, Sir Amb., 184.

Gerrard, Gilb., 35, 157, 181, 196.

Gerves see Jarvys.

Geslyng, Anne, 90; Ellen, 13; Rd., 90; Th., 13.

Gess(h)am see Gaysham.

Geste, Dor., J., 159.

Geyre, Rt., 35.

Gibson (Gy-), Ag., Edm., 233; Geof., Joan, 111.

Gilbert (Gylbart, -berd), Al., 94; Dor., 90; Edw., 94; El., 174; Jerome, 44, 68; Joan, 140, 197; J., 174; Rd., 34, 90; Th., 99, 130, 140, 179, 197.

Gilbert *alias* Hale, Joan, J., 48.

Gilbert *alias* Bilberde, Amb., 64.

Gilbourne (-barn), J., 151; W., 171.

Gilder (Gy-), Ag., 212; Anne, 195; Edw., 195, 212; Joan, 186; J., 33; Th., 186.

Gilgate, Ar., Mgy., 238.

Gill(e) (Gyll), Anne, 38, 44, 71; El., 65; Geo., 38, 44, 69, 71; J., 152; Leo., 32, 65.

Gillam (Gyllam), Salperswicke *alias* see Salperswicke.

Girdeley, Ag., Pe., 107.

Gladwyn, Mary., Th., 203, 214.

Glas(se)co(c)k(e), Ag., 108; Anne, 148; Edw., 127, 144, 153, 188; Frances, 121; Grace, 105; Hy., 233; Joan, 31, 51, 188; J., 6, 22, 31, 38, 51, 66, 79, 105, 106, 112, 133, 134, 142, 146, 148, 160, 167, 176, 189, 200, 217; Kath., 112, 142, 146, 167; Lau., 171; Mgt., 66, 79; Mary, 38, 172; Philippa, 209, 213; Rd., 5, 66, 79; Rt., 121; Th., 34, 74, 160; W., 6, 63, 68, 106, 126, 163, 172, 209, 213, 224.

Glassenbye, Mgt., 53.

Glenham, Frs., Lettice, 100.

Glover, Ag., 18; Jane, 143; J., 18, 143.

Godbolde, Mgy., 32.

Godday see Goodday.

Goddyng see Gooding.

Goddyshalff see Godsalff.

Godfrey, Al., 47, 58, 111; J., 74; Rd., 5, 8, 14, 47, 58, 111; Th., 30, 130, 232.

Godman, Anne, 172, 205; Innocent, 172, 190, 205. See also Goodman.

Goldsalff (-ave), Al., 219; Sir J., 16, 219, 233; Th., 93, 101, 118, 130, 236.

Godson, Anne, Ph., 224.

Goff, Frances, Lau., 137, 145.

Goldan, J., 16, 97.

Golding(e) (-yng(e)), Adrea, 21; Al., 100, 118, 150, 216; Ar., 220; El., 116, 119, 131; Edw., 205; Geo., 220, 229, 237; Hy., 110, 118, 131, 150, 197; Joan, 66, 100, 148, 219; J., 2, 66, 100, 148, 170, 241; Mgt., 208; Mary, 237; Rd., 28, 67, 116, 181, 186, 193, 208, 219; Rt., 21; Sir Th., 2, 13, 116, 119, 120, 131, 139; W., 218, 231.

Goldyngham, Dor., Th., 138, 176, 181, 182.

Goldsmythe, Frs., 83.

Goldwell, Anne, J., 6.

Golston, Ag., 179; Rt., 129, 179.

Gombersall, W., 172.

Gooche, Th., 141.

Goodchilde, Ag., J., 175.

Good(d)ay(e) (Good(h)ey), Joan, 81, 241; J., 17, 30, 77, 84, 110, 118, 131, 143, 159; Mary, 77, 159; Rt., 39, 241; Rog., 235; Rose, 119; Th., 81, 119, 179.

Goodheye *alias* Goodaye, J., Mary, 112.

Gooddere, Frances, Hy., 190.

Goodeve, Joan, J., 20, 138.

Goodewe *alias* Farthing, Edm., Joan, 50.

Gooding(e) (-yn), Dan., 231; Ja., 113; Mgt., 84. See also Goodwin.

Goodman, Th., 146. See also Godman.

Goodryck, Chr., Rd., 74.

Goodwyn, Ag., 23, 110; Anne, 9-10, 122; El., 111, 141-2, 164, 196; Ellen, 142; J., 9-10, 66, 91, 111, 113, 130, 196; Mgt., 64-5; Mark, 206-7; Rd., 23; Rt., 142, 217-8; Th., 148-9, 163-4, 201-2; W., 6, 10-11, 12-3, 14-5, 17, 24-5, 35-6, 109-10, 121. See also Gooding.

Goslyng (Gosylinge), Helen, Rh., 172, 191.

Gosnold, Mat., 179; Rd., 50.

Gosse, W., 10, 39.

Gourney, Rd., 159, 191, 207.

Gover, J., 216.

Gower, J., 200.

Gowge, W., 40, 156.

Grabyn, W., 136.

Grace, Mgt., Rog., 47, 53, 81; Rd., 60.

Gracebye, Rt., 137.

Gratay, J., 161.

Grave, J., 52, 152; Kath., 169; Mgt., 152; Rog., 169; W., 162.

Graveley, J., 59, 143.

Grave, Anne, 161; Hy., 161.

Graygose, Kath., Wal., 155.

Gregill, Th., 24, 39, 76; W., 3, 6, 15, 58.

Gregill *alias* Grigge, Al., 113, 173; Olive, 76, 215; Th., 76; W., 105, 113, 173.

Gregory, Joan, J., 155.

Gre(e)n(e), Ag., 20; Alinora, 110; And., 114; Barthelet, 43; El., 34, 35, 48; Fredeswida, 229; Geo., 177; Helen, 193; Hy., 115, 122, 189; Jane, 115, 124; Jerome, 42, 50, 115, 124; Joan, 19, 115, 127, 137, 166, 189; J., 34, 35, 36, 48, 99, 109, 136, 141, 198; Kath., 141; Law., 70, 225; Mgt., 165, 225; Martha, 198; Pe., 122, 127, 137; Rd., 17, 109, 127, 131, 133, 137, 166,

198, 208, 212, 224; Rt., 24, 130, 221, 229; Rochus, 99, 110, 151, 158; Th., 19, 54, 231; W., 165, 193.

Grenacres, Frances, 213; Rd., 193, 213.

Grenestrete, Joan, Th., 57.

Gres(s)ham, Dame Isabel, 21; Sir J., 37.

Gresswell, Nic., 21. See also Creswell.

Greves, Edw., 170.

Grevyle (Gryvell), Fulk, 206, 223.

Grey(e) (Gray), Al., 24, 50; And., 82, 84, 168, 200; Anne, 161; Hy., 54, 161, 176, 178; Ivo, 112, 138; J., lord, 178; Mary, 176, 178; Th., 24, 50, 59, 61, 103; W., 6, 61.

Griffin (Gryffyn), Edm., 200, 206, 221, 227, 233; Edw., 38, 42, 136.

Griffith (-yth), Hugh, 63, 67, 163.

Grigg(es) (Gryggys), Al., 224; Brt., 205; Joan, 46; J., 55, 224; Mgt., 205; Rt., 46; Th., J., 147, 205; W., 86 115, 129, 205.

Griggs, Grigle *alias* Al., W., 173.

Grigge (Gryggs), Gregill *alias* see Gregill.

Grigle (Gryggle) *alias* Griggs. see Gregill.

Gro(o)me, Rog., 30, 64; Th., 165; W., 240.

Grose, Rt., Thomasina, 123.

Grove, J., 94.

Grymesdyche, El., J., 82; Th., 152.

Gryme(e)wa(r)de(e), Al., 141; Hy., Joan, 154; J., 141.

Grymston, Edw., 226.

Grys, le, Chas., Esther, 184.

Guldeford, Hy., 146.

Gunson, Benj., Ursula, 135.

Gurdon, Rt., 2, 7, 15, 65, 91, 146, 238; Rose, 2, 7, 15, 65.

Gutter, Jane, 46; Th., 39, 46.

Guye, Joan, Rt., 192.

G(u)y(o)n (Gwyn), J., 12, 14; Mgt., 12; Rd., 63, 67; Rt., 14.

Gybbes, Ja., Joan, 140; Rd., 5; Th., 198.

Gyfford, Rh., 46.

Gylbanke, W., 49.

Gylbarn see Gilbourn.

Gyldard, Joan, J., 98.

Gyler *alias* Spendlove, Hy., 79.

Gyllett, J., 39.

Gylman, Clemencia, J., 175.

Gylson, Mgt., W., 131.

Gymlett, Clem., 95, 210; Mgt., 210.

Gyne(s), Faith, 115, 124, 130, 135, 142, 148, 163; Rt., 95, 115, 129, 164; Th., 115, 124, 130, 135, 142, 148, 163, 221; Ursula, 115.

Gyon see Guy(o)n.

Gyppes (Jeppes, Jyppes), Ag., 127; Al., 122; J., 98, 122; Mgt., Nic., 8; Th., 127.

Gysse, Rog., 89, 115, 121.

Gytton(s), Emma, 78, 161; Rog., 78.

Gyver, Al., 141; And., 189, 197; Joan, 197; J., 141, 217; Rd., 88; Th., 80, 197, 217.

Hache, Mgt., Ste., 40.

Hackett, Th., 154.

Hackston, J., 114.

Haddon, Th., 105.

Hadley, Geo., 42-3, 69, 103; Joyce, 69.

Hadstock, Rog., 23.

Hagar(the) (Hagar), Beatrice, 37; Geo., 163, 181; J., 37; W., 135.

Hale, Anastacia, 241; J., 120; Th., 26, 98, 144; W., 26.

Haledaye, Ja., 62.

Hales (Hayles, Halys), Edw., 93; El., 40, 54, 60, 70, 88, 149; Hy., 207; Jane, 93; J., 133; Ste., 23; Th., 40, 54, 60, 70, 88, 123; W., 19.

Half(fe)hide (-hed), J., 208; Rt., 28, 62, 65.

Hall(e) (Hawle), Ag., 189; Anne, 105; Ant., 118; Ar., 218, 241; Edm., 121; El., 82; Etheldreda, 44; Geo., 229; Hy., 119; Jane, 118; Joan, 71, 186, 218, 223, 241; J., 8; Kath., 8; Mark, 186; Mary, 166, 229; Rd., 71, 105, 215, 226; Rt., 44, 71, 135, 137, 196, 223; Th., 39, 105; W., 82.

Hall(s), J., 171-2; Mgt., 172.

Halmer, Hy., 71; Mgt., Th., 31, 112.

Halsall, Hugh, 140.

Hame, Brt., Hy., 61.

Hamlyn, W., 61, 116.

Ham(m)ond(e) (Haw-), Edw., 170, 202; El., 107, 124, 130; Geo., 62; Hy., 229; J., 1, 6, 40, 55, 61, 93, 119, 187; Mgt., 170, 202; Rd., 55, 59, 61, 130, 179; Rt., 224; Th., 124, 129; W., 62, 101, 107.

Hamnare, Edw., 133.

Hampden, Hy., 9, 38; Sir J., 9; Philippa, 9.

Hampton, Barnard, Kath., 90.

Hanbery, W., 186, 199.

Hanchett, Brt., J., 27; Th., 67, 117, 121, 168.

Hanco(c)k(es), Ag., 154; El., 140; Geo., Grace, 108; Nic., 140; Th., 154.

Hansard (-sharte), Frances, Rd., 65, 86.

Hapten, J., 186.

Harbottell, J., 168.

Harby(e), Christina, Rd., 3; W., 1.

Harde, Dor., Th., 80.

Hardekyn, El., J., 128.

Harding(e) (-yng), Jane, 175; Joan, 20, 54, 156, 239; J., 20, 175; Rd., 156, 161; Th., 54, 239; W., 68.

Hardson, Anne, Hy., Rd., 2.

Hardy(e), Chr., 223; Kath., Ste., 171.

Hare, Frs., 196; Joan, 45; J., 175, 196; Mgy., 175; Marion, 148; Rd., 148; Rt., 45; Th., 46, 87, 91; Wd., 142; W. 55.

Harecrofte, J., Kath., 28.

Harford, J., 137.

Harker, Rd., 166.

Harlakenden, Mgt., 177.

Harman, Garrett, 40; Habakkuk, 224; Kath., 21; Mary, 224; Th., 21, 143. See also Herman.

Harper (-ur), (Sir) Geo., 11; Hy., 170; J., 80; Rd., 44.

INDEX OF PERSONS

Jo(h)nson, Ag., 34; Anne, 90; Cecily, 25; Dor., 55, 153; Effa, 108; El., 43; Geo., 35; Hy., 31, 55, 108; Hilary, 88; J., 32, 34, 56, 90, 97; Justinian, 90; Kath., 35; Mgt., 31, 47, 144; Mary, 34, 144; Pe., 34, 144; Rd., 37, 43, 47, 203; Sebastian, 56; Th., 25; W., 34, 132, 225.

Johnson, Cornelius *alias* see Cornelius.

Jol(l)y(e), Anne, 185; Joan, J., 128, 225; Th., 207, 238; W., 185.

Jon, Feltwell *alias* see Feltwell.

Jones, Hy., 53, 61; Jasper, 59.

Jordan, Joan, Rt., 72.

Jos(s)(e)lyn, Anne, 103, 124, 130, 133–4, 176, 214, 226; Dor., 38, 41, 57, 59, 89; Frances, 89; Hy., 103, 124, 130, 133–4, 136, 152, 176, 214, 219, 226; Helen, 136; J., 27, 89, 103, 124, 178, 238; Mgt., 170; Si., 34, 170; (Sir) Th., 5, 17, 38, 39, 41, 57, 59, 89.

Josua, Rd., 93, 108.

Joye, Hy., J., 183; Mgt., W., 126.

Joyer, J., 14.

Joynour, And., 136.

Judde, W., 208.

Judye (Judie), Lau., 54; Mgt., Si., 231; Rose, 54.

Justanus, Anne, J., 205.

Justyce, J., 153.

Jyppes see Gyppes.

Kaye, Geo., W., 114.

Ke(e)ler, Ag., Chr., 151; Edith, 154; Rt., 151, 154; Th., 151.

Kegyll, Anne, Rt., 9, 10.

K(e)ightley, Frs., 136; Th., 128, 160, 184.

Kellogge (Kellocke), Marion, Th., 81, 90.

Kellogge *alias* Ryche, Cecily, Edw., 106.

Kelmache, W., 194.

Kelsey, Geo., Joan, 48.

Kelton, Rd., 121.

Kember, Wal., 2.

Kemp(e), Ag., 90; Ar., 25–6; Bart., 113; Joan, 187; J., 90; Rt., 69, 78, 120, 129, 141; Th., 187.

Kempe *alias* Whythe, Ag., Th., 103.

Kemys *alias* Morgan, Anne, Chr., 207.

Kendall, Anne, 163, 185; Mic., 132; W., 163, 185.

Kene, Joan, W., 49, 60.

Kenne, Chr., El. (*alias* El., Beckwith), 234.

Kenester, Anne, Th., 71.

Kennett, Al., 161; J., 115, 161.

Kent(e), Hy., 109; Joan, 109, 175; J., 90, 104, 107, 117, 118, 120, 125, 126, 128–9, 133–4, 136, 145, 167, 175, 178, 180, 189, 202, 215, 235; Nic., 57; Rd., 93; Susan, 133; Th., 90; W., 133.

Kent, Reignold *alias* see Reynolde.

Kenynden, Mgt., Rd., 8, 15.

Kequick, W., 211.

Kervyne, Hum., Joan, 182.

Ketcher, Aug., 223.

Kettell (Kettle), Ag., 202; J., 58, 83, 202; Kath., Rt., 67.

Key(e), Barb., 186, 218; Th., 113; W., 186, 188, 218.

Keyle (Keyll), J., 60, 65.

Keyme see Kyme.

Kightley see Keightley.

Kinge (Kynge), Al., 132, 177; And., 51; Anne, 233; Chr., 56; David, 223; Geo., 177; Joan, 46, 56, 225; J., 44, 46, 71, 109, 111, 115, 141, 157, 182, 225; Kath., 112, 127; Lettice, 24, 34, 135; Mgt., 109, 115, 145; Raymond 118, 152; Rd., 122, 143, 145, 214; Rt., 5, 24, 26, 34, 98, 135, 141, 223; Th., 5, 7, 132; Thomasina, 127, 146; W., 7, 29, 36, 63, 72, 106, 109, 112, 127, 141, 146.

Knight, Ag., 53; Anne, 131, 145; Grace, 231, 241. Rd., 53, 131, 145; Th., 8; W., 231, 241.

Knight (Knyght), Eglam *alias* see Eglam.

Knightley, Geo., 148, 235.

Knotte, Kath., 202; Th., 141, 202.

Knyffe, J., 144.

Knyghtbrydge, Rabardgia, W., 193.

Knyghton, Frs., Kath., 86.

Knolles, Mary, Th., 64, 72.

Kyddermynster, Ag., 136.

Kylhogg see Kellogge.

Kyllycke, Al., J., Th., 119.

Kyllyngworth, Geo., Jane, 217.

Kymbold, Mgt., Th., 45.

Kyme (Keyme), Hy., 167; J., 21; Mary, 167; W., 53.

Kympton, Edw., 213.

Kyne, Greg., 191.

Kyng(e)sman, El., 2; J., 24; Mgt., Th., 144.

Kynwelmarshe, Anne, 221; El., Giles, 61; Hum., Mary, 129; Rt., 221.

Kyr(k)by, Ag., 204; El., 78, 100; J., 78, 100, 204.

Kyrle, J., 163.

Kyrton, Frs.,, 66.

Kytchyn, Anne, 228; Rd., 140, 228.

Kytson, Ant., Mgt., 120.

Lacy(e), J., 106, 229, 240; Mgy., 229, 240; Rd., 29.

Lagden, J., 159.

Lake, Thomasina, 50; W., 193.

Lakes, Osmund, 226.

Lakyn, Miles, 75, 117, 160, 238.

Lambarde (-art, -erd, -ert), Elr., 94; Emma, 138, 204; Joan, 38; J., 38, 75, 138, 170, 204, 227; Lewis, 22; Nic., 236; Rt., 71, 77, 111, 122; Th., 233; W., 94.

Lambert, Olyff *alias* see Olyff.

Lam(b)e (Lam(m)e), Joan, 94; J., 77; W., 94, 105.

Lancaster, Hugh, 134, 220, 221; Th., 220.

Lane, Hy., 207; Th., 233.

INDEX OF PERSONS

Mars(s)he (Mers(s)he), Al., 93; Hy., 107;
  J., 25, 38, 40, 93, 210; Maud, 206;
  Th., 26, 184; W., 206.
Marshall (Mer-), Anne, 162; J., 149, 161,
  165, 171; Mgt., 194; Rd., 117; Rt.,
  162, 173; Th., 194; W., 75, 174, 225.
Mars(t)on, Ag., Nic., 171, 193.
Marten (-yn), Al., 211; Ant., 199; Dorcas,
  120; El., 186, 203; Geo., 219; Joan, J.,
  168; Maurice, 184, 211; Nic., 183, 187;
  Rd., 17, 120, 131; Rt., 30; Rog., 17,
  74, 83, 115, 131, 152, 175, 186, 232;
  W., 81, 139.
Martin (Martyn) *alias* Wenden, J., 185.
Martin (-yn) *alias* Wignall, Al., Rd., 137.
Marven (-yn), Anne, 208; J., 31, 208; Th.,
  10, 203.
Mary, Queen, 63.
Maryon, Rd., 201.
Mascall (Maskall), David, Joan, 15; Kath.,
  127; Rt., 15, 127; Th., 45.
Mason, Ag., 165; Anne, 23; Nic., 23, 165;
  Rd., 123, 125.
Massingberd, Dor., J., 166, 168, 181.
Massye, W., 233.
Master (Mayster), Anne, 157; J., 17, 88;
  Roland, 157.
Mathew(e), Cecily, 70; Emma, 36; J., 70,
  200; Rd., 225; Th., 36.
Maule (Mawle) see Malle.
Mawldon, Anne, J., 216.
Mawter, Ag., W., 90.
Maxey (Maxye), Ant., 99, 111, 143, 155,
  159, 169, 175, 205, 233, 235; Dor., 99,
  155, 219, 225, 233, 235; Edw., 10;
  Geo., 4, 186; Hy., 77; J., 154, 220;
  Mgy., 186; W., 99, 179.
May(e), Christina, 61; Geo., 211; J., 36, 61,
  84; Lucy, 36, 169, 173, 180; Mgt., 30;
  Rt., 11, 30, 38; Susan, 180; W., 55,
  137.
May(de)stone, Geof., 151; J., 11; Rt., 113.
Mayer (Mayre), J., 63; Si., 57.
Maygate, E., W., 125, 133.
Maykyn see Machyn.
Mayle, Al., Geo., 205.
Maynard (-erd), Anne, 68, 241; Dor., 158;
  Edw., 68; Hy., 158; J., 39, 158; Mgy.,
  Rh., 164; Rd., 36; Rt., 18; Th., 156;
  W., 146, 152, 241.
Mays, J., 12.
Mayster see Master.
Mayston see Maydestone.
Me(a)d(e), Barbara, 45, 206; Edw., 135,
  189, 225; Geo., 120; Joan, 135, 225;
  J., 58, 68, 105, 162, 176, 217; Mgt.,
  120; Mary, 105, 135; Reg., 45, 115,
  135, 206, 222; Rd., 24, 135; Th., 45,
  46, 70, 129, 134, 163, 199, 202, 219,
  221, 228.
Meakes *alias* Pope, Hy., 120.
Medowe *alias* Mede, J., 108.
Medley, Hy., 160.
Mee, Th., 39.

Me(e)ke, Al., 152; J., 80, 152.
Melborne see Milborne.
Meller see Miller.
Melsoppe see Mylkesoppe.
Mered(d)eth, Magdalen, 174; Martha, 88,
  114; W., 88, 114, 174.
Merell (-yll), El., 43; Mary, Mic., 45; Nic.,
  43.
Merke, Rd., 6; Th., 56; W., 35.
Mershall see Marshall.
Mers(s)he see Mars(s)he.
Merytt, Ankerius, 21.
Mesante, J., 188.
Metcalf(fe), Al., 33; J., 216; Nic., 169;
  Th., 33.
Methold, W., 84.
Metyns, Rd., 120.
Mewtys, Hercules, 138.
Michell (My-), Alvered, 20; Anne, 30; Frs.,
  63, 96, 132; Jane, 63, 96, Joan, 63; J.,
  25; Marion, 20; W., 30.
Mid(d)leton (My-), Al., 92; Geo., 92; Rt.,
  29, 50, 73, 180, 187, 189.
Milbo(u)rn(e) (Myl-, Mel-), El., 55; Elr.,
  74; Geo., 225; Helen, 77; Joan, 237;
  J., 74, 77, 135, 161, 210, 225, 237;
  Rt., 55, 61, 77, 90, 124.
Mild(e)may(e) (My-), Ag., 11; Frances,
  184; Hy., 130, 192, 196, 210; Jane,
  192, 196, 210; Mary, 210; (sir) Th., 2,
  5, 6, 71, 102, 118, 155, 183, 184, 195,
  227; Sir Wal., 11, 32, 87, 132, 181,
  184, 191, 240; W., 11, 32.
Miller (Myller, Meller), Ag., 24; Al., 20;
  Edw., 235; Elr., 127, 189; El., 235;
  Hy., 67; Ja., 24; J., 20, 27–8, 211;
  Mary, 120; Rose, 67; Th., 20, 120, 127,
  189, 211.
Miller (Meller) *alias* Sawman, Al., J., 104.
Moigne (Moy(g)ne), Al., 57; Edm., 1, 20;
  J., 13, 20, 181; Mgt., 36, 181, 236;
  Nic., 226, 236; Reg., 36. See also
  Moynes.
Mone see Moone.
Mongey *alias* Mountioye, W., 177.
Mon(c)ke (Mounk), El., 237; Hy., 107,
  227; Leo., 92; Rt., 22.
Monoux, El., Geo., 82; Th., 96.
Monynges, Anne, Geo., 152, 172.
Moodye, Ag., J., 154.
Mo(o)ne, Benet, 207; Edm., 32, 138;
  Edw., 207; Gilb., 155; J., 155; Susan,
  32.
Moore, El., 24, 80; Rt., 196; Th., 24, 80;
  W., 25.
Mooteham see Moteham.
Mor(r)ant, Clara, 87; Edm., 132; W., 87.
Morda(u)nt(e), Ag., 8, 22, 30, 33, 47, 59,
  64; Barb., 25, 75, 105; Edm., 8, 11, 17,
  22, 30, 33, 47, 59, 64, 70; El., 151,
  180; Hy., 163, 193; dame Joan, 87,
  105, 106, 137, 145; Sir J., 46, 64, 72,
  106, 121, 131, 137, 145, 151; Lewis,
  105–6, 151; lord, 180; Mary, 25; Ph.,

Riggs (Ry-), Anne, 51; Joan, J., 103; Th., 103; W., 47, 49, 51.
Ro(a)des, Rd., 97., 97, 140, 223.
Robert(e)s (Robartes, Roberdys), Clem., 2, 36, 38, 135, 211, 215; Edm., 102; Geo., Joan, 93; Mgt., 102; Mary, 2, 211, 215; Si., 226.
Robertson, J., 134.
Robgent (Robiant), Edw., 236; Rt., 126.
Robyns alias Robynson, Kath., Th., 200.
Robynson, Ag., 230; Anne, 185; Chas., 221; Edw., 100, 171, 189; Mgt., 207, 230; Nic., 3; Susan, 230; Th., 185, 230; W., 17, 207.
Roche, Joan, 152; W., 152, 184, 212, 217.
Rochell, Joan, 193; J., 110, 232; Lau., 108, 148, 169, 193, 226-7.
Rochester, Ag., 41; Dor., 123, 127, 206; Edw., 195, 199; Hy., 41; J., 195, 199; Mgt., 206; Rt., 11; Th., 123, 127, 206; W., 11, 18, 28, 40, 109, 206, 236.
Rockaden, Hy., 6.
Rockyngham, Hy., 72.
Rodea see Roades.
Roger(s), Charity, 184; Frs., Helen, 143; Joan, 195; J., 19, 20, 43, 60, 96, 193, 238; Rd., 193, 200; Rog., 184; W., 115, 171, 193, 195.
Rogers, Phicksall alias see Phicksall.
Rokewode, Nic., 4.
Rolf(f)(e), El., 35; Eustace, 209; Gilb., 231; Joan, 126, 209; J., 28; Th., 103, 126; Winifred, 55; W., 35.
Rolles, J., 1.
Roo, Ant., 34, 60; J., 222.
Rookes, Joan, 36; Nic., 36, 153; Rt., 210.
Roper (Rooper), Ag., 88; Annabel, 23, 39; Ant., 205, 240; Geo., 88; Th., 23, 39, 205, 240.
Roote, Rt., 139.
Rose, Ant., 221; Joan, Ste., 29.
Rosewell, Pet., 101, 220.
Rosse (Roose), Edw., 61, 68; Joan, Polidor, 64.
Rossheton, Joan, Nic., 10.
Rotheman, Mgt., W., 79.
Rottour, Ag., 221; Ant., 227; Edw., 221; Jane, 227.
Rought, Philippa, Rd., 40, 45.
Rowbothum, Ja., 218, 236.
Rowe, El., 24; J., 24, 159, 161; Th., 111, 123; W., 111, 203, 239.
Rowell, J., 226.
Rowley, J., 227.
Roydenhurst, W., 161.
Roys, El., Wal., 97.
Roydon (-en), J., 223; Mary, 29, 44.
Rudde, W., 69.
Ruse see Rewse.
Russell, Brt., countess of, 157; Frs., earl of 92, 157, 230.
Russell (Rushell), dame Frances, 64; Jas., 204; J., 230; Sir Th., 64; W., 81.
Russhe, Ant., 72, 222; Elr., 72.

Ruste, Ag., 216; Edw., 169; J., 216.
Rusticens, Camillus, Mgy., 214, 231.
Rutland, Nic., 31.
Rutland, earl of, see Manners.
Rutte, W., 12.
Rutter, Philippa, 85; W., 18, 22, 58, 85, 86, 98, 116.
Rutter, Hewman alias see Hewman.
Ryche see Riche.
Rychold (Rytcholl), Al., 142; Sigismond, 214; Rt., 142.
Rycheman, J., 125.
Ryder, Edw., J., 233.
Rydgeley, Al., W., 8.
Rydnall, Edm., Joan, 198.
Rydesdale, Hy., Joan, 113.
Rye alias Raye, Joan, Rd., 82.
Rynger, Th., 60.
Ryngland, Joan, 68.
Ryppyngale, Wal., 24.
Rypton, El., 201.
Ryse (Ryce) see Rice.
Ryvers, El., 212; Etheldreda, 114; Ja., 212; Th., 114.
Ryvett, J., 90, 156. See also Revett.

Sabbesforde, El., Rd., 175.
Sabryght, Joan, W., 8.
Sabyster alias Sapister, J., 215.
Sache, J., 144.
Sa(c)kvile, Cecily, lady Buckhurst, 211, 222; J., Sir Rd., 107; Th., lord Buckhurst, 211, 222, 224-5; Th., 107.
Sad(e)ler (Sadiller), Augustine, 88; J., 227; Magdalene, 88, 114; Mgy., 126; Sir Rh., 84; Rog., 88, 114; Th., 126, 149, 152, 230.
Sadlyngton, Th., 117.
Saffowe, Th., 60.
St. Clere see Seyntclere.
St. John, J., Nic., 191; Oliver, lord, 152.
Salisbury, countess of, see Pole.
Salisburye, Maud, Th., 233.
Sallowes, Anne, J., 202.
Salmon(d) (Salman), Ag., 53; Joan, 31, 141; J., 7, 53, 82, 91, 189; Rt., 32, 240; Th., 106, 141, 193; W., 31, 165.
Salper(s)wicke alias Gillam, Frs., Joan, 127, 189, 220; J., 220.
Salter, And., 59; Blaise, 170; Joan, 24.
Saltonstall, Rd., 181, 204.
Salyng(e), Edm., 81; Joan, 119; Mgy., 81; Th., 119; W., 35.
Samborn, J., 31.
Samer, J., 209, 230.
Sam(m)es (Sammys), Edw., 180; Grace, 180, 204, 215; Hy., 35, 215; J., 180-1, 204; Rd., 54; Rt., 194, 231; Th., 35, 65, 82, 207; W., 54, 158, 180, 204, 215.
Sam(pe)ford (-forth(e), -furthe, Stampford), Ag., 91, 148; Edw., 188; El., 188; Ellen, 92; Joan, 3, 6; J., 6, 147;

Westwood(e), Chr., 71; Mgy., 34, 124; Rd., 31, 34, 79, 124, 129.

Westwyke, Dor., 24; El., J., Rd., 14; W., 24.

Wethers, J., 193.

Wethersby, El., 42.

Weylde see Welde.

Whale, Nic., 147. See also Wale.

Wheler (Whea-), El., 94; Joan, 87; Rd., 94; Rt., 87; W., 82.

Wheler, Cowper *alias* see Cowper.

Whepyll, Mgt., Th., 3.

Whetcroft, Th., 229.

Whet(e)ley, Th., 226; W., 146.

Whet(e)n(h)all (Whytnall), Al., 47; Dor., 202; Edith, 180; Geo., 29, 47; Th., 202, 221; W., 180.

Whetstons, Rt., 38.

Whitbread (Whytbread), Jane, Reg., 46; Th., 83, 227.

Wiffyn (Why-), Al., 180; Geof., 125; Geo., 175; J., 180.

White (Why(gh)te, Whytt(e)), Ag., 46; Al., 141, 170; David, 46; Dor., 132, 166; Edm., 117; El., 211; Geo., 45, 105, 116, 127, 132, 141, 207, 210, 213, 216; Hy., 211; Hum., 132, 166; Joan, 140; J., 44, 48, 113, 115, 125, 132, 139; Kath., 45, 207, 210, 213; Mgt., 233; Mgy., 125; Nic., 56; Pe., 167; Rd., 15, 233; Rt., 26; Rose, 170; Si., 26; Th., 15, 37, 122, 170; W., 54, 69, 131, 137, 140, 156, 211.

White *alias* Cowper, J., Juliana, Th., 31.

White Wythe), Kempe *alias* see Kempe.

Whitehand, Th., 122.

Whiter, J., 17.

Whithed (Why-), Ag., Edw., 237; Mgy., W., 15, 35.

Whitley (Why-), Joan, 140; J., 75, 140; Mgt., 75.

Whitteston, Barnard, 151.

Whittingham (Why-), Anne, 215; Edw., 191, 194, 215.

Whood, Hy., 152. See also Wood.

Whorwood see Horwood.

Whyacres, J., 240.

Whyne, Ag., W., 193.

Whytherell, Joan, Rh., 47.

Whytlocke, J., 135.

Whytnall see Whetenhall.

Whytte see White.

Whytyng, J., Mgt., 40.

Wigleswood (Wykylsworth), Ag., 143; Joan, 31; W., 31, 75.

Wignall, Martyn *alias* see Martyn.

Wilbore (Wel-, Wyle-), Mic., 12, 14, 15, 17; Nic., 58, 111, 127, 173, 223.

Wilbr(ah)am, Th., 139, 157.

Wilcocks, Joyce, Rd., 189.

Wildon, Edw., 92.

Wilford (Wyl-), Ag., 92, 117, 142, 148, 149, 169, 175; Joan, 24; J., 9; Mary, 206; Th., 76, 206; W., 92, 117, 142, 148, 149, 169, 175.

Wilkyns, W., 195.

Wilkynson (Wyl-), Anne, 48, 72; Beatrice, 146; Dor., 4; El., 191; Ja., 4; J., 146; Paul, 26, 37, 48, 72; Rd., 219.

Willett (Wyl-), Ag., 70; Al., 209; J., 4; Mary, 178; Th., 15, 178, 209.

Williams (Wyl-), Ag., 183; Anne, 66; Aubrey, 11; Etheldreda, 212; Giles, 183; Griffin, 157; Jane, 237; J., 66, 131, 148, 235; Mgt., 11; Mgy., 214; Mic., 147; Ph., 212; Rt., 237, 241; Si., 11; Th., 214.

Williamson (Wyl-), Edm., 103; Joan, 202; Kath., 28, 46, 71; Th., 28, 30, 31, 46, 59, 71; W., 202.

Wil(l)mer, Geo., 111, 223, 240.

Willowes (Wyl-), Geo., 102; Joan, 174; J., 44, 59; Th., 23, 45; W., 44, 132.

Wilughby, El., 223; Sir Frs., 223.

Wilsemer, Ja., 184.

Wilson (Wyl-), El., Hugh, 205; Jane, 221; Joan, 116; Th., 98, 123, 127, 131, 148, 158, 161, 221, 233; W., 183.

Winchester, marquess of, see Paulet.

Wincoll, Anne, 27, 66; Isaac, 238; J., 27, 66; Rog., 54.

Wind(h)am (Wy-), Brt., 208; Frs., 194; Hy., 157, 166, 208.

Wingfe(i)ld (Wy-), Ant., El., 225–6; Rt., 94.

Winton, St. Mary see Oxford New College.

Wiseman (Wy-), Ag., 28; Dor., 113, 115, 168, 222; Edm., 127; El., 124, 240, 242; Geo., 125, 147, 161, 165, 174; Jane, 151, 154, 224, 225; Joan, 16, 18, 20, 22, 129; J., 1, 8, 16, 18, 20, 22, 28, 33, 43, 46, 124, 125, 174, 198, 239; Martha, 147, 165, 174; Rd., 124; Rh., 124–5, 159, 168, 240, 242; Ste., 115; Th., 30, 33, 61, 73, 113, 115, 124, 129, 139–40, 150, 151, 154; W., 172, 203.

Wittham (Wytt(h)am), Ag., 198; Al., 18; Barnard, 105, 213, 241; Joan, 158; Pe., 233; Th., 18; Thomasina, 241; W., 158, 198.

Wolbar(te), Wal., 143; W., 13.

Wolgrave *alias* Wollard, Joan, Rd., 178.

Wollard, Wolgrave *alias* see Wolgrave.

Wolman, Th., 26.

Wolmer (-ar), Al., 4; J., Kath., 221; Th., 4; W., 139.

Wolvur *alias* Albar, Joan, Nic., 43.

Wood (Wood(de)), Al., 167; Edw., 24, 58; Geof., 139; Geo., 54, 229; Hy., 147, 226; Joan, 24, 54, 55, 61, 108, 119, 142, 159, 170; J., 54, 158, 178, 184, 201; Mary, 139, 201; Rd., 24; Rt., 54, 55, 108, 119, 127, 142, 159, 170, 207, 231, 235; Th., 54, 61, 142, 131, 167; W., 35, 119, 121. See also Whood.

Woodam, Ag., Th., 43.

Woodcock(e) (-coke), Ag., 168; Ja., 168, 208; Mary, 208; Rd., 62.

Wooddall (Woodhall), Ja., 70, 194; Joan, 70.

INDEX OF SUBJECTS

If one or more references on a page this is denoted by '(2)'. See Introduction for further details.

Advowsons (rectories, vicarages), *passim*. See also tithes.

Bakery, 38.

Chapels, free, 120, 186, 190.
Commons, 2, 63, 182.
Common of pasture, 2, 3, 13, 30, 32, 57, 64, 68, 82, 83, 89, 93, 96, 98, 100, 108, 112, 120(2), 126, 146, 153, 156, 159, 161, 166, 168(2), 172, 179, 182(2), 185, 188, 191, 193(2), 196, 198, 199, 203, 208(2), 209(2), 211, 213, 214, 217, 226, 228(2), 230, 233, 236, 237, 241. See also Foldage.

Dovecotes *passim*.

Fairs, 126, 187, 209, 238.
Ferries, 80, 85, 88, 103, 114, 120, 121, 128, 171, 215.
Field-names, 11, 14, 15, 24, 26, 29, 36, 40, 41, 47, 50, 51, 57, 63, 65, 67, 68, 72, 74, 77, 91, 93, 97, 107, 118, 127, 128, 129, 135, 139, 143(2), 155, 161, 167, 173, 178.
Fields, common, 93(?), 161(?).
Fisheries, 33, 43, 58, 62, 63, 82, 84, 115, 116, 121, 148, 149, 150, 154, 164, 166(2), 172, 174, 186, 192, 201(2), 205, 208, 221, 229, 232, 235, 240(2). See also weirs.
Fishpond, 107.
Fish house, 37.
Foldage (sheepwalk), 45, 120, 148, 151, 172, 222, 233. See also common of pasture.
Ford, 58.
Forest, 60, 100, 156, 159.
Forge, 154.
Frankpledge, 52, 58, 63, 104, 130, 161, 179, 196, 201, 206, 208, 214, 222, 236, 239.

Inns(?) see messuages.

Kitchen, 13.

Manors *passim* (indexed under their parishes in Index of Places).
Markets, 126, 187, 209, 234.
Meadow, first crop, 204.
Messuages (houses), named, 8, 13, 14, 19, 21, 25, 36, 40, 48, 50, 52, 60, 65, 67, 75(2), 82, 88, 89, 95, 110, 115, 119, 129, 140, 141, 160, 161, 162, 186, 191.

Mills, 11, 16, 26, 28, 43, 51, 63, 73, 79, 81, 92, 98, 99, 110, 113, 117, 121, 128, 132, 133, 140, 148, 154, 157(2), 164, 169, 181(2), 187, 189, 193, 204, 206, 208, 217, 221, 222, 234, 235(2), 236, 237(2), 238, 241.
Fulling, 39, 47, 77, 143, 194.
Water, 2, 32, 41, 43(2), 57, 58, 59, 61, 62, 69, 77, 82(2), 88, 89, 91, 94, 98, 100, 104, 108, 111(2), 117, 121, 122, 126, 130, 143, 145, 148, 154, 162, 163, 164(2), 166, 175, 177, 181, 190, 191, 192, 194, 205, 208, 209, 213, 214, 225, 230, 233, 239.
Wind, 2, 20, 69, 85, 89, 100, 102, 105, 114(2), 133, 167, 168(2), 180, 185, 187, 189, 195, 196, 199, 204, 219, 233, 241.
Monasteries, 11, 16, 70, 126, 186, 225.

Occupations see trades.

Parks, 8, 89, 90, 157, 181, 190.
Pensions, 40, 70.
Priory, 77.
Priory, site of, 70, 121, 200.

Quays, 37, 81, 240.

Rectories see advowsons.

Salt, salthouses, 37, 84, 224.
Sheepwalk see foldage.
Shops, 17, 71, 174, 221.
Stall (market), 234.
Swamp, 1.

Tithes, 16, 59, 60(2), 70, 93(2), 100, 102, 104, 124, 131, 136, 137, 141, 148, 151, 153, 156, 157, 160, 170, 174, 176, 184, 186(2), 191, 194, 200, 214, 224, 236.
Trades and Occupations:
  alderman of London, 37(2), 181; attorney general of the Queen, 38, 157; baker, 38; chancellor of the exchequer, 181; citizen and alderman of London, 21, 31, 34, 44(2), 48, 51, 96, 98, 105, 111, 123, 151, 181, 183, 188, 189, 193, 194, 195, 202; barber-surgeon of London, 65; butcher of London, 120; carpenter, 37; clothworker, 35, 146; cooper, 42; draper, 47(2), 66, 80, 97, 108, 151, 159; fishmonger, 80, 88, 131; glover, 34; goldsmith, 26, 70, 97, 116; grocer, 7, 35, 37, 146, 168, 242; haberdasher, 8, 20, 25, 82; husband-